HITLER'S FIRST WAR

HITLER'S FIRST WAR

HITLER'S
FIRST WAR

ADOLF HITLER, THE MEN
OF THE LIST REGIMENT, AND
THE FIRST WORLD WAR

THOMAS WEBER

OXFORD
UNIVERSITY PRESS

OXFORD
UNIVERSITY PRESS

Great Clarendon Street, Oxford OX2 6DP

Oxford University Press is a department of the University of Oxford.
It furthers the University's objective of excellence in research, scholarship,
and education by publishing worldwide in

Oxford New York

Auckland Cape Town Dar es Salaam Hong Kong Karachi
Kuala Lumpur Madrid Melbourne Mexico City Nairobi
New Delhi Shanghai Taipei Toronto

With offices in

Argentina Austria Brazil Chile Czech Republic France Greece
Guatemala Hungary Italy Japan Poland Portugal Singapore
South Korea Switzerland Thailand Turkey Ukraine Vietnam

Oxford is a registered trade mark of Oxford University Press
in the UK and in certain other countries

Published in the United States
by Oxford University Press Inc., New York

British Library Cataloguing in Publication Data

Data available

Library of Congress Cataloging in Publication Data

Data available

Typeset by SPI Publisher Services, Pondicherry, India
Printed in Great Britian on acid-free paper by
Clays Ltd., St Ives plc

ISBN: 978-0-19-923320-5

2

For Edna Cooper and Kay and Morry Rotman
and
In loving memory of Irving Cooper, Heinrich and Marianne
Wantier, and Günter and Margarete Weber

Acknowledgements

This book started its life one day in 2004 in the Senior Common Room of Pembroke College, Oxford, when Adrian Gregory first suggested to me the idea of writing a book on Hitler's regiment in the First World War. I was immediately enthused by his suggestion. As Adrian paced up and down the SCR, consuming a seemingly bottomless cup of black coffee, the idea for this book took shape, as we sketched out how the book could be researched and written. My greatest thanks are thus due to Adrian Gregory.

On the long road from the inception of the book to its completion, I was helped and inspired by a great number of extraordinarily generous, enjoyable, and intelligent people, without whom I could not have possibly reached the end of the road.

I should particularly like to single out the help I received from a number of outstanding research assistants: without the good humour, stamina, and detective work of Kolja Kröger, I would have never found half the sources on which this book is based; Kacey Bayles and Alec Ofsevit helped with the painstaking, almost impossible task of checking hundreds of names against the Nazi Party membership records; Kristen Pagán did much to help me to make sense to the military justice files of the List Regiment and much more. Daniel Rittenauer undertook the monumental task of helping to compile a database of the soldiers of 1st Company of Hitler's regiment, and Dominik Witkowski made his way with unfaltering energy through countless denazification records as well as many other files. I would also like to thank Kristen Pagán, Helen Kincey, Sarah Davidson, Hannah Starritt, and my wife Sarah for help with translations of quotations from German and French into English.

I have greatly benefited from the comments of Jackson Armstrong, Alexander Watson, and my wife, who all read the manuscript of this book. Others who have read and commented on parts of the book or my initial research and book proposal include Anne Allmeling, Hendrik Kafsack, Kolja Kröger, my father, Conan Fischer, Sir Ian Kershaw,

William Mulligan, and James Wilson. I am also grateful for the reports of the anonymous expert readers of Oxford University Press. Special thanks are also due to Niall Ferguson—to whom I owe most intellectually as a historian—for having been an inspiring and unfaltering mentor for more than a decade.

The following people will find many of the ideas, or at least echoes of the ideas, they put in front of me over the last few years represented in the pages of this book: Richard Abels, Alan Allport, Simon Ball, Annette Becker, Chris Boot, Michael Brenner, Frank Bialystok, Sandra Bialystok, Joseph Blasi, Philip Bullock, Caroline Bynum, David Cannadine, Justine Childers, Tom Childers, Nicola di Cosmo, Martin Eisner, Annette and Carsten Fischer, Moritz Föllmer, Detlef Garz, Philipp Gassert, Robert Gerwarth, Martin Geyer, Michael Geyer, Geoffrey Giles, Udi Greenberg, Thomas Gruber, Dagmar Herzog, Gerhard Hirschfeld, Peter Holquist, Harold James, Heather Jones, Yosef Kaplan, Peter Klein, Barbara Kowalzig, Thomas Kühne, Alan Kramer, Ferdinand Kramer, Daniel Krebs, Christiane Kuller, Irving Lavin, Jörg Lau, Elizabeth Macknight, Charles Maier, Avishai Margalit, Peter Meyers, Amos Morris-Reich, Philip Nord, Phil O'Brien, Muireann Ó Cinnéide, Cormac Ó Gráda, Peter Paret, Robert Jan van Pelt, Steven Pfaff, Hartmut Pogge von Strandmann, Sönke Neitzel, Helke Rausch, Chris Reed, Sven Reichardt, Andreas Rose, Ben Shepherd, Hilary Silver, Mishka Sinha, Thomas Sonders, Heinrich von Staden, Nick Star-gardt, Jonathan Steinberg, David Stevenson, Fritz Stern, Yael Sternhell, Christof Strauß, Kristen Stromberg Childers, Frank Trommler, Bernard Wasserstein, William Whyte, and Daniel Ziblatt. Without the people mentioned here, this book would be a much poorer one. Needless to say, I alone am responsible for any remaining limitations.

Audiences at research seminars and conferences at the University of Pennsylvania, the Institute for Advanced Study in Princeton, the Center for European Studies at Harvard, the History Department of Princeton University, the Hebrew University, the University of Aberdeen, Strathclyde University, the University of Tübingen, and the University of Waterloo were also extremely generous, incisive, and far more patient than I deserved in their feedback on the ideas on Hitler's regiment that I put in front of them.

While researching and writing this book, I was fortunate enough to have been given an intellectual home and been welcomed in turns at the University of Chicago, the University of Pennsylvania, the Institute for Advanced Study in Princeton, Harvard University, and the University of Aberdeen.

I would like to thank my colleagues in Chicago and at Penn for providing a perfect testing ground for my research on Hitler's regiment as it evolved. It was humbling and intellectually stimulating to be surrounded for a year by some of world's brightest minds amidst the tranquil beauty and excellent cuisine of the Institute for Advanced Study. Harvard's Center for European Studies and the riches of Harvard's libraries provided the perfect place to write most of the manuscript of this book. I would also like to thank Diana Eck and Dorothy Austin for inviting me to join Lowell House at Harvard as a resident scholar. They got it exactly right in how they set up an inter-generational academic community that knows equally well how to work and how to celebrate. Since arriving in Aberdeen, its Department of History has proved a wonderfully welcoming and dynamic place.

I also owe an immense debt of gratitude for the hospitality I received on my research trips to Munich to Anke and Rainer Fischer, Dorothea and Johannes Friedrich, Constanze and Steffen Metzger, Eva and Florian Weig, Andreas and Anne-Katrin Rose, and Magdalena and Boris Schmid-Noerr. Moreover the staff of the following archives and libraries have been greatly supportive: the Bayerisches Haupstaatsarchiv (and, in particular, the Kriegsarchiv), the Staatsarchiv, the Stadtarchiv München, the Institut für Zeitgeschichte, the Archiv des Erzbistums München und Freising, the Provinzarchiv der Bayerischen Kapuziner, and the Archiv der Ludwig-Maximilians-Universität in Munich; the Landeskirchliches Archiv der Evangelischen Landeskirche von Bayern in Nuremberg; the Evangelisches Pfarramt Feldkirchen; the Stadtarchiv Augsburg; the Bundesarchiv Militärarchiv in Freiburg; the Stadtarchiv Braunschweig; the Archives Départementale du Nord in Lille; the National Archives of the United States of America in College Park, MD; the Leo Baeck Institute in New York City; Yad Vashem in Jerusalem; the Royal Norfolk Regimental Museum in Norwich; the Bayerische Staatsbibliothek; the Stadtbücherei München; the library of the Historicum of Munich University; the libraries of the universities of Bochum and Essen; Locke Library, Robarts Library, and the Toronto Reference Library in Toronto; Regenstein Library at the University of Chicago, van Pelt Library at Penn; Firestone Library at Princeton University; the History and Social Sciences Library of the Institute for Advanced Study; Widener Library at Harvard; the Devon County Council Library in Exeter; Aberdeen's Queen Mother Library; the University Library of Edinburgh University, the National Library of Scotland; and the Bodleian Library at Oxford.

I am also grateful to the *St Louis Post and Dispatch* and the *Münchner Merkur* for publishing my calls for primary sources on the List Regiment. Johann Benkner, Martin Cambensy, Maria Anna Ekert, James Fleischmann, Beverly, Karen, and Rohn Grant, Linda Hagen, Ekkehard Müller, Ursula Paszkowski, Ernst Richter, Johann Schlehuber, Andrés Strauss, Manfred von Tubeuf, Wolo von Tubeuf, Marvin Verman, and Katharina Weiß and her family generously provided material or information on individual members of the List Regiment.

I gratefully acknowledge the funding I have received for this book from the American Philosophical Society, the Gerda Henkel Stiftung, the Herodotus Fund of the Institute for Advanced Study, the Mellon Foundation, the Minda de Gunzburg Center for European Studies at Harvard, as well as the School of Divinity, History and Philosophy and the College of Arts and Social Sciences at the University of Aberdeen.

My thanks go to my superb and inspiring agent Clare Alexander, who helped me to give this book a home at Oxford University Press, to Luciana O'Flaherty and Matthew Cotton for being such patient, good-humoured, and incisive editors, to Mary Worthington for so ably copy-editing my book, to Shaun Doody, Karl Schabas, and my father-in-law Jerry Cooper for casting fresh eyes over the proofs and to Claire Thompson, Emma Barber, Mary Payne, and Hayley Buckley for seeing it through the production process.

This book owes most to my beloved wife, Sarah Yael Cooper Weber, who countless times read and improved on drafts of the book in its various incarnations, accompanied me on research trips across two continents, and put up with my occasional bouts of absent-mindedness; without her support and love, this book would not have been possible. This book is dedicated to our grandparents, whose lives were influenced by Private Hitler in myriad ways. They are, and they were, the best grandparents we could have hoped for.

Contents

List of Plates

1. Adolf Hitler attending the patriotic gathering in Odeonsplatz in central Munich the day after the outbreak of the First World War, 2 August 1914 (Bayerische Staatsbibliothek, Fotoarchiv Hoffmann, Munich).

2. King Ludwig III of Bavaria inspects the List Regiment in the Türken barracks in Munich, 8 October 1914 (Stadtarchiv München, Photoarchiv, Postkartensammlung).

3. Watercolour by Hitler depicting the ruins of Messines monastery in the Ypres Salient, December 1914 (Max Amann, *Ein Leben für Führer und Volk* (Berlin: Großdeutscher Verlag, 1941)).

4. Adolf Hitler in Fournes, May 1915 (Fridolin Solleder (ed.), *Vier Jahre Westfront: Geschichte des Regiments List R.I.R. 16* (Munich: M. Schick, 1932), 168; photographer Korbinian Rutz).

5. Adolf Hitler (front row, first left) and his fellow dispatch runners in Fournes, September 1915 (privately owned postcard, Thomas Weber).

6. Hitler amidst the 'Kapelle Krach', undated (Balthasar Brandmayer, *Meldegänger Hitler 1914–18*, 2nd edn (Munich, 1933), 65).

7. Hitler amongst his fellow dispatch runners from regimental HQ in Fournes, 1915 (privately owned, Katharina Weiß).

8. Adolf Hitler, Max Amann, and Ernst Schmidt revisit the garden in Fournes where they were photographed in 1915 (Heinrich Hoffmann, *Mit Hitler im Westen* (Munich, 1940), 11).

9. Jakob 'Jackl' Weiß, prior to his departure for the front, 10 October 1914 (privately owned, Katharina Weiß).

10. The combat zone close to the village of Biache-Saint-Vaast to the east of Arras, May 1917 (privately owned, Maria Anna Ekert).

11. Max Amann and Alois Schnelldorfer at regimental headquarters of RIR 16, 1915 (privately owned, Maria Anna Ekert).

12. A trench on Vimy Ridge, late 1916 or early 1917 (Adolf Meyer, *Mit Adolf Hitler im Bayerischen Reserve-Infanterie-Regiment 16 List* (Neustadt/Aisch, 1934), 27).

13. Albert Weisgerber and his men from 1st Company shortly before his death in the Battle of Fromelles, 9 May 1915 (Bayerisches Hauptstaatsarchiv, Kriegsarchiv, München).

Abbreviations

SB	Stadtarchiv Braunschweig
SM	Stadtarchiv München
SP	Schnelldorfer papers, in private hands, Inning, Bavaria
SPD	Sozialdemokratische Partei Deutschlands (Social Democratic Party of Germany
SS	Schutzstaffel (Protection Squad)
YVD	Yad Vashem Database

Prelude

I found him on page 168. I had been browsing through the book in front of me for quite a while, and was surprised at how long it took me to find a trace, any trace of him at all. Now I had found him. He walked across the picture at the centre of page 168 of the official 1932 history of the List Regiment (see Plate 4) in his long grey coat, a spiked helmet on his head, and a rifle hanging off his right shoulder. He walked right in the middle of a cobble-stoned street, seeming not to pay much attention to the small, urban brick houses and the soldiers in the background. He walked quickly enough for the bottom of his coat to be blown open and lifted by the wind. Yet he did not seem to be walking anywhere in particular.

Had it not been for the caption below the picture, I would not have recognized him. The picture was of such poor quality that all I could make out of his face was his moustache. Had it not been him, I would have laughed at such a sight—a face with apparently no mouth, eyes, or nose but only a moustache. Yet the caption told me that he it was: 'War volunteer Adolf Hitler, dispatch runner of the regiment, May 1915. Phot[ographer] Korbinian Rutz.'[1] Later I found two other brief references to Hitler in the regimental history which, it is important to remember, was published only months before Hitler came to power. The second reference, to which we shall return later, was a brief mention of Hitler's supposed role in saving the life of one of the regimental commanders. The first reference was merely a perfunctory mention of him in the book's introduction, which I had missed the first time I had flicked through the book: 'The picture of the List Regiment would not be complete without a mention of the historical fact that the war volunteer Adolf Hitler, who later became the founder and leader of one of the strongest political parties in Germany, served in its ranks for four years.'[2]

This was very odd indeed. Ever since an Austrian historian had demonstrated in the mid-1990s that the old story (that Hitler had been politicized and radicalized in pre-First World War Vienna) borders on fiction,[3] historians had pointed to the First World War and his experience in the List Regiment as the chief explanation of why he was to become one of the most infamous dictators the world has ever seen. For instance, as a recent double biography of Hitler and Stalin argues: 'The war made Hitler, as revolution made Stalin.'[4] Elsewhere, we read that for Hitler 'the formative episode of his life was service in the Great War.'[5] Of the two great classic Hitler biographies, meanwhile, one argues that it was the war, not the revolution, which made all the difference for Hitler's political radicalization.[6] The other posits that 'the war, and the impact of war upon the individual lives of million of Germans, were among the essential conditions for the rise of Hitler and the Nazi Party.'[7] Moreover, the most influential book on military leadership published in the last third of the twentieth century tells us how much it mattered that Hitler had served in the List Regiment, arguing that his 'selection for the 16th Bavarian Reserve must be seen as a key ingredient of Hitler's life'.[8] When the first book specifically on Hitler's war years in the List Regiment was published in 2005, it told us that his regiment had been Hitler's 'university'[9]—a claim based in part on his own protestation that the war had been his university[10] and the 'greatest of all [his] experiences'.[11] The obvious question that follows from this is: if Hitler's war service in this specific regiment was supposed to have 'made' him, why did he only feature in the form of a moustache on an empty face in a blurry photograph and a perfunctory reference to him in a fat, thick regimental history of almost 500 pages?

The 2005 book on Hitler and the List Regiment does not provide any persuasive answer to this question. It presents a picture of Hitler, socialized in the supposedly Pan-German, *völkisch*, anti-Semitic, Social-Darwinist climate of his all-volunteer regiment, turning from a lazy failed artist into a political activist. According to the book, the experiences of 1916 and 1917 transformed him into a pathological anti-Semite. In the regiment, he experiences solidarity and bonding. Many of the men of the regiment, the book tells us, rose together with him to the apex of the Third Reich, most notably Rudolf Hess, Hitler's deputy—a claim that had also been made in Alan Bullock's magisterial Hitler biography. In short, the book tells us that the war and the regiment 'made' Hitler.[12] If this portrayal were true, we would expect Hitler to have been the central character of the 1932 regimental history, not an awkward side figure depicted in a photograph which bordered on the insulting.

Even arguably the greatest among the Hitler biographies, Ian Kershaw's *Hitler*, raises more new questions about Hitler's war years than it provides answers to the question of the role of the war and of Hitler's regiment in creating Hitler (which is, of course, the book's strength rather than its weakness). While arguing that 'the war . . . gave him for the first time in his life a cause . . . and—more than that—a sense of belonging', and that the List Regiment 'became home for him',[13] Kershaw is very cautious in his treatment of Hitler's war years. Even though describing Hitler's First World War experiences as probably the most formative of his life,[14] he does not disentangle the question of whether the war itself or its aftermath created Hitler but treats the two periods as one entity, arguing in rather unspecific terms: 'The War and its aftermath made Hitler.'[15] This leaves the question open as to what the impact of the war itself was and if the political future of Hitler and of Germans at large was still open in late 1918.

As to the role of Hitler's regiment in his transformative war experience, Kershaw merely mentions that 'his immediate comrades, mainly the group of dispatch runners, respected him, and, it seems, even quite liked him'.[16] Anybody checking the sources available to historians on Hitler's war years will immediately realize that there are very good reasons for Kershaw's reluctance to disentangle Hitler's war from his post-war revolutionary experiences and to discuss the role the List Regiment played in Hitler's life. With the exception of a handful of letters, postcards, and photographs (mostly from the first half of the war and mostly lacking political content), Hitler's military ID, and a tiny number of similar documents, only post-war accounts have been available to historians. Chief amongst those are Hitler's own semi-fictional *Mein Kampf*[17] and the hagiographical memoirs of people close to him.[18]

The obvious problem with these accounts written long after the event is that they tell us much more about the attempt by Hitler and his comrades to reconfigure their war experiences for political (and commercial) ends. Books that have not accepted the limitations of these accounts have, at best, reproduced almost every cliché and stereotype about Hitler and the First World War, as has the 2005 book on Hitler and the List Regiment. Its author did not visit any German-language archive and thus did not even realize, for instance, that Rudolf Hess never had been in Hitler's regiment.[19]

Books that have recognized the limited value of the memoirs of Hitler and his associates have still not been able to shed much light on the role of the First World War and his regiment in forming Hitler. Even though the one-time contention of *Commentary* magazine that Adolf Hitler would not find many biographers[20] has long been proven spectacularly wrong, Hitler's time as a dispatch runner during the First World War has remained a blank spot due to the absence of easily available contemporary material. This means that we know with certainty next to nothing about the period that most historians now see as Hitler's formative years.

A handful of letters, postcards, photos, and personal documents simply cannot possibly tell us if the First World War 'made' Hitler. And if the war did 'make' him, they cannot possibly tell us whether his regiment as a whole, the group of men immediately around him, or influences beyond his regiment formed him. Nor can they shed light on how typical Hitler was of his regiment. Equally, they cannot disentangle the respective influence of the war and the revolutionary period following the war. If we thus rely on Hitler's wartime documents and try to steer as clear as possible of mythical and semi-mythical post-war accounts, the image we are left with is the equivalent of the photo of Hitler in the 1932 regimental history: the blurry image of a man without a face.

The only way to navigate through the almost complete absence of wartime documents on Hitler and thus to bring him back into focus is to look at his regiment as a whole. If we can tell the story of the wartime experience of the List Regiment, we can see how Hitler fits into the picture. If the information we have specifically on Hitler allows us only to gain a blurry out-of-focus image of him, but we can get a sharper picture of the regiment as a whole (in other words of the bigger picture from which the image of Hitler has been cropped out), then we can reconstruct a fairly accurate in-focus image of Hitler from this time. The huge amount of information this approach is likely to produce will also allow us to test to a much greater degree which parts of post-war accounts provide reliable information. In other words, this approach provides us with the tools to include post-war recollections (the reliability of which we hitherto could not determine) in our attempt to reconstruct an accurate in-focus image of Hitler. In short, Hitler's regiment will allow us to determine what role his First World War experience played in 'making' him.

A few weeks after first encountering the photo of Hitler in the 1932 regimental history, I sat on a plane to Munich, the city which was home to the List Regiment, the city that the Nazis saw as their spiritual capital, which today is one of the most pleasant, liberal, and prosperous places on earth, and home to the Bavarian War Archive and thus to the papers of the List Regiment. When I first arrived at the War Archive, I was worried: did the fact that nobody had ever written about Hitler's regiment using wartime sources imply that no useful files existed or survived? As I leafed through the search aids for the regimental papers, I could see why nobody had ever really used the regimental papers. The listings were few and the titles of the listings sounded forbidding. However, when the archivist placed in front of me the search aids for the Brigade and Division to which the List Regiment belonged, I rejoiced. Here was a treasure trove of papers on Hitler's regiment. As I untied each of the fragile threads that held together the bulky piles of files, covered in dust and undisturbed for almost nine long decades, the picture of Hitler's regiment became ever sharper. The one big disappointment, though, was that I could not find any military justice files or letters of ordinary soldiers. This disappointment lasted only until my next visit to Munich when one day the War Archive's main archivist told me that the regiment's justice files had indeed survived, including numerous confiscated letters and testimonies of both soldiers and officers. They had just never been catalogued and sorted and, yes, I was welcome to use them if I could make my way through the mountain of unsorted files.

From the moment that I first stepped off the plane in Munich on my first research trip to Bavaria's capital, one find led to another. As I cast my net wider, new information about the List Regiment appeared almost everywhere I looked, as long as I dug deep enough and was not put off by the daughter of a leading Nazi, who hung up on one of my research assistants, or by dubious vendors on antique markets, who either wanted to sell SS paraphernalia to me or would not make their holdings available as I did not look like a Nazi sympathizer. What emerged from the holdings of Munich's various archives, from letters[21] that had sat in attics for decades in the Bavarian countryside, from the Nazi Party membership files as well as the files of the FBI and the predecessor of the CIA in the US National Archives, from the collections of the Leo Baeck Institute in the busy streets of New York City and of Yad Vashem in the tranquil hills of Jerusalem, was the amazing story of the men of Hitler's regiment in the First World War and what became of them once their former comrade turned into the most infamous leader Germany ever produced. This book tells their story as well as that of Hitler's wartime years. It tells the story of how they got caught up and entangled in the transformation from the relative political stability of the nineteenth century to the bloodiest period of history the world has ever witnessed. The book chronicles their lives both on the Western Front and

in Private Hitler's Third Reich. It seeks to answer the question of what roles
the men of the List Regiment played in 'making' Hitler.

Hitler's First War unravels the battle experience of Hitler and the men of his
regiment and tells their story at the moment when the nineteenth-century
world of empires died and the modern age of destruction, total war, and
genocide was born. Part I of this book tells the story of the impact on Hitler
and the men of the List Regiment of four years of combat. It follows Hitler
and his comrades from the days when the outbreak of war uprooted them
from their communities across Bavaria, through the muddy trenches of
Belgian Flanders and northern France, to defeat and their chaotic return
home in 1918. Part II shows what role Hitler's war experience and what role
the men of the regiment played in the rise of Nazism to power, in Hitler's
empire, as well as in American-occupied Germany.

   This book also raises the question of whether the war was the breaking
point, or—as George F. Kennan famously put it for Europe as a whole—'the
seminal catastrophe'[22] in German history. For a long time, historians believed
that since the Enlightenment Germany had been radically different from any
other European country and that the roots of the Third Reich reach back
deep into German history.[23] At the time, explaining Hitler and the course of
German history was relatively easy. Today, however, few historians would
still subscribe to this view. The new consensus (even though a significant
number of historians still hold onto the old view) is that until the First
World War, Germany had really not been all that different from Britain or
France and that Germany was, at any rate, more liberal than tsarist Russia.
This all begs the question of what effect the First World War had not just on
Hitler but on Germans at large. The jury is still out on this question. The
battle of ideas now rages between a view that puts most of the blame on the
war experience—positing that Germany had been destabilized by the war to
such an extent that the rise of right-wing extremism was highly likely—and
one that argues that Germany had not been politically in almost terminal
decline since 1918. In short, recent debates have revolved around the
questions whether the war itself radicalized Hitler and his comrades and
turned them into would-be Nazis, whether Hitler and his comrades were left
with a choice as they returned from the war in late 1918, or whether their
political convictions were by 1918 already fully formed.

   To summarize: at the core of the book are five questions: did the war
politically radicalize Hitler and his comrades, in other words, did the war

turn the men of the regiment into would-be Nazis (who would not inevitably but easily be turned into Nazis); or were they politicized only by their post-war experiences in the form of extreme economic volatility, fear of Communist revolution, the perceived injustices of Versailles, and right-wing take-over? Were the majority of the men of the regiment politicized by experiences during or after the war at all? What role did the men of the regiment and the myth about them play in the establishment of the Third Reich and in keeping Hitler's Germany running? Finally and maybe most importantly, the book raises the question of how typical a product Hitler was of his regiment.

The final question is essentially the same question raised by Stephen Fry's *Making History*. In this book by the British writer, wit, and comedian, a young Cambridge Ph.D. history student and a Cambridge scientist whose father had carried out medical experiments in a concentration camp set out retrospectively to change the course of history. The protagonists build a time machine that allows them to send substances back in time and poison the well in the street in which Hitler's parents lived. Hitler senior becomes impotent and Hitler junior is never born. Yet the alternative history the characters in Fry's book have unwittingly unleashed is more horrible than the history they tried to prevent from unfolding. For Hitler's place is taken by a young officer in Hitler's regiment. Gloder, the young officer, is less of a procrastinator and a better organizer than Hitler. Gloder fills the vacuum created in Germany by the First World War and its aftermath, taking on the role Hitler would have performed. What follows is a more 'perfect' Holocaust.[24]

Needless to say, Fry's book is not intended to be serious but the idea he uses is. The question it raises is whether anybody from the List Regiment could have taken Hitler's place, if he had not existed. Or differently put, whether Hitler was a typical product of the List Regiment and would have turned out differently had it not been for his war experience in the regiment. The implication of the book is clear: anybody who went through the same political and mental socialization as Hitler and who had the same war experience would fit the bill to take Hitler's place. Yet what is still unclear is whether the regiment was full of Gloders and Hitler clones, or whether it included a certain number of Gloders and would-be Hitlers among a number of men with very different political convictions. In the former case, the story would be relatively straightforward, particularly if we accept that the List Regiment was representative of German society at large.

In other words, the great majority of members of the List Regiment and of Germans in general would then be all but mutations of the same political creed. In the latter case, we are still left with the question whether and why the Hitlers and the Gloders of Germany were politically transformed or 'made' by the war experience in regiments like the List Regiment, even if the same experiences had a different impact on other men in these regiments.

Another question is—even if it turns out that Hitler was not a typical product of his regiment—why he found an audience in the Germany of the 1920s and 1930s, that is to say why a situation arose in which Hitler could thrive. This question has, of course, been raised a million times. However, this book uses the microcosm of the veterans of the List Regiment to show why an increasing number of Germans with political attitudes that were often far from identical with those of Hitler decided to support him. How in other words a diverse regiment and a sectarian Weimar Republic[25] turned into a collectivist dictatorship, and why Germany ended up with Private Hitler, rather than a Mussolini, Franco, Piłsudski, Horthy, or Metaxas, while France's collectivist authoritarian tendencies[26] did not produce a right-wing dictator. In short, the book explains how collective action (and inaction) came about in the List Regiment during the war and in German society after the war. *Hitler's First War* challenges the thesis according to which German society collapsed because it had the wrong kind of civil society following the First World War.

The contention of the book is that little of what we thought about Hitler's regiment is true but equally that the real history of the List Regiment that looms darkly under the mythical cloak woven by Hitler and his propagandists is pivotal for understanding the collapse of the relatively stable and peaceful nineteenth-century first age of globalization and Hitler's meteoric rise to power.

PART
I

I

A Crowd in Odeonsplatz

1 August–20 October 1914

They were born within a day of each other exactly ten years apart. They both grew up in small towns; both were mediocre students who aspired to be artists. Both ultimately ended up in Munich, the German Mecca for artists. After the outbreak of war, both were assigned to the same regiment the day it was set up. Both loved their regiment: the 16th Bavarian Reserve Infantry Regiment (RIR 16), commonly called the List Regiment after its first commander Julius von List. Both were fully committed to the war. Yet this is where the similarities between Albert Weisgerber and Adolf Hitler stop—and not just because Weisgerber, unlike Hitler, was accepted by the arts academy and became one of Germany's most successful painters; nor was it just because Weisgerber became one of the celebrated heroes of the official 1932 history of the List Regiment, while Hitler was barely mentioned.

While Hitler's pre-war friends came from the Pan-German nationalist milieu, Weisgerber's friends included Theodor Heuss, the towering figure of German Liberalism and West Germany's first President after the fall of Hitler. Whereas Hitler's friends would become pawns of his regime, one of Weisgerber's closest friends and collaborators, Rudolf Levy (a war volunteer), became a Holocaust victim in 1944. Moreover, whilst Hitler's relationship with women was troublesome, Weisgerber was married and his wife would be labelled a 'Half-Jew' once Hitler's Nuremberg Laws came into effect. Whereas Hitler had never travelled beyond a small section of German-speaking Austria and southern Bavaria, Weisgerber had spent a year in Paris, where he met Matisse. While Hitler painted third-rate postcards in the streets of Munich, Weisgerber became President of the Neue Secessionisten—the most avant-garde group of Expressionists, whose paintings would be branded 'degenerate art' in Hitler's empire.[1] Weisgerber's and Hitler's biographies thus immediately illustrate the dangers of drawing too direct a line from service in and love for the List Regiment to the evolution of Nazi Germany.

Before we follow Adolf Hitler and Albert Weisgerber to the Western front, we will encounter the two men and their would-be comrades in the streets of Munich at the moment when news reached the Bavarian capital that Germany was at war. We will be introduced to their regiment and the society from which RIR 16 had sprung before witnessing how the men of Hitler's regiment were hastily trained in a manner that inadvertently turned them into likely perpetrators of war atrocities once they were to arrive at the front.

Once war came in the summer of 1914, both Hitler and Weisgerber willingly followed the call to arms. On Sunday, 2 August 1914, the day after war had broken out, Hitler hurried to Odeonsplatz in central Munich to attend the huge patriotic gathering taking place there that day. While assembling in front of the Feldherrenhalle, the city's imposing edifice honouring past Bavarian military commanders, Hitler found himself sur-rounded by many of the men who would serve with him in the First World War. In a photograph depicting the scene (Plate 1)—a photograph that would become one of the most iconic photographs of the twentieth century, we see Hitler amidst a sea of cheering people.[2] The image, we have been told time and time again, clearly demonstrates two things: that Munich was infected with public enthusiasm for the war and that Hitler was representative of the average and ordinary Munich population.[3] The whole of Germany, it was long believed, could not wait for the First World War to break out.[4]

Among the people in Odeonsplatz who were to serve with Hitler in the First World War was Fridolin Solleder, a trainee in the Bavarian State Archive. In the early 1930s, he recalled of the gathering in Odeonsplatz that 'all the noble passions that people had internalized now seemed to come out. The melodies, warrior songs, and enthusiastic words heard that day sounded like the song of songs of German strength, of German confidence... It was a celebration of brotherhood; for many it was a last farewell. I shook the hand of many a man who would lie in foreign soil within a year.'[5]

Similarly, Hitler, while imprisoned in Landsberg Fortress in the 1920s, fondly looked back on the weekend the war had broken out. For him, it had been the best weekend ever: 'I am not ashamed to acknowledge today that I was carried away by the enthusiasm of the moment,' he wrote in *Mein Kampf*, 'and that I sank down upon my knees and thanked Heaven out of the fullness of my heart for the favour of having been permitted to live in such a time.'[6] Like millions of Germans, Hitler recalled, he had been looking forward to the war: 'The War of 1914 was certainly not forced on the masses; it was even desired by the whole people.' In a moment of 'excessive enthusiasm', the German people 'looked forward to a radical settlement of accounts. I also belonged to the millions who desired this.' In *Mein Kampf*, Hitler saw the outbreak of war as an 'inexorable test' that 'the hand of the Goddess of Destiny' set for nations to determine their 'truth and sincerity', concluding that 'just as millions of others, I felt a proud joy in being permitted to go through this test.'[7]

If we are to believe Hitler, who only a year earlier had moved from Vienna to Munich almost certainly in an attempt to dodge the Austrian draft,[8] he volunteered to serve in the Bavarian Army as early as the day following the patriotic assembly in Odeonsplatz. Hitler's enlistment in the Bavarian Army as an Austrian citizen was unusual. He later claimed that he had petitioned the Bavarian king to be allowed to serve in the German armed forces. According to Hitler, it only took a day before he received special dispensation to serve in the Bavarian Army. In *Mein Kampf*, he recalled how he supposedly received the letter from the cabinet's office of the king: 'I opened the document with trembling hands; and no words of mine could now describe the satisfaction I felt on reading that I was instructed to report to a Bavarian regiment.... For me, as for every German, the most memorable period of my life now began.' Hitler claimed that his gratitude and feeling of joy had no bounds.[9]

By mid-August, Hitler, who had turned 25 in April, was admitted to the Sixth Recruit Depot of the 2nd Bavarian Infantry Regiment. From there, on 1 September 1914, he was transferred to the 1st Company of the newly established List Regiment.[10]

Hitler tells us that there was nothing unusual in his volunteering, reminding us 'how more than two million German men and youths voluntarily joined the colours, ready to shed the last drop of their blood for the cause'.[11] Similarly, Solleder contended in 1932 that following the patriotic gathering in Odeonsplatz that Hitler and he had attended, crowds of men had flocked to recruitment centres and more often than not ended up in the same regiment as did Hitler and he himself:

> In front of the recruiting centre the stream of war volunteers was forming a crowd. Munich's deputy mayor Dr Merkt stepped out onto the balcony and gave a speech. Spontaneously, the volunteers responded with the German song of defiance, 'The Watch on the Rhine'. Most of the volunteers present were sent into the field a few weeks later with the List Regiment.[12]

One of the volunteers whom Solleder might have seen outside the recruiting centre was Arthur Rödl. A locksmith trainee in Munich, Rödl—who thirty-one years later was to commit suicide for his involvement in the crimes of Nazi Germany—was one of the youngest volunteers in Hitler's regiment. Having turned 16 only in May, young Arthur had to lie about his age, making himself two years older than he really was, when he volunteered the same day that Adolf Hitler attended the patriotic assembly in Odeonsplatz.[13]

The List Regiment was one of the new volunteer regiments; or at least this is what all Hitler biographies, the official 1932 history of the regiment, as well as numerous other publications tell us.[14] It was, as Adolf Meyer, who was to serve with Hitler in the war, put it in his flattering 1934 memoirs of Hitler's and his war years, 'the first Bavarian volunteer regiment to arrive at the Western Front in October 1914'.[15] The implication of RIR 16 being a volunteer regiment is, of course, that Hitler would immediately appear as representative of the whole regiment and, by extension, of all Bavarians and Germans who readily endorsed the war.

Postcards available to members of the List Regiment who wanted to write home encouraged them to see the List Regiment as a volunteer regiment. One such card reproduced a poem that the father of Karl Naundorf, a 24-year-old war volunteer in RIR 16, had written for his son shortly after he had volunteered:

> Now strap on your sword, my son,
> Go willingly into the field!
> God willing, you'll come home a victor.
> If not, you'll die a hero,
> For our beloved precious Fatherland,
> And as a reward I'll tell you:
> You were, you are, and you'll always be,
> A brave German son.[16]

Furthermore Valentin Witt, an officer who acted as an army recruiting officer after the outbreak of war and who was to serve in RIR 16, claimed in a late 1915 pamphlet about the war service of the List Regiment up to that time that after the outbreak of war his recruitment office had been swamped with volunteers: 'An hour ago I had a poster put up on the door to the school, which henceforth will be the home of the battalion, which said: "Volunteers being recruited". The space in front of my office is already uncomfortably full. . . . There's pushing and shoving all around me as I ask for documents; everyone wants to be first, everyone is afraid he won't make it to the front of the queue.' Witt wants us to believe that all of Munich desperately tried to volunteer and none more so than the city's youth:

> They hurried away from school, the office, the factory, to come to the aid of the Fatherland. All professions were represented. In particular, many men of the arts and sciences reported for duty, to whom Munich chiefly owed its famous name and importance. The sons of the best families in our city are signing up for duty . . . Rich and poor, without distinction. Being called to duty, they have responded. The love of the Fatherland showed the men the way—to arms.[17]

Like Witt, numerous Nazi propagandists would later claim that the regiment was full of students, artists, and university graduates.[18] We are indeed told by a leading authority that the huge number of students and university graduates in the regiment were of pivotal importance in the 'making' of Hitler.[19] Valentin Witt also wants us to believe that the plan to augment the List Regiment with old experienced soldiers was abandoned once the Bavarian military authorities realized the exceptional quality of the volunteers to the List Regiment: 'The ranks of the new regiments were to be mixed with [experienced reservists]; they wanted to assign to them experienced soldiers who had completed their mandatory military training.' However, as the superiors watched the 'Listers' during the drills, they were found to be fully-fledged soldiers who could be sent out confidently and without a 'chaperone.'[20]

Powerful though the accounts by Hitler, Solleder, and Witt are, they are little more than fiction. Hitler's rendering of how as an Austrian citizen he managed to be admitted to the Bavarian Army is particularly problematic as it was not in the remit of the office of the king's cabinet to issue special dispensations to serve in the Bavarian Army. Even if the office had had the power to grant requests of foreigners to volunteer for the German armed forces, it would have had more important business to attend to on the day after the outbreak of war than to consider a petition of a 25-year-old Austrian postcard painter.[21] At any rate, Hitler's case was not as exceptional as sometimes believed; he was indeed not the only Austrian soldier in the List Regiment.[22] It is likely that Hitler was accepted into the Bavarian Army either simply because nobody had asked him if he was a German citizen when he first volunteered or because the recruiting authorities on the ground were happy to accept any volunteer and simply did not care what Hitler's nationality was, or because he might have told the Bavarian authorities that he intended to become a German citizen. We cannot know.

Far more important than the details of how Hitler managed to be admitted into the Bavarian Army is his claim that his attitude and behaviour were representative of the men of his regiment and of the masses; in other words, that his response to the outbreak of war was typical of the German response to the war.

It is true that in the days prior to the outbreak of war, brass bands had played patriotic songs in the streets and cafés of Munich. Students and a rowdy crowd had smashed up a café that was perceived as insufficiently patriotic.[23] Yet, it is difficult to ascertain the degree to which these cases of patriotic outbursts were representative of the general population, as the loudest and most visible responses to the outbreak of war do not neces- sarily equate to the most widespread responses to war. In fact, only a minority of Germans were initially genuinely enthusiastic about the war.[24] Anxiety, fear, and grief were the initial responses. A young Heinrich Himmler, who experienced the outbreak of the First World War in Landshut in Lower Bavaria, complained on 27 August of the lack of popular enthusiasm for the war in Lower Bavaria. He noted with disdain in his diary that Landshut had been full of sobbing and weeping people. There is, in fact, a vast discrepancy between immediate responses to the war as the one described by Himmler and accounts that were published later on in an attempt to give the war meaning retrospectively.[25] This is why we need to treat post-war recollections of August 1914 with a huge grain of salt. The same is true of the photograph of Hitler amidst crowds in Odeonplatz from 2 August (Plate 1).

The photograph, in actuality, does not in any way support Hitler's claim that he was representative of the population of Munich, nor of the would- be members of the List Regiment, nor of the German population at large. The photo tells us more about why its photographer, Heinrich Hoffmann, would later become Hitler's personal photographer than anything about

the mindset of the German people at the outbreak of war. During the Third Reich, it would be his masterful photographs and Leni Riefenstahl's magnificent propaganda movies that would create the public image of Hitler and of a young, energetic, and forward-looking Germany.

On 2 August, only a tiny fraction of Munich's near 600,000 residents[26] attended the patriotic assembly Hoffmann depicted. On Hoffmann's photo, the entire square appears filled with cheering people. However, a film clip that has survived of the scene and that, unlike Hoffmann's photo, did not zoom in onto the crowd immediately in front of the Feldherrenhalle gives us a very different impression. Parts of the square are not filled with people. There is even enough space for a tram to move at normal speed across the square. When the film camera started filming the crowd, we see restless people. Only when they become aware that the camera is filming do they start to cheer and to raise their hats. At that very moment, Heinrich Hoffmann, standing close to the camera crew, took his photo. And thus the myth of central Munich overflowing with cheering and warmongering crowds was born. There is even some indication that Hoffmann might have 'doctored' his photograph to place Hitler in a more prominent position, for in the film clip Hitler stands in a less central position than in the photo. And where there are crowds of people in front of Theatiner Church in the background of the photo, there are far fewer people at the same spot in the film clip.[27]

Even if the List Regiment had been a volunteer unit in a strict sense, it would not necessarily have consisted of men with uniform attitudes to the war. The cases of Eduard Abtmayr, a hardened criminal, who volunteered for the List Regiment almost certainly to avoid having to go to prison,[28] or of Georg Ferchl—a 19-year-old technician and war volunteer who, while still in Munich, ran off for almost two weeks from his recruit depot because he felt he had been paid insufficient attention by his superiors[29] (which was a widespread feeling)—are cautionary tales against automatically equating voluntary enlistment for the war with hyper-nationalist, chauvinistic, and militarist political attitudes.[30]

At any rate, contrary to conventional wisdom, Hitler's regiment never was a volunteer regiment. We do not know how many of the men Solleder had witnessed outside Munich's main recruitment centre ended up in the List Regiment. But we do know that they did not typify a representative cross section of the regiment. The regimental history of RIR 16 contains a reproduction of a painting of the masses of volunteers outside Munich's recruitment centre that Solleder described.[31] Unlike Hoffman, the painter did not even require the skill of a Heinrich Hoffmann to distort reality. With his brush, he could simply project onto the canvas his post-war fantasies and longing for the popular enthusiasm and unity that had supposedly existed in Germany in August 1914.

Even at the beginning of the war, only a minority of the men of the List Regiment had been volunteers. Of the soldiers who had joined the unit by the end of 1914, no more than three out of ten were volunteers.[32] In Hitler's 1st Company, the figures were even lower. More than 85 per cent of the men of his company were, unlike him, not volunteers, but conscripts.[33]

The group that came closest to the Nazi claim that the Hitler's regiment was a volunteer unit was ironically Jewish, men like Leo Guggenheim, who had recently returned from Italy, where he had spent six months learning Italian, and immediately volunteered on the outbreak of war. In total, three of the six Jews in RIR 16 in 1914 were volunteers. However, the high volunteering rate among Jews was merely a result of the extraordinarily high educational and social background of the Jews in the List Regiment. Compared to Protestants and Catholics of a similar social status, the volunteering rate of Jews was not out of the ordinary. Contrary to the public image of the regiment, only a relatively small number of the volunteers were either university or high-school students (less than 5 per cent.) However, it is worth pointing out that the number of volunteers among all students in the regiment was staggering (72 per cent), irrespective of their religious background.[34]

To be sure, the great majority of the regiment (more than 70 per cent) had, unlike Albert Weisgerber but like Adolf Hitler, received no previous military training.[35] However, they were not volunteers at all. They had been members of the *Ersatzreserve* or supplementary reserve. All adult men in Imperial Germany had in theory been subject to conscription. In reality, however, the German armed forces lacked the capabilities and financial resources to call up more than 55 per cent of the male population each year.[36] The majority of those who did not serve would simply never be called up. However, a minority among those who did not serve had initially been called up but had been put straight into the *Ersatzreserve*.[37] Recruits assigned to the supplemantary reserve were generally men who were deemed insufficiently fit to serve in the army in peacetime but still sufficiently fit to be called up in the event of war. The List Regiment thus did not consist of cheery volunteers like

Hitler but of a medley of half-fit men, formed in a last ditch attempt by the German armed forces to scramble together an army big enough to knock out France before the anticipated war with Russia.

In mid-August, Hitler and the men of RIR 16 started training in locations across Munich. They now had less than two months to prepare for their baptism of fire in what would be the First Battle of Ypres. On 8 September, Colonel Julius von List, the 49-year-old career soldier who had just been appointed regimental commander, spoke the following words of welcome to Hitler and his fellow recruits:

> Comrades! I welcome with all my heart and full of confidence all officers, doctors, and officials, all Offiziersstellvertreter, NCOs, and troops. The Regiment, whose men for the most part are untrained, is expected to be ready for mobile deployment within a few weeks. This is a difficult task, but with the admirable spirit which animates all member of this regiment, not an impossible one.... With God's blessing, let's begin our work for Kaiser, King, and Fatherland![38]

Life in Munich, Hitler and his new comrades soon realized, had dramatically changed since the beginning of the war. The Bavarian authorities had even cancelled Munich's famed Oktoberfest because of the war.[39]

The only thing the Munich-based List Regiment shared with a volunteer unit was that its men were utterly unprepared and untrained for the realities of warfare. As Munich's military barracks had no space for all the new recruits and volunteers, Hitler, Solleder, Weisgerber, and the men who would become their comrades were housed in several schools that had been hastily transformed.[40] Hitler now wore the first uniform of his life—a simple greenish-grey uniform, with an 'RIR 16' sown in red onto his epaulettes and a red stripe down the side of the trousers, which he was under strict instructions not to pleat. He had to tuck the trousers into his new leather boots and to put a thick belt around the jacket of his uniform. As the supply of helmets and of army knapsacks had run out, Hitler and his comrades were kitted out with ordinary rucksacks and oil-cloth hats with a grey cotton cover that was supposed to give the hats the appearance of helmets. The men of Hitler's regiment thus were to go to war with hats that provided next to no protection and that, as they were to find out, looked from a distance to other trigger-happy German troops like British helmets.[41] As their poor equipment made blatantly clear, Weisgerber and Hitler were in a regiment that was, and would

continue to be, not very high up the pecking order in the Bavarian
Army.

While training in Munich, Hitler and the other previously untrained men
in the List Regiment soon learned how their regiment functioned and what
its place in the German armed forces was: it was one of more than 400
infantry regiments, part of the newly set up 6th Bavarian Reserve Division
(RD 6), which included a total of 4 reserve infantry regiments, as well as
cavalry and artillery units (the 6th Bavarian Reserve Cavalry Regiment and
the 6th Bavarian Reserve Artillery Regiment), and over time also an engineers'
company (the 6th Bavarian Reserve Pioneers Company). The Bavarian
Army, which since the foundation of Imperial Germany in 1871 had
remained a semi-autonomous army under the umbrella of the German
armed forces, now, unlike in peacetime, was under the supreme command
of the German Kaiser. The troop contingents of the smaller German states
had long been integrated into the Prussian Army but the bigger states had
kept their own armies, which meant that the German armed forces consisted of the separate armies of Prussia, Bavaria, Saxony, and Wurttemberg.
The sister infantry regiments of the List Regiment were RIR 17, RIR 20, and
RIR 21, which were regiments of a similar social make-up as the List
Regiment. Each of the regiments had been established in one of Bavaria's
military districts. However, even though the majority of men of each
regiment tended to come from within its military district, all four regiments
also received very significant numbers of recruits from beyond their own
military district, giving the regiments an all–Bavarian character. As Hitler's
brothers-in-arms soon realized, each of the two reserve infantry regiments
were teamed up as brigades: RIR 16 and RIR 17—the two South Bavarian
regiments—formed the 12th Bavarian Reserve Brigade (RIB 12); and RIR
20 and RIR 21 from Franconia in northern Bavaria made up the 14th
Bavarian Reserve Brigade.[42]

Once it was ready to go into battle, the regiment consisted of three
battalions which were each subdivided into four companies. Each of
the battalions included a thousand men. Yet the total number of men
who passed through the regiment during the war is far higher. The rolls
of service include up to 16,000 names of soldiers who were members of the
regiment at some point between 1914 and 1918. However, the actual
number of men who served in the regiment is smaller since many men
were listed in more than one company of the regiment. There are, for
instance, two entries for Hitler: one for 1st Company in which he served

during the first year of the war, and another one for the rest of the war when he served in 3rd Company.[43] The battalions and companies were commanded by experienced officers, including Julius Graf von Zech auf Neuhofen, a former Governor of German-Togo who had not led a military unit for seventeen years but was now in charge of Hitler's battalion.[44]

Up to early October, Hitler and the men of the regiment underwent a crash course for soldiers in Munich, learning to shoot, set up tents, and how to boil drinking water at the front.[45] However, due to shortage of supplies and as yet another sign that RIR 16 was close to the bottom of the food chain of the German armed forces, the List Regiment was trained with outmoded rifles that functioned differently from the rifles that the regiment was to use once at the front.[46] For most of the men, including almost certainly Hitler, this was the first time they had touched a gun.

Hitler was typical of his regiment in that the median age of the soldiers of the List Regiment came very close to Hitler's, who was 25 when war broke out. Almost 60 per cent of soldiers were born within five years of Hitler's own birth. The oldest men were born in the 1870s but their numbers were extremely small, while 18.5 per cent were born after 1895. Hitler's unit was dominated by farmers, agricultural workers, tradesmen, and crafts-men. Close to a third worked in agriculture and around 40 per cent were tradesmen or craftsmen; 7.5 per cent were blue-collar workers, 7.7 per cent white-collar employees, 4.9 per cent ran their own businesses or were property owners, just under 2 per cent were university or high-school students, 3.6 per cent were professionals or academics, while another 3.6 per cent were non-agricultural servants or day labourers.[47] The regiment was primarily made up of recruits from Munich and southern Bavaria (80 per cent). However, only just over half of the unit's members came from Upper Bavaria itself. Hitler was not the only soldier who had grown up or lived outside Bavaria. In total 4.4 per cent came from regions outside Bavaria (of whom approximately half came from abroad).[48] More than half of the men of Hitler's regiment came from rural communities. A quarter even came from villages with fewer than 100 inhabitants. Just over one in ten soldiers came from towns of small to medium size, while a third of the members of RIR 16 lived in bigger towns and cities, the great majority of whom lived in Munich. In total two out of ten soldiers came from the Bavarian capital.[49] Many of the soldiers from the countryside and from Munich had lived in worlds far apart from each other.

Life in southern Bavaria outside Munich and the bigger towns was rural and traditional. It was a region of small towns and villages and, in the foothills of the Alps, of lonely farms or villages consisting of a handful of dairy farms, an inn, and a church. Unlike northern Bavaria or many parts of Prussia, farms continued to be small family enterprises as they had been for hundreds of years. In 1907, fewer than 40 per cent of farms in southern Bavaria used any machinery. Rural life was dominated by local farmers who were patriarchs in their communities. Life in rural Bavaria was more akin to those Sicilian villages that had given birth to the Mafia than Munich, let alone Berlin or the industrial cities of the Ruhr. More than half the Bavarian population lived in places with less than 2,000 inhabitants, compared to only about a third of the population in the entire German Empire. In Lower Bavaria almost 70 per cent of the population still worked in agriculture. Much more than was the case in the rest of Imperial Germany, people in the Bavarian countryside still lived in a world that was dominated by the local, or at best the Bavarian. Locals saw themselves as Bavarians and as people from a particular village, and as Catholics, but not predominantly as Germans. If they thought of their monarch, their Bavarian king and Mad King Ludwig's castles came to mind, not the German Emperor and the palaces of Potsdam.[50]

The population of rural regions of southern Bavaria were mostly apolitical, habitually voting for the Catholic Centre Party at every election.[51] After the outbreak of hostilities, the population not only in Himmler's Landshut but also in the countryside responded to the war with fear and anxiety. When Balthasar Brandmayer, a 22-year-old construction worker from rural Upper Bavaria who would serve with Hitler, received his call-up order in the post, his mother and sister did not rejoice but burst into tears. They were not able to utter a single encouraging word.[52] In the collective memory of the rural population of southern Bavaria negative memories of war competed with and often prevailed over the memory of the victorious war over France in 1870/1. Farmers worried about what would happen to their farms if they were called up, particularly since Russian agricultural labourers across southern Bavaria had to leave their posts after the outbreak of war. There were widespread reports of tearful wives and mothers. Some younger, unmarried men saw the outbreak of war as an opportunity to go out and see the world but the overwhelming response was one of pessimism. As a result, the Bavarian government felt compelled to plant rumours to whip up a bellicose mood, such as that the French had bombed a railway line close to Nuremberg and that there was widespread espionage. In an effort to increase support for the war among churchgoers, Catholic priests across southern Bavaria read out a letter from the Bavarian bishops during Mass telling them that the war was a defensive one that had been forced upon Germany.[53]

While life in the Bavarian countryside was thus still dominated by farming and Catholicism as it had been for hundreds of years, and while there was a relative lack of enthusiasm for war in the rural regions of Bavaria, Munich had been transformed in the late eighteenth and the nineteenth centuries into an elegant capital city. By the eve of the First World War, art deco buildings, both municipal and private, had been mushrooming, while both Liberalism and Social Democracy had been flourishing. The vote for the Social Democrats and the liberal parties was so large in Munich that even overall in Upper Bavaria, despite its rural regions that were anything but conducive to liberal or socialist political ideas, the Social Democrats received 33.6 per cent in the Reichstag election, while the different liberal parties received 17.2 per cent of the vote. Munich's art scene made it possibly the most liberal and cosmopolitan of Germany's cities. Lenin, who had lived in Munich a few years before Hitler, had been attracted by its left-wing political subculture. Under the aegis of a benevolent and—compared to existing alternatives—progressive royal house, the Munich of *fin-de-siècle* artists and of Lenin peacefully coexisted with traditional, Conservative ways of life and with a growing number of industrial workers. It was only the extreme political and economic volatility of post-war Munich that would provide explosive fodder for communal relations and thus create the conditions under which National Socialism could flourish. In the 1912 Reichstag election in Upper Bavaria no radical right-wing party received any number of votes worth speaking about. Even the Conservative Party received less than half a per cent of the vote.[54]

The majority of Hitler's comrades in the List Regiment came from the hinterland outside Munich. Under 20 per cent came from Bavaria's capital itself. Most men came from the villages and towns that lay in the hinterland of Munich and in the foothills of the Alps. The members of the regiment were from all professions and walks of life, including a good number of intellectuals and artists, such as the writers Georg Kleindienst, Josef Pflügl, and Heinrich Schnabel, and Albert Weisgerber.[55] However, claims that a great number of the men of the regiment were university students are not supported by the facts. Of the men who joined RIR 16 in 1914, less than 2 per cent were either university or high-school students.[56]

The men of the regiment, unlike Hitler, were ordinary Bavarian men. Just over 60 per cent of the men of RIR 16—unsurprisingly because of the regiment's age structure—were unmarried. Typical of southern Bavaria, but untypical of the German Empire as a whole, the overwhelming majority were Catholic (approximately 88 per cent). A very small minority were Jewish (0.8 per cent) and the rest were Protestants.[57]

In total, fifty-nine Jews would serve in the List Regiment,[58] among them three men from Ichenhausen, a picturesque southern Bavarian town of some 2,700 inhabitants. At the beginning of the war, Germans of almost all political persuasions celebrated how well and successfully Jews had integrated into mainstream German society and how willing Jews were to pull their full weight for the German war effort.[59]

To be sure, early twentieth-century Bavaria was home to some considerable low-level old-fashioned Catholic and Protestant anti-Semitism. Moreover, modern racial anti-Semitism had also started to rear its ugly head in some subsections of Bavarian society.[60] However, as made clear, for example, in an article Fridolin Solleder wrote about the history of Jewish–Gentile interaction in Lower Franconia, published in 1913, racial anti-Semitism was still confined to the fringes of Bavarian society. Solleder argued that many Jews of Lower Franconia had possessed negative traits during the middle and early modern ages, including greed and a frequent falseness of character. However, those traits, he posited, were a result of the discrimination to which Jews had been subjected, of treating Jews as foreigners in their own country. Solleder reserved his most negative words for those Christians who persecuted Jews. He detailed how the 'mob' killed 'Jewish martyrs' during the crusades and how 'the blinded and distraught public' resorted to murder during the time of the Black Death. Meanwhile, he celebrated those who had acted as 'powerful patrons of the Jews' and had undermined anti-Jewish policies. He argued that the problems that had existed for hundreds of years had been successfully resolved through the process of Jewish assimilation into German life. The nineteenth century, 'the age of the great liberation movements', he concluded, had brought the 'emancipation and civil equality' of the Jews, which allowed them, with all the talents they possessed, to contribute 'in a fruitful manner' to trade and the professions.[61]

On the balance sheet, things had indeed been moving in the right direction for the Jews of Bavaria. German Jews prided themselves on being the most assimilated and successful Jews in the world. As a symbol of their self-confidence and pride, the Jewish community of Munich had erected a magnificent synagogue in central Munich, which on its opening in 1887 had been the third biggest Jewish temple in Germany.[62]

Contrary to a long-held belief, in Imperial Germany German Jews had just as many career opportunities in the professions as well as in public life as their British counterparts across the English Channel.[63] The one sector of society into which Jews had only temporarily managed to break was the Prussian Army. A significant number of Jews had become officers in the Prussian Army during the Franco-Prussian War. However, between 1885 and 1914, no practising Jew had been promoted to the officer class (though 300 Jewish converts to Christianity had become officers including at least one general), while by 1910 France had 720 Jewish officers amongst its numbers. However, this stark Franco-Prussian contrast cannot possibly explain what was to happen to German Jews during the Third Reich. The situation of Jews in the pre-war Bavarian Army—in other words, the army in which Hitler would serve and which supposedly 'made' Hitler—and the British Army and Navy was virtually the same. Thanks to its relatively progressive, enlightened political class, Bavaria—together with Germany's other southern German states—generally afforded Jews even more oppor-tunities than the rest of the Reich. Unlike the Prussian Army, the Bavarian Army continued to have (practising) Jewish officers right up until 1914. In 1909, there were 88 Jewish officers in the Bavarian Army, while, in 1910, the combined figure for the much larger British armed forces (i.e. the Royal Navy, the Regular Army, the Militia, the Yeomanry and Volunteers, and the Reserve of Officers) was 182.[64]

In principle, in Germany Reform and secular Jews in urban, Protestant regions were the most integrated. However, the Orthodox Jews in Catholic rural regions who would serve in units such as the List Regiment defied this principle. In 1800, Ichenhausen had a higher percentage of Jews among its population than Jerusalem; by 1900, Ichenhausen still had in relative terms a larger Jewish population than New York City. Jews were heavily repre-sented in the local assembly, in prominent positions in local clubs and societies, and even in the veterans' association of the Franco-Prussian War. In 1913, the town even awarded honorary citizenship status on the chairman of the Jewish community. At the beginning of the war, the Catholic priest and the Jewish rabbi of Ichenhausen walked together from door to door to collect money for serving soldiers. The case of Ichenhausen might have been an extreme example. Yet it was an extreme, rather than an atypical example.[65] After the outbreak of war many Jews were among the most fervent supporters of the German war effort.

On 8 October, Hitler and his new comrades paraded in front of King Ludwig III of Bavaria in the Prince Arnulf Barracks in Munich, who then personally bid the men of RIR 16 farewell.[66] However, before being deployed to the front, Hitler, Weisgerber, and the other men of RIR 16 trained for ten days on the Lechfeld north of Munich, the site of the medieval battle in which Emperor Otto the Great had defeated the Magyars. During a service held on the Lechfeld, the Protestant divisional chaplain, Oscar Daumiller, who himself had served in the German Army following his university studies, told the soldiers of the List Regiment that they were about to face 'a holy war for the just cause of our people'. Daumiller also told them to be prepared 'should they be called by God to a holy death'.[67]

If anybody had thought that young Hitler and the List Regiment were ready to go into battle when Ludwig III had inspected the regiment, any such hopes were crushed on the Lechfeld. Hitler even whined about how strenuous it had been to get to the Lech Valley: 'As I told you,' Hitler wrote to Anna Popp, the wife of his landlord in Munich, 'we left Munich on Saturday. We were on our feet from 6.30 a.m. until 5 p.m. and during the march we took part in a major [exercise], all in pouring rain. We were quartered in Alling. I was put in the stables and I was wet through. Needless to say I could not sleep a wink.'[68]

Once at their training site on the Lechfeld, without having any Magyar (or British and French) warriors to face, the men of the regiment were experiencing fatigue before even reaching the front. Hitler wrote to Anna Popp that 'the first 5 days in the Lech valley were the most tiring of my whole life. Each day a longer march still, more strenuous exercises and night marches up to 42 kilometres followed by brigade manœuvres.'[69] By contrast, Ludwig Waldbott Count Bassenheim, a Bavarian aristocrat born in Jersey and an officer in the List Regiment, noted in his war diary on the same day Hitler wrote his letter that the exercises had not been particularly strenuous, but that 'discipline had grown very bad due to [the] marches and over-exertion'.[70] Once close to the front, Bassenheim would complain that the troops had not trained hard enough and had wasted their time on the Lechfeld.[71]

The only consolation was—if we are to believe the accounts of Hitler and of the official regiment history—how well received the regiment was by the local population. If true, it would be testimony of how well the public supported the regiment and the German war effort. Hitler wrote to Anna Popp that the local population had 'almost stuffed [them] with food'.[72] In the official regimental history, Franz Rubenbauer, an officer in the regiment who was also briefly regimental commander in early November 1914, similarly noted that,

> we still gratefully remember the warm welcome we received from the local population in the places where we had our living quarters. When in the afternoon the units came back to their living quarters after the exhausting daily exercises on the vast Lechfeld or from the practice firing range in the meadows of the Lech, singing marching songs with high and clear voices, old and young were out and about and marched with us. After we were dismissed for the day, they took us back into their homes, where the food waited ready for us on their stoves.[73]

Rubenbauer's post-war account is belied by Count Bassenheim's war diary. He confided to his diary that the local farmers 'are exceptionally unfriendly. Colonel List had to act with utmost firmness because we could obtain no food or heating materials at the inn.' One day, two companies were only fed half portions because local farmers had provided the regiment with rotten meat.[74]

It is common wisdom that armies plan for future wars by refighting the previous one. Ever since Germany's last major war, the Franco-Prussian War, Germans had been obsessed by the danger the *francs-tireurs*—the French partisans—had posed in 1870/1. The solution to the problem was for the officers of the List Regiment to hand out ropes to the troops. Bassenheim noted that his 'Company provided the troops with ropes to hang *franc-tireurs*; every three men receive a readily prepared noose. The ropes are heavily sought after by the men.'[75] When Bassenheim had handed out the ropes for use for *francs-tireurs*, or partisans, to inexperienced, ill-trained troops, who were trying to make up for their inexperience with a gung-ho mentality, he had, as we shall see, inadvertently set up a self-fulfilling prophecy.

2

Baptism of Fire

21 October–Early November 1914

I n the early hours of 21 October, their bags stuffed with apples, cigarettes, and candy, the men of the List Regiment left Bavaria. Many never returned. Friends and family stood on the platform as their trains left Munich's goods station.[1] The previous day, Hitler, who after the outbreak of war only corresponded with the family of his landlord and one other acquaintance but not with surviving members of his family or former friends, had written to Anna Popp that he was 'tremendously excited'.[2] The men of RIR 16 still did not know for certain where they were to be deployed, but many hoped that it would be against 'England'.[3] Soon after Britain had entered combat, 'perfidious Albion' began to be held responsible for the war. The day before the regiment left Bavaria, Hitler had written to Popp: 'I hope we shall get to England'.[4] Similarly, Weisgerber had written to his wife a few days earlier: 'It would be splendid if we could be part of the high point of the war—the invasion of England'.[5]

After Hitler's and Weisgerber's trains had pulled out of Munich, they headed north-west. Weisgerber reckoned that this indeed implied that they were to be taken to Calais, and from there across the English Channel.[6] Wherever the trains transporting the regiment stopped en route to the Belgian border, the men of the regiment were greeted by cheering crowds. In one of the trains sat Father Norbert Stumpf, a short, stocky, and well-fed Capuchin monk with a thick, black beard and a calm and serious appearance, who now was the Catholic army chaplain of Hitler's division and who, only hours before, had celebrated his forty-first birthday. In the opening paragraph of his war diary, Norbert noted with delight that on their first stop after leaving Munich they had been fed Bavarian Weisswurst and beer. Smiling women in Red Cross uniforms everywhere welcomed the men of the List Regiment and of its sister regiments.[7] This was all a great adventure for young Hitler. When his train stopped briefly in Ulm, Hitler hurriedly sent a postcard to Joseph Popp, his landlord, sending him 'best wishes from Ulm on my way to Antwerp'.[8]

Hitler reported that 'after a glorious journey down the Rhine', as they left Aachen, the last German city before the Belgian border, 'we were given an enthusiastic send-off by thousands of people, and much the same thing happened throughout our journey.'[9] Similarly, the commander of the 6th Bavarian Reserve Division to which the List Regiment was attached, Max Freiherr von Speidel, noted in his diary: 'Our train has been warmly welcomed by the population everywhere; at every stop we have been given refreshments . . . cigars, and cigarettes.'[10]

The support the local population gave to the passing trains, draped in the colours of Munich, Bavaria, and Germany, should not necessarily be taken as a sign of widespread popular enthusiasm for the war. It was support of the kind that was put on for the short period a passing train remained in a station. However, prior to the arrival and after the departure of the trains in locations along the line between Munich and the Belgian border, the mood was different. When a refreshment station for transit troops had been built in Heidelberg a few weeks before Hitler and his comrades passed through the town, Karl Hampe and Hermann Oncken, two professors of history at Heidelberg University, were disappointed by the lack of enthusiasm in Heidelberg. Hampe noted in his diary: 'Tonight I went with people from the Red Cross to the goods station, where barracks had been built for the catering of passing troops. Oncken and I were disappointed. Order and spirit [among the people] were not first class. Perhaps things are always like this during mobilization, and we simply lack any point of comparison.'[11] Rather than being an expression of enthusiasm for war, support shown to units like the List Regiment was thus meant as support for 'their boys' who were about to put their lives on the line.

As we have seen, the majority of the men of the List Regiment had not volunteered. Yet now almost three months into the war, and after several weeks of training, many were eager to get to the front to defend, as they thought, their Fatherland. As the men of RIR 16 left Bavaria, Count Bassenheim described their mood as excellent. When crossing the Rhine and passing the Niederwald Statue, an enormous statue of Germania with a sword and the crown of the German emperor in her hands, erected high above the banks of the

Rhine after the Franco-Prussian War, the troops of the List Regiment reportedly broke out into singing 'The Watch on the Rhine'.[12]

The song—which would be sung again and again at the front—was the unofficial national anthem of Imperial Germany. Today maybe best known from the famous scene in the Hollywood classic *Casablanca* in which German soldiers sing the song in Rick's Café and prompt the regular guests of the bar to chant the Marseillaise in response, its message was defensive in character. Written in the aftermath of the Napoleonic occupation of Germany, it calls Germans to be ready to defend Germany from foreign occupation, rather than to start on a quest for world domination:

> to the Rhine, to the Rhine, to the German Rhine! | . . . Firmly and devoted stands the watch, the watch on the Rhine! Through hundreds of thousands it quickly twitches, and everybody's eyes brightly flash; the German honestly, piously, and strongly, protects the sacred land. . . . As long as a drop of blaze still glows, | a fist still draws the dagger | and one arm still holds the rifle, | no enemy will here enter your shore! . . . Firmly and devoted stands the watch, | the watch on the Rhine![13]

The attitude of Bavarians towards the song perhaps best epitomizes Bavarian, German, and European society on the eve of the First World War. A militarized society it was to be sure. Yet it was a society that by and large did not actively push for war but was prepared to take up arms if called to duty when their country was under siege.[14] And the song was certainly no more militaristic than the Marseillaise, the French national anthem.

Prior to the war, anti-French feeling had not been at the core of German nationalism. The essence of pre-1914 nationalism had not been, as sometimes claimed, the creation of the 'other', that is other nations, as enemies.[15] To view pre-1914 nationalism as a mutually antagonistic force that would sooner or later make a major European war almost inevitable is to read history backwards in an attempt to make sense of the two world wars.[16] However, once war had broken out, a German defensive nationalism redefined pre-war nationalism, blocking out elements that allowed for a peaceful coexistence of the nations of Europe, and trying to make sense of the conflict. This is why the men of the List Regiment, as they sang 'The Watch on the Rhine', now focused on the cultural legacy of resistance to French invasion. They saw themselves as members of a mythical tradition following those who had, in their minds at least, tried to defend Germany against the hordes of Louis XIV when Heidelberg Castle was destroyed in the seventeenth century, against French revolutionary troops in the wake of the French Revolution, then against the Napoleonic invasion, and in what was seen as a pre-emptive defence against the perceived aggression of Napoleon III in 1870.

Britain, however, was an unexpected adversary in the war. It is sometimes forgotten that in the hundred years leading up to the outbreak of the First World War, Britain had been at war with all her major allies in the Great War (France, Russia, and the United States) but not with any of her main adversaries (Germany and Austria-Hungary). Indeed Germany and England (or Britain) had never faced each other on a battlefield prior to the First World War. Despite pre-war Anglo-German tensions, few Germans had thought that Britain would join France and Russia against Germany: hence the feeling of betrayal and outrage at Britain's declaration of war, and hence probably Hitler's hope to face Britain on the battle front. Weisgerber had already referred to the British as 'English dogs' in mid-September.[17] Moreover, where British and French POWs had been transported together to Germany in the early weeks of the war, public anger had been directed much more at the British than the French POWs to the extent that food and drink had been given to groups of travelling French POWs but denied to British soldiers.[18] When the men of the List Regiment saw a train full of British POWs while passing through Aachen, talk spread that the Bavarian troops would indeed be sent to England, which was greeted by the troops with great joy.[19]

As the List Regiment crossed the Belgian border in the early morning of 23 October and as Hitler thus left German-speaking lands for the first time in his life, troops shouted 'Hooray' and broke into song. Lights had to be kept switched off on the trains, as they were now in imminent danger of bombardment by enemy fighter planes. By the early afternoon, the troops were ordered to keep their weapons ready at all times, as *francs-tireurs* had been reported in the region they were passing through. For the next day, the trains containing the soldiers of the RIR 16 crawled through the ruins of Belgian cities.[20] Twenty years later, Ignaz Westernkirchner, who was to become one of the closest comrades of Hitler, was to remember: 'The country seemed awfully flat and monotonous; the only villages we passed were nothing but heaps of gaping ruins. Dead horses blown up like balloons lay in the ditches.'[21] Hitler himself recalled of the train ride: 'At 9 a.m. we arrived in Liège. The railway station was badly damaged. The traffic was tremendous. Army transport only, of course. At midnight

we arrived at Louvain. The whole town is a heap of rubble. Via Brussels
we went on to Dournay.'[22] Hitler wrote of this early part of the journey:

> our journey went fairly well and peacefully but then we had nothing but
> trouble. In some places the rails had been prised loose despite the closest
> watch, and then we came across an ever greater number of blown-up bridges
> and smashed railway engines. Although our train was moving at a snail's pace,
> we kept grinding to a halt more and more often. From the distance we could
> hear the monotonous roar of our heavy mortars. Towards evening we arrived
> in a fairly badly damaged suburb of Lille. We got off the train and then
> lounged about our piled arms. Shortly before midnight, we at long last
> marched into the town along an endless, monotonous road with low factory
> buildings on either side, and an endless row of sooty and smoke-blackened
> tenements.[23]

Lille, the unofficial capital of northern France, rather than the port city of
Antwerp as Hitler had anticipated, was thus the final destination for the men
of the List Regiment. It was now clear to Weisgerber and Hitler that Britain
had not been their destination after all. Hitler and his comrades, who had
grown up in the relative peace of the long nineteenth century, now saw the
destruction of war at close range for the first time in their lives. How they
interpreted what they saw was determined by their ability to empathize
with the suffering of others, of which Father Norbert was well capable and
young Hitler utterly incapable.

Occupied by the Germans since 12 October, 'Lille, and in particular the
central station, was a terrible sight', noted Father Norbert in his diary. 'The
entire train station was a shambles. The wounded lay everywhere. 1,200
houses were said to have been destroyed by the bombardment, most of
them grandiose buildings. There were burnt-out gables and smoking piles of
rubble everywhere, along with crying and begging women and children, and
withdrawn, sullen men.'[24] Equally, the Bavarian Crown Prince Rupprecht,
the commander of the Bavarian troops, felt 'compassion for the hard-hit city'
on his visit after it had fallen to the Germans.[25] Hitler, meanwhile, wrote to
Joseph Popp: 'Lille is a typical French town. Parts of it have been shot up or
burnt down by us. By and large, however, the town has suffered little.'[26]

Spy fever had erupted on both sides of the front. A few days prior to the
arrival of RIR 16 in France, the *Toronto Globe* reported that 'the shooting of
batches of [suspected German] spies takes places daily' in northern French
towns unoccupied by the Germans. 'In the last three days there have been as
many women shot as men. It is most hard for the veteran who loathes the

task of shooting women but, according to the laws of war, it must be done. They are lined up with men, often young girls or women of refinement, at the zenith of their charm and beauty.' Spy fever had soon turned into paranoia: 'So many spies have been caught in France recently that the possession of papers, apparently in good order, avails a man or woman nothing, once an accusation has been made or a suspicion levelled.'[27] Equally, Hitler's division suspected, rightly or wrongly, that it was surrounded in Lille by spies and guerrilla fighters: 'In the military hospitals, of which there are 15 in the city,' wrote Father Norbert, 'lie about 4,000 soldiers, most of them seriously wounded, but no clergymen; the French priests are not allowed to visit the injured due to fear of espionage.'[28] The Germans and the French had thus converged in their spy paranoia.

In a letter to his wife, Weisgerber, meanwhile, described how in Lille the wine flowed freely: 'Our war is still beautiful. But every day we see and hear a little bit of the real war.'[29] Lille was so packed with German soldiers that the men of Hitler's company had to sleep their first night in the city under the open sky:

> We spent the night in the courtyard of the Bourse. The pompous building has been left unfinished. Since we had to bed down with all our gear—we were on alert—and since it was freezing cold on the cobble-stones I did not sleep a wink. Next day we changed our quarters. This time we were put into a very large glass building. There was no lack of air, quite the opposite as only the iron framework had been left standing. The blast of German shells had shattered the glass into a million fragments.[30]

At night, Hitler sang with his brothers-in-arms. By day, he had a chance to explore his new surroundings: 'During the day we did a little training, visited the town and admired the huge army machine that had left its stamp on the whole of Lille and now rolled past our astonished eyes in gigantic columns.'[31]

During Hitler's third night in Lille, the men of the List Regiment were abruptly woken up. 'No one knew precisely what was happening, but we all believed it was a kind of drill. It was a very dark night,' wrote Hitler.[32] Soon Hitler and his brothers-in-arms realized that this was the real thing; they were finally going to the front. Yet before they could leave the city and start marching towards the Belgian frontier in the direction of Ypres (Jeper), they were delayed at first. The reason was that several troops had lost their way on their way to their meeting place.[33]

As the men of the regiment were soon to find out, while they were not to go to England, as Hitler and Weisgerber had hoped, at least they would face the British Expeditionary Force. In a field order from late October, the Bavarian Crown Prince Rupprecht told the soldiers of Hitler's 6th Army who their enemy was, in case there had been any doubt:

> Soldiers of the Sixth Army! We now also have the pleasure of facing the English before us, the front-line soldiers of that nation whose envy has for years been hard at work to encircle us with a ring of enemies, in order to strangle us. It is above all [to England] that we owe this bloody, terrible war. . . . let us seek retribution for such hostile cunning, for the many heavy casualties![34]

The task of the List Regiment was temporarily to join the 54th (Wurttemberg) Reserve Division and support the German assault on the British positions around the Flemish city of Ypres, just to the north of the Belgian–French border, in an effort to break through to Ypres in what would later be known as the First Battle of Ypres, or simply as 1st Ypres.

Ypres was famed for its medieval beauty, but had long been reduced to a quiet country town.[35] In strategic terms, however, a successful breakthrough at Ypres would have allowed the Germans to win what was to become known as the Race for the Sea. The German plan to move swiftly through Belgium, as the only good and viable natural route into France, and rapidly invade and defeat France before turning to Russia, had come to a standstill on the right wing of Germany's invading formation earlier in the autumn.[36] Almost all seemed lost. However, the German High Command still had one hope. At the far end of their right wing lay the Belgian coast with only weak defences. The calculation was that if German forces managed to race to the North Sea, they could still break through there, envelop enemy troops, and move rapidly towards the heart of France. The Belgians, however, thwarted this plan. They opened the floodgates at the Belgian port of Nieuwpoort at high tide on 27 October (the day the men of RIR 16 received their marching orders in Lille), flooding the lower-lying land and closing the floodgates before low tide set in.[37] The only option left for the Germans now was to try a desperate breakthrough at Ypres some 30 kilometres inland. And it was here that the List Regiment was to be thrown into battle.

After marching for a full day towards the front from Lille, Hitler was still restless: 'At 9 p.m. we were handed our rations,' he reported.

I couldn't sleep, alas. There was a dead horse four paces in front of my palliasse. It looked as if it had been dead for two weeks at least. The beast was half decomposed. Just behind us a German howitzer battery fired two shells over our heads into the dark night every 15 minutes. They kept screaming and whistling through the air, followed by two dull thuds in the far distance. Everyone of us listened out for them. We had never heard anything like it before. And while we lay pressed one against the other whispering and looking up into the starry sky, the distant noise drew closer and closer, and the individual thuds of the guns came faster and faster until finally they merged into one continuous roar. Each one of us could feel his blood pound in his veins. We were told the English were making one of their nocturnal attacks. Unsure of what was really going on, we all waited anxiously for the next move. Then everything died down until finally the hellish din stopped completely, except for our own battery which kept spitting its iron salutes into the night every 15 minutes.[38]

Contrary to the post-war portrayal of the regiment as well disciplined,[39] even with only a few miles to go to the front, the men of the List Regiment still showed no sign of being so. Count Bassenheim recorded in despair: 'The indiscipline happily acquired on the Lechfeld finds its expression now as the men try to kill the chickens of Le Halois with their bayonets, all the while running a high risk of injuring each other. I have forcefully restored order and as punishment I will have the men pay the farmers for the chicken.'[40] Later in the day, after a messenger on a horse had been shot and injured reportedly by a *franc-tireur*, the regiment received a divisional order to arrest all locals in the village in which they were staying that night.[41] The men of Hitler's regiment were eager to hang them. Yet to the disappointment of Bassenheim and his troops, they were not allowed to hang them.[42] But why did the men of RIR 16 feel the urge to go on a killing spree in the first place? And how typical of the German armed forces were Hitler's comrades in this behaviour? Does the willingness to execute the Belgian villagers suggest that pre-war German culture and political attitudes had set the men of the List Regiment on a path of destruction and had infused them with a deeply ingrained hatred of their French and British adversaries?

By the time the List Regiment arrived at the front and in contrast to the first weeks of the conflict, German military authorities were trying to curtail excesses in counter-guerrilla warfare. They thus stopped the men of the List Regiment from going on a killing spree of suspected *francs-tireurs*. However, as we have seen, the rudimentary and hurried military training the men of the List Regiment had received in Bavaria had conditioned them to expect encounters with *francs-tireurs* as soon as they entered the combat zone. In the first few weeks of the war, the German armed forces had indeed used excessive force to quell the involvement in the war of *francs-tireurs* or what we would call today guerrillas, partisans, irregular troops, or unlawful enemy combatants. The German counter-insurgency strategy included the summary executions of illegal combatants as well as of hostages, the burning of the houses of suspected guerrillas, and deportations. The Germans also used human shields in an attempt to keep pace with a hectic timetable. In the event, in at least 130 episodes German troops killed more than ten Belgian or French civilians each. Most of these episodes happened during an eleven-day period from 18 to 28 August and they occurred in Belgium rather than in France. In total, German troops killed an estimated 6,400 civilians and destroyed between 15,000 and 20,000 buildings. The rationale behind this heavy-handed approach was to prevent a repetition of the Franco-Prussian War of 1870–1, in which approximately 60,000 *francs-tireurs*, or guerrillas, had tied up a quarter of all German troops outside Paris, resulting in up to a thousand German casualties. In fact, objectively speaking, German troops encountered only very few irregular troops in 1914. However, the expectation of encountering guerrilla fighters made them see *francs-tireurs* everywhere, with lethal consequences. In many cases of 'friendly fire' directed by German troops on other German troops or on occasions when German troops could not work out the direction of enemy fire, the existence of illegal enemy combatants was immediately assumed with devastating and disastrous results. To make matters worse, the Belgian Garde Civique—or home guard—that had been deployed particularly during the first few days of the war (and thus immediately prior to the eleven-day period in which most atrocities took place) did indeed not wear regular uniforms. Moreover, the Garde Civique lacked sufficient numbers of tunics, armbands, and national cockades to mark new volunteers as even belonging to the Garde Civique.[43] The willingness of the men of the List Regiment to liquidate the inhabitants of an entire village was thus well in line with German attitudes at the beginning of the First World War.

The reason why Hitler and his comrades did not become grass-root perpetrators of the summary execution or hanging of civilians was due to one simple fact: namely that the German armed forces had realized that the situation had got out of hand and that the reports of German conduct had had a devastating effect on public opinion in the United States and other neutral states. Yet the question remains why Hitler's comrades were so ready to participate in war atrocities? And why were German counter-insurgency measures so heavy-handed?

We will not be able to answer these crucial questions and thus to take our story forward without briefly looking at whether the behaviour of Hitler and his comrades was part of an evolving German national and military culture that was becoming ever more radical, ruthless, and 'absolute'.

The standard answer to the questions raised here is to blame a combination of situational and cultural factors for the growing violence. There is not much dispute about the situational factors at play here, such as the nervousness and anxiety of hastily mobilized, largely untrained civilians, panic, or the slippery slope from requisitioning to looting and pillaging. More problematic are the cultural factors that supposedly interacted with situational ones and generated a lethal dynamic which is said to have fuelled the atrocities. These cultural variables, which are claimed to have produced a delusional and self-induced paranoia about the existence of *franc-tireurs*, were said to be a deeply ingrained anti-Catholicism, a demonizing 'war culture', and a culturally produced fear of invasion, racism, and social Darwinism directed at a predominantly Catholic Belgian and French population.[44]

If only troops from Protestant regions of Prussia or Franconia had been involved in the massacres, an explanation based on anti-Catholic feeling would have potentially something to offer.[45] However, this fails to explain why the List Regiment, composed predominantly of Catholics (85 per cent of the men of Hitler's company were Catholic), would be eager to kill and humiliate other Catholics. Another problem with the conventional explanation is that even the supposedly 'predominantly Protestant' troops who—according to the standard work on the subject—were driven by a 'markedly anti-Catholic' sentiment (the 1st, 2nd, 3rd, and 4th Armies and the Wurttemberg units of the 5th Army)[46] were not predominantly Protestant at all. In fact, an equal number of Protestants and Catholics lived in the recruiting area of the 1st Army, while the 2nd Army included not only North German Protestant troops but also the troop contingents from Westphalia and the Rhineland, where almost two thirds of the population was Catholic. Even in Wurttemberg, 30 per cent of the population was Catholic.[47] Due to the existence of conscription, the 1st–5th armies thus consisted of a mix of Catholic and Protestant soldiers, rather than being a more or less homogeneous Protestant unit out to target Catholics.

Moreover, resorting to cultural explanations such as anti-Catholicism, social Darwinism, and the demonizing of the enemy to account for the

German atrocities in 1914 does not explain why, with the notable exception of Kalisz on the German–Russian border,[48] no large-scale atrocities
took place on the Eastern Front in predominantly Catholic Poland. Nor
does it explain why social Darwinism did not translate into widespread
anti-Slavic atrocities in the East. Furthermore, the existence of a deep-
seated cultural drive behind the 1914 atrocities would not explain why, by
late 1914, atrocities had all but ceased. If German culture cannot then
sufficiently explain why the men of RIR 16 wanted to hang Belgian
civilians on their arrival at the front, how do we make sense of the
behaviour of Hitler's brothers-in-arms?

One answer is to point to the evolution of a specifically institutional
culture of the German military that is said to have led time and time again
to atrocities and 'absolute destruction'. The idea here is that cultural-
ideological factors such as anti-Catholicism, hyper-nationalism, or social
Darwinism mattered relatively little. Rather, what counted was an institutional culture within the German armed forces that supposedly always
pushed for the most extreme measures. The starting point for this proposition is the statement that all military institutions will push for the most
extreme of alternatives, following the developmental logic of military
culture. The argument is that the military is driven by the power of its
own potential, an inherent logic which, if unchecked, pushes it to extremes,
always to invoke military necessity, to the repeated and unlimited use of
violence, towards an idealization of risk, violence, and fear. The almost
inevitable result, if the military is left to its own devices, is the emergence of
policies of 'absolute destruction', 'annihilation', of decisive victories, and of
total or 'final solutions'. In the German case, these results were the 1914
atrocities in Belgium, the massacre of the Herero and Nama in German
South West Africa in 1904/5, the Schlieffen plan (the strategic plan for a
two-front war involving a defeat of France with lightning speed before
Germany would turn towards Russia), the harsh occupation and scorched-
earth policies during the First World War, the German instigation and
condoning of the mass killings of Armenians in the eastern reaches of the
Ottoman Empire in 1917, and ultimately Nazi genocide and warfare.[49]

Was the mindset of Hitler's comrades thus different from that of the
soldiers they were to face in their preparedness to participate in a massacre?
Not necessarily, if the theory of Germany's military institutional culture as
the instigator of 'absolute destruction' is correct. Germany was different
from other countries, the theory tells us, for one simple reason that had little,

if anything, to do with ideology or political convictions: a lack of civilian oversight of the German military. While the political sphere and the public in other countries supposedly stopped the armed forces from gravitating towards 'absolute destruction' and 'final solutions', the German armed forces were constitutionally autonomous and independent in Imperial Germany. They were thus isolated from criticism and external challenges. A good example of this, we are told, is the different way Britain and Germany dealt with the maltreatment of Dutch settlers in the Boer War and the massacre of the Herero and Nama.[50] In fact, the comparison reveals something rather different, indeed something that helps us understand why the List Regiment had become so close to perpetrating a massacre: on one level, the comparison is highly problematic as it compares a case of ill-treatment of white European settlers with one of natives.[51] Yet on another level, the comparison is very instructive in explaining German behaviour in general, as well as the conduct of the List Regiment in particular: the main difference between the Boer War and German South West Africa does not lie, as claimed, in the responses to the two crises (which were ultimately very similar) but in the different timescale in which the crises unfolded and in which German and British authorities responded to them.[52]

The real difference lay in the speedy conduct of military affairs in the German case. Even though the reversal of German policy against the Herero, following an outcry in political circles and the press, came, in fact, much faster than in the British case, it ultimately came too late as Lothar von Trotha, the German general in charge of the campaign against the Herero, had already managed to kill a large percentage of the Herero population. Germany was thus not different because of a purported lack of civilian oversight of the military but because of her speedy conduct of war.

The speedy German conduct of war was a result, not of German constitutional arrangements, but of Prussia's historical experience of relative financial and military weakness and of its geographical position in the heart of Europe. The lessons of Prussia's emergence and survival as the smallest of Europe's great powers since the seventeenth century was that Prussia could only win wars against powers with superior financial resources and manpower if she defeated them swiftly and if she developed tactical and operational supremacy. The inherent logic of this policy, as opposed to the logic of National Socialism, was the rapid annihilation of an opponent's military capability rather than of the opponent itself.[53]

In addition, the German military had to face a parliament that was progressively less willing to grant the armed forces the levels of funding military planners thought that they required. By contrast, a more militaristic German society would have thus ironically created a military that would have felt less inclined to go for extreme measures.[54]

This is what conditioned the Schlieffen plan; this is also what conditioned the German atrocities in the late summer of 1914, and what almost turned the men of the List Regiment into perpetrators of a massacre. In other words, the perception of the existence of Belgian guerrilla warfare implied that the German armed forces would be held up which, in turn, endangered a swift Prussian-style victory. The results were extreme and harsh measures as the seemingly only fast and effective way of dealing with guerrilla warfare and of creating a deterrent for the future.[55] Nevertheless, the policy of resorting to extreme violence as a counter-insurgency strategy during the invasion of France and Belgium was too short-lived for the theory of the German Army always going for 'absolute destruction' to be true. The policy should not have been stopped until the 'final solution' of the destruction of partisans and a German breakthrough through French and British lines had been achieved. Yet the opposite was the case; the atrocities were curtailed.

What, then, explains the urge of the men of RIR 16 in late October to hang the population of a small Belgian village? It was the convergence of six factors which we can only lay out here but not discuss in detail. The first was the expectation of guerrilla warfare that was borne out of the historical experience of 1870/1 (and in the case of the List Regiment had been instilled in the minds of its soldiers during the rushed training on the Lechfeld); the second, the perceived need for a swift annihilation of France's military capability (but not of France or the French), borne out of Prussia's historical experiences; the third, Germany's relative military and financial weakness; the fourth, the fact that most men of RIR 16 had been ill-trained as soldiers; the fifth, 'friendly fire' that was perceived as enemy fire; and the sixth, stronger than anticipated Belgian resistance during the German advance as well as the brief deployment of tens of thousands of Belgian soldiers in unusual uniforms (or no uniforms at all) that created a perfect storm. It was the kind of tempest that would almost have turned the men of the List Regiment into grass-root perpetrators of the massacre of civilians. However, whether it was just a question of time before Hitler and his comrades became involved in atrocities against civilians and enemy soldiers, and whether thus there was to be a straight line from the conduct of the List Regiment to Hitler's subsequent beliefs, still remained to be seen. As yet, on 28 October, it was time for them to prepare themselves for their first battle.

On 28 October, the troops were still in exuberant spirits. That day, they also tried to shoot down a plane, not realizing that the plane at which they were aiming was in fact a German one.[56] Father Norbert, meanwhile, reported that they were surrounded by spies: 'Because the enemy received intelligence from the church tower, through signs and the chiming of the hour and the direction of the hand, the clergymen were arrested and were not allowed to enter the rectory again.' He himself, in his long brown monk's habit, which he preferred over the uniforms available to army chaplains, was mistaken for a spy and *franc-tireur*. 'My accoutrement, or monk's habit, excited everywhere a great commotion amongst friends and foe alike. I was even to be arrested as a spy as a result of my dress. For five hours, I was closely watched by a constable and 15 men, until the mistake was cleared up.'[57]

As night fell, the troops of the List Regiment no doubt wished they had been allowed to kill the chickens from the previous day, for the field kitchen unit had been incompetent enough to get lost during the day. The men of Hitler's regiment thus had to go to sleep hungry on the eve of their first battle.[58]

In the early hours of 29 October, 349 men of the List Regiment woke up for the last time in their lives. Awakening to a still dark night, they marched silently for four hours towards the flickering light of burning villages in the combat zone. Many men were eagerly awaiting their initiation into combat. For others, the anticipation of battle, the stress, and the heavy load they had to carry was just too much. Quite a few of them suddenly stumbled to one side and let themselves fall into the roadside ditch.[59]

As dawn approached, the men still could not see. They were surrounded by heavy fog, with a visibility of less than 40 metres. The troops went into battle still wearing their cotton hats and rucksacks.[60] The good news was that new supplies of the Gewehr 98, the standard battle rifle of the German armed forces, had finally arrived three days before Hitler and his comrades left Bavaria. However, it was only good news for the British troops whom the men of RD 6 were going to face during their first day of battle, for as Bassenheim confided to his diary, the men of the regiment did not have any clue about how to use the Gewehr 98.[61]

Around 6 a.m., Hitler and his comrades reached their destination. They assembled behind the top of a small hill just behind the front. As Hitler loaded his rifle and attached a bayonet to it, he was surrounded by fresh German graves on top of which lay the helmets of the fallen soldiers—a clear sign that finally Hitler's first war had begun. Fridolin Solleder, who fought in 12th Company, later recalled that his company leader sent them off into battle with the words: 'Men, we must attack! Conduct yourselves bravely! Good luck!' The objective for the List Regiment was first to get past the hill, then to face the enemy in the hollow beyond, and finally to fight their way up the next hill. The primary goal was to throw the British out of the Flemish village of Gheluvelt on top of the hill and to break through towards Ypres.[62] Gheluvelt, with its eighteenth-century castle, lay a few kilometres to the east of Ypres on the Menin road, the street that ran straight from the German positions to Ypres. The German armed forces put all their effort into breaking through the enemy lines here. Kaiser Wilhelm was waiting a short distance behind the front, ready to enter Ypres in triumph.[63]

Probably in an attempt to ensure that the men of RIR 16 would readily advance, they had been told, as a soldier from 11th Company wrote home, that 'the Englishmen do not have any ammunition left, and their positions would have to be attacked today'.[64] Hitler and his comrades, meanwhile, could hardly make out where their opponents were. Bassenheim noted: 'We can barely see anything of our own troops, or of the enemy because of the fog'.[65] Not only was the vision of the men of the List Regiment impaired by the heavy fog but the landscape, dotted with hedges, fields, little forests, farm buildings, and the buildings of the village, made it well nigh impossible to see the British. As Weisgerber wrote home, in order to advance they had to squeeze through holes in thick hedges across dead bodies .[66] Adolf Meyer, who served in 11th Company, later recalled that he had to storm past 'mortally wounded comrades, and the torn cadavers of horses and cattle'.[67]

When the regiment came under artillery fire, still a good distance from the British positions, Bassenheim speculated that the fire had been directed at them by those locals whom they had not been allowed to hang the previous day.[68] In fact, the British knew of the impending attack because they had intercepted a German radio message the previous afternoon.[69]

Once the List Regiment started to attack the British positions, shells started to rain down on Hitler and his comrades. Yet an awesome barrage of fire from the Germans allowed the regiment to advance.[70] Early in the battle, Ludwig Klein of 11th Company smoked one of his last two 'Münchner Havanna' cigars, as if he were a convict eating his last meal before his execution. However, as yet the shelling could do nothing to dampen the high spirits of Klein and his fellow soldiers from RIR 16.[71] They still thought that all this would be jolly good fun. Hitler would later claim that, as shrapnel was exploding around his comrades, they shouted 'a wild "Hurray" ... in response to this first greeting of Death.'[72] Weisgerber reported: 'It started up again right away, with "Hurrays" across the fields.'[73] Hitler's claim is also supported by a diary entry of Count Bassenheim, who recorded of the first shelling in his diary that 'the troops enjoy themselves and joke about the grenades that come down everywhere around us.'[74] The behaviour described here might well be understood as a release of the tensions and anxieties that had built up in the run-up to the battle. One might also interpret the jokes of the men of the List Regiment as a coping mechanism for dealing with fear through gallows humour rather than any sign of confidence.

Due to an order the troops of the regiments of RD 6 had received, there is good reason to believe that the shouting of 'Hurray' in the battle by the men of the List Regiment should not be taken as evidence either for or against the existence of enthusiasm among the men of RIR 16. The chanting of 'Hurray' was, in fact, not necessarily a sudden and genuine expression of the feelings and attitudes of the soldiers of the List Regiment; Hitler and his comrades were under orders to shout 'Hurray' as soon as they entered enemy positions.[75]

The men of the regiment recklessly charged forward. As they crossed the British trenches they failed to check whether the trenches had already been cleared, which resulted in British soldiers shooting them from both the front and from behind.[76] The officer in charge of Klein's platoon kept on shouting: 'Jump up. March—March!'[77] At some point when his company was ordered to move backwards, Weisgerber, clearly ignoring the order, shouted at his men: 'Stay, fire!' He recalled: 'There were about a hundred men all around me who followed my order and opened rapid fire on the Englishmen.'[78] However, the fact that men kept on charging forward, not turning round, was in part due to the fact that they could not bear the thought of having to look into the faces of their comrades. Weisgerber told his sister: 'It was terrifying the way my comrades fell all around me with ghastly injuries. I couldn't face any of it, so I kept looking forward and never backward.'[79]

Hitler would later claim in *Mein Kampf* that amidst close-quarter fighting they heard soldiers chanting what would become the German national anthem in 1922: 'Deutschland, Deutschland über alles, über Alles in der Welt'.[80] a song that would send shudders across the world from 1939 to 1945. Hitler claimed that 'with a burning love of the homeland in their hearts and a song on their lips, our young regiment went into action as if going to a dance.'[81] While there is indeed some evidence that German soldiers sang patriotic songs at the front early in the war,[82] Hitler's claim that they sang 'Deutschland, Deutschland über alles' is not credible. In no contemporary descriptions of the battle, nor in a 1915 pamphlet about the List Regiment containing detailed battle reports about 1st Ypres, is there any reference to the song.[83] Even in the two letters that Hitler wrote in December and February to acquaintances in Munich that describe the battle in great detail (and in far more detail than in *Mein Kampf*), there is no reference to the song.[84] The only reference to soldiers singing during the battle is Solleder's account in the official regimental history. However, here the reference is to 'The Watch on the Rhine' and the claim is that soldiers sang the song to recognize each other in the chaos of the battle,[85] a practice that was also used by the sister regiment of the List Regiment.[86] Similarly, according to a late 1915 account, soldiers from the List Regiment sang 'The Watch on the Rhine' during the first ceremony during which Iron Crosses were awarded on 8 November 1914.[87] Meanwhile, in the 1932 report of the same event from the official regimental history, the song had mutated into 'Deutschland, Deutschland über alles'.[88]

Hitler's claim in *Mein Kampf* and the account which appeared in the official 1932 regiment history, according to which enthusiastic young German volunteers marched into machine-gun salvos at Langemarck (the German term for 1st Ypres) with 'Deutschland, Deutschland über alles' on their lips, as they were mown down by British machine guns, have to be understood as stemming from the post-war nationalist myth.[89]

The good mood among the Bavarians did not last long. As they ran across the fields outside Gheluvelt, casualties were mounting. A British machine-gun squad based inside the windmill of Gheluvelt had a field day gunning down members of the List Regiment,[90] as had British soldiers who, from the cover of a tobacco field just outside the village, shot the advancing Bavarian soldiers one by one.[91] However, due to the acute shortage of machine guns in the British Expeditionary Force, most of the slaughter of German soldiers in 1st Ypres was a result of rifle fire,[92] a fact that Hitler chose not to mention.

In a letter to Ernst Hepp, an acquaintance from Munich, Hitler wrote that he and his comrades did not have any protection against British fire: 'Because we had no cover, we simply had to press on. Our captain was in the lead now. Then men started to fall all around me. The English had turned their machine guns on us. We flung ourselves down and crawled through a gully.'[93] Throughout the day, the men of the regiment would now be involved in man-to-man combat, often with bayonets and rifles used as clubs.[94] In Hitler's letter to his acquaintance in Munich, this all sounded very heroic and victorious: 'We crossed the fields at lightning speed and after many bloody hand-to-hand skirmishes we cleared the lot of them out of their trenches. Many came out with their hands up. Those who did not surrender were mown down. And so we cleared trench after trench.'[95]

The reality was less heroic. The Bavarians benefited from the fact that their opponents—units from the York Regiment, 1st Coldstream Guards, 1st Black Watch, 1st Grenadier Guards, and 2nd Gordon Highlanders—[96] had run out of ammunition and energy after weeks of combat. However, in man-to-man combat, the men of the List Regiment with their two months of training, no battle experience, and cotton hats were still no match for tired but experienced professional British soldiers. Hitler claimed that on 29 October, 'we lost nearly all our officers and our company was only left with [illegible word] vice-sergeant majors'.[97] He also stated that he was the only soldier of the group (*Haufen*) with which he fought who survived the day.[98] This was a huge exaggeration. In fact, the total number of soldiers from Hitler's 1st Company killed on 29 October was 13—barely more than a squad. This means that if all the members of Hitler's squad other than him had died that day, all the other squads of his company would hardly have lost a man, which is extremely unlikely.[99] At any rate, it is unlikely that Hitler survived because of his superior combat abilities. He was rather a weak young man with scant military training, who had been rejected for military service by the Austrian authorities because of his poor physique less than a year prior to the outbreak of the war (they had eventually caught up with him after his attempt to dodge the draft). Hitler thus almost certainly just tried to stay alive, knowing when to duck, rather than attempting to fell any battle-hardened Highlanders.

In his letter, Hitler claimed that when, after several hours of combat, he and his comrades had found the Major in charge of them—Julius Graf von Zech, the former Governor of German-Togo[100]—'lying on the ground with his chest torn wide open, and a heap of bodies all round him', they had been 'boiling with rage'. Hitler maintained that all of them had yelled at Zech's adjutant, Lieutenant Bernhard Piloty, the son of a prominent professor of law, who was the only officer still around: ' "Lieutenant, lead us into the attack." . . . And so on we went to the left of the wood, for we couldn't possibly make it on the road. 4 times we advanced only to be thrown back.'[101] This was most probably an example of Hitler boasting and embellishing a story more than three months after the event. Evidence from the day of the battle suggests that, after several hours of fighting, with many casualties, the men of the List Regiment found that their nerves did not allow them to fight the war that they wanted to fight. Their baptism of fire was indeed not like the one they had fondly imagined during their training marches through the Lechfeld.

After witnessing the death of his best friend, Eugen Roth's attitude towards the war was transformed. While earlier in the day he had willingly charged forward, Roth now just threw himself to the ground and waited for the battle to end.[102] When, towards evening, Count Bassenheim ordered his company to go forward again, he had to give the order no fewer than three times before his men began to move.[103] Furthermore, during the battle, several men of Hitler's 1st Batallion went AWOL and only returned to the regiment a week or so after the end of the battle.[104]

The British troops who were trying to thwart the advance of the List Regiment on 29 October received unsolicited help from other German units: many men of the List Regiment were killed by 'friendly fire'. The reason for this was that other German troops had mistaken the men of RIR 16 as British troops because of their grey cotton hats.[105] As Hans Raab from 12th Company, who would later be caught in a gas attack with Hitler in 1918, recalled in 1939: 'It was the first black day for us, when our Wurttembergers and Saxons mistook us as English troops because we had been put into battle in the front line and because we wore Landsturm [i.e. units comprising untrained conscripts and very old reservists] hats with a [grey] cover (just like the List Regiment as they marched into battle). They mistook us for the enemy and we were shot at by them from behind, hence the great number of casualties.'[106]

That any men of the List Regiment survived the first day of battle was due to the shortcomings of the British, which rivalled those of RIR 16. At times, the British troops fighting in the vicinity of Gheluvelt and the List

Regiment seemed to have been competing to be the more ineffectual and incompetent. The British troops were dug into defences and trenches that were unconnected in and around the village. There was virtually no communication between the different contingents. Moreover, two machine guns that had been supposed to keep the Bavarians at bay jammed, and a large number of cartridges that had been issued to the British troops at Gheluvelt were too big and did not fit into their rifles. Furthermore, the artillery had only nine shells per gun. With the battle already fully under way, the reserves of the 1st Grenadier Guards who were stationed close to the village were sent back to the rear for breakfast since the Grenadier Guards did not know what was going on.[107]

Following the first day of battle, at the close of which Hitler and the men of his company had to move backwards, 'crawling slowly, flat on the ground',[108] the List Regiment fought at Gheluvelt and a neighbouring village for another three days. By the end of the second day of combat, which was rainy and cold, Hitler's battalion had fought its way halfway up the hill to Gheluvelt. Yet his battalion was barely still the size of a company. Its new commander, Captain Franz Rubenbauer, argued in vain on the evening of 30 October that the men of Hitler's battalion were utterly exhausted. Continuing the attack the following day, he argued, would surely result in the death of most of his men.[109] Rubenbauer was ignored, as listening to him would have meant an admission that Germany had lost the Race for the Sea and that there would be no breakthrough towards Paris. The battle had to continue, and continue it did.

On 31 October, the men of the 3rd Battalion of RIR 16, in a joint effort with Wurttemberg and Saxon troops, managed in savage close-quarter combat to occupy Gheluvelt. Later in the day, the 3rd Battalion was caught by surprise, resulting in many casualties, when suddenly troops of the 2nd Worcesters tried to retake the park of Gheluvelt Castle, lying just outside the village. A British Major later recalled the grounds of the castle being 'littered with bodies and debris of equipment, rifles, caps and helmets of the discomforted enemy'.[110] The day's casualties included the commander of RIR 16, Colonel Julius List, who was killed while entering the park of Gheluvelt Castle, as well as the regimental adjutant, Lieutenant Philipp Schnitzlein, who was injured.[111] Hitler and the men of his battalion had been luckier. While their comrades from 3rd Battalion were fighting from house to house, Hitler and the men of 1st Battalion spent the attack on Gheluvelt inside the relative safety of a former British trench outside of the park of Gheluvelt Castle.[112]

Gheluvelt was now under German control, but the German objective to take Ypres was never to materialize. The British would later refer to the fighting around Gheluvelt between 29 and 31 October as the 'Three Great Days',[113] realizing that German success at Gheluvelt could have changed the outcome of the war but that the British had withstood the Bavarian-Saxon-Wurttemberg attack. The front now stretched all the way from the Swiss border to the English Channel. By 11 November, the front near Gheluvelt had advanced not more than 3 kilometres towards Ypres. There it would more or less remain until at least the second half of 1917. Static warfare had begun.

After the first few days of battle, Oscar Daumiller, the Protestant chaplain of RD 6, was overwhelmed by the horrors he had seen. He was also awed to observe how profoundly combat had changed the men of Hitler's regiment and its sister units: 'It is horrible to see the torments, the indescribable injuries; it is horrible to see how the strife that has not gone on for long yet has shattered the hearts [of the troops].' Yet Daumiller desperately tried to find meaning in all the horrors of war, noting: 'It is, however, joyful to see how they all have a longing for God. . . . The devotion with which they all listen to the prayers is beautiful to see. . . . Again and again one hears the words: We will gladly endure everything, if only it means that our Fatherland will be safe.'[114]

During the battle, the troops of RD 6 had experienced a steep learning curve as to how they viewed their opponent, concluding, as Father Norbert noted in his diary, that 'the Englishmen are surprisingly brave and skilled soldiers'. The result was that neither side had benefited from the battle: 'One moment our troops went forward, the next they had to go back.'[115] That did not stop Hitler from selling the battle as a triumph. 'We beat the English,' he claimed in a letter on 3 December.[116] Similarly, the regimental commander Colonel Julius List had announced on 29 October, the evening of the debacle at Gheluvelt: 'Enemy thrown out of all his positions, several hundred prisoners.'[117] The List Regiment was desperate to sell its failure as a triumph lest the casualties of the first four days of battle appeared to have been in vain. And the casualties had been staggering.

Weisgerber wrote to his wife: 'Half the regiment is dead or wounded.'[118] According to Hitler, casualties had run even higher. 'By the end of the fourth day of fighting,' he wrote, 'our regiment had been reduced from 3,600 to 611 men. For all that, we beat the English.' This amounted to an 83 per cent casualty rate.[119] Hitler was not far off the mark with his numbers: in fact the regiment had been reduced by roughly 75 per cent from approximately 3,000 to 725, and the number of officers from 25 to 4.[120] According to Adolf Meyer, the regiment had been reduced to the size of a battalion.[121] Weisgerber, who was now 36 years old, still believed that ultimately Germany would win the war.[122] He wrote to his wife that he was coping well with the war: 'I endure everything as well as the youngest man, maybe even better. Hopefully it will continue this way. Now two days rest. Then back under the free sky with its shell fire.'[123] Yet to his friends he wrote less sanitized letters. He told one friend that he had to endure 'four terrible days', concluding: 'What I have experienced would be enough.'[124] To another friend, he worried about how many men were still to die in the war and what lay ahead.[125]

The high casualty rate among the men of the List Regiment resulted, of course, from injuries rather than from deaths. Among the injured were Hans Raab, Arthur Rödl, the 16-year-old war volunteer from Munich, and Fridolin Solleder, who had been hit in the stomach by a bullet. Lucky ones like Count Bassenheim had simply fallen sick and were sent home. Ludwig Klein wrote home that he was taken from hospital to hospital in Lille as all of them were hopelessly overflowing with the casualties of 1st Ypres. As all the drinking water from the wells in the region had been depleted, dying and thirsty injured soldiers from the RIR 16 now had to drink water that looked like liquid manure.[126]

Their baptism of fire had been totally different from what the men of the List Regiment had expected. Nearly a quarter of all German losses in 1914 occurred at 1st Ypres.[127] On the first day alone 349 men of the List Regiment died but the remaining days of 1st Ypres were no less bloody. By 24 November, the end of 1st Ypres, as many as 725 men of the regiment—or approximately one in four men—had died. Hitler, though, was still alive. Hitler's survival was in part due to his assignment to 1st Company. Had he joined any of the companies of 3rd Battalion, he would have been twice as likely to die during the first seven days of combat. Had he been put with Ludwig Klein in 11th Company, the chances of him today being buried in some grave in Flanders and of a dramatically different twentieth century would have even been three times higher than the odds he faced through his service in 1st Company.[128] The Highlanders of the Black Watch and the Coldstream servicemen had missed their golden opportunity to kill Hitler on the List Regiment's first day of battle.

Soon Hitler's position in the regiment was to change in a way that would set him apart from the front-line soldiers of RIR 16. By the end of 1st Ypres it was still unclear whether the experience of seeing hundreds of their comrades killed or injured by British servicemen was to lead to a brutalization and politicization of the men of RIR 16. At the height of the Second World War, Hitler, at any rate, would claim that it was this experience that made him start to believe 'that life is a constant horrible struggle'.[129]

3
Two Tales of One Christmas
Early November 1914–31 December 1914

P resents kept on arriving at the front in the days leading up to Christmas 1914. They were a sign that the war would not be over by Christmas, as soldiers had imagined on the outbreak of hostilities in August. German military authorities had grown increasingly worried over how the men of the List Regiment, as well as their comrades along the Western Front, would react to this blow to their expectations and dreams. Yet at first it seemed that the worries were unwarranted.

After weeks of wet weather, Christmas Eve had brought a sharp frost and had cleared the air. The men of the List Regiment—survivors of 1st Ypres as well as new reinforcements—were thrilled that they could spend Christmas, if not with their loved ones at home in Bavaria, then at least not in the trenches but in the Dutch-speaking Belgian village of Messines (Mesen). Lying to the south of Ypres, Messines lay on top of a low ridge overlooking the positions from which the regiment had faced British and French troops since the end of 1st Ypres in late November. A few hundred metres outside the village lay the rather appropriately named Bethlehem Farm which had housed the command post of regimental HQ the previous month. Hitler described the outskirts of Messines as 'partly flat and partly undulating and covered with countless hedges and straight rows of trees'.[1]

For centuries, Messines had been dominated by an imposing medieval monastery which had been turned into an orphanage in 1492 and which Hitler sketched in late 1914 (see Plate 3).[2] In Hitler's words, 'Messines is a village of 2,400 inhabitants, or rather it was a village, for now nothing is left of it except an enormous heap of ash and rubble.'[3] The combat of the previous weeks and months had indeed reduced Messines and its monastery to rubble. Father Norbert fittingly referred to the village as 'the ruins of Messines'.[4] However, compared to the trenches, Messines seemed like paradise. After their sister regiment, the 17th Bavarian Reserve Infantry Regiment, had relieved them the previous day amidst light snow, the men had found shelter in the cellars of bombed and burnt-out houses. As night fell over Messines on Christmas Eve, which for Germans is the most important day of their Christmas celebrations, three companies gathered in the ruins of the village's former monastery. There they recreated some of the magic of the traditional Bavarian Christmas celebrations, gathering round a festively decorated and lit Christmas tree. Also present at the Christmas celebrations, under their feet in the crypt of the former monastery, were the remains of the mother-in-law of the last successful invader of their adversaries' country, William the Conqueror. After singing 'Silent Night' and praying that Christmas would bring peace, the men of RIR 16 opened presents donated by companies, clubs, schools, and ordinary citizens from Munich in a room adjacent to the monastery's cloister, while they drank the Bavarian beer that Munich breweries had shipped to the front.[5] As Weisgerber opened his present, he became very excited: 'Every package was a success,' he reported. 'We had a Christmas tree as well and the mood was thus really festive. We have sparkling wine here too, almost every day. What else could one want?'[6] On Christmas Day, it was the turn of some of the remaining companies to join in the festivities.[7]

By all accounts, Adolf Hitler was highly critical of religion. Unlike almost all of his comrades, he did not drink and did not particularly like receiving presents from friends and family.[8] He had indeed long lost touch both with his family, including his sister Paula, and with friends from his childhood and youth.[9] Yet there is no reason to believe that he would not have joined in the Christmas festivities in the ruins of Messines's former monastery.[10]

Hitler and men like him had accepted the reality that war would not end as swiftly as had been predicted. Victories on the Eastern Front, celebrated with beer shipped in from Munich,[11] had helped to fuel their continued morale. Unreservedly still supporting the war, they had, in many cases, volunteered for the war, been prepared to kill perceived *francs-tireurs*, had pulled through 1st Ypres, and had put up with the weeks of mud and incessant warfare until Christmas had brought them temporary relief. In the letters to his local Protestant pastor in the south Bavarian village of Feldkirchen, the Commander of the Military Police unit of RD 6, Georg Arneth, acknowledged the bad conditions and tough combat the men of the division had had to face. Yet he maintained that 'our position in the war remains good', stating that the men of RD 6 fought with 'true defiance of death'. He told his pastor that he had no doubt that victory would be theirs.[12]

As Hitler celebrated Christmas, he was no longer a simple infantryman. His experience as a combat soldier and a regular infantryman had lasted only a few days longer than those who had died in the fields and hedges of Gheluvelt. Soon after the List Regiment's initiation into the war, on 3 November (but retrospectively effective from 1 November), at a time when the List Regiment was desperately short of officers, NCOs, and troops of higher rank—when virtually all NCOs and higher-ranking NCOs had been promoted to fill the vacant ranks (as was Albert Weisgerber, who had become a Offiziersstellvertreter, or warrant officer)—Hitler had been promoted to Gefreiter.[13] This was a promotion in the Bavarian Army still within the rank of Private in the US or British armed forces.[14] It was a rank that did not provide Hitler with any power of command over other soldiers—as the rank of Corporal or Lance Corporal (which English-language publications tend incorrectly to apply to Hitler)[15] would have done. Another event which occurred around the same time transformed Private Hitler's war to an even greater extent, an event without which Hitler's life and that of the world he made would have been very different. Eleven days after arriving at the front, on 9 November, Hitler was made a dispatch runner and was assigned to regimental headquarters.[16] The full impact of this turn of events, affecting how Hitler would view the war, how he would fit into the List Regiment, and, in due course, how he would develop politically were to become apparent only much later.

The men at regimental headquarters were rapidly becoming an ersatz family for Private Hitler. He displayed steadfast and often courageous loyalty towards his superiors. Indeed when, in the later stages of 1st Ypres, RIR 16 had to storm a heavily defended forest a few kilometres to the north-west of Messines, Hitler might well have saved his commander's life. According to one report, in an attack that would cost the lives of 122 men, Hitler and his fellow dispatch runner Anton Bachmann saw how the List Regiment's new commander, Lieutenant Colonel Philipp Engelhardt, had foolishly stepped out of his cover on the edge of the forest. Engelhardt immediately drew French fire. If we can believe a 1932 report by Georg Eichelsdörfer, the former regimental adjutant, Hitler and Bachmann dramatically leapt forward, covering Engelhardt's body and taking him back to safety.[17] The gist of the story is supported by a report of the same event, published in late 1915 in a commemorative brochure celebrating the List Regiment's war service to date. The differences between the 1915 report, written at a time when Hitler was a nobody, and the report published the year before Hitler came to power are, however, as interesting as the similarities. The 1915 report describes four dispatch runners, rather than just Hitler and Bachmann, stepping forward to protect Engelhardt. In this report, Engelhardt himself is not actually under fire but the dispatch runners are worried that the heavy fire of the battle might move towards him. Interestingly, the hero of the 1915 report is not Hitler but Bachmann who is credited with having crawled 30 or 40 metres out of the trenches and then carrying a wounded man of the List Regiment through French fire to safety.[18]

On 17 November, two days after Hitler may have saved his commander's life, Hitler and Engelhardt only narrowly escaped death when their battle regimental post—a simple makeshift hut—was hit by a shell. Hitler had reportedly left the hut only five minutes before it was shelled. He described the incident as 'the worst moment in my life'.[19] The men who were still with Engelhardt had been less lucky. Seven of them were killed. Engelhardt himself was hit by shrapnel in the hand and legs, piercing the main artery of his leg. He believed that he was going to die but lived to tell the tale.[20] Indeed the tales he was to tell in the inter-war years about Hitler's wartime service, whom he encountered for a mere seven days during the entire war, would assist in establishing the 'Hitler myth' and help to silence Hitler's many critics.

By the time Hitler and Weisgerber sat under a Christmas tree in Messines, the two men were among the few members of the List Regiment who had already been decorated with the legendary Iron Cross 2nd Class, the second highest military honour for men of their rank. All four dispatch runners who had stepped forward to alert Engelhardt to the danger he had faced in mid-November, had—on the recommendation of the regimental adjutant Georg Eichelsdörfer—been among the sixty recipients from RIR 16 of Iron Crosses on 2 December.[21] Hitler recorded the following day: 'Yesterday, on 2 December, I finally received the Iron Cross. It was the happiest day of my life.'[22]

Few of the other men of his regiment experienced their existence in the trenches close to Messines as the happiest days of their lives. Their experience of both the weeks leading up to Christmas and of Christmas itself was very different to Private Hitler's. An acute shell shortage following the big battles of the autumn had turned the conflict south of Ypres into a low-level one. It was dominated by snipers, occasional fusillades of rifle fire, and typically two daily rounds of shelling around lunchtime and dinnertime.[23] As Hitler recalled in 1942, 'in general, the battles on the Western Front had come to an end by the end of November/beginning of December. Then it suddenly began to rain and to snow, and the entire story was washed away.'[24]

In the period between 25 November and Christmas fewer than two members of RIR 16 a day were killed in action.[25] Low-level though the conflict was, the artillery fire was heavy enough to make it often impossible to recover injured soldiers: 'Some wounded soldiers lie in pain for days in the fields, exposed to shellfire, without being found,' noted Father Norbert. 'Once the wounded have been placed in the casualty station, they have to lie in wet cellars or destroyed houses because of the difficulty of evacuation, abandoned to the shell fire and to adverse exposure.'[26] The cumulative number of casualties had been enormous. By Christmas, only thirty of the original men of 12th Company, Fridolin Solleder's company, were still with the regiment:[27] in other words, almost 86 per cent of the men who had left Munich with 12th Company two months earlier were either injured or were slowly decomposing in Flanders' fields. The regiment also rapidly started to change character with the arrival of the new recruits following 1st Ypres.[28]

In the month leading up to Christmas, the men of the List Regiment found themselves fighting not just the British and French forces but also the elements. 'The old Landwehr men must suffer terribly with the constant wet and cold weather, and with the difficult food rations,' recorded Father Norbert. 'Rheumatism, enteritis, cases of typhus fill our infirmaries.'[29] Many men had to be treated for frostbite to their feet.[30] Weisgerber wrote to his wife:

> We are now rotated out of the trenches every three days, as the troops would not be able to endure staying there any longer. They stand up to their knees in muck and water. The men build themselves hollows like cavemen, but the rain presses against the walls at night and everything falls in on itself. Some of the soldiers have been killed this way. The water is disgusting and surges everywhere inside both from above and below—we can't do anything about it. The rain of bullets is more tolerable. The men must shovel out the trenches day and night without pause. There are no dry feet here, much less dry clothing.[31]

The region around Ypres, like most of Flanders, is characterized by high ground-water and an abundance of rain and fog. The name Flanders is believed to have originally meant 'flooded land' for good reason.[32]

For centuries, a system of drainage ditches and water-courses had kept the water at bay. It was, however, a system ill-prepared for the combined on-slaught of heavy rain in one of the wettest late autumns and winters recorded in history, and the enormous damage continued combat had inflicted on the drainage system. Soon the men of the List Regiment found themselves living in a morass of water and liquid mud. They were almost constantly cold and wet, as their winter coats proved to be too thin to afford any protection against the chilly and wet weather. Their woollen blankets were equally useless as they had no means of keeping the blankets dry. Moreover, they had to eat wet bread, as their bread bags had turned out not to be waterproof. The walls of the trenches constantly collapsed and the water in them often stood for days more than knee-high. The only consolation was that conditions were even worse in the British trenches, which lay lower than the Bavarian ones.[33]

The men had to alternate between spending generally three or four days in the mud-filled filthy trenches, where they only received food after nightfall, followed by four days in Messines, and an occasional reprieve in a former industrial plant in the town of Comines on the French–Belgian border, a few kilometres behind the front.[34] According to Weisgerber, while in the trenches, 'we live like moles and only come out to attack'.[35] The troops had to be relieved so often, wrote Weisgerber, 'as the men would not be able to endure being there any longer'.[36] Life in Comines, meanwhile, Weisgerber at least thought, was very pleasant, particularly since food and alcohol were still plentiful (a result of the requisitioning of 70,000 bottles of wine in the town)[37] in 1914: 'These 3 days rest [in Comines] have been beautiful, except for the hours of periodic shell fire in the area. The evenings are pleasant.... We do not want for anything; there is more than enough sparkling wine and food.'[38] However, on their way from Messines to Comines, the men of the List Regiment had to pass the rotting corpses of British colonial troops, mostly from India, which still could not be buried due to the heavy enemy fire.[39]

In the wet and dark nights, the men of the List Regiment started to see enemy soldiers everywhere. One night, dark shadows were moving slowly towards them. The men of RIR 16 sensed an imminent enemy attack. Soon they sent a formidable barrage of fire at the shadows. Yet strangely enough not a single shot was returned. They were soon to find out why. As the sun rose the following morning, the area ahead of their front was littered with dead bodies—the dead bodies of a herd of cattle that had gone astray during the night.[40] This was not the war that they had expected.

It was not just the old men who had been drafted into the List Regiment whose morale was low. Contrary to the image created by post-war mythical publications about Hitler and the List Regiment and contrary to how Military Police officers such as Georg Arneth might have viewed the war, the harsh, miserable, and brutal experience of 1st Ypres and its aftermath had killed any romantic ideas that some of the men might have harboured about going to war. As the commander of the sister regiment of RIR 16 noted, the troops had been ill trained for the conditions they were now encountering. One might add that, in reality, they had been ill trained for any conditions. The commander also thought that his own men were inferior to their British counterparts in their combat ability to make use of the terrain around them.[41] The officers of the 12th Reserve Brigade concluded in late November that increasingly often soldiers from RIR 16 and RIR 17 tried to get away from the front by any means, noting:

> The strain put onto the men in the last few days produced a fairly high incidence of absence due to illness. However, many soldiers also tried to remove themselves from the unit under false pretences. It was thus decreed by the brigade that troops might only leave the unit if they had a pass that had been issued by an officer.[42]

Around the same time, Father Norbert observed: 'As a result of their terrible days at war—made worse by adverse weather conditions . . . , our troops are very dispirited.'[43] Many soldiers, wrote Norbert, were upset that officers constantly addressed them 'in harsh military voices' even when talking to soldiers with injuries.[44] In early December, Father Norbert realized that the dramatic fall in morale was not limited to older, married men; on the contrary, he noted: 'Even the young volunteers were no match for the strains that the winter campaign brought. It is particularly these young men who . . . make a pitiful impression. Everyone yearns for peace, our beautiful Christmas present.'[45]

The fall in morale among the Bavarian troops had been so radical that an officer of another Bavarian Division that was also stationed in Comines thought that the only solution was to force them into combat by making the price of disobedience so high that men would rather go into combat than face the consequences. In a private letter, he wrote in December:

> For two days now the British have been attacking fiercely. They are brave men, far better than the French, better, I fear, than our old Landwehr men with whom we have to plug the gaps. . . . The fearful effects of modern

artillery and infantry fire have to be combated with an even more threatening compulsion to obey the will of the leadership so that cowardly men are more afraid of what awaits them behind the lines than the fire from the front. . . . The long time spent lying in the trenches and shelters has damaged the morale of the men. They only care about staying under cover, and they forget that there are moments when that thought has to be dropped.[46]

Even men such as Weisgerber, whose career had advanced rapidly within the List Regiment and who had been much more positive about the war than many of the troops were longing for peace. Even though earlier that month Weisgerber had written that 'to take part in a storm attack and live creates a feeling of exhilaration that I will hopefully never lose'[47] and that he had enjoyed it 'when a direct hit impacts the trenches [of the enemy] and the chaps scatter from the force',[48] he wrote on Christmas Day: 'We would gladly have peace! Peace! When will the day come?'[49] The falling morale evident in the List Regiment in the winter of 1914/15 was not limited to Hitler's military unit but visible throughout the German and British forces. Going by the prevalence of self-inflicted wounds, the winter of 1914/15 was the British Army's real period of crisis, rather than 1916 or 1918.[50]

The individuals of the List Regiment responded very differently to the first two months of the war. Hitler's experience was very different from Weisgerber's, and both their experiences were very much unlike that of many ordinary front-line soldiers. However, the most common response to the war among the men of RIR 16 was to turn towards religion. As Oscar Daumiller soon realized, the only men in RD 6 who were actively dismissive of religion were some of the army physicians who thought of 'the Christian religion only as antiquated junk'. On one occasion, a young army doctor told one of the Protestant ministers who worked under Daumiller and who 'prepared a dying soldier for his death, to do something else, as the dying man would pass away anyway.'[51] Yet with the exception of these cases, a religious renaissance was almost universal within the List Regiment. As a soldier from Hitler's regiment wrote home in the aftermath of his experience of combat: 'Quite a few of the men told me after the battle that they rediscovered their long-forgotten prayers to God.'[52] This was also how the Catholic population in rural southern Bavaria—for whom religion had remained at the centre of their daily lives anyway—responded to the war for the first half of the First World War. As in France, the revival in religion often became allied with the German national cause in the war.[53]

However, as we shall see, this nationalism tended to be defensive in character. In other words, the increased religious interest in the regiment was not to translate into hyper-nationalism.

The services held for the 6th Reserve Division were overcrowded, as many soldiers were attending services for the first times for years.[54] Father Norbert noted, in recording his impressions of the services for soldiers of RD 6: 'Low sobbing and crying interrupted the sacred stillness during the sermon, and many an Ave Maria of the rosary was choked in the throat during the holy mass.'[55]

There is no doubt that the relationship between Bavarian occupiers and the French and Belgian local population was extremely volatile and uneasy, as evident in the forced labour of local men and the requisitioning, not just of wine, as we have already seen, but also, among other goods, of all vehicles, horses, firearms, wood, and farm produce. Nevertheless, the soldiers of the units of RD 6 and the local Belgian population did sometimes even attend services together. On one occasion, 'after the mass, the Belgian civilians present expressed their repeated approval of the pious Bavarians'. On another, soldiers from RD 6 attended the funeral of a local civilian.[56]

Similarly, a soldier from the List Regiment wrote home in November 1914 that the French people with whom he had been quartered in Lille had been 'very [nice people], who were anything but fervid chauvinists'.[57] A French doctor working in the ophthalmology ward of a hospital in Lille which had been taken over by German military authorities, meanwhile, had noted days prior to the arrival of the List Regiment in Lille: 'Two German soldiers have started to work at the hospital, good fellows who were delighted finally to have a break; they exhaust themselves with politeness and smiling expressions now.... We can in no way complain about the behaviour of the German military doctors.'[58]

In fact, German military authorities tried to keep tensions with the French and Belgian population to a minimum. For instance, after a German cavalry officer had tried illegally to requisition large amounts of jam and chocolates in Comines, as well as levying a fine on the municipality, the French local representatives felt confident that reporting the officer to the German occupation force would help their case and indeed it did. The French complaint resulted in a shouting match between a German official from RD 6 and the cavalry officer, which the latter lost. As a result of this, the illegal act of requisitioning was revoked. Furthermore, in December 1914, the German Commander of Comines, Rittmeister von

Faber, felt compelled to write a letter to the French mayor of Comines in which he told him that he was stunned at the lack of interest the French mayor had shown in handling welfare provisions for the poor people of Comines. Von Faber urged the mayor to get his act together as he did not want the local population to suffer on his watch.[59] Whatever Faber's real intentions, he had decided that it was preferable to deal with, rather than to ignore, the plight of the population under occupation.

Father Norbert also noted that soldiers from his division were helping local nuns to care for old, sick civilians, concluding: 'Incidentally, the soldiers are full of heart-felt care for the poor people.'[60] At least for the moment, the sentiment that had seen *francs-tireurs* in all enemy civilians had died. It had indeed been a short-lived phenomenon of the first weeks of the war, rather than an expression of a deeply ingrained German culture. 'The coexistence of the local troops with the returned population is a very good one,' wrote the French-speaking Father Norbert in his diary on 3 December 1914.[61] Three days later, on St Nicholas Day 1914, he noted: 'It is being said by the soldiers serving in the first line that the Frenchmen often throw cigarettes to the Germans, while the Germans throw chocolates back in return . . . until suddenly fire is ordered and the situation once again takes on an antagonistic character.'[62] The Christmas of these men was to be very different from that of Private Hitler.

On Boxing Day, which Germans still consider to be part of Christmas, the combat troops of RIR 16 had to return to the trenches at 3 a.m. On taking their positions, they learnt from the troops of their sister regiment, which they were to relieve, that during the previous two days something miraculous had happened. On Christmas Eve, the men of RIR 17 and of the Devonshire Regiment on the other side of the trenches had taken turns to sing Christmas hymns and carols. The men of RIR 17 put up Christmas trees. Soon a member of RIR 17 stepped out of the trenches, shouting: 'You no shoot; we no shoot. It is your Christmas. We want peace. You want peace.' Scores of English and Bavarian men had now emerged from their trenches, leaving their weapons behind. They had met each other in the no man's land between their trenches, exchanging little presents.[63] In the sector right next to the one of RIR 17, between two and four hundred British and German soldiers, including their officers from the Norfolk Regiment and from a unit of RD 6 or its neighbouring division, had met in no man's land conversing and singing hymns together.[64]

The company leaders of the List Regiment had tried to prevent a reoccurrence of this Christmas Truce on Boxing Day, but to no avail. As the first rays of light turned night into what would become a frosty but very bright day, Josef Wenzl, a soldier in 2nd Company from rural eastern Bavaria, saw British soldiers emerge out of their trenches, waving at him and his comrades. Wenzl's brothers-in-arms took this as an invitation to put up a Christmas tree on the parapet of their trench. They lit its candles and rang its bells as if in invitation to their British counterparts. Soon the men of the List Regiment and of the Manchester and Devonshire Regiments shook hands, engaged in simple conversations in German and English, and exchanged presents. When Wenzl decided to join his comrades, as he wrote home, a British soldier immediately approached him, shook his hand and gave him some cigarettes. He reported: 'Another gave me a handkerchief, a third signed his name on a field postcard, a fourth wrote his address in my notebook. The soldiers chatted with each other, as much as they could, getting along with each other well. An Englishman played a German comrade's harmonica, others danced, and still others were extremely proud to try on a German helmet.' Wenzl's comrades from RIR 16 and their British counterparts now assembled around the illuminated Christmas tree and sang Christmas carols. Wenzl wrote home that as many as half of the men of his platoon mixed with British soldiers,[65] while Weisgerber reported: 'We even celebrated a cheerful Christmas. Today we exchanged greetings with the Englishmen. There was no shooting, and instead all of the soldiers came out of the trenches and sang and danced together. It is a strange war.'[66] Max Herold from 8th Company, meanwhile, received several Christmas wishes from British soldiers that they had hastily scribbled on the back of photos of themselves or postcards. One read: 'Wishing you a very happy Christmas and to a speedy ending to the war. L.A. Praer, 15. Devonshire.' The following day, on 27 December, the British troops were relieved by other troops from the Manchester Regiment and the Norfolk Regiment. This did not put an end to the Christmas truce, as the men of Hitler's regiment now also exchanged presents with them too.[67]

The Christmas Truce between the List Regiment and troops from three regiments of the 5th Division of the British Expeditionary Force was not an isolated event. The truce did not spring up everywhere, to be sure. Yet it did occur on about two thirds of the stretch of the Western Front on either side of the Belgian–French border that was manned by British forces.[68] While in the case of the List Regiment, the Christmas Truce was initiated by British troops, elsewhere it originated at least as often with German troops as with British ones.[69] One British serviceman from the 1/5 Londons reported of his conversations with Saxon soldiers during the Christmas Truce that 'none of them seemed to have any personal animosity against England and all said they would be fully glad when the war was over'.[70] Elsewhere, German soldiers told members of the 2nd Royal Dublin Fusiliers: 'We don't want to kill you, and you don't want to kill us. So why shoot?'[71] According to some reports, German and British soldiers played football against each other; elsewhere soldiers from both sides of the English Channel swapped barrels of German beer for plum pudding and buried their dead together.[72]

The perplexing question is why the Christmas Truce did not continue? The answer lies in a change in the weather and in orders that were issued, which had nothing to do with the political convictions and cultures of the combatants. As the war diary of 1st Battalion recorded on Boxing Day, 'Attempts at fraternization between the Englishmen and our own men were energetically opposed.'[73] The day following Boxing Day, a break in the weather had brought back the soaking Flemish rain and turned the ground back into a sea of mud. Two nights later brought one of the worst winter storms with thunder, 'a terrific gale of wind and sheets of rain'. A British officer nearby recorded: 'Even in the tropics I have never seen lightning more vivid.'[74] The atrocious weather and fiercely worded orders from their superiors thus finally put an end to the Christmas Truce of 1914. On 28 December, the regimental leadership of the List Regiment ordered the men to shoot any British soldiers leaving their trenches.[75] This was followed by a German army order and a similar British instruction the following day, prohibiting any and all fraternization and approaches to the enemy in the trenches as high treason.[76] By New Year, killing as usual had returned.

The British novelist Henry Williamson, who had participated in the Christmas Truce a few miles from the position of the List Regiment, later saw the Truce as the single most transformative event of his life. As he drifted more and more into the arms of British Nazi sympathizers in the 1930s, he fantasized about Hitler having participated in the Truce just a few kilometres up from where he himself experienced the Christmas Truce of 1914. He tried in vain to convince a 1930s British public that Hitler was some sort of hybrid of his friend Lawrence of Arabia and himself. The war, Williamson wrote, had turned Hitler into an idealist who wanted to create a new and better world and to avoid another war. According to Williamson, neither Hitler nor the Nazi Party possessed a 'war mentality'.[77] Like millions of Germans, Williamson projected his own hopes and dreams onto Hitler.

The only thing, though, that Williamson perceived correctly was that Hitler wanted to create a new world. Hitler certainly did not participate in the Christmas Truce. For one, his role in the support staff of regimental HQ would have rendered any participation almost impossible. For another, if we can believe the 1940 testimony of Hitler's fellow dispatch runner Heinrich Lugauer, Hitler had abhorred the Christmas Truce and was enraged by the behaviour of the men of his regiment. Lugauer reported in 1940: 'When everyone was talking about the Christmas 1914 fraternization with the Englishmen, Hitler revealed himself to be its bitter opponent. He said, "Something like this should not even be up for discussion during wartime." '[78] Even if we treat Lugauer's testimony with a pinch of salt, the fact remains that Hitler adored the officers of regimental HQ and behaved in a reverential way to them throughout the war. It is thus inconceivable that he would not have shared the critical attitude among the officers of regimental HQ towards the Christmas Truce, whose job was to curtail it whatever their private thoughts were on the matter. However, the question remains how to make sense of the fact that soldiers from the List Regiment—who had been prepared to become perpetrators of the summary execution of civilians, who had cheered when finding out that they were facing the British, and who had displayed a gung-ho mentality in the run-up to their first battle—fraternized with British soldiers during Christmas of 1914. After all, unlike Hitler, at least half of the men of the List Regiment participated in the Christmas Truce.

The problem in answering this question is that, ever since news of the truce broke in early 1915, there has either been a tendency to downplay the importance of the truce, to see the German soldiers involved as unrepresentative of Prussian-dominated Germany, or to romanticize the Christmas Truce. The 'romantic' school of thought has had a tendency to see what one book on the Christmas Truce has called 'the best and most heartening Christmas story of modern times'[79] as an expression of universal bonds of humanity against a militarist elite. The central theme of a recent scholarly book on the Christmas Truce indeed is 'whether the episode had the slightest chance of bringing hostilities to an end'.[80] Similarly, the lavishly filmed, Oscar-nominated *Joyeux Noël* tried to tell the tale of the Truce as some kind of modern version of the great inter-war pacifist novel and film *All Quiet on the Western Front*.[81]

At the other end of the spectrum, the Christmas Truce has been dismissed as 'simply . . . a festive interlude in a war that needed to be won'[82] and as primarily driven by an urge to bury the dead.[83] Another idea that has been put forward, that the German soldiers who participated in the Truce were 'good Germans' who were unrepresentative of Germany as a whole, is based, meanwhile, on the observation that Bavarian and Saxon troops, rather than Prussian ones, were the protagonists of the Truce. They were supposedly culturally more prone to participating in the Truce, rather than nationalist and militarist Prussians.[84]

This interpretation does not explain why, when accounting for the Christmas Truce, suddenly in this context Saxons (and their culture) should be grouped together with Bavarians as the 'good' Germans in opposition to the 'bad' Prussians, when, as we have seen, the Saxons (and their pre-war traditions) had been associated with Prussians as the 'bad' Germans in opposition to the South Germans in the context of the war atrocities in August and September 1914. This interpretation ignores one simple fact: that the behaviour not of German units but of British, French, and Belgian ones made all the difference. Despite the chocolate and cigarettes that had crossed the lines in the sector of RD 6 in early December and even though some cases of Franco-German and of Belgo-German fraternization occurred during Christmas 1914, they were the exception that proved the rule. Fraternization involving British and German units, meanwhile, was extremely widespread. The reason for this lay quite possibly in the different motivations for fighting the war and of the place of Christmas in the military cultures of British, French, and Belgian soldiers. For one, Christmas had a higher importance in British than in French and Belgian military culture. For another, the war was, according to one argument, a much more concrete and personal war that was fought on home soil with most of Belgium and some of France under German occupation and with its population terrorized.[85] Whatever explains the difference in behaviour of British, French, and Belgian soldiers, the important point here is that almost all cases of fraternization during Christmas took place on the rather short section of the front that was held by the British Expeditionary Force between German and British soldiers.

Facing the British section was the 6th German (predominantly Bavarian) Army with which some Saxon and a small number of Westphalian (Prussian) units also served temporarily. Little surprise then that it was primarily Bavarian and Saxon, rather than Prussian, units that participated in the Christmas Truce.

Significantly, the Prussian units that did serve with the 6th Bavarian Army opposite the British sector did also participate in the Truce, while the Bavarian, Saxon, and Prussian troops that faced French, rather than British, troops at the southern end of the sector of the 6th Bavarian Army only were involved on rare occasions. Equally, the French troops who faced the men of the List Regiment at one end of their sector did not join in the Truce. Unlike the British troops on the other side of Hitler's regiment these 'Frenchmen continued to shoot', according to a note sent from 1st Battalion to regimental HQ on Boxing Day.[86]

In short, what determined German behaviour during the Christmas Truce were not cultural, ideological, and political variations between Prussia and the rest of Germany. What mattered was whether German units faced British, French, or Belgian ones.

Similarly, if the Truce had almost exclusively been driven by an urge to bury the dead, it should have been a much more sombre affair and should have excluded episodes of the men of the List Regiment dancing with their British counterparts or of British soldiers temporarily wearing the helmets of Hitler's regiment. Likewise, the 'romantic' school clearly poses the wrong question. The question is not *if* soldiers were prepared to continue fighting or not. The real question is *why* the Truce took place and *why* soldiers were willing to continue fighting.

If the orthodox view of pre-war European society being rife with militarism and hyper-nationalism was true, the Christmas Truce should not have taken place. According to this view, the collapse of the pre-war European society was, more or less inevitable because European 'men of violence' were yearning for war.[87] According to one authority, pre-1914 Europe was a 'torn, conflicted world caught up in the grip of an arms race that one might well have called suicidal'.[88] Furthermore, it has often been argued that there was a constant rise of Anglo-German antagonism and hatred at both the popular and political level[89] which supposedly explains an outburst of public Anglophobia in the autumn of 1914, with Bavaria being the centre of anti-English agitation throughout the war.[90]

If these explanations were correct, they might well explain the German war atrocities in August and September 1914, the expression of joy among the men of the RIR 16 upon learning that they were to face the British, as well as their gung-ho behaviour in combat during the first few hours of their baptism of fire. However, if these explanations were correct, we will be left with no answer as to why at least half of the men of the List Regiment participated in the Christmas Truce.

The involvement in the Christmas Truce of the men of the List Regiment and so many other British and German soldiers indeed suggests the possibility that the men of RIR 16 were not fighting because of pre-war cultures of militarism, hyper-nationalism, an aggressive masculinity in crisis, or deep-seated Anglophobia. The events of Christmas 1914 indicate that the cultural similarities of the men on either side of the trenches—which went well beyond the fact that British Christmas traditions had been heavily influenced by German ones—might well have been stronger than any kind of culturally driven hatred. The involvement of the men of RIR 16 in the Truce raises the question of how deep the anti-British sentiment of Hitler's comrades in late October 1914 really ran. Anti-British manifestations after the outbreak of war had indeed often been a sudden expression of a feeling of betrayal by the British at the beginning of the war.[91] The Christmas Truce suggests that the extreme form of Anglophobia from the first weeks of the war did not even survive until Christmas. Worse still, the behaviour of the front-line combat soldiers of the List Regiment showed that all the anti-British propaganda in the German trench newspaper, the *Liller Kriegszeitung*, had not worked. Likewise, all the atrocity propaganda about German soldiers being brutish monsters, more akin to animals than to humans, did not stop the men of the Manchester, Devonshire, and Norfolk regiments from fraternizing with the men of the List Regiment. This is not to say that British and German soldiers did not associate any negative connotations with each other's countries. Far from it; moreover, the British blockade of Germany did not make the United Kingdom any more popular in Germany. However, the Truce suggests that militant versions of Anglophobia as expressed by intellectuals, official propaganda, and the radical right[92] failed to resonate with the majority of ordinary soldiers, or at least that it was not directed at enemy soldiers on the ground.

By contrast, it has been argued that, whatever cultural proximity might have existed prior to the war, the war had turned into an ideological war, a 'war of ideas', by late 1914 which was 'embraced' by the populations of Europe. This was now supposedly a war, as far as ordinary combat soldiers and intellectuals alike were concerned, of liberalism against militarism, individualism against community, anarchy against order, and of capitalism against state socialism: 'The determination of the belligerent state to appropriate the "ideas of 1914" suggest that they were also what the people wanted to hear. Soldiers' letters, not only of 1914 but later in the war, frequently mouthed the phrases and ambitions of the academics' outpouring.'[93]

One argument against this view is that it is based primarily on rather selective compilations of war letters, including one that was originally published during the war[94] and was meant, according to the editor of the compilation—who also was the editor of the army newspaper of 7th Army, as well as a speaker for Patriotic Instruction events on the home front, and the recipient of an Iron Cross for his propaganda work—to serve both as a 'national document' and 'particularly as propaganda in neutral foreign nations'.[95] These compilations of letters tell us more about German war propaganda and the culture wars over the legacy of the Great War in inter-war Europe than about the mental state of combatants in late 1914. More-over, the great majority of postcards that both the men of the List Regiment and of the German armed forces at large sent home during the war neither tended to celebrate violence nor to be propaganda postcards full of patriotic slogans which were readily available to the men of the regiment. They were rather postcards that had been produced prior to the war for tourists, depicting panoramas of towns, street scenes, and churches.[96] The soldiers who sent postcards like these home wanted to share with their friends and family where they were and what places they had visited, not spread the 'ideas of 1914'. Wartime evidence as well as a critical reading of post-war sources indeed suggest, as we shall see, that the majority at least of the men of the List Regiment were not fighting for the 'ideas of 1914'. Nor does the available evidence suggest that most men now subscribed to a Hitlerite view of 'life [as] a constant horrible struggle'.[97] They rather suggest, as another historian has put it, 'the lack of rancour between many front-line soldiers'.[98]

Whether this Christmas 1914 mentality was to persist, or whether the experience of continued warfare was indeed to politicize, brutalize, and change opinions and thus make the great majority of the men of the List Regiment more similar to Hitler (or at least to those views Hitler would express after the war), was an open question, as the men of RIR 16 returned to the business of killing in the final days of 1914.

4

Dreams of a New World

1 January–May 1915

By early 1915, the war had started to wear down even Private Hitler. In December, he had already written to his Munich landlord Joseph Popp: 'Sometimes I have a great longing for home.'[1] Now, in January, he wrote:

> We are still in our old positions and keep annoying the French and the English. The weather is miserable; and we often spend days on end knee-deep in water and, what is more, under heavy fire. We are greatly looking forward to a brief respite. Let's hope that soon afterwards the whole front will start moving forward. Things can't go on like this for ever.[2]

In a separate letter from the same day, Private Hitler wrote: 'Our daily losses are often relatively severe, despite our defensive position. The strain is tremendous.'[3] Hitler, who had to alternate between the regimental HQ posts in Messines and Comines, reported a few days later that 'what is most dreadful is when the guns begin to spit across the whole front at night. In the distance at first, and then closer and closer with rifle fire gradually joining in. Half an hour later it all starts to die down again except for the countless flares in the sky. And further to the west we can see the beams of large searchlights and hear the constant roar of heavy naval guns.' Hitler told Popp that 'because of the eternal rain (we have had no winter), the closeness of the sea, and the low altitude, the meadows and fields look like bottomless swamps, while the roads are covered ankle-deep in mud.'[4] On one occasion, when Father Norbert had to ride from Comines towards Messines, his horse occasionally disappeared up to its stomach in water and mud.[5] The almost constant rain, Solleder would later recall, turned the men of RIR 16 into 'walking clay monsters'.[6]

On 5 February, Hitler wrote to Ernst Hepp, a Munich acquaintance: 'I am very nervous right now. Day after day we are under heavy artillery fire from 8 a.m. to 5 p.m. and that is bound to ruin even the strongest of nerves.'[7] As Georg Arneth, the Commander of RD 6's Military Police, reported to his Protestant pastor at home: 'Combat rages here day and night. Every metre of terrain must be fought over. The wretched war will probably continue for a long time and many of our brave men will have to bite the dust.'[8] Small raids, persistent artillery fire, and sniping continued throughout the winter of 1914/15. In a four-day period in early January alone, British units fired an estimated 8,000 shots at the section of the front occupied by RD 6. Artillery fire also destroyed the post of the regimental HQ in Messines. However, this was far from being the only hazard the men of RIR 16 had to endure, each of whom had to guard a two-metre stretch of the trench. For instance, the bodies of the soldiers were infested with lice. By February, disease was mounting.[9] Indeed, typhus soon proved a worse foe than enemy snipers and artillery, as Gustav Scanzoni von Lichtenfels, the commander of RD 6, concluded: 'If one bears in mind that all men suffering from typhus will probably be out of action for the rest of the war, then our losses during these quiet times are higher through illness than through the enemy weapons.'[10] Similarly, as the officers of the List Regiment learned from a diary found on the body of a dead British soldier, more British troops were incapacitated by frostbite and sore feet than by Bavarian fire.[11]

The landscape on either side of the front looked beautiful now only during cloudless nights, when the silvery light of the moon created flickering reflections on the sea of mud and water. The rest of the time it looked desolate, bleak, and miserable. The knee-deep water in the trenches and the dugouts was hated by everyone but the insects who laid their eggs in it. By March, the regiment had to battle an infestation of flies.[12]

In spite of this hardship, Private Hitler remained steadfast in his support of the war: 'But nothing on earth can ever shift us from here,' he wrote to Joseph Popp: 'Here we shall hang on until Hindenburg has softened Russia up. Then comes the day of retribution!'[13] Through Hitler's letters shines a man who is deferential to authority and relishes concepts like revenge.

Hitler put his hopes in the arrival of new recruits. They were supposed to replenish his regiment, which in early 1915 was standing at 1,794 men rather than the 3,000 men a regiment was supposed to have,[14] and was seriously undermanned:

A few kilometres to our rear the place is teeming with fresh young Bavarians. Every Belgian pocket now has young German troops. They are still being pampered and trained. I don't know for how long, but then the fun is bound to start. As for our old volunteers, they are a bit low right now. The constant fighting has claimed a great many victims, and then there is the cold and the wet.[15]

Hitler now started to dream of a new better world. As he wrote to Hepp, a better world for him meant a world in which Germany had emerged victoriously from the war and, more importantly, a world with a less cosmopolitan Germany:

I often think of Munich, and each one of us has only one wish: that he might soon get a chance to even scores with that crew [mit der Bande; i.e. the British], to get at them no matter what the cost, and that those of us who are lucky enough to return to the fatherland will find it a purer place, less riddled with foreign influences, so that the daily sacrifices and sufferings of hundreds of thousands of us and the torrent of blood that keeps flowing here day after day against an international world of enemies will not only help to smash Germany's foes outside but that our inner internationalism, too, will collapse. This would be worth much more than any gain in territory.[16]

Hitler's letter is so important because it provides us with the clearest wartime statement we have about his ideology. Unlike all his post-war statements, or statements by people he encountered during the war, this is the only letter which we know beyond any doubt really represents his wartime political thinking; or, one should add, his thinking at the beginning of the war. Hitler's wish for a return to a pure, less cosmopolitan Germany was expressed in language that had been commonplace among the radical Right in both Imperial Germany and the German lands of the Habsburg Empire. The significance of the letter is that in it he aligned himself with the political fringes of German politics. It should really be read as a bitter attack against pre-war mainstream German political thought. It might also well be read as a scathing criticism of those of his comrades-in-arms in the List Regiment who only a few weeks earlier had fraternized with British soldiers.

Events in 1915 would show whether the majority of the men of the List Regiment would, like Hitler, channel their war experience to date into a steadfast and unqualified support of the war. More importantly, events in 1915 would reveal whether they would support the war for the same reason as Hitler did. In other words, the coming months would reveal whether the men of RIR 16 would, like Hitler, see as their goal a less international and cosmopolitan Germany—in short, whether they would become in their political aspirations more like Hitler—or whether they would channel their war experiences in different directions. Finally, events in 1915 would show how typical Hitler's war service was of the regiment at large and what front-line soldiers thought about him.

The reinforcements which Hitler put all his hope in and who kept arriving in the first few months of the year had, in fact, been very poorly trained and, according to the officer who kept the war diary of the 12th Reserve Infantry Brigade, still could not even shoot straight by the time they arrived in Belgium and France.[17] However, many new young recruits compensated for their lack of training, at least until they had gone through their baptism of fire, with a hawkish eagerness to prove themselves in the front line: 'The young replacement troops appear impatient, as they have to drill all the time and are not yet allowed to go to the trenches,' observed Father Norbert in early March.[18] At least some of them, no doubt, displayed the kind of attitude towards the war that had been characteristic of Nikolaus Denk, a 28-year-old son of a farmer in 1st Company. While dying on 5 March from injuries he had incurred the previous nights, he breathed, 'Germany must prevail, Germany will pre-vail, Germany prevails!', as the regimental physician Max Riehl scribbled in his diary.[19]

This incident suggests that Hitler's hopes about the new recruits were justified. However, contrary to his perception, neither the men in his regiment who had already been with RIR 16 for several months nor the older men among the regiment's recruits shared Denk's attitude.

It was now that the first cases of self-mutilation occurred in the army group to which RIR 16 belonged. Sometimes men would leave their unit, inflict a wound on themselves, and then report to another unit in the hope of being transported to an army hospital or even home.[20] Falling morale was not limited to those who mutilated themselves. Father Norbert noted that discontent with the war had been brewing among the men who had already spent several weeks or months in the trenches and among the older men of the reinforcement troops: ' "If only the war were over! If only it were suddenly peacetime!" This is what one hears everywhere, particularly from the older reservists.'[21] In short, as yet, there had been little sign of agreement in the attitudes of Hitler and the majority of the men of his regiment. Then again, the big bloody battles of 1915 (and the impact of the battles on the men of

RIR 16 with their potential for a brutalization and radicalization) still lay in the future.

The officers of the List Regiment, meanwhile, had to face the problem of how best to deal with the growing levels of discontent in the regiment in an attempt to sustain morale among the men of RIR 16.

Bavarian military planners and the officers of the List Regiment used both sticks and carrots to keep up morale among the soldiers and to make them continue to believe that this was a war worth fighting (and if necessary dying) for. Initially at least, the emphasis lay on using incentives in an attempt to combat any growing discontent in the regiment. In fact, at no time in the war would German military authorities use disciplinary measures as relentlessly as the British, French, and Italians. While, for instance, 307 British servicemen, approximately 700 French soldiers, and up to 900 Italian soldiers were executed, the Germans carried out the death penalty only on 48 of their men.[22]

The efforts to maintain high morale among the men of the List Regiment included visits to the front by both King Ludwig III of Bavaria and Crown Prince Rupprecht. King Ludwig's visit was for the soldiers, as Father Norbert noted in his diary, 'a day that would go down in history'. Ludwig even came to visit the men of Hitler's regiment in their rest quarters in the Galant factory in Comines, shaking the hands of many men from RIR 16—most of whom had never imagined that their position in society would ever allow them to meet their monarch in person—and telling them how important the service of every single soldier was.[23] Privately, Rupprecht, however, had huge doubts about the men of RD 6, noting: 'During the parade, the differences between the individual sections became quite conspicuous. One could clearly see which of the men were trained soldiers and which were members of the *Ersatzreserve* or war volunteers. A few of these who had spent a long time in the forward line and had just come out of the trenches made a truly haggard impression.'[24]

The officers of the List Regiment also tried to give their men short, albeit very infrequent, periods of leave in which they could return home and visit their families and, later in the year, help to bring in the harvest.[25] Another element of the attempt to keep up morale was the establishment of soldiers' messes, set up in Comines for Catholic soldiers by Father Norbert and for Protestant ones by Oscar Daumiller. They were extremely popular with the troops while they were on reserve duty in Comines. It provided them with a space for social life, a sense of normality, and a home from home.

'The soldiers gather in these messes for cheerful get-togethers,' wrote Father Norbert into his diary one day. 'There were newspapers and magazines. . . . For a small payment, coffee, food, and cigars were handed out. Our mess was situated in the theatre room of an institution run by the Soeurs de Notre Dame. The nuns who had stayed on here eagerly lent us a hand with the preparation of the food and drink.'[26]

The war experience at Gheluvelt and Messines led a great number of soldiers from the List Regiment to turn to gallows humour as a coping mechanism that helped them to interpret their predicament more positively,[27] as Father Norbert noted: 'Our soldiers use it to deceive themselves about their dangerous situation.'[28] However, unlike irreligious Private Hitler, beyond resorting to jokes, an increasing number of men turned towards religion for guidance, rather than dreaming of the kind of Germany Hitler had envisioned in his letter to Hepp. For many throughout the German forces, religion gave meaning to the war and was a source of strength,[29] as men either imagined that God would protect them, or at least that their fates lay in his hands, rather than in those of the enemy on the other side of the trenches.

On 15 January, for instance, almost all Catholic soldiers of RIR 16 attended a service held for the regiment,[30] while on Sundays, the two churches of Comines, with a combined capacity of more than 9,000, still did not provide enough room for the Bavarian soldiers staying in Comines. Sometimes hundreds had to follow the services from outside the two churches.

Among the churchgoers was Alois Schnelldorfer, one of the young new recruits, who wrote to his parents: 'I was at church in the morning[;] I wish that you too could see something so celebratory some day. The windows are blown out. There was a German sung mass being held in which about 500–800 men took part. What a sound that made! During the breaks one could always hear the thunder of cannons. Our army chaplain always gives a beautiful sermon as well. There is seldom anyone there without a rosary.'[31]

The men of the List Regiment attended services, first and foremost, not from boredom but out of a sense of strengthened religious feeling; they prayed in private using their rosaries and flocked not just to the services but also to confession and to the other Catholic sacraments. Father Norbert had to deal repeatedly with overcrowded confessionals. In a context in which a huge number of people in the recruitment regions of RIR 16 saw the war first and foremost as divine punishment, Norbert, together with army chaplains on both sides of the trenches along the Western Front, skilfully connected in his sermons and addresses faith in the nation with religious faith. In his services, Norbert alternated between prayers and hymns with no connection to the war and ones that prayed for guidance and protection in battle, such as the Niederländisches Dankgebet (Dutch Prayer).[32] First used as a prayer by Dutch troops in the late sixteenth century, the third verse of the Niederländisches Dankgebet was meant to reassure the men of RIR 16 that God was on their side and that victory was theirs: 'Beside us to guide us; Our God with us joining; Ordaining, maintaining; His kingdom divine; So from the beginning; The fight we were winning; Thou, Lord, wast at our side; All glory be Thine!'[33]

Protestant army chaplains across the German armed forces took support for the war one step further. While Catholic chaplains were priests of a global and universal Church, Protestant chaplains were members of an essentially national Church. It was thus much easier and much more tempting for them to stress the national mission of the war. As we have seen, Oscar Daumiller had told the men of the 6th Bavarian Reserve Division before their departure from Bavaria that they were going to fight a holy war for Germany. Similarly, Robert Hell, who acted as Protestant chaplain in one of the military hospitals of the division, told his patients in an address he delivered in the spring of 1915: 'Everything that is un-German in our people shall yield, everything that is not true, not genuine, what is contrived and smug, what is only outer appearance without inner truth.'[34] Hell sometimes also signed private letters he sent from the front: 'With true German greetings.'[35] Similarly, Wilhelm Stählin, who served from November 1914 to March 1915 as one of RD 6's Protestant army chaplains under Daumiller, had declared at the beginning of the war that a warrior 'has God's will to do'.[36]

The fundamental message of Protestant theology during the war was that the conflict was not merely being fought in self-defence but that the fighting would purge, renew, and redeem the German people. The domestic war aim was to destroy and replace a corrupt society, to combat materialism, and to unite a divided and fractured society.[37] In its ideals, Protestant war theology came ostensibly close to Hitler's wish expressed early in 1915 for the war to change radically German society.

And yet there is no easy equation between Hitler's conception of the war and that of Protestant war theology, as the approach of German Protestant theology towards the war was not a German peculiarity. Indeed there was little difference between the wartime theology of German and British Protestant army chaplains. Both shared a common ideal of the nation's mission and the meaning of the war and both shared a common moral language.[38] As, however, Britain did not follow a path towards Fascism in the twentieth century, we should be extremely cautious about drawing too direct a parallel between Hitler's aspirations and Protestant war theology.

Even though both Hitler and Protestant army chaplains might have wished to cleanse German society through the war, their visions of a perfect society Hitler and the Protestant army chaplains of RD 6 wanted to achieve were rather dissimilar. Oscar Daumiller, for one, saw the war as a test God had set for the people to enable them to become more pious rather than to create a new less cosmopolitan and international Germany: 'Despite the long duration of the war,' he noted in May 1915, 'our people have not come as far as God would have wanted them to. Our people and we as individuals must devote ourselves much more wholeheartedly and completely to Him, to the only one who can offer solace, relief, and salvation.'[39] Wilhelm Stählin, for another, had been more than a little worried when a fellow attendee at a conference of field clergymen expressed 'that religion was now coloured by nationalism and that the Fatherland was now religious'. Stählin noted: 'I must admit that this train of thought seems very dangerous to me. This close association between religious and *völkisch* sensibilities may be justifiable from time to time on special occasions; generally, I would, however, advocate emphasizing that God is eternally, changelessly peace-loving.' Stählin also thought that God's kindness and love should be brought to the fore rather than the future of the nation. He firmly believed that it was important 'to point out that God is the father of all men and uses very different standards from those that we humans use'. At any rate, Stählin had come to the realization that the majority of soldiers were objecting to services that were used as a 'rally to battle'.[40]

Yet the invocation of religion was not the only measure used to try to entice soldiers to keep up their morale. Announcements put up about successes on the Eastern Front, and the practice after victories on the Eastern Front to have the church bells rung in the villages in which the List Regiment and its sister units were stationed, were also meant to boost the morale of the troops.[41] As Alois Schnelldorfer concluded in early March: 'If America remains blessedly neutral, peace will come soon.... When we received the good news from Russia, it was one in the morning, the officers had us cheer Hurrah three times.'[42] Selling the war as a defensive endeavour was another strategy to reinforce support. At the funeral of Karl Naundorf, a 24-year-old war volunteer and battalion dispatch runner killed by a British infantry bullet striking right through his heart, the commander of 2nd Battalion, Emil Spatny, told his men that they were fighting a defensive war: '[Naundorf] died as a hero in the most loyal fulfilment of duty for the preservation and greatness of our Fatherland.'[43]

The real test of how morale among the men of Hitler's regiment had developed in early 1915 and how they now viewed their enemy would, of course, lie in how they would cope with a major new battle.

As the winter in wet, cold Flanders drew to a close and as the ranks of the regiment were replenished, the men of the List Regiment expected the new season to bring a Franco-British spring offensive. However, they thought that first they would have some time to rest and sleep when on 8 and 9 March they were finally taken out of the section of the front near Messines and away from Comines, where they had lain since early November. The men of RIR 16 and their brothers-in-arms in RD 6 were in a boisterous and cheery mood: 'All night long one could hear the singing regiments and troop units pull through the streets,' reported Father Norbert.[44] 'We moved out of Comines like moving away from home. The French people and the remaining German troops stood in the street everywhere to wish us farewell. People were waving after us from all the windows.... Naturally we were in a cheery mood, as we were moving towards a better future.'[45]

After four months in Belgium, during which time 819 members of RIR 16 had been killed, Hitler and his fellow soldiers were taken back across the French border to Tourcoing, an industrial town nestled between Lille and the Belgium border. Once the men of RIR 16 had arrived at the spinning mill which had been transformed into the 'Kronprinz Rupprecht barracks', their most urgent need was to sleep. After rising late in the morning, and receiving a warning from both Father Norbert and Oscar Daumiller about 'the dangers of city life',[46] they started to frequent the bars of the town anyway, drinking cheap liquor, and strolling through the local shops. The men of Hitler's regiment were looking forward to two weeks, maybe more, of such an existence.[47] Yet the spring offensive came much, much faster than expected.

Since February the French had already been trying to pierce the German front further south. On 10 March, it was the turn of the British to try to break through the German front and shatter the stalemate. The British identified the German front next to the once sleepy medieval farming village of Neuve Chapelle, lying amidst flat and soggy farmland 25 kilometres to the south-west of Lille and approximately 15 kilometres south of the Franco-Belgian border, as the spot where they had the best chance of breaking through the German lines. The British plan was to obliterate the German front along a 2-kilometre stretch. They tried to accomplish this by firing more shells than they had during the entire Boer War on an approximately 4-kilometre-long section of the front close to Neuve Chapelle. British troops were then supposed to move swiftly through the gap in the German front. In the event, the British botched the attack by advancing too slowly. They had only been able to advance just over a kilometre on a 2-kilometre wide stretch before German forces brought the advance to a standstill.[48] Yet the situation was still precarious. The German armed forces feared that over the next few days the British would continue their onslaught. This is when the German high command decided that the best defence was a counter-attack. For that, they needed new troops and they needed them fast. This brought an abrupt and sudden end to what the men of RIR 16 thought would be a time of recuperation and training.

At 3 p.m., the List Regiment received their orders. As Jakob Schäfer, a 21-year-old mechanic from Munich and a war volunteer in 2nd Company who had been with the regiment since January noted, the call to arms came as a total surprise and was the source of great annoyance and complaint among his comrades. Yet within minutes they had packed their rucksacks, assembled outside their quarters in the spinning mill, and were ready to go.[49] They still did not know where they were to be deployed but they knew to where they wanted to be sent. Wilhelm Schlamp, the Commander of 9th Company told one of his NCOs: 'Albert, now that we have fought against the English and the French, we shall strike the Russians as well.'[50] This was a common sentiment in the List Regiment. It is today sometimes forgotten that the war that mattered in the minds of Germans in late 1914 and 1915 was the war on the Eastern Front where Germany had to date usually been victorious. Unlike the fear that being sent to the Eastern Front instilled in any German soldier in the Second World War, the men of the List Regiment thus now wished, not for the first time during the war, to be sent to the Eastern Front.[51] Yet this was not to be.

After having had to encounter the excited French population who imagined that they were about to be liberated by British troops, the men

of the regiment boarded a train to Don at 5.30 p.m., one of the stations close
to Neuve Chapelle. The next day was spent in hurriedly preparing for the
counter-attack, planned for the following day, 12 March 1915. Two battalions of RIR 16 had received the order to form the third wave of a Prussian-led
attack, while the third battalion was to be kept in reserve.[52] This was supposed
to be a return to a classic battle of movement, in which soldiers ran forward
with bayonets attached to their rifles, rather than living like moles underground. On the eve of the battle, Weisgerber would later write to his wife,
'every man made closure with his earthly life once again, like so many times
before'.[53]

It is worth looking at how the battle unfolded for ordinary front-line
soldiers, as it provided them with combat experiences very different from
those of Hitler.

Josef Wenzl from 2nd Company later wrote home that they had been
'full of confidence' going into battle. Yet almost from the start of the
counter-attack in the early hours of 12 March, it was doomed because of
poor preparation, a lack of coordination between different military units,
and atrocious battle and weather conditions. Previous days still had seen the
occasional fall of snow. While Private Hitler spent the battle in the command post of regimental HQ in the de Biez Farm a few hundred metres
behind the front, the men of the List Regiment had to cross the du Bois
Forest, which had turned into a swamp, before facing British troops. Inside
the small forest, many soldiers had to abandon their boots, which had stuck
in the mud, and move forward barefoot. Others threw off their combat gear
in an attempt to get through the muck. Once they had passed through the
forest, the Garhwal (Indian) Brigade and other British units greeted them
with an awe-inspiring wall of fire produced by artillery, machine guns, and
rifles. The soldiers of RIR 16 ran into a wall of fire. From each of the British
machine guns, 600 rounds of fire a minute streamed at the advancing
Bavarians and Prussians. They ran straight into the line of fire of a British
gunner from the 2nd West Yorkshire Regiment: 'I saw another mass come
out of the wood, what a target. One could not miss. It was just slaughter.
A third lot came out of the wood further down, but there was no escape,' he
recalled. Wenzl, meanwhile, experienced the moment the men of RIR 16
emerged from the forest: 'The entire area was wrapped in a single cloud of
smoke.... I believed that my last hour had struck; the apocalypse itself could
not have been worse.' As the holes in the ground and trenches were all filled
with water, it was next to impossible to find adequate shelter from the

British bullets and exploding shells. However, even heavily wounded soldiers threw themselves into the smelly, dirty, and cold water, trying to keep their head above the surface. Soon the uniforms of the men of the List Regiment turned yellow from the acid gas emanating from British shells. By the end of the battle, 243 men from RIR 16 had died. In some companies the fatalities were as high as those incurred at Gheluvelt in late October. In 9th Company, for instance, fifty soldiers died, or more than one in four. The overall casualty rate in 1st Battalion stood at 19 per cent and at 25 per cent in 2nd Battalion.[54] Alois Schnelldorfer had been among the lucky ones who survived the battle unharmed. Shrapnel had pierced his eating utensils but had narrowly missed his body. After the battle he proudly wrote home: 'I have now been properly baptized by fire.'[55]

After a huge number of soldiers had, as we have seen, fallen into British hands as prisoners, the men of 10th Company believed that the British had tricked them unfairly during the battle. Survivors from 10th Company alleged, maybe self-servingly, that some British troops had worn German helmets and uniforms.[56] This sentiment was widespread among German participants of the Battle of Neuve Chapelle who often believed that the British had used illegal dumdum bullets and that Indian soldiers had acted in a particularly treacherous fashion.[57] Whether these claims are true or not, the impression that their British counterparts were fighting in a deceitful manner left its mark on the minds of the men of the List Regiment, potentially transforming the Christmas 1914 image of British soldiers into an object of personal hatred.

As made clear by the case of the battalion that had originally been kept in reserve during the battle, coercion, rather than simply an unquestioning conviction in the purpose of the war, became an increasingly dominant motivator for Hitler's brothers-in-arms continuing to fight: two companies of the battalion (7th and 8th Company) were ordered almost instantly to join the battle. Their task was to stop the retreat of troops from the Prussian 104th and 139th Regiments, who—according to a British officer—had experienced a 'slaughter [that] was prodigious' to the south of the du Bois Forest, and to lead them back into the German counter-attack.[58] One regiment was thus pitted against another to prevent soldiers from fleeing the scene.

The reality of what happened in the battle did not fit the carefully choreographed picture which the Nazis subsequently painted. The monumental losses of the List Regiment as well as the attempts to pit one German unit against another in an effort to prevent soldiers from retreating do not feature at all in Adolf Meyer's Nazi-era memoirs of Hitler's and his own war experience. In it, he reduced the Battle of Neuve Chapelle to a successful repulse of the British attack, 'during which many Indian troops bled to death in front of our ranks'.[59]

The Battle of Neuve Chapelle came to an end as night fell, when the British aborted their attempt to break through the German lines. At a cost of more than 11,000 British and a similar number of German casualties[60]—equal to the population of a university town such as Tübingen—the battle ended in a draw and brought neither side any military advantage.

During the night of 13/14 March, RIR 16 was relieved and taken out of the Neuve Chapelle section of the front. For the following three days, the List Regiment regrouped in villages behind the front, trying to transform the survivors of the Battle of Neuve Chapelle, who were, in the words of Father Norbert, 'deeply shaken', back into a cohesive unit, shuffling men from company to company.[61] It was still unclear what impact the battle had had on the attitudes and political mentalities of Private Hitler and the men of his regiment. The battle had certainly not changed Alois Schnelldorfer. He was very proud of having earned battle experience. Now, he reasoned, he would always be a veteran who had risked his life for his fatherland. Yet Schnelldorfer had no taste for a prolonged or cataclysmic war, telling his parents: 'I hope that there will be peace soon but there is still no sign.'[62]

As it turned out, the men of RIR 16 were to stay in the vicinity of Neuve Chapelle for the foreseeable future. Their task was to relieve a Prussian regiment at the section of the front outside the village of Fromelles just 5 kilometres to the north-east of Neuve Chapelle.[63]

As the men marched for the first time into the village on the evening of 17 March, the moonlight dimly showed the jagged ruins of the church tower of Fromelles. That was all that they were to see of the village for the moment, as they were taken straight to their new trenches, lying some 3 kilometres to the north-west of the village.[64]

The following morning, as night turned to day, it was time for the men to inspect their new 'home'. Their 'neighbours' on the other side of the trenches were still British troops, as Alois Schnelldorfer observed: 'The enemy (Blacks, Scotsmen, and Englishmen) is only 60–80 or 100 metres away from our new positions.'[65] If Schnelldorfer carefully sneaked across the parapet of his regiment's new trench, he could see, behind no man's land

and the British trenches, meadows, brooks, drainage canals, occasional trees, and a small forest in the distance.[66] The men of the List Regiment thus still had an opportunity to take revenge on the British for any real or imagined British acts in 1st Ypres and at Neuve Chapelle; in other words, as Hitler had put it in early February, 'to even scores with that crew, to get at them no matter what the cost'.[67] If Schnelldorfer and other front-line soldiers turned their back on their British opponents for a moment, the landscape awaiting them was one of more meadows, willow trees, bushes, and ruined farms lying at the foot of the heavily damaged village of Fromelles, which sat on top of a very low ridge (the Aubers Ridge).[68] It was, as Father Norbert observed, a once glorious region: 'We find ourselves in a magnificent area. . . . We are surrounded by lovely rolling hills with many small towns and villages, as well as numerous castles in magnificent parks. . . . Naturally not everything remains in its ideal condition. The villages and castles are sad ruins, the parks are laid waste in parts. Everything speaks of former grandeur and lost glory.'[69]

The men of RIR 16 now did what many soldiers do in alien environments. They gave familiar names to locations in their segment of the front, thus trying to recreate a miniature version of Bavaria as well as a sense of familiarity and belonging. One dugout was christened 'Löwenbräu' after Munich's famous brewery; a position just behind the trenches was christened 'Wasserburg' after the Upper Bavarian town of the same name; others were called 'Dachau' or 'Schwabing', while the makeshift tram-railway line that zigzagged through the rear area of RIR 16's section of the front was called 'Isartalbahn' after the river that runs through Munich.[70]

In the weeks after their arrival in Fromelles, the men of RIR 16 drew little fire during the day. At night, they were subjected to machine-gun fire and occasional artillery fire that crossed the German artillery fire in mid-air. This was a relative quiet time; on average, approximately one soldier from the List Regiment was killed every day and a half during the first month and a half at Fromelles.[71] It was so quiet that the leaders of Private Hitler's division bothered to worry about accidents that were occurring when the more absent-minded among its soldiers were getting off the train. They urged the men of its units to remember 'that on Belgian and French railroads the platforms are usually on the left'.[72]

There are many reasons why the men of Hitler's regiment continued to fight. First, even disgruntled men in most wars tend naturally to believe that their national cause is just, or, even if they have doubts, that winning the war is still preferable to losing it. Therefore a far better question to ask, than simply whether or not the men of the regiment would continue to fight (since the general expectation for soldiers in any war is that they will perform), is to enquire about concrete battle motivations and the underlying ideological and cultural assumptions that drove their continued participation in the war.

One of the reasons why the regiment continued to perform as well as it did is that motivation for the tasks individual soldiers had to perform was driven both by their abilities and their attitudes towards the war. Disgruntled or less able men only had to man the trenches or to upgrade the trench system and, other than that, were allowed to keep their heads down. This was still an extremely dangerous task. It was also considerably more dangerous than Hitler's task, as we shall see. However, in-between battles and based on a day-to-day calculation, the cost of continuing to perform was considerably lower than the potential cost of protest and disobedience. In the former case, soldiers, of course, ran the risk of being killed, while in the latter case the likelihood of being subjected to the death penalty was, as we have seen, almost non-existent. However, the odds of a soldier in the List Regiment being killed on any one day in January stood at approximately 1:2,000. The risk of being killed for soldiers who did not, for instance, volunteer for patrols was even lower than that. Meanwhile, the likelihood that an act of desertion would bring disgrace, a prison term, and a cessation of welfare provisions for family members was close to 1:1.[73] The rational choice of action for men in the List Regiment, particularly for dissatisfied soldiers who had further minimized their risk of being killed by not volunteering for dangerous tasks, was naturally to continue to perform, as long as they calculated their risk on a short-term, rather than a cumulative, basis.

Men with a very positive attitude towards the war, meanwhile, were asked to participate in far more dangerous tasks. For instance, they were urged to join hand-grenade platoons. As an order from 1st Battalion decreed: 'Every company has to form a hand-grenade troop from each platoon. It should be made up of volunteers and led by a particularly spirited NCO.'[74] Later volunteers were used to form storm troops—mini-units which would pierce and infiltrate the front. Volunteers were also sought for patrol missions. Two such patrols were formed in early May exclusively from volunteers for this task under the leadership of Albert Weisgerber, who by then, to his great delight, had been made commander of 1st Company.[75]

This division of tasks would gain significance retrospectively in the inter-war years both when the official regimental history and semi-mythical accounts of Hitler and his regiment were published. They took those soldiers who had been most positive and brave in their war service as *pars pro toto* of Hitler's regiment, thus editing out the war performance and experience of the majority of men of the regiment. Yet even the subsection of the regiment on which Nazi propaganda would focus was, in reality, a heterogeneous group. Albert Weisgerber's involvement in the two patrol operations is a reminder that a positive attitude towards the war and a willingness to volunteer for dangerous tasks far from equates a proto-Fascist Hitlerite political attitude or even politicization at all. Weisgerber wrote to his wife in early April: 'You see, I don't believe that the war alters men, or alters anything in the world at all. However, I do believe that some people become more simple and direct.'[76]

The new routine for the List Regiment was to rotate troops between active duty in the combat trenches, stand-by duty in the reserve trenches or the brewery at Fromelles and other buildings in and nearby Fromelles, and going on reserve in Fournes, a village 4 kilometres to the south-east of Fromelles, or in two other villages, La Bassée and Santes. The tedious and mindless reality for the next few weeks was for the men of RIR 16 to spend more time reinforcing their position and drilling than shooting at the British. All front-line trenches had to be upgraded, concrete dugouts built, barbed wire put out in front of the trenches, support trenches dug, support lines and paths created, bridges across creeks constructed, new living quarters for the soldiers put up, drainage trenches dug, and tram tracks laid. Some days, the existence of the men of the List Regiment was more akin to construction workers than to soldiers.[77]

Either from ignorance or driven by an urge not to admit that he was not fully in control of the men of the List Regiment and its sister units, the Commander of RD 6's military police, Georg Arneth, wrote to his Protestant pastor in Feldkirchen that the troops were happily putting up with the tasks put before them: 'Our troops are blessed with high spirits. They are treated well and receive good provisions. . . . They march through the towns and villages to their trenches at the front singing the usual soldier songs that one would hear at home or in the garrisons.'[78]

The reality was rather different. By late March, Schnelldorfer complained: 'I wished the troops were treated a bit better.'[79] Alexander Weiß, a soldier in RIR 16, meanwhile observed: 'It was just an unpleasant rotation between standing guard, filling sacks of sand, and working as a Sherpa.' His fellow soldiers, noted Weiß, became increasingly 'embittered' around Easter 1915.[80]

Their bitterness was not simply translated into hatred towards the British or the French. There was also growing animosity against the nation which the Bavarians had last faced on the battlefield in 1866, only five years earlier than their last military clash with the French: the Prussians. This animosity is often forgotten by historians writing about the uneasy legacy of the Franco-German War of 1870/1. Anti-Prussian feeling was indeed now rampant, which did not go unnoticed by the local population. The ophthalmologist from Lille confided to his diary a few days before Christmas: 'Recently a small difference of opinion arose at the Café Belle-Vue between Bavarian and Prussian officers. The Bavarians complained that their turn to take up the artillery position came too often. There is talk of many Bavarian deserters.'[81] Now in early 1915, the men of the List Regiment blamed Prussia increasingly often for the predicament they found themselves in. The nagging doubt that the war was not a result of the perfidy of Britain, French 'revanchism', and Russian expansionism but also of decisions taken in Berlin had indeed for many turned into a firmly held belief. After many cases in which soldiers of the List Regiment and its sister regiment had insulted, sworn at, and threatened soldiers they encountered from non-Bavarian units, the men of Hitler's regiment were told at the daily roll-calls on three successive days that their behaviour 'befitted neither the German camaraderie nor the reputation of the division'. They were warned that if their behaviour continued they would be 'most severely punished'.[82] The rise in anti-Prussian feeling in the List Regiment, which was symptomatic of the entire Bavarian Army as well as of the home front,[83] is clear evidence that the national unity after the outbreak of war—the *Burgfrieden*, in which nationalist feeling transcended all other loyalties of class, religion, or regional origins—had only temporarily existed and had already been eclipsed. For the rest of the war, the German war effort had to be based on pragmatic and temporary alliances full of potential tensions.

Hitler would later blame anti-Prussian feeling in his regiment exclusively on British propaganda leaflets, dropped from aeroplanes. The leaflets told Bavarian soldiers that the war was directed solely at Prussian militarism and that no hostility existed towards Bavaria.[84] Hitler again did not comprehend that the harshness of trench life, rather than superior British propaganda, led the men of the List Regiment to distance themselves from the war and from Prussia. Moreover, many soldiers in the List Regiment did not buy into the kind of stories and news coverage aimed at inspiring soldiers and at sustaining their morale. As Alois Schnelldorfer told his parents, he found much of the newspaper coverage of the war laughable:

> While reading the papers I discovered so many 'new' things [and learned] how wonderful the war and life in the trenches was.... Such news comes mostly from people who are five hours behind the front, who hear shooting, ask someone about it, and then explain everything... as if they had taken part in it. What I am writing to you only presents part of the truth, telling you about how *well* it's going here for me. But it's not like this every day.[85]

Officers like Wilhelm von Lüneschloß, the 52-year-old commander of 3rd Battalion who had lost an eye in 1st Ypres at Gheluvelt, did not help to make the men of the regiment feel more at ease. One day, he saw a man from RIR 16 urinate in the driveway of the house in which his horse was kept in Fournes. He lost his temper, took out his horse whip, and struck it across the back of the soldier.[86] This case was just the tip of the iceberg in the deteriorating relations between officers and troops, as revealed by evidence from units across the Bavarian Army.[87]

Josef Stettner, a soldier in RIR 16, would later recall of this time: 'the wet, indescribably bad position at Fromelles and Aubers turned the once so proud regiment into an embittered and grumbling community that was unhappy with God, the world, and itself, that performed its tough duty out of loyalty and a survival instinct. Our primary enemy in that position was... the water, mud, and the rats.'[88]

This was a period when the List Regiment and their British opponents were not trying to antagonize each other. Quite the contrary, rather than actively seeking opportunities for revenge against the British, they operated a 'live and let live' strategy, generally ignoring each other as best as they could. It was behaviour that was endemic all along the Western Front and was the result of a realization among small units facing each other for extended periods of time in trench warfare that the benefits of mutual cooperation outweighed those of aggression. In other words, soldiers understood that they operated under what game theorists call a relative simple case of a prisoner's dilemma under stable conditions in which tit-for-tat behaviour offers the highest chance of survival: if they either did not shoot at all or, when ordered to shoot, deliberately tried not to aim at the soldiers of the unit facing them, the chances were high that their adversaries would behave in the same way.[89] Very occasionally, the men of the List Regiment even tried to communicate with each other across the lines. One day, for instance, British soldiers shouted across the lines—amidst singing, whistling, and mouth-organ music—in impeccable German: 'Germans, do you still have bread? Would you like cigarettes? Do you have beer? Sing us a song!'[90] Partially as a result of this informal cooperation, only very few fatalities occurred in-between battles. For instance, just as in January, less than one soldier died on average each day in February and in April.[91] However, potentially every new battle would make the 'live and let live' approach less sustainable. Every battle would bring the possibility of more real or imagined cases of maltreatment, treachery, and massacres. After a sunny April in which, as Weisgerber reported to his wife, 'the men lie around half naked [in the trenches] and sunbathe',[92] precisely such a battle was not far away.

May brought an increase in artillery fire and in bombs dropped from British planes but it also brought a decrease in machine-gun fire.[93] Above all, it brought the glories of May to the region around Fromelles and Fournes, when Western Europe looks its most beautiful, thus lifting everybody's mood: 'The wonderful spring days have spread a rare natural glory over our region. Everything is green and blooming; the birds sing and chirp,' wrote Father Norbert. Were it not for the war and all the traces of destruction, 'one could feel completely happy where we are'.[94]

For the men of the List Regiment, 9 May was supposed to have been just another day of 'war as usual' with some intermittent fire, maybe some patrols, and possibly some more mockery from their British counterparts. RIR 16 had been lucky enough not to have been thrown into 2nd Ypres, which had started in April. Albert Weisgerber and his men from 1st Company, now in reserve for a few days while the men of 2nd and 3rd Battalions were manning the trenches, were preparing for another day of relative comfort in Fournes behind the front. But at 5 a.m. shells started to rain down heavily on Fournes. Forty-five minutes later the distant sound of heavy barrages of fire was a tell-tale sign that this day was to be different for Weisgerber and his men. Fifteen minutes later, the soldiers of 1st Company could see the men of regimental headquarters, possibly including Private Hitler, racing off towards the advance post of regimental HQ at Fromelles Castle. As night turned into a glorious, sunny May day, the heavy bombardment continued. The fire created havoc among the troops of 2nd and 3rd Battalions at the front. Otto Bestle of 8th Company saw how, a few metres away, a British shell tore the body of his comrade Josef Meisl into two pieces, severing the lower part of the body from the upper half.[95]

At 7 a.m., Bestle and Weisgerber heard an ear-splitting detonation, caused by the explosion of two mines that British troops had placed in a tunnel they had dug right under the position of 10th Company; among them was Adolf Meyer who had been transferred to the company. A pillar of fire erupted. Fountains of soil, rubble, as well as dozens of men from 10th Company were catapulted into the air. Unlike scores of his comrades, Meyer had been lucky enough to stand away from the explosion. Together with other survivors of the explosion he was encircled by British troops all day before he was freed late at night. Of the eighty-nine soldiers from 10th Company who died that day, the bodies of only forty soldiers were ever recovered from the craters of the explosion. Many of the bodies did not show any wounds, a clear sign that they had either had been killed by the air pressure from a shell explosion or suffocated, buried under metres of soil and debris. Back in the battle, British troops from the 8th Division of the BEF, who had lain hidden in the yellow rape fields behind the British trenches, poured forward. Each of them carrying 200 bullets, waterproof blankets, and food supplies for two days, they now quickly moved through the gap created in the front under the cover of the black and yellow smoke of the explosion. As the soldiers of the List Regiment were later to find out, the attack was part of the Battle of Aubers Ridge, a sideshow British troops were putting on to ease the French attempt to break through German lines further south. Many groups of men from RIR 16 were now trapped by British troops.[96] Some fell into the hands of the British, among them Engelbert Niederhofer from 9th Company. Niederhofer and his comrades had been at the centre of the heavy shelling that preceded the British advance. He had twice been buried alive. After his comrades had rescued him the second time, only eight men of his squad were still alive. Their ordeal was, however, far from over. They found themselves surrounded by British soldiers who took them prisoner. A few days later, while giving evidence to his officers after his eventual lucky escape from the British, Niederhofer recalled of the occasion:

> The Englishmen came into our trench and took the eight of us prisoner and led us towards the right to the rear of the position. Injured Englishmen lay there on the ground who immediately shot at us from all sides when we arrived

there. 2 of my mates collapsed straightaway. I jumped, so as to duck, into a hole, as did two fellow soldiers who, however, were hit in the event, one in the foot, the other in the shoulder.

Now the three of us lay still on our stomachs in the hole. After approximately half an hour, my mate to the right of me moved. Immediately a fatal shot hit him in the head, another hit me in my left buttock. When after approximately two hours my other mate lifted his head slightly, he was shot too and was instantly killed: all shots came from injured Englishmen who lay about 5 metres away. Then I was hit by a second shot at the same spot as before but I am not sure if I was hit by an infantry bullet or a shell splinter.

I remained lying on the ground as if dead for the entire day. At night, around midnight I removed my coat and crawled through the [position] past the injured and the dead. A gap in the trench created by a shell allowed me to get back here without being noticed by the British. Around 1 a.m. I reached the German position.[97]

It was at least partly for fear of enduring such an ordeal that the men of the List Regiment ferociously and aggressively fought back during the British assault. The hand grenades and machine guns in the possession of the men of the List Regiment gave them the tools and the confidence to resist forcefully. They indeed used the machine guns and hand grenades to great and lethal effect, thus slowing down the British attack. Chaos reigned wherever troops from RIR 16 and British troops engaged with each other. On many an occasion, close-range bayonet combat ensued. In a scene depicted in a photograph that became one of the most reproduced images from the List Regiment (Plate 13) Weisgerber and his men, meanwhile, were waiting all day under the trees of the park of Fournes Castle, thus being protected against detection by British planes, ready to be deployed. As dusk was approaching, Weisgerber and his men, as well as the other companies of 1st Battalion, were finally ordered to move forward, joining the fierce combat that had gone on all day. After heavy fighting throughout the night, the German lines were back in the possession of Hitler's regiment by 5 a.m. on 10 May. A total of 142 British soldiers had fallen into the hands of the List Regiment, while countless British soldiers lay dead. Yet the price the men of RIR 16 had to pay for this was enormous. On 9 and 10 May, 309 men of the List Regiment died, a figure almost as high as during the first day of battle in November. The total number of casualties ran to approximately 600. Among the dead were Albert Weisgerber and thirteen of his men, who in the middle of the night had got lost on the battlefield and had been ambushed. Weisgerber, who was 37, had been killed by two bullets, one of which had hit him in the temple.[98]

The death of Albert Weisgerber, one of Bavaria's most famous and successful painters as well as the commander of the company of which Hitler was still nominally a member, became a symbol of the sacrifices of the men of the List Regiment in the war.[99] For him, the policy of burying fallen soldiers in France, rather than taking dead bodies home to Bavaria, was not followed. After he had initially been buried by his brothers-in-arms in Fournes, his body was exhumed, taken to Munich, and buried there in early June in the presence of many soldiers and artists of the avant-gardist Neue Sezession.[100] Newspapers, meanwhile, celebrated him as 'the model of a brave soldier, a leader with incomparable courage [*Schneidigkeit*], a man of most noble character'.[101] Even in the regimental history of 1932, Albert Weisgerber was to be the celebrated hero of the List Regiment, while only perfunctory lip-service was to be paid to that other painter from 1st Company, Adolf Hitler.[102]

It took a long time after the battle before any kind of normality returned to the trenches. The massacre of Niederhofer's comrades after they had been taken prisoner by the British no doubt helped to instil into the minds of the men of the regiment a realization that continuing to fight was less dangerous than surrendering.

The claim by Adolf Schmidt, an NCO in 4th Company, that in the early hours of 10 May 1915, when recapturing a German trench, his squad had found mutilated bodies of German soldiers had a similar effect on the troops. Schmidt's superior investigated the report and concluded that, in fact, the allegation had resulted from an optical illusion due to the half-light in the recaptured trench.[103] However, the real point about these episodes is not whether they really took place. It is that soldiers of the List Regiment thought that they had occurred. Some publications directed at soldiers encouraged them to believe that they really had occurred. One such had already asked in March: 'Who will punish the fiendish criminals who cut out the eyes of our defenceless wounded?'[104]

It should also be added that a strong disincentive for soldiers to surrendering to the enemy was not just the fear of the enemy, but also of their own peers who might interpret a fellow soldier's surrender as an act of personal betrayal and treason. What could happen in that event was illustrated by the example of two British soldiers who tried to surrender to a combined unit of troops from the List Regiment, RIR 17 and RIR 20, just over a week after the battle of 9 and 10 May: 'Early on 15 May 1915, two people approached my left-wing troops,' reported an officer from RIR 17. 'I immediately realized that the two wanted to defect and gave the patrol, which had been dispatched in the meantime, the order not to shoot the two people who kept getting closer and closer to my men. As the first of the two Englishmen was still only twenty steps away from my patrol, he was shot in the head from the English side.'[105] There was nothing to choose between British and German behaviour in this regards, as a similar incident had happened in February. At the time, snipers from RIR 17 shot dead a German soldier, who had surrendered to the British, when they caught sight of him inside the British trenches.[106] Furthermore, on 6 May Albert Weisgerber had written to his wife in his last letter before his death that his men had shot dead British soldiers who had tried to surrender: 'The E[nglishmen] were on an advance post [vorgeschobenem Horchposten] and wanted to give themselves up, but as [our men] did not understand them they shot them all. The English artillery will probably avenge its fellow soldiers today.'[107]

It has been argued that it was the fear of falling into the hands of an enemy who simply takes no prisoners that really did change the combatants of the First World War and led to a brutalization of warfare. Both the perception and the reality of the execution of prisoners and other acts of violence is said to have given birth to mutual hatred and erased any sense of common origins and of a common predicament. The result supposedly was an ever faster spinning cycle of violence and an unleashing of primitive impulses such as revenge and bloodlust on the battlefield. This was, the argument goes, the end of the sentiment that had made the 1914 Christmas Truce possible. A repeat of the Truce was supposedly henceforth inconceivable.[108] This was, however, as we shall see, not quite what was to happen once Christmas 1915 came, even though 1915 was to be the most murderous year of the war. If we can believe Father Norbert's observations, the anger of the men of the 6th Reserve Division towards the English resulting from the battle did not translate into maltreatment of the British who had been taken prisoner (at any rate not once they had been led away from the battlefield): 'The bitterness against the Englishmen is terrible; however, the prisoners are being treated well.'[109] Moreover, several soldiers of RIR 16 and its sister regiments handed in personal belongings of fallen British soldiers, so that they could be returned to the families of their fallen adversaries.[110] By mid-1915 there were as yet no signs that the majority of men of the List Regiment were supporting the war for the reasons Hitler had stated in February, nor that they had become more like Hitler.

5

Of Front-Line Soldiers and 'Rear Area Pigs'

May 1915–31 December 1915

After the battle of 9 and 10 May, even the physical landscape had changed. The orchards, fields, hedges, and trees behind the trenches of RIR 16 had been turned from their spring splendour into a scorched landscape. Days after the battle, hundreds of dead bodies of British soldiers still littered the no man's land between the trenches. Worse still, for days the moans of the badly injured soldiers who lay in no man's land, doomed to die, could be heard on both sides of the front. With every day that passed, the smell of the decaying bodies left out in the ever-warmer weather worsened. The bodies were covered with flies that had laid their eggs on the bullets' point of entry. Next, the bellies of the fallen soldiers started to bloat. Then carnivorous beetles started to attack the corpses. As Alois Schnelldorfer wrote to his parents in early June: '500 Englishmen lie dead near us just over the front line, black in the face and stinking up to a kilometre away. They are horrible to see and yet men on patrol missions have to crawl close by them and even grope their way along them!'[1] When six weeks after the battle Father Norbert visited the trenches of RIR 16, the smell of the decomposing bodies was almost unbearable: 'The air is full of the stench of the putrescent bodies that after six weeks remain unburied between our trenches and those of the enemy.'[2] While Private Hitler spent his time in the relative comfort of Fournes or Fromelles, the front-line soldiers of his regiment had constantly to endure an odour that was akin to the smell of decaying fish, 'dense and cloying, sweet but not flower-sweet. Halfway between rotting fruit and rotting meat.'[3] After several weeks, the smell was so bad that soldiers crawled up to the decomposing bodies, which lay on soil sodden with the liquids of human decay, and injected a cresol solution into the corpses as a disinfectant.[4]

After the battle, Private Hitler, meanwhile, could settle back into his routine as dispatch runner for regimental headquarters rather than having to endure the intense smell of decomposing bodies. It still remained to be seen whether the recent battles had changed the mental outlook of the majority of the men of the List Regiment in a way that made them more similar to the views expressed in Hitler's letter to Ernst Hepp.

Private Hitler's assignment as dispatch runner for regimental HQ was very dangerous, as was any assignment in his regiment. By the time RIR 16 moved to its section of the front near Fromelles, it had its fourth commander, excluding one temporary fill-in. Colonel List himself had been mortally wounded. As we have seen, Hitler might well have died together with Philipp Engelhardt, the regiment's second commander, back in November. A few days prior to the incident involving Engelhardt, Hitler had already narrowly escaped death when he had been lucky enough not to have been present at the combat post of regimental HQ in Bethlehem Farm, when the post was shelled by the French forces. At the time, a piece of a French shell had flown through the door of the farm, grazing the regimental adjutant Valentin Witt and killing the divisional doctor.[5]

Hitler, however, claimed that his job was not just very dangerous but that it was more dangerous than any other assignment in his regiment. In early December 1914, Hitler had already written to Joseph Popp of his post as regimental dispatch runner: 'Ever since [being appointed dispatch runner], I have, so to speak, been risking my life every day, looking death straight in the eye.' From that, Hitler concluded: 'It is a sheer miracle that I am hale and hearty.'[6] In February, he had written to his Munich acquaintance telling him that his assignment as dispatch runner for regimental HQ was 'slightly less dirty work but all the more dangerous'.[7] Hitler was already an incorrigible embellisher of his own war service. For instance, in January 1915, he wrote to his Munich landlord of the German capture of Messines in 1st Ypres:

> First we stormed the place. The English put up a desperate defence. Only when our heavy artillery opened up and our 21-cm mortars produced craters, each large enough for a hay-cart to turn round in without difficulty, and only when the whole village with its great monastery went up in flames, did our regiments manage to take it amidst streams of blood.[8]

Hitler clearly implies here that his own regiment was involved in the capture of Messines, not volunteering the information that at the time of the fall of Messines, the List Regiment was still fighting close to Gheluvelt.

Hitler's job in the war was all the more dangerous, as Nazi school textbooks and other propaganda accounts would recount, because he had to take messages through machine-gun fire from trench to trench, while ordinary front-line soldiers could find some protection from enemy fire inside the trenches. For instance, the 1935 children's book *Die Geschichte von Adolf Hitler den Deutschen Kindern Erzählt* (*The Story of Adolf Hitler Told for Children*) gives an account of young Hitler constantly fighting his way through collapsing trenches, infantry fire, and exploding shells,[9] concluding:

> Hitler was always one of the bravest soldiers in every battle. His comrades at that time later said that they often marvelled that Hitler had not met with a bullet long ago. Because he was so brave and dependable, he was made a dispatch runner. He had to run straight through gunfire and bring news from one officer to another. This was a very dangerous job but Hitler always performed it courageously and quietly. For this, the Kaiser first gave him the Iron Cross Second Class, and after that even the Iron Cross First Class, which only the very bravest soldiers were given.[10]

In the same vein, Karl Lippert, the NCO in charge of the regimental dispatch runners, claimed in 1940 that during one of their missions in early 1915 Adolf Hitler, Anton Bachmann, and he himself 'ran into . . . heavy machine-gun fire' at 'the street intersection in Messines'.[11] Similarly, in 1940, Hitler's fellow dispatch runner Heinrich Lugauer told the Nazi Party archive, which for propaganda purposes was recording testimony of Hitler's former comrades: 'I specifically remember his perpetual readiness for duty in the delivering of dispatches near Fromelles in early 1915. He would regularly take up the more dangerous routes for his married comrades. Actually we shook our heads often enough in disbelief that he managed to return completely unharmed, particularly during the advance on the Marne.'[12] Ignaz Westenkirchner, one of Hitler's other fellow dispatch runners, tried to underline how dangerous Hitler's and his task was by pointing out: 'Generally two of us were sent out together, each bearing the same dispatches, in case anything happened to either of us.'[13] Meanwhile, Hans Mend, a cavalry dispatcher in the List Regiment, claimed in the introduction to his quasi-hagiographical account of Hitler's war years, first published in 1930, that Hitler was 'brave, fearless, outstanding'.[14]

Similar characterizations were provided by Balthasar Brandmayer in the 1930s when he told a heart-warming story about how Hitler volunteered to take over his job for two weeks in addition to his own, so that Brandmayer could visit his family in Germany.[15] Similarly, Max Amann, the Staff Sergeant of regimental HQ, told US interrogators in May 1945: 'Hitler was courageous and stood up well under strain; even then he showed a passion for war.'[16]

These accounts would indeed suggest that Hitler's war service was very similar to that of front-line combat soldiers, and possibly even more dangerous. They would also suggest that Hitler and the men of his regiment formed a band of brothers. But are these accounts reliable?

According to much of the literature on Hitler they are indeed trustworthy. In fact, they have informed much of what historians have written about Hitler and the role the First World War had in 'making' him. One of the most popular books on the First World War from the 1990s, for instance, tells us that Hitler had to carry 'messages up and down the front line through barrages and bullets' and that his job was thus 'one of the war's most dangerous assignments'.[17] Elsewhere we are told that Hitler was a 'battalion runner' (which was a considerably more dangerous post),[18] rather than a runner for regimental HQ. We are also told that the fact that Hitler 'survived for four years, while he watched thousands of his colleagues killed, was mere chance'.[19] According to one of the standard Hitler biographies, Hitler had to take messages to the forward positions of the List Regiment and any doubts that were later expressed about his bravery were just politically motivated.[20] A 1990s TV documentary for the BBC and PBS, meanwhile, characterized Hitler's job as 'extremely dangerous . . . because it involved subjecting yourself to artillery fire and to machine gun fire'.[21] Another Hitler biography tells us that Hitler showed 'exceptional courage' during the war and 'escaped death an inordinate number of times'. Evidence for this characterization included the fact that at 1st Ypres, 'under heavy fire Hitler, now a regimental dispatch carrier, found a medic and the two dragged the deputy [regimental commander] back to the dressing station'.[22] Hitler also was, we are told, the epitome of a combat soldier: 'As he slouched around, rifle in hand, helmet askew, moustache drooping, "a lively glow" in his eyes, he was the picture of the front-line fighter.' We are also told that Hitler survived three months in the Battle of the Somme, one of the bloodiest battles of world history.[23] Hitler was, 'as brave as the next man and a good deal more conscientious'.[24]

The key message of all these accounts of Hitler's war service is that he was an exceptionally brave and heroic soldier and that he had been seen by the men of the List Regiment as one of their own. It is this view that lies at the core of the conventional view about Hitler's years in the List Regiment during the First World War according to which the regiment was the 'university' that formed him.

The reality of Hitler's war existence was rather different. Private Hitler had to alternate between three day shifts at the advance post of regimental HQ inside Fromelles Castle and three day shifts at the regular regimental headquarters in Fournes, where the administrative support of the regiment was based.[25] Fournes lay an hour's walk from Fromelles behind the front. Even though British and French artillery fire had inflicted severe damage on the church, school, and the rest of the village in October 1914[26] and even though pre-war guidebooks had warned tourists of the 'primitive provincial characteristics' of inns and 'watering places' in places like Fourmes,[27] Private Hitler's domicile seemed like heaven to the soldiers of RIR 16. The popular claim that Hitler 'knew what it meant to live in the mud and the slime of the Western Front'[28] is thus quite wrong.

Fridolin Solleder would later recall that life in Fournes was totally different from the life in the trenches: 'The lovely summer sun in Flanders and the cool breeze that blows from the sea lets the infantrymen—who are staying a good hour away in the quiet quarters behind Fromelles, where French children play "shop" with grenade splinters and play with balls of shrapnel—soon forget the horrors of the trenches.'[29] Fournes, which had existed for a millennium, was well past its prime, mostly consisting of long rows of modest brick buildings. Yet the elegant eighteenth-century castle, the bandstand at the centre of the village, as well as the little chapel opposite the bandstand similar to the kind that could be found in every village in Catholic regions of Bavaria gave Fournes a charm and a sense of home and belonging that stood in stark contrast to life in the trenches. While the chateau housed the HQ of the 12th Reserve Brigade, the regimental HQ of RIR 16 was located in the home of the local public notary, which was one of Fournes' most elegant houses. Private Hitler and his fellow dispatch runners had been assigned a room in the building attached to the rear of the main building.[30]

As a dispatch runner for regimental HQ, Hitler's main task was to take messages to the headquarters of the regiment's battalions. The job to take messages to the trenches was generally left to dispatch runners of battalions and of companies. This is not to say that he never made it to a trench but this was not normally his job. The primary danger for Hitler was artillery fire behind the front and not machine-gun and rifle fire or any of the other grave hazards of trench life such as from mines explosions right under German trenches. Karl Lippert's 1940 claim that Hitler and he had been subject to heavy machine-gun fire at the crossroads in Messines is fictitious. No concerted machine-gun fire could have reached all the way to Messines from the British positions at the bottom of Messines Ridge.[31] Similarly, Ignaz Westenkirchner's 'proof' of the extraordinary danger of Hitler's post—namely that two dispatch runners had to be deployed in order to make sure that at least one runner would get the message through—needs to be treated with great caution. In fact, according to Hitler's superior, Fritz Wiedemann, sending two dispatch runners was standard procedure which due to the shortage of men during the war was rarely followed in the List Regiment.[32] Moreover, Brandmayer's claim that Hitler took over his duties for a fortnight is bogus. Even if Hitler had volunteered to do so, it would have simply been impossible for him to carry out the duties of two dispatch runners unless he had gone totally without sleep for two weeks.

It is difficult to find anything accurate in the statement from one of the standard Hitler biographies about Hitler's rescue of the deputy regimental commander at Gheluvelt in late October, according to which, as we have seen, 'under heavy fire Hitler, now a regimental dispatch carrier, found a medic and the two dragged the deputy [regimental commander] back to the dressing station.'[33] For a start, Hitler was not yet a regimental dispatch carrier when the List Regiment fought at Gheluvelt and thus not attached to regimental HQ. Moreover, the deputy regimental commander—Hitler presumably refers to the regimental adjutant, Lieutenant Philipp Schnitzlein, here, as there was no such rank as a deputy regimental commander—was injured on 31 October in Gheluvelt.[34] On that day, however, Hitler's company spent its time in the relative calm of a former British trench outside of the park of Gheluvelt Castle.[35] Hitler was thus not anywhere near Schnitzlein and could not possibly have been in a position to save Schnitzlein 'under heavy fire'. Furthermore, the portrayal of Hitler as 'the picture of a front-line fighter' is more akin to the kind of description Nazi propaganda liked to give than to an accurate rendering of the appearance of a dispatch runner. Furthermore, Hitler was not to spend three months in the Battle of the Somme. In fact, as we shall see, Hitler was only to spend four days in that battle.

One might still wonder though, as historians repeatedly have,[36] whether the early award of an Iron Cross 2nd Class to Hitler, as well as the award of an Iron Cross 1st Class in 1918, did indeed suggest that Hitler's job had been exceptionally dangerous and that he had been unusually brave and heroic in his service. It was, we are told, 'a rare achievement for a corporal' to receive both Iron Crosses.[37] One of the standard Hitler biographies also points out that the new regimental adjutant, Fritz Wiedemann, and the regimental Staff Sergeant, Max Amann, had even proposed Hitler for an Iron Cross 1st Class in November 1914: 'Wiedemann and Sergeant Amann now had time to make up the decoration list. They recommended Hitler for the Iron Cross, 1st Class, but since he was on the staff put his name at the bottom of the list. For this reason alone Hitler was turned down and instead given a 2nd Class award'.[38]

This story is little more than fiction, as Wiedemann was still serving with RIR 17 at the time and did not join RIR 16 and become its regimental adjutant until 1915.[39] There are good reasons to doubt even the proposition that the award of the Iron Crosses suggests extraordinary bravery on Hitler's part compared to the rest of the List Regiment. While certainly an award for bravery, the Iron Cross being awarded to Hitler does not necessarily prove that he was more courageous than most men in the front line. Often the award of an Iron Cross signified rather how well connected soldiers were to regimental headquarters than serving as an absolute measure of a soldier's bravery. In other words, Iron Crosses tended to go either directly to officers, such as the Commander of RD 6's military police unit, Georg Arneth, or to those soldiers who were familiar with the officers who had the privilege to nominate soldiers for awards. It was thus little surprise that the sixty recipients of Iron Crosses on 2 December included the four dispatch runners of regimental HQ. At the same time, Father Norbert (who himself had been awarded an Iron Cross in mid-November which he proudly wore attached to his monk's habit) had recorded in the aftermath of the baptism of fire of RD 6 the disappointment many soldiers felt at having not been honoured.[40] In short, the mere fact that Hitler was assigned to regimental headquarters, rather than his commitment and dedication, increased his chances of receiving an Iron Cross. That combat soldiers were less likely to receive Iron Crosses than men behind the front was even posited by Fridolin Solleder in the official 1932 regimental history:

> In fairness towards the comrades who stood in the first line of fire year long without anything but wounds to show as decoration, we have to say that the

healthy belief of our Bavarian Crown Prince—that Iron Crosses should above
all be awarded to combat troops—unfortunately was not acted upon. Among
combat troops themselves, in which so few ranks could ever be decorated, it
was only natural that there were hardly any left for the plain front-line
soldiers.[41]

The resentment front-line soldiers still felt years after the war about the
privileged award of Iron Crosses to non-combat soldiers like Hitler found its
expression in the fact that Hans Ostermünchner, a sniper in RIR 16,
underlined the above passage in his own copy of the regiment's history.[42]

One might, of course, raise the question of how we explain that, as Nazi
propaganda wants us to believe, almost all officers, as well as virtually all
veterans of the List Regiment, irrespective of their political convictions,
stood by Hitler when newspapers questioned his version of his war service
in the 1920s and early 1930s.[43] The answer is that the claims made by Nazi
propagandists are simply not true.

Ostensibly the claim made by Hitler's spin doctors appears true if we
look at a number of instances in which soldiers and officers of the
regiment gave testimony in support of Hitler's vendettas in German
courtrooms against the newspapers that questioned his account of his
war service. For instance, Wilhelm von Lüneschloß, the one-eyed
former commander of 3rd Battalion, was to testify in 1922 that Hitler
'was a dispatch runner for the staff of [RIR 16] and had truly proved
himself as such. Hitler never failed and was particularly suited to the
tasks that one could not give to the other dispatch runners.'[44] Similarly,
on the same occasion, Friedrich Petz, who had commanded RIR 16
during the first war winter, was to declare: 'Hitler was an exceedingly
diligent, willing, conscientious, and dutiful soldier, and he was also
unfailingly reliable and truly devoted to his superiors. He proved himself
to be mentally very active and physically fresh, deft, and strong. Particularly stressed should be his personal grit and the ruthless courage with
which he confronted the most dangerous circumstances and the perils of
battle.'[45] Two other former regimental commanders, Emil Spatny and
Anton von Tubeuf, were to express similar views.[46] Yet, it was the
testimony Michael Schlehuber, a committed Social Democrat and
trade unionist, was to give in support of Hitler in 1932 that is apparently
the best piece of evidence that there was no substance in the claim that
Hitler's real war service had been significantly different from Hitler's
mythical version. Schlehuber was to declare:

I've known Hitler since our deployment [*Ausmasch*] with the Bavarian Reserve Infantry Regiment 16 and was with him in the Bethlehem-Ferme in mid-November 1914, likewise during combat ordinance. I knew Hitler as a good soldier and an impeccable comrade. I never observed Hitler trying to shirk his duties or holding back from danger. I was within the division from deployment to the return home, and I never heard anything unfavourable about Hitler even later on. I was astounded to read adverse reports about Hitler's accomplishments as a soldier in the newspapers. Politically, I stand at the other end of the spectrum from Hitler and am giving this opinion only because I think highly of Hitler as a war comrade.[47]

The claim that the officers and troops of his regiment almost universally stood by him also appears to be supported by the facts, if we look at a collection of letters in the Nazi Party archives that were sent by veterans of the List Regiment to Hitler. A number of these letters indeed offer Hitler assistance against newspaper accusations against him.[48]

Looking exclusively at this set of sources, however, is a case of an observational selection fallacy. In plain English, this means that by focusing on these pieces of evidence we look only where the Nazi propagandists wanted us to look. Hitler would hardly have asked soldiers who disagreed with him to provide evidence for him in legal proceedings. Moreover, we would hardly expect to find soldiers critical of Hitler to write to him and for those letters to be housed in a collection of the NSDAP archive called 'Reports and Statements of Former Front Comrades'.

However, if we track down the newspaper articles critical of Hitler's version of his war years we soon realize that they were often written by veterans of the List Regiment. One such article was published by the *Volksfreund*, a Social Democratic newspaper in the north German city of Braunschweig, when Hitler ran unsuccessfully for the German presidency in 1932. The state of Braunschweig, incidentally, had also finally given German citizenship to Hitler earlier that year without which he could not have run for the presidency and could not have been appointed Chancellor in 1933.

The article was written by Josef Stettner, whom we have encountered before. Through Stettner's eyes, Hitler's war experience looked like a life of plenty. This did not endear Hitler to Stettner:

Hitler had worked out for himself how to get out of the line of fire on time. He had already managed to get a small post as regimental dispatch runner behind the front at the end of 1914. At first he lay with the regimental staff in the underground vaults and basements of Fromelles. For months, the infantry companies that lay in reserve behind the front and pioneers that had specially been deployed for this task had to make the shelters of the regimental staff bomb-proof. While we had to lie in the wet trenches at the front line for seven to ten days without a break or while we stood up to our stomachs in the mud, Hitler lay on a warm, lice-free stretcher and had several metres of protective stone above his hero's body.

But it did not take very long before the entire regimental staff set itself up even more comfortably in Fournes, approximately 10 kilometres behind the first line. There for more than a year the dispatch runners had a room of their own in a former Estaminet (small pub or café). Every one of us in the trench would have given his eye teeth to swap with the hero Hitler even just for eight days.

. . . The front experience of Private Hitler consisted more in the consumption of artificial honey and tea than of the participation in any combat. He was separated from the actual combat zone by a zone some 10 kilometres deep. Thousands of family fathers would have filled Hitler's little post behind the front just as well as him: however, at the time Hitler did not display any sign that he felt driven towards military front-line action, as he is trying to tell the blinded German youth today. He did, as we front-line soldiers used to say at the time, 'keep his position'.[49]

Josef Stettner reminds us that as a dispatch runner for regimental HQ, rather than for a battalion or a company, Hitler rarely had to cross the line of fire:

Some worshippers of Hitler have pointed out now that the job of a dispatch runner was more dangerous than that of a soldier in the trenches. While the troops in the first line could calmly lie under cover, it is said in Hitler's defence, the dispatch runners would have been much more exposed to enemy fire while on duty. However, I can accept that only for dispatch runners of companies or maybe also of battalions. In the worst-case scenario, the regimental dispatch runner had to go to the dugout of a battalion which still lay far behind the first line. And even in those cases, it was for the most part the dispatch runners of the battalion themselves who had to pick up the messages at the regimental headquarters, particularly when things were getting dangerous. All the duties of a regimental dispatch runner lay outside the dangerous zone of machine-gun fire.[50]

Even the command posts of the battalions were well behind the front, as Fridolin Solleder's account in the official regimental history confirms.[51] Most of Stettner's claims are confirmed by other sources produced both during and after the war. The gist of his account is also verified by an article by another veteran of the List Regiment which was to appear in the *Echo der*

Woche, the weekend edition of a Social Democratic newspaper in Hamburg, and by the accounts of a medic who joined the List Regiment in September 1915 and who was to serve from then until the end of the war with Hitler in regimental HQ.

The *Echo der Woche* article—the contents of which closely mirrored Stettner's account—was to become the subject of a legal battle between Hitler and the paper which, as we shall see, Hitler brilliantly exploited in his attempt to falsify the historical account of his war record. The great obstacle for the defence team of the *Echo der Woche* was that the paper had decided that in order to protect his safety it would not disclose the identity of the veteran who was the author of the bitter attack on Hitler's war record. This made it much easier for Hitler to dismiss the article as politically motivated and as having been fabricated from thin air. The only information we have about the identity of the article's author is that he had started the war as a reservist, that he came from the Bavarian mountains, had been a member of the same company as Hitler at the beginning of the war, that he continued to serve in the same company throughout the war, that he received Iron Crosses of both classes, and that he was heavily injured during the war.[52] Unlike Hitler in 1932, we can today match these pieces of information with the muster rolls of 1st Company and the records pertaining to the Iron Crosses awarded to members of RIR 16 and thus identify the author of the article.

The only member of 1st Company who fits all criteria is Korbinian Rutz. Rutz was not just any soldier. On the contrary, the teacher from the Upper Bavarian countryside during the war was the photographer of the blurry, borderline insulting photograph of Hitler used by the 1932 regimental history. Furthermore, Rutz was the Commander of 1st Company. He had begun the war as a battalion dispatch runner in the List Regiment but by 1916 had become the Commander of 1st Company[53] and was known during the war 'for his exemplary intrepidness and sangfroid'.[54] As a former dispatch runner and as the commander of the unit of which Hitler was a member for the first half of the war, Rutz thus knew perfectly well what he was writing about.

The medic whose account also supports Stettner's recollection, meanwhile, was Alexander Moritz Frey, a writer of grotesque, satirical, fantastic novels and short stories, whose friends included Thomas Mann as well as Franz Marc. In 1946 Frey recalled of his encounters with Hitler: 'Although we were assigned different duties, we encountered one another quite often.

Taken out of our companies, we were both assigned to regimental HQ.' According to Frey, their tasks were as follows: 'As a subordinate, Hitler had to bring news and the like to the battalion HQs. I worked for the regimental doctor at the casualty station, or as a scribe in the resting quarters.' Frey recalled that service even in Fromelles was still considerably less dangerous than that in the trenches, not least since artillery fire tended only to rain down at Fromelles in a predictable pattern: 'The Englishmen bestowed the "evening blessing" upon us every day [in Fromelles]; three shots came from long-distance cannons every day almost to the same minute. Three shells exploded in the already crushed ruins of the village. We knew that and holed ourselves up at that time.' Frey thought that Hitler had neither been a hero nor a coward: 'Claims that he was cowardly are untrue. But he was also not courageous—he lacked the requisite composure. He was always alert, ready for action, conniving, very much caring about himself; all comradeship was a façade, put on in order to make himself popular and to make a striking impression.' Frey, who was eight years Hitler's senior, concurs with Stettner that Hitler's and his service had been rather different and rather safer than that of front-line soldiers in the trenches. Even at the price of non-promotion, Frey argued, the members of the support staff of regimental HQ were eager to keep their posts:

> Without a doubt Hitler could have re-enlisted with a company and done trench duty with the goal of promotion. But he did not seem to have wanted that; there were certain positions, so treasured that if troops got hold of them, they would not want to give them up, as they had certain automatic advantages. In this case, these were better quarters and better food than infantryman in the trenches had. I had to resist the urging of my company commander that I leave my post in the medical service (since I was not a doctor, I couldn't go much farther in this particular field) and take part in an officer training course. I did not want to leave my field of work—probably for the same reasons that Hitler did not want to leave his. Measured against the dreadful hardship of trench duty, our posting was a small alleviation, combined with small comforts.[55]

Frey made the privileged war experience of Hitler and himself also the subject of a novel published in 1945 as *Hölle und Himmel* (*Hell and Heaven*):

> We received reasonably decent meals, at least some of the time, even into 1918, along with Sergeant Bähmann [as Amann is called in the novel], Corporal Wurm, and two dozen other men. All the while, the others, who spent their time outside in the trenches, had long ago received nothing much better than filth to eat. We still had the better uniforms and the dryer quarters

than all the others. We were cleaner on the whole. No wonder, as we were in the constant company of the officers of Regimental HQ. . . . I don't want to say that it was easy for us, but Severin [Hitler's name in the novel], it was better for us than for the most people, of whom you expected to keep going until they had no trousers on their backsides and no barley in their stomachs. They then have to stand across from your picture-perfectly clothed and well-nourished form in this state . . .

You (should have) gone into the trenches at the time, because then you would have had to . . . say goodbye to the quarters of regimental HQ and their covered saucepots . . . Do you know what the trench soldiers, these exhausted and tired-out men, occasionally said, after you gave them a pep talk when they reached us in our quarters? 'Severin [i.e. Hitler] shouldn't hang around here. He should join us in the real shit.' Now you haven't dodged your duty, you have carried out your duties in a soldierly manner, but you did so from behind the trenches and like me, with a degree of security. Wherever high-ranking officers (colonels and so on) had to do their duty, there was always still a remnant of outward order, of soap, edible food, of a roof above one's head. We got to enjoy that.[56]

The fact that even Frey was to be awarded an Iron Cross 2nd Class in late 1917,[57] even though he had tried as hard as he could to stay out of harm's way, is yet another proof that Iron Crosses were more an indicator of how close soldiers were to the officers who proposed men for such awards than of how dangerous and courageous the conduct of the recipients of the crosses really was. It is also of note that Frey's short stories and novels—such as 'Der Pass', published in 1915, which is highly critical of the spy fever and the blindness of the masses in wartime Germany and which features the metamorphosis of the story's protagonist from a German into a French-man[58]—did not stop Frey from receiving his Iron Cross. In other words, the award of Iron Crosses to Hitler and Frey as men with very different political convictions suggests that the award of Iron Crosses to Hitler should not be taken as a sign of similarity of political attitude between Hitler and the officers of the List Regiment.

The question, of course, still remains how representative Stettner's and Frey's accounts are of the views held by members of RIR 16. Stettner, who clearly had Social Democratic leanings, tried to discredit Hitler as much as he could in his article to prevent Hitler from being elected German president, while Frey, who had to spend the long years of the Third Reich in exile, clearly had an axe to grind.

However, even Adolf Meyer inadvertently confirms the validity of much of Stettner's and Frey's claims in his 1934 memoirs. While emphasizing the extraordinary courage of Hitler in certain sections of his book, his account of his first two encounters with Hitler, when Meyer—at the time an NCO—was still serving with 10th Company in the trenches, gives credence to Stettner's account. Both encounters took place in the troops' living quarters, consisting of corrugated iron huts rather than dugouts, a few hundred metres behind the front. On one occasion, Hitler had just returned from a mission to the List Regiment's sister regiment rather than from the trenches. During the encounter, there was a fundamental divide between the front-line soldiers and Hitler over how they perceived an existence a few hundred metres behind the front. Hitler had rolled up his epaulettes to avoid identification of his unit by the enemy as was required in combat zones, whereas the men of 10th Company wore them openly on display because they considered their living quarters to lie outside the combat zone. Hitler thus genuinely perceived an area that front-line soldiers thought belonged to the rear area, as lying in the front-line combat zone.[59]

Alois Schnelldorfer's letters to his parents also testify to the gulf in the war experience that existed between men serving in the trenches and those serving like Hitler with regimental HQ. Schnelldorfer himself had been transferred from his service in the trenches to regimental HQ in early April. Ever since then, he had been assigned to serve with the signal units. Like Hitler, he now divided his time between regimental HQ in Fournes and the advance post of HQ in Fromelles. Like Hitler, he also had to operate in the open in the area behind the immediate front line as he had to check daily and repair the telephone lines of the regiment. After being transferred, he told his parents: 'Was transferred to the signal unit today. This is very different from being a sapper. I sit in a chair and wait for news . . . You see that things are getting better for me all the time. By the end, I'll probably have absolutely nothing to do. But I will still be here a long time.'[60] A week later, he elaborated on his service: 'I am now, as I wrote before, with the signal unit. It's going very well for me there. My task is to sit in an armchair and make calls like a postmistress . . . . Then there are the patrols at night, mending wires, etc. . . . Today I slept on a mattress until 10 in the morning. I wasn't allowed to do that with my old company. It was like being at home.'[61] By the end of the month, he still could not believe his luck at being able to serve with regimental HQ: 'It is now so different; being a signal technician or telephonist I don't have to do physical work any more, I don't have to stand guard . . . I'm also always well groomed and my hands are clean so that I look respectable when I bring [news] to a company commander or to regimental HQ.'[62] Schnelldorfer also told his parents that men like him received more generous provisions than the men in the trenches: 'I don't need to go hungry, thank God. You will have seen from my last letter that I'm doing very well with the signal unit. . . . It is very good in Fournes. I can drink a litre of beer under a shady walnut tree. . . . I have free rein in Fournes as a telephonist.'[63] When Schnelldorfer encountered two soldiers in early July with whom he had trained as recruits but who were still serving in the trenches, he immediately realized how different the impact of service with regimental HQ had been compared with service in the first line of fire. He told his parents that 'most people think that I have just arrived since I look so well', while the two soldiers with whom he had been trained 'looked pretty bad. I look the complete opposite.'[64]

We can find watertight confirmation that Stettner's and Frey's views were widely shared by members of the List Regiment where we would least expect it, namely among the letters veterans sent to Hitler that found their way into the archive of the Nazi Party. However, this particular letter is not housed with the collection of quasi-hagiographical letters to him grouped under 'Reports and Statements by former Front-line Comrades'.[65] It is hidden away in a miscellaneous collection of letters.[66] The letter was written by Ferdinand Widman, who had served with Hitler at regimental HQ. Formerly a musician, by the early 1930s he was a low-paid local official in the Lower Bavarian village of Mengkofen. Widman felt compelled to write to Hitler in 1932, when Hitler was engaged in furious legal activity against anybody who questioned his war record. In the letter, he told Hitler that he should know well that the essence of the attacks against him was almost identical with that of the consensus view among combat front-line soldiers in the List Regiment during the war, namely that 'all the soldiers in the trenches thought that those serving with regimental HQ were [already] rear area pigs [*Etappenschweine*]'. He went on to recall how there had been a 'general outcry' in the regiment when the regiment's dispatch runners had received holidays. 'Millions think so and the job as dispatch runner is thought little of by all these men,' he wrote to Hitler. He concluded that while both he and Hitler had, of course, served honourably, much of the criticism directed at them was not without merit, telling Hitler that he could not deny that the conditions under which they had to serve had been very different and indeed better than that of front-line combat soldiers:

> It cannot be ignored that life was indeed better at regimental headquarters than with a company. Adolf, we can't deny that we were regimental staff members. The belief that no infantry or machine-gun bullet could have struck a dispatch runner is the opinion of these people. However, they don't mean this in an ill manner, because whoever did not lie in a trench achieved nothing in their minds. You are not to be held responsible for your residence in the basement of the monastery in Messines, or in the secure shelters in Fromelles and Fournes. You also were not the one to decide that these shelters should even be built.[67]

There was thus indeed a growing gulf between Private Hitler and the men of regimental HQ and front-line soldiers, rather than a convergence of attitudes and experiences of Hitler and the majority of the men of the regiment following the Battles of Neuve Chapelle and Aubers Ridge. The full significance of that growing gulf for the development of Hitler and his rise to power was to become apparent only much later.

Between mid-May and the end of the year, the List Regiment was not involved in any major battles. As Georg Arneth noted in a letter to the Protestant pastor of Feldkirchen in late August, the men of RD 6 were very lucky that their opponents did not realize quite what bad a state their units were in:

> If our enemies knew how weak we were here, they would certainly have handled themselves differently. . . . It is a huge secret, and speaking of troop movements etc. is harshly punishable. Everything is in the East. . . . I mentioned how I found out from a officer who had been on leave that in Munich it is often said that the brave army stands in the East, and the fire department is fighting in the West.[68]

The one time the List Regiment was involved in battle between May and the end of the year was in the Battle of Loos—the failed renewed British attempt to break through the German lines that took place some 10 kilometres south of the section of the front occupied by the List Regiment. Only two companies from RIR 16 were deployed at Loos. However, they were involved in very fierce combat. Seventy-four, or almost 28 per cent, of the soldiers from RIR 16 who fought in the battle became casualties.[69] 'Our military hospital was overflowing with the wounded, both serious and minor cases,' noted Robert Hell, one of the Protestant divisional chaplains. 'A hall in Ward 1 was and is still a picture of misery: nearly all are victims of bullets in the head. One can speak to very few of them. They dream, and gasp for breath.'[70] Among the soldiers killed in action at Loos was Leopold Rothärmel, a Catholic volunteer with a citation for bravery on a patrol and a musician seventeen days short of his eighteenth birthday.[71] His body was to be excavated eight decades later by a British TV crew and rather bizarrely given the identity of a Jewish soldier for dramatic purposes.[72]

Even though Rothärmel was not Jewish, the case of the Jewish soldiers from RIR 16 in the Battle of Loos testifies to the, by and large, continued amicable relationship between Jews and non-Jews in Hitler's regiment and its division. One of the two officers in charge of the contingent from RIR 16 deployed in Loos was Hugo Gutmann, the adjutant of 3rd Battalion, a Jew from Nuremberg nine years Hitler's senior who had joined the regiment in early 1915. Hitler's and Gutmann's interaction at the end of the war was to influence each other's lives dramatically once Hitler had risen to prominence.[73]

Prior to the Battle of Loos, Oscar Daumiller had held brief services for the men of the division. In his official report for 1915, he was full of praise for the behaviour of a Jewish company commander (whose name he does not provide) during these services. He recalled of the occasion: 'As I [illegible word] and prayed with two companies in the monastery garden in Beau-camps, where they stood ready to move out, a Jewish company leader came to me and asked me to come to his company; [he told me that his men] stood in the other courtyard; I responded: "I was just about to come anyway, but I'm happy that you asked me personally." '[74]

With the exception of the Battle of Loos, this was a period of low-level conflict, in which every day, on average, between one and two soldiers were killed and in which, at times, the 6th Reserve Division noted that their British counterparts were seriously short of both infantry and artillery ammunition. At night the men of the List Regiment now had busily to reinforce their positions, to try to dig tunnels under enemy positions, and to guard the trenches. With dawn came the highest risk of attacks and fire. Once the sun had risen, with the exception of a few men who had to act as guards, it was time for the men to go to sleep. During the day, snipers or artillery would only occasionally fire across the trenches. In the heat of the summer of 1915, as planes became an increasingly common sight in the skies above the trenches close to Fromelles and as wells dried up, the men of RIR

16 were kitted out with their first, still very primitive, gas masks, as the British had recently introduced gas into their arsenal following the French and Germans. (All three nations had already experimented with the military application of gas prior to the war.)[75]

The realization had spread that the war would not be over any time soon. In June, Alois Schnelldorfer came to the conclusion that 'I think we should be happy if we don't have to fight World War [19]14–[19]15–[19] 16.'[76] By early July, Schnelldorfer told his parents: 'Until now there has still been damned little hope for peace.'[77] Even though the men of the List Regiment did realize that the war was going to last longer than anticipated, they always assumed that it would be over within a manageable time-frame. This explains why the realization that this was to be a longer war than anticipated did not lead to a widespread drop in morale. What has been said about the attitude of the French people to the war can also be applied to the men of Hitler's regiment: 'they found that each new phase brought with it the hope that this would be the last. They were like the mountaineer who, at every peak, discovers another rising beyond.'[78] The men of RIR 16 simply did not foresee how long and how cruel an ordeal the war was still going to be.

What gave the men of the List Regiment confidence and a continued willingness to fight beyond this was the arrival of good news from the Eastern Front which made it possible for soldiers to imagine that the war would be over within a manageable time-frame and thus that their chances of personal survival were very high (even though the entry of Italy into the war on the side of the British, French, and Russians was source of some concern in the regiment).[79]

In late May, Schnelldorfer had already come to the conclusion that the war in the East would be decisive: 'With the situation here and with all the attacks of the Englishmen, there is still no peace in sight. The whole thing will be decided in Russia, I think, and when we get troops from there, we'll be able to break through here too....'[80] In June, he wrote: 'When it's all over in Russia then it will happen the same way here. General offensive. March, march to Calais. Then to England for all I care; this would give me the opportunity to go there.'[81] By 25 July, Schnelldorfer thought that the war in the East was almost won: 'By the time you get this letter, Warsaw will have fallen. Then the offensive will come here.'[82]

However, as we shall shortly see, what boosted the willingness of the men of the List Regiment to fight above all was the availability of hand grenades, which the men were busily being trained to use.[83] The hand grenades helped to overcome the feeling of impotence and the perception that the enemy had an advantage in the use of weapons available to them.[84] It was those feelings which lay at the heart of fear among soldiers. The new ready availability of hand grenades gave many combatants of RIR 16 new hope of victory and allowed them to subdue their fear and to continue to perform.

The flipside of the new heavy reliance on hand grenades was, as Emil Spatny, the Commander of 2nd Battalion, concluded after the Battle of Loos, that a 'lack of hand grenades immediately arouses the feeling of insecurity in a troop that finds itself in battle, and can lead to panic in certain circumstances'.[85] The downside of hand grenades was also that accidents were almost unavoidable. In the battle of 9 and 10 May, for instance, a soldier from 8th Company had thrown his hand grenade too early, giving a British soldier time to throw it back, thus tearing the German soldier to pieces.[86] On another occasion, a soldier dropped a bag full of hand grenades during a practice session behind the front, killing himself as well as three of his comrades and injuring another twenty soldiers.[87] Yet accidents like these were rare. The men of the List Regiment tended to look at the positive side of having hand grenades, as a battle report from the Battle of Loos reveals. According to the report, hand grenades gave the men a sense that they could really overpower their opponents in an attack. In the Battle of Loos, hand grenades made all the difference to the men of the combined unit from RIR 16 and RIR 17. The 5,000 hand grenades they threw gave them the courage to charge forward and clear out British trenches in what the battle report of the List Regiment called a 'vehement' fashion.[88] Yet it should be borne in mind that hand grenade attacks were often performed by soldiers who had volunteered for the task. The gung-ho confidence hand grenades instilled in men was thus arguably a phenomenon primarily among a self-selected subgroup of the men of the regiment.

The same is true of the brutalization of members of RIR 16 and of the Bavarian Army in general. Brutalization had certainly occurred among some men of the regiment. Interestingly, however, the most gung-ho anti-British attitude emanated not from the men in the trenches but, as at least one case suggests, from the relative safety of the support staff of regimental HQ. On 4 August, Alois Schnelldorfer wrote to his parents:

I keep waiting with baited breath to see when we will start to fight and enforce peace [obs nicht bald losgeht, den Frieden zu erkaempfen]. I don't believe that the Englishmen would give up so easily without actually being beaten. . . . but then they won't have anything to laugh about, because everyone here has a fanatical hatred of the enemy.[89]

Schnelldorfer had reserved special hatred towards Indian soldiers, referring to them as 'damned devils' and 'fanatical dogs' whom 'one should never take prisoner; they should all be killed'.[90] At least for the time being, however, only a minority of the men of the regiment had shown signs of lasting and sustained brutalization. It is not clear anyway why a widespread brutalization should have only happened in 1915 or after, if it occurred at all. If wartime brutalization resulted from the experience of mass death, it should have occurred in 1914, as the first few months of the war were among the bloodiest of the entire conflict. The casualty rate of September 1914 in the German armed forces stood at almost five times the monthly rate of the period from mid-1915 to mid-1916.[91] Moreover, as we know from Prince Rupprecht, acts that could have easily translated into a tide of brutalization had certainly repeatedly occurred in the Bavarian Army in 1914. With a clear-headed mind, Rupprecht had noted in his diary that these acts were the result not of a deep-seated antagonistic attitude but of the chaos of war. Rupprecht saw no difference between the behaviour of Bavarian, French, and British soldiers. On one occasion he noted:

> Once again it happened that several Englishmen were killed. The reason for that was that after the majority of them had raised their hands in surrender, others started to fire again, which exceedingly angered our men, who saw this behaviour as an insidious ruse. The situation was actually much simpler: The cowards raise their hands, the brave ones continue to fire after a brief respite, and the cowards follow their example, as they fear they would otherwise be killed.[92]

On another occasion, Rupprecht noted: 'Today it happened again that wounded French soldiers shot at the stretcher-bearers! Clearly somebody had told them that the Germans would kill all wounded that they came upon. The result of this foolish behaviour is that our stretcher-bearers really do leave wounded French soldiers lying on the battlefield since they don't trust them not to shoot.'[93]

Widespread brutalization should thus have already occurred early in the war, there should have been no Christmas Truce in 1914, and the war atrocities against perceived guerrilla fighters from the early weeks of the war should not have abated.

To be sure, maltreatment and the killing of POWs certainly did happen in the List Regiment and in the Bavarian Army as a whole in 1915. Moreover, brutalization and kindness can and does, of course, coexist in individuals. However, what mattered was, first, how widespread brutalization was, in other words, to what extent collective 'brutalized' action of a majority of the men of the List Regiment occurred; and, second, whether brutalized behaviour was condoned or even encouraged by fellow soldiers as well as by the Bavarian military authorities. At least on the evidence of a case from October 1915, there was no widespread condoning of violence towards POWs. In that month, a pastor from an unidentified Bavarian location wrote to Crown Prince Rupprecht, bringing an incident to his attention that one of his parish members had told his family. According to the pastor, the soldier had witnessed one of his comrades cutting the throat of a British POW. Challenged on why he had killed the POW, his response was: 'I just felt like it.' He also reported and criticized cases in which British POWs had died of heat stroke, which was a common euphemism for the killing of POWs.[94]

Two of the reasons why incidents like these did not turn into a mass phenomenon were that, thus far, no universal and lasting mutual personal hatred existed between British and German soldiers, discounting necessary antagonism in the heat of battle, and that the Bavarian military authorities tried all they reasonably could to prevent the killing and maltreatment of POWs. In mid-October, the Commander of RD 6, Gustav Scanzoni von Lichtenfels, used the incident that had been drawn to Rupprecht's attention to instruct the List Regiment and all the other units of the division to do all they could to prevent the maltreatment of POWs:

> I will use this opportunity once again to state clearly my abhorrence of any mistreatment of prisoners. All superiors are obligated to the harshest intervention, when suspicion arises of such activities, which are not worthy of a German soldier and only perpetrated by bestial hordes. Every soldier of the division must know that offences in the treatment of soldiers are judicially prosecuted without mercy, even when these may lead to a murder charge.[95]

Bavarian civil society as well as checks within the Bavarian Army thus pre-emptively blocked any risk of Bavarian soldiers going for 'absolute destruction'[96] in the second half of 1915. There is good reason to doubt that the enormous losses at Neuve Chapelle, Fromelles, and Loos had created a lasting anti-British hatred that fuelled a vicious circle of violence. Most of the interaction between German and British soldiers in the summer and autumn was a repetition of the mocking treatment seen in the spring. Soldiers from RIR 16 who were on patrols left notes in the barbed wire in front of the British trenches reading, for instance, 'Greetings from Munich!',[97] while British soldiers, amidst much cheering, put up posters, announcing the loss of German battleships or of Russian victories. On one occasion, they shouted across the trenches in German: 'Konstantinopel ist kaput (sic!), der Krieg ist bald beendet.' ('Constantinople is in pieces, the war is almost over!')[98] Sometimes, the chanting across the lines was in a less boisterous mood. In mid-November, for instance, British soldiers shouted across the trenches in German, asking the men of the List Regiment 'if [they] wouldn't get to go home soon'.[99]

The continued willingness to fight was not necessarily a result of an ever growing anti-British drive among the majority of the soldiers of RIR 16. Father Norbert, at least, referred to the British in his diary in the summer of 1915, in an ironic manner as 'the "evil enemy"',[100] in the same manner that the British students of an elitist British boarding school in Heidelberg had referred to the German students they were to face in a rowing regatta a few weeks prior to the outbreak of war as 'our friend "the enemy"'.[101] Similarly, in his diary he had nothing but kind words for a British officer killed in action whom he had to bury in late June: 'The body made a very agreeable impression in its impeccable uniform. The Englishman must have been a grand man. Even in death, the look in his open blue eyes was a most peaceful one.'[102] Looking at the views and attitudes of a Catholic military chaplain is, of course, not necessarily the best way to identify the brutalizing and radicalizing effect of war. However, it needs to be said that the funeral of the British soldier attracted a huge number of soldiers from RD 6 who acted most respectfully towards the dead British officer. The funeral 'proceeded in a very dignified manner', noted Father Norbert.[103] As the behaviour of the soldiers attending the funeral reveals as well as their conduct once Christmas 1915 came, the majority of the men of the List Regiment did not continue to fight the British out of personal hatred. They had not dehumanized the British but continued to fight them because they believed that Germany's cause was just or at the very least because they deemed that the cost of ceasing the fighting was too high.

The war experience of 1915 translated less into violent Anglophobia and a brutalizing cycle of violence than in a heightened sense of religiosity, even compared to the spring.[104] In mid-June, Father Norbert noted:

'Since Easter the troops have so frequently gone to the sacraments that one can hardly keep up with the confessions.'[105] Nothing had changed by November: 'Barely manageable confessional work,' noted Norbert. 'The gravity of our days brings people very close to our Lord God.'[106] Make-shift altars and crucifixes now mushroomed in the dugouts of the List Regiment, while front-line soldiers carried on them rosaries and medal-lions blessed by priests.[107] Oscar Daumiller also reported well-attended services among the Protestant soldiers of RD 6.[108]

Father Norbert observed increasingly often that the men of the List Regiment were 'in a sombre mood', anticipating that it might be their turn to die next.[109] With the exception of a subsection of the younger recruits, this was also true of the new troops that kept on arriving as reinforcements at the front. As early as late April, Norbert reported of a service for new recruits:

> This ceremony made a deep impression on the soldiers, who were very solemn from the funeral preceding the ceremony. Only three days earlier had they said goodbye to their homes, now they were already so close to the serious realities of war.... So many tears roll down the faces of the young and also the old, as we have many Landwehr men among our replacements. Deeply shaken, the comrades now receive the general absolution.[110]

In *Mein Kampf*, Hitler also was to acknowledge that by the second half of 1915, his romantic enthusiasm for war had given way to feelings of fear and horror. Yet for him, if his claims in *Mein Kampf* are to be trusted, it did not translate into either religiosity, indiscipline, low morale, or a questioning of the war but into something higher and better than romantic enthusiasm. It was a transformation, he tells us, which not only he but his entire regiment and the whole German Army underwent:

> A feeling of horror replaced the romantic fighting spirit. Enthusiasm cooled down gradually and exuberant spirits were quelled by the fear of the ever-present Death. A time came when there arose within each one of us a conflict between the urge to self-preservation and the call of duty. And I had to go through that conflict too. As Death sought its prey everywhere and unrelent-ingly a nameless Something rebelled within the weak body and tried to introduce itself under the name of Common Sense; but in reality it was Fear; which had taken on this cloak in order to impose itself on the individual. But the more the voice which advised prudence increased its efforts and the more clear and persuasive became its appeal, resistance became all the stronger; until finally the internal strife was over and the call of duty was

triumphant. Already in the winter of 1915—16 I had come through that inner struggle. The will had asserted its incontestable mastery. Whereas in the early days I went into the fight with a cheer and a laugh, I was now habitually calm and resolute. And that frame of mind endured. Fate might now put me through the final test without my nerves or reason giving way. The young volunteer had become an old soldier. This same transformation took place throughout the whole army. Constant fighting had aged and toughened it and hardened it, so that it stood firm and dauntless against every assault.[111]

The reality in 1915 was rather different. As Father Norbert wrote in a letter to Bishop Michael von Faulhaber in October 1915: 'These have become hard times for our men, especially since we have hardly any young men who on active military duty in [our] Reserve Division. Instead we have mostly Landwehr and Landsturm men.'[112] These were clearly neither the kind of soldiers that the officers of the List Regiment had been hoping for, nor did they display any of the characteristics described by Hitler.

Eduard Ziegler, the 35-year-old Commander of 10th Company, had been full of disdain for and frustration with the quality of the men in the List Regiment as early as May. A lawyer in peacetime and a drunkard with extreme mood swings at the front, Ziegler walked the trenches, slapping soldiers in the face for falling asleep, for being disrespectful to superiors, or for not showing up for tasks they had been ordered to do. Ziegler explained that he had no choice in the matter, as 'the majority of the company... consists of replacement troops who do not have any sense of discipline and who can be brought to some kind of order only with exceeding difficulty. In addition, they take no particular joy in the hard labour that in the present time must necessarily be demanded of the men.' Ziegler's opinion was shared by one of the platoon leaders, Martin Kuisle. He said that 'The company consists for the most part of people who, after their short military education, still have no sense for order and discipline, who don't like to work and to whom one must pay close attention.'[113] Needless to say, none of these tensions made it into the 1934 memoirs of Adolf Meyer, who served under Kuisle during this time.[114]

The complaints voiced particularly by troops recently arrived at the front that they were not adequately fed and that the food was distributed unfairly and unevenly among the men of the regiment were only one of the minor problems the officers of the regiment had to face.[115] Far more worrisome was the fact that the expectation that they would not survive the war had gained currency among some of the recruits by May 1915, as the key to the resilience of soldiers to date had lain in the ability of soldiers to deceive themselves and to overestimate their chance of survival.[116]

As he was leaving for the front, Hans Amnon, a 20-year-old mechanic from Nuremberg, wrote to his girlfriend: 'They say that not every bullet will be aimed at me but there will be one that will put my life to an end.'[117] The previous month, Father Norbert had already noted at one of the frequent solemn and well-attended funerals at the new German military cemetery in Fournes, which had to take place at dusk, for fear of artillery fire and aerial bombardment:[118] 'Every man present was conscious of the fact that he could be the next to be buried. It was thus quite to be expected that we were all in a solemn mood, and that some tears were shed during my address.'[119]

Soon patriotic addresses were ordered for recruits, as the perception that they had no sense of what they were fighting for gained currency. Significantly, the talks were entrusted to the divisional chaplains, rather than the officers of the division—a clear sign who recruits were trusting: 'Patriotic addresses in front of 450 recruits in Santes about "A soldier's duties"', noted Father Norbert in early August. 'These newest recruits are mostly between 36 and 44 years old. With them, the drills alone are insufficient; their belief in the necessity of their current tasks must first be awakened and then maintained.'[120] Other topics for the talks included 'The Meaning of Military Obedience' and 'Comradely Loyalty.'[121] Furthermore, the commander of RIB 12 contemplated in September publishing a weekly newspaper for the men of the List Regiment and of RIR 17, which was meant to mark, reward, and draw attention to soldiers who, for example, had participated in patrols.[122]

Soldiers from Hitler's regiment who were critical of the horrors of the war, meanwhile, had no inhibitions about voicing their opinions. In late June, men from 4th Company erected an altar for a service for 1st Battalion with which they expressed their belief that the horrors of their war were an insult to God, as Father Norbert realized when inspecting the altar:

> Only one thing was surprising, the pedestal of the altar cross. On it is namely a larger-than-life (½ m), beautifully painted Sacred Heart with a crown of thorns, and pierced by a Bavarian [illegible word] bayonet bearing the sword knot of 4th Company. As I attempted to criticize the depiction a bit and asked how 4th Company had offended the Sacred Heart, the soldiers present were astounded at my ignorance about the symbols they had used. The heart pierced by a military bayonet was supposed to signify that the Sacred Heart had been insulted by the atrocities of war; the sword knot of

the 4th Company, however, was supposed [merely] to declare to the world
that the altar artist belonged to 4th Company of Reserve Infantry Regiment
16.[123]

The fact that the military court of RD 6 accepted the testimony of a soldier
who had run off from RIR 16, according to which he had not tried to desert
but only to report to the military authorities in Munich in order to be
deployed to a different military unit, shows in what low esteem service in
Hitler's regiment was held.[124]

By late September 1915, Gustav Scanzoni von Lichtenfels, the commander of RD 6, felt compelled to warn the commanders of RIR 16 and
its sister regiments about a new escape ruse front-line soldiers would
sometimes use by seeking permission to see the doctor. However, rather
than reporting to the doctor, they left the front.[125] Furthermore, Jakob
Schäfer, the twice-injured war volunteer from 2nd Company—after telling
his girlfriend in a letter that 'Freedom is an ideal. Only an idiot allows
himself to be enslaved'[126]—tried in September to run away from the
regiment out of annoyance that despite his two serious injuries he had not
been allowed to visit his loved ones back in Bavaria. However, he had to
realize that 'all streets and alleys were occupied by the military and I could
not find passage without a pass'. German authorities had felt compelled to
set up a chain of military policemen behind the combat zone of RD 6 to
prevent soldiers from deserting and to set up a huge disincentive even
to attempt to run off.[127] Military policemen also patrolled all trains going
back to Germany for deserters as well as the train stations of Bavarian cities
upon the arrival of trains from the front.[128]

As a military policeman of RD 6 had to learn the hard way one November
night, indiscipline was fast rising among the soldiers of the division. That
night, he entered the canteen of the living quarters of RD 6 units that were in
reserve in a factory in Santes. On telling the crowd that it was closing time, a
soldier from either RIR 16 or one of its sister regiments threw a bottle at him.
When he tried to find out who had thrown the bottle, all the soldiers present
surrounded him and one of them hit him hard with a military kettle, injuring
him close to his eye. The bartender managed to arrest the soldier who had
thrown the bottle but when he handed him over to two NCOs they let him
go as soon as they had left the building, rather than taking him to the next
military police station.[129]

The transformation that had taken place in Hitler's regiment thus had little in common with that 'habitually calm and resolute' fighting spirit that 'stood firm and dauntless against every assault' which Hitler claimed he as well as German soldiers in general had felt during this period.

After a warm and sunny early October, the dreadful rainy and foggy weather that is the hallmark of Flemish winters returned to the region of Fromelles. With the return of the bad weather came the return of rising water levels in the trenches. Only for the men of regimental HQ like Hitler or Schnelldorfer was the situation half-tolerable, as they at least could keep themselves dry, as Alois Schnelldorfer told his parents: 'It has rained here . . . for days on end. We telephonists at least have the opportunity to dry ourselves off or change clothes.'[130] What had looked like beautifully constructed trenches in the spring now filled with water. By mid-November, the reserve trenches stood one metre under water. Some trenches simply collapsed under the onslaught of water and mud. Others filled so completely with water that they had to be abandoned. Meanwhile, the soldiers of the List Regiment had to perform the almost impossible feat of trying to stay dry by avoiding the bottom of the trenches without exposing themselves to British fire. Furthermore, the men of the regiment subjected themselves to the imminent danger of contracting diseases when, out of desperation, they started using their eating utensils to bail water out of their trenches. Much of the leather equipment of the men of RIR 16 now was covered in a green layer of mould. The happiest inhabitants of the trenches were rats and mice who had the rather disconcerting habit of nibbling at the strings and the covers of the hand grenades that were stored in the trenches.[131] There was no sign that things would improve any time soon, as Georg Arneth wrote to the Protestant pastor of his home village in mid-December, a month prior to Arneth's unexpected death from heart disease:

> The rumbling and groaning of cannonry and the cracking of impact have ruled over us for a long time. Only one who has survived it could describe it. One is tempted to believe that no man will survive. But these murderous bullets and shells do not strike everyone, thank God. Many will have to die a hero's death before the final peace, and this peace is still far off.[132]

As it turned out, the battles at Neuve Chapelle, Fromelles, and Loos had not led to a lasting brutalization of the men of Hitler's regiment. By December, the sentiment that had given birth to the Christmas Truce 1914 returned to the trenches close to Fromelles. As Hitler was spending his time away from the trenches in his own little world in regimental HQ, maybe reading the architectural history of Berlin he had purchased in late November,[133] British soldiers shouted across the trenches on 8 December: 'Bavarians! Don't shoot!'[134]

On Christmas Eve, a grey and rainy day, massive machine-gun fire had been ordered to prevent a reoccurrence of the 1914 Christmas Truce. However, during the morning of Christmas Day, the British soldiers on the opposite side of the trenches started to wave with their hats at the men of the List Regiment and its sister regiment. The soldiers facing the List Regiment, amidst singing and accordion playing, tried to make contact with the men of Hitler's regiment, shouting: 'Bayern' ('Bavarians') and 'Kameraden' ('Comrades') across the trenches. The British servicemen in the sector opposite RIR 17 and the German unit that lay to the left of RIR 17, lying right to the left of the sector of RIR 16, actively tried to fraternize to the delight of the men of the sister regiment of RIR 16.[135] 'A few of our people have, enticed by similar incidences in the left neighbouring regiment, left our trenches and wanted to approach the Englishmen,' reported the war diarists of RIR 17.[136] These were not isolated events.

Next to the 6th Bavarian Reserve Division lay the 14th (Prussian) Infantry Regiment which fraternized with soldiers belonging to the British Guards Division, among them Private William Tate of the 2nd Coldstream Guards. In a scene reminiscent of the previous year, Tate saw how the Prussian soldiers 'came out of their trenches and walked towards our line. We did not fire on them as they had no equipment or arms of any sort. Some of our fellows went over to meet them. They shook hands and exchanged greetings, they also exchanged money and cigarettes.'[137] To the dismay of the Earl of Cavan, the commander of the Guards Division, similar scenes occurred with the 13th Bavarian Reserve Infantry Regiment. He had to report 'that in spite of special orders there was communication held between the lines occupied by the Guards Division and the 13th Bavarian Reserve Regiment this morning. I have seen the Brigadiers who were on the spot within 20 minutes of hearing of the episode and our men were back in the trenches within 30 to 40 minutes after first going out.' Just as in 1914, German reports tended to state that attempts at fraternization had originated with the British, while British reports, of course, claimed the opposite: 'Large parties of unarmed Germans were the first to appear,' the Earl of Cavan wrote, 'but this is no excuse, and I regret the incident more than I can say.'[138]

Why then did the scenes of the Christmas Truce 1914 not repeat themselves on a larger scale? There is a simple answer to this question that has nothing to do with a brutalizing cycle of violence in 1915: the British fired shrapnel on the units of the 6th Bavarian Reserve Division and the Bavarian soldiers 'were ordered back and punished' as soon as grass-roots attempts to repeat the Christmas Truce 1914 started to get off the ground.[139] Furthermore, despite the slightly foggy weather on Christmas Day, British fighter planes constantly circled over the sector of RIR 16.[140] Moreover, the Grenadier Guards who were facing the List Regiment sent a patrol out during the day of Christmas Eve which, of course, was inevitably followed by orders from the officers of RIR 16 to shoot at the patrol, resulting in the deaths of two Guards soldiers.[141] As Christmas 1915 was approaching, the commanders of British units had been reminded of 'the unauthorized truce which occurred on Christmas Day at one or two places in the last year'. They were now ordered to make sure 'that nothing of the kind is allowed on the Divisional front this year'. To help this along, 'the artillery will maintain a slow gun fire on the enemy's trenches commencing at dawn' and 'snipers and machine guns are to be in readiness to fire on any German showing above the parapet'.[142] As Alois Schnelldorfer wrote to his parents on Christmas Day: 'There was no attack[,] just terrible artillery fire.'[143] At no time in December had the British artillery fired on the positions of the List Regiment and its sister units as strongly as during the period immediately following Christmas. The villages in which the reserve battalions and the headquarters of the regiments, brigades, and division lay, were indeed only shelled on three days in December: on 7 December, the day before Christmas Eve, and on the evening of Christmas Eve itself.[144] Father Norbert reported that vigorous artillery could be heard throughout the Christmas Mass he celebrated with soldiers on leave in the church of Beauchamps. Three days later, when he celebrated another Christmas service with soldiers from an RD 6 unit in a cowshed within the combat zone, the shed was struck by a direct hit, destroying the space where the altar had stood.[145]

It was thus direct orders, punishment, as well as the awesome lethal force of thousands of shrapnel balls erupting from anti-personnel artillery shells, rather than growing mutual hatred or wartime brutalization, which prevented a reoccurrence of the Christmas Truce of 1914. What had changed was not so much the mindset and combat motivation of the men of the List Regiment and their British counterparts but the response by the military authorities behind the front to any nascent attempts to strike up a Christmas Truce. The key factor which explained why Christmas 1915 was so different from the previous year was thus official policy and not grass-root opinion.

The question, however, remains how to explain the ferocious combat in March at Neuve Chapelle, in May at Fromelles, and in September at Loos on the one hand, and the relative lack of hatred towards the British after the battles of 1915 as well as the attempt at a reoccurrence of the Christmas Truce in 1915 on the other.

The fact that the profound Anglophobia of the early months of the war was driven by an acute sense of betrayal rather than deep-seated traditions of mutual antagonism might well explain why there was no sustained Anglophobia among the men of RIR 16 and why the Christmas truces were possible. However, this does not explain the ferocity of combat in the three major battles in which the regiment was involved in 1915. The answer might well lie in the presence of a common anthropological response to combat among Hitler's comrades, in which the natural fear of death is translated into a 'fight or flight' impulse, which in turns leads to a release of copious amounts of adrenalin and ultimately of aggression and feelings of exuberance, euphoria, exhilaration, and elation during the act of killing—in short, to a 'combat high'. Success in combat, which is ultimately measured in either the maiming or killing of one's opponent, is the best inhibitor of fear. There has been a taboo in the Western tradition to speak about this aggression during combat, sometimes labelled 'blood lust'. However, much of the research carried out on combat motivation over the last century or so strongly suggests that soldiers across extremely varied national cultures and ideologies have the same experience in that once they have overcome their fear of going into battle, during combat they, at least temporarily, lose all, or almost all, inhibitions about aggression, often feeling a thrill when killing an opponent. However, this loss of inhibition does not necessarily translate into a brutalization of warfare. Even the celebration of the act of killing within military units does not automatically equate to a lasting hatred of the enemy. Combat aggression does not necessarily survive after the end of the battle. Once all the adrenalin is gone, remorse, and subsequently a rationalization process sets in. With the exception of a very small number of sociopaths, hatred and aggression towards the enemy is only sustained by factors other than combat aggression such as ideology or feelings of revenge.[146] In the relative absence of those factors among most of the soldiers of the List Regiment, there was no contradiction between the ferocious combat performance of many men of RIR 16 in the three big battles of 1915 and the relative lack of rancour towards British soldiers of the front line for the rest of the year. This is why only orders from above prevented the reoccurrence of a widespread Christmas Truce in 1915. Differently put, combat aggression, where it existed among the men of the List Regiment (it needs to be pointed out that not all front-line soldiers of RIR 16 even displayed combat aggression), did not equate to a change of the political mentalities of the men of the regiment.

Since, in February 1915, Hitler had provided in his letter to Ernst Hepp a blueprint of his attitude towards the war and of his utopian vision of a future Germany in his letter to Ernst Hepp, there had thus been, at least in 1915, no apparent convergence of attitudes towards the war between the majority of the men of the List Regiment and of the ideas expressed by Private Hitler in his February letter. Unfortunately, beyond Hitler's letter from February little is known about his attitudes and perceptions of the war in 1915.

Despite the heavy losses 1915 had brought on all sides—by the end of 1915, 47 per cent of all fatalities in the List Regiment and more than 50 per cent of all wartime fatalities in the French Army had already occurred,[147]—there had been surprisingly little change in the attitudes of the men of the List Regiment between Christmas 1914 and 1915. This was to cause a problem for Hitler after the war when he was to try to tell the story of how the war experience had changed him, the men of the List Regiment, and German society as a whole for good. The most traumatic battle of the war, however, had not yet occurred.

6

Occupation

January–July 1916

During the relatively quiet period between New Year and the summer of 1916, at a time when elsewhere Germany waged its futile all-out attack on Verdun in Lorraine, aimed at bleeding the French Army to death, it became routine for Hitler and his immediate comrades to go into Lille every time they received leave. On the way to northern France's cultural and administrative centre, Private Hitler and his comrades sat huddled together in the tram that ran from one of the neighbouring villages of Fournes along endless rows of simple suburban brick houses to Lille. The visits to Lille of Hitler and his brothers-in-arms as well as the time they spent in places such as Fournes and Haubourdin inevitably brought them in contact with the local French population. Their interaction with civilians provides a fascinating glimpse of their evolving view of the world.

Hitler's trips to Lille had been made possible because the command of RD 6 realized the need to set up incentives that would ensure that young Hitler and the men of his regiment would continue to fight and perform at a time when the war had already lasted much longer than anticipated. On a visit to RD 6, it was not lost on Crown Prince Rupprecht in what dire a state the men of Hitler's division were in and how important it was to set up incentives aimed at making the men feel appreciated: 'One can clearly see the stresses of the past weeks in the deployed troops, especially those who came from the left wing of the forward position. Many have a sallow colour to their faces, a sign of sleep deprivation.'[1]

Another predictably Bavarian strategy to keep men happy had been to ship beer from Munich in special beer wagons to the front to ensure that each soldier would get his daily ration of half a litre. The division frequently corresponded with other military authorities and with Munich breweries

regarding complaints such as that the beer had arrived too warm or complaints from troops that they wanted to get draught beer rather than bottled
beer.[2] Unlike Private Hitler who was a committed teetotaller, the men of
RIR 16 had a reputation for drinking to excess, particularly when they lay in
reserve behind the front. When a butcher from the foothills of the Alps was
arrested one January night after he had assaulted a guard in Santes while
rearing drunk, investigations revealed that he had first consumed between
six and seven litres of beer and then finished a bottle of cognac with two of
his comrades.[3]

After their arrival in central Lille during their outings, Hitler's immediate
comrades would dash straight to the nearest bar. From time to time, Hitler,
together with some of the men from regimental headquarters, attended
theatre performances put on by the 'Deutsches Theater Lille', set up in
Lille's Théâtre de l'Opéra in 1915. However, on trips to Lille that did not
feature visits to the theatre, Hitler and his comrades went their separate
ways. As the others drank away their sorrows, Hitler walked the streets of
Lille.[4] Hitler thus missed the opportunity to meet ordinary front-line
soldiers and to hear how they saw and experienced the war. As we have
seen through the episode in which Hitler believed, unlike the soldiers
whom he met, to be in the combat zone and had rolled up his epaulettes,
Hitler, of course, did encounter ordinary soldiers from his unit while on
duty. However, there is no record that gives any hint of him mixing socially
with ordinary front-line soldiers.

Occasionally, while in Lille, Hitler sat down on walls or benches and took
out his sketch pad. As he sketched street scenes in the same style he had
drawn postcards in Munich prior to the war,[5] some of Hitler's comrades
graduated from local bars to the brothels that had been mushrooming since
the beginning of the German occupation,[6] which for a few Marks, the men
of Hitler's regiment could buy sex.[7] As a wartime French novel put it, the
German occupiers felt that 'they had a double right to the favour of all
women and girls, being at once lords and conquerors'.[8] Hitler, meanwhile,
was dismissive of soldiers who were sleeping with prostitutes or local
women, as were many of the married Catholic soldiers from the Bavarian
countryside.[9] The often-told tale that Hitler fathered a son during the war is
indeed a hoax.[10]

Hitler's brothers-in-arms had no difficulty in fulfilling their sexual desires.
As the French ophthalmologist had already noted in late November 1914, '[the

German soldiers] have great love for their uniforms, and I must admit that they wear them very well. The fairer sex thus [behaves towards the German soldiers in a way that brings] about no high opinion of their "love of their Fatherland" or of the dignity of the women of Lille. I quote the following opinion of an officer from the City Commander's Headquarters: "All the women here are harlots." '[11] Oscar Daumiller, meanwhile, had noted in early 1915: 'The long spell in one and the same place allows the men to get to know the town and village inhabitants and affords them the possibility of building relationships with local girls and women.'[12]

Trashy wartime novels—with titles such as *Kriegsbräute* (War Brides), *Die Schwester des Franktireurs* (The Sister of the Franc-Tireur), *Deutsche Hiebe, Deutsche Liebe* (German Thrashing, German Loving)[13]—also inspired the soldiers of RIR 16 to strike up amorous encounters with local women in Lille and in the villages and towns behind the front. When Hermann Münderlein, one of the Protestant army chaplains in RD 6, had to write a report about his work to date, he was not complimentary about the behaviour of the men of the List Regiment and its sister units. He thought that the units of RD 6 were rife with problems of 'alcohol, promiscuity, aggression and unkind criticism, theft, disobedience, materialism, descent into indifference, and apathy'. The officers of the units, he thought, were just as bad. Not only did they display an 'antisocial behaviour towards the men' but they consumed alcohol in excessive quantities and were just as lecherous and sexually promiscuous as the troops.[14]

So widespread was the problem that the Command of the 6th Army had felt prompted to establish special wards for men suffering from VD in army hospitals behind the front.[15] In the villages that the men of the List Regiment frequented, military authorities had put up notices warning Hitler and his comrades of the perils of VD: 'Warning: Soldiers! Protect your health! All prostitutes, waitresses, and loose women are infected!'[16] The army doctors of the List Regiment even had to compile a secret list of men to whom condoms had been handed out, so as to be able to punish anybody who had contracted VD who had not used condoms. Soon allegations arose that French doctors deliberately did not treat prostitutes and other women suffering from VD properly in order to use them as a secret weapon against German soldiers.[17] As Oscar Daumiller claimed, 'one woman boasts that she has "delivered" more Germans than many French soldiers at the front.'[18] The 6th Reserve Division was quite worried about the extent of prostitution and of the attempts of the soldiers of its units to make advances towards

French women behind the front. By January 1915, special military police patrols walked the streets of Comines to prevent soldiers of the List Regiment from striking up relationships with local women or from frequenting brothels.[19]

With war had come, of course, also the danger of rape committed by soldiers. Rape during the First World War was not the result of wartime brutalization specific to the Great War.[20] Rape has indeed been the hallmark of all military conflict throughout history and it occurred on all fronts during the First World War. While war tends to bring a general increase in criminal behaviour among soldiers, the rise is generally higher for sex crimes.[21] It is impossible to tell how widespread a problem rape was among the men of RD 6. However, we do know of at least one case that was to happen in early 1918 in Picardy, when a soldier of one of the sister regiments of the List Regiment was to rape an 11-year-old girl and was to try to rape another woman in the same village.[22]

The frequenting of brothels by Hitler's comrades while Hitler walked the streets of Lille is a reminder that trips to Lille, as well as life in the villages and small towns behind the front, such as Fournes or Haubourdin, brought regular interaction with the local population. The history of this encounter is both a fascinating and a precarious one. Even the deployment of foreign troops in 'friendly' countries inevitably led to tensions with the local population, as evident, for instance, in the ransacking and setting ablaze of the red-light district in Cairo by Australian troops on Good Friday 1915.[23] Yet any encounter of occupying troops in a hostile environment necessarily unleashes forces—collaboration, resistance, as well as the temptation of heavy-handed occupation policies—that are far more explosive.

It is utterly unsurprising that many of Hitler's brothers-in-arms were whoring and drinking their way around Lille in the spring of 1916. More revealing of the development of their political mentalities and their opinion of the enemy is their relationship with the local French population on a day-to-day basis.

For the men of the List Regiment, their relationship with the local French population had to bridge the gap between the need felt by German military planners, for example, to coerce local men to work for them and to persuade the local population to cooperate with them (particularly since the German goal was to operate as much as possible through indigenous institutions) and not to engage in any activity that was likely to be used by foreign propaganda against them.[24] The potential for tension was increased through the necessity for the German occupation forces essentially to live off the land as the Germans had to experience a far more acute shortage of resources than their adversaries. This relative shortage was a result of the smaller economic output of Germany and her allies compared to that of her enemies as well as of the Allied blockade of Germany. The Germans thus faced the agonizing dilemma whether too lenient a treatment of the population in the occupied territories would unduly drain Germany's resources and thus increase the likelihood that Germany was going to lose the war.

For the French locals, their relationship with the men of the List Regiment was coloured by the difficulty of juggling between competing bonds of loyalty in weighing up how best to come through the war while protecting the interests of their families, as epitomized, for instance, by the case of a Frenchman at Fournes. The man had agreed to contribute to the *Gazettes des Ardennes*, the newspaper the German occupation force published in France. However, ever since starting to work for the Germans he was worried, as he told the German occupiers in November 1915 that he might be 'lynched by his fellow countrymen' at Fournes.[25] Similarly, the unidentified physician and diarist in Lille had been outraged by the behaviour of some of his compatriots: 'I'll mention in passing the loathsome behaviour of our local policemen. They kowtow before the German officers and conduct themselves during the requisitioning operations of the Germans with a servility that is comparable to complicity.'[26] Other collaborators operated in cities and villages other than their own,[27] to prevent reprisals by their neighbours.

As in all wartime occupations, local officials had to face the agonizing decision about whether collaboration, cooperation, or resistance best served the interests of their communities. And as in all wartime occupations, local officials were unlikely to receive gratitude for the difficult and impossible decisions they had to take, as the wartime mayor of Comines, Paul Le Safre, was to find out after the war when an official investigation was launched into his wartime activities.[28]

As we have seen, the beginning of the war had been marked by overzealous, inexperienced German soldiers who in the chaos of the first months of the war saw *francs-tireurs* everywhere. Even once atrocities of the early weeks ceased, the war was still marked by tensions between German occupiers and the French and Belgian populations.

Signs of tension were everywhere. In 1915, anti-German graffiti appeared on walls in Haubourdin. In the late spring, just after the arrival of the List

Regiment in Haubourdin, locals were forced to turn in their bikes. Some owners, however, threw their bikes into the canal rather than hand them over to the Bavarians. There were also cases of alleged espionage by civilians. The prohibition against civilians leaving their villages at night[29] also did not help to ease tensions. Neither did the case of Josef Leclerq. A native of Fournes, which had been badly looted by German soldiers prior to the arrival of the List Regiment,[30] he had deserted his regiment after the fall of Lille in October 1914. His wife had then burnt his uniform and thrown his rifle into an outhouse. After a few weeks in hiding in Lille, he moved to Haubourdin where he was hidden in the local brewery. The German authorities eventually got wind that his wife in Fournes sent parcels to him through Césarine Bouchacourt, a tall, slender woman with dark blond hair, who had a German permit to take goods from Fournes to Haubourdin. On New Year's Day 1916, German military policemen wearing civilian clothes secretly followed Bouchacourt to Haubourdin, ultimately arresting Leclerq. He now received a draconian sentence of fifteen years in prison, as German authorities treated all Frenchmen who were in the French Army but found without uniforms as spies.[31] Similarly, notices put up in the villages in which the List Regiment was stationed informed the local population in late July 1915, that six men and women residing in Lille had been condemned to death for hiding and sheltering a French soldier. Moreover, in the first half of 1916, locals in Haubourdin were forced to help construct the makeshift tramline behind the German lines and to dig graves in the graveyard; others were deported to the Ardennes to carry out forced labour there.[32]

All the tensions described here indeed seem to support the common argument that the essence of the German occupation of northern France and Belgium—both on the level of German military institutions which formulated policy and at the grass-root level at which soldiers carried out policy and personally encountered civilians—was its brutality: a brutality that was part and parcel of the general brutalization and radicalization brought by the Great War and that was particularly pronounced in the German case. For German policy makers and soldiers on the ground alike, it is said, terror and violence became tools intentionally to humiliate the population under occupation in an attempt to prevent the French from ever waging war against Germany again.[33]

If this view were true, Hitler's comrades would have not been trying to have sex with French women for the same reason that Australian troops had frequented the brothels of Cairo but in order to humiliate and terrorize the local population and thus to target the enemy by different means in the same way as they were trying to target the British troops on the other side of the trenches at Fromelles.

However, there is a danger of overstating the level of tension and of hostility towards the local population among the men of Hitler's regiment. Tension and heroic resistance are omnipresent in the collective and individual memory of all traumatic wartime occupations, while recollections of collaboration and cooperation and the tough choices a population under occupation had to face tend to be edited out of the story.[34] Furthermore, even during the war British and French propaganda had a vested interest in presenting German soldiers as irredeemable rapists as a device for recruiting and for boosting morale in order to persuade hesitant French and British men to fight the Germans. Any suggestion in wartime novels such as Marguerite Yerta's 1917 Les six femmes et l'invasion (Six Women and the Invasion) that French women were sleeping with German soldiers voluntarily or even only for the sake of feeding their children was censored.[35] But a fair number of French women did sleep with the enemy. For instance, in 1916, Madeleine Le Safre, the daughter of the mayor of Comines, bore the child of one of the officers who lodged with the mayor's family.[36] A 36-year-old woman in Haubourdin, meanwhile, engaged in a sexual relationship with the cook of the 2nd Batallion of RIR 20 in the spring of 1916. She seems neither to have been coerced into the relationship nor received any financial rewards for sleeping with the chef.[37] Indeed, in reality, wartime occupations produce, as one historian has put it, 'more complex relationships than those of brutal oppression' between occupiers and the local civilian population than the collective memory of the occupied will ever allow.[38] Maybe surprisingly, over time the German occupiers of northern France and the French local population grew closer together.[39] Military necessity had dictated that the men of Hitler's regiment find a modus vivendi with the local civilian population that would allow them to interact with the population under occupation.[40] The French population had an equal interest in a working relationship with the Germans. As our ophthalmologist and diarist from Lille had noted in February 1915:

> The enemy has always conducted himself appropriately since occupying the city. After the people of Lille and the German Army had regarded each other with hate and distrust for a few weeks, gradually people reached a state of

indifference and even felt the beginnings of 'sympathy', in the etymological sense of the word. One does not live unaffected side by side if entrenched in the same unfortunate situation: finally one starts to find this situation bearable and to set about making mutual concessions. . . . The common people who live with the soldiers by necessity and house them will eventually fraternize with them. Both parties, the victors and the conquered, succumb to circumstances and have a chance to understand one another. Thus one can observe everywhere situations like the following: a young beggar follows a soldier who finally gives him some money after speaking some broken French to him; or one sees soldiers ordered to escort requisitioning wagons secretly giving poor women several pieces of coal or a small quantity of petrol. . . . The soldiers who have been billeted in private homes make themselves useful as much as they can, and even share the food that they bring home with the people with whom they stay. As a result, many workers ask to house soldiers. As far as the officers (with whom the town is teeming) are concerned, they are measured, polite even, when one has to come into contact with them.[41]

More than that, it was very much in the interests of the men of Hitler's regiment and its sister units to strike up good relations with local civilians as the civilians, in effect, constituted a human shield against British attacks. While the List Regiment was still lying on the French–Belgian border close to Messines, Father Norbert noted in his diary:

> While the troops in Warneton [a neighbouring village of Comines] stay by day in their cellar rooms and are only allowed to slink along the house walls on necessary errands, the civilians can move freely through all the streets and squares. The goal in this is to deceive the enemy about the presence of troops and to deter the enemy from bombardment out of consideration for the inhabitants. Enemy planes circle constantly over Warneton for surveillance purposes.[42]

The 6th Reserve Division was also careful to prevent the appearance that its units were engaging in cultural destruction. In a divisional order of 13 February 1915, the command instructed its units not to confiscate church bells and church apparatus and to hand over ownerless damaged church goods to church parishes which were still active.[43] The attempts to ease the relationship with the local population under occupation did not stop there. For instance, by late 1915, French courses were held twice a week in the soldiers' mess.[44] Moreover, unlike in other military conflicts, rape was not used as a weapon, nor was rape tolerated as it was, for instance, arguably by the officers of some American units in Vietnam.[45] Suggestions that German military authorities gave tacit justification to rape by dehumanizing the

French and Belgian local population as *francs-tireurs*[46] or that they 'system-atically humiliat[ed]' women and girls, making them 'the chosen subject in total war'[47] are not supported by the experience of the 6th Reserve Division. On the contrary, after the incident in which a soldier from one of the sister regiments of RIR 16 raped an 11-year-old girl, her mother reported the case to the officer in charge of military justice in RIR 17. The fact that she reported the rape to the German authorities is significant in itself. It suggests that at least some among the French local population felt that they could get justice from the German military authorities. The officer immediately embarked on an extensive investigation that ultimately failed to identify the rapist but that sent the strongest possible message to the soldiers of RIR 17 that rape and the maltreatment of the local population was absolutely unacceptable. He first investigated the place where the rape had taken place. Next he ordered all men of his regiment who had been in the village to be examined by the regimental doctor the same day for traces of blood on their clothes or any other signs that would identify the rapist. A few days later, he lined up the 118 men of his regiment who potentially fitted the description of the rapist. However, neither the raped girl nor the women who had narrowly escaped rape could identify their attacker. The military court of RD 6 abandoned the investigation a few days later only after another line-up of about half the 118 men still had not produced the rapist.[48]

Crown Prince Rupprecht was particularly sensitive to the need to treat the local French population with as much respect as possible. When he visited Haubourdin in the summer of 1916, local military authorities had put the local French population under a strict curfew, forcing them to keep all their doors and windows shut. When Rupprecht heard of this, he immedi-ately revoked the order and allowed locals out of doors.[49]

Despite all the tensions and in spite of the official harsh post-Somme occupation policies that still lay in the future, over time the treatment of the local population by ordinary soldiers became, in fact, less, not more, severe. The relations between French civilians and German occupiers thus devel-oped in a direction which was contrary to what was to happen in the Second World War.[50] In a divisional order from late February 1915, the command of RD 6 had already felt compelled to tell the soldiers of its units not to give any bread to civilians.[51] By May 1915, another divisional order complained that there had been a growing number of cases in which soldiers of the division had volunteered to receive letters for locals and pass them on to them.[52] For instance, the husband of a French woman from Wattignies (a village in the region occupied by RD 6), who stayed in the unoccupied part of France, sent letters to the Zurich-based wife of Robert Weber, a Private in RD 6's Reserve Artillerie Munitions Kolonne 10 who was stationed in Watignies. Weber's wife then forwarded them to her husband, who passed them on to the local French woman.[53]

Furthermore, in June of 1915, the commander RD 6 issued an order reminding soldiers of the need 'to exercise strict restraint with regard to the French population in speech as well as in the rendering of personal favours'. The order also warned them not to deliver letters for the local population, not to engage in 'careless conversations', and, in general, not to display 'a misguided appearance of friendliness'.[54] The shared Catholic identity of occupiers and occupied also helped, at least in some cases, to find ways of coexistence in the face of the tensions caused by wartime occupation. In mid-January 1915, Father Norbert noted of the people with whom he was quartered in Comines: 'My new hosts are an 80-year-old man with his around 50-year-old daughter. Both are members of the Third Order. That I am most heartily welcome in my new quarters I need not even mention.'[55]

The improvement in the relationship between German occupiers and the French local population was not limited to the interaction of soldiers of RD 6. For instance, the president of the Comité des Réfugiés du Departement de la Somme had concluded in May 1915 that 'according to the statements of those who have returned to their Fatherland, the Germans no longer conduct themselves with the arrogance and conceit that they displayed at the beginning of the war. They don't want to be treated like "barbarians", and they comport themselves properly with the occupied population. In the villages of the region, there has been no more devastation since the second occupation.'[56] By February 1916, the complaint was that some soldiers of RD 6 in Santes were trading with French women to their mutual advantage, giving food to the women and receiving thread and other items that were in short supply back in Bavaria, which they sent home.[57]

The reality of the encounters of the men of the List Regiment with the local French and Belgian populations during their time in the region of Comines, Messines, Fournes, and Fromelles does not support the thesis that German policies and conduct of soldiers at the grass-roots level were driven by an urge to terrorize, humiliate, and shock the local population.

German conduct was often harsh, sometimes brutal. However, the aim of the policy towards the civilian population was not to destroy forever France's capability of waging war. In reality, the official policies were

driven, first, by an attempt to win the war under conditions of 'total war'—
in which the ideal is to apply all military and economic resources to the
conflict—and, secondly, by the shortage of resources the Germans and her
allies were facing. Within these parameters and at least until 1916, German
military authorities tried—but due to adverse conditions often failed—to
treat the population in the occupied territories in an acceptable manner.
These policies were not necessarily driven by a love for the French but by a
cost benefit calculation according to which it was not in the interest of the
Germans to antagonize the local population any more than was deemed
militarily absolutely necessary. The conduct of the men of the List Regiment
was driven by similar considerations. However, by the spring of 1916 the
surprising consequence of the continued encounter with the local French
population was that, if anything, many men of Hitler's regiment had
become less anti-French, rather than more. The deep-seated anti-French,
anti-Belgian, anti-Catholic German nationalism that was supposed to have
driven German soldiers both during the atrocities in 1914, as well as
throughout the war, was simply not a majority sentiment in the List
Regiment.

The behaviour of Hitler's brothers-in-arms during their trip to Lille as
well as their continued preparedness to fight should thus not be read as
giving evidence of wartime brutalization or a political radicalization of the
majority of the men of Hitler's regiment. At any rate, as several pieces of
evidence suggest, by the first half of 1916 the fervour with which the men of
the List Regiment and Bavarians in general were supporting the war effort
was no longer what it had once been.

As was not lost on Alois Schnelldorfer, the German authorities desperately tried to make the German population look at the war through rose-
tinted spectacles: 'But naturally pains were taken so that nothing negative
reached the home front. Thus letters were opened, vacations were denied,
etc.,' he wrote to his parents. 'A deputy of the Bavarian Parliament came to
see us once, naturally after prior notification had been given . . . There was
roast beef with potatoes and beer, and, as you know, when a Bavarian has
beer, he laughs. Photographs were then taken and snapshots were made of
the good spirits of the troops. . . . In reality, life is less splendid than we are
allowed to describe.'[58]

Bavarian civil and military authorities were indeed aware that the situation was precarious. In early 1916, several local authorities in the recruitment region of the List Regiment had complained that soldiers had sent

letters home requesting their family and friends to stop buying war bonds, in the hope that the German Empire would run out of money to fight the war.[59] Moreover, in February, the Bavarian War Ministry had sent a rather alarmist secret letter to the commanders of the Bavarian divisions according to which 'in some circles on the home front, the will to persevere at all costs has been abating' because of 'reports from soldiers in the field army and stories from soldiers on leave about real and claimed injustices, grievances etc., that poison the morale of whole communities'.[60]

In the List Regiment, the behaviour of some soldiers indicated that the officers of RIR 16 could no longer take it for granted that their soldiers would either be fully committed to the war or at least deem the cost of disobedience higher than that of obedience. For instance, in March one soldier from 2nd Company refused to follow a direct order he had received from one of his officers, telling him in reply: 'I don't care if you shoot me, I'll even give you the bullet to do it, even though I have a wife and children at home.'[61] Then in April, the officers of the sister regiment of the List Regiment complained that its troops displayed a lack of respect towards the regiment's officers and performed their duties in a lax manner.[62] In May, an NCO refused to adjust his hat when ordered by a military policeman, adding: 'I don't care if I am imprisoned; then I won't have to go into the trenches!'[63]

In June, Dominikus Dauner, an NCO from 1st Company, expressed what many NCOs and officers really thought about the men of Hitler's regimemt. He told two soldiers who had joined the regiment earlier in the year, in terms that could hardly have been less flattering: 'You are useless. If you (he said to Grundwürmer [who was one of the two soldiers]) were good for anything, you would have a commendation. You fit in well with the regiment. It is full of shirkers and good-for-nothings. You are scallywags. You've never done anything of value.'[64]

The mood described here among both soldiers and civilians at home created an extremely volatile situation that was to explode in the second half of 1916. However, the fact that no major battles had taken place for almost half a year was central to why most soldiers continued to perform for the time being. The sector of the front occupied by the List Regiment was, in fact, so quiet and manned by such poor troops compared to the rest of the British sector of the Western Front that the Australian contingents of the British armed forces, which only started to pour into Europe in 1915, used it as a 'nursery' to introduce new formations of trench warfare. From April 1916, RIR 16 faced the I Anzac Corps that had just arrived in Europe.[65]

Another reason why the men of the List Regiment continued to perform was that, like their peers along the Western Front, they had spent only a fraction of their time in the front line. They spent at least as much time drilling, resting, training, on transportation, or on leave as they spent in the trenches.[66] It has been said that the characteristic act of men at war is 'killing';[67] in fact, in the First World War most men spent far more of their time 'waiting'. Boredom was a more common feeling among the men of Hitler's regiment than either acute excitement or horror.

Escapism was another coping mechanism. Rather than consuming the propaganda books that were shipped to the regiment,[68] soldiers were longing for books that would provide some escape and books that would allow them to see normality and wildlife amidst the horror they were experiencing. For instance, Arthur Janzen, a 30-year-old soldier in Hitler's 1st Company, asked the divisional mobile library to acquire a book on water birds. Others requested books on free thinkers or on *Liebesleben in der Natur* (Love Life in Nature). No soldier in the List Regiment requested a book of a remotely political character.[69] The soldiers of RIR 16 were in the habit of shunning the kind of books propagandists wanted them to read, just like the German soldiers in general. Light entertainment, humorous literature (particularly Wilhelm Busch's books), and novels and novellas were most sought after, while instructional reading was the least popular genre. For instance, not a single soldier from the 105th Prussian Infantry Regiment took out from their regimental field library *Bismarck's Speeches*, *The Address to the German Nation* by the high priest of German nationalism Johann Gottlieb Fichte, or Martin Luther's *To the Christian Nobility of the German Nation*. Meanwhile, the great classics of Germany's erstwhile enemies, including the works of Leo Tolstoy, Fyodor Dostoyevsky, Victor Hugo, and Charles Dickens, were popular choices.[70]

We have seen how important religion was in helping the men of the List Regiment to cope with their war experiences in 1914 and 1915. Father Norbert, Oscar Daumiller, and the chaplains working under them had also tried to instil a high morale into the men of the regiment. However, by the second half of 1915 religion had started to lose its central place in the hearts and minds of at least some of the men of Hitler's regiment. How did this change affect how the men of the List Regiment viewed the war? Was it a result of a wider change of attitude, whether political or otherwise?

We do not really know how Father Norbert assessed the situation in 1916, nor for that matter later in the war, as his diary that is kept in the archives of his religious order suddenly ends in early 1916.[71] However, several other sources reveal how religious the men of RIR 16 were in 1916. The long war, at least for some, had led to new doubts about how God could allow the continued horrors of the war to happen. Both Catholic and Protestant army chaplains across the Bavarian Army reported in 1916 that fewer soldiers were flocking to services than in 1914 and 1915. Sometimes Catholic chaplains were branded among the troops as war-mongers.[72] The distancing from religion, where it happened, did not tend to imply a hardening of support for the war from an anti-religious hyper-nationalist perspective as advocated by National Socialist ideology after the war. It suggested rather a distancing from hyper-nationalism or indeed sometimes a rise in fatalism. As Hermann Körnacher concluded in January 1916 of his work since May 1915 as a divisional chaplain under Oscar Daumiller: 'Our work here will become harder the longer the war lasts. One comes across those who have become completely indifferent or fatalistic because of their war experiences.'

Yet there is a danger of exaggerating the extent to which religiosity was on the wane. In absolute terms, religious attendance and interest had, as several reports confirm, remained higher than in peacetime both among Catholic and Protestant soldiers.[73] Moreover, the soldiers of RIR 16 did not display any signs of their religious beliefs becoming more nationalistic during the war, despite attempts particularly in Protestant war theology to link religion with a call for a national renewal. There was little taste for nationalistic sermons. Religion continued to equip soldiers with a mechanism for coping with the strains of war, rather than with a vehicle to express nationalist sentiments. Oscar Daumiller, at any rate, did not detect any change in the religious beliefs of the Protestant soldiers of RD 6 in 1916, noting: 'What I have heard in occasional conversations with comrades and during my Bible hours, as well as what I have heard from my officer friends about the beliefs of their men, have led to the following judgement: The substance of their faith is the same as it was before the war, but spiritual life has deepened and become more internalized.'[74]

Significantly, while the upsurge of religiosity in 1914 and 1915 as well as the continued religious beliefs of a large number of the men of RIR 16 helped them to deal with the war and structured how they saw the war, Private Hitler in regimental HQ had been largely isolated from this religious revival. The reason for this was that the officers of the units of RD 6—in other words the figures at the centre of the milieu in which Hitler lived during the war—were rather lukewarm in their attitude towards religion. Several of the Protestant chaplains in RD 6 agree on this point. Hermann Körnacher was full of disappointment about the officers of the division when he sat down one day in late 1916 to pen his report about his activities to date in RD 6:

> The participation of the officers and doctors, and in general of the educated ranks, in religious services and in religious life has been less than impressive. Most of them don't participate at all. First of all, there may be many external reasons why this is; however, according to the *Weltanschauung* and attitude towards life of many, many officers, which I have got to know a bit better, nothing else is to be expected. It was only the war that has revealed how much materialism has crept into the educated classes.[75]

Hitler thus moved in a microcosm in which, unlike in the regiment as a whole, many, at least among the officers, were critical of religion. It is important to repeat here that throughout the war he looked up to his officers and acted towards them in a deferential manner. This is not to say that the political ideology of the officers of RIR 16 was necessarily the same as Hitler's. Indeed the memoirs of Fritz Wiedemann, the regimental adjutant, a Swabian career officer who had joined the List Regiment in 1915, suggest that, unlike discussions with his immediate comrades, Hitler did not talk about politics with his officers: 'What [Hitler] said at the time was no different from what was expected that any decent soldier during the first years of the war would say.'[76] However, Hitler's service in regimental HQ and his submissive attitude towards the officers of his regiment, whom he saw as the heads of his ersatz family, did mean that his lack of exposure to religion deepened the gulf between himself and the front-line soldiers and their mental attitudes. Hitler was thus divorced from religion, and religion was one element that explains how front-line soldiers approached the war. There was little chance that he would turn towards religion as a strategy for dealing with the war, when many of the officers of his regiment were full of disdain for religion. Hitler was thus, arguably, more receptive to alternative ideologies than soldiers in the trenches.

After his brief stint as a combat soldier, Hitler, who was characterized by Max Amann as 'a homely, pale soldier',[77] had indeed more interaction with officers and their support staff at regimental headquarters than with ordinary combat soldiers. Hitler was thus removed from the realities of the trenches and the camaraderie of front-line soldiers.

As Alois Schnelldorfer kept reminding his parents in the first half of 1916, as a member of regimental HQ he was much better off than the men in the trenches: 'As a telephonist, I have it pretty good here,' he wrote on one occasion.[78] Unlike the men who lived in the dirt of the trenches, Schnelldorfer and his fellow members of regimental HQ had the luxury of worrying about how they were groomed: 'Once again, I have been able to get a shave and a haircut. At the moment I thus have a handsome, smooth, youthful face.'[79] Schnelldorfer, Hitler, and their comrades even had their own allotment, as Schnelldorfer reported to his parents: 'Everything in *our* vegetable garden is growing beautifully. I can't wait to taste the first radish.'[80]

The men serving with regimental HQ consisted of, in Alexander Moritz Frey's words, 'a relatively small group immediately subordinate to the wishes of the officers'.[81] Regimental HQ consisted of four officers (a commander, a regimental adjutant, a physician, and a quartermaster) and approximately fifty NCOs and troops.[82]

The deepest emotional feeling Hitler felt for any other being during the war was for a British deserter—a dog, which had belonged to a British unit and which he christened Foxl, or 'little fox'. Teaching the white terrier tricks, Private Hitler enjoyed the extent to which Foxl obeyed him.[83] Even though he had reserved his most affectionate feelings for a dog, Hitler also felt at ease among the men of the support staff in regimental headquarters, as he never had since the death of his mother. He was closest to two other dispatch runners, Ernst Schmidt and Anton Bachmann, and it was with Bachmann that Hitler had reportedly saved Engelhardt's life in November 1914. Hitler was also on good terms with the other dispatch runners. They included Jakob 'Jackl' Weiß, Josef Inkofer, Balthasar Brandmayer, Franz Wimmer, and Max Mund. He was also close to Karl Lippert, an NCO who until 1916 was in charge of the regimental dispatch runners,[84] and Franz Mayer, a cyclist dispatcher, for regimental HQ.[85]

According to Hans Mend, a cavalry dispatcher in the List Regiment from 1914 to 1916, Private Hitler was not just close to Schmidt—a decorator exactly Hitler's age who had spent the two years preceding the war in Switzerland, France, and Austria—but was in fact his lover. In a December 1939 meeting with Friedrich Alfred Schmid Noerr, an academic and philosopher who then was a member of the conservative resistance circle around the chief of the German military intelligence service, Admiral Wilhelm Canaris, Mend was to tell of his time with Hitler in the First World War:

> Meanwhile, we had gotten to know Hitler better. We noticed that he never looked at a woman. We suspected him of homosexuality right away, because

he was known to be abnormal in any case. He was extremely eccentric and displayed womanish characteristics which tended in that direction. . . . In 1915 we were billeted in the Le Fèbre brewery at Fournes. We slept in the hay. Hitler was bedded down at night with 'Schmidl,' his male whore. We heard a rustling in the hay. Then someone switched on his electric flashlight and growled, 'Take a look at those two nancy boys.'[86]

Tantalizing though this account is, it is, of course, impossible to tell for certain whether Hitler was homosexual or not. However, Mend's claim of Hitler's homosexual activity at the front is not credible. In fact, not a single word uttered by Mend can be believed unless supported by other sources.

First and maybe least important, Mend's behaviour and actions from the end of the First World War to his death in a Nazi prison in 1942, as we shall see, make him an unreliable witness. The fact that he was convicted ten times prior to 1933 mostly for fraud, harassment, embezzlement, and the forgery of documents[87] does indeed suggest that he was not the most trustworthy of witnesses. Second, the two accounts of Mend and Hitler's war years by Mend totally contradict each other. The first is a hagiographical account of Hitler and his war service, published first in 1930 as *Adolf Hitler im Felde*,[88] while the second is the report of Mend's conversation with Schmid Noerr, known as the 'Mend Protocol'.[89] Both accounts are totally over the top, the former in its celebration of Hitler and the latter in the criticism of his former comrade. How do we know which, if any, of the accounts we should believe? As we shall see, Mend and Hitler fell out shortly before Hitler came to power and from the day Hitler came to power, Mend was targeted by the Nazis, which does not make him exactly a reliable witness. Finally, both accounts are full of verifiably wrong statements. For instance, Mend claimed in his conversation with Schmid Noerr that 'it was also Lieutenant [Hugo] Gutmann who got him his Iron Cross 2nd Class at Christmas 1914'.[90] In fact, as we have seen, Gutmann did not even join the List Regiment until early 1915.

Moreover, Mend tells his readers of his encounter with Hitler in regimental headquarters on the eve of the List Regiment's baptism of fire in 1914, when he saw him among the dispatch runners, noting that Hitler 'walked leaning slightly forward and with a smile on his face'.[91] He also reports that the other dispatch runners at regimental headquarters told him, while the battle of Gheluvelt was still raging, that there was general agreement that Hitler was one of the most fearless and reliable dispatch runners. Inconveniently for Hans Mend, Hitler was not a dispatch runner for regimental headquarters at that time. Furthermore, Mend narrates in dramatic terms a conversation he claims to have had with Colonel List,[92] ignoring the fact that at the time the conversation was supposed to have taken place List was already dead. Furthermore, on almost every page of his book Mend gives very long, detailed verbatim quotes which he could not have possibly remembered almost twenty years after the event. Both as a source for Hitler's sexuality and for writing the wartime history of the List Regiment, Mend's book is thus absolutely useless. It should be seen as part of the post-war rewriting of the history of RIR 16.

Even among the support staff at regimental headquarters, Hitler was something of an outsider, but a well-respected one. In the six wartime group photos that depict Hitler with his immediate comrades, he looks comfortable but, with the exception of one photo, always chose to stand or sit at the edge.[93] His trips to Lille were also symptomatic of his relationship with his immediate comrades. He would attend theatre performances with them and he would give them as presents some of the drawings and pictures he produced while they were out and about in town[94] but he would not bond with them over beer and wine in the bars of Lille and thus did not quite fit in with the rest of the support staff of regimental HQ.

Even those closest to him would later describe him as reclusive, at a time when they had no incentive to distance themselves from him. They also saw him as a bookworm who was not always very practical. As Alois Schnelldorfer later remembered, they joked that Hitler would starve to death in a canned food factory, as unlike them, he did not succeed in opening a can of food with a bayonet.[95] Heinrich Lugauer, another dispatch runner, recalled Hitler in a report he gave to the Nazi Party central archive in 1940 as a man distanced from his peers: 'Every free minute he used to read. Even in the forward position he sat in a corner, his cartridge pouch attached and his rifle in arm, and read. He borrowed some book from me once; it was Nietzsche, as far as I can remember.'[96] In the same year, Karl Lippert, the NCO who had until 1916 been in charge of Hitler and the other dispatch runners of the regiment, reported that 'as soon as there was a so-called quiet day in the command post at Fromelles or at Fournes, Adolf Hitler busied himself with drawing or reading. He particularly liked works on the history of Germany and Austria. Almost every man in regimental headquarters was sketched by him, some also as caricatures.'[97] Lugauer and Lippert's verdict was shared by Hans Bauer, a telephonist at regimental HQ who had been assigned to regimental HQ in May 1915 and who took some of the photos we have of Hitler during the war. Bauer described Private Hitler as a 'lonely man' who spent his spare time reading, while maintaining that his 'relationship with Hitler as a comrade [was] the same as with all of his comrades.'[98] According to another member of regimental HQ, Hitler spent his free time memorizing historical dates from a study guide,[99] while, according to Jackl Weiß, Hitler either constantly talked about history or paced up and down a patch of grass in Fournes, thinking and studying.[100] Ignaz Westenkirchner, one of Hitler's fellow dispatch runners, meanwhile, recalled that he 'was always the one to buck us up when we got down-hearted: he kept us going when things were at their worst. . . . He was one of the best comrades we ever had.'[101] The only suggestion that everybody around Hitler found him 'intolerable' and that 'all cursed him' was made in Hans Mend's unreliable account.[102]

There is hence no reason to doubt, even though nobody took him particularly seriously, that Hitler seems to have loved the company of the support staff of regimental HQ, trying in his own way to get on everybody's good side. There is also no reason to doubt that, even while being seen as an oddball, he was well liked among the support staff of regimental HQ. To the officers of regimental HQ, meanwhile, Private Hitler was submissive, trying to anticipate their wishes, and thus making himself popular with his superiors.

An amicable relationship with the officers was not unusual among the men of regimental HQ. 'All of the active officers here are very kind and friendly, and one can put absolute faith in them,' Alois Schnelldorfer told his parents. 'Among them is Colonel Spatn[y]. Have sent a picture of him home before. [He] is our regimental commander.'[103]

Hitler got on particularly well with Max Amann, the staff sergeant of the regiment who was two years his junior. Amann was the most important of the lower staff of the regiment. A short man with blonde hair and a moustache, who was, as has been remarked, 'strong and active looking, with a heavy head and a short neck almost lost between his shoulders', Amann was the logistical brain of regimental HQ. The Office of Strategic Services (OSS), the predecessor organization of the CIA, would, in 1943, come to the conclusion that Hitler modelled himself on the Amann he had got to know during the First World War: '[Amann] is the typical militarized commonplace man and knows himself to be commonplace. He has the assurance to proclaim his right to decide all questions, even such as are beyond his horizon. He is typical of the sergeant sub-Fuehrer type on which Hitler has based his power.'[104] Likewise, Frey recalled of Amann: 'He had the regimental office under his control, he was in the ranks of a staff sergeant, he was small, entreating, fawning, and clever in the treatment of his superiors, and brutal in his treatment of his underlings.'[105] Hitler also got on well with Adolf Meyer, the regiment's reconnaissance officer, and with Fritz Wiedemann, the regimental adjutant, who thought of Hitler as 'brave and reliable' and as 'a particularly quiet, humble, and dependable subordinate' with an 'unmilitary demeanour and a slight Austrian accent'.[106]

In 1947, Max Amann described Hitler during the First World War: 'He was obedient, zealous, and modest.... He was always devoted, always loyal.... He was always ready for duty.' Amann recalled that when during the war he had entered the room of the regimental dispatch runners in the middle of the night 'and cried: "Dispatch", no one moved; only Hitler leapt to action. When I said: "It's always you", he replied: "Let the others sleep, it is no problem for me." ... He was a good and eager soldier, who also never blew his own trumpet.'[107]

Private Hitler, throughout the war, received commendation for his behaviour towards his superiors.[108] Regimental HQ became for Hitler, in the absence of friends and family ties, his ersatz family.

The image we get of Hitler from his comrades is one of a loner sitting in the corner, constantly drawing and reading (art guidebooks to Berlin or Brussels and above all newspapers rather than Schopenhauer and Nietzsche, as Hitler and one of his comrades later were to claim),[109] occasionally mixing with the men around him. According to Max Amann, everyone in regimental HQ referred to Hitler as '[the] painter' or '[the] artist'.[110] Even that favourite pastime of First World War soldiers, letter-writing, was an activity Hitler indulged in little. Other than the family of his landlord in Munich and one other acquaintance with whom he was not even on first-name terms, he had nobody to write to. As Max Amann would tell his US interrogators in 1947: 'He was the poorest soldier. He had no one who would send him a care package.'[111]

As the war progressed, Hitler did not even write to his acquaintances any more. His evolving but still confused and shifting world-view was informed as much by the reading he did as by the views of his immediate comrades among the support personnel of regimental HQ. His behaviour and personality was such that it was little surprise that he was never promoted during the war above the rank of Private, even though his conscientiousness and commitment would earn him the highest German military orders available to men of his rank, the two Iron Crosses.

Rather implausibly and nonsensically, Max Amann was to tell US interrogators after his capture in 1945 that Hitler 'was not promoted because there was no opening.'[112] Equally nonsensically, Bruno Horn, who for a while was the officer in charge of the dispatch runners in regimental HQ, was to declare when giving testimony for Hitler in a libel case Hitler brought in 1932 against a newspaper that had questioned his war record: 'Had Hitler been promoted to NCO, he would not have been able to remain a dispatch runner and the regiment would have lost its best runner.'[113] The obvious flaw in Horn's reasoning is that had Hitler been seen as talented as claimed by Horn, the regimental commander would have clearly preferred to use his talents for a more important and senior post than that of dispatch runner.

It has also been suggested that Hitler did not want to be considered for promotion for fear of having to leave his regiment.[114] However, this was almost certainly not the case as a promotion did not necessarily entail a transfer, as made clear by the cases of Alexander Moritz Frey and Adolf Meyer, among many others, who were promoted and yet stayed in RIR 16.

In direct contradiction to his own testimony in 1945, even Amann confirmed to his interrogators in 1947 that Hitler could have been promoted within RIR 16, which is also confirmed by Wiedemann's memoirs:

> One day I proposed him as a candidate for the post of NCO. Our NCO in charge of the dispatch runners had been wounded and I said: we'll take the next one, Private Hitler, he should have long been up for promotion. That's why I proposed him to Wiedemann . . . I had him brought to me and said: 'Congratulations, you are a NCO from now on.' He looked at me completely in shock and said: 'I would like to ask you not to promote me. I have more authority without laces than with them.'[115]

Another suggestion has been that the class structure of German society made a promotion impossible,[116] which would explain why Hitler did not become an officer but would not resolve why he did not at least become an NCO as there were a good number of NCOs from social backgrounds similar to that of Hilter. Meanwhile, Alexander Moritz Frey claimed, as we have seen, that the most likely reason why Hitler was not promoted was that, like Frey, Hitler did not want to leave the relative security of life at regimental HQ.

In fact, no record exists of Hitler ever even trying to get promotion. His lack of social skills and eccentricity might also have explained why he never became so much as an NCO.[117] Wilhelm Diess, who for a while was the

officer in change of Hitler during the war, told a student of his in post-Second World War Munich while teaching in the Faculty of Law at Munich University that the reason why Hitler was never promoted was that he had been too quarrelsome and self-opinionated, always thinking that he was right.[118] Furthermore, the reality, ironic though it is, was that Private Hitler did not display any leadership qualities during the war. Another one of Hitler's superiors, at any rate, could not detect in him any 'leadership traits' nor any talent for leading other soldiers. Moreover, Hitler's 'posture was lazy', according to Fritz Wiedemann, 'and his answer, whenever someone asked him something, was anything but militarily short. He usually had his head cocked somewhat to the left.'[119]

While it is not too difficult to figure out what Hitler's position in regimental HQ was by 1916 and how the political mentalities of the men of the List Regiment at large had developed, it is much more difficult to locate Hitler on the political radar in 1916 due to the absence of contemporary documentation.

In *Mein Kampf*, Hitler claims that during the war he stayed well clear of politics: 'I was then a soldier and did not wish to meddle in politics, all the more so because the time was inopportune. . . . I despised those political fellows and if I had had my way I would have formed them into a Labour Battalion and given them the opportunity of babbling amongst themselves to their hearts' content, without offence or harm to decent people.' Yet Hitler maintains that his war experience slowly and gradually politicized him: 'In those days I cared nothing for politics; but I could not help forming an opinion on certain manifestations which affected not only the whole nation but also us soldiers in particular.'[120] Hitler contends that he now already formed quietly all the ideas that he would express in *Mein Kampf*.[121] He also claims to have conversed with his brothers-in-arms in regimental HQ about the need to set up a new nationalist classless party: 'I frequently discussed that want with my intimate comrades. And it was then that I first conceived the idea of taking up political work later on. As I have often assured my friends, it was just this that induced me to become active on the public hustings after the War, in addition to my professional work. And I am sure that this decision was arrived at after much earnest thought.'[122] Ignaz Westenkirchner and Ernst Schmidt would later also claim that Hitler talked about either becoming an artist or a politician, even though, it needs to be pointed out, Westenkirchner was an unreliable witness, as we shall see. Equally, Jackl Weiß would tell Fritz Wiedemann, once Hitler had come to power: 'Well, he did occasionally give us political lectures. We had thought that maybe he could one day become a deputy of the Bavarian Parliament, but Reich Chancellor—never!'[123] However, unlike Hitler, even Westernkirchner, Schmidt, and Weiß do not claim that Hitler had a clearly formulated world-view.[124] According to Max Amann, Hitler's politicking was limited to criticizing the Habsburg monarchy: 'He was always spouting off to the other men about the condition of Austria, that it was decayed, that it was lucky the war had come as long as the Emperor was alive, etc.'[125] As, with the exception of Mend's fabricated memoirs,[126] neither Hitler's comrades nor his superiors recall the kind of conversations Hitler claims had taken place, we can be pretty certain that they simply did not happen.

Rather than conversing with his comrades about how to create a new nationalist, classless world, Hitler did, however, according to Frey, have a reputation for wildly railing against the 'impudence' of the 'stupid Englishmen' and of the 'French swines' and to argue whatever his superiors wanted to hear. So doing, he 'talked, scolded, decried and distorted the true state of affairs with a certain cunning deftness', Frey claimed in 1946, concluding that during the war one could already see all the hallmarks of his later style of propaganda and politics.[127] However, his wildly articulated ideas had not yet made the transformation from merely bitterly extolling the stupidity of a military enemy and the House of Habsburg towards expressing National Socialist ideas as found in *Mein Kampf*. In short, Hitler might have acquired most of his subsequent rhetorical style by this point. He might also have harboured fantasies about a political career. His political ideas, as expressed to others (as opposed to whatever ideas Hitler might have silently and secretly harboured) were, it seems, still limited to an expression of some Pan-German ideas and to a venting of frustration about the battlefield adversaries of the List Regiment.

7

Collapse

July–October 1916

I n the first half 1916, the war of Hitler and his brothers-in-arms only
started to change in little ways. In February, the food rations for the men
of the List Regiment were reduced—a clear sign that the long war and the
allied blockade of Germany were taking their toll and a warning that time
was working in favour of Germany's adversaries. The army cooks of RIR 16
had to attend special courses on how to cook without meat, as the meat
ration had been reduced from 375 to 300 g.[1] Gas attacks were also becoming
more frequent. However, the effectiveness of gas warfare was still very
limited in 1916 due to technological limitations that were overcome only
towards the end of the war. At this point, gas clouds would only slowly
crawl towards the men of the regiment and they would have time to put on
their gas masks and to try to find shelter.[2]

Despite the growing hardship, the experience of RIR 16 compares well
with that of many other German units on the Western Front, for the
men of the List Regiment had successfully avoided becoming fodder for
the Battle of Verdun, which had been consuming soldiers faster than new
reinforcements could be brought in. In the summer, they were also not
rushed to the Somme, after the British and the French had embarked on
their all-out attempt to break through the German front and end the war.
Their continuing task was to guard the quiet sector of the front close to Lille
where they had lain now for well over a year. This was a task appropriate for
a regiment not particularly high up the pecking order.

It had not escaped the attention of the British forces that German troops
were stretched dangerously thin at quiet sectors of the Western Front. They
thus decided to strike at the weakest link as a diversion to the Battle of the
Somme. That link was the sector occupied by RIR 16.

The attack, on a front of nearly 4 kilometres, was left to two inexperienced British divisions: the 61st (2nd South Midland) Division and the 5th Australian Division. On the evening of 19 July 1916, after a heavy three-day bombardment, the men of 3rd Battalion, who were manning the first line, suddenly saw British troops go over the top and storm towards them.[3]

The attack was a total failure. The BEF soldiers ran straight into the machine-gun and infantry fire of the List Regiment and were mown down. RD 6 turned out to be a much more resilient opponent than their adversaries had expected. Retreating BEF troops were hit by German shrapnel. However, the sister regiments of RIR 16 were less lucky. Australian troops broke through the Bavarian lines on either side of the List Regiment. The men of Hitler's unit faced the immediate danger of being trapped.[4]

This is when the units of RD 6 started their counter-attack. Luckily for the Bavarian troops, the Australian troops who had broken through got stuck once they reached the German rear trenches which, to their dismay, turned out to be filled with water. RIR 16 was under strict orders not to start a frontal attack but to move into the vacated German first line and cut the enemy off. It was now the Australians who were trapped. Chaotic close-range combat ensued and lasted the entire night. In the chaos and darkness of a foggy night, there were instances of soldiers from RIR 16 throwing hand grenades at each other. Yet as night turned into morning, the List Regiment and its sister regiment had managed to reconquer most of the lost territory. This was due in no small degree to the energetic combat performed by hand-grenade and storm troops—mostly led by volunteers such as Georg Dehn of 1st Company, a student of archaeology who had been close to Albert Weisgerber. What also helped the men of Hitler's regiment was that many of the attacking Australians were drunk.[5] Bavarian soldiers seemed to close in on the Australians from all sides. An Australian Sergeant saw 'dead bodies lying in all directions, just as they had fallen, some without heads, other bodies torn apart minus arms or legs, or pieces cut clean out of them by shells'.[6] The battle came to an end when huge numbers of Australian soldiers surrendered after being trapped and fired upon by friend and foe alike. RIR 16 had emerged victorious from the Battle of Fromelles at a cost of more than 340 casualties, of which 107 were fatal.[7]

The casualties the List Regiment had incurred, however, were small compared to those of their opponents. The Australians alone had incurred more than 5,500 casualties, of which almost 2,000 were fatal. It was the single darkest day in Australia's military history. The English casualties, meanwhile, ran at more than 1,500. Following the battle, the ground between the first Bavarian line and the rear trenches was covered with countless dead Australian and English soldiers.[8]

After the battle, some Australian soldiers stated that they had seen Bavarian soldiers shooting injured Australians.[9] According to Australian reports, Bavarian soldiers let an Australian soldier who had been blinded stumble in circles before they shot him.[10] A report by 1st Battalion of the List Regiment agrees that the laws of 'civilized' warfare had been broken. However, the villains of the RIR 16 report were Australian, not Bavarian: 'Under these conditions the recovery of the large number of prisoners has become extremely dangerous for us. The number of our losses incurred while undertaking this task is a result of the perfidiousness of the enemy, as they first feign surrender and then resume combat when we come close to them.'[11]

How widespread the practice of shooting injured or surrendering soldiers was is almost impossible to say; we also do not know if soldiers shot injured soldiers out of mercy or out of revenge and hatred. At least some soldiers, no doubt, were driven by a growing hatred of the British. Alois Schnellorfer, for instance, had already written to his parents from regimental HQ a few days before the battle: 'My only wish is that God will punish England.'[12] Furthermore, several British soldiers believed that the killings had been motivated by revenge. As a soldier from the Royal Engineers who had fought at Fromelles recounted years later, the result was that he and his comrades stopped taking prisoners.[13] Perceptions were thus as important as the reality in feeding the circle of violence.

The reason why prisoner-taking during the war was precarious and why it is difficult for us today to determine how widespread wartime brutalization really was is that acts of decency and of treacherous violence coexisted and were sometimes combined. One such incident occurred at the end of the Battle of Fromelles, when two Bavarian soldiers carried an injured Australian soldier back to the Australian trenches, saluted the injured soldier, and then, as they walked back towards German lines, were shot by other Australians who probably simply were oblivious to what had happened.[14] Another tragic incident occurred when an officer from the 14th Australian Infantry Brigade decided to surrender to the Germans on 20 July 1916, after he had realized that the situation of his unit had become hopeless. He thus gave himself up to two Bavarian soldiers from RD 6 (we do not know from which regiment). He ordered his men to surrender too. However, in defiance or in ignorance of their superior, they now shot the two Bavarian soldiers dead.[15]

It seems, however, that acts of decency in the aftermath of battle were more common than acts of brutality. POWs later recorded that on arrest they were not treated at all brutally. Similarly, with some exceptions, injured soldiers reported that German medical teams treated them very well. So readily forthcoming had been the help afforded to injured Australian and English troops by the men of RIR 16 that the commander of the List Regiment felt compelled to issue the order that the men of Hitler's regiment were only supposed to help their Anglo-Saxon counterparts once their own injured soldiers had been taken care of. He also felt the need to remind them that captured soldiers, rather than the men of the List Regiment, were supposed to carry injured Australian and English soldiers to the rear. Furthermore, on 2 August, less than two weeks after the battle, twenty to thirty Australian soldiers who faced either RIR 16 or RIR 17 climbed up the parapet of their trenches and tried to fraternize.[16]

The Battle of Fromelles had not led to a collapse of morale in the regiment. On the contrary, it had boosted the willingness of many of the men of the regiment to continue fighting as it had brought their first victory for a long time. For the rest of the summer, while new reinforcements were arriving, calm returned to the sector of the front of Hitler's regiment. In addition to their trips to Lille, the men of 3rd Battalion were taken on a day trip to the seaside resort of Heyst in an attempt to boost their morale. This was the first time that many men of Hitler's regiment ever saw the sea.[17]

Yet not everything was moving in a favourable direction for the List Regiment and the Germans. In late August, for instance, Romania joined the ranks of Germany's enemies, a fact that the troops facing the List Regiment and its sister units rubbed in by sending a grenade-dud with a piece of paper attached to it announcing the entry of Romania to the war.[18] The case of two NCOs from 10th Company was also the source of some concern. They thought that their company commander, Lt. Bachschneider, was a 'complete and utter swine' for not having joined them in the trenches but having stayed in his fortified dugout during the Battle of Fromelles. Their resentment had grown to such an extent that after a drunken night in mid-August, one of the NCOs told the Commander of Santes that he was going to desert to the British: 'Screw you, I'm going to do whatever I want to do.'[19] The case of the two NCOs revealed that many of the front-line soldiers, as well as some of the NCOs—unlike Hitler who was full of admiration for the officers of RIR 16—were starting to resent their officers for, as they thought, keeping their heads down, while they put their lives on the line.

Another source of concern was that a growing number of soldiers were becoming impatient for still not having been given leave to visit their families in Bavaria. Alois Schnelldorfer claimed that soldiers started to worry that if they were denied home leave, their wives would start to sleep with prisoners of war.[20] Sometimes the frustration of soldiers became so intense that they simply refused to continue to perform and went AWOL, as did, for instance, Heinrich Munzer, an NCO from Munich, in early September. The patience of the soldiers was wearing increasingly thin. Some started to snap over the smallest of incidents, regardless of the consequences. For instance, when an officer asked Xaver Christl, an infantryman in 6th Company, to put out and throw away the cigarette he was smoking during a roll-call, Christl told his officer to get lost.[21] On another occasion, an infantryman from 8th Company said to his NCO, when ordered to continue to move forward on a march: 'Kiss my arse; you can carry my knapsack yourself.'[22] All these cases indicate that the situation in the regiment remained extremely volatile and that the recovery of morale was very fragile and likely to break with any major change in the tasks that the men of Hitler's regiment were asked to perform.

Throughout the summer, the men of RIR 16 could hear the distant sound of the Battle of the Somme raging some 70 kilometres to the south. From the reports the soldiers read, but more importantly from stories troops returning from the Somme were telling, the Battle of the Somme seemed increasingly like a giant black hole that kept on sucking in new troops. More and more, the men of RIR 16 sensed that it would only be a question of time before the Somme would consume them too. The letters Alois Schnelldorfer sent to his parents in 1916 clearly show that he did not think that the war was going well. On 19 September, for instance, he wrote: 'I am certain that we have not gone through the worst yet; things will still get worse. Unfortunately, once war has started, it cannot easily be stopped. . . . the war will not end any time soon. It is inevitable that we will have [another] Christmas at war.'[23]

As word reached Hitler's comrades, both sides had made wide use on the Somme of gas, which killed soldiers, horses, and rats indiscriminately. The sight of men in gas masks caused mules to panic and stampede. In September alone, the Germans incurred 135,000 casualties on the Somme. According to reports from the front, the British and French kept pushing forward relentlessly. And the first use of the 'caterpillar machine-gun destroyer'— soon to be known as tanks—by the British in September was causing dumb horror among German troops. To the dismay of the Germans, the British finally seemed to be on the move, managing to capture as much ground in the second half of September as they had done in the first two and half months of the battle. The constant rain of September transformed the battleground on the Somme into a sea of mud in which corpses—on which rats were feeding—served as stepping stones. It was a battle in which ultimately three million men fought.[24] By late September, at a time when British newspapers such as the *Daily Post* believed that 'the killing of Germans is the only way to peace',[25] rumours were spreading that the List Regiment was about to be deployed on the Somme.[26]

The news that the men of Hitler's unit were about to join the German forces on the Somme abruptly ended the fragile and volatile recovery in morale that had occurred in the aftermath of the Battle of Fromelles. By August, Gustav Scanzoni von Lichtenfels, the commander of RD 6, had already concluded: 'Recently, the number of cases in which soldiers went AWOL for both shorter and longer periods of time has increased.'[27] Yet once the men of RIR 16 knew that deployment on the Somme was imminent, the problem escalated.

After artillery soldiers had told Ludwig Reininger from 11th Company what to expect on the Somme, Reininger decided he had had enough. In the event, on 26 September, as his company stood ready in Haubourdin for its deployment on the Somme, Reininger and his friend Jakob Reindl, who like him was in his thirties, came from rural Lower Bavaria, and had not served in the military prior to the war, and two other soldiers just walked off. They made their way to Tournai, where Reininger and Reindl separated from the two other soldiers and boarded a train to Munich. There they split up and both walked to Lower Bavaria. They kept their heads down until they heard from comrades in the List Regiment who were on home leave following the end of the Battle of the Somme that the battle was over. They both now walked to the closest office of the *Ersatz* unit of their regiment and turned themselves in. Reindl stated: 'I didn't want to go into the trenches because I was afraid of the shooting.'[28]

Reiniger and Reindl's case suggests that it was the core, or primary, groups to which soldiers belonged, rather than their company or the regiment at large that would determine both the individual and collective behaviour of soldiers. It was there, among their immediate comrades, that soldiers talked about their fears and about their attitude towards the war. It was to their primary group that soldiers felt a sense of belonging. To be sure, the majority of primary groups decided that they would continue to fight for various reasons; and it was loyalty to the members of one's core group that tended to act as an inhibitor against desertion. It was thus as a web of loosely interconnected primary groups that the List Regiment continued to perform. However, the case of Reindl, Reininger, and their two co-conspirators was far from isolated. Indeed nineteen cases of desertion, absence without leave, and other offences relating to disobedience—more than the combined figure for the first six months of 1916—were deemed significant enough eventually to make it to military court of RD 6. In almost all of the eighteen cases, the soldiers tried had been motivated by the fear of being deployed on the Somme. And these cases do not include those that occurred in early October *en route* to the Somme. The common feature of the soldiers who deserted was that they looked pale and distraught, had trembling hands, and that they deserted jointly or had at least talked with comrades about their plans or had received help from others. Some had been buried alive in previous battles and were unable to keep their balance when closing their eyes.[29]

The cases of insubordination included that of Anton Haimbacher, an agricultural worker from rural Upper Bavaria and infantryman serving in 2nd Company with reddened eyes. He went AWOL on 24 September, walking to nearby Aubers, where he hid among Prussian soldiers in their barracks and dugouts for fourteen days, being supplied all the while with food by the Prussian soldiers. Haimbacher's case suggests that the vast number of soldiers who chose not to go AWOL and to continue to perform understood well those men who had deserted. They no longer saw them as traitors but as comrades in need of their help. When Haimbacher eventually was arrested, he declared that he had deserted because of his fear of the Somme. He also stated that his primary allegiance was to Mintraching, his village. He was indifferent to national identities, professing: 'I don't care whether [after the war] I'll be Bavarian or French.'[30]

Note that the choice Haimbacher allowed was between being Bavarian or French, not even mentioning a national German identity. His case is a reminder that at least some German soldiers from the rural countryside, like their counterparts from rural France, still had no concept of nationality.[31] For many Bavarian farmers, their regional identity was still the only one that mattered, as is evident from the opening sentence of an undated manuscript of a talk given for the purpose of 'Patriotic Instruction' during the second half of the war: 'The farmers often say that they don't care if Alsace-Lorraine stays German or becomes French, because they would continue to sow their seeds, harvest their grain and their potatoes, and plough their fields, regardless of whether the French or the German flag waved over Strassburg.'[32]

The very significant number of soldiers going AWOL on the eve of the Battle of the Somme, as well as their testimony, and the help they received from other soldiers suggests that, even though most soldiers did not desert, the underlying reasons for desertion were widely shared among the men of Hitler's regiment. Such reasons were a fear of the Somme, growing fatalism, and a feeling of disenchantment with the war, rather than a lasting distancing from the political system of Bavaria and Germany, in spite of the case of Anton Haimbacher and in spite of occasional critical voices among Bavarian soldiers that the Bavarian king was too submissive to the Prussians.[33]

Fear more than anything else led to a collapse of morale and discipline on the eve of the Battle of the Somme. As we have seen, fear can be translated into aggression in combat as long as soldiers still feel that they can still in some way control the dangers of the battle through their own behaviour. However, the bottom line of all the rumours about the Battle of Somme was that this was a battle in which soldiers had lost all sense of control. Furthermore, enemy artillery fire was on the rise in September which resulted, as the war diary of 1st Battalion recorded, in an increase of 'incidents of strained nerves'.[34] It was precisely this state of being an impotent and vulnerable target for heavy shelling and bombing without the ability to strike back that put a larger strain on soldiers than many forms of close-range combat.[35] The breakdown of discipline on the eve of the Battle of the Somme thus resulted from the kind of fear occasioned by incessant long-range fire as well as from the expectation of being deployed in a battle in which the men of RIR 16 had no control over their own survival.

It was no secret that units like the List Regiment were simply not up to the task that awaited them on the Somme and that a collapse of morale in units like RIR 16 was to be expected. However, in the absence of other available troops, the German High Command felt that there was no alternative but to deploy units such as RIR 16 on the Somme. As Crown Prince Rupprecht noted on 4 September 1916, 'unfortunately, our troops at the Somme front are for the most part not the best, and those who will come to relieve them will not be any better. The ranks of veteran officers and troops are being constantly diminished, and the large quantities of *Ersatzreservists* have not enjoyed the same soldierly education and are for the most part physically lacking.'[36]

On the night of 24–5 September, the 19th Bavarian Infantry Regiment, just having returned from the Somme and full of stories about the horrors of the battle, replaced the men of the Hitler's regiment in their position close to Fromelles. The men of the List Regiment were given two days to rest behind the front in Loos and Haubourdin.[37]

In the early hours of 27 September it was time for Private Hitler and the troops of RIR 16 to board the trains that would carry them to the Somme. Alexander Moritz Frey recalled how Max Amann constantly talked to him on the train, while Hitler sat opposite them, fast asleep with his mouth open. Several hours later, they got off their trains and marched through rolling hills to two villages just to the east of Bapaume, the old medieval town at the most north-eastern point of the territory on which the Battle of the Somme was fought. By this time, the battle had already been raging for three months.[38]

Initially, the men of the RIR 16 were lucky. Rather than being thrown into the battle, they had to help build a new line of defences to the east of Bapaume. At night, the men watched in awe the artillery fire of the nearby battle that illuminated the night. At night, they also endlessly played cards and smoked to calm their nerves. The men of the List Regiment now received steel helmets, each weighing 1.25 kg, which signalled the end of the German spike helmet.[39]

After four days of helping to build the new German defence line, the men of RIR 16 ran out of luck. They were told that the following day, on 2 October, they were to be thrown into the battle.[40]

The Germans had tried to stop the continued British advance and put up a defence line on the Warlencourt Ridge in the farmland just to the south of Bapaume. The task of the men of the List Regiment was now, in rainy weather, to defend and reinforce the new defence line which lay close to the old Roman street running from Albert to Bapaume on ground that had already been the stage for fighting in the Franco-Prussian War of 1870/1. Regimental HQ, and consequently Hitler, as well as the battalion battle posts were set up in the tiny village of Le Barque, approximately 2 kilometres behind the front. On the evening of

2 October, the men of the regiment arrived at the front in pouring rain. A few hours later, they relieved RIR 21. The front-line defences into which the men of the List Regiment marched looked like a scene from hell. The constant shelling of the previous days and weeks had turned the once rich farmland and gentle hills into a desert of shell craters, a landscape more reminiscent of the moon than the earth. There were dead bodies of men and horses everywhere; shell-holes had filled up with foul-smelling water. The position of RIR 16 included of trenches that were often only a metre deep; in other cases, the trenches merely consisted of shell holes that had been linked up. The only communication to the front line was through runners, whose task was hellish.[41] Luckily for Private Hitler it was not the job of regimental dispatch runners to take messages to the trenches.

British artillery fire on the Somme, however, brought danger even to relatively privileged soldiers behind the immediate front, such as Private Hitler. And indeed, on 5 October—on the List Regiment's fourth day in the Battle of the Somme, Hitler, together with his fellow dispatch runners Anton Bachmann and Ernst Schmidt, was wounded for the first time in the war, when a British shell hit the dispatch runners' dugout in the village of Le Barque.[42] When the dugout had been constructed, its entry had been set up so that it could not be hit by artillery fire. However, due to a change in the front line that had occurred earlier in the battle, this was no longer the case. Now on 5 October, a small grenade exploded right outside the entrance to the dugout, firing splinters right into the entrance. A shell splinter hit Hitler in his left upper thigh, while several of his fellow dispatch runners were injured too, though none of them was killed, contrary to the story told by Nazi propaganda.[43] He was neither hit by a shell splinter in the face, nor was he in a front-line dugout, as we sometimes still read.[44]

According to a Polish priest, who claims to have had conversations in the 1960s with the medic who treated Hitler after his injury, Hitler lost one of his testicles in the battle. The medic, Johan Jambor, had allegedly told him of Hitler: 'His abdomen and his legs were covered in blood. Hitler was injured in the abdomen and had lost his testicle. His first question for the doctor was: "Will I still be able to have children?"' A friend of Jambor claimed that Jambor had given him a similar account: 'Jambor and his friend searched for injured soldiers for hours. They called Hitler "the screamer". He was very loud and shouted "Help, Help!"'[45]

Maybe Jambor really believed in this version of events, however self-serving the telling of the story was. Yet his testimony should certainly be treated as fiction.[46] Even if we ignore the fact that none of Hitler's military and medical records mention an injury to the abdomen and that Hitler did not have to be 'found' as he was not injured on the battlefield but in the dugout of the support staff of regiment headquarters, Jambor's account is less than convincing. Even if Hitler really had lost one of his testicles and was saved by Jambor, why would he have remembered the fate as well as the name of this particular still totally unknown, insignificant soldier, when he must have encountered hundreds, maybe thousands, of injured soldiers during the war?

If we can believe the memoirs of Fritz Wiedemann, Hitler was worried that the injury meant that he had to leave the regiment, telling Wiedemann: 'It's not so bad, Herr Lieutenant Colonel, eh? I can stay with you, stay with the regiment.'[47] Hitler's injury was indeed only a light wound, as the casualty list of his Battalion, the official Bavarian casualty list, as well as Wiedemann's recollections make clear,[48] but it was serious enough to warrant being sent home.

When Hitler described the incident in *Mein Kampf*, the real account of his injury was not dramatic enough for the aspiring dictator. In typical fashion, he embellished the story:

> At the end of September 1916 my division was sent into the Battle of the Somme. For us this was the first of a series of heavy engagements, and the impression created was that of a veritable inferno, rather than war. Through weeks of incessant artillery bombardment we stood firm, at times ceding a little ground but then taking it back again, and never giving way. On October 7th, 1916, I was wounded but had the luck of being able to get back to our lines and was then ordered to be sent by ambulance train to Germany.[49]

Similarly, Ignaz Westenkirchner would incorrectly claim in 1934 that in the shelling of 5 October, 'four of us lay dead, and seven others lay hideously wounded spouting blood on the ground. A splinter had gashed him in the face.' According to Westenkirchner's fictional account, Hitler still fought for another week on the Somme when 'he ran such a gauntlet between exploding mined and burning houses, that for the most part his own clothes singed on his back'. The conditions were so bad that 'it took six runners now to get a message through'. It was supposedly only Hitler and Schmidt who still volunteered to bring messages forward, which led to Hitler's injury: 'This time only Schmidt got back. Hitler had been hit in the left leg. Later on the regimental stretcher-bearers brought him in . . . .'[50] A similar, equally fictitious account was provided by Balthasar Brandmayer in his unreliable pro-Hitler memoirs.[51] Brandmayer's and Westenkirchner's testimonies are probably the real origin of Jambor's story, as their memoirs claim—as does Jambor's account—that Hitler was injured on the battlefield rather than inside a dugout.

The truth is that, Hitler, who at no point in *Mein Kampf* mentioned that after the first battle he was a dispatch runner rather than a front-line soldier, had not lived through weeks of 'incessant artillery bombardment'. By the time he was injured on 5 October (not on 7 October as Hitler himself stated),[52] he had spent only four days engaged in the Battle of the Somme. Hitler also lied about where he was injured, stating that he had to get back to the German lines, implying that he was wounded as a front-line soldier rather than in regimental headquarters in a village 2 kilometres behind the front.

Moreover, because of the intense rain between 2 and 7 October, British air observers had been grounded and the British artillery was thus severely hampered. While Hitler was on the Somme, British troops, guns, tanks, and supplies could barely be moved due to the atrocious weather conditions. Serious British operations against the List Regiment thus did not start until 7 October. When on 7 October, in a futile attempt to break through the German lines, British shrapnel, exploding gas shells, and infantry fire wiped out the lives of 104 men of the List Regiment and when soldiers pretended to be injured just to be taken away from the Somme, Hitler, Bachmann, and Schmidt were already safe in an army hospital at Hermies well behind the front. As British shells tore to pieces men like Heinrich Langenbach, a Jewish soldier and opera singer, or buried them alive, the commander of 1st Battalion warned that morale was so low that he could not guarantee that his men would still resist any future enemy attack.[53] Moreover, as the soldiers of RIR 16 gained the impression that they would only be replaced once the casualty rate of their unit exceeded 50 per cent,[54] Hitler was already on a hospital train to Germany.

Despite the horrific conditions that RIR 16 had to endure, it was still not taken out of the battle as the German battle plan demanded that each infantry division deployed on the Somme had to hold the line for two weeks before it could be relieved, whatever the cost.[55] Crown Prince Rupprecht described the predicament of German troops on the Somme thus: 'The enemy's almost complete air superiority until recently, the superiority of their artillery in accuracy and number, and the extraordinary quantity of ammunition they have, allow them utterly to pulverize our defensive positions. . . . Our men can only lie in shell-holes, without barriers or shelters. . . . Also, the men often cannot eat in the forward lines because of the smell of corpses, and they cannot sleep either.'[56] It was not just the shrapnel emanating from the explosion of grenades and mines that made the heavy artillery fire so deadly. It was also so lethal because of the shock waves of the explosions which destroyed the body's most easily compressed tissue, which is situated in the lungs. Damage to this tissue, in other words, 'the tiny, delicate air sacs where the blood picks up oxygen and drops off carbon dioxide', has been described in the following way: 'An explosive shock wave compresses and ruptures these sacs. Blood then seeps into the lungs and drowns their owner, sometimes quickly, in ten or twenty minutes, sometimes over a span of hours.'[57]

With every day the situation worsened. On 9 October, 1st Battalion noted: 'Morale low. The nerves [of the soldiers] are shot.' Moreover, 'mental depression' was on the rise. On 10 October, the battalion recorded: 'The troops become unreliable if replacements do not arrive. . . . Even during moderate artillery fire, [the men] conduct themselves as if they were crazy.' The assessment of the following day was: 'The troops in the first line do not all seem to be dependable. . . . The new men are also mentally too weak. . . . The new replacements are worthless in this fire.' On 12 October, soldiers of the regiment abandoned their positions in droves, clearly feeling abandoned to their fate by their commanders. In one case, fifteen men from 4th Company jointly walked to the rear. Military police had to be ordered in to stop men from leaving their posts and to return the deserters to the front.[58] Even Emil Spatny, who had been regimental commander of RIR 16 since the spring, broke under the strain of the battle and maybe also under the responsibility he felt for the deaths of so many of his men. Finding solace in the bottle during the Battle of the Somme, Spatny was almost constantly so drunk that he was often in no state even to sign the regimental orders that his adjutant had prepared for him. On the urging of the officers of RIR 16, Spatny was eventually released from his post the following spring, as he had become an unsustainable liability.[59]

Oscar Daumiller also experienced the meltdown of morale among the troops of RD 6 during the Battle of the Somme. He noted that by 10 October, 'the state of the morale of the men was alarming.' That day,

Daumiller recorded, 'I have heard that of 300 men [from one Battalion] about 100 men deserted during the advance.' During the battle, as Daumiller realized, the soldiers were no longer responding to patriotic slogans: 'During the Battle of the Somme, resorting to patriotic slogans did not help to comfort the soldiers; only the word of God helped.' Daumiller concluded that the men of Hitler's division had great difficulty in finding any meaning in their involvement in the battle: 'When the drum of gunfire continued in the first line with unyielding intensity for hours, when renewed misery arose in the tents of the casualty stations, when we stood in the open trenches for 8 to 10 hours a day, then doubts clouded the faces of many.' Long gone were the days when Daumiller had described the war as a holy war and supported the German national cause unreservedly:

> The days on the Somme have taken on great meaning for my own thinking [about the meaning of life]. The truth of Psalm 90: 5–7 became frighteningly clear to me, just like the emptiness of our entire famed culture of the peoples of Europe. Men and entire peoples went bankrupt and One alone has remained fearless in his holy majesty and has again become a helper in love and in mercy for those who finally listen to him, God, the Living.[60]

Daumiller, however, did not, or at least not immediately, share these thoughts with the survivors of the Somme. Rather than sharing his honest opinions, probably out of a feeling of responsibility or duty, he told them in a service honouring the fallen of the battle that the deceased had 'found a hero's death in the battle trenches at the hand of a rifle or machine-gun bullet or of an artillery projectile. About them it is appropriate to say: "There is no more beautiful death in the world than to die at the hands of the enemy and fall upon green meadows in the open field." The battlefield has become their grave.'[61]

The battle had even changed the physical appearance of the men of the List Regiment and its sister units. As one of the officers of RIR 20 noted, 'the appearance of most of the men was sallow, their features were strained, vacant, their cheeks and eyes sunken. In addition, many men were in shock from having been buried alive.'[62] Futhermore, the skin of the survivors of the battle was, as the war diarist of 1st Battalion noted, covered with 'scabs, boils, and abscesses', stemming from the constant scratching of their skins which was an inevitable result of 'a lack of opportunity for hygiene [and the] constantly lingering plague of lice'.[63]

The cost of the battle for the men of RIR 16 was astronomical. Of all the men of the List Regiment killed on the Somme, 78 per cent were killed after

Hitler had been transported to safety. In total, 335 soldiers from RIR 16 had died on the Somme and 827 men had been injured, which amounts to a casualty rate of more than 50 per cent. Among the injured was Hugo Gutmann, who had received a wound to the head in the early hours of RIR 16's last day on the Somme. By 13 October, the List Regiment had shrunk to such a degree that it could no longer function and it was hurriedly withdrawn.[64]

8

In the Shadow of the Somme

October 1916–31 July 1917

After his injury on the Somme, Hitler had been taken to an army hospital at Beelitz, near Berlin, where he remained for a little less than two months. He had not been to Germany since October 1914 and was shocked by what awaited him. In *Mein Kampf*, he drew a picture of a stark difference between the morale of the men in the List Regiment and of the patients in the army hospital at Beelitz: 'The spirit of the army at the front appeared to be out of place here,' wrote Hitler. 'For the first time I encountered something which up to then was unknown at the front: namely, boasting of one's own cowardice. . . . loud-mouthed agitators were busy here [in the hospital] heaping ridicule on the good soldier and painting the weak-kneed poltroon in glorious colours.' He recalled of his time at Beelitz:

> A couple of miserable human specimens were the ringleaders in this process of defamation. One of them boasted of having intentionally injured his hand in barbed-wire entanglements in order to get sent to hospital. Although his wound was only a slight one, it appeared that he had been here for a very long time and would be here interminably. . . . This pestilential specimen actually had the audacity to parade his knavery as the manifestation of a courage which was superior to that of the brave soldier who dies a hero's death. There were many who heard this talk in silence; but there were others who expressed their assent to what the fellow said.[1]

It is extremely difficult to find out what Hitler really thought of the changes happening all around him in 1916, as no letters or other documents survive to give an indication of how he responded to the signs of collapsing morale. A postcard Hitler sent to Franz Mayer, the cyclist dispatcher for regimental HQ, indicates that, while in Beelitz, his focal reference point is likely to have remained the support staff of regimental HQ.

Meanwhile, there is no indication that he corresponded with anybody, either on the front proper or on the home front, who was not a member of regimental HQ. Unfortunately, the brief message he scribbled on the postcard—'Dear Mayer. Warm congratulations on the Iron Cross. I'm pleased that they finally thought of you. Warmest Greetings A. Hitler'— does not tell us anything about Hitler's political attitudes in the autumn of 1916.[2]

We do know, however, what Hitler retrospectively claimed, while writing *Mein Kampf* in the 1920s, his response to the fall of morale during the war was. We have already seen that in *Mein Kampf* Hitler blamed superior British propaganda as cause for the pessimism among many at the front. The culprits which Hitler added through his account of 1916 in *Mein Kampf* were women. According to him, they were sending defeatist letters to the front. Contradicting his own protestation that the spirit of the army was intact in 1916, he wrote:

> The whole front was drenched in this poison which thoughtless women at home sent out, without suspecting for a moment that the enemy's chances of final victory were thus strengthened or that the sufferings of their own men at the front were thus being prolonged and rendered more severe. These stupid letters written by German women eventually lost the lives of hundreds of thousands of our men.[3]

Although Hitler claimed that there was a profound difference between the morale of the men of his regiment and that of the men he encountered in the army hospital, in reality Hitler's description of the soldiers he came in contact with at Beelitz closely resembles that of the men of the List Regiment during the period of his absence, as the cases of soldiers such as Friedrich Hofbauer make clear.

Hofbauer's superiors had never had a problem with the 38-year-old innkeeper and livestock trader from Passau in Lower Bavaria. Serving in the 2nd Machine Gun Company of the List Regiment, he had always done what had been asked of him. However, the horrors of the Somme had left deep scars on this father of two.[4]

Nobody knew how men such as Hofbauer would perform in the post-Somme world, as the survivors of the battle were taken to their new segment of the front, where they would remain until early February 1917. Hofbauer now found himself in the German trenches halfway up Vimy Ridge, some 30 kilometres south of Lille. Unlike the ridges of Messines or of

Fromelles, this one was formidable. Their opponents likened it to a giant whale. From the regiment's position on the slope facing the enemy, Adolf Meyer, who had recently become the reconnaissance officer of regimental HQ, could on a clear day look deep into unoccupied France, as Vimy Ridge suddenly rises out of an almost flat terrain. He could see a panorama of industrial towns, surrounded by fields and forests, and dotted with church and mine towers, and with slag heaps, which from the distance looked almost like sugar cones. The regiment was now close to the heart of one of France's most important coal basins. So devastating had the British and French fire on the ridge been during previous attempts to capture it that the new 'home' of RIR 16 looked, as had the battlefield on the Somme, in places like a lunar landscape; on top of the ridge nothing but the charcoaled remains of tree-trunks were left standing. Some craters were so vast that Bavarian and enemy snipers took positions on opposite sides of the crater's lip.[5]

Hofbauer and the men of RIR 16 still faced British positions which were manned by Canadian troops. Their time on Vimy Ridge started out as a relatively quiet period which was wholly appropriate for a depleted, medi-ocre and average regiment. There was little fire, as both sides tried to conserve ammunition on 'quiet' sectors of the front.[6] However, on 28 October, just over two weeks after Hofbauer had been pulled out of the carnage of the Battle of the Somme, he snapped. Ordered to stand guard on the edge of one of the mine craters, he repeatedly refused to follow the instruction, saying that he would not have his head blown off. The NCO who had issued the order now tried to intimidate him into doing as he was told. He called Hofbauer a 'sad clown' (*trauriger Hanswurz*) and a 'weed' (*Schlappschwanz*), and told him that he would shoot him dead unless he followed the order. The intimidation did not work. Hofbauer's only response was: 'What do you want? To shoot me? I don't believe you could do it.'[7]

Hofbauer's case was far from isolated. Josef Leicher, whose disciplinary record had been 'excellent prior to the Somme', had already stopped performing their duties two days earlier than Hofbauer. The soldier, whose two brothers had been killed in action, simply refused to go into the trenches, stating that he did not want to end up the same way his brothers had.[8]

Despite the fact that 'only' sixteen men were killed in November, cases like these did not go away. Alois Müller, a worker from Munich, for instance, told the company clerk of his unit while in reserve that 'under no circumstances would he go to into the trenches'. The following day, his company commander personally ordered him to go into the trenches later that day. In the event, however, Müller chose to remain in bed. Upon then being ordered to report to the company commander, he just lay down in front of all his comrades who stood ready to march into the trenches and repeated that he would not join them.[9] Müller did not show any sign of concern that he might be seen as a traitor for his action.

Müller shared this sentiment with many of his peers. For instance, when Max Bentenrieder, a 21-year-old soldier from the Bavarian countryside serving in 1st Company, went AWOL he was helped by his comrades, just as had been the case with many of the soldiers who had deserted on the eve of the Battle of the Somme. The first night, one of Bentenrieder's comrades in the 3rd Machine Gun Company of RIR 16 put him up and hid him in his living quarters in a village behind the front, while Bentenrieder spent the following day with soldiers from his own company in nearby Douai before boarding a Germany-bound train. On a stop in Luxemburg, he was arrested. A few weeks later, his brother wrote a letter to him, telling him what the people in his village thought about the war and reassuring him of their support: 'It's just a big fraud through and through; everyone says so. Hugo [Sieder] wrote to me and told me so. He praises you. If the war doesn't end soon he'll do the same as you.'[10] Meanwhile, another soldier told his officer that he no longer wanted to serve in the List Regiment: 'I want to go to jail. I'd rather be there because there I don't have to risk my life.'[11]

Discontent was brewing even in regimental HQ. Alois Schnelldorfer wrote to his parents that if after the hardships of the Somme—he had to fix telecommunication cables under heavy fire for days on end—he did not receive leave to visit them soon, 'I won't go forward in the next battle'. He told his parents that 'since the Somme', he was 'a changed man', particularly since he felt that those who could sweet-talk their way up with the officers would receive all the honour, while those who really risked their lives were almost ignored. Two days later he wrote that he wanted those who were responsible for the war themselves to experience the front line, concluding: 'To the devil with the war. . . . Down with the military, we don't need them.'[12]

Even under the relatively quiet conditions of Vimy Ridge in the late autumn of 1916, there was thus little that indicated that Hitler's regiment had recovered from the Battle of the Somme. And the quiet conditions were not going to last forever. Unbeknownst to the men of RIR 16, even though only thirteen men were killed in December, the plans the British and French were drawing up for Vimy Ridge were intended to end the 'quiet' in this sector. December saw heightened enemy activity. The busy trench mortar fire, the very active enemy aerial reconnaissance, as well as the sound of the digging of enemy tunnels underground, were a clear sign that something was afoot close to the regiment's new 'home'. In the first week of December alone, 4,000 mortar shells were fired on the positions of RIR 16.[13] None of this was likely to help restore morale.

In December, conditions on the slopes of Vimy Ridge grew progressively and rapidly worse. With the wet winter and the heavy bombardment, the walls of the trenches or the access to dugouts of the List Regiment collapsed increasingly often, each time bringing the risk of burying the soldiers in the trenches alive under mounds of mud. Moreover, at night, unnaturally fat rats would run across the sleeping bodies of the men of RIR 16 or feed on dead bodies. The glutinous mud that covered the entire terrain made it almost impossible to walk. It did not take long before the temperature dropped and the bitter frost turned the mud as hard as granite. There were instances in which men were wounded by flying chunks of earth. Throughout the winter, wet, cold fog, snow, sleet, and rain were constant companions of Bavarian and Canadian soldiers alike.[14]

One day, a few days before Christmas, Karl Hackspacher decided that he had had enough. The conduct to date of the 26-year-old dental technician from just outside Munich had been excellent. He also had recently been proposed for an Iron Cross. Yet on a patrol the week before Christmas 1916, Hackspacher, who had a pale face and blonde hair, suddenly ran off from the patrol and surrendered to the British. Soon he wrote to his parents from a POW Camp in England, telling them: 'I am well, my health is first rate.'[15] One of the hitherto most reliable and brave soldiers had thus decided that the cost and danger of surrender was lower than that of continuing to fight.

In late December, another soldier went AWOL after grenades had rained down on his platoon, because, as he stated, he could no longer control himself when he had to experience close-range detonations.[16] Furthermore, on 30 December, two soldiers in their early twenties from 5th Company with no previous disciplinary problems told the NCO in charge of them that 'they would no longer go into the trenches; they no longer dared to do so'.[17] These cases suggest that even though few men of the List Regiment had been killed in action since arriving on Vimy Ridge, morale had never-theless not recovered.

Between the end of the Battle of the Somme and the end of the year, a total of twenty-nine cases of desertion, disobedience, AWOL, self-mutilation, and cowardice occurred that were deemed serious enough eventually to make it to the divisional court. Countless other cases of insubordination were not sent to the court but were dealt with at the regimental level. Remarkably, the conduct in the war of well over half of the twenty-nine soldiers tried by the court of RD 6 had previously been excellent (*sehr gut*) or good (*gut*), while only less than a quarter had a record of bad or inadequate conduct. It is also noteworthy how many of the younger soldiers were among these twenty-nine soldiers. Their average age was 25.4 years. The mean age was even two years lower than that, as eight of the twenty-nine soldiers were still only 21 or younger.[18]

The common feature of many of these cases was that soldiers openly told NCOs or officers that they would no longer do as they were told. These cases also indicated a deteriorating relationship between ordinary soldiers and their junior officers and NCOs that had previously provided much of the glue holding the List Regiment together.[19]

The rapid increase in cases of infringements of the code of military justice in the form of desertions, going AWOL, self-mutilations, disobedience, and cowardice thus did not, as Hitler claimed, only become a problem in the regiment with the influx of recruits that were would-be 'November criminals' in the final year of the war.

In no period of the war to date had so many cases been brought before RD 6's military tribunal than in the second half of 1916, at a time when the home front by and large still supported the war. It was thus the experience of the trenches and of bloody battles, and in particular the experience of the Battle of the Somme, that made the men turn their back on the German war effort. The case of Hitler's regiment thus suggests that internal strains in the German armed forces had already begun in mid-1916, and not only in 1917 or 1918, as usually believed.[20]

Of course, only a minority of soldiers were taken to court. The number of soldiers from RIR 16 tried for desertion and other disciplinary offences is minute compared, for instance, to the 9 per cent of all Union Army soldiers who deserted during the American Civil War.[21] Yet it would be a mistake to see the cases of the men of RIR 16 who were tried by the divisional court as constitut-ing an unrepresentative section of Hitler's regiment. As many letters and memoranda make blatantly clear, the cases of desertion and of absence without leave were just the tip of the iceberg in terms of the fall in morale in RIR 16. And it needs to be repeated that, by comparison to the British and French armed forces, German officers and military courts were far less harsh. During the Christmas Truce of 1914, British soldiers had indeed complained to the men of 1st Battalion about 'the strictness of [their] officers.'[22] Due to the relative leniency of the German military justice and disciplinary system, the men of Hitler's regiment were far less likely to be tried than their counterparts on the other side of the trench. This means that, unlike what would have been the case had RD 6 been a unit in the French or British forces, only the most severe cases are represented in the figures provided in Figure 1. In fact, not only were far fewer German soldiers executed than in the forces of her enemies but the minimum sentence for various forms of desertion and going absent without leave was also reduced twice in 1916 and 1917 at the urging of the Reichstag;[23] this was also a sign that the checks and balances between civil and military institutions in Germany worked at least sometimes and that wartime Germany was not a military dictatorship.

In the German case, the majority of cases of insubordination were dealt with on the level below military courts as it was seen as preferable to hand out disciplinary detentions rather than to try soldiers in court.[24] Moreover, company and regimental commanders had every reason to try to deal with cases of insubordination themselves rather than pass them on to the court martial, as they were worried that if too many of their men were tried by

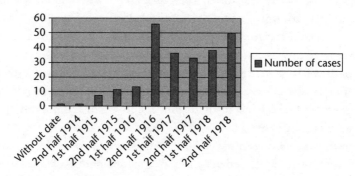

Figure 1. Cases relating to morale measured in six-month periods.

Note: the disciplinary offences represented here include desertion, absence without leave, self-mutilation, cowardice, disobedience (both *Ungehorsam* and *Achtungsverletzung*). Also included are two specific cases of defamation.

court martial, they would be seen as not having their units under control and thus as incompetent. Many also thought that it would be counter-productive to try soldiers who had only temporarily lapsed. They thus often deliberately ignored cases of insubordination and absence without leave.[25]

If we look at how the officers and NCOs assessed the situation in the regiment internally, rather than at the semi-mythical memoirs of Hitler's comrades according to which there was 'no room for shirkers and deserters' in the List Regiment,[26] one thing becomes clear. It is that the cases brought to the military court indeed constitute only the tip of the iceberg and that soldiers were trying to circumvent orders where they could in an attempt to stay alive.

The sentiment that had led to an explosion in the number of deserters was more often channelled into a growing sense of fatalism, apathy, and resignation among German soldiers than into open acts of protest. When a German psychologist surveyed the coping strategies of servicemen, he found that almost one in four German combatants had adopted fatalism as their mindset at the front.[27]

Another reason why the absolute number of cases that made it to the court martial of RD 6 under-reports the extent to which the men of RIR 16 had become disenchanted with the war was that strong disincentives to desert existed, such as the prospect of being ostracized by their families and communities in Bavaria, factors that are unrelated to how positively or negatively a soldier saw the war. Jakob Schäfer, the war volunteer who had tried to desert in 1915, for instance, urged the military court of RD 6 not to write to his parents about the punishment he would receive, as he was sure 'that the sorrow would send them to their graves'.[28] Another disincentive was that family members of deserters lost their right to welfare provisions back home, which explains why the overwhelming majority of deserters were unmarried. Moreover, the many military checkpoints and military police patrols behind the front also made it difficult to desert, thus serving as another obstacle to desertion.[29] This is why it is more useful to look at the change in frequency of cases that made it to the divisional court, rather than their absolute number.

While Private Hitler—who missed what was happening on Vimy Ridge—thought that the collapse of morale really only occurred on the home front but not in his regiment, in reality, the attitudes of the men in the hospital in Beelitz and in his regiment were thus almost interchangeable in the aftermath of the Somme.

When Hitler was finally released from hospital, he encountered for the first time the realities of the home front. Soon he was forced to realize that the kind of behaviour he had experienced at Beelitz and that he could have experienced among the men of his own regiment on Vimy Ridge, had he been a front-line soldier, was ubiquitous.

The first place he visited was Berlin, where he arrived in early December. Previously, he had never been to the city that would eventually become both his capital and his grave. However, his well-thumbed art guide to Berlin that he had purchased the previous year in Fournes had prepared him thoroughly for his stay. While the front-line soldiers of his regiment in Vimy busily tried not to be buried alive by mud from collapsing walls and positions, the museums and the architecture of Germany's metropolis enthralled Private Hitler. However, if his account of his visit to Berlin in *Mein Kampf* is to be trusted, he soon realized to his great dismay that the mood among the population 'was much the same as in our hospital'.[30]

Hitler had arrived in Berlin during the 'turnip winter', the worst winter in Europe for twenty-one years, in which many Germans died from malnutrition. During the course of the entire war, according to some reports, between 500,000 and 700,000 Germans died from the indirect effects of malnutrition, such as tuberculosis. In other words, far more Germans died from malnutrition during the First World War than from the bombing of German cities in the Second World War, which would cost the lives of approximately 400,000 civilians. Urban unrest resulting from food shortages and other factors in Berlin had started as early as late 1914. By the summer of 1916, the streets of Berlin were rife with food-related discontent, as the food intake of many urban Germans stood at 40 per cent of pre-war levels, 25 per cent below the standard of necessary consumption. The deteriorating material conditions in Berlin, and the unrest that was a product of it, was primarily the result of Germany's limited food resources, which were considerably worsened by the Allied blockade.[31]

The problem Germany faced was that, as the world was moving towards total war, ultimately production capacity and access to raw materials had become the deciding factor in winning. The combined resources of the British Empire, France, their Allies, and their supporters in the USA exceeded those of Germany by so much that, short of a miracle, in the long run no degree of German dedication and military genius could have made up this shortfall. Germany had thus been fighting a war in which the odds were heavily stacked against it from the very day Britain had entered the conflict. As long as Germany's enemies did not lose their will to fight and as long as they did not make any fatal mistakes in the way they conducted the conflict, the question was not if Germany would lose the war but when.[32] Hitler, of course, did not see it that way and after the war would embark on a crusade to identify those elements on the home front that were apparently responsible for Germany's worsening predicament in the war.

Hitler, meanwhile, was allowed only very briefly to stay in Berlin as he had to report back to the *Ersatz* unit of his regiment in Munich. While in Bavaria's capital, where he would remain until returning to the front in March, Hitler's health had not fully recovered yet. As a result, as Hitler bitterly complained, he was not allowed to eat jam, his favourite food during the war. He wrote to Balthasar Brandmayer, one of his fellow dispatch runners: 'Am suffering from hunger-induced typhus because I cannot eat bread; additionally I am adamantly denied any sort of jam.'[33]

During his time in Munich, Private Hitler met up with Bachmann and Schmidt, who had also been released from hospital, as well as two other dispatch runners, Max Mund and Franz Wimmer, with whom Hitler celebrated Christmas 1915.[34] Even in Munich, Hitler's main social contacts were thus the members of his core group at the front, in other words the support staff of regimental HQ, rather than pre-war acquaintances and family, as would have been the case for most soldiers on leave. He was thus relatively isolated from the home front even while he was in Munich. He superficially observed the collapse of morale on the home front without understanding it.

On Vimy Ridge, meanwhile, as the men of the List Regiment were getting ready to celebrate Christmas, there was little indication that the slaughter on the Somme had finally led to a brutalization, heightened nationalism, and growing hatred of the British among the men of the List Regiment. Rather remarkably, Bavarian and Canadian soldiers on either side of the trenches on Vimy Ridge attempted a repeat of the Christmas truces of the previous two years.

In the run-up to Christmas 1916, British and German commanders on Vimy Ridge had tried everything to prevent attempts at initiating a new Christmas truce, particularly as the experiences since October strongly suggested that a new Christmas truce was in the offing. When Canadian troops had first reached Vimy Ridge in October, around the same time that the List Regiment arrived, German soldiers—we do not know from which unit—held up a sign from their trenches reading: 'Welcome Canadians'. Another German sign told the Canadian soldiers: 'Cut out your damned artillery. We, too, were at the Somme.'[35] There had also been cases of Canadian and German soldiers waving at each other in the run-up to Christmas. Canadian wartime letters and war memories indeed suggest that, as one historian has put it, 'for the Germans, most private soldiers felt no emotion other than a mild curiosity'. They shot at the Germans because they shot at them, but not as a personal matter.[36] The mortality among the men of the List Regiment in months in which no battles took place had remained stable throughout 1915 and 1916. If we take out of the equation the three months in 1915 and the two months in 1916 in which RIR 16 was involved in major battles, on average almost exactly 'only' one member of Hitler's regiment a day was killed in 1915 and 1916 alike. In December 1916, the mortality rate was even lower than that.[37] In the light of this evidence, it thus seems that cooperation across enemy lines was a more widespread phenomenon than brutalization.

As in the previous years, military authorities were trying to prevent a Christmas truce from occurring through increased combat activity. For instance, British planes dropped bombs on the villages behind the front at Vimy, in which the command posts and reserve troops of RD 6 were stationed.[38] Some Canadian officers had been so worried about a repeat of the Christmas truces of the previous years that they had cancelled the daily rum ration for Christmas Day. However, the officers of the Princess Patricia's Canadian Light Infantry Regiment had doubled the rum portion of their men. Whether a result of the double portion or not, soon the men of the Princess Pats embarked on a truce with their German opponents. All attempts to prevent a truce had been futile. The men of the Princess Pats and the Germans facing them met in no man's land, conversing with the help of a Canadian soldier who spoke German. We do not know if it was the List Regiment or one of the other German units at Vimy Ridge that was involved in this incident. However, we do know that the war diary of the sister regiment of RIR 16 also recorded attempts at Christmas fraternization. Both incidents were put to an end by orders from above, as well as by the heavy artillery fire that erupted, the explicit intention of which was to prevent the truce from spreading. As the war diary of the RIR 16's sister regiment noted on Christmas Day: 'Attempts at initiating fraternization by...of the enemy (calling out, raising of hands, etc.) are immediately quashed by the snipers and artillery men who had been ordered in and had stood ready to fire.' Just as in the previous year, Christmas Eve and Christmas Day brought increased British patrol activity, which inevitably led to a lively exchange of fire between Hitler's regiment and its sister units on the one side and Canadian troops on the other.[39] Bavarian and Canadian officers had indeed not trusted their men for good reason and it was only their policies that prevented a widespread repeat of the Christmas Truce of 1914.

As the behaviour of the men of the List Regiment thus reveals, while morale in the regiment had been at a critical level ever since the eve of the Battle of the Somme, the men of RIR 16 did not display any likelihood of responding to Germany's worsening situation in the same way that Hitler claimed in *Mein Kampf* that he did.

Hitler's time in Munich was a huge disappointment to him, a city which like Berlin was suffering from catastrophic material shortages and where soldiers on leave had started to resort to begging the previous winter. The realities in the city he had chosen as his home in 1913 had little in common with the Munich of his dreams. Like Berlin, Munich had seen food riots the previous summer, at the height of which 2,000 people demonstrated outside Munich's city hall and had broken its windows. The previous winter, the first flyers had already appeared in Munich calling for a revolution.[40] In *Mein Kampf*, Hitler recorded that the conditions in Munich were far worse even than those in Berlin and Beelitz: 'Anger, discontent, complaints met one's ears wherever one went. . . . the general spirit was deplorable. The art of shirking was looked upon as almost a proof of higher intelligence, and devotion to duty was considered a sign of weakness or bigotry.'[41]

Hitler felt ill at ease in Munich, as he hated the attitudes of people towards the war. What is more, he was again a nobody. He thus longed to get back to the front; not to the front proper, but to the support personnel at the regimental headquarters of his regiment. On 21 December, he had written to Balthasar Brandmayer from Munich: 'A transport left a few days ago for the regiment. Unfortunately, I could not get on it.' He wrote to Brandmayer at least three times from Munich.[42]

Unlike Hitler, other men from his regiment on leave in Bavaria had no urge to board a train to the front. Between the end of the Battle of the Somme and the time Hitler returned to the front in early March, nine soldiers overstayed their home leave to such a degree that they were tried by the military tribunal of RD 6.[43] Similarly, another eight soldiers of Hitler's regiment were desperate to travel in the opposite direction from the one that

Hitler desired. After going AWOL, they tried to make it back to Germany. However, as German military police were constantly patrolling trains going to Germany for deserters, only three successfully made it to Bavaria.[44]

In *Mein Kampf*, Hitler reported that he experienced anti-Prussian feelings everywhere in Munich: 'The work of inciting the people against the Prussians increased. And just as nothing was done at the front to put a stop to the venomous propaganda, so here at home no official steps were taken against it. Nobody seemed capable of understanding that the collapse of Prussia could never bring about the rise of Bavaria. On the contrary, the collapse of the one must necessarily drag the other down with it.'[45]

Even Hitler knew that in spite of the possibility that British propaganda had had a considerable effect on soldiers at the front, it could not possibly explain what he had been experiencing in Beelitz and Berlin and what he was witnessing in Munich. Even 'stupid' letters written by women were at best a symptom of the deepening crisis and a vehicle for transporting attitudes from the home front to the front proper, rather than an explanation of the crisis. Hitler was in need of an explanation that would account for all the signs of crisis. While incarcerated at Landsberg fortress in the 1920s, he was to identify the work of Jews behind all of Munich's and Germany's problems:

> Government offices were staffed by Jews. Almost every clerk was a Jew and every Jew was a clerk. I was amazed at this multitude of combatants who belonged to the chosen people and could not help comparing it with their slender numbers in the fighting lines.
>
> In the business world the situation was even worse. Here the Jews had actually become 'indispensable'. Like leeches, they were slowly sucking the blood from the pores of the national body. By means of newly floated War Companies an instrument had been discovered whereby all national trade was throttled so that no business could be carried on freely.
>
> Special emphasis was laid on the necessity for unhampered centralization. Hence as early as 1916–17 practically all production was under the control of Jewish finance. But against whom was the anger of the people directed? It was then that I already saw the fateful day approaching which must finally bring the debacle, unless timely preventive measures were taken.[46]

In *Mein Kampf*, Hitler was to see a Jewish ploy even in the anti-Prussian feelings in Munich: 'In it I could see only a clever Jewish trick for diverting public attention from themselves to others,' he argued. 'While Prussians and Bavarians were squabbling, the Jews were taking away the sustenance of both from under their very noses. While Prussians were being abused in Bavaria the Jews organized the revolution and with one stroke smashed both Prussia and Bavaria.'[47] Hitler's recollections in *Mein Kampf* of wartime Munich thus centred around a long tirade against Jews whom he blamed in 1924 for all the ills of wartime Germany.

According to conventional wisdom, Private Hitler frequently engaged in 'violent attacks on the Marxists and Jews' already during the war.[48] Hugo Gutmann, the Jewish officer from Nuremberg, it is claimed 'was generally unpopular with the men' of the regiment and 'detested by Hitler.'[49] It has also been said that 'there is no reason to presume . . . that [Hitler's] account of his anti-Jewish feelings in 1916 was a backwards projection of feelings that in reality only existed from 1918-19 onwards.'[50] This view concurs with the message Hitler and some of the post-war hagiographical accounts of his war years tried to convey for political reasons, namely that he had been a full-blown and open anti-Semite by 1916 and that anti-Semitism was ubiquitous in both the List Regiment and in German society at large. Yet the question remains whether Hitler's account in *Mein Kampf* about his feelings during the 'turnip winter' of 1916/17 is a truthful reconstruction of what he really felt during the war.

Whatever Hitler's views on anti-Semitism were in late 1916, he, no doubt, experienced an outpouring of anti-Semitic hatred while visiting Germany. Germany's faltering war fortunes in 1916 had provided fertile ground for the radical Right. The rise of radical right-wing groups would culminate in their union in 1917 through the foundation of the Fatherland Party. Throughout 1916, vicious anti-Semitism, very much along the lines sketched out by Hitler while writing *Mein Kampf* after the war, was one of the focal points of their political agitation. Up and down the country, claims were heard that the Jews were not pulling their full weight and that they were profiteering from the war. The peak of anti-Semitic agitation was in mid-1916 when voices blaming the food shortage on Jewish profiteers were on the rise in Germany's urban centres.[51]

The claim that Jews were not pulling their full weight in the German war effort prompted the German armed forces to conduct a Jewish census in the German military in October 1916, officially at least to refute claims that Jews were dodging front-line duties. The decision not to publish the results of the census aroused anti-Semitic suspicion to an even greater extent.[52] In Hitler's regiment, the census identified, in addition to Hugo Gutmann, who, like Hitler, spent Christmas 1916 recuperating in Bavaria, six other

Jews in RIR 16, two of whom had been volunteers. Three of the seven had received Iron Crosses and three would be killed in action during the war.[53] Over the course of the entire war, more than 30 per cent of all Jews in RIR 16 were honoured for their bravery, while 17 per cent of all Jews serving in Hitler's regiment would be killed in action.[54] Hitler's post-war claims were thus far off the mark. In fact, the Jews of the regiment had pulled far more than their own weight. Calculations carried out after the war showed that nationwide almost exactly the same percentage of Jews as gentiles had served in the German armed forces during the war.[55]

The war experience of the Jews of the List Regiment should not be viewed through the prism of the genocide Private Hitler was to trigger in the 1940s. The increase in anti-Semitism in Germany during the Great War indeed needs to be put in context. Unlike in Britain, where, for instance, in 1917 anti-Jewish riots in Bethnal Green in north London involved a crowd of 5,000, and in Leeds another 1,000, amidst claims that British Jews were pulling strings to be excluded from conscription,[56] no anti-Semitic riots or large-scale street violence occurred in wartime Germany.

The anti-Semitism of 1916 in Germany did not tend to be proto-Fascist and racial. Far fewer people than is sometimes claimed, even though producing a lot of noise, expressed the kind of anti-Semitism favoured by Hitler after the war.[57] As wartime reports from various districts in southern Bavaria reveal, the kind of anti-Semitism associated with the 1916 'Jewish census' was very rare in the countryside.[58] Significantly, Hitler said in Mein Kampf that in Munich people were anti-Prussian during the 'turnip winter'. Even he did not say that they were anti-Semitic. Also the fact that the German Chancellor, Theobald von Bethmann Hollweg, of all people, was accused by radical anti-Semites in Germany of being the 'chancellor of Jewry' and a 'servant of the Jews'[59] clearly indicates that the political ideologies of the proto-Fascist radical Right and of the governing elite and mainstream German conservatism were far apart during the war.

The majority of anti-Semitic voices being heard in wartime Germany used terms such as 'Jewish gouger' (swindler) to represent anyone engaged in the act of profiteering. It was not linked to the heritage of a person and functioned alongside other expressions of class antagonism.[60] Furthermore, as we have seen, Jewish converts to Christianity had become officers even in the pre-war Prussian Army, which is another sign that, where it existed, anti-Semitism was not primarily racially motivated.

Some of the tensions between Jews and Christians in Germany at the time were of the same kind as the tensions that existed between Catholics and Protestants, and should not thus be viewed through post-Holocaust lenses. As the mother of one of the soldiers serving with the List Regiment wrote to her former Protestant pastor in Feldkirchen, she found it very difficult after moving away from Feldkirchen to have to live among Catholics, whom she did not even consider Christian: 'As I was raised Christian, it is a very difficult thing to have to live with these Catholics.'[61]

It would take the experience of revolution for anti-Semitism to become a widely and persistently used and accepted currency in southern Bavaria. Furthermore, the Jewish census was, initially at least, conducted to refute, not to incite, anti-Semitic agitation. Moreover, to say that radical right-wing groups were on the rise, and that the Prussian military felt a need to respond to them, is not the same thing as to demonstrate that a majority of Bavarians or of Germans agreed with these groups. Note that the Fatherland Party was to be formed against the majority of Reichstag parties which also happened to be the parties that had received the overwhelming majority of the votes in the recruitment region of the List Regiment.

The German armed forces were not a hotbed of radical anti-Semitism either. In fact, of the 754 wartime letters which the director of the Reichenheimisches Waisenhaus, a Jewish orphanage in Berlin, received from the front from 81 different individuals, the great majority of whom had grown up in his institution, only one single letter recorded an incident of anti-Semitism. And even in this instance, the case is based on hearsay, not on the personal experience of the correspondent.[62] This obviously is not to say that no anti-Semitism existed in the German armed forces. However, it does suggest that, more often than not, anti-Semitism was not a central feature of the German military.

During the war, the German armed forces tried to make special arrangements for its Jewish soldiers to observe Jewish high holidays on the front and in cases in which Jewish soldiers were due for home leave to allow them to return home for these festivals.[63] On the Eastern Front, meanwhile, where German troops encountered the several million strong Jewish populations of Poland and the Baltic that the SS was to target for destruction less than thirty years later, the Germans presented themselves, not without reason, as the liberators of Jews from tsarist oppression. It is certainly true that during the occupation of Poland and the Baltic some anti-Semitic officers and soldiers found confirmation for their hatred of Jews. However, the majority of German soldiers on the Eastern Front shunned anti-Semitism.[64] As one authority put it, during the war, 'Jews on the eastern front fled from the ravages of the Russian Army to the civilized embrace of Austria or Germany.'[65]

The German armed forces went so far as to tell their soldiers that if some of the Eastern European Jews they encountered appeared dirty or behaved as crooks, they should know that this was only a result of having lived under Russian occupation for so long. As two articles from the army newspaper of the 10th Army told its readers in early 1916, at their core the Jews of Eastern Europe had kept a 'truly astounding vitality and moral fortitude', 'a strong and selfless idealism', and 'a deep and honest thirst for knowledge and education driven by great intelligence, sobriety, temperance, thrift, and a goodness of character'. Furthermore, the Jews' 'adherence to the German language' was another indicator that Jews and Germans ultimately had interchangeable characteristics and values. All it needed for Eastern European Jews to lose any negative traits they might possess, the articles concluded, was for the Germans 'to free the captives from their chains'. In short, Germany's mission in the war was to liberate the Jews of Eastern Europe, to 'bring freedom and light to millions of unfortunate people'.[66]

As we have seen earlier, in total fifty-nine Jews served in Hitler's regiment during the war. Even more soldiers had Jewish family links, such as Albert Weisgerber, who had been married, as we have seen, to a Jew. The regimental papers of the List Regiment do not provide any suggestion that the Jewish soldiers of Hitler's regiment were subject to anti-Semitism. Oscar Daumiller's interaction with a Jewish company commander before going to battle at Loos in 1915, as we have seen, rather suggests amicable Jewish–gentile relations in Hitler's regiment. Moreover, a far higher percentage of Jews serving in the List Regiment were officers than was the case for Christian soldiers. For instance, Ludwig Rosenthal, the deputy commander of 1st Battalion in mid-1918, was Jewish. While almost 12 per cent of the Jewish servicemen in RIR 16 were officers, the overall figure for the regiment was only approximately 2.5 per cent.[67] Neither Hugo Gutmann's career in the List Regiment nor the evaluations Gutmann received from his superiors both up to 1916 and, as we shall see, later in the war suggest the existence of particularly deep-seated anti-Semitism.

Born in Nuremberg to Emma and Salomon Gutmann, Hugo Gutmann's pre-war life had been an example of the ever-growing assimilation of Jews into Bavarian and Imperial German society. Young Hugo had made the most of his opportunities. The son of a merchant, he carried out his military service together with the educated elite of Nuremberg in 1902 and 1903, being promoted to NCO. By the time war broke out, he had set up his own company in Nuremberg. Soon after his transfer to RIR 16 in early 1915, Gutmann was promoted to Lieutenant of the Landwehr 1st Class. On the occasion of his promotion, he was praised for his exemplary character and behaviour in the war to date. Gutmann's Jewish background did not seem to bother any of the officers in Hitler's regiment who unanimously voted in favour of his promotion. By January 1916 Gutmann had been awarded the Iron Cross 1st Class, for his 'distinguished service' in general, and his 'prudent conduct' during the Battle of Loos in particular. Following the Battle of the Somme, the Commander of 3rd Battalion, Wilhelm von Lüneschloß, singled out Gutmann for his 'energetic and fearless action' and his 'exceptional discretion and great courage'. Lüneschloß commended him as a role model of perfect behaviour under heavy fire, pointing out that Gutmann had gone to great lengths during the battle to ensure that the troops in the first line of fire received warm food. Lüneschloß thought that Gutmann's performance as his adjutant during the battle had been so exemplary that he deserved another honour on top of his Iron Cross 1st Class: 'Lt. Gutmann distinguished himself in a way above and beyond the call of duty during the Battle of the Somme (2–13 Oct. 1916). . . . Lt. Gutmann contributed to the success of the battalion in such an outstanding way that I hereby propose him for a particularly honorific award.'[68] As we shall see from the case of a Jewish soldier who was to join the regiment in August 1917, anti-Semitism did not feature in his war experience either. Meanwhile, another Jew, Siegfried Heumann from Munich, had joined the List Regiment in January 1917, whose patriotic lyrics of songs with titles such as 'The Old Colours' (Die alten Fahnen) or 'The Bavarian Lions' (Die bay'rischen Löwen) had been printed on postcards in 1916. One linked the Franco-Prussian War with the First World War and was meant to inspire Bavarians to fight in the war and to be 'proud, that I can be a German in my Bavaria'. Another one with a strong anti-British undertone included the refrain: 'God be with you, Land of Bavaria, with loyal heroes, we renew this plea, for the brave Bavarian lions.'[69]

There is good reason to believe that even Hitler had not grown into a full-blown and overt anti-Semite by early 1917. In fact, no contemporary sources exist recording any wartime anti-Semitic expression by Hitler. Other than Hitler's own mythical claims in *Mein Kampf*, the only indicators that suggest that Hitler had already turned into an open anti-Semite are three hagiographical accounts by former comrades (Balthasar Brandmayer, Hans Mend, and Ignaz Westenkirchner) that were published only in the 1930s.[70] Westenkirchner, for instance claimed: 'Two things seemed to get his goat—what the papers were saying at home about the war and all, and the way the government, and particularly the Kaiser, were hampered by the Marxists and the Jews.'[71] Their accounts are hardly the kind of descriptions of Hitler that would point out flaws and contradictions but were wholly in keeping with Hitler's self-construction in *Mein Kampf*. In fact, Westenkirchner is just as unreliable a witness as Mend is as evident, for instance, in Westenkirchner's verifiably wrong account of Hitler's injury on the Somme. Similarly, as we shall see, once we encounter how Nazi propaganda kept on rewriting Brandmayer's memoirs in the 1930s, Brandmayer's account is barely more trustworthy than Mend's. Significantly, Brandmayer even contradicts himself by claiming at one point in his book that during the war he and the other dispatch runners of RIR 16 had despised Gutmann for his Jewish traits while claiming a few chapters later that he himself had not been anti-Semitic at that point but full of sympathy for the plight of the Jews.[72] Furthermore, according to Fritz Wiedemann, the interaction Hitler had with Jewish officers in the List Regiment during the war did not suggest that he was already anti-Semitic.[73] Had Hitler already been an overt anti-Semite during the war, we will have, as we shall see, huge difficulty in explaining Hugo Gutmann's behaviour towards Hitler during the summer of 1918.

Back at Vimy Ridge late in 1916, there was thus almost certainly relatively little open anti-Semitism that went beyond the traditional but low-level anti-Semitism of the Catholic regions of Europe. The war experience of 1916 had translated neither into widespread anti-Semitism nor into a growing hatred of the British or into brutalization. After more than two years of fighting and after a dramatic fall in morale, the majority of the men of the List Regiment had not significantly changed their pre-war outlook on life. Nor had the war brought a widespread questioning of the legitimacy of pre-war society and Bavaria's reformist political settlement. This is not to say that the war experience of all front-line soliders was the same. Nor is it to doubt that some soldiers might well have harboured deeply anti-Semitic, anti-British, and anti-Western sentiments, might have adored violence, or have subscribed to radical revolutionary thoughts. However, sentiments of this kind were at best undercurrents within a majority culture in the regiment that was not prone to a fervent and lasting hatred of Jews or even of the British or to acting in a brutalized fashion. At any rate, they failed to bring about collective action among the majority of the men of RIR 16 consistent with wartime brutalization or strong forms of anti-Semitism or Anglophobia.

Had Hitler been allowed to return to the front and go to Vimy Ridge just before Christmas 1916, he would thus have escaped the kind of political attitudes which he so desperately wanted to avoid in Munich only by returning to the bubble of regimental headquarters, rather than to the trenches on the slopes of Vimy Ridge. Even that might not have done the trick, as Alois Schnelldorfer's growing discontent with the war indicated that even among the support staff of regimental HQ the mood had started to change.

As 1916 turned into 1917, the situation for the men of the List Regiment on Vimy Ridge did not improve. Far from it; by January, the British forces stationed there were shooting with devastating torpedo mines at the positions of RD 6. Even walls of dugouts that were several metres thick did not provide protection against them. Furthermore, on two occasions, mines rolled down the steps of dugouts, causing havoc among the troops inside. Heavy artillery fire grew stronger as January gave way to February, as did the frequency of Canadian patrols as well as the activity and alertness of Canadian snipers.[74] The constant noise caused by the digging and blowing-up of tunnels by Canadian sappers led to, as a report by RIB 12 from February 1917 put it, 'quite a worry among the men in the trenches' of the List Regiment and of RIR 17.[75] According to an assessment made by 3rd Battalion of RIR 16 in the spring of 1917, the regiment was even then still under the spell of the horrors of the Battle of the Somme: 'For months on end, the immense demands of the Battle of the Somme took their toll on the troops both mentally and physically.'[76]

While the majority of the men of the List Regiment did not show signs of radicalization (at least not of the radical right-wing variety), the Imperial political and military leadership did. Ever since Paul von Hindenburg and Erich Ludendorff, the celebrated heroes of victories on the Eastern Front, had been appointed to direct the German war effort in the summer of 1916, they tried to concentrate all military and civil power under them and channel it in a totalitarian manner towards winning the war.[77] They had realized that the emergence of total war had fundamentally changed the rules of the game.

Unlike Hindenburg's predecessor, Erich von Falkenhayn, who had believed that total war was unwinnable and that ultimately the war could only be ended at the negotiating table, the conclusion Hindenburg and

Ludendorff drew was that if Germany uncompromisingly applied all her resources towards the war effort and conducted the war in a more ruthless manner than hitherto had been the case, a war of annihilation of the enemy's military capabilities was still possible. Driven in no small degree by desperation, Hindenburg and Ludendorff believed that Germany could only still win the war through totalitarian means, including a dramatic reversal of policy in the occupied territories of France and Belgium. The Germans now ruled there as if in conquered land.[78]

When, in the second half of 1916, Hindenburg and Ludendorff decided, that they would shorten the Western Front and thus free up troops, they meticulously drew up a plan in cold blood for a scorched-earth policy. The plan for Operation Alberich, named after the spiteful dwarf from the Nibelungen saga, was to turn the area from which the Germans were to retreat into a desert that would minimize the ability of the Anglo-French forces to attack the new shortened front line.

The policies carried out in the abandoned territories during Operation Alberich stand in stark contrast to the treatment of the French population behind the line in places such as Fournes or Comines. Houses and churches were razed, bridges blown up, and orchards cut down in preparation of the shortening of the front. Up to 150,000 civilians had to leave their homes and were shipped away, while towns such as Bapaume were almost obliterated. It had taken hundreds of years to build Bapaume. The city had survived the onslaughts brought by the Hundred Years War, the French invasion of 1641, the Napoleonic Wars, as well as the Franco-Prussian War. The Germans now destroyed the town within forty-five minutes, through a series of explosions and 400 fires. This was total war.[79]

While stationed on Vimy Ridge, the List Regiment was deployed just to the north of the region that was vacated. However, RD 6 was ordered to participate in the implementation of Operation Alberich. In a dramatic reversal of the policy of RD 6 to go out of its way to tell the soldiers of the List Regiment and its sister units to avoid the destruction of churches and other cultural symbols, the division now was instructed to draw up a plan systematically to destroy behind its lines all buildings of potential strategic value: 'In the event of a retreat to the second or to any line even further back, it will be necessary to destroy all architectural structures of art-historical value that could be used by the enemy for combat purposes or for transport and supplies.'

Among the candidates for destruction were 'mine towers, chimneys, water towers of mines and church towers . . . dugouts fortified with iron-reinforced concrete, strategically important streets, and power stations.'[80] Once the implementation of Operation Alberich started on 9 February, it is possible that the companies from the List Regiment which were on reserve at the time had to carry out some of the destruction in the region to the south and south-east of Vimy Ridge.

The construction of the new trench system for the shortened front line and the implementation of Operation Alberich has been seen as nothing less than the 'the invention of the war of annihilation or in any case of one of its central aspects: scorched-earth warfare'. It was supposedly here that the German Army started to mutate into the Wehrmacht of the Nazis; and it was here that Germany developed a 'totalitarian syndrome' and embarked on its 'path towards the war of annihilation'.[81] This proposition clearly overstates the case. Scorched-earth policies were hardly an innovation of the First World War, nor were they exclusively a German phenomenon during this war. The people on the receiving end during the sacking of Carthage, the Russian retreat during the Napoleonic War, or the burning of farms and infrastructure during the Boer War, to name but three examples, would have certainly been surprised at the proposition that scorched-earth policies were still to be invented. Moreover, during the First World War, the Russians had already implemented a scorched-earth policy while retreating in 1915.[82] Furthermore, the suggestion that Germany acquired a 'totalitarian syndrome' in the winter of 1916/17 essentially tells a story of the twentieth century that cuts the period of 1918 to 1933 out, when German policy makers most certainly did not employ totalitarian policies.

Operation Alberich and the policies of Hindenburg and Ludendorff have also been seen as part of Germany's 'tendency to go to extremes', and as a continuation of Germany's approach to colonial warfare and of the war atrocities in 1914. Operation Alberich was supposedly part of a 'spiral of extremity' that was uniquely German because of a lack of civilian oversight over the German armed forces. The claim also is that Germany was different from the other warring powers of the First World War in that, in 1917 and 1918, the Germans are said to have supposedly only sought a tactical solution to a strategic problem, that is, that they had no strategy other than to knock out the enemy by military means. Germany's conduct of the war in 1917 and 1918 is said to have also been uniquely German because German military planners did not reflect on, for instance, the Russian scorched-earth policies of 1915 when drawing up their own extremist policies. In other words, they did not 'learn' from Russian policies but only from Germany's own past conduct of the war.[83] This is an odd argument as the existence of scorched-earth policies on both sides, irrespective of whether either side learned from the other, suggests the existence of a parallel development towards total war, rather than a unique German phenomenon. Moreover, as we have seen, under pressure from the Reichstag, the German Army lowered the minimum sentence for desertion in 1917 which demonstrates that it was unable always to go for the most extreme measure and that civilian oversight did have an impact on the military.

It might be more useful to put the German war effort in early 1917 into a global context. It is indeed difficult to see how the German strategy during the last two years of the war, namely to knock out her enemies militarily at all cost, was any different from the strategy of the French and the British. At any rate, by means of Operation Alberich and their other policies, Hindenburg and Ludendorff were following the inherent logic of total war in an industrial age, as did Germany's enemies and allies. Despite important differences in intentions, ethical considerations, and outcomes, the British in their attempt to starve Germany through a naval blockade, the Russians with their forced deportation of approximately 200,000 ethnic Germans, at least 500,000 Jews, 300,000 Lithuanians, 250,000 Latvians, and 743,000 ethnic Poles from tsarist Poland and the Baltic to the East, and the Turks with their policies of ethnic cleansing towards the Armenians, to name but three examples, were ultimately and increasingly often following the logic of modern total war in their conduct.[84] The end point of the inherent logic of warfare in this kind of conflict in an industrial age was the 1940–1 Blitz of English cities, the 1945 bombing of Dresden, the Nazis' industrialization of killing, and the 1945 dropping of the atomic bombs on Hiroshima and Nagasaki, though not necessarily the Holocaust.[85] This is, of course, not to say that there is a moral equivalence between all these actions; nor that the Second World War was inevitable. It is merely that it was only once a new world war had broken out that all belligerent powers developed the full potential of the inherent logic of total war.

Even though the German conduct of war in the First World War was not more extreme than that of her adversaries and allies, the men of the List Regiment were sucked into Germany's new policy of totalitarian destruction through the involvement of their division in Operartion Alberich. And yet there is no indication that the men of RD 6 participated in these policies for any reason other than those that had kept the men fighting since the beginning of the war. Yet the radicalization of the German military and political war effort inevitably changed the conditions under which the men of the List Regiment operated. By following the men of RIR 16 to the locations in which they were deployed, we will see whether the radicalization initiated by Hindenburg and Ludendorff as well as the radical Right in Germany ultimately pulled the men of the List Regiment along and radicalized them too.

By the time RIR 16 was withdrawn from Vimy Ridge in February, the men of the regiment still did not know why their sector of the front had been so unexpectedly active. Only for two weeks in February did they now have a chance to recuperate some 15 kilometres behind the front from the stressful and taxing months on Vimy Ridge.[86]

On 4 March, they had to take up their new positions close to La Bassée, about halfway between Vimy Ridge and Fromelles. The following day, Hitler's wishes to return to the front were fulfilled. Initially Hitler had been ordered to report to the 2nd Bavarian Infantry Regiment after his recovery. However, he had successfully begged Fritz Wiedemann, the adjutant of RIR 16, to be allowed to return to his ersatz family, to his place in the regimental HQ of the List Regiment, writing to Wiedemann, 'it is my urgent wish to return to my old regiment and to my old comrades'.[87]

The new positions of the regiment lay right by the La Bassée Canal in flat, swampy land. In the almost two months that Hitler's unit spent in its new position, little combat took place, with the exception of fairly frequent patrols and occasional mine explosions. Just as at Fromelles, their opponents, still British units, used the section of the Western Front guarded by the List Regiment as a nursery to introduce new troops to the front. Opposite RIR 16 and its sister units lay drunken British troops who distinguished themselves by singing and yelling loudly.[88]

Hitler had thus missed most of the Battle of the Somme as well as the extremely unpleasant months on Vimy Ridge and returned to the front only after the regiment had been moved to a relatively quiet sector. He had thus also been oblivious to what had been going on in the regiment which made him arguably more susceptible to right-wing propaganda and hence more likely to blame the subsequent defeat of Germany on Jews, Socialists, 'traitors', and women on the home front. Hitler had missed the period when his regiment was stabbed in the front on the Somme and on Vimy Ridge, not in the back by traitors on the home front as Nazi propaganda would have it.

By 9 April, it had finally become clear what the Canadians facing the List Regiment had done all winter while Hitler was in Germany. They had dug an impressive system of tunnels that has survived to the present day in preparation for a major assault on the German lines. On 9 April, what has been called the 'epic Canadian assault'[89] began. After an awesome rain of 2.6 million British shells had been dropped on the German positions on Vimy Ridge, the four Canadian divisions, fighting together for the first time, and being aided by other British units, managed to dislodge the Germans from Vimy Ridge and thus from the positions that had been inhabited by the men of RIR 16 throughout the winter. The victory on the ridge marked the beginning of the Battle of Arras and Vimy Ridge and it was, above all, a stunning victory in a year that was generally a disastrous one for the Allies.

After the fall of the ridge, British forces managed to break through German lines to a depth of 10 kilometres before German forces brought the advance to a halt. The British, however, desperately tried to press on since a gain of a territory that was a mere 10 kilometres deep was hardly likely to make a significant change in the war. As a result, the German forces threw all their units at their disposal at the position where the British advance had come to a standstill. Consequently, Hitler's regiment was brought back to the region to the east of Vimy Ridge on 25 April. For the first sixteen days, RIR 16 managed for the most part to avoid direct involvement in the battle. However, when moved into the German positions to the east of Vimy Ridge in the night of 11/12 May, it had to withstand a massive British attack. After intensive bombardment, British troops started a frontal assault on the positions of RIR 16, managing to break through with eighty men and machine guns. The machine-gunners stopped 40 metres into the position of 1st Company, turned round and started to fire at the men of Hitler's regiment from behind. Soldiers of RIR 16, however, managed to take out the machine-gunners with hand grenades, which led the surviving British soldiers to flee back to their own lines. The men of RIR 16 also managed successfully to withstand a renewed British attack the following day.[90]

On 19 May, on the day that the regiment was finally pulled out of the battle, Franz Pfaffmann, a soldier from Feldkirchen, wrote to his Protestant pastor back home that in the wake of the battle everyone in Hitler's regiment hoped that the war would be over soon: 'It is quiet right now, but all hell was let loose here a few days ago. Hopefully it will all be over soon; that is everybody's fondest wish out here.'[91]

The price the List Regiment had to pay in the Battle of Arras and Vimy Ridge was terrible: 149 men were killed and hundreds wounded.[92] However, if we can trust the recollections of Anton von Tubeuf—an energetic officer in his late forties with an authoritarian streak who had been the new commander of RIR 16 since late April—the success in withstanding a series of British attacks had finally helped to boost morale in the List Regiment, as the men of the regiment felt that they were superior to the British troops.[93] By 17 May, RD 6 had indeed concluded that the British had been wavering for some time now and had run out of steam.[94] During the battle, Hitler had been most impressed by the performance of the German air force. At the height of the Second World War, Hitler would recall that 'during the Battle of Arras, the Richthofen Squad cleared out the entire sky. . . . I myself saw some of this, [and witnessed] how each and every one of [a squad of] 10 aircraft was brought down. Then we had free rein.'[95]

Even though Vimy Ridge had been lost, the Germans had prevailed strategically over the Allies by the end of the Battle of Arras and Vimy Ridge. Despite its status as 'the greatest achievement of Canada as a nation in that war' and as one of the foundation stories of modern Canada,'[96] the Canadian success at Vimy turned out to be a Pyrrhic victory. The front had merely been moved some 10 kilometres to the east over a stretch of maybe 50 kilometres. As we have seen, the Germans had shortened their front line and given up a lot of territory anyway through Operation Alberich to free thirteen divisions to fight in the East. Moreover, the Allies inflicted casualties on the Germans that exceeded their own only by less than 12.5 per cent. In the great scheme of things, the Battle of Arras and Vimy Ridge had produced only minute strategic advantages for Britain and France.[97] Furthermore, the number of cases of desertion and other disciplinary offences brought before the military court of RD 6 was lower throughout 1917 than it had been in the second half of 1916. This was unusual compared to the German armed forces as a whole, where the number of desertions had increased hugely between 1916 and 1917.[98] This does not mean, however, that morale in the List Regiment had fully recovered since the number of cases remained at a high level. The relative decline in numbers was a result of the absence of major battles in which the List Regiment was involved in 1917. In periods of low-level conflict, different strategies of expressing low morale existed, as then the life-saving pay-offs of simply resorting to apathy and fatalism were not much lower than that of desertion, while the price of desertion was much higher.

Anton von Tubeuf's self-serving post-war claim that by the spring of 1917 morale had been restored and was high throughout the regiment as a result of the Battle of Arras and Vimy Ridge cannot be trusted. As a matter of fact, the commander of 1st Battalion, Karl Leeb, complained in an internal report on 21 May 1917 of 'very lax troops' who only under duress continued to carry out their duties, concluding:

> Repeatedly incomprehensible cases of refusals to follow orders occurred here.... There is an urgent need for Imperial Military HQ to issue a decree stating that deserters cannot count on an amnesty after demobilization. The men are counting too heavily on an amnesty. It must also be made known that, after the war, the Regional Commands will pursue every single case of desertion.[99]

In total, eighteen cases of insubordination that occurred between Hitler's return to the List Regiment and the time when the unit was pulled out of the Battle of Arras and Vimy Ridge made it to the level of the divisional court. The fact that soldiers who had gone AWOL continued to receive support from their comrades is a good indicator of how widespread dissatisfaction with the war was. For instance, a soldier from the 1st Machine Gun Company, who did not return from his leave home in March, spent several months in Munich before being arrested. Throughout this time, he was in touch with comrades from RIR 16 who were recuperating from injuries and illnesses in Munich.[100] In mid-April, another soldier who pretended to be suffering from toothache in order to avoid having to go back into the trenches, told his superior: 'I'm not going to build trenches; I'm going to the dentist. I don't want to construct trenches, even if I'll get shot for it!'[101] Another soldier refused to go back into the line of fire during the Battle of Arras and Vimy Ridge, saying that he had to stay alive as he had to provide for his family after the recent death of his father, since two of his brothers had been killed in action, while a third had been gravely injured.[102] There had thus been little change in the behaviour and attitudes of the soldiers of Hitler's regiment since they had left Vimy Ridge.

We have seen that there was no one reason why the men of the List Regiment had continued to fight for more than two and a half years. Neither enthusiasm for war, militarism, Anglophobia, Francophobia, other pre-war political and cultural mentalities, nor a brutalization of the soldiers of the List Regiment can sufficiently explain why they continued to perform. To be sure, all these factors had served as motivators for subgroups of soldiers but none constitutes a single factor that would explain why the men continued to perform. Looking at the first three years of the war, it was factors that do not suggest a politicization of the men—such as simple cost benefit calculations about the price of continuing to fight, the fear of the consequences of defeat on the home front, a willingness to fight a defensive war, a division of labour of tasks according to what individual soldiers were prepared to give—that explains why the men continued to fight. However, if we are to believe Nazi propaganda, there was indeed one element that drew all the men of the regiment together: that one element is supposed to have been a sense of *Kameradschaft* and *Frontgemeinschaft*, which can loosely be translated as 'comradeship' or 'camaraderie' and the 'community of the front'. However, none of these translations quite capture the German terms. The idea was that there existed an *esprit de corps* in German regiments that transcended all rank and class divisions. According to Nazi ideology, it was this idea of *Kameradschaft* and *Frontgemeinschaft* that had given birth to a German *Volksgemeinschaft*—a classless German society, the full realization of which became the goal of the Nazi movement.[103]

It is, of course, true that in wars throughout history loyalty to one's mates has been one of the prime battle motivators. To state the obvious, continued support from their peers in combat is indeed the best life insurance for soldiers. However, in the case of military units such as the List Regiment, the idea that soldiers were driven primarily by an *esprit de corps* and by ideas of *Kameradschaft* and *Frontgemeinschaft* transcending the entire regiment is mythical at best. Due to the high fluctuation rate of soldiers in the List Regiment and similar Bavarian units, even those soldiers who did stay in their unit for a long time did not tend to serve together with the same group of men for long. This inhibited many soldiers from fully identifying with their unit and explains the growing fragmentation of the List Regiment.[104] In May 1915, Crown Prince Rupprecht had already realized that this was a problem that affected the entire Bavarian Army: 'Not even the regimental commanders know all their officers, and trench warfare makes it difficult even for a battalion commander to get to know his officers and influence them. Under these circumstances, feelings of unity, mutual understanding and trust are suffering.'[105] Rupprecht's assessment, of course, refers to middle and lower-ranking officers. However, ordinary soldiers did not form a *Frontgemeinschaft* either.

As a soldier from Augsburg, serving in a different Bavarian unit, wrote home in July 1917, 'the so-called camaraderie [*Kameradschaft*] exists only on paper. Nowhere have I ever found as much selfishness as here in the military.'[106] Similarly, Justin Fleischmann, who would join the 7th Company of the List Regiment in August 1917, reported in his war diary in the autumn of 1917 that the different companies of Hitler's regiment stole from each other and amidst enemy fire competed for the best dugouts: 'We take over the emergency dugouts during constant shell fire. 1st Company comes over as well and tries to force us out. We stay. People from 1st Company steal into our dugout. . . . It gets light; 5th Company comes to our dugout and tries to toss us out (carrying a military order to the effect). We stay. 5th Company backs off.' Similarly, he would record in the spring of 1918 that another company of RIR 16 stole a machine gun from his company. If there ever had been an *esprit de corps* in RIR 16, it had long evaporated by the second half of the First World War.[107]

Competition and envy among soldiers over promotions were also common. Furthermore, as in all the armies in the First World War,[108] many men who had been drafted resented, and often hated, war volunteers (like Hitler). Cases in which conscripted men tried to load all tedious tasks on volunteers were frequent sources of tension.[109] One soldier in the 32nd Bavarian Infantry Regiment, for instance, noted in May 1917 how happy he and all his peers were after one of the war volunteers of his unit did not return from a patrol: 'Everyone was happy because the war volunteer Gesicht had been taken prisoner. The French are very fair; they even did not take us under barrage.'[110]

There was thus no particularly deep-running *esprit de corps* or sense of *Kameradschaft* among the men of the List Regiment that transcended the entire regiment. A soldier from 8th Company declared after his arrest following his unsuccessful desertion in early June 1917 that all he wanted was to get out of the List Regiment 'because I don't like being in this regiment'.[111] However, as we saw while encountering small groups of soldiers going AWOL both on the eve and during the Battle of the Somme, it was small groups of peers that determined both individual behaviour and collective action in the regiment. Soldiers from rural backgrounds in particular formed small groups with men from their communities, which also gave them a sense of familiarity and home. As in the regiments of the armies of all warring nations during the First World War, small, or primary, groups made up the true structure of the List Regiment.[112]

After the end of the Battle of Arras and Vimy Ridge, the List Regiment spent the rest of May recuperating and training behind the front in what Oscar Daumiller described as the 'glorious region to the East of Douai'.[113] This period of rest, which was also meant to help restore bonds of solidarity between the men of the regiment after the battle. The Intelligence Section of the US General Staff concluded that, while training in 1917, RD 6 was turned into an attack unit.[114] This was absolutely not the case. The division remained a unit whose purpose was to man a small piece of the Western Front and hold the line. What the List Regiment and its sister units did train for were counter-attacks in the event of an enemy attack.[115] Around this time, soldiers also started to worry that the home front no longer supported them. As Anton Haimbacher—the soldier who did not care if his village was French or Bavarian after the war—wrote to a friend in May, while early in the war soldiers on home leave had been held in high regard, the word was that that was often no longer the case.[116]

In early June, when Messines Ridge—which Hitler's regiment had defended in the winter of 1914/15—fell to the British amidst what has been called 'history's greatest man-made non-nuclear explosion',[117] the regiment spent another few days manning a section of the front to the east of Vimy Ridge. Here they came under heavy artillery fire and had to endure gas grenades, while Hitler was based in the regimental command post in the village of Quiérny la Motte, a few kilometres behind the front.[118] The 6th Reserve Division concluded that following British gas attacks an extraordinary number of troops from the List Regiment and its sister units needed replacement. The men of RD 6, who had grown more and more irritable and nervous as a result of the constant shelling, injuries, and danger of being buried alive,[119] had to be reminded that there was no point trying to escape gas: 'Drivers of horse-drawn vehicles and horsemen have got to be briefed thoroughly that it is dangerous and pointless to step up the pace to escape a gas cloud. The gas will get to them anyway and moreover they endanger the horses of their patiently waiting comrades, who will get nervous and will throw off their gas protection.'[120] Despite all the death and suffering he had seen since 1914, it was taxing for Oscar Daumiller, who was finally to leave RD 6 in the summer, to have to deal with soldiers who had been gassed: 'It is a heartbreaking sight to see these poor men, struggling for air,' he wrote.

'Sometimes one of them would seem to be on the road to recovery, and I would speak with him; a few moments later, I would turn back and look at him again, and there he would lie, already dead.'[121] The growing irritability of the men of RIR 16 had also found its expression in the behaviour of a soldier from 7th Company, who had been buried alive during the Battle of the Somme. In late May, he had told the NCO in charge of him: 'Leave me alone, or I'll run you through with my bayonet!'[122]

Despite Anton von Tubeuf's claim to the contrary in the official 1932 regimental history,[123] morale continued to be far from excellent in the List Regiment. In fact, it was close to rock bottom. In Hitler's regiment, it had been the custom for some time to remove the epaulettes from the uniforms of the men of the regiment to prevent the enemy from identifying their units. However, as Tubeuf complained internally in 1917, the men in Hitler's regiment had also worked out that if the enemy could not identify them, neither could other Germans: 'During combat the absence of identification numbers makes shirking extremely easy. It allows the troops to mix themselves with men from any other unit as they please. The concealed identification numbers are also an impediment to maintaining discipline.'[124]

After a ten-day stint behind the front in the region to the east of Vimy,[125] RIR 16 was finally moved out of the region on 24 June and was moved back into the Flemish plain. Late that day, the List Regiment crossed the Belgian–French border for the first time since March 1915. Franz Pfaffmann was thrilled to leave France: 'Thank God we are out of filthy France which just has suffered too much under the war. We are being deployed to where the blood of so many 16ers had already been spilled in 1914/15. . . . Hopefully, peace for which we have longed so much is near.'[126]

The List Regiment was clearly in no state to be deployed anywhere. It was thus taken to two villages in Flanders well behind the front where they would remain until mid-July. There the regiment celebrated a summer party with free beer and a competition 'in hand-grenade-throwing, sprinting, relay running, sack racing, [and] tug-of-war'. No records have survived of a sack-racing Private Hitler. In his recollections in the official regimental history, written in a heroic mode of remembrance, Anton von Tubeuf describes what a glorious time the men of the regiment had enjoying the Flemish summer.[127] However, the omissions in Tubeuf's account are as significant as what he does mention. For instance, he edited out of the story the fact that during this period the regiment did not have sufficient wheat to feed the men of the regiment adequately, nor was there sufficient mineral water.[128]

What made the shortage of food for the troops even worse was that some soldiers illegally sold food to Russian forced labourers behind the front. Moreover, the complaint was that the men of the List Regiment and its two neighbouring regiments treated the local population too leniently.[129] This was a sign that Hindenburg's harsh post-Somme policies of running the war, had not changed the attitude of the men of the List Regiment towards the local populations. It was also a sign that the radicalization of the German war effort triggered by Hindenburg and Ludendorff had not the altered the political and cultural mentalities of the men of Hitler's regiment on the ground, in other words that they had neither acquired a totalitarian syndrome, nor that they had been infected by a culture of destruction. If we look at the level of official policy and the institutional culture of the High Command, the argument that there was 'a radicalization of war with a tendency towards systematic, total exploitation of enemy civilians and the resources of the conquered territory'[130] may well be true. However, for the men of Hitler's regiment this radicalization did not occur. Indeed even in March 1918, German military authorities would still complain that surprisingly often French women who had been deported to Belgium received visits from German soldiers on short-term leave from the combat zone in France from which the women had been deported.[131]

The behaviour of the men of Hitler's regiment in the First World War indeed suggests that there was little specifically German which would explain why the men of the List Regiment continued to fight in the war. In other words whatever changes had or had not occurred at the policy-making level, they did not bring a sea change in how soldiers in RIR 16 viewed the war at a grass-roots level.

Soldiers also proved more or less immune to ideological indoctrination, as suggested by their reading habits, the fact that they were more likely to send postcards depicting local sights than ones with patriotic slogans, and their lukewarm response to Patriotic Instruction, particularly in the second half of the war. This is not to say that they only fought because of 'timeless' anthropological group processes, a division of tasks according to the preparedness of soldiers to carry them out, a cost—benefit calculation of the advantages of continuing to perform, or a fight or flight instinct. All these factors could only work well because they were supported by an essentially defensive nationalism, a militarism that did not encourage a gung-ho mentality but conditioned men to follow calls to duty, a model of masculinity that celebrated military virtues, and a conception of religion that promoted military participation of men or at least helped them to deal with the strain combat entailed. There existed a symbiotic relationship between these anthropological, military-institutional, ideological, and societal factors. The societal and ideological factors at play in all the armies engaged in the First World War emanated from different national and regional cultures. Yet they were all part of a common European culture, even if combatants at the time did not always perceive it that way. The common trends in different European national cultures explain why men across Europe fought in the war and continued to perform for more than four years; however, they also explain the relative absence of excesses of warfare, of atrocities, and of brutalization at the grass-roots level of combat.[132]

The new post-Somme policies of the German High Command also did not change the political mentality of Matthias Erzberger, the leader of the Catholic Centre Party, the all-dominant political party in the recruitment area of the List Regiment. On 6 July, as Private Hitler's brothers-in-arms trained and recuperated in Flanders, Erzberger dropped a political bomb-shell in the Reichstag, directly assaulting the German High Command. He told a stunned public that Germany's submarine campaign had failed, that Germany's allies were on the verge of collapse, and that the military situation was close to hopeless. The leader of the most popular party in the communities from which the men of RIR 16 came concluded that Germany should immediately start to negotiate for peace and forsake any territorial gains.[133] Erzberger's views were a clear sign that even the prag-matic and temporary alliances on which the German war effort had been based after the fall of the short-lived intense sense of national unity at the beginning of the war were no longer holding.

Erzberger's propositions were fully supported by Philipp Scheidemann, the leader of the Social Democrats in the Reichstag, who for the radical Right was a traitor of the first rank. After the war, the Nazis were to target Scheidemann as one of the prime 'November criminals' for having proclaimed the Republic and for having become Germany's first demo-cratically elected Reich Chancellor. When in early September Wilhelm Stählin, who, as we have seen, had been one of the Protestant army chaplains of RD 6 earlier in the war, met Scheidemann, Stählin was immensely impressed by him. He was, Stählin thought, 'very charming'. Scheidemann, who was to survive a right-wing assassination attempt after the war, Stählin concluded, 'makes a very clever and thoroughly agreeable impression'.[134] Stählin also thought that any comparison between the period of the Reformation and the World War which had been suggested by German propaganda was ill-advised for several reasons. He confided to his diary that, unlike the war, the Reformation had supported 'individualism' rather than 'collectivism', stating: 'With that we must recognize the distressing point that, under censorship, we can hardly sing songs in praise of freedom of thought, or in praise of the mighty word.'[135] Despite the national mission of the war and the domestic war aims that many Protestant war chaplains stressed, Stählin was thus politically closer to Hitler's future enemies than to him.

Soon after Erzberger's intervention, the Centre Party, the Social Democrats, and the Left Liberals teamed up and openly challenged the German High Command. On 19 July, the majority parties in the Reichstag voted with a majority of 212 to 126 votes (62.7 per cent) in favour of a peace without annexations. The parties that had received overwhelming support in the recruitment area of the List Regiment disapproved in their peace resolution of calls for territorial expansion and believed in international arbitration of conflicts, in other words in the kind of internationalism against which Hitler had spoken up in his letter of February 1915.[136] It stated: 'Germany took up arms in defence of her freedom, her independence, and the integrity of her soil. The Reichstag strives for a peace of understanding and a lasting reconciliation of peoples. . . . The Reichstag will actively promote the creation of international organizations of justice.'[137]

To be sure, some Bavarian politicians of the Centre Party had been critical of Erzberger's initiative. However, an assessment of attitudes among both Bavarian soldiers and civilians on the home front makes it blatantly clear that the overwhelming majority of Bavarians both on the front proper and the home front supported Erzberger's stand.[138] Proto-Fascists, meanwhile, saw the hand of Jews in the Reichstag vote. Yet the parties that were seen as 'Jewish', unlike the groups that were to found the radically right-wing Fatherland Party, received the support of the great majority of Germans as well as of the overwhelming majority of the people in the recruitment area of RIR 16.

Of course, the men of the List Regiment themselves could never vote specifically on these matters during the war. However, there is a very strong likelihood that the mainstream political opinions of the men of Hitler's regiment and the way they viewed the war were much closer to the ideals expressed in the Reichstag peace motion than to the goals of the German

High Command for one simple reason: that the Reichstag had been elected by universal male suffrage and that, due to the existence of conscription, the List Regiment was more or less a mirror image of the communities from which the regiment was recruited.

The three parties behind the peace resolution had received 75.3 per cent of the votes in the 1912 Reichstag election. Support in Upper Bavaria for the three parties had even stood at 82.7 per cent and in the Oberpfalz at 92.6 per cent.[139] This would suggest that the majority of the men of the List Regiment had indeed voted for the parties that were behind the peace initiative. It needs to be pointed out that the left wing of the Social Democrats had broken away from the Social Democratic Party and had voted against the peace initiative. However, they only voted against the peace initiative because it was not radical enough for them. They were thus even more critical of the High Command.

As we shall see, the election results of the first post-war election in southern Bavaria strongly suggest that the majority of Germans continued to support throughout the war, not the Fatherland Party, but the parties the radical Right was deriding as 'Jewish' parties, in other words, those parties that had been in favour of the peace initiative. Until after the war, the ideas Hitler expressed in *Mein Kampf* thus remained out of line with mainstream Bavarian opinion and with the men of his regiment.

Significantly, the Bavarian royal family was closer in their attitude to the war to the men of the List Regiment than they were to Hindenburg and Ludendorff. Crown Prince Rupprecht had internally challenged the policy of absolute destruction during Operation Alberich[140] and criticized the harsh deportation policies, noting on 13 February 1917: 'Most regrettable is the fate of the French civilian population, which, in the implementation of [Operation] Alberich, has been ordered to be moved out of the area to be vacated prior to the destruction of their towns and villages. While travelling to the Command of the Third Army, I came across several groups of these unfortunate people, who trudged, laden with bundles, to the available rows of automobiles or trains.'[141] He had been critical of the degree to which the war impacted on the civilian population right from the beginning of the war. On 3 May 1915, he had noted in his diary: 'These bombings of cities, which both sides are now engaging in, are barbarous nonsense.'[142] When the plans for Operation Alberich were drawn up in the autumn of 1916, Rupprecht, meanwhile, had written in his diary that he disapproved of the idea that the region that was to be vacated should be laid waste: 'This order reminds me of the one that Louvois once gave for the destruction of the Pfalz.... [The order] seems extraordinarily harsh to me.'[143] The Bavarian Minister President, Georg von Hertling, a former Professor of Philosophy now in his mid-seventies, was also highly critical of Hindenburg and Ludendorff's radicalizing conduct of the war. In a closed meeting of the Finance Committee of the Bavarian parliament, Hertling had declared: 'Excellency Ludendorff...is making peace in the West impossible with this U-boat war.'[144] In the run-up to the 1917 peace initiative of Pope Benedict XV, Hertling also liaised with and fed information to Eugenio Pacelli, the papal nuncio to Bavaria and future Pope Pius XII.[145]

Despite the hardships of the Flemish summer behind the front, the period in Flanders was, nevertheless, infinitely better than what had preceded it and even more blissful compared to what followed. For RIR 16 was about to face among the worst losses it was to incur during the whole war right where it had had its baptism of fire in 1914, in Gheluvelt. However, few of the soldiers of RIR 16 who had been with the regiment at the time were still with the unit. Among them were Adolf Hitler and Adolf Meyer.[146]

The time of the men of Hitler's regiment close to Gheluvelt started out calmly enough. For the first half of the ten-day stint in the new position, the soldiers had to endure nothing worse than what they were used to from all the previous sectors of the Western Front that they had been manning. However, on 18 July—the day of the Reichstag peace resolution—the British whom the List Regiment were facing embarked on a heavy artillery bombardment of the German positions to the east of Ypres. The bombardment would last for ten days. The men of RIR 16 knew perfectly well that this meant that the British were 'softening up' the German defence system for a major battle. The men of RIR 16 expected a British attack to start at any moment. In the event, that attack did not come until after they had left the Gheluvelt sector of the front. However, so heavy was the British artillery bombardment that the List Regiment incurred a staggering 800 men in casualties in the ten days the regiment spent in the Gheluvelt sector. The British forces had now twice as many heavy guns and howitzers at their disposal than the previous year. They used them to devastating effect. Between 16 July and 31 July, the British fired a total of 4.3 million shells on the German troops deployed in the Ypres Salient, employing as many gas shells as possible in an attempt to neutralize the German troops. Even the soldiers who did not become casualties suffered extreme fatigue, exhaustion, and nervous strain.[147] Anton von Tubeuf reported that his regiment was close to melt down:

> The troops were unable to sleep or rest at all. Due to the shortage of troops in the trenches, at night everyone had to carry out either sentry or sentry relief duty. Because of the constant gas and mine attacks, it was impossible to rest at any rate. . . . The repeated gas mine and gas grenade attacks really shattered the nerves [of the troops].

The men of the regiment had lost all trust in the effectiveness of their gas masks: 'Various men claim that, despite having put their gas masks on in time, they still breathed in the gas and fell ill from it. . . . The men stated: "Now even the masks are no longer of any use to us." ' Tubeuf continued: 'The constant sight of horribly mutilated bodies, of the badly injured, of those sick from the gas (those with particularly aggressive symptoms), and of those killed by the gas, had a very depressing effect on the men. . . . The men of the regiment [are], at this time, both physically and mentally finished.'[148]

Tubeuf concluded: 'The company commanders are convinced that the physical and mental stamina and capacity [of the men] at this moment are not up to the challenges that fresh action would bring with it. Considering the low number of rifles and the physical and mental condition of the remaining men, I cannot but conclude that the regiment has no combat value at present.'[149] A sign of the desperation of the officers in charge of Hitler's regiment was that they did not even arrest men such as Anton Markl, an infantryman from 10th Company. On 23 July, Markl yelled at his company commander in the presence of all the soldiers of his platoon: 'I don't want to do this any more! I don't care about anything any more. Do you really think that I'll have myself killed because of you? I'd rather go to jail.' The following day, Markl told the Commander of 3rd Battalion: 'You get to stuff yourself with good food and booze while I have to fight for you.' Markl was still not arrested. He was not even arrested when another two days later, he told his company commander during the roll-call of 10th Company that 'he didn't want anyone to tell him what he had to do, he wanted to have his peace, or else he'd rather be imprisoned or shot.' Markl managed to force his own arrest only after he had deserted as his company was about to return to the trenches, walked to a nearby town, and turned himself in.[150] It is less Markl's actions than the response of his officers that is remarkable. The inaction of Markl's superiors, in the face of Markl's repeated and provocative expressions of disobedience (in the presence of his comrades), indicates that the officers in charge of Markl thought that the feelings he expressed were ubiquitous throughout the regiment; in other words, that it was pointless or even counter-productive to clamp down on him.

Due to the mounting problems in RIR 16, Tubeuf thus requested an immediate withdrawal of his regiment from the Ypres Salient on 24 July, the same day that, as a sign of how 'total' the war had become, the church bells of Ichenhausen were removed from the local church and designated to be melted down and turned into weapons. Tubeuf's request for withdrawal, however, was turned down as the German Army did not yet have new units at its disposal.[151]

After just three days, the regiment was put back into the line, now at another sector in the Ypres Salient, a few kilometres to the north of Gheluvelt, where the conditions were almost as bad. Yet the anticipated British attack still had not occurred. Soon after, German military authorities finally decided that the units of RD 6 had been decimated to such a degree that they were immediately to be taken out of the line of fire. As a result of that decision, two of the three battalions of the List Regiment were successfully moved out of the Ypres Salient before the British attack finally came. Second Battalion, Hitler, and the men of regimental HQ were less lucky. Before it could be pulled out of the battle zone, it had to endure the first day of the all-out attack of the 5th British Army on a 25-kilometre stretch of the front.[152]

Adolf Meyer claims that that day he himself, Private Hitler, and six other men from regimental HQ only narrowly escaped death, when they had to lead reinforcements to the combat zone and suddenly found themselves exposed to both British artillery and machine-gun fire. How close they came to death is difficult to verify. However, the fact that all eight men returned unharmed to regimental HQ, on a day that brought epic losses for RIR 16, indicates that there might well have been a considerable gulf between how Meyer perceived the situation and the actual reality.[153]

After the battle, RD 6 had to conclude that it was difficult to determine 'how exactly the fighting went in the first line because only few of the combatants who fought there returned [to tell the tale]'. To be sure, the machine gunners of the units of the division managed to kill a considerable number of British soldiers. However, there were just far too many British soldiers and tanks that kept on creeping towards the men of the List Regiment. On 31 July, the British did indeed manage to break through the lines of 2nd Battalion as well as elsewhere in the Ypres Salient.

This British success marked the opening day of what would come to be known as 3rd Ypres, or simply as Passchendaele, a battle that continued until November whilst the British were stubbornly trying fully to break through the German lines as well as cutting off the German submarine bases in the English Channel. This was to be the final great battle of attrition in the war. Around half a million German and British soldiers were to become casualties of the battle. However, this was clearly not the kind of battle in which the List Regiment in its current state would have been of any use to the German war effort. In the evening of the day on which 3rd Ypres started, 2nd Battalion and regimental HQ were also withdrawn. The List Regiment was moved away from Ypres as far as possible. It ended up in the section of the Western Front that was the most peaceful. RIR 16 was now moved back to Germany to Alsace—that territory hotly contested between France and Germany—for two and a half months. At the end of seventeen days of action in Flanders, 318 men of the division had been killed, 101 men were missing, and 2,516 were wounded, two thirds of whom had been gassed.[154] Hitler, meanwhile, was most distraught at the loss of Foxl, who was nowhere to be found when it was time to leave Flanders. Even while fighting the Second World War, Hitler told those present at one of his 'table talks' in January 1941: 'The swine who took him from me doesn't know what he did to me.'[155]

9

Blinded

August 1917–11 November 1918

O nce arrived at their new destination in the rolling hills west of
Mülhausen, the List Regiment had to guard the only section of the
front on German soil. The men of RIR 16 were thrilled temporarily not to
be deployed in occupied foreign territory: 'I am happy to be on German soil
once again, and to be able to speak with German civilians,' Franz Pfaffmann
wrote home. As he reported, this was an extremely quiet segment of the
front: 'Maybe 5 rounds from the artillery all day. Up there in Ypres, there
were barrages of fire all day and all night. . . . Everyone is being accommo-
dated in houses here with the exception of those in the first line. I think a
mutual accord exists, based on allowing weary troops to rest here.'[1]

Of course, sporadic fire was exchanged between French troops and the
List Regiment, killing twenty-two men from RIR 16 over two and half
months. Yet compared to Vimy and Third Ypres, life was bearable. No
battles were expected in Alsace and unlike during the run-up to 3rd Ypres,
hardly any cases of desertion occurred in RIR 16 whilst in Alsace. Their new
position, which was surrounded by orchards, was so quiet that the men of
the regiment had to be reminded not to go into the trenches without their
weapons.[2] It was here that Justin Fleischmann, an 18-year-old Jewish recruit
from Munich who had recently left grammar school, joined Hitler's regiment.[3] The deceptively quiet conditions of Alsace allowed him still to see
the war as an adventure for grown-up boys. This was quite common among
young men from educated middle-class backgrounds who had gone
through the grammar schools and universities of Wilhelmine Germany.
Their socialization had encouraged them to combine defensive patriotism,
martial manly values, and a deep sense of duty and honour. The resulting
mentality explains the very high participation rate of high-school and

university students in the First World War in the forces of all the warring nations.[4]

As Fleischmann, whose two brothers also served in the war (see Plate 14),[5] recorded in his diary, his service in the List Regiment began with an 'easy stroll' for his battalion. His 7 August entry was: 'Stole apples. Tried out revolver.' He spent the following day 'reading, writing, etc.', while on 11 August, he encountered 'beautiful orchards, plums and mira-belle prunes'. On 13 August he had 'cheerful drills until 6 o'clock'. Five days later, he was quite obviously excited to have had 'thrown 2 live hand grenades' that day. On 29 August, he enjoyed the 'good life in Oberspeck-bach. Big orchard. Roasted apples and enjoyed eating pears.' The first day of September brought some more excitement: 'rat and mouse hunting with revolver', while the highlight of the day on 15 September was when he 'saw through my binocular: French civilians who were working, etc. No news other than that.' On many days, his only diary entry was: 'Nothing of importance'. The worst hardship for Fleischmann, while in Alsace, was posed by his heavy luggage: '9:30 p.m.—terribly exhausting march with full luggage to the forward positions'.[6]

There is no indication that his Jewishness bothered any of his fellow soldiers in Hitler's regiment. Just like the hundreds of letters that the Director of the Reichenheimisches Waisenhaus in Berlin had received from Jewish soldiers at the front, Justin Fleischmann's war diary does not record any anti-Semitism or even tensions with fellow soldiers. Indeed the only explicit reference to his Jewishness in his diary is to the Jewish high holidays. On 17 September, on Rosh Hashanah, he scribbled into his diary 'New Year'. And a week later, he and Julius Mendle, a fellow Jewish soldier in 7th Company, received two days' leave to celebrate Yom Kippur: 'On leave to Mühlhausen for Yom Kippur. Marched with Mendle to Brunnstadt, from there took the tram to Mühlhausen. Looked for the synagogue.... Found lodgings in the "Zum goldenen Lamm"... Went for dinner in the Traubengasse: Potato soup, mashed potatoes, 2 helpings of beef with sauce, mixed vegetables. Compote. Synagogue at 9 o'clock.'[7]

The deceptive quietness in the new sector and subsequently in Picardy—the easternmost part of the Paris Basin, where the List Regiment was stationed next—as well as the relatively easy life behind the front proper, is likely to have lulled Hitler into exaggerating out of all proportion how strong his regiment and the other German units on the Western Front still were. It made it easier for Hitler subsequently to put all the blame for

Germany's defeat in 1918 on Communists, Socialists, Democrats, Jews, striking munitions workers, and all kind of other 'traitors' on the home front. As Hitler would tell his post-war audiences time and time again, they all had stabbed Germany's army in the back on the brink of victory.[8] Hitler failed to see, or did not want to see, the bleak state of his regiment. In fact, had RIR 16 been deployed at a more serious section of the front, there would have been no way even for Hitler of escaping the realization that his regiment was in dire straits by the winter of 1917/18. In that sense, the stab-in-the-back myth—so popular among the political Right in Weimar Germany—had its origin for Hitler, not only in subsequent events, but also in the deceptive conditions of late 1917 and early 1918.

Meanwhile, the big question facing the officers of the List Regiment was whether a stint back in Germany would help recover morale and ensure that the unit was going to continue to perform and not collapse.

The health of the men of the regiment was restored relatively quickly in Alsace. However, Hitler seems to have been oblivious to the fact that the regiment now faced a new problem: unlike Fleischmann, the majority of the reinforcements that RIR 16 received were grumbling old men who either had never served in the army at all or who had trained many years before. For the moment, few young recruits would be put into as mediocre a unit as the List Regiment. RIR 16 had to report that the new men displayed 'a strikingly low spirit'[9] and that the only thing the old disgruntled reinforcements were capable of was performing drills. Their combat training, particularly for trench warfare, had been dismally bad. As the regiment complained, it was next to impossible to form one coherent group out of the existing troops and the new arrivals. Moreover, RIR 16 was seriously short of officers.[10]

Fleischmann, who unlike Hitler encountered 'ordinary' soldiers from the List Regiment on a daily basis, soon came to understand that it was not just old men who displayed low morale. He recorded of the survivors of the prelude to Passchendaele: 'Low morale among the men.' One day in early October, Fleischmann also noted 'at 1 a.m., infantryman [Haass] who is in my company shot himself in the foot with his own gun.'[11]

In paternalistic fashion, the officers in charge of the regiment did everything they could to improve the spirits of the men, talking to them for hours, bribing them with cigarettes, and, most important of all, giving them liberal amounts of leave to visit their families in Bavaria.[12] Moreover, the command of one of the sister regiments of the List Regiment suggested that 'in order to preserve the morale and high spirits' of the regiment, twenty-five soldiers of each company of Hitler's division should be allowed, while in reserve, to go to Mülhausen and attend a concert or see a film or a play.[13]

This was the first time that Hitler, who had recently been honoured with a Bavarian Military Medal of Honour 3rd Class, applied for regular leave during the war. In late September, together with Ernst Schmidt, who was also on leave, Hitler first visited Brussels, Cologne, Dresden, and Leipzig. Then he went by himself to Berlin, the capital of Prussia, staying with the parents of Richard Arendt, a comrade from regimental HQ until 17 October.[14]

Political turmoil was brewing in Germany's capital during Hitler's stay there. For instance, the Minister of War, General von Stein, was howled down in the Reichstag. Long gone were the days of the *Burgfrieden*—of the political truce following the outbreak of war, as the different political parties and organizations and their publicity machines increasingly turned on one another.[15] All over Germany, there were signs of fragmentation in state and society, of declining morale, of growing levels of political rancour, and of deteriorating material conditions. As early as 1916, children in Germany had been encouraged to go barefoot.[16] However, Private Hitler had no eyes for the escalating crisis, nor for other aspects of the grim reality. As he wrote to Ernst Schmidt on a postcard depicting one of Berlin's most famous museums, he visited the city's cultural institutions and adored its imperial splendour: 'The city is magnificent, a real metropolis. The traffic is tremendous even now. I am out and about almost the whole day. At last I have the chance of getting to know the museums a bit better. In brief: I am short of nothing.'[17]

The only other correspondence that has survived from Hitler's trip consists of three postcards of Berlin sights (with perfunctory greetings scribbled on them) that he wrote to the staff sergeant of his regiment, Max Amann.[18] Hitler's visit to Germany was thus most unusual compared to the behaviour of ordinary servicemen. While almost every other soldier on leave visited friends and family, Hitler went sightseeing in Berlin. The reason for this was that he perceived his 'family' to be at the front and that he had no home to go to, as made blatantly clear by the fact that his only correspondence was with other men of regimental HQ. Significantly, Hitler did not visit Munich, of which he was apparently not fond, contrary to claims by Nazi propaganda[19] and the subsequent designation of Munich as 'The City of the Movement' and contrary to Hitler's own claim in *Mein*

Kampf that he '[was attached to Munich] more than to any other spot on this earth'.[20]

Nor did he visit the homes of his comrades in Bavaria. He had not forgotten his hatred of the anti-Prussian feeling in Munich and of Bavaria's Catholicism during his previous visit to Munich. He did not display any desire to go back to Bavaria.

By mid-October, it was time for the regiment to leave the relative peace and tranquillity of Alsace. Even with the new arrivals, the List Regiment was still well over 300 men short. Even towards the end of their stay in Alsace, the men of RIR 16 had been deemed incapable of anything other than being deployed in static trench warfare. However, the men's mood had changed for the better towards the end of their stay in Alsace.[21]

As Justin Fleischmann noted, in 'very bad weather', which soon left him and the men of RIR 16 'completely soaked', the List Regiment was now moved back to France to the border region of Picardy and Champagne, the region about 150 kilometres to the north-east of Paris in the vicinity of Rheims, where Fleischmann's company stayed in a 'huge farm in a very barren area in Champagne, about 30 km from Rheims'.[22] It was here that Private Hitler rejoined the regiment. This was a slightly more dangerous section of the Western Front than the one in Alsace. Yet luckily, particularly since the new recruits of the regiment still had been insufficiently integrated into the unit, the regiment did not see any action in the less than two weeks in which it stayed there. However, after the French had broken through the German line to the south-west of Laon on 22 October, not far from where RIR 16 was stationed, Hitler's regiment was moved back into action. In the attack, the French had forced the Germans off the strategically pivotal Chemin des Dames, the famous ridge between the valleys of the Aisne and Ailette rivers named after the road running across it, necessitating a rushed German retreat behind the Oise–Aisne Canal.[23]

When the men of the regiment arrived at the rather narrow canal during the night of 25/6 October, close to the villages of Lizy and Anizy-le-Château, they had to guard the northern bank of the waterway in a muddy and swampy terrain that was essentially still unfortified. By the time they arrived at their new location, they were utterly exhausted. Justin Fleischmann recorded of the final march towards their new position: 'Our company became separated from the rest and got lost; strenuous march; Gruber collapsed unconscious. Another two or three follow him. A swift march along a street that is under a barrage of enemy fire. About 20 half-decayed horses lay all around. Disgusting stench. . . . We were completely soaked with rain and sweat and were terribly cold.'[24]

During the first few days, when regimental HQ was based inside a cave on a hill behind the front (thereafter the regimental command post was hidden inside a forest),[25] the front-line men of the regiment, who could not stay in the safety of a cave, were subject to heavy French fire. For several nights, Justin Fleischmann and his comrades had to sleep in holes in the ground that they had dug and covered with branches to avoid detection by French planes. One night, even that was not possible, as he recorded in his diary: 'We set up posts and slept on the ground.' A few days later, he reported: 'Spent the night in a shell crater.' Throughout these days, Fleischmann and his peers were 'completely exhausted and famished'.[26] By contrast, Anton von Tubeuf, who was almost universally disliked by the front-line soldiers of RIR 16, decided one day that he would go hunting in the forests behind the front, using the men of the support staff, including Hitler, as beaters. In other words, while the front-line soldiers of RIR 16 were risking their lives, experiencing cold and hunger, and being exposed with little protection to the French on the other side of the canal, the primary danger Hitler had to face was posed by wild boars. On 29 October, one of the regiment's barrack camps, which included a depot of gas grenades, received a direct hit, setting the depot on fire and thus killing seven members of RIR 16 and injuring another forty. However, soon after this tragic event, combat in the List Regiment's sector of the front died down almost completely. For the following weeks as well as for most of the winter of 1917/18, the men of the regiment spent more time reinforcing the German defences to the north of the canal than actively fighting the French.[27] An exception was Justin Fleischmann, who, after being promoted to NCO and having completed a training course as a machine-gunner in November, had to man a machine gun dangerously close to the French. The young Jewish soldier from Munich showed exceptional bravery almost daily: 'I was with 4 men in the NCO post which is situated on the war-ravaged bridge over the Oise-Aisne Canal,' he reported on 5 December. 'We are only 30 metres away from the Frenchmen.' On 6 December he had a '7-hour-long stay on the bridge in fairly intense cold'; the same on 9 December: 'At 6 p.m., I went with 8 men to the NCO post on the bridge. We were on guard there from 6 p.m. to 8 a.m., and returned to the shelter on the railway embankment completely exhausted.'[28]

Hitler's regiment spent a very quiet Christmas on the Oise–Aisne Canal.[29] This time, there was no attempt at a Christmas truce. The reason for this was, first, that a waterway divided the men of RIR 16 from their opponents, and second, that Hitler's brothers-in-arms faced French, rather than British, troops who had always been less prone to engage in Christmas truces.

That the morale of the men of the regiment had been restored to some extent by the time the List Regiment arrived in Picardy was not just the result of the Alsatian air and visits home. Suddenly everything seemed to move into the right direction for Germany. With the Italian Army, including the 32-year-old Benito Mussolini, almost knocked out of the war and the Russian armed forces on the brink of collapse, Hitler felt elated, if we can believe his account of late 1917 in *Mein Kampf*:

> Towards the end of 1917 it seemed as if we had got over the worst phases of moral depression at the front. After the Russian collapse the whole army recovered its courage and hope, and we were gradually becoming more and more convinced that the struggle would end in our favour. We could sing once again. The ravens were ceasing to croak. Faith in the future of the Fatherland was once more in the ascendant.
>
> The Italian collapse in the autumn of 1917 had a wonderful effect; for this victory proved that it was possible to break through another front besides the Russian. This inspiring thought now became dominant in the minds of millions at the front and encouraged them to look forward with confidence to the spring of 1918. It was quite obvious that the enemy was in a state of depression.[30]

This is one of the few fairly accurate sections from *Mein Kampf*—or at least it mirrored the official perception of regimental HQ, as we know from a report about the morale among the men of the List Regiment and its sister regiments from late October: 'The spirit among the troops is high and confident,' the report stated. 'The news of victory from the Italian front had a particularly reinvigorating effect on the morale of the troops.'[31]

In the event, the regiment spent five months in Picardy, guarding the Oise–Aisne canal until mid-January, and again from mid-February, against the elusive French troops on the other side of the waterway. In between the two stints on the canal, RIR 16 spent several weeks more than 30 kilometres behind the front where it was retrained for the imminent German spring offensive that was to bring an end to the German strategy of employing a defensive, static stance on the Western Front. It was during this period, that

Erich von Ludendorff, Germany's chief strategist since 1916, attended a field exercise of RD 6.[32] Private Hitler, still an insignificant dispatch runner, of course, did not meet Germany's third most powerful man on that occasion. Yet within five years, Ludendorff was to become one of Hitler's followers.

Throughout the winter, when munitions workers in Munich, Berlin, and other German cities went on strike, demanding a negotiated end to the war, morale in Hitler's regiment remained at a higher level than it previously had been. After the losses of the first week in Picardy, only another thirteen men would die during this period.[33] In *Mein Kampf*, Hitler described this time as 'the calm before the storm'.[34]

There is no indication, however, that the temporary restoration of morale changed the general attitude towards the war of the men of the regiment and of the people in the communities from which the soldiers of RIR 16 came. Morale remained at a critical level, as is evident in cases in which soldiers of the List Regiment told their officers, for instance, that they no longer saw any sense in the war, or that they would rather go to prison or even be shot than to return to the trenches.[35] Moreover, most Bavarian soldiers were full of disdain for the annexationist goals of the Fatherland Party, as they thought that the policies advocated by the party would serve to prolong the war.[36] The party was so unpopular among wide sections of the Bavarian population that the Bavarian War Ministry tried to prevent meetings of the Fatherland Party from taking place for fear that the activities of the party would put popular support for the war in jeopardy.[37]

On his daily walks through the Englische Garten in Munich, Max von Speidel, the former commander of RD 6, who now worked in the Ministry of War, experienced the meltdown of morale in Munich in late 1917 and early 1918. He was frequently stopped by people in the park, who complained to him about the lack of food and asked how soon the war would be over. Speidel had to realize that people remained unimpressed by his answers. The former commander of Hitler's division also noted: 'If one boarded a tram and tried to take a soldier to task for continuing to smoke his cigarette without taking notice of the officer present, one could feel that all of the passengers, including the conductor, would take sides with the soldier.' Speidel thus concluded: 'The discipline of the troops in Munich went to hell at an alarming rate. Attempts to boost it have been unsuccessful. It has also become increasingly obvious that the Munich populace has been worn down by the length of the war and the lack of provisions.'[38]

Throughout the winter, the List Regiment was short by hundreds of men. By spring, conditions improved slightly with the arrival of a group of 18-year-old recruits, as RD 6 had once again become eligible to receive significant numbers of young reinforcements. But even then, conditions started to look only slightly rosier after an accounting trick had lowered the criteria of what was considered a fully manned regiment. According to the original criteria, RIR 16 remained seriously under-manned even by spring. Moreover, the new troops had still been insufficiently integrated. For most of the winter, the regiment was thus deemed suitable at best for static trench warfare. Even in the absence of serious combat, RD 6 managed only with enormous difficulty to maintain the health of its soldiers. Furthermore, food, new uniforms, and equipment were extremely difficult to procure. There were barely enough facilities to delouse the units of the division.[39]

Unlike Hitler, the German High Command knew perfectly well by the spring of 1918 that—despite recent successes in the East—time was running out fast for the Germans: new American troops kept on flooding into Europe, Germany's resources had almost dried up, and morale among soldiers and civilians alike was difficult to maintain. Objectively speaking, time had already run out for Germany. In February, Crown Prince Rupprecht thus embarked on a futile attempt to convince the Kaiser that peace with Britain was possible and necessary.[40]

Yet Paul von Hindenburg and Erich Ludendorff did not listen to the Crown Prince or the men of the List Regiment. Now that Russia had been knocked out of the war, which finally ended the German nightmare of a prolonged war on two fronts, the two men decided on one last gigantic reckless gamble. It was so huge that it was reminiscent of the hazardous plan in 1914 to knock out the French within weeks. And as in 1914, things at first seemed to go according to plan.

The plan was to leave only a limited number of divisions on the Eastern Front and to use up all of Germany's remaining resources to try to break through the Allied lines with lightning speed, to finish off the British forces, and ultimately push towards Paris. In the event, a million German soldiers were transferred from the Eastern to the Western Front. By the time that the offensive started on 21 March, the Germans had managed to field fourteen more divisions on the Western Front than the Allies. But the problem was that the Allies had more guns, aircraft, and tanks. German tactical military ingenuity, decentralization, and trust in officers at low echelons of command, and a superior ability for self-reform, however, made up for that disadvantage. By 5 April, the German armed forces had already gained 1,000 square miles, dwarfing the modest Allied gains after the Canadian attack on Vimy Ridge a year earlier. By the time the spring offensive had come to a standstill, German troops had come dangerously close to Paris. The problem for the Germans, however, was that they had lost troops too quickly. On the first day of the offensive alone, they had lost far more men—78,000 men—than the British did on their most fateful day of the war, the first day of the Somme.[41]

The List Regiment took part in countless operations in the German spring offensive in Picardy and Champagne. It operated in the wake of 'real' combat units. Its task was an auxiliary one.[42] Everywhere the men of RIR 16 went they saw the traces of heavy combat that had just taken place. 'Here lay bodies on top of bodies,' observed Franz Pfaffmann, the soldier from Feldkirchen whom we encountered earlier. 'Our gas must have worked fatally, because most of them lay quite blue on the ground with their gas masks still on. . . . Well, it's good that it isn't summer yet, or the stench would be unbearable.' Pfaffmann was shocked at the destruction the war had brought to local villages, sympathizing with the French: 'And the towns and villages, how they look! La Fere, Roor, and many villages [have been reduced to] heaps of rubble. Many times I've wondered about the thoughts of a Frenchman as he is led through [what is left of] his towns and villages.' After Pfaffmann encountered abandoned British lines, he no longer believed the claims made by German propaganda that the British would not be able to continue their fight for long: 'By now, I doubt that there is a lack of food in England because of all that falls into the hands of our troops. The finest meat products, chocolate ([and] the town of Mondichy is teeming with wine).'[43]

The abundance of food the men of RIR 16 associated with British units epitomized the general perception that the war had become unsustainable for the Germans, particularly since the List Regiment itself had run out of food during the spring offensive. On the same day that soldiers in Regensburg, the capital of the Oberpfalz, were heard shouting, 'Three Cheers for England, down with Germany!'[44] an NCO from RIR 16 wrote to the mayor of his home village: 'where the advance came to a standstill, we had nothing left to eat, as our provisions had run out and no more were coming from the rear. There was no coffee at all and in the evening we only had potato soup or "warm water", whatever one wants to call it.'

Soldiers who had been injured were sometimes deliberately given only small quantities of food in army hospitals and were told: 'If you are given too much, you are not returning to the front at all.'[45] Around the same time, a soldier from RIR 16, who was a member of the Social Democratic Party, and who was on leave in Munich, together with other front-line soldiers, stormed and disrupted a Pan-German pro-war meeting and demanded an end to the war.[46]

In late March and for most of April, the task of Hitler's regiment was to help set up a new line of defence to protect the newly gained territories. Even though RIR 16 was by no means an attack unit, it had incurred monumental losses in its new position to the west of the medieval town of Montdidier in Picardy. In contrast to the men of regimental HQ, who stayed in the deep cellar of a chateau behind the front, there was hardly any protection against the heavy French artillery fire. There was a total absence of the kind of dugouts and trenches to which soldiers had grown accustomed.[47] On 17 April, Justin Fleischmann recorded: 'Night of 16–17 April: terrible artillery fire. Heavy gas bombardment around morning. Severe losses. In the evening, we marched to the most forward line with only 40 men [left] . . . We got lost and ran into heavy artillery fire.'[48]

The List Regiment lost almost half its men through death, injury, and illness in April, including Fleischmann who was hit on his head by shrapnel. When the men of RIR 16 were relieved on 26 April, they stank indescribably as they had not washed or had had a change of clothes for almost seven weeks. On the four-day march east through the wasteland of the Battle of the Somme and of Operation Alberich, some men collapsed from exhaustion. After a few short days which were supposed to help them regain their strength, the men of the regiment were back in their old positions on the Oise–Aisne Canal. They remained there under fairly heavy artillery fire for ten days, followed by another ten days behind the front. The day the men of RIR 16 arrived at the canal, their Crown Prince tried in vain to persuade Ludendorff that Germany should immediately begin negotiations for an armistice. Ludendorff, however, would not hear of it.[49]

Even though the List Regiment was only the size of half a regiment by then, RIR 16 soon had to rejoin the offensive. The next stage of the operation was to attempt a breakthrough to the south of the already gained territories. Like gamblers who are close to broke, Hindenburg and Ludendorff threw their last coins away in a final act of desperation.

Hitler's regiment was supposed again to operate at the rear of combat units. However, due to unforeseen circumstances, it briefly found itself in the first line of attack in late May. In the hilly region of southern Picardy, it luckily had to face only weak French forces, among whom the List Regiment took many prisoners. Nevertheless, on 28 May alone, fifty-nine men were killed in action.[50] The high losses were in no small degree due to the inadequate length of time allowed for integrating reinforcements into the regiment. As Hitler would recall during the Second World War, some of the new arrivals had to engage in combat during the spring offensive within less than twenty-four hours of joining his regiment: 'We set off for the second offensive in 1918 on the night of the 25th. On the 26th we spent the night in a forest, and on the morning of the 27th we reported for duty. At 5 o'clock in the morning we departed. The day before, during the afternoon, we received the reinforcements for the big offensive at the Chemin des Dames.'[51]

By 1 June, the day on which Rupprecht unsuccessfully tried to persuade the Chancellor that Germany could not possibly defeat her enemies and that peace negotiations should begin immediately, the German advance came to a halt. For most of the first half of June, the regiment now had to set up a new line of defence on the Aisne River close to Soissons. By then, the men of Hitler's regiment had to fight not just the French but also the outbreak of the Spanish Influenza, which ultimately would take more lives than the First World War. Hitler's brothers-in-arms lay shivering in their positions or inside the wet caves behind their new lines of defence.[52] Among them was Franz Pfaffmann who did not really know what to make of the new mysterious pandemic. He wrote to his pastor back home that he had 'lain in a fever for four weeks already. A type of malaria that now has moved to my lungs and that I contracted during the last offensive.'[53] By 7 June, as a result of both the spring offensive and the Spanish Influenza, the companies of RIR 16 consisted of only twenty to twenty-five men each.[54]

The regiment spent the rest of the month in Picardy behind the front, during which time the German Foreign Secretary, Richard von Kühlmann, who had been the enthusiastic architect of pre-war attempts to improve Anglo-German relations, voiced scathing criticisms of the High Command in parliament. To the outrage of Hindenburg and Ludendorff, he told the German public that the war could not be won by military means alone. Moreover, *Vorwärts*, the newspaper of Germany's most popular party, the

Social Democratic Party, told its readers that there would be 'No End to the War by Military Decision'. (The result of the speech and the article was the sacking of the Foreign Secretary and the banning of the SPD newspaper.)[55]

One of the still most reliable men in the List Regiment was Justin Fleischmann. He was thus awarded an Iron Cross 2nd Class on 19 June and sent on an officer's training course a few days later from which he only returned on 19 October. On his return, the young Jewish soldier remarked that the officer training course had been for him 'a splendid time' and that he had been given a 'rousing send-off'.[56] His Jewishness did not to seem have bothered them at all.

Following its brief stint behind the front, RIR 16 was moved to Champagne close to Rheims, where the High Command planned to throw all its available divisions into battle in a last-ditch attempt to break through towards Paris. By the time the attack came on 15 July, the unit had been replenished with 900 new men, consisting equally of extremely young new recruits and of soldiers only half-recovered from injuries and illnesses. The new arrivals were undisciplined and thus worse than useless. When an officer, who inspected a group of men in a recruitment depot in Bavaria, including recruits for the List Regiment, remarked that their hair needed to be cut, several soldiers started to yell: 'We are not prisoners, we won't allow ourselves to be insulted.'[57] And when another group of soldiers travelled in mid-June to the front as reinforcements for RD 6, they started to fire from their train as soon as they had reached the border of Bavaria and Wurttemberg. At the next stop, they stormed a local pub and helped themselves to beer. As their train pulled through Ludwigsburg, just outside Stuttgart, some of the new soldiers of RIR 16 and of its sister units climbed onto the train's roof, shooting with live ammunition right into the city.[58]

In the event, the attack of 15 July, commonly known as the Second Battle of the Marne, was a colossal failure. It is true that for the first three days German troops managed to gain some territory and to cross the Marne River. The List Regiment participated in this attack in a supporting role in the rolling hills, vineyards, and forests to the south-west of Rheims. Yet the French had been well prepared for the German attack. What is more, 28,000 fresh American soldiers had joined them and by the fourth day of battle, the Franco-American forces started their counter-attack. Private Hitler and his comrades had to run for their lives. As they rushed back across the Marne on a make shift bridge, made from doors and whatever else they could get their hands on, several soldiers are said to have lost their balance on the slippery surface of the bridge and drowned. Even Ludendorff, Hindenburg, and the Kaiser finally came to the realization that the German spring offensive had run out of steam and that it had failed.[59] Depleted of resources, Germany had lost the war. Hindenburg and Ludendorff, however, stubbornly pressed on.

The spring offensive had cost the lives of 482 men in the List Regiment. In total, the German Army had lost more than 880,000 men between March and July 1918.[60] The offensive had left the men of the German armed forces burnt out. However, unlike the crack and serious combat units and also unlike the front-line soldiers of RIR 16, the support staff of regimental HQ of the List Regiment had been kept away from the worst combat. It was thus possible for Hitler to portray the German spring offensive of 1918 as a glorious and epic endeavour. In *Mein Kampf*, he claimed that 'once again the lusty cheering of victorious battalions was heard, as they hung the last crowns of the immortal laurel on the standards which they consecrated to Victory.'[61] By contrast, Germany's 6th Army reported in mid-April that 'the troops will not attack, despite orders. The offensive has come to a halt.'[62]

Hitler did not see the ultimate failure of the German war effort in the spring and summer of 1918 as the logical consequence of an offensive that due to Germany's limited resources, had arguably been doomed from the beginning.[63] In 1918 the Allies had indeed six times as many motor vehicles available as the Germans. Similarly, Germany's ninety tanks in 1918 were dwarfed by the thousands of tanks at the disposal of Britain, France, and their Allies.[64] The spring offensive had been a hazardous all-or-nothing plan that was not sustainable for months on end. As the Command of the army group directed by Crown Prince Rupprecht had noted in the run-up to the spring offensive, 'it is out of the question that we will undertake a war of attrition like the one perpetuated by the British and French on the Somme and at Arras. Months of fighting is not an option for us. We must break through promptly.'[65]

The spring offensive was thus lost on the front proper, not the home front. However, Hitler, at any rate from the vantage point of his imprisonment following his failed 1923 *coup d'état*, did not perceive it that way. Rather, in the post-war world he would accuse striking German munitions workers, the German press, and Socialist and Democrat politicians calling for a negotiated peace, of 'spiritual sabotage' and of treacherously having stabbed the German Army in the back.[66] He did not realize that even without any industrial unrest on the home front, the German attack could have been sustained at best for another few days.

Rather than pulling the plug when it was still possible, Hindenburg and Ludendorff had employed the List Regiment in an offensive that had ultimately been doomed from the beginning, or at least from the moment that it had become clear that the Germans had failed to knock out either the British or the French Army in one lightning strike. As a result of this all-fated decision, the moderately high morale among the men of RIR 16 from early 1918 had all but evaporated by the end of the spring offensive. Discipline and morale among the men of Hitler's unit was dropping dramatically and was never to recover.

Morale on the home front was no better. For instance, the owner of a cinema in Munich realized in the summer of 1918 that propaganda movies would no longer work as people did not wanted to see images of war.[67] The Bavarian Ministry of War, meanwhile, had come to the conclusion that 'the people's power to resist and their willingness for sacrifice suffers ever more; alarming set backs from month to month. . . . This is not only the case in cities and towns but—according to indisputable evidence—particularly in the countryside.' The Ministry saw 'widespread pessimism' everywhere. All attempts to counter the fall in morale had been futile due to the negative reports from soldiers of Bavarian units that had made it back to the recruitment region of the List Regiment:

> Using any means necessary, the military and civil authorities on the home front are working to raise morale and *convince* the homeland of the unavoidable necessity of its perseverance. Unfortunately, this work is constantly met with the indisputably proven resistance of *field soldiers on home leave*, whose stories about everything concerning the war still continue to find absolute belief at home.' The War Ministry had come to the conclusion 'that a large number of men abuse this authority given them by the home front to dish out the most foolish stories about the Kaiser, about the food on the front, about the lives of the officers both at and behind the front, about losses . . . and about their relationship with the non-Bavarian contingents.[68]

Following the end of the spring offensive, RIR 16 spent the rest of July helping to hold the new line of defence on the site of the failed Second Battle of the Marne. The German Army was forced now to revert to a defensive strategy against the quick succession of tactical Allied blows that were to become the hallmark of fighting on the Western Front for the remainder of the war. In late July, an exhausted and decimated RIR 16 was taken out of the line of fire and moved north to Le Cateau, some 40 kilometres to the east of where the regiment had fought during the Battle of the Somme.[69] It was here that on 4 August 1918 one incident would occur that more than anything else created the myth of Hitler as a brave and extraordinary soldier: Hitler was awarded the Iron Cross 1st Class, the highest honour in the German armed forces available to men of his rank.[70] During the years of the Third Reich, the only military decoration which Hitler would wear was his Iron Cross.

To the present day, Hitler's Iron Cross 1st Class has commonly been seen as evidence of how dangerous his life as a dispatch runner had been.[71] In fact, it does not show that at all. To be sure, the award of an Iron Cross 1st Class to troops below the rank of NCO was extremely rare. According to a newspaper report, by the summer of 1918 more than 51,000 Iron Crosses 1st Class had been awarded to officers and another 17,000 or so to NCOs, compared with a mere 472 Iron Crosses 1st Class to troops. Ordinary soldiers would normally at best receive an Iron Cross 2nd Class. Eighty-seven men of the List Regiment had received Iron Crosses 1st Class between November 1914 and May 1918. Of those, only two went to Privates. In all other units of RD 6, only another six men below the rank of NCO received an Iron Cross 1st Class during that period.[72]

All this would suggest that Hitler had been an extraordinarily brave soldier, more so than almost any other men in the regiment. Josef Stettner, however, pointed out in his 1932 newspaper article that such a reading of Hitler's award is flawed. In fact, he tells us, Iron Crosses 1st Class for ordinary troops were most often awarded to support staff behind the lines who had sweet-talked their way up in regimental HQs rather than to combat soldiers:

> Among real front-line soldiers it has never been a secret that the Iron Cross and, in particular, the Bavarian honours could be earned far more easily with the staffs behind the front than in the trenches at the front-line. I know particularly in our regiment these officer servants (Offiziersburschen) and dispatch runners at the rear command posts who were more likely to get the 'usual' decorations even than brave officers in the trenches.[73]

Stettner, of course, had an axe to grind with Hitler in 1932. Yet his observations of how Iron Crosses 1st Class were awarded were correct.

Of the only two recipients of the Iron Cross 1st Class among men below the rank of NCO between November 1914 and May 1918, one went to a dispatch runner. (The other one went Private Johann Stepper who had repeatedly volunteered for dangerous patrols).[74] Hitler's Iron Cross 1st Class was thus less a sign of bravery than of his position and long service within regimental headquarters.

Hitler had initially, albeit unsuccessfully, been proposed for an Iron Cross 1st Class by Max Amann and Fritz Wiedemann, Hitler's two most fervent supporters among the officers and NCOs of RIR 16.[75] That Hitler finally did receive the Iron Cross 1st Class was not due to the intervention of Amann and Wiedemann, who were to become the men of the List Regiment who rose the highest in Hitler's Third Reich. For his award, he tragically had to thank Hugo Gutmann, who by that time had risen to be regimental adjutant. After Hitler had delivered a dispatch to front-line units of RIR 16 on a particularly dangerous occasion, Gutmann took up Hitler's case and advocated the award of the Iron Cross 1st Class to him.[76] Emmerich von Godin, who had just become regimental commander, then officially proposed Hitler for the award, writing that 'as a dispatch runner he was a model in sangfroid and grit both in static and mobile warfare', stating that he was 'always prepared to volunteer to deliver messages in the most difficult of situations under great risk to his own life'.[77] Hitler's Iron Cross had also been made possible by an order, probably originating from Kaiser Wilhelm II himself, according to which a higher percentage of Iron Crosses 1st Class were to go to ordinary troops.[78] Yet the main facilitator of Hitler's Iron Cross had been the regiment's highest serving Jew.

Once Hitler had made a career as a politician and demagogue on anti-Semitic diatribes and once he had embarked on the Holocaust, Hitler, for obvious reasons, edited out of his autobiography Gutmann's role in facilitating his Iron Cross. Moreover, Hitler would then also disparage Gutmann. His own and Balthasar Brandmayer's 1930s account would claim that Gutmann had been universally detested in the regiment.[79] In his hagiographical account of Hitler's war years, Hans Mend recalled an incident in which Hitler and Gutmann allegedly had openly clashed. Mend claimed that one December morning in 1915 Mend had run into Hitler on a street behind the front. As they were talking to each other, they saw Gutmann approaching. According to Mend, Hitler now quickly jumped off the street, hiding behind a tree, as he did not want to have to salute Gutmann:

> [Hitler], however, had been seen by [Gutmann] and was asked to explain why he was hiding. Hitler just stared at him in response. His expression appeared to reveal something else, as the snobbish G[utmann] grew more and more upset and eventually rode off, after threatening to report Hitler for punishment. As Hitler walked back over to me, he said, 'I recognize this Jew as an officer only in the field. Here he readily gives voice to his Jewish impertinence, [but] when, once in a while, he really has to go into the trenches, he just crawls into a hole and does not come out; then he does not care if he is saluted.'[80]

Many Hitler biographies have also adopted Hitler's post-war characteriza-tion of Gutmann.[81] They have tended to see the alleged negative attitudes towards Gutmann as evidence of mounting anti-Semitism both in Hitler's regiment and in German society. However, this reading misses the point that beyond Hitler and Brandmayer's post-war claims there is no evidence that supports such an interpretation.

If Hitler had really been a fervent, overt, and active anti-Semite by 1918, it seems odd, to say the least, that a Jewish officer would go out of his way to propose him for an Iron Cross. Furthermore, all wartime evaluations of Gutmann by his superiors, as he rose through the officer ranks of the List Regiment to eventually become regimental adjutant, praise Gutmann's char-acter. For instance, Wilhelm von Lüneschloß, the commander of 3rd Battal-ion, had described him in 1917 as 'very gifted' and 'conscientious' and pointed out that he had a 'first-class character' and 'always thought about the well-being of the troops'. In the summer of 1918, Gutmann received a similarly positive evaluation from the regimental commander of the List Regiment.[82]

The story that would be told by Nazi propaganda was, of course, not that of a Jew nominating Hitler for his Iron Cross. Curiously, Hitler himself was rather silent on the details of how he had earned his Iron Cross. Nazi propaganda was not. According to an article in a regional Nazi newspaper in 1932, Hitler had personally taken an entire group of British soldiers prisoner:

> As a dispatch runner, Hitler had come under a barrage of fire en route to battalion headquarters; he assumed that the battalion lay behind [the next] hill, rushed up the slope, and ended up in a mine crater occupied by Englishmen, who immediately ordered him to surrender. Hitler pulled out his pistol, which was his only weapon, and with it not only kept the Englishmen at bay, but also managed to take them prisoner and lead them to his regiment's headquarters.[83]

The article does not share with us why the British soldiers simply surrendered to Hitler rather than piercing Hitler's body with hails of rifle bullets the moment he took his pistol out.

Another version of the story was the one told to schoolchildren in the Third Reich according to which Hitler single-handedly took twelve French soldiers prisoner in early June 1918,[84] an account that is seconded by Ignaz Westenkirchner's 1934 account.[85] This story has hitherto been dismissed as National Socialist propaganda. In fact, the incident really did take place. However, the entire regimental staff was involved in the episode. And its hero was not Adolf Hitler but none other than Hugo Gutmann.

The capture had taken place during the last two days of May in Picardy during the spring offensive. The objective for the List Regiment at the time had been to occupy the villages of Vézaponin and Épagny. While the battalions of RIR 16 had still been fighting French troops to the north of one of the villages, the regimental staff had rushed ahead to occupy the bridge to the south of Vézaponin. Anton von Tubeuf, the regimental commander, noted in a letter dated 4 August, the date of Hitler's award of the Iron Cross:

> While I had the twelve Frenchmen that I had taken prisoner restore the blown-up bridge to the south of Vézaponin, I divided the regimental staff into two groups to occupy the bridge and to hold the bank of the brook. Lieutenant Gutmann volunteered for the latter assignment. Even though the enemy retreated to the west, the patrol led by Gutmann managed to inflict considerable casualties on the enemy.—On 31 May 1918 Gutmann again went on a voluntary patrol on his own to the northern side of the bank of the Aisne that was still held by the enemy; he personally took prisoners and as a result of his reconnaissance report the regiment could continue to advance to the bank of the Aisne.

Gutmann's role had been such that Tubeuf proposed that Gutmann, who, as we have seen, had already been awarded an Iron Cross 1st Class long before, should be honoured in a special way. As on many previous occasions, Gutmann was praised for his 'extraordinary drive and caution', for being tactful, and for having acted 'in a self-sacrificial way'.[86]

On 15 August, the time of Private Hitler and his brothers-in-arms in Le Cateau came to an end. They were taken a few kilometres to the north, where the regiment continued to exercise and drill. On 20 August, the regiment was suddenly given marching orders, as British troops were trying to run against the German positions to the north of Bapaume, within walking distance of the village in which Hitler had been injured in 1916. For a week, the men of RIR 16 had to endure British shells as well as repeated tank and infantry attacks. Hitler, however, missed this week of fighting that was to be among the worst in the war as he had left for Germany on 21 August to attend a signal training course in Nuremberg.[87]

After Hitler had left the Western Front for Bavaria, a British all-out attack on the position of RIR 16 ensued for several days. The exhausted and dispirited regiment was no match for the Australian troops it had to face. While the air was impregnated with black smoke, the smell of poisonous gas, and projectiles, the regiment lost 700 men through close-range combat, illness, artillery fire, and prisoner-taking to the north of Bapaume.[88]

As the Commander of 1st Company, Lieutenant Ernst Rombach, found out, even now pre-war attitudes—the belief in the coexistence of nationalism and European transnationalism which had been, for instance, propagated by British and German elites studying at universities such as Oxford and Heidelberg[89]—had not been wholly replaced by wartime brutalization and radicalization. On 25 August, Rombach was severely hit twice amidst heavy combat. Rombach lived to tell the tale due to the actions of a British officer who had studied in pre-war Heidelberg. The officer stumbled across the critically wounded Rombach, personally put bandages on the four wounds from which he was bleeding heavily, and then had him carried away by medical orderlies.[90] The same day that Rombach was injured, Otto Rosenkranz, the Commander of 3rd Company, was taken prisoner by the British. While he reported that en route to the POW Camp in England both the French and English population yelled at him, he also noted after the war on his return to Germany that 'the behaviour of the Englishmen was generally proper'.[91]

By the time the List Regiment was relieved during the night of 26/7 August, morale in RIR 16 had been collapsing rapidly. The cumulative strain and exhaustion of the troops led to an explosion of cases of desertion. In August twenty-three cases of desertion and disobedience (three times the figures of June) were deemed serious enough to warrant proceedings by the military tribunal of RD 6. The sentiment of the men who were tried is summarized well by the statement one of them made in court. He stated that he had lost control of himself, thus not being able to bring himself to go forward.[92]

So mediocre was the performance in battle of German regiments during this period that one historian has concluded that the German armed forces were in the grip of a 'covert military strike', arguing that as a result of exhaustion, discontent, and hunger, soldiers had decided that they would not throw their lives away in a conflict that could not be won.[93] German soldiers irrespective of the units in which they were serving were exhausted and apathetic. Lax discipline reigned supreme. Soldiers now were totally uninterested in Patriotic Instruction and other attempts by officers to explain the war to them. A report had come to the conclusion that the level of bitterness among German troops was 'incredible'. Soldiers were either abandoning their positions and making their way home on their own, or were surrendering to enemy troops in droves. Similarly, the population of southern Bavaria firmly believed by that time that victory was no longer possible and that the war was lost. In short, both the Bavarian soldiers on the Western Front and the society they had come from had lost the will to fight.[94]

As Private Hitler was away from RIR 16 for most of the time between the end of combat to the north of Bapaume and the end of the war, he again failed to understand why morale was collapsing so quickly among the men of his regiment. In *Mein Kampf*, Hitler stated that 'in August and September the symptoms of moral disintegration increased more and more rapidly, although the enemy's offensive was not at all comparable to the frightfulness of our own former defensive battles.'[95]

As far as his own experience is concerned, Hitler's assertion is, without a doubt, accurate because he was in Germany far away from the front during the most fearful battles that the List Regiment had to fight in the summer and autumn of 1918. So for him, unlike his comrades, the experience of earlier battles had indeed been more terrible. Hitler thus saw in the collapse of morale only the work of traitors on the home front.[96] This was little surprise for a man who, during this period, spent more time on the home front than on the Western Front and when on the Western Front could more often than not be found a few kilometres behind the front.

After completing his signal training course in Nuremberg, Hitler took regular leave. Rather than setting foot in Munich, he chose to leave Bavaria as fast he could and spend a couple of weeks in Berlin where he witnessed the twilight of Imperial Germany. In Berlin, revolution and the imminent fall of the House of Hohenzollern was now the talk of the day.[97]

In *Mein Kampf*, Hitler would leap to the conclusion that there existed a causal link between what he had experienced back in Germany and the morale among the men of his regiment. He asserted, as did post-war right-wing propaganda, that young recruits had infected the regiment with low morale.[98]

Once back on the Western Front on 27 September—the List Regiment had in the meantime been moved back to the Ypres Salient in Flanders to where the regiment had stood in 1914—Hitler had only enough time to witness, but not to understand, the disintegration of the regiment. For instance, on 30 September, an NCO in the 3rd Machine Gun Company simply refused to follow a direct order, telling his superior to his face: 'I'm tired of this war.'[99]

The day after Hitler's return, a British attack forced the regiment to retreat from its positions close to Comines, where the regiment now had to guard the Lys River.[100] It was close to here that Hitler's war ended during the night of 13/14 October, which saw heavy British artillery fire.[101] That night, Hitler was exposed to poisonous gas in the company of his fellow dispatch runners Heinrich Lugauer and Hans Raab and of signal personnel on a hill behind the front near Werwik, a town on the French–Belgian border just to the east of Comines.[102] The incident is alluded to in the 1932 regimental history: 'The Englishmen tormented the post with their artillery fire and particularly with gas, the result of which is that there are now casualties to bemoan—among them a large number of men from regimental HQ.'[103]

During the trial following his failed 1923 coup, Hitler would tell the judge that 'three of my comrades were killed immediately, others were permanently blinded'.[104] Hitler's comrades would also embellish the story, suggesting that they were immediately blinded and only survived because they clung to each other and were led back to regimental HQ by a comrade who had been slightly less blinded.[105] This account does not ring true as the gas they were exposed to, mustard gas, only affects the eyes after a few hours.[106] Even Hitler stated in *Mein Kampf* that he started to feel pain only towards the morning. However, once the pain had set in, the symptoms were anything but pleasant: 'Towards morning I also began to feel pain. It increased with every quarter of an hour; and about seven o'clock my eyes were scorching as I staggered back and delivered the last dispatch I was destined to carry in this war. A few hours later my eyes were like glowing coals and all was darkness around me.'[107]

And yet Hitler had been lucky, just as he had been in 1916 on the Somme. He had been exposed to a non-lethal quantity of gas that would not leave any long-term medical effects but that ensured that he was knocked out for the rest of the war. However, it was not the gas as such that brought an end to Hitler's first war. The quantity of gas to which Hitler was exposed was, in fact, so small that it would not even have necessitated an extended stay in an army hospital. Hitler's blindness was not physical but psychosomatic.[108]

As RIR 16 collapsed under British attacks, Hitler was safely on a hospital train en route to Pasewalk, 100 kilometres to the north-east of Berlin in Pomerania, where he was to be treated for 'war hysteria' in the hospital's psychiatric department, not the ophthalmology ward.[109] According to a US intelligence report based on an interview with one of the doctors from the psychiatric department at Pasewalk, Hitler was diagnosed as a psychopath with symptoms of hysteria.[110] According to one speculation, Hitler was put into a hypnotic trance as part of his treatment, from which his doctor failed to release him as the doctor was discharged from his post before completing Hitler's treatment. This unfinished treatment, we are told, explains Hitler's radical change of personality from a fairly unremarkable and deferential soldier to a man with a self-confident *über*-personality.[111] Be that as it may, within a little more than a fortnight of returning to the front from his leave in Berlin, Hitler had been caught in a gas attack and was back in Germany being treated for a mental disorder. In stark contrast to the story he would tell of himself after the war and that would become the core of the Nazi myth, even though he had shown an astonishing degree of resilience during four years of war, he was eventually no longer able mentally to withstand the realities of war.

Hitler was not to return to Flanders until 1940. He thus missed the horrors of Flanders at the end of the war with its relentless British attacks when, for instance, Josef Gabriel, a 24-year-old machine-gunner who had tried to find a shelter in a hole was careless enough to raise his head for a few seconds. The next thing his mate Eugen Schneider saw was Gabriel lying next to him, with a bullet hole both in the back and the front of his head and with the remains of his brain scattered all over the ground.[112] The day after Hitler had been injured, the regiment had to retreat, the first of several retreats that, by the time Armistice Day came on 11 November 1918, would bring the List Regiment to the village of Sint Goriks-Oudenhove, 30 kilometres to the west of Brussels. That day, the regiment received notification at 10.50 a.m. that by noon the war would be over.[113]

Hitler only found out a day later that the war was over, when the hospital chaplain called an assembly of all patients, telling them the news of the armistice, that revolution had broken out, and that the Kaiser had gone. Hitler claimed in *Mein Kampf* that on receiving the news, he went blind again and started to cry: 'As my eyes once again went dark, I fumbled and felt my way back to the dormitory, threw myself on my bed, and buried my burning head in my pillow and the duvet. I had not cried since the day I had stood at my mother's grave. Now I couldn't do anything else.'[114]

Hitler's war service as regimental dispatch runner for regimental HQ had set him apart from the rest of the regiment. What also set him apart was his unusually long service in the war. He had served on the front for approximately forty-two of the just over fifty-one months that the war lasted, which was well above the average of other soldiers from the List Regiment.[115]

It was time to count the dead. By the end of the war, 3,754 men of the List Regiment had been killed, 8,795 injured, and 678 had been taken prisoner.[116] It is difficult to compare the figures for Hitler's regiment with those for the German armed forces as a whole, as the exact number of soldiers who served with the List Regiment during the First World War is hard to determine. However, we can confidently say that the war had been far bloodier for the List Regiment than for the German armed forces as a whole. While about one in four of the men of the List Regiment had been killed, the figure for the German armed forces as a whole was one in six. Similarly, the casualty rate in the List Regiment stood at approximately 80 per cent, as opposed to just under 50 per cent nationwide. The percentage of soldiers who became POWs, however, at approximately 4 per cent, was below the national average of about 7.5 per cent.[117] The men of Hitler's regiment who had fallen into the hands of the British or the French had been lucky, all things considered, as the French and British generally treated POWs well, which is not true for German POWs in Russian hands. While, in total, 91 per cent of German POWs returned home alive, a staggering 40 per cent of POWs on the Eastern Front died in captivity.[118]

The national casualty figures given here, however, include the large number of soldiers who had served in Germany in the *Heimatheer* or who were involved in the running of the occupied territories in both East and West. If we take out of the equation those soldiers serving in the *Heimatheer*, approximately a third of all soldiers at one time[119] (even leaving those soldiers serving in the occupied territories in the equation), the national average was that approximately one in four soldiers were killed, which is exactly the same figure as for the List Regiment. Compared to other German units that had served at the front, the war of Hitler's regiment had been no more and no less bloody.

However, the experience of Private Hitler as a dispatch runner for regimental HQ had been much safer than that of the front-line soldiers of both his regiment and the German armed forces at large. In 1915, Hitler was photographed together with Balthasar Brandmayer, Anton Bachmann, Max Mund, Ernst Schmidt, Johann Sperl, Jakob Weiß, and Karl Tiefenböck (see Plate 7). Of the eight people in the picture, only Bachmann did not survive the war. Bachmann, however, was not killed while serving with the List Regiment but only after he was transferred to a unit deployed in Romania. It is not even clear that Bachmann was then still a dispatch runner and, if he was one, whether he served with regimental HQ or with a company or battalion. In other words, in their post of dispatch runner for regimental HQ of RIR 16, the survival rate of the men with whom Hitler was depicted in 1915 was 100 per cent. This provides the final proof that Hitler's task had been considerably less dangerous than he, as well as Nazi propaganda, were to claim time and time again. Moreover, Karl Lippert, the NCO who until 1916 had been in charge of the regimental dispatch runners, Heinrich Lugauer, Hans Mend, and Hans Raab (who had served with regimental HQ since May 1915), were also still alive.[120] As Hitler thus never experienced the destruction of his own *Frontgemeinschaft*, which was highly unusual for German soldiers, it arguably became subsequently much easier for him to idealize life at the front.

PART
II

IO

Revolution

11 November 1918–Early 1919

When Adolf Hitler was released from the military hospital at Pasewalk on 17 November 1918, the world around him had changed. On the way back to Bavaria, he had to pass through Berlin, which had been in the grip of the revolution since 9 November. That day Philipp Scheidemann, the Social Democratic politician whom Wilhelm Stählin had so admired, had proclaimed Germany a republic.

During the war, the Social Democrats had been divided over the question of whether a future Germany should take the form of a constitutional monarchy or a republic.[1] However, the demand of President Woodrow Wilson of the United States that he would not accept peace with Germany unless the monarchy was abolished had settled that question. The same day that Scheidemann had proclaimed the republic, Max von Baden, the pro-reform last Imperial Chancellor and heir to the throne of the south-west German state of Baden, had thus announced—against the wishes of Wilhelm II—the abdication of the Imperial royal family. Max von Baden had also named Friedrich Ebert, the leader of the Social Democratic Party, as his successor as Chancellor.[2]

Despite the fondness that Adolf Hitler had developed for Berlin during the war, the now 29-year-old Private did not stay in Germany's capital this time. He quickly made his way to Munich, where the revolution had swept away the House of Wittelsbach, rulers of Bavaria for more than 800 years. Revolution in Bavaria had occurred even earlier than in Berlin, on 7 November, the anniversary of the Bolshevik Russian October Revolution. That day, Kurt Eisner, the leader of the Bavarian Independent Social Democrats, who had quit the Social Democratic Party out of frustration with the party's lack of revolutionary zeal, had declared Bavaria a

Socialist Republic. The revolution in Bavaria had thus been spearheaded by the radical Left, while in Berlin centrist reformist Social Democrats led the political transition of Germany.[3]

In the years to come, Hitler was to claim that he was utterly appalled and disgusted by the revolutionary events unfolding all around him in Pasewalk, Berlin, and Munich in late 1918. In *Mein Kampf*, he was to state, for instance, that he had left the hospital in Pasewalk a changed man, vividly describing how he had become outraged by the defeatist attitude in the hospital and how he had broken down on hearing of the revolution. From the vantage point of 1924, he recalled that behind the revolution had lain a 'gang of despicable and depraved criminals' consisting mainly of Jews, and that it was there and then that he decided to go into politics.[4]

Is this how Hitler really experienced the revolution, as he returned to Munich on 19 November? Even though there is general consensus that he embellished the details of his stay at Pasewalk for propaganda purposes and that it is questionable whether he had already decided to go into politics there, the gist of his account of late 1918 and early 1919 has been widely accepted as true. To date, there has been near universal consensus that the general foundations of Hitler's world-view had been laid by the time he returned to Munich. In other words, the war had supposedly 'made' him. What was still unclear, as Hitler came back from the war, was not the general shape but the exact design of the edifice that he would erect on those foundations. The implication is that the world war had put in place all but the precise details of Hitler's world-view. The post-war period in Munich is said merely to have solidified and rationalized his political views.[5] This interpretation is essentially based on Hitler's own account of his life between 1914 and 1919. However, curiously, his account of the end of the war and of the five months following the war is full of silences and contradictions. It indeed raises more questions than it answers.

Even Hitler's reasons for his decision to return to Munich and to stay there do not ring true. This was a city he had for so long avoided coming back to and a place he had quite obviously disliked during the war. Why then did he return to Munich, rather than staying in Berlin, a city which had enthralled him from his first visit?

Hitler almost certainly returned to Munich not because of any particular liking for the city but because of one simple reason: he had to return to Munich, as the demobilization unit of his regiment was based there.[6]

And he is likely to have stayed only because his sole social network at the end of the war was the support personnel of the regimental staff of RIR 16 and one or two of his officers and NCOs. Private Hitler simply had no friends or family with whom he was still in touch, no job, or life to which to return. With the end of the war and the imminent decommissioning of his regiment, Hitler thus also faced the imminent disintegration of his personal world. In order to avoid the collapse of his social network, he thus had to stay where his 'ersatz' family was to be demobilized. That Hitler would stay in Munich for several years and that the city would become the 'City of the [National Socialist] Movement' was arguably only a result of these factors and of subsequent events.

Once back in Munich, Hitler did indeed immediately try to recreate his social network from regimental HQ. He soon met up with Ernst Schmidt, his closest acquaintance among the support staff of the List Regiment, who had been discharged from hospital shortly before him. In February 1919, he also tried unsuccessfully to visit Karl Tiefenböck in rural southern Bavaria.[7] After the war he also re-established his acquaintance with Max Mund, with whom he had been wounded on the Somme, occasionally meeting up with him in local bars.[8]

Two weeks after Hitler's arrival in Munich, Schmidt and Hitler, who both opted against being decommissioned, were sent to Traunstein, close to the Austrian border, not far from where Hitler would set up his favourite residence whilst in power. There, they guarded the main gate of a POW camp for French and Russian soldiers, which was about to be disbanded and which was run by a soldiers' council in support of the Bavarian revolution. In late January or early February, the two returned to Munich. From 20 February, they had to perform guard duty at Munich's central railway station for two weeks, using their meagre income to attend opera performances whenever possible.[9] Hitler's service in Traunstein and at Munich's central station does not call into question his claim to have returned politically fully matured and ready to become a National Socialist even though technically at least he was now serving the revolution. However, he was soon to engage in activity that stands in direct contradiction to the story he was to tell in *Mein Kampf*.

On Hitler's return to Munich, his regiment, meanwhile, was still deployed in Belgium. After the end of the war, it had remained there for almost two weeks.

On 13 November, RIR 16 marched into Brussels. The Belgian capital was full of looting, drunken soldiers. The task of the men of RIR 16 was to help restore some kind of order in the city and to guard two railway stations. Significantly, the men of the List Regiment decorated the regiment's vehicles and their machine guns with Bavarian blue-and-white flags, rather than with German ones.[10] In the hour of Imperial Germany's defeat, for which they had fought for more than four years, their primary allegiance— or at least the one put on display—lay with Bavaria, not with Germany.

The commanders of RD 6 and its units now faced the agonizing choice of how to behave towards the new regimes in Germany and how to respond to the revolutionary Socialist Soldiers' Council in Brussels.[11] Like the German Army as a whole, they decided to cooperate with the new governments in Berlin and Munich, both of which had for the time being proved fairly moderate. In this decision, they were largely driven by anti-Bolshevik convictions and the consideration of how best to channel the disaffection of soldiers in their units, particularly those from Munich, away from Bolshevism towards more moderate ideas. As the Commander of the 6th German Army, General Ferdinand von Quast, had put it, the aim now was to cooperate with the moderates to prevent 'terrorist Bolshevism from spreading all over Germany'.[12]

The most urgent question Maximilian von Baligand, the regimental com- mander of RIR 16 since mid-August, had to face while in Brussels was how the men of his unit would respond to the revolution. The choice of the List Regiment as a unit to help restore some minimal order in Brussels suggests a lack of radical left-wing revolutionary fervour in Hitler's unit. Had German military authorities perceived RIR 16 as a hotbed of militant Socialist revo- lutionary activity, it would hardly have been chosen for this task.

On 17 November, RIR 16 was the last German regiment to leave Brussels. Unlike in October 1914, when the men of the regiment had travelled by train in the opposite direction in excited anticipation of their baptism of fire, the men of the regiment had to march eastwards for a week towards the German border past the ruins of Louvain and Liège. On the march back to Germany, red flags, the colour of the revolution, suddenly appeared on the List Regiment's military equipment. In a contribution for the 1932 regimental history, von Baligand was to claim that Prussian soldiers had been behind these revolutionary flags on the regiment's equipment. This claim was part of the self-serving tale, which was also disseminated by Nazi propaganda, according to which RIR 16 had been a disciplined regiment and thus an island of order in a sea of chaos in Brussels and on the retreat.[13] Baligand's 1932 tale, however, has little in common with how he had really perceived the situation in 1918. In the event, he reported that the List Regiment had 'rapidly deteriorated' and that it had been rife with 'growing indiscipline'. Furthermore, in a letter to his superiors, he did not blame Prussian soldiers but an NCO from RIR 17 for the red flags that had appeared on the regiment's equipment.[14] Indiscipline was not just rife in Hitler's regiment but all over the Bavarian Army. Crown Prince Rupprecht was appalled by the behaviour of German troops in Belgium: 'An unutterable revulsion overtook me; for the first time in my life, . . . I was ashamed to be German. What the Belgians must think of us and how they must despise us!'[15]

Despite the growing indiscipline, as the election results to the revolutionary soldiers' councils that took place all over the German armed forces in the wake of the revolution reveal, the majority of the men of RIR 16 did not support the actions of the NCO who was responsible for the red flags. By late November, Maximilian von Baligand could report that the formation of a Soldiers' Council in RIR 16 had been a success. The men of Hitler's regiment had elected men critical of the radical Left, or as von Baligand put it, 'people with the right kind of convictions, who exert a positive influence on their men'.[16] Radical Socialists thus did not have any wide-ranging support in RIR 16, as the men of the regiment were about to return home from the war.

The List Regiment crossed the Belgian–German border on 24 November. Once RIR 16 was back in Germany, Hitler still had to wait for a while for the return of his comrades to Munich. The German demobilization plan stipulated that the units of RD 6 were not moved straight back to Bavaria, primarily to ensure an orderly return of the masses of military units flooding back into Germany. The List Regiment was ordered to make its way to Barmen, the industrial town south of the Ruhr where Friedrich Engels, Marx's brother-in-arms, was born and where the men of Hitler's regiment were about to witness revolutionary turmoil.

On 3 December 1918, Hitler's regiment arrived in Barmen, a town which lay in the constituency of Friedrich Ebert, who as the first post-war Chancellor, and subsequently as the first democratically elected President of Germany, was to do more than quite possibly anyone to move Germany towards becoming a liberal and parliamentary democracy. However, in

Barmen local delegates of Ebert's own party had broken with him. They had left the Social Democratic Party during the war to join the breakaway radically left-wing Independent Social Democratic Party, which was, of course, the party that had led the Bavarian revolution under Kurt Eisner. Just after Ebert had become the head of the German government and was in the process of organizing the election to a National Constitutional Assembly, the delegates of the Independent Social Democrats in Barmen and in the region grew ever more radical, campaigning against the establishment of a National Constitutional Assembly and for the dictatorship of the proletariat. The belief was that the entire region stood on the brink of a Bolshevik revolution. The practice of deploying non-local troops such as the List Regiment in German cities was meant to help to prevent a Bolshevik revolution from breaking out and to stop troops from fraternizing with local revolutionary forces. Before complaints by the local population put an end to this practice, the men of the List Regiment had been ordered to guard Barmen—which was full of red flags—with rifles fitted with bayonets. Throughout the entire region, soldiers from RD 6 and other divisions—whether under orders or driven by grass-roots initiatives is difficult to establish—removed red flags amidst the cheers of the local population. The deployment of RIR 16 and of other Bavarian units was indeed seen by local revolutionaries as evidence that the SPD had joined forces with the counter-revolution, which led one local Independent Social Democratic leader to call for an end to all prevarication and for the introduction of a dictatorship. Similarly, in a neighbouring town, local revolutionaries threatened civil war, while in another town in the region a list of hostages of local dignitaries was drawn up by radical revolutionaries that was meant to force units such as RD 6 out of the region and to entice the local population to submit themselves to a Bolshevik revolution.[17]

The first experience of the men of the List Regiment after their return to Germany was thus with a city in which calls for a Bolshevik revolution could frequently be heard. Significantly, they originated in members of the same party that had spearheaded the revolution in Bavaria. We can only speculate about the degree to which this experience influenced how the men of the List Regiment were to view the political situation in Bavaria and in Germany in the months to come.

It has often been remarked that the likelihood of a Bolshevik revolution in Germany was rather remote, as moderates among German Socialists outnumbered radicals.[18] This argument is not necessarily wrong; however, it does have the benefit of hindsight. At the time, the fear of revolution seemed real enough.[19] It is also important to remember that the Russian revolution had also initially produced a liberal and democratic government and that the Bolsheviks managed to seize power in their subsequent revolution, which really was a *coup d'état*, without majority support.[20] In other words, with the information available to historical actors in late 1918 and with the experience of what had happened in Russia the previous year, Barmen indeed appeared to be on the verge of revolution when the men of Hitler's regiment were deployed there. And the men of the List Regiment were to see in Munich a few months later what could happen if a determined, revolutionary group decided to seize power even without popular support.

In the early hours of 10 December, almost a month after the end of the war, the first contingent of the List Regiment finally left Barmen for Bavaria. Between 12 and 15 December, the trains carrying the men home arrived in Grafing, outside Munich, where they were given a warm welcome by the local population and then quickly demobilized.[21] On 12 December, Maximilian von Baligand issued the last order to his men, which gave credence to the legend according to which the German armed forces had not suffered military defeat:

> Men of the Regiment!
> From the glorious storming of Wytschaete ... to the heated battles of 1918 close to Montdidier ..., and once again on blood-soaked Flemish soil, the Reserve Infantry Regiment 16 has added glorious chapter after glorious chapter to the book of its history. ... The regiment that knows itself to be free from guilt about the disastrous outcome of the war can always look back on its actions with pride.
> You will now take up new civic duties. Honour them as well as our heroes have honoured their duties in the field! ... Live well, comrades! In your strength and discipline, in the pureness of your hearts, there lives the pledge for a better future. My best wishes will go with you. May God be your protector, and let dutifulness and true patriotism adorn all the days of your lives.[22]

For the men of Hitler's regiment, the war was finally over. The question arose now whether they were going to mentally demobilize too or whether the attitudes and views they had acquired during the war made them prone to carry on their fight whenever possible. This question was swiftly and decidedly answered in the first half of December when volunteers were sought for 'Grenzschutz Ost' units. These were semi-official or *Freikorps* units that were supposed to protect Germany's eastern border. In reality, they were also supposed to guard German interests in the multi-ethnic borderlands to Germany's east that boiled over in a frenzy of violence after the First World War. Even though the men of the List Regiment were deployed in Barmen when the calls for volunteers were being issued and thus exposed to calls for a Bolshevik revolution, the overwhelming majority of the men had no desire to join *Freikorps* that would fight 'Bolsheviks' in the East. In fact, no more than eight men from the entire regiment, all of whom came from the Trench Mortar Company, volunteered to serve in 'Grenzschutz Ost' *Freikorps*.[23] The great majority of men, not only in the List Regiment but also in the German armed forces as a whole, just wanted to get home and return to civilian life. A desire for peace and a return home trumped everything for Bavarian soldiers. Few soldiers were receptive to voices on the radical Right who—like Hitler in the years to come—blamed Germany's defeat on traitors on the home front.[24]

There were, of course, exceptions. In particular, some members of regimental HQ, including Adolf Hitler and Ernst Schmidt, resisted decommissioning. Max Amann also stayed in the army for the time being, taking up a position in the Bavarian Ministry of War. In 1947, Amann would tell US interrogators, consistent with his rather implausible line of defence of having always been an apolitical man, that he only stayed in the army out of loyalty to one of his superiors: 'We were redirected to Grafing and there demobilized. The Lieutenant Colonel then begged me and said: "I still urgently need you." I told him that I had already been a soldier for 6 years and that he should let me go, as I was planning to get married. He told me that it would last 6 months more, and that he had a position that he needed me for.'[25]

However, even men such as Hans Bauer, who later became Nazis, had no taste for staying in the army. Bauer was demobilized as early as 16 December.[26] Fritz Wiedemann, the regimental adjutant from 1915 until the time he was succeeded by Hugo Gutmann and moved on to serve with the HQ of RD 6, meanwhile, left the army after a short stint on the staff of the 3rd Bavarian Infantry Regiment in December. After serving in the Bavarian Army for eight years, the 27-year-old enrolled at Munich University to study economics.[27]

It is, of course, impossible to identify and quantify the political convictions of the men of the List Regiment in the months after its demobilization beyond stating that in the aftermath of the revolution the overwhelming majority of the members of RIR 16 had voted for candidates in the Soldiers' Council elections who were not radical Socialists and that they had shunned radical right-wing *Freikorps* fighting in the East. This all suggests a relative absence in the regiment of political radicalization on either side of the political spectrum. This was also a sign that throughout more than four years of war, the majority of the men of RIR 16 seem to have kept their pre-war outlook on life, in other words that the war had remarkably little effect on the political attitudes of the men of Hitler's regiment.

Moreover, when the election to the National Assembly took place on 19 January 1919—from which Private Hitler as an Austrian citizen was, of course, excluded—the men of RIR 16 voted almost certainly overwhelmingly for the parties that had supported the Reichstag Peace Resolution and that would form the Weimar Coalition, in other words, for the parties that formed the bedrock of the new republic: the Bavarian People's Party (as the Bavarian arm of the Catholic Centre Party was called after the war), the Social Democratic Party, and the Left Liberals. As voting was secret, we cannot obtain an exact breakdown of the vote for the National Assembly for the men of the List Regiment. However, between 80 and 85 per cent of voters in the recruitment region of RIR 16 voted for the three parties most supportive of the new republic in the election for the National Assembly.

Was this very high support for the parties of the Weimar Coalition a result of a politicization that had been generated by the war; in other words, a politicization that did not produce radicalism but one that implied a shift of political attitudes from an authoritarian monarchy to a democratic republic? Conventionally, this question has been answered by pointing towards a claimed fundamental break with an authoritarian, semi-feudal monarchy in favour of a liberal democracy and republic. There has been a tendency to ignore or explain away the election results of early 1919 and to argue that due to the claimed radical change occurring in 1918, the Germans were faced with too liberal and democratic a political system for which they were not ready.[28] In fact, this answer falls far wide off the mark.

A comparison of the combined pre-war election results for the parties of the Reichstag Peace Resolution and of the Weimar Coalition with the results for the election to the National Assembly in the recruitment areas of RIR 16 reveals that for the great majority of the electorate a fundamental shift of political attitudes simply did not occur during the war. The combined election results for the Social Democrats, the Bavarian arm of the

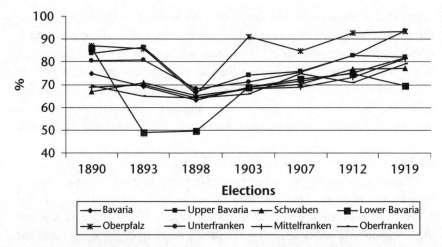

Figure 2. Support for the Centre Party, the SPD, and Left Liberals in national elections, 1890–1919.

Source: http://wahlen-in-deutschland.de; Mitchell, *Revolution*, 187.

Note: Votes for the Bavarian People's Party are counted as votes for the Centre Party.

Centre Party, and the Left Liberals in 1912 and in 1919 were almost identical (see Figure 2). Indeed, if we track the election results for the three parties between 1890 and 1919, it is astonishing to see how little impact the war had on the combined vote for the three parties most in favour of a negotiated peace during the war and the strongest proponents of the Weimar Republic post-war. What stands out is not the period of 1912 to 1917 but the late 1890s when during the agrarian crisis of this era the Catholic Centre Party temporarily lost the confidence of many farmers. This crisis of the 1890s thus had a deeper impact on the political attitudes of Bavarians than the First World War. Remarkably, the war thus had no discernible impact on the political attitudes of the vast majority of Bavarians.

The election results of the period 1890–1919 leave us with the apparent contradiction that, after the war, the vast majority of Bavarians and almost certainly also of the men of the List Regiment supported, through elections, the same political parties they had before the war, yet in 1919 gave legitimacy to a political system at the voting box very different from the one they had voted for before the war. However, this apparent contradiction dissolves if we look at the underlying values and characteristics of the political systems of the pre-war monarchy and the post-war republic in Bavaria. The two systems were in fact far less different than commonly assumed.

Even though pre-war Bavaria, and pre-war Germany in general, had semi-autocratic political systems, on the balance sheet pre-war Bavaria possessed a reformist political system that had been very slowly moving towards more democracy, liberalism, and equality. It was crucially also a reformist system that the Bavarian royal house had by and large supported, although not always enthusiastically. There is thus no contradiction between support for the pre-war political system, a relative lack of criticism for Crown Prince Rupprecht and Ludwig III among the men of the List Regiment during more than four years of war, and support for the Weimar Republic in early 1919. When Ludwig had been criticized during the war in Bavaria, he was generally (only) criticized for giving in too easily to the Prussians, while calls for an end of the monarchy had been limited to a very small, but very vocal, minority. Even though most of Rupprecht's criticism of the German conduct of the war had occurred behind closed doors, his critical stance towards Hindenburg and Ludendorff had been common knowledge and much appreciated in southern Bavaria, as evident in rumours that had been circulating in rural parts of Upper Bavaria and Swabia in the early summer of 1918 that Crown Prince Rupprecht had refused to continue to sacrifice his troops in a war that was already lost and had thus shot Hindenburg dead in a duel. Furthermore, when the official regimental history of RIR 16 was published in 1932, Hans Ostermünchner, from the 3rd Machine Gun Company, approvingly underlined in his copy of the book all references to Rupprecht's criticism of the German conduct of war.[29] In short, by late 1918 the monarchy had not lost all its legitimacy. The Centre Party advocated a reformist monarchy. As the war drew to a close, many Social Democrats, including their leader, were promoting, often for pragmatic reasons to be sure, the transformation of Bavaria and Germany to a constitutional monarchy, rather than a revolution.[30]

Rupprecht's track record suggests that he would probably have made a good constitutional monarch, and that the Bavarian military and administrative elite would have supported him, had the Allies not insisted on an end to the monarchy in Germany. For instance, Rupprecht had confided to his diary during the war: 'That [Chancellor Bethmann Hollweg] is bitterly hated by the Prussian Conservatives for his support for the extension of the Prussian suffrage speaks for him.'[31] This was a sentiment that was shared by the Bavarian Minister of War, General Philipp von Hellingrath. Similarly, Alfons Falkner von Sonnenburg, the director of the Press Office of the Bavarian War Ministry, and thus in charge of censorship, passionately advocated democratic reform.[32] Even Max von Speidel, the former commander of RD 6 and a staunch monarchist, was willing for pragmatic reasons to cooperate with Kurt Eisner during the revolution, by which time von Speidel was a high-ranking civil servant in the Ministry of War. Three days after the revolution erupted, Hitler's former superior met up with Eisner and offered him his support. The same day, he drove, together with revolutionary delegates, to the castle at which Ludwig III had stayed on the outbreak of revolution to persuade the Bavarian king to release the officers of the Bavarian Army from their oaths of allegiance to him. As the king was not to be found, von Speidel decided the following day to issue a decree himself urging the officers and soldiers of the Bavarian Army to cooperate with the new government.[33] Furthermore, in the aftermath of the Munich Soviet Republic, von Speidel was to advocate an amnesty for Communist leaders.[34]

Moreover, Rupprecht's grandfather had already shown in 1912 that the House of Wittelsbach was prepared to accept a gradual transformation towards democratic and parliamentary government, when he appointed a politician from the largest party in the Bavarian parliament as Minister President. This politician was Georg von Hertling, who had previously been leader of the parliamentary group of the Centre Party in the Reichstag. When Hertling was eventually appointed Reich Chancellor in November 1917, even though he was highly critical of Ludendorff, he initiated the first steps towards a constitutional reform of the Reich and also appointed several parliamentary leaders to government positions. Similarly, the 1906 and 1908 election reforms of Bavarian and local elections had catapulted Bavaria into the international vanguard of progressive and democratic electoral systems.[35]

The willingness at least to accept liberal and democratic reforms was not limited to the pre-war Bavarian governing, administrative, and military elite but was also prevalent among many members of the Prussian ruling circles.[36] For instance, Hermann Ritter Mertz von Quirnheim, whose son would become one of the brains behind the attempt to assassinate Hitler in 1944, had advocated the introduction of universal suffrage in Prussia during the Great War.[37] Moreover, when in 1920 the co-founder of the Fatherland Party, Wolfgang Kapp, attempted a *coup d'état* against the Weimar Republic, it was not, as the radical Left tried to convince themselves, a general strike that prevented a takeover of the radical Right but the refusal of government civil servants to cooperate with Kapp. Kapp's daughter had, in fact, to type 'government' decrees on a typewriter which putschists had to requisition from a shop in central Berlin, as no one in the Reich chancellory was willing to follow Kapp's orders. Moreover, most militias based in regions close to Berlin refused to join ranks with him. (The radical Left, meanwhile, used the coup attempt as an excuse for an anti-democratic takeover attempt of their own, establishing a 'Red Army' 50,000 men strong in the industrial region of the Ruhr, which was only put down after civil war-like combat had occurred, which resembled a bloody civil war.)[38]

There is thus no evidence that the majority of the men of the List Regiment had been politically radicalized by their experiences in Belgium and France between 1914 and 1918 or that the war had fatally undermined the legitimacy of the pre-war reformist political system and society. The acceptance of the collapse of Bavarian state institutions including the monarchy in 1918 was not the result of a revolutionary politicization of soldiers and civilians alike but of collective cumulative exhaustion and an urgent desire for peace, which had created apathy, not anger across the German armed forces.[39] There is no evidence for the claim that the monarchy in Germany fell as a result of popular pressure from below, which supposedly foreshadowed the *Volksgemeinschaft* of the National Socialists.[40]

The political pre-war attitudes of the men of the List Regiment had not changed much; they had no taste for political radicalism on either side of the political spectrum. The preference for the majority of the men of RIR 16 probably would have been for a constitutional monarchy, or, like the leaders of the Social Democratic Party, they would have at least accepted a consti-tutional monarchy. Hardly any voices in the List Regiment had questioned the institution of the monarchy during the war. However, few among the men of RIR 16 were hardcore diehard monarchists. The members of the List Regiment were thus, by and large, prepared to live with Wilson's demand for an abolition of the monarchy. They were ready to support the new republic, particularly since it promised, just as a constitutional monarchy would have done, to generate the same benefits towards which the pre-war political system in Bavaria had slowly been moving. Crucially, the new republic was run by the parties that had already received most of the votes in Bavaria prior to the war. In other words, the great majority of the men of the List Regiment and of Bavarians in general embraced, or at least accepted, the new republic because it stood in the tradition of the pre-war political system of Bavaria.

The exact form and shape that the post-war democratic settlement of Bavaria and Germany took had emerged for most of the actors involved— who possessed a multitude of different goals that were only distantly related to each other—unintentionally out of conflict amongst each other. However, this is the general rule rather than the exception of how new political systems and institutions come into being.[41] The important point here is that the overwhelming majority of Germans supported the new political order, despite all their differences over how they viewed the world.

The sometimes expressed idea that 'perhaps even a majority' of Germans had shown 'downright hostility' towards democracy from the republic's 'very founding'[42] is thus baseless, as is the argument that the end of the First World War had 'merely marked a relative respite' before the people of Europe and America had to return 'to fight again to contain German aggression'.[43] Neither of these ideas is supported by the development of the political attitudes of the men of the List Regiment and of the Bavarian population at large.

However, the Bavarian electorate left no doubt that while it supported the Weimar Republic it did not embrace Kurt Eisner's Socialist Republic. When Bavarian elections took place the week prior to the election for the National Assembly, only 2.5 per cent of the vote went to Eisner's party, while 82 per cent voted for the three parties that would form the Weimar Coalition. In the countryside hardly anybody voted for Eisner's party. In Ichenhausen, home to some of the men from RIR 16, for instance, a mere five voters gave their vote to his party. Even in Munich, Eisner's party only received 5.1 per cent of the vote, compared to 46.7 per cent for the Social Democrats. The fate that befell the party of the self-appointed Bavarian leader a week later in the national election was just as dire.[44] Only one in twenty Bavarians supported Eisner but more than four out of five embraced the parties in support of the Weimar Republic. The radical right-wing successor parties of the Fatherland Party, which itself had dissolved at the end of the war, received hardly any votes in Bavaria at all in early 1919. Even Balthasar Brandmayer, who eventually was to become a committed National Socialist, claimed in his 1932 memoirs that initially he had welcomed the republic.[45]

Bavaria and Germany's future looked bright. Unlike for eastern and south-eastern Europe, the First World War was, for Bavaria at least, far less of the 'seminal catastrophe of our century' than George F. Kennan thought it was.[46] Among mainstream society, political radicalism had been

1. Adolf Hitler attending the patriotic gathering in Odeonsplatz in central Munich the day after the outbreak of the First World War, 2 August 1914. Nazi propaganda reproduced this cleverly staged photo countless times. Its photographer blocked out the parts of Odeonplatz that were far less crowded.

2. A royal farewell: King Ludwig III of Bavaria inspects the men of Hitler's regiment in the Türken barracks in Munich not long before their deployment to the front, 8 October 1914.

3. Hitler's favourite pastimes at the front were painting and reading. He painted this watercolour of the ruins of Messines monastery, in the Ypres Salient, in December 1914.

4. A man without a face: This out-of-focus photo bordering on the insulting – taken by one of Hitler's main adversaries from the regiment in May 1915 – was the only photo of Hitler included in the official 1932 regimental history of the List Regiment.

5. A well-liked loner amongst his immediate peers: Adolf Hitler (front row, first left) and his fellow dispatch runners in Fournes, September 1915. Note that Hitler looks comfortable amongst his peers but tends to place himself on the edge of group photos.

6. Hitler (back row, first left) amidst the members of 'Kapelle Krach', undated.

7. Hitler (front row, first left) and his fellow dispatch runners in the garden of regimental HQ in Fournes, I: 1915.

8. Hitler and his fellow dispatch runners in the garden of regimental HQ in Fournes, II: 1940 – A Nazi propaganda book, with a print-run in the hundreds of thousands, reproduced the image from 1915 and that from 1940 next to each other.

9. One of Hitler's closest wartime friends and fellow dispatch runners: Jakob 'Jackl' Weiß, prior to his departure for the front, 10 October 1914.

10. Hitler generally had to operate behind the immediate combat zone in areas like this, close to the village of Biache-Saint-Vaast to the east of Arras, May 1917.

11. 'Rear area pigs': This is how frontline soldiers from the List Regiment characterized Hitler and his fellow members of regimental HQ – among them Max Amann (front row, first right) and Alois Schnelldorfer (front row, first left).

12. A trench on Vimy Ridge, late 1916 or early 1917. Soldiers in the trenches showed little appreciation for the dangers of Hitler's task during the war.

13. The painter-turned-soldier: Albert Weisgerber (sitting on the end of the tree trunk) and his men from 1st Company before being deployed in the Battle of Fromelles, in which he would meet his death, 9 May 1915. Between 1915 and 1933, Weisgerber—whose wife had to flee Hitler's Germany as a 'half-Jew' and whose friend was to become the first democratically elected President of post-Second World War Germany—was the List Regiment's most celebrated soldier.

14. Justin Fleischmann and his brothers Ernst and Martin (from right to left), 1918. The young Jewish soldier from Hitler's regiment noted in his wartime diary to experience 'a splendid time', not reporting any anti-Semitic sentiments or incidents.

15. Unlike many other Jewish soldiers in the List Regiment, Justin Fleischmann (first left) survived the Holocaust and emigrated to the United States, where he was photographed with his brothers, *c.* 1967.

16. Indian soldiers killed by the List Regiment in the Battle of Fromelles, 9 May 1915. Despite the almost constant experience of killing and seeing peers being killed, the men of Hitler's regiment did not undergo a lasting brutalization and political radicalization.

Verwund. engl. Flieger 9/III. 16.

17. Soldiers from RIR 16 taking a British pilot prisoner, March 1916. Members of the List Regiment were involved in war atrocities but POWs were more often than not treated with respect.

18. A soldier from RIR 16 plays cards with his French hosts with whom he is quartered in Somain. Over time, the relationship between the men of Hitler's regiment and the local population improved, rather than worsened.

19. Father Norbert Stumpf, the Catholic chaplain of Hitler's 6th Bavarian Reserve, visiting the trenches, 1915. To his left is Emil Spatny, the commander of RIR 16 in 1915. Unlike Hitler, the men of the List Regiment tended to turn to religion in their attempt to find meaning in the war.

20. The commemorative window honouring the service of the List Regiment in Munich's City Hall. Hyper-nationalists—among them members of the regiment—argued that it made the members of RIR 16 look apathetic and that it failed to represent the heroism of the List Regiment. Nevertheless, it was chosen as a full-page illustration, facing the title page, of the official 1932 regimental history.

21. Jakob Weiß (standing next to Hitler) meets Hitler, mid-1930s. Most of Hitler's fellow dispatch runners stood by Hitler after 1933 and thus helped Hitler to create the myth of how the List Regiment had given birth to National Socialism.

Der Führer als Tierfreund

22. One of Jakob Weiß's most treasured possessions: This postcard, personally signed by Hitler, gives an indication of how his immediate peers viewed Hitler.

23. A propagandistic article about Jakob Weiß and Adolf Hitler from the Süddeutsche Sonntagszeitung, 2 April 1933. Articles like this one were aimed at widening Hitler's public appeal at a time when the majority of Germans still did not support Hitler.

24. Service held in the Türken barracks during the reunion of the List Regiment on the twentieth anniversary of the outbreak of the First World War, Munich, October 1934. The Nazi propaganda machine staged the reunion full of pageantry and placed photos from the event in glossy magazines all over Germany, avoiding the fact that Hitler had chosen to stay away from the event.

25. Jakob Weiß (first row, first right) and Iganz Westenkirchner (standing behind Weiß) attending the 1934 reunion of the List Regiment. The wife of one Weiß's wartime comrades used this photo as a postcard which she sent to Weiß the day after the reunion. She wrote: 'I hope that the day will come soon when Hitler can stay with his loyal comrades. My heart is bleeding that there are still comrades who lack the holiest and inner conviction that the future lies with Hitler. This is why Hitler cannot attend [reunions of the List Regiment]. I understand this all even though I am just a woman.'

26. Fritz Wiedemann, the former regimental adjutant of RIR 16 and one of Hitler's adjutants from 1934 to 1939, during his time as German Consul General in San Francisco, 1939. Soon thereafter, he secretly met with British intelligence to discuss how best to remove Hitler from power.

27. Hugo Gutmann during the First World War. The highest-ranking Jew in Hitler's regiment took this photo with him when he fled Germany and emigrated to the United States and kept it all his life, despite never talking about his life in Germany.

28. Gutmann also took with him a photo of Hitler amongst his fellow dispatch runners taken in 1916.

largely curtailed. The hyper-nationalist and proto-Fascist groups in Bavaria's capital were about to return to where they had been before the war, to the fringes of politics. Hitler was close to having to return to drawing second-rate postcards of Munich's sights in order to eke out a living. However, with one stroke things went horribly wrong. Within months, the Bavarian political landscape was drastically to change and to radicalize, giving Hitler a cause and an audience.

The events that would limit the prospect of a peaceful and reformist future in Bavaria were triggered on 21 February 1919 when Kurt Eisner was assassinated by Count Anton von Arco-Valley, a radical right-wing former officer who, according to some reports, felt that he needed to prove himself after being turned down for membership of the proto-Fascist Thule Society because of the Jewish ancestry of his mother. As a response to the assassination, Eisner's Independent Social Democrats refused to hand over power to the parties that had found such overwhelming support among the Bavarian electorate. In total disregard of the electorate, they convinced leftist elements among the Social Democrats, who were in a dilemma about what course of action to follow, to join them in setting up a 'Central Council of the Bavarian Republic', under the leadership of Ernst Niekisch, a left-wing Social Democrat who would soon cross floors to the Independent Social Democrats[47] and whose path would cross Hugo Gutmann's in the 1930s.

The Social Democrats, meanwhile, feverishly negotiated behind the scenes with all political parties and tried everything to save the Republic. After the SPD finally managed to gather support for a new legitimate government under the leadership of the SPD, even including the Independent Social Democrats, Niekisch's revolutionary council showed its true colours and refused to hand over power. In the wake of Eisner's assassination, the council had already ordered hostages to be taken from amongst the numbers of Munich's notables. Soon both Liberal and Catholic newspapers were suppressed in Munich.[48] The Communist epidemic had spread to Bavaria and, unlike in Berlin where a Communist attempt to overthrow Ebert's democratic and liberal government and to prevent elections from taking place had failed after four days of street fighting in mid-January, it created havoc in Munich and continued to spread. By 21 March, Bela Kun had established a Soviet Republic in Hungary which was to last until August.[49]

The new Bavarian government headed by centrist Social Democrats under Johannes Hoffmann, who had started his political life as a Liberal, meanwhile, had fled to Bamberg. With every day, the democratically elected government grew more worried about how to regain power from the illegitimate, undemocratic revolutionaries in Munich. On 14 April, the day revolutionary troops militarily defeated the Republican Militia (*Republikanische Soldatenwehr*), which had tried to return Munich to liberalism and democracy,[50] an official in the Ministry for Military Affairs in Bamberg warned all other ministries and the command of the Bavarian troops that 'the situation in Munich has worsened since last night. . . . A Red Army is being formed.'[51]

The situation escalated further still. The revolution devoured its own children. Following the fighting of 13 April, hardliners unseated Niekisch and proclaimed a Bavarian Soviet Republic, modelled on Bolshevik Russia and calling for a dictatorship of the 'Red Army' which had been formed out of 20,000 workers and soldiers in Munich. The Soviet Republic also spread through the south Bavarian countryside. Despite almost non-existent popular support, the decisiveness of Communist revolutionaries allowed them to seize control of an array of towns in the region between Munich and the Alps, including Miesbach, Rosenheim, Kolbermoor, and Kempten.[52]

The experience of this second Bavarian revolution was later utilized to the full by Nazi propaganda. Even when interrogated after the Second World War, Max Amann would still tell a mythical version of his experiences during the revolution. When the Munich Soviet Republic was suddenly established, Amann was still working in the Ministry of War. He claimed during the days of the Soviet Republic to have 'observed the march of the Bolshevists and the shooting of hostages in Munich'.[53] It is, in fact, most unlikely that Amann's claims are true as the only execution of hostages occurred inside a school.

On 17 April, the Social Democratic-led Bavarian government, the Bavarian Soldiers' Council, and the Bavarian armed forces issued an urgent appeal for all former members of the Bavarian Army to join up immediately and form a people's army to liberate Munich:

> Appeal to all former members of the Bavarian army!
> . . . The government is calling all trained men to protect the homeland, rescue our German brothers, and fight against terror. . . . Therefore . . . join the

ranks of those fighting for the government regardless of age, class, or political party! Register at the local recruitment centres (*Wehrstellen*) for the fight for freedom and justice, and for the redemption and rescue of our brothers!

For the Soldiers' Council: Rothfuß

For the [Bavarian] government: [Wirseling]

For the Command of the 2nd Army Corps [Joil][54]

The Bavarian government assured men that it would not require them to serve beyond the unseating of the revolutionaries in Munich: 'Fixed-term enlistments in the militia (*Volkswehr*) are accepted. For 14 days, for example.'[55]

Did the veterans of the List Regiment follow the call to arms by the government for which the great majority of Bavarians had voted? Unfortunately, we do not know how many answered the call. In general, in the regions of southern Bavaria where there was no actual or perceived immediate danger of a Communist takeover, such as in parts of Swabia, few local men joined up, while in regions where Communist takeovers had occurred in some towns, men were far more likely to volunteer. However, as a report from the district administration of Chiemgau to the south-east of Munich made clear, where there was a willingness of men to serve it was indeed strictly limited to the goal of preventing a Communist takeover: 'There was willingness in late April to join up for a few days to meet the danger of Communist rule. Beyond that, men do not want to commit themselves to anything.'[56] Even though we cannot know the exact number of those of the RIR 16 veterans who joined up, we do know that, while the attempt to recruit members of *Freikorps* fighting in the Baltic among the men of the List Regiment had been a resounding failure, a considerable number of men enlisted now. In total 19,000 men were enlisted in Bavarian *Freikorps* and local militias during the campaign against the Soviet Republic.[57] Considerable though the number was, it was minuscule compared to the total number of Bavarian veterans of the Great War. It was barely greater than the total number of men who at some point or another during the war had been members of Hitler's regiment.

One of the *Freikorps* volunteers among the veterans of the List Regiment was a former war volunteer, Private (*Gefreiter*), and dispatch runner. This veteran was not Adolf Hitler, who had no intention at all of joining a *Freikorps*; it was Arthur Rödl, the war volunteer who had lied about his age in 1914 in order to be allowed to serve in the war. After his injury in 1st Ypres, he had soon returned to the List Regiment, ultimately becoming a dispatch runner by 1916. Now in 1919, Rödl joined the Freikorps Oberland.[58] Among the veterans who joined a *Freikorps* was also Fritz Wiedemann. The student of economics had left Munich after the assassination of Kurt Eisner. In Kempten, in the south-west corner of Bavaria close to the Alps, he joined the Freikorps Schwaben, in which he served from May to June 1919 as the commander of a company. In the event, his *Freikorps* was only deployed in Kempten itself. It consisted almost exclusively of local men from the region, who were driven by an urge to defend their homes rather than by ideology.[59] Fridolin Solleder, meanwhile, commanded a deployment of eighty *Freikorps* men who helped to put an end to Communist rule in Landshut and Kolbermoor.[60]

Another officer from RIR 16 who joined up was Karl Frobenius, a Protestant pastor who had been commander of 4th Company until he lost his eye in the Battle of Fromelles of 1916. Frobenius now became a staff officer in Freikorps Epp, which also included a whole host of future top Nazi leaders, including Ernst Röhm as quartermaster, Hans Frank, Rudolf Hess, and Gregor Strasser as well as his brother Otto.[61] Philipp Engelhardt, the former regimental commander whose life Hitler might have saved in 1914, meanwhile set up his own *Freikorps*, the Freikorps Engelhardt, in Erlangen in Franconia.[62] Ludwig von Vallade, the former commander of RIB 12 and a friend of Rupprecht von Bayern, meanwhile served as a Bavarian liaison officer in a non-Bavarian unit (*Gruppe Friedeburg*) during the campaign against the Munich Soviet Republic.[63]

It is impossible to get an exact profile of those among the RIR 16 veterans who joined *Freikorps* since the muster roles of the *Freikorps*, at any rate those held by the Bavarian War Archive, do not include details about previous military units of which *Freikorps* recruits had been members.[64] A much higher number of veterans of the List Regiment—such as Hans Ostermünchner, a former sniper in RIR 16 and a farmer living close to the Bavarian Alps—is likely to have joined the local militias (*Einwohnerwehren*) that had been set up in the wake of the Communist revolution in Bavaria and were meant to defend the republic and prevent a radical left-wing takeover of Bavaria. Ostermünchner, for instance, together with the other men from his local militia, had to guard a bridge against Communists in nearby Penzburg. By 1920, as many as 300,000 Bavarians had joined local militias, which answered to the Bavarian government. However, as a result of the Versailles Treaty the militias were disbanded in 1921.[65] Yet, with the full knowledge of local authorities, many kept their weapons anyway. Ostermünchner, for instance, hid six machine guns on his farm.

Whatever the exact number of veterans joining *Freikorps* and militias in the spring of 1919 was, unlike in late 1918, some, maybe many, of Hitler's former brothers-in-arms were willing to join paramilitary units now. Protecting their own homes against the perceived or real threat of Bolshevism at the instigation of their own democratically elected government was quite a different matter from fighting in the East. The case of Hitler's regiment thus does not support the idea that the activities of *Freikorps* in post-war Germany were unequivocal evidence of a general wartime brutalization of front-line soldiers generated by the First World War. It was the dynamic and logic of the post-war conflict, rather than either general wartime brutalization caused by the First World War or some longing for unity or *Volksgemeinschaft* among the German bourgeoisie, as has sometimes been claimed,[66] that explains the relative popularity of *Freikorps* and militias—and their willingness to employ violence—in the Germany of 1919.[67] If it were true that veterans, as has been said, 'shifted their brutal front-line practices to the home front and went on waging war'[68] and that virtually all members of *Freikorps* were 'ideologues and agitators'[69] the men of the List Regiment would not have waited to join *Freikorps* until being urged by Bavarian authorities to defend their communities against Bolshevik revolutionaries. And if the argument were true that the vision of all *Freikorps* and of all its members 'stood completely opposed to democracy; it was, instead, a Fascist ethos that they espoused and practised',[70] we are left with no answer as to why DDP members such as Fridolin Solleder, and even some Jewish veterans, had fought in a *Freikorps*. Even the Freikorps Oberland, sections of which were later to form the nucleus of the SA, included not only Heinrich Himmler and Arthur Rödl, who, as we shall see, was to become a Concentration Camp Commander, but also several Jewish members.[71] Even Himmler's politicization towards Fascism was only to take place in 1922. There was thus no direct line from service in a *Freikorps* to a politicization towards radical right-wing Fascism.

It is worth repeating here that the appeal for veterans of the List Regiment and of other Bavarian units to join up derived from the fact that they were to defend, rather than assault the post-war democratic political settlement. What caused them to join *Freikorps* units was thus not the war experience of a long brutal war but the urging of the centrist parties that had been the parties of choice for Bavarians before and after the war to defend Bavaria against Bolshevism.

On 1 May, regular army units, militias, and *Freikorps* that had been amassed around the city started to move in on Munich. The men in these units had been reminded time and time again that the Republic could only be saved from Communism if they acted ruthlessly.[72] They were told that the federal Minister of Defence, Gustav Noske, a Social Democrat, had issued an order in early March, according to which 'any person who is found fighting government troops with a weapon in hand will be shot on sight'.[73]

The Bolshevik experiment in Bavaria ended amidst the cheers of Munich's population when a 'White' Armada of regular and irregular troops defeated the 'Red Army' in a sea of blood and violence, resulting in the deaths of between 550 and 650 men and women, with men of Hitler's regiment fighting probably on both sides of Bavaria's very brief but ferocious civil war. The 'Red Army' managed to inflict between approximately forty and sixty deaths on the troops ordered in by the legitimate government of Bavaria, while it itself lost around a hundred men. The majority of deaths, however, occurred when in the aftermath of the combat that had taken place, regular troops and *Freikorps* tried to hunt down real or imagined Communist insurgents.[74] Bloody though the end of the Munich Soviet Republic was, we should resist the temptation to exaggerate the brutality of either the 'White' or 'Red' forces. The truth is that more than 98 per cent of all 'White' and 'Red' troops (the figure just for 'Red' troops is approximately 97 per cent) survived the end of the Communist regime in Munich.

Robert Hell, who during the war had served as one of the Protestant divisional chaplains under Oscar Daumiller, experienced the end of the Soviet Republic in Perlach, a working-class suburb of Munich, where Hell was Lutheran pastor. On 1 May, the Lützow Freikorps arrived in Perlach. The leader of the unit, Hans von Lützow, stayed in Hell's house, where he was welcomed with open arms, while the men of the *Freikorps* tried to arrest real and imagined Communist revolutionaries and put up posters requesting under the threat of the death penalty that all guns be handed in. As it became clear that the *Freikorps* would stay in Perlach only for a few hours, Hell's wife grew worried, confronting Lützow with her fear of Communist reprisals after the departure of the *Freikorps*. Lützow told her not to worry, reassuring her that he and his men were only one phone call away. In the three days following the departure of the *Freikorps*, Hell and other 'Whites' in Perlach received several threats for having aided the Freikorps Lützow. There were also reports, whether based on fact or fiction is next to impossible to ascertain, about 'Red Army' activity. These included claims that farms had been set alight and that clandestine 'Red Army' meetings had taken place in a forest close to Perlach. Hell's name had also appeared on a list of local dignitaries allegedly drawn up by Communists as possible hostages. Whether out of paranoia or not, Hell and his wife feared for their lives by 4 May. Hell's wife thus took Lützow up on his offer to call him if necessary. The ultimate result of this fateful phone call was that a few hours later a deployment of the Lützow Freikorps arrested fifteen suspected Communist revolutionaries. When the officer in charge of the arrests confirmed the names of the arrested men in the late hours of 4 May, Hell told him: 'They make no bones about it; they just line them right up against the wall.' As the officer was leaving Hell's house, he told Hell that the arrested men would not return alive. The fifteen men were taken to Munich, where the following morning they were shot in the courtyard of one of Munich's foremost beer halls, the Hofbräukeller.[75]

For men among the veterans of Hitler's regiment like Hell, it was not the war, but rather the experience of the short-lived Soviet Republic that had been the seminal event of their lives. If we can believe a mid-1920s article published in *Vorwärts*, the Social Democratic flagship paper, Robert Hell's response to the Soviet Republic was typical of a huge section of Bavarian society. Hell was for the paper the personification for everything that had gone wrong during the revolutionary period.[76]

The legacy of the short-lived Munich Soviet Republic was to be tragic for Bavaria, as it helped the fortunes of the radical Right and undermined the Social Democrats. There has long been a taboo against discussing the degree to which the attitude of Germans towards National Socialism and other radical right-wing movements was centrally driven by anti-Bolshevism and the experience of radical Socialist revolutions across Central and Eastern Europe, lest historians were seeking to exculpate 'ordinary' Germans for their support of the Third Reich and trying to provide an apologia for the crimes of National Socialist Germany.

Pace the participants of the heated 1980s debate over the nexus between Communism and National Socialism (the *Historikerstreit*), to allow the central importance of anti-Bolshevism in the rise of Nazism is merely to enter the minds of 'ordinary' Germans, not to justify their behaviour. Nor is it to equate Bolshevik violence with the Holocaust or to ignore the

Freikorps' own violence after the war. To explain is not to excuse; to empathize is not to sympathize. Even though the existence of the Munich Soviet Republic was a *conditio sine qua non* for the growing acceptability of proto-Fascist groups in Munich in the spring of 1919, it does not remove any responsibility for subsequent events from radical right-wing groups and their supporters.

In their origins National Socialism and Fascism were intellectually neither a response to Bolshevism nor a product of the First World War.[77] However, the involvement of radical right-wing and Fascist political groups in containing Bolshevism in Bavaria brought increasing legitimacy, but not large-scale outright support for their political goals, to groups that previously had been confined to the fringes of the political spectrum. In other words, the Soviet Republic allowed radical right-wing groups to become a serious political force in so far as people perceived them as a bulwark against Communism, while not necessarily looking too closely at what the real political goals of Fascism were. To be sure, it had been a moderate government that had ordered the removal of the Soviet Republic. However, after the crushing of the Communist regime the paranoia of the radical Right about Bolshevism, at least ostensibly, appeared as less crazy. Moreover, an increasing number of Bavarians, who never were to vote for radical right-wing parties in free elections, started at least to respect hyper-nationalist groups as defenders of Bavaria against the Socialists and Bolsheviks, even if they did not agree with all of the policies of proto-Fascist groups. It was thus due to the legacy of the Soviet Republic that an increasing number of Bavarians would start to see groups on the radical Right as reliable tools, or, one might say, as useful idiots, to further their own political ideas, even if they did not actively support the core of the ideology of these groups. From a 1920s perspective, the experiences of the Bavarian Soviet Republic and of Bolshevism in Russia were real (even if the likelihood of a Bolshevik takeover of Germany was pretty slim at best), while the horrors of the Third Reich still lay far in the future. Fear of Bolshevism hardened into paranoia and blinded many Bavarians towards the violence of the radical Right.

Radical anti-Semitism also saw a breakthrough now, as the extreme Right portrayed Eisner's government, Niekisch's council, and the Bavarian Soviet Republic as a Jewish ploy, which was made easier by the fact that Eisner and most of the prominent leaders of the Soviet Republic had been Jewish. Ironically, however, two of the three parties of the Weimar Coalition and of the Reichstag Peace Resolution had been the traditional political homes of German Jews, rather than the groups that supported the Soviet Republic. Moreover, one of the 'White' hostages shot by the 'Red Army' was Jewish. Yet in the nationalist mind of a growing number of Bavarians—and of an increasing number of Eastern and Central Europeans around the same time—Bolshevists and Jews became interchangeable. For instance, on Theresienstraße, not far from where Hitler had lived prior to the war, pieces of paper, the size of a business card, were stuck to the walls of houses in July 1919 reading: 'Racial disgrace! German women, beware of the Jews! They will treat you like a commodity and defile your blood!! Do you want Jew children?'[78]

Yet compared to the disintegrating parts of the former tsarist empire—where during the revolutionary period and the ensuing civil war more than 150,000 Jews were killed,[79] relatively little physical violence to-wards Jews occurred in post-war Germany.[80] While many farmers in the southern Bavarian countryside started to complain about Jewish swind-lers and profiteers during the revolutionary and post-revolutionary period, they also tended to exclude local Jews in their own communities from that criticism. Racial anti-Semitism, meanwhile, was almost absent from the southern Bavarian countryside. Nor did the rural population blame the loss of the war on the Jews.[81] Despite his membership of an anti-Communist militia in 1919, Hans Ostermünchner continued to have good business relationships with local Jewish cattle traders through-out the 1920s.[82] Arnold Erlanger, the son of Levi Erlanger, who had served in 6th Company during the war, claims that, during the years of the Weimar Republic, his father did not run into any trouble when he was travelling on the train while praying with hand-tefillin (the Jewish prayer boxes), wrapped around his arms. He recalled in his memoirs that Jewish–gentile relations had been amicable in Ichenhausen when he grew up in post-war Germany:

> I cannot recall any inappropriate or anti-Semitic remarks or even any other kind of incidents. . . . Whenever [Christian] processions took place, we watched and behaved respectfully. We children greeted the Catholic priest Sinz most respectfully and were proud to be allowed to shake his hand. I must also point out that during the service on the eve of the Day of Atonement, Christian men, women, and children sat in the gallery of the synagogue and listened. . . . On 1 January, our rabbi went to Father Sinz to wish him a happy New Year. The priest also came to wish our rabbi all the best on our New

Year's Day. In short, most of the people in Ichenhausen respected us and we respected them. We were German but could live Jewish lives. It was only with Hitler's rise and the 'seizure of power', that that all changed.[83]

Racial anti-Semitism in Munich was also limited to a small, but extremely vocal, minority. In fact, next to the racially anti-Semitic slurs put up on Theresienstraße, other pieces of paper had appeared in response: 'Not the Jews, but the war profiteers and the Fatherland Parties are to blame for our misfortune. They are, in reality, the betrayers of the Fatherland. (See Erzberger's revelations.) . . . Racial hatred is idiotic. . . . Your megalomania was Germany's downfall.'[84] Even Heinrich Himmler, who was a student at the Technical University of Munich at the time, was not yet a racial anti-Semite during the revolutionary and post-revolutionary period.[85]

While the number of RIR 16 veterans joining the radical Right in early 1919 was small, the number of those joining the extreme Left was even smaller. Just as it is impossible today fully to lift the cloud of history from the involvement of veterans in *Freikorps*, it is equally difficult to establish how many men of the List Regiment exactly served the revolutionary government in the spring of 1919. However, both the election results of the Soldiers' Council elections among the men of RIR 16 in late 1918 and the election results of the Bavarian and national elections in January strongly suggest that the number of veterans supporting the revolutionary government was very small. Yet we know with certainty of at least one veteran serving the revolutionary regime. He was a former member of the support staff of regimental HQ. This man was none other than Private Hitler.

Perhaps surprisingly, once back in Munich, Hitler did not act in any way consistent with his later beliefs. In fact, his actions during the five months after his return to Bavaria did not show any consistency at all. They were full of contradictions and reveal a deeply disorientated man without a clear mental compass to steer him through the post-war world. Hitler, who in painstaking detail described all other periods of his life in *Mein Kampf*, skated at great speed over the first five months after his arrival back in Bavaria, including the time of the Bavarian Soviet Republic, as though he were hiding something—and he had a lot to hide.

In the spring of 1919, as a soldier based in Munich, Hitler served a government that he was later to deride as treacherous, criminal, and Jewish in *Mein Kampf*. And he did not keep his head down. Soon, he had been elected to the Soldiers' Council of his military unit, the Ersatz Battalion of the 2nd Infantry Regiment, and was based in military barracks in Oberwiesenfeld, close to where Munich's Olympic Stadium stands today. More precariously, on surviving film footage of Eisner's funeral we see Hitler with a few men from his unit walking behind Eisner's coffin in the funeral procession of the Bavarian leader. We clearly see Hitler wearing two armbands: one black band to mourn the death of Eisner and the other a red one in the colour of the Socialist revolution.[86] Similarly, Hitler appears on one of Heinrich Hoffmann's photographs of the funeral procession for Eisner,[87] taken shortly before Eisner was eulogized: 'Kurt Eisner, the Jew, was a prophet who fought relentlessly against the fainthearted and wretched, because he not only loved mankind, but believed in it and wanted it.'[88] While Hitler could easily have joined, for instance, the Thule Society, which had inspired Eisner's assassination and which was full of future National Socialist leaders, such as Alfred Rosenberg, Rudolf Hess, or Hans Frank, Hitler chose publicly to show his support for Eisner.

Even two days after the Soviet Republic had been proclaimed, Hitler stood for election again, when the new regime conducted an election among Munich's soldier councils to ensure support for the Soviet Republic by Munich's military units. Hitler was now elected Deputy Battalion Representative and remained in the post for the entire lifespan of the Soviet Republic. His task included liaising with the Department of Propaganda of the new Socialist government.[89]

All explanations that are normally given to make sense of Hitler's behaviour during this period—ranging from assertions that Hitler really was a Socialist at the time to one that argues that he was merely superficially hiding his true self and really was the spokesperson of Pan-German nationalist counter-revolutionaries[90]—are unsatisfactory.

If he really had been a committed dyed-in-the-wool Pan-German anti-Socialist, anti-Semite, and hyper-nationalist and had only overtly cooperated with the new regime to steer the men around him away from Communism and Social Democracy, why did he not join a *Freikorps* with his comrades prior to the defeat of the Soviet Republic? Furthermore, Ernst Schmidt was demobilized during the days of the Soviet Republic[91] which clearly indicates that Hitler could have left his post if he had so desired. Otto Strasser, the Nazi leader, indeed later asked after he had broken with Hitler, why Hitler had not like him joined the forces that put an end to the Soviet Republic: 'Where was Hitler on that day? In which corner of Munich did the soldier hide himself, he who should have been fighting in our ranks?'[92] If Hitler really had been hiding his true colours and had been the champion of all the other anti-revolutionary men in the unit who were also keeping their heads down, why did none of those men make a statement to that effect once Hitler had become famous? If Hitler really had been trying to undermine the revolution by staying in his post, why did he not brag about it in *Mein Kampf* instead of keeping silent about this time? Meanwhile, if he really was a Socialist after the war, how do we make sense of his anti-Socialist expressions during the war (for which contemporary sources exist at least for 1915)? How do we make sense of his closeness to and adoration of officers among the regimental staff who clearly were not Socialists?

What most Hitler biographies, which tend to argue that Hitler's political outlook and prejudices had almost fully developed by the end of the war,[93] did not fully take into account is that the whole point of Hitler's behaviour in the month after the end of the war is that it was inconsistent. It is impossible convincingly to arrange the existing evidence from Hitler's time after the war in a way consistent with either a portrayal of Hitler as a Socialist or as the hyper-nationalist Pan-German anti-Semite that he was to become for one simple reason: he was neither.

Hitler was confused and his life could have still developed in different directions. The experience of revolution as such thus did not radicalize him. Hitler retrospectively invented a revolutionary experience to suit his subsequent radicalization. To be sure, during the revolutionary period, Hitler was not a man without qualities and without a biography who could have developed in any direction. The directions into which he could have developed were limited by the often contradictory political and social influences: the pro-Bavarian sentiments from his time in Munich in 1913/14 and reinforced by his social network among the support personnel of the regimental staff versus his anti-Bavarian sentiment resulting from his visits to wartime Munich, his wartime reading, his pre-war company in Munich and Vienna, the anti-Bolshevik, pro-Ebert policy of his superiors whom he adored, his own anti-monarchist stance, and his belief in a classless society, to name but a few. Hitler was torn between these often contradictory poles. Over time, some influences would have to be eliminated at the expense of others if he was ever to make the leap from being politically disoriented to having a clear political world-view. However, it was not preordained which of these influences were to be eliminated. This implies that the influences on him could have been put together in different ways and could have produced different political mentalities, which included, but was by no means limited to, National Socialism.

It does not require too much of a stretch of the imagination to see how under different circumstances Hitler could have been attracted by Ernst Niekisch's idiosyncratic anti-Western National Bolshevism that promised to merge nationalism with socialism;[94] by other Social Democratic groups, including some elements in the 'Reichsbanner Schwarz-Rot-Gold' (the paramilitary group that was to be set up in defence of the republic), which attempted to merge nationalism, anti-materialism, and socialism;[95] or by centrist Social Democrats who advocated the importance of both patriotism and socialism (but probably not by the Catholic BVP, Liberals, or monarchists.)

It is likely that Eisner's and Niekisch's regimes, with their acceptance of the nation state, had been acceptable to Hitler in a way that that was not true of the Soviet Republic. One possibility is that Hitler had missed jumping ship after Niekisch's demise because at the time he had deemed continuing to serve with his unit as advantageous over any existing alternative but that he had never been fully comfortable with the internationalism of Soviet leaders such as Ernst Toller. In his approach to the Munich Soviet Republic, he might thus have acted in a way similar to the behaviour of those Germans who never fully supported Hitler after 1933 but either saw support for him as advantageous over existing alternatives or deemed the potential price of resistance to be too high.

The suggestion that Hitler might conceivably have developed in the same direction as either Niekisch or even mainstream Social Democrats is not to equate either Niekisch or Social Democracy with National Socialism, which would be absurd. It is merely to argue that Hitler's future was undetermined and that he could have moved in the direction of diametrically different political movements as long as they combined the promise of a classless society with some kind of nationalism.

Hitler's undetermined political future becomes even less surprising if we bear in mind that the intellectual origins of Fascism share central tenets with the non-Marxist Left. According to one argument, despite its eventual collusion with the conservative Right once Fascism tried to come to power, early Fascism had been in its promises, rather than in its eventual application, more socialist than capitalist, more plebeian than bourgeois.[96]

Two interlocking factors determined which of the influences on Hitler would prevail: the way his acquaintances would develop politically and post-war conditions. At this point in his life, Hitler adapted to the people around him, as he was in the process of building up an 'ersatz' family (that was built on, but was not identical with the men of regimental HQ of RIR 16). To please the people of his social network was paramount for him at this point, as he did not have a life outside the support personnel of the remnants of the regimental staff of the List Regiment. The company of men that Hitler's acquaintances such as Ernst Schmidt—who was a member of a trade union backed by the Social Democrats[97]—mixed with after their return to Munich would also become Hitler's company. To which political circles Hitler was exposed thus largely depended on the choices made by his acquaintances.

Later, once Hitler had fully developed his political ideas and become the dictator of the Third Reich, people around him would 'work towards the Führer',[98] trying to develop and implement policies that would please Hitler and go hand in hand with his general ideas. At this point, however, the process worked in reverse: Hitler worked towards his acquaintances and because their political ideas and development depended on post-war conditions and events, Hitler's future had not been predetermined by the time he had returned to Munich.

In short, at the time he returned from the war, Hitler was a man unsure about his future and his identity. He was a man who even now could have been swayed in different directions. His confused ideas about the world could have still been composed in different ways. Hitler and the men from his regiment still had a choice. When Hitler returned to Bavaria in late 1918, his future was still wide open.

11

Hitler's *Kampf* against the List Veterans

Early 1919–1933

Karl Mayr was heavily overworked. Running the counter-revolution propaganda unit of the army in Munich had fully consumed him for most of the five months since the defeat of the Munich Soviet Republic. He really had no time to attend to the kind of letter he had just received. The long tedious letter culminated in the question: 'Are the Jews not the threat that they are seen to be, is their corruptive influence being overestimated, or is the government misjudging the danger, or is the government too weak to take action against the dangerous Jewry?' Rather than answer the question himself, Mayr scribbled a note on a piece of paper which he put together with the letter into an envelope addressed to one of his most reliable men, none other than Private Hitler.[1]

On receiving the letter, Hitler learned that Mayr wanted him to answer the letter on his behalf. He was happy to oblige. Just as in regimental HQ of RIR 16, he was still excelling at pleasing his superiors. However, more than that, now he had to quell any doubts about his behaviour during Niekisch's regime as well as during the Soviet Republic. Hitler sat down to compose the letter Mayr had asked him write: 'Anti-Semitism as a political movement should not and cannot be driven by emotions but by facts. The fact, however, is that first of all, the Jewry is a race, not a religious community.' In terms that include all the hallmarks of the vile anti-Semitism that he would preach in the years to come, Hitler elaborated that Jews could not be Germans, stating further: '[The Jew is a] leech upon the peoples of the world.... And from this follows: [the end goal of] rational anti-Semitism must be, without any compromise, the removal of the Jews. Only a government of national will can be capable of both.'[2]

Five months prior to composing the letter, Hitler had still been serving the Soviet Republic. Relatively little is known about his time in the final days of the Bolshevik republic and its immediate aftermath. Hitler made sure figuratively and quite possibly also literally to burn any traces of his activities during this period. Whatever these had been, it did not take long before he had swiftly turned on some of his comrades from those fateful days in April by becoming an informer on Communist activities in his unit for an investigation commission into the Munich Soviet Republic. Whether true or not, Amann would later claim that he had to face Hitler when being discharged, as Hitler's task was to interview members of his demobilization unit about their involvement in the Soviet Republic.[3] No evidence has survived that would allow us to tell whether Hitler became an informer because he had been given the choice either to turn on his comrades from the days of the Soviet Republic or to be targeted himself, or whether he volunteered, ready with a story of how he had supposedly hidden his true self under Communist rule.

From his position as informer, he had proceeded to take one of Mayr's courses that trained soldiers to carry out counter-revolutionary education among the troops, though not as an education officer as he wants us to believe in *Mein Kampf*, or as Max Amann would tell US interrogators after the Second World War.[4] After completing his course, Private Hitler started to work for the propaganda unit of the army in Munich, where he discovered that his confused and disoriented political ideas could flourish. The unit allowed him to distance himself from his apparent flirtation with left-wing ideas during the revolutionary period through a 100 per cent commitment to political ideas at the other end of the political spectrum. It was also there that the mutually contradictory parts of his political make-up were channelled in a direction which were soon to lead him into the lap of the National Socialists. Yet as Captain Mayr's own political future would reveal, the path from the propaganda unit in which Hitler served did not inevitably lead to a Fascist future. In fact, as we shall see, even when Hitler was writing his spiteful letter in September 1919, he was among a group of men whose political futures were still wide open, as long as they combined some kind of nationalism with forms of collectivism.

Unlike the majority of the men of the List Regiment who had long been discharged and had returned to their civilian lives, Hitler stayed in the army until March 1920. However, it would be wrong to portray those who like

Hitler were not immediately demobilized as proto-Fascist Hitler clones. Infact, in the Bavarian election of 1919, for which special election districts had been set up for soldiers who were still based in military barracks and military hospitals, the overwhelming majority of soldiers voted for the Social Democrats (72.5 per cent). Eisner's party received only 7 per cent of the vote, while the radical Right received virtually no votes at all.[5] In other words, proto-Fascist ideology did not resonate with the overwhelming majority of soldiers still in the army. The election results from the special election districts also shed further light on Hitler's own political convictions. The fact that hardly any soldiers voted for radical right-wing parties in the Bavarian election (which was secret) and that at the same time the soldiers of Hitler's unit elected him as one of their representatives on two successive occasions in early 1919 strongly suggests that Hitler's peers did not view him as standing on the extreme right at that point. In contrast to this time, once he had started to work for the counter-revolutionary unit, Hitler was out of step with most of the men who had stayed in the army, if we can believe the testimony Max Amann would give to US interrogators in 1947.

Amann recalled a chance encounter with Hitler in Munich in the post-revolutionary period. On that occasion, Hitler had told him of his post as a propagandist in the army: ' "I give talks against Bolshevism." I asked him if they interested the soldiers. "Unfortunately not", said [Hitler], "it's pointless. I don't like doing it on a continuing basis." ' According to Amann, Hitler had said that officers, in particular, had no ears for his warnings about the dangers Germany was apparently facing. 'They interested the soldiers more than the old majors, whom they didn't interest at all.' Hitler clearly must have thought that even ordinary soldiers were not particularly interested in his endeavours as otherwise he would not have deemed his talks useless. His point was that the officers disapproved of his talks even more than ordinary soldiers, stating: 'I give talks to groups of soldiers up to the size of a battalion, [but] the majors do not enjoy them at all. They would prefer if I entertained the soldiers with a dancing bear, but that I don't like and that is why I will leave.'[6]

Private Hitler's job in Mayr's unit included the observation of the activities of small political groups. On 12 September 1919, Mayr ordered him to monitor a meeting of an obscure little party: the German Workers' Party. Hitler immediately fell in love with the party and joined it within a week.[7] The party provided Hitler with a new arena for his activities and it offered him a way out of his current post in the army that he had quite obviously not enjoyed because of the uninterested response to his speaking engagements. Furthermore, his joining of the German Workers' Party helped Hitler to avoid encroaching solitude as most men from regimental HQ of the List Regiment were no longer in the army and had returned to their respective civilian lives. The unit which he had served as a councillor after the war, meanwhile, had been compromised through its involvement with Niekisch's regime and the Soviet Republic. To be sure, Hitler tried as far as he could to stay in touch with his immediate former comrades in regimental HQ, to whom he had shown affection, and would continue to do so, by giving them paintings, drawings, photographs, or later presents such as watches. Moreover, for a while after the war, when Hitler had nowhere else to go he stayed in the apartment of Hans Mend. He also visited Josef Inkofer, one of his fellow dispatch runners, several times, as well as on two occasions Franz Küspert, who had served with him in regimental HQ.[8] However, he was fighting a losing battle in his attempt to resurrect his 'family' from the war, as the support staff of regimental HQ no longer formed a cohesive social network since its members were scattered all over Bavaria. Hitler's 'families' from the war and the revolutionary period did not exist any longer, while the post-revolutionary army had ultimately proved insufficiently welcoming to him and had lost its appeal. On 31 March 1920, Private Hitler was thus formally discharged after spending more than 2,050 days in the army.[9]

In the German Workers' Party, Hitler found a new home and social network. Soon after joining it, he had become the star of the party, soon to be renamed National Socialist German Workers' Party (NSDAP). Hitler had finally found his calling. With great talent, within three years Hitler turned the NSDAP from one of the many radical right-wing political groups that had been mushrooming on the political fringes of Munich in the aftermath of the Soviet Republic into Bavaria's leading right-wing protest party.

It still needs repeating that Hitler's path from the end of the war to right-wing extremism by late 1919 was atypical not only of his regiment, but also of those veterans who, by the time of the first anniversary of Armistice Day, like Hitler, had ended up at the far right of the political spectrum. While they tended to have served in *Freikorps* units against the Munich Soviet Republic, Hitler had—at least formally—served both Niekisch's regime and the Munich Soviet. His decision to join anti-revolutionary hyper-nationalists might thus well have been driven as much by opportunism as by deeply held political convictions. The best life-saving strategy for anybody involved in the Soviet Republic was naturally to join their strongest opponents.

While building up the Nazi Party, Hitler turned to the members of regimental HQ for advice and support. He now set out to recruit them and thus to merge his old and new 'families', that is, the men of regimental HQ and the inner circle of his party. This might be read, first and foremost, as an attempt not to lose his 'ersatz' family from the war but it was likely to have been more than that. The organizational structure of regimental HQ was the only functioning organization Hitler had ever encountered. He thus tried to replicate in his new party the way regimental HQ had been run and for that he needed to recruit the men of regimental HQ.

Soon Hitler had persuaded Ernst Schmidt and Max Amann to enlist in the NSDAP. As early as 1 March 1920, Schmidt joined as party member No. 858, while at the same time continuing to be a member of a Social Democratic trade union.[10] Like Hitler, Schmidt, who had been his closest associate during the revolutionary period, was thus fluctuating between collectivist ideologies of the Left and the Right.

Hitler also visited Jackl Weiß at his home in the Upper Bavarian countryside in the late autumn of 1919 whom he had not seen since the end of the war and asked him to join his political movement. If we can believe a propaganda account of the visit from 1933, Hitler said to his former comrade: 'Jackl, I already have seven men and soon I'll have a million.'[11] Amann, meanwhile, had started to work for a small mortgage bank after his discharge from the army in August 1919. In the early summer of 1921, Hitler approached Amann and asked his former superior from the war to join him and run the machinery of his new party, telling him that his current staff was incompetent. Hitler had some persuading to do, as Amann was worried about losing a safe job and a pension to support his wife and young son. After a long monologue by Hitler about the imminent danger of Bolshevism, stressing that his pension would not be safe anyway in the event of a Bolshevik revolution, Amann gave in. Hitler had won over the staff sergeant of RIR 16, who now could help to model the organization of his new party on regimental HQ of the List Regiment. Hitler made Amann the managing director of the NSDAP. A year later, in 1922, Amann also became managing director of the Franz Eher Publishing House, the publishing house of the party, and turned it into a propaganda machine. He now spent the mornings with the publishing house and afternoons in the party administration.[12] Adolf Hitler and Max Amann, the two men from regimental HQ of the List Regiment, had teamed up to construct the party that would bring war and genocide to Europe: Hitler knew how to speak and incite, Amann how to run a business.

Hitler also recruited Arthur Rödl for his movement. Unlike other veterans who only temporarily served in a *Freikorps* during the revolutionary period of 1919, Rödl had found his calling in the Freikorps Oberland in which he was to serve until 1927. Furthermore, in 1921, during the 'Polenaufstand' Rödl was to serve in Upper Silesia in the contested German–Polish borderlands.[13] Unlike the majority of the veterans of RIR 16, Rödl really did fulfil all the stereotypes of a veteran brutalized by the war,[14] who had developed a permanent war mentality.

Hitler also managed to recruit Karl Ostberg, who had served with him in the same company at the beginning of the war. Ostberg, a policeman in Munich, became one of the first members of the NSDAP. Holding the highly prestigious membership No. 56, he joined the party as early as March 1920. When a Nazi Party court was set up in 1926, Hitler appointed him as one of its three judges. During the 1920s, Ostberg also made a name for himself as one of Munich's foremost National Socialist thugs. For instance, in 1928 he stormed into an opera performance of which he disapproved and threw stink bombs at members of the orchestra. On another occasion, he was injured in a brawl with political opponents. Ostberg was also notorious for secretly putting up anti-Semitic posters, calling for anti-Jewish violence, all over Munich. The city's police found as many as 300,000 anti-Semitic pamphlets in his apartment during a house search in 1929.[15]

Max Amann, meanwhile, offered in vain the post of arts editor of the Nazi Party newspaper, the *Völkischer Beobachter*, to Alexander Moritz Frey, to whose anti-war novel and short stories Amann must have been oblivious.[16]

Despite the setback of Frey's refusal to join their ranks, Hitler seems to have genuinely believed that after the war and the revolution, the men of his regiment saw the world the same way as he did. With this in mind, he attended a reunion of the veterans' association of the List Regiment in 1922. In the run-up to the reunion, he had already contacted his immediate former comrades and asked them to attend the function.[17] However, at the get-together, he encountered resistance in his attempts to recruit the men of RIR 16 for his cause, to an extent he had not anticipated. For instance, he approached Fritz Wiedemann, who had become a farmer in rural Bavaria. Hitler asked the former regimental adjutant, for whom he had, according to an FBI report, 'developed a dog-like affection and adoration' during the war, if he wanted to help build up the SA. Wiedemann flatly turned down the offer.[18]

The officer whom Hitler most vigorously tried to enlist for his new party was Anton von Tubeuf, who had led RIR 16 for much of 1917 and 1918. Since 1919, Tubeuf had lived in retirement in Bad Aibling, halfway between Munich and the Austrian border, attending to his orchard, his roses, and his bees.[19] While most of the front-line soldiers of RIR 16 had hated him and while one of the commanders of RD 6 had stated that he possessed a 'a slight trait of malevolence',[20] Hitler adored him, possibly for his 100 per cent dedication to the war and for his willingness always to go the extra mile, and his decisive leadership at a time when the regiment had been on the verge of collapse. Even once in power, Hitler always sent him a telegram on his birthday.[21] During the Second World War, Hitler was to say that only once Tubeuf had joined RIR 16 'did we finally [get] a regimental commander of calibre'.[22] Hitler's praise for Tubeuf, of course, is also a good indicator of what he really thought of all the other regimental commanders of the List Regiment.

Hitler's and Tubeuf's esteem for each other was mutual. Tubeuf had been impressed by the dedication and conscientiousness of Hitler's service as a dispatch runner.[23] In 1922, he stated: '[Hitler] became closest to me out of all the men, and in private conversation I was happy to hear his great love of the Fatherland, as well as his fair, well-reasoned patriotic views. I wish him all the best in life.'[24] Nevertheless, Tubeuf's staunch conservatism and Hitler's political convictions only partially overlapped. Unlike Amann and Schmidt, Tubeuf proved resistant to the offer to join ranks with Hitler and continued to be so once Hitler was in power.[25]

Private Hitler did not prove any more successful in his attempts to recruit other officers from the List Regiment than he had been with Wiedemann and Tubeuf. Whilst sometimes encountering sympathy, Hitler ran up against a brick wall in his efforts to talk them into joining his party. The great majority of the officers of RIR 16 never were to join the Nazi Party.

At the 1922 reunion, Hitler also tried to recruit RIR 16 veterans who came from beyond the numbers of the officers of his unit and the men of regimental HQ, in other words from beyond his personal contacts from the war. However, as he came to realize, most of the veterans cold-shouldered Hitler the 'rear area pig' and had no intention of becoming his brothers-in-politics.

While lending no ear to Hitler, the veterans present at the reunion, meanwhile attentively listened to Wilhelm Diess, who delivered the main address at the event. They were captivated by Diess, a gifted storyteller and lawyer and, in many ways, the quintessential non-Hitler: educated, good-humoured, and a non-racist Bavarian and German patriot. After the war, Diess, whose wartime posts had included that of military commander of Fournes and officer in charge of the dispatch runners of RIB 12, including Adolf Hitler, married a woman, who according Hitler's criteria was a 'half-Jew'. During the Second World War, as we shall see, Diess was to join an anti-Hitler resistance group. While the veterans of RIR 16 were enthralled by Diess, their response to Hitler was so lukewarm that the aspiring dictator never again attended a meeting of the veterans' association of the List Regiment.[26]

The 1 November 1920 issue of *Das Bayerland*, a bi-weekly magazine publishing articles about the history and culture of Bavaria and edited by Fridolin Solleder, could have already given Hitler a hint that the men active in the veterans' association of RIR 16 were politically heterogeneous and not likely universally to embrace his ideology. The issue published the war memories of eight veterans of the List Regiment. The articles were also published as a stand-alone publication, which celebrated Albert Weisgerber, rather than Adolf Hitler, by placing his photo on the cover (see Plate 13). The articles were also to form the nucleus of the much more extensive regimental history published in 1932. They described the war in many different and varied voices. One article was by Adolf Meyer, who later was to single himself out with his staunchly pro-Hitler memoirs. However, another article celebrated the Christmas Truce, which Hitler had treated with disdain. Two of the remaining articles were written by Wilhelm Diess, and by another of Hitler's opponents during the years of the Third Reich: Georg Dehn, Albert Weisgerber's friend, who was to emigrate to South America during the years of Hitler's power. Fridolin Solleder, meanwhile, was from 1919 to 1933 a member of the pro-Weimar German Democratic Party (the DDP).[27]

Even once the Nazi Party grew in popularity, the great majority of the men of the List Regiment stayed well clear of Hitler's party. While most of his immediate comrades from regimental HQ joined the Nazi Party,[28] their behaviour is not representative of the regiment at large.

There have been some attempts to look at the careers of Nazi leaders and to conclude from them that the First World War had turned the veterans of the Great War into Nazis, as a great number of National Socialist leaders had served in the First World War. Rudolf Hess, Hitler's deputy, for instance, had been, like Hitler, a war volunteer in a Bavarian unit during the Great War.[29] Rudolf Höss, the future commander of Auschwitz, meanwhile, had served in a German unit in the Middle East in the First World War and after the war became a committed *Freikorps* soldier, and joined the Nazi Party as early as 1922.[30] However, the flaw in looking at the biographies of leading Nazis to identify the origins of National Socialism is that, of course, the great majority of Nazis born before 1900, just as the great majority of German men born before the turn of the century, had served in the Great War. The important point here is that these men were born prior to 1900 and thus subject to military service during the war. While almost all Nazi leaders born before 1900 naturally served in the war, the majority of men who fought in the war did not join the Nazi Party later in their lives.

In fact, the generation that had been too young to fight in the First World War, men such as Werner Best, the future Nazi administrator of occupied Denmark in the Second World War who had been born in 1903, were far more likely to join the Nazi Party than the veterans of the First World War.[31] It was thus non-service in the war and a feeling of having been cheated from an opportunity to serve, rather than the experience of combat and an alleged brutalization during the First World War,[32] which increased the likelihood of German men joining Private Hitler's party. As Erhard Auer, the Bavarian Social Democratic leader during the revolution, was to remind pro-Republic war veterans on 22 February 1931, unlike their own party, Hitler's party primarily consisted of people 'who during the war had not even yet attended school'.[33]

Of a sample of 623 veterans who had served in the 1st Company of the List Regiment, only 17 per cent of veterans joined the Nazi Party at any point between 1919 and 1945.[34] In total approximately 10 per cent of the German population joined the Nazi Party. However, the overwhelming majority of party members were male.[35] If we thus exclude women and boys who were not old enough to join Hitler's party, the percentage of List veterans who became members of the NSDAP was well in line with the adult male population of Germany. It is likely to have stood even slightly below the national average. This figure clearly disproves the idea that the regiment as a whole 'made' Hitler or that Hitler's political radicalization was typical of the men of the regiment.

Even fewer members of the regiment joined the SS. Of a sample of 984 veterans who served in 1st Company, only two joined the SS at any time during the existence of the SS.[36] One of the two veterans was Karl Ostberg, the fellow dispatch runner and early follower of Hitler. The former policeman and NCO in RIR 16 was indeed one of the most important men in the early history of the SS. By 1932, he had risen to become a Sturmbannführer in the 1st SS Standarte and was in charge of political indoctrination of the unit.[37] Unfortunately, it can no longer be established how many veterans of RIR 16 joined the SA.[38]

The overwhelming majority even of those veterans of Hitler's regiment who did join the Nazi Party did so only after 1933. Of the sample of 623 veterans from 1st Company under investigation, only two men joined the Nazi Party prior to 1923, that is, between the foundation of the Party and the Hitler putsch. The two men were Hitler himself and Karl Ostberg. Between 1925, when the ban on the Nazi Party was lifted, and Hitler's rise to power in 1933, only another eleven of the 623 men under examination joined the NSDAP. In other words, prior to the birth of the Third Reich, only 2 per cent of all veterans of RIR 16 underwent a politicization that matched that of Private Hitler. Neither the politicization of Hitler, nor the evolution of National Socialism thus have their roots in the List Regiment or in similar German First World War units.

With the exception of Hitler's immediate peers from regimental HQ,[39] factors such as class and religious affiliation, rather than the war experience in RIR 16, were decisive for those veterans who chose to join the Nazi Party. The military rank of soldiers or the act of war volunteering did not significantly affect the probability of veterans joining the NSDAP. There is hardly any variance between veterans of different rank as far as the likelihood of joining the Nazi Party is concerned. Men of Hitler's rank (Gefreiter) were no more, and no less likely, to join the Nazi Party than men of any other rank. War volunteers were even marginally less likely than conscripted men to enter the Nazi Party. Furthermore, there was no discernible difference between NCOs and privates (both infantrymen and Gefreite) in their likelihood of joining Hitler's party. In other words, if we understand promotion in the war and the act of war volunteering as an indicator of the attitudes of soldiers towards the war, then these figures strongly suggest that different war experiences and attitudes of soldiers towards the conflict did not influence their decision to join, or not to join, Hitler's party.[40] Maybe surprisingly, there is no significant correlation either between the age of soldiers and their likelihood of joining the Nazi Party. Even the youngest among the men of RIR 16 were not more likely to join ranks with Hitler than the average.[41]

However, the religious background of soldiers had a huge impact on the odds that veterans would become members of Hitler's party. For instance, Protestant veterans were almost twice as likely to become a member of the NSDAP as Catholic ones. The regional background of veterans also strongly influenced the likelihood of members of RIR 16 joining the Nazi Party. While there was little variance between the behaviour of soldiers from southern Bavarian and other Catholic regions of Bavaria—the figures for these regions are slightly below the regimental average of 17 per cent—one in three of the veterans from predominantly Protestant Upper and Middle Franconia joined the NSDAP. In fact, more than half (55.6 per cent) of the Protestant veterans from Upper Franconia joined the Nazi Party, while only 15.8 per cent of Catholic veterans from Lower Bavaria joined. Put differently, between 80 and 90 per cent of those veterans from Lower and Middle Franconia who joined Hitler's party were Protestant. Significantly, due to Hitler's Austrian background, the likelihood of soldiers residing abroad joining the Nazi Party was well in line with the regimental average.[42]

The general rule was that the more rural the background of a soldier, the less likely it was that he would join ranks with Hitler. 13.9 per cent of the RIR 16 veterans who came from villages (the figure for villages with less than 100 inhabitants was even only 12.0 per cent) joined the Nazi Party, while 16.1 per cent of soldiers from small to medium-size towns became members of NSDAP. The figure for bigger towns and cities was 20.5 per cent, which was also the figure for Munich. We see again here that factors unrelated to a soldier's war experience determined the likelihood that a veteran would join Hitler. However, it needs to be stressed that the overwhelming majority of veterans from rural and urban backgrounds alike did not enter Hitler's party.[43]

There was a huge variance between veterans in their likelihood of joining the Nazi Party according to their occupational background: while only 8.5 per cent of agricultural labourers, and 9.2 per cent of farmers joined the Nazi Party, the figure for business and property owners was 33.3 per cent, for professionals and academics 26.6 per cent, and for white-collar workers 25.5 per cent. The figure for tradesmen and craftsmen, meanwhile, was 18.6 per cent, for blue-collar workers 21.7 per cent, and for non-agricultural servants and day labourers 4.5 per cent. None of the university and high-school students within a sample of 623 soldiers from 1st Company joined the Nazi Party.[44] The variance we see in these figures cannot be explained in detail here. However, it underlines the fact that social class (and religion), rather than service in Hitler's unit, determined the likelihood that veterans would join the party of their former brother-in-arms. National Socialism was at its core a social movement,[45] which explains why religious and class affiliations, rather than the experience of war and violence, determined the likelihood that the men of Hitler's regiment would join his party.

Despite the fact that the NSDAP had been founded in Munich and even though the home of the List Regiment would be celebrated during the Third Reich as the 'City of the Movement', the great majority of the Munich populace, like the veterans of RIR 16, shunned Private Hitler's party. Even a 1936 National Socialist guidebook to Munich alludes to the fact that initially little love was lost between the inhabitants of Munich and the Nazi Party. It claims that the populace of Munich preferred to listen to foreign (*volksfremde*) rather than to National Socialist ideas, concluding: '[Munich] was the city that refused, out of its conservative smugness . . . the offer of salvation in Adolf Hitler's movement.'[46]

Even though the majority of Hitler's peers from the war displayed no interest in joining ranks with Hitler, his star continued to rise in the early 1920s. The Treaty of Versailles, the punitive peace treaty Germany was forced to sign in late June 1919, further helped his fortunes. However, it was neither the harshness of the treaty nor France's staunch stand towards Germany that helped Hitler most decisively. Hitler could only thrive because the powers on the winning side of the war managed to agree to harsh peace terms and to make the new German government sign up to them but then disagreed over whether the terms should really be implemented. The victorious powers had thus inadvertently weakened the German government as it was now easy for Hitler to portray the members of the German government as traitors to their own people for agreeing to terms that, as it seemed, even the British and Americans deemed excessive.

The letter that one of Hitler's former comrades from regimental HQ wrote to Hitler in April 1923 is emblematic of Hitler's rising fortunes: 'My dearest Hitler, whoever has had the opportunity to follow you from the foundation of the movement until today cannot hide their adoration of your character. . . . You have achieved what no other German man could have achieved, and we your comrades from the front stand ready to serve your will. Thousands upon thousands of men feel the same.'[47] Hitler shared with the veteran who had written to him a grossly inflated sense of how much support he had among the German population. In November 1923, he thus felt so assured of his support that he decided the time was ripe for a *coup d'état*.

Inspired by Mussolini's march on Rome, Hitler planned a march on Berlin, which took off from one of Munich's beer halls on 9 November 1923. Hitler was joined in his putsch by Erich von Ludendorff, Germany's third most powerful man during the second half of the war. By coincidence, Alois Schnelldorfer was in Munich on the day of Hitler's attempted putsch, as he had to run errands in the Bavarian capital. At the time, Schnelldorfer did not know much about Hitler's policy goals. However, he considered joining Hitler on his march once he heard that his former comrade from regimental HQ was in the city to try to seize power. He thus waited in the square in front of Munich's City Hall for Hitler's march to arrive. Yet once Hitler arrived in the square, Schnelldorfer changed his mind about Private Hitler and his plan of joining him when he saw Ludendorff, whom he despised. Schnelldorfer decided that a political movement supported by Ludendorff could be up to no good and just walked off, never to join the Nazi Party.[48]

Within minutes of Schnelldorfer's decision to keep his distance from his erstwhile wartime comrade, Hitler's march on Berlin turned into a farce. It ended after just another few hundred metres when Bavarian police—commanded by Michael Freiherr von Godin, the brother of the former commander of Hitler's regiment who had awarded the Iron Cross 1st Class to Hitler—opened fire on Hitler and his followers extremely close to the spot where Hitler had stood on Odeonsplatz in 1914 on the outbreak of war. A number of Nazis were shot dead, while many of Hitler's co-conspirators, including Erich von Ludendorff, were arrested. Hitler himself was put in custody the following day.[49]

At his trial, Hitler made the most of his service in the war. He used the Munich courtroom in which the proceedings against him took place as a stage to tell the world how dangerous his service had been and how the First World War had given birth to National Socialism. In the event, Hitler's sentence was light, only five years' imprisonment, of which the last four and a half years were suspended.[50] When Max Amann was eventually also tried for his involvement in the putsch, he claimed that he was an apolitical businessman and escaped with a mere fine of 100 gold marks, or ten days' imprisonment, for an 'illegal assumption of official authority'.[51]

While Hitler received an astonishingly light prison term for his attempt to bring the Weimar government down and while both Bavarian state institutions and the Bavarian People's Party (which headed the Bavarian government from 1920 until 1933) included individuals who only half-heartedly accepted modern democracy and occasionally were openly hostile to it, it is also true that the Bavarian police was the only German state authority ever to shoot at Hitler and that the Nazi Party was outlawed after the failed coup. Even though Bavarian state authorities tended to rein in radicals on the radical Left far more harshly than radicals at the other end of the political spectrum, ultimately, successive Bavarian governments successfully met the challenges posed to the Weimar Republic by both the radical Left and the radical Right between 1918 and 1933.

As a result of his involvement in Hitler's putsch, Karl Ostberg, for instance, had to leave his post in the Munich police in early 1924. Meanwhile, Arthur Rödl, who was to be awarded a 'Blutorden' (the highest Nazi Party decoration) for his role on 9 November 1923, had to leave the army. Even those within the BVP who did not fully embrace the Weimar Republic tended to dream of a Bavaria run by Crown Prince Rupprecht in the tradition of Bavaria's pre-war reformist political order rather than a state run by Hitler. Rather than join forces with the Nazi Party, the BVP decided that it was preferable to form a coalition in Bavaria with the liberal-conservative DVP, the party of Gustav Stresemann, the Nobel Peace Laureate and defender of the Weimar Republic. Furthermore, after his release from prison in 1925, the Bavarian government issued a ban on Hitler speaking in public, which was in effect until 1927. After the initial widespread support for the centre Left in Bavaria after the revolution had evaporated, a shift had taken place among the Bavarian electorate towards the centre Right, rather than the far Right. Once the National Socialists seized power in Bavaria away from the BVP-led government in March 1933, they did so by force, unlike at the national level.[52] To label Bavaria in the years of 1920 to 1933 as an 'eldorado for radical right-wing organizations'[53] is thus highly misleading.

Whilst serving his prison sentence in Landsberg fortress, not far from where he had undergone his training in the autumn of 1914, Hitler was visited by Ernst Schmidt, who since moving to the Bavarian countryside in 1922 no longer saw Hitler as often as he once had. Around the time of his visit, Schmidt completed his political journey away from Socialism and Social Democracy to National Socialism. As we have seen, both Hitler and Schmidt had been equally disoriented after the war and had been torn between the promises of different versions of Socialism and nationalism.

However, while Hitler had fully embraced Fascist socialism within months of the fall of the Soviet Republic and had broken with competing political ideologies, Schmidt's political future had remained open for much longer. It was only in the spring of 1924, as Hitler was imprisoned, that Schmidt finally left the Social Democratic trade union and founded a local branch of the Völkischer Block[54] which carried the torch of National Socialism during the period in which the Nazi Party was outlawed (which lasted from 1923 to 1925).

Meanwhile, in Landsberg fortress, Hitler sat down to write *Mein Kampf*. In it, he codified his war experience as the foundational myth of the Nazi movement. He claimed that his four years on the Western Front had provided him with prophet-like revelations that would allow him to lead Germany away from the trauma of defeat, inflicted on a militarily unbeaten nation by 'November criminals', consisting of Socialists, Democrats, and Jews, to salvation: a renewed, classless, and powerful Germany.

In the years to come, Nazi propaganda was to use the post-war story of the men of the List Regiment along the lines sketched out in *Mein Kampf*: namely as the story of a united and heroic band of veterans who supported Hitler. The claim was that the war experience in Hitler's regiment had given all the veterans of RIR 16 the same revelations as Private Hitler and that he was thus a typical product of his regiment. This myth has proved surprisingly resilient to the present day.

In *Mein Kampf*, Hitler used his First World War experience as a rallying cry for the establishment of a new German Empire that would last a millennium: 'For a thousand years to come nobody will dare to speak of heroism without recalling the German Army of the World War. And then from the dim past will emerge the immortal vision of those solid ranks of steel helmets that never flinched and never faltered. And as long as Germans live they will be proud to remember that these men were the sons of their forefathers.'[55] *Mein Kampf* is in many ways Hitler's *Bildungsroman*. The experience of the First World War and the lessons he drew from it provide both the Alpha and the Omega of National Socialism. Written in a terrible, almost unintelligible prose, it, however, provides little more than a laundry list of his convictions, grievances, and prejudices. Distilled down to its essence, his 'laundry list' of why Germany had lost the war was as follows:

• that Jews, Socialists, Democrats had stabbed a victorious army in the back,
• that during the war, 'the Kaiser held out his hand' to 'Jewish' Marxism,
• that the Reichstag had been defeatist and politically fractured,

- that the German press had undermined the German war effort by 'dampening the public spirit', and
- that Germany's universities were 'Jew-ridden'. German universities thus had supposedly fed political and military leaders with erroneous ideas about how to fight a war.[56]

The lessons of defeat and of his own war experience included the following revelations:

- The state has to proceed against Marxism as a Jewish ideology 'leading humanity to its destruction'. Hence there is a need 'to exterminate this vermin'.
- In wartime, there can be no truce or cooperation, not even a tactical one, with Socialists, or any other political group, 'that [is] opposed to the national spirit'. It is 'the duty of any Government . . . to . . . mercilessly [root]' them out.
- Ideologies such as Marxism cannot be destroyed by 'the application of force alone' but can only 'be broken by the use of force [if] this use of force is in the service of a new idea or *Weltanschauung* which burns with a new flame'. The fight against Marxism will thus only succeed if a new *Weltanschauung* based on positive ideas that go beyond the defence of the status quo will employ force 'systematically and persistently'. Without the 'spiritual conviction' of a new ideology, there will inevitably be episodes of 'hesitation' and 'tolerance' which will be counter-productive and ultimately serve to strengthen rather than weaken Marxism because Marxists 'will not only recover strength but every successive persecution will bring to its support new adherents who have been shocked by the oppressive methods employed'.
- The only way to fight Marxism is to set up a new classless nationalist party aimed at rallying the entire German people behind the fight against Marxism, as Hitler thought that the 'proletarian masses' would never join bourgeois parties.
- Parties should be abolished in wartime. Parliament has got to be 'brought to its senses at the point of the bayonet, if necessary' and ideally be 'dissolved immediately'.
- 'When public [war] enthusiasm is once damped, nothing can enkindle it, when the necessity arises. This enthusiasm is an intoxication and must be kept up in that form.' The role of the press thus is 'to raise the pitch of public enthusiasm still higher' in order to 'keep the iron hot'.

- War-waging nations should not care about what 'foreign opinion' thinks about the way they conduct the war and should present their case for war to their own people.[57]

In short, Hitler presented his war experience as having provided him with two sets of revelations: the first one was about how successful wars ought to be waged ideologically, in other words, how, for instance, the press and propaganda have to be directed in wartime and that parties have to be abolished and parliament 'brought to its senses at the point of the bayonet'.[58] The second set is ultimately the more important, as Hitler uses his war experience as the revelatory source of the core of his ideology: namely that a new powerful, classless, and prosperous Germany can only be established if Germany rids herself and the world of Marxism and the Jews, for, as Hitler put it, 'there is no such thing as coming to an understanding with the Jews. It must be the hard-and-fast "Either-Or".'[59]

Ever since the day *Mein Kampf* was delivered to the first bookshop, there has been fierce disagreement over the significance of Hitler's book. Positions range from the belief that *Mein Kampf* provided a blueprint for the Third Reich, the Second World War, and the Holocaust that was systematically and gradually implemented over time, to a position according to which Hitler's positions and policies evolved only gradually. According to the latter view, Hitler had only laid out a rough programme that was often contradictory in character and used strong, metaphorical language that was at that point still bare of any genocidal intent.[60]

An equally interesting question as the one about what objectively Hitler's intent was at this point, is what other people including the veterans of the List Regiment—few of them actually ever read the extremely tedious and long-winded *Mein Kampf* even if they owned a copy—thought Hitler's intent was. Whatever Hitler's real intent, most Germans did not take *Mein Kampf* literally, at any rate not his anti-Semitism. Hitler was to come to power not because of, but in spite of his crude and virulent anti-Semitism.[61]

In late 1924, Hitler was released from prison and shortly thereafter, the ban on the NSDAP was lifted. As a foreigner, Hitler, however, had to fear deportation from Germany, as he was now an ex-convict. Yet Hitler's Iron Cross, above everything else, saved him from repatriation to Austria. Whatever the real background behind his Iron Cross had been, it allowed him to make the claim that he was German. He declared that since he had risked his life for more than four years serving in the German Army, he had already earned German citizenship and therefore would refuse to beg for it.[62] The Austrian authorities, meanwhile, argued that they would not admit Hitler back into the country on the grounds that he had lost his citizenship by serving in a foreign army during the war.[63]

Once the threat of deportation had been averted, Hitler immediately set out to rebuild his party. However, he soon realized that his ideas still failed to resonate with the German public. In the 1925 presidential election, the candidate backed by the Nazis only won the support of 1 per cent of the German electorate, while in the 1928 Reichstag election, Private Hitler's party received a mere 2.6 per cent of the vote. When the former British ambassador to Germany, Viscount d'Abernon, published his memoirs in 1929, he thought that Hitler had by then been reduced to an irrelevant footnote in history, noting that Hitler had had his fifteen minutes of fame during the Beer Hall putsch of 1923. Hitler, d'Abernon observed, 'was finally released [from Landsberg fortress] after six months and bound over for the rest of his sentence, thereafter fading into oblivion'.[64]

If one thing was clear to Hitler after 1925, it was that he urgently needed to broaden his popular appeal. To that end, he set out to write a new book as well as to start using language in his speeches that would resonate with a larger section of the German population than he had to date. The former endeavour turned into a fiasco but the latter one ultimately proved spectacularly successful, due to Hitler's clever use of the war myth of the List Regiment.

In the book, he set out to explain his foreign-policy goals, including an absurd plan for an Anglo-German alliance that was meant to allow Britain and Germany to divide the world between them.[65] Hitler was either persuaded, or realized himself, that his new book would do more harm than good and that, at any rate, even *Mein Kampf* would not sell well. For instance, in 1928, a mere 3,015 copies of *Mein Kampf* were sold. In the event, Hitler's new book was never published during his lifetime.[66] However, he proved extremely successful in identifying and integrating into his rhetoric those elements of the war experiences of Germans that had an appeal across political and class boundaries.

The single most successful such element was the invocation of the *Frontgemeinschaft* and *Kameradschaft* that had supposedly been the hallmark of the relationship of German soldiers to one another during the war. It was used by Germans of diverse political convictions, ranging from regimental veterans' associations to left-wing groups critical of war as an instrument in international politics (but who still maintained that a *Kameradschaft* of ordinary Germans in opposition to Germany's military and political leadership had existed), as a model for overcoming the fractured, and often sectarian, society of Weimar Germany. *Kameradschaft* was used by some as a rallying cry for a new, strong Germany, and by others as a call for friendship with France, Britain, and America, and for support of the League of Nations. It was indeed celebrated by liberals, conservatives, and the Left alike.[67] In the past, the National Socialists, however, had been strangely absent from this celebration of the virtues of *Frontgemeinschaft* and *Kameradschaft*. Their ideal had been that of a heroic lone warrior.[68]

After his release from Landsberg, Hitler realized how valuable a tool references to *Kameradschaft* and *Frontgemeinschaft* were in broadening his appeal and in propagating the Nazis' own dream of a *Volksgemeinschaft*—or classless community. Soon, talk about the comradeship amongst soldiers in the trenches as the origin of Hitler's vision of a future society took centre stage in National Socialist propaganda.[69] An invocation of *Kameradschaft* was also a perfect tool to further the one idea that the Communist, National Socialist, and other right-wing collectivist revolutions shared: to bring an end to the conflicting nature of human society; in other words to eliminate the liberal credo that conflict is part of human nature and a source of human progress.[70] The irony, of course, was that Communism and Fascism believed far less in compromise and non-violent conflict resolution than Liberal Democracy did. However, the Communist and Fascist habit of seeing any compromise as rotten but at the same time preaching a world free of conflict was perfectly consistent. While Liberal Democracy believed in a fruitful dialectic of conflict and compromise, collectivist ideologies of the Left and the Right believed that a conflict-free universal or nationalist egalitarian world was only possible if competing ideologies were wiped off the map of the earth.[71] When Communists, Liberal Democrats, and Fascists thus invoked the ideals of wartime *Kameradschaft* they hence ultimately meant very different things. However, all played towards a general popular longing for a less fractured society. This allowed ideologues on either side of the political spectrum to appeal to sections of society who hitherto had not been seduced by the temptations of right-wing or left-wing extremism.

It was hence here in the constant celebration of *Kameradschaft* that the war myth of the List Regiment became more central than it had ever been in the early years of the Nazi Party. Hitler shamelessly invented a version of his experiences in the List Regiment during the war that allowed him to recount how he himself had experienced the comradeship of the *Frontge-meinschaft* and how he had used these experiences to develop his ideas about what form Germany's future should take. This is the reason why, over time, invoking Hitler's war experience became more and more central for Nazi propaganda. And this is one of the reasons why the Nazis were to be so assertive in trying to discredit or silence anybody who pointed out that the reality of life in the List Regiment had been rather different from what Private Hitler made it out to be and that, in fact, his regiment had been a heterogeneous, often disunited, unit.

It was thus really in the period of 1925 to 1933 that the myth of the List Regiment took centre stage in Hitler's rhetoric and that his references to the war in general increased. For instance, in the foreword that he provided for a nationalist book in 1931, he described 'the western front [as the place] where the belief in the old Reich was shattered on barbed wire and in drum-fire—and where, out of the crater fields in blood and fire, in hunger and death, the new belief in a better Germany was born.'[72]

Nazi propaganda now preached up and down the country that Hitler's service as an ordinary front-line soldier who had bravely met the challenges of combat for more than four years gave him special legitimacy to speak for the generation that had served in the war and to make himself heard in politics. As a Nazi regional newspaper put it, it was in the First World War 'that Adolf Hitler earned the right, with blood and mire, to speak for the generation that had served at the front and to fulfill the legacies of the two million killed in action.'[73]

Hitler and Nazi propaganda were aided in their attempt to widen Hitler's public appeal by a shift that had occurred in Western thought in the late eighteenth century. Until then war had been understood, first and foremost, in religious terms. Defeat and victory in battle had been seen as signs of God's displeasure or grace. Even some Catholic soldiers in RIR 16 from the Bavarian countryside still had believed the war to be God's punishment, as we have seen. However, since the late Enlightenment, combat was increasingly understood as a revelatory experience, which had hitherto never been the case. This allowed Hitler to claim that his war experience had revealed a higher truth about himself and about the world, which he believed privileged him as a leader.[74]

The myth of Hitler's war record was now propagated in a myriad of ways. One core element in the propaganda strategy was the publication of memoirs by some of Hitler's comrades. One such memoir was Hans Mend's quasi-hagiographical account of Hitler's war service which was published in 1930 under the title *Adolf Hitler im Felde 1914/18*.[75] In the run-up to Christmas 1931, it was repeatedly praised in the *Völkischer Beobachter* as 'the finest Christmas gift for any supporter of Hitler'[76] and the following year it was widely circulated during the campaign for Hitler's unsuccessful bid for the German presidency.[77] Memoirs such as the one by Mend use the conventions of *Bildungsromane*, telling how the experiences of the First World War 'made' Hitler and how he rose from the ranks of the regiment to save Germany. They also all follow a similar pattern in their insistence that they were apparently apolitical in character. The authors of the memoirs tended to claim that they had been outraged by public accusations against the accuracy of the story Hitler told about his personal war experience, that they were apparently not driven by political considerations at all, and that they simply wanted to put the record straight. Hans Mend wrote in the introduction to his memoirs: 'With this book, I hope to give the German people true and unadorned information about "Adolf Hitler, the front soldier". . . . It is far from me to want to support any particular party in this book, as I myself do not belong to any one of them.'[78]

While the myth of Hitler's war record became ever more central to the attempt to broaden the NSDAP's appeal after 1925, the veterans from RIR 16 who had played an important role in the development of the Nazi Party up to 1923 became marginalized after the rebirth of the Nazi Party in 1925. The reason for this was that they were out of their league in the running of a political party, which is particularly true of Max Amann. Even though he was given the highly symbolic and prestigious membership number 'No. 3' when new NSDAP membership cards were issued in 1925, Amann lost his post as manager of the Nazi Party but stayed at the top of the Nazi publishing empire.[79] Amann's diminished role was a result of his personality, rather than a distancing of Hitler and Amann. Amann always remained at heart the staff sergeant he had been in the List Regiment, which made him a successful businessman but a miserable politician. This became evident when Amann, to whom Goebbels referred behind his back as 'Sergeant director',[80] became National Socialist city councillor in Munich.

During council meetings, Amann had no talent whatsoever as a speaker and debater. Newspapers referred to him as 'the brawling city councillor'. Superficially jovial in character, he could not contain his outbursts of anger towards friends and foes alike, calling anyone he disliked 'Schweinehund',

'Sauhund', or 'Schweinekerl'. He was so excitable that the Munich police refused to issue him a gun permit. In City Hall, he would threaten his political opponents: 'Just wait, fellow—when we come to power, you will be the first to go.' Even fellow Nazis disliked him because of his aggressive, rowdy behaviour. In 1925, they had been adamant that he was not to be reappointed as managing director of the Nazi Party. Amann was feared by his subordinates for his domineering, brutal, and bullish behaviour. He frequently hit or kicked subordinates and shouted at them; on one occasion he even attacked Hermann Esser, Hitler's former propaganda chief, with scissors. His behaviour became such a spectacle that people would stop outside the windows of the Eher Publishing House to watch the former staff sergeant of the List Regiment.[81]

Whereas Max Amann at least did not pose any threat to the evolving myth of Hitler's war experience, the same cannot be said for the majority of the veterans of the List Regiment. As we have already seen, 98 per cent of List veterans did not join Private Hitler's party prior to 1933. Unfortunately, only fragmentary evidence has survived about those veterans who never joined the Nazi Party or one of its organizations. The papers of the veterans' association of the List Regiment (*Vereinigung der ehemaligen Angehörigen des Listregiments*) no longer seem to exist. They were quite possibly destroyed in a Second World War air raid on Munich which inflicted heavy damage on the collections of the Bavarian State Library, where some of the association's papers seem to have been kept. Moreover, the membership files of political parties other than the NSDAP and of national veteran associations have not survived either. However, scattered in collections around the world, sufficient evidence about the veterans of Hitler's regiment still exists, which once put together produces a conclusive picture of a heterogeneous body of veterans that does not live up to the myth Hitler was trying to propagate.

We have already seen, while discussing both the 1922 RIR 16 reunion and the 1920 *Bayerland* articles commemorating the war service of the men of the List Regiment, that those veterans who joined the official regimental veterans' association were heterogeneous in their backgrounds and convictions. Furthermore, Fridolin Solleder, even though a member of the staunchly pro-Weimar DDP, was the deputy chairman of the veterans' association,[82] which further supports the idea that the men of his regiment were not politicized by the war in the way Hitler claimed. The veterans' association also included Siegfried Heumann, the Jewish soldier who had written the lyrics for patriotic songs during the war. Heumann was also active in the 'Reichsbund jüdischer Frontsoldaten', the veterans' association of Jewish soldiers founded in 1919 which at its height had 30,000 members, as well as of the Order of B'nai B'rith, the Jewish community and advocacy organization.[83] His membership provides further evidence that the veterans' association of the List Regiment was politically disparate and was not quintessentially anti-Semitic. Heumann's case, it should be added, was not isolated. For instance, the local veterans' assocation at Ichenhausen, the 'Veteranen-, Krieger und Soldatenverein Ichenhausen', also admitted Jewish veterans.[84] Moreover, in many communities across Germany, Jews and Christians were listed together on local war memorials,[85] while Hugo Günzburger from Memmingen in Swabia, a Jewish owner of a knitwear company who had served together with Hitler in 1st Company at the beginning of the war, was a member of the local rifle club, the 'Kgl. Priv. Schützengesellschaft Memmingen'.[86]

When just before Christmas 1931 the official regimental history of the List Regiment finally appeared, an additional challenge emerged to the foundational myth of Hitler and the Nazi movement. Edited by Fridolin Solleder and following the same formula as the special issue of *Das Bayerland* in 1920, it told the story of the List Regiment through the eyes of various members. Containing extended and rewritten versions of the *Bayerland* articles,[87] it also included an abundance of new contributions, as well as a listing of all 3,637 members of Hitler's regiment who had fallen during the war or died in captivity or as a result of accidents. It also reproduced an order from Gustav Scanzoni von Lichtenfeld, the uncle of the defence lawyer of one of Hitler's opponents. Moreover, the regimental history reproduced, facing the title page, a full-page photo of the memorial window for the List Regiment (see Plate 20) that had been installed in Munich's city hall during the First World War. The inclusion of the memorial window in such a prominent position in the book is remarkable given the criticisms hyper-nationalists had voiced against it during the war. They had found the window distasteful and distorting the truth, arguing that it made the members of RIR 16 look apathetic and that it failed to represent the heroism of the List Regiment. Significantly, one of the protesters, Eugen Roth, did nevertheless contribute and article to the regimental history. It thus included both supporters and critics of the interpretation of the war experience of Hitler's regiment offered by the memorial window.[88] The book also included a number of contributions by Fritz Wiedemann, who in the future was to become one of Hitler's closest allies, and by Georg Eichelsdörfer, who was to join the NSDAP in 1941. With contributions by Solleder, Wiedemann, Meyer, Dehn, and Diess, it thus included both future supporters and staunch opponents of Hitler. Furthermore, Hugo Gutmann, the Jewish officer who had proposed Hitler for his Iron Cross, was mentioned twice in very positive terms. As we have seen earlier, with just over a year to go before Hitler was to come to power, Albert Weisgerber was eulogized in the regimental history, while Hitler was barely mentioned. The awkward and blurred image of Hitler included in the book, meanwhile was taken by Hitler's political adversary Korbinian Rutz, the commander of 1st Company.[89] Another contributor to the regimental history, August Haugg, was a passionate advocate of the Weimar Republic. In 1924, he had published a pro-republican pamphlet entitled *Deutsche Heraus*. In it, he described the Weimar constitution as 'the best constitution that has ever been created'. He argued that the Weimar Republic was the logical end product of two millennia of Germanic traditions of freedom. He also advocated that Germany should further her national interests through trade, rather than through war.[90]

The case of the veterans' association of the List Regiment thus suggests that, just like in France,[91] there was no direct line from the trench experience of German soldiers, via veterans' associations, to Fascism. The politically heterogeneous character of the veterans' club also challenges the idea that post-war Germany had the 'wrong' kind of civil society—in other words, a robust and strong civil society that supposedly helped bring down the Weimar Republic. It is said to have weakened the post-war republic because German voluntary organization had been set up 'within rather than across group boundaries' and were the result of frustration 'with the failures of the national government and political parties'. This is said to have provided fertile ground for the Nazis with their 'unifying appeal and bold solutions to a nation in crisis'.[92] The veterans' organization of the List Regiment, by contrast, had been set up across political boundaries. It is likely, however, to have included only a minority of the veterans of RIR 16—in other words, a self-selected largely middle-class group (in which officers were heavily overrepresented) that was politically diverse but felt a common bond of allegiance through their service in the same regiment.

The majority of veterans of RIR 16 probably either did not join any veterans' associations, were members of associations critical of war, or they were active in the local veterans' associations of the villages and towns in which they lived. This was partly a result of the great distances that veterans would have had to travel to attend reunions of the List Regiment at a time of economic hardship. Maybe more significantly, a large number of veterans are likely to have felt no particular *esprit de corps* towards RIR 16 as they served with the regiment only for a short period of time. Furthermore, during the war the men of the List Regiment had felt, as we have seen, allegiance and attachment to the men of their core groups rather than to the regiment as a whole. It is also highly likely that many soldiers had not forgotten those instances when soldiers of one company had stolen from those in another and had competed for the best dugouts. Many RIR 16 veterans in communities across Bavaria thus had more in common with other veterans from their own communities than with the men of the List Regiment. The relative low attendance of the reunion of the List Regiment that was, as we shall see, to take place in 1934 on the twentieth anniversary of the establishment of the regiment, indeed suggests that the veterans of the List Regiment always remained a heterogeneous, disunited group. The regimental veterans' association constituted thus a self-selected subgroup of the members of Hitler's regiment. That the activities of the List Regiment were dominated by the officers of the regiment is unsurprising not only because of the hierarchical character of military units but also because the regiment's officers were more likely to feel an *esprit de corps* towards the regiment than ordinary soldiers, as, unlike them, officers had always been members not only of a company but also of the officer corps of the entire regiment.

A significant number of veterans of the List Regiment were also likely to have been members of the paramilitary groups that stood politically close to the Bavarian People's Party and the Social Democrats. These groups had been set up specifically in response and opposition to the activities of Private Hitler and other extremists on either side of the political spectrum. In the early 1930s, the 'Bayernwacht', the BVP-backed paramilitary group, had a membership of 30,000.[93] Unfortunately, today it is impossible to tell how many RIR 16 veterans joined the 'Bayernwacht'. The same is true for the 'Reichsbanner Schwarz-Rot-Gold', founded in 1924. Standing close to the Social Democrats, it understood itself as a 'Bund republikanischer Kriegs-teilnehmer' (League of Republican Combatants). By the time of its first official meeting in early July 1924, the Munich chapter of the Reichsbanner already had 2,500 members, and consisted of 27 subsections. By the early 1930s, membership had swollen to 2,800. The Reichsbanner thus had more members in the city that was the home of Hitler's regiment than the SA, which had a membership of approximately 2,400 in 1932. As the Munich police concluded in 1931: 'A growth in the Reichsbanner is making itself known everywhere.' Local groups of the Reichsbanner were also set up in towns and villages across Bavaria. For instance, by the early 1930s, the local Reichsbanner chapter in Hausham, a village on the outer reaches of the Alps, had between forty and fifty members. The goal of the Reichsbanner was to foster international cooperation, collective security, and the prevention of future wars. It was by far the most successful veterans' association of inter-war Germany. Within a year, it had attracted a million members. According to some estimates, the membership was even higher than that. The Reichsbanner was even backed by the Centre Party until the end of the 1920s, while the Left Liberals were also in support of it; in other words, the Reichsbanner was supported by the parties that in 1919 had found such overwhelming support in the recruitment region of the List Regiment.[94]

Rather astonishingly, one of the men who joined the Reichsbanner was the man often seen as Hitler's political mentor.[95] This man was Karl Mayr, Hitler's commanding officer from the propaganda unit of the army in Munich who also joined the Social Democratic Party. Mayr eventually became one of the leading and most outspoken voices of the *Reichsbanner-Zeitung*, the periodical of the association. Hitler's former boss argued time and time again that the lesson of the First World War was that the European nations could only solve their future in cooperation with each other, rather than by war.[96] While Mayr and Hitler had once been politically close, Mayr's political journey thus had ultimately led in a very different direction from Hitler's, even though Mayr continued to describe himself as a 'national Socialist'—but as one spelt without a capital 'n'.[97] Like Hitler and Ernst Schmidt, after the war Mayr had been torn between anti-Semitic right-wing collectivism and left-wing ideas.[98] However, unlike Hitler and Schmidt, Mayr ended up in the SPD-backed veterans' association that had been formed in defence of the Weimar Republic. Mayr's and Schmidt's political journeys thus underline the argument that Hitler had been part of a political milieu after the war that had not been fixed and allowed its members, within certain limits, to develop in different directions. An important subsection of radicals on either side of the political spectrum had indeed displayed a fluidity of ideas in the early years of the Weimar Republic.[99] While Hitler and Schmidt had ultimately ended on the extreme Right, Mayr became a defender of the Weimar Republic.

When in early 1931, republicans grew increasingly worried about the danger of a renewed Nazi *coup d'état*, Mayr passionately addressed the Munich branch of the Reichsbanner on 22 February. So many members had come that day that two parallel meetings had to be held in two of Munich's biggest beer halls, which were decorated in the colours of the Republic for the occasion. According to police reports, between 2,100 and 2,500 people attended the two meetings. Amidst frantic applause, Mayr spoke for fifty minutes. In a clear allusion to Hitler's mythical war experience, but draped in language that would not allow Hitler to take him to court, Mayr said that Hitler's 1923 coup had been carried out primarily by those 'who had never seen the trenches, rear area "combatants", men serving with general staffs, profiteers, and poseurs'. The Reichsbanner, by contrast, was full of veterans 'who had experienced all the horrors of modern warfare in the trenches'. The Reichsbanner was directed, he said, against both Bolshevism and Fascism. It was, Mayr told an enthusiastic audience 'the torch-bearer of true nationalism' and 'of the true European alliance of peace'.[100]

It would be wrong to see regimental veterans' associations politically in direct opposition to the Reichsbanner.[101] In reality, the veterans' association of RIR 16 was, as we have seen, a politically heterogeneous entity. It included men, who like the members of the Reichsbanner, were staunch supporters of the Weimar Republic. The tensions that institutionally existed between regimental veterans' associations and the Reichsbanner did not result from irreconcilable attitudes towards the Weimar Republic and democracy; the disagreement was over what role power and military force should play in international relations.

Even though the events of 1919 had brought legitimization to the radical Right and had turned Hitler into a Fascist demagogue, the war had thus not turned the majority of the men of the List Regiment into proto-Fascists, which was well in line with German veterans at large. Indeed twice as many German veterans of the Great War joined the anti-war Reich Association of War Disabled, War Veterans, and War Dependents (including the List veteran who had disrupted a Pan-German meeting in Munich in the spring of 1918) as became members of the *Freikorps*. The great majority of German veterans of the Great War joined neither a *Freikorps* nor a veterans' association.[102] Many agreed with Ferdinand Widman, Hitler's wartime comrade who, as we have seen, confirmed that there had been a growing gulf between the soldiers of regimental HQ and front-line soldiers. In 1932, he wrote to Hitler: 'I hate the war and all that is associated with it; my job has been taken from me, during the inflation my money was taken from me; and to be blamed is only the war, the megalomania [of Germany's leaders], Wilhelm-The-Vanished, and that we did not have a revolution but only a collapse.'[103]

Nazis among the veterans of Hitler's regiment often ran into trouble for their political convictions among their peers. Georg Hammerl, for instance, who lived in a small village 30 kilometres to the north of Munich, complained in 1932 that 'whenever I go to the pub, I get into a political argument because I am a member of the Frontkriegerbund and read the National Socialist Landpost'.[104] Similarly, in 1932, Balthasar Brandmayer claimed that prior to 1931 nobody in his village was attracted to National Socialist ideas and that even then the local farmers were continuing to shun Hitler.[105] Many veterans as well as their peers from the communities in which they lived had thus not been politicized or radicalized even by the traumatic experience of the Soviet Republic. Rather they just continued to live their lives, only sporadically attending meetings of veterans' associations. Furthermore, unlike Hitler, many veterans did not invoke their war experience to justify their political demands. In fact, many of the veterans of the List Regiment only spoke about their time in the war in the presence of their former comrades or of other men from their villages who had served in the war. Other than that, the war was seldom brought up. Many veterans would have agreed with Oscar Daumiller on the subject: 'Everyone has his own wartime experiences. One does not discuss them gladly. But when former comrades get together, then the old memories come to life once again.'[106]

Even though veterans were allowed to visit First World War sites and the graves of their comrades in France from 1924 onwards and even though from 1927 veterans could go on specially organized trips to the locations where they had fought during the war, the great majority of veterans and of the families of fallen soldiers had no urge to visit First World War sites. In fact, only the families of three in every hundred German soldiers killed in the war even enquired to the agency in charge of war graves about the whereabouts of their fallen relatives in the decade between 1920 and 1930.[107]

As Hitler's war years had become so central in his attempt to broaden his public appeal after 1925, it did not take long before his political adversaries began to look for holes in his war tales in an attempt to expose him as a fraud.[108] Hitler's propaganda machine, meanwhile, embarked on a clever and uncompromising campaign in defence of his mythical war experience, realizing how important it was for his political fortunes and legitimacy.

The attack on Hitler's war record intensified during his unsuccessful 1932 campaign for the German presidency, when Upper Bavarians were among the least likely to vote for Private Hitler. As part of the assault on Hitler's war record, on 29 February 1932, the Hamburg Social Democratic newspaper *Echo der Woche* published an article bearing the title 'Kamerad Hitler', that pointed out, as we have seen earlier, that most of Hitler's war stories were fictional. As we have also seen, in order to protect his safety, the *Echo der Woche* did not reveal that the article was written by Korbinian Rutz, the former Commander of Hitler's 1st Company.

Rutz's article argued that Hitler had been an Austrian deserter. Other than that, it closely mirrored Josef Stettner's article in the Braunschweig Social Democratic *Volksfreund*, which was published shortly after the *Echo der Woche* article, stating that Hitler had spent the war in the relative safety of regimental HQ rather than fighting in the first line of fire, that he had probably not fired a single shot himself during the war, and that he had received two Iron Crosses only because he was on intimate terms with the people who had the right to propose soldiers for honours.[109]

Hitler, immediately realizing the great threat to his legitimacy posed by the article, lost no time in bringing a libel suit against the *Echo der Woche* in early 1932. He emerged victorious from the lawsuit, due to his smart legal and propaganda strategy, thus turning a potentially extremely dangerous situation into a triumph. He concentrated on the one glaring error in the article, namely that he was allegedly an Austrian deserter. Even though he had indeed initially tried to dodge the Austrian draft, he had eventually made himself available for an army medical examination in Salzburg in early 1914, which he could easily prove. Furthermore, his lawyer cleverly argued that the unwillingness of the *Echo der Woche* to disclose the name of the veteran who had written the article implied that in fact the veteran simply did not exist.[110]

The Nazis also used the honour code of the military to their advantage, as the code served as a huge disincentive to any current or former member of the military publicly to question the courage of other soldiers. Until at least the First World War, accusations against the courage of other soldiers if made by officers resulted either in a duel or in very risky proceedings in the Honour Courts of the German officer corps. The potential cost of questioning the honour of other soldiers thus was prohibitively high. Because of this tradition, Hitler could be fairly certain that only very few veterans of RIR 16 would publicly speak out against his war record, even if privately they were full of disdain for it.

The only officer in the trial in Hamburg who thus did speak out against Hitler was a lieutenant of the name of Reinhardt. The lawyers representing the *Echo der Woche* started their court proceedings by reading out a telegram from him. In it, the officer from RIR 16 declared that Hitler had never served in the trenches.[111] However, as Reinhardt was the only officer prepared to give testimony against Hitler in a court room and as the lawyers of the *Echo der Woche* could only disclose that the article had, in fact, been written by an officer too but could not name him, it was easy for Hitler's lawyers and propagandists to dismiss Reinhardt's verdict.

In short, due to the high cost of making accusation against a former comrade, very few veterans critical of Hitler were prepared to speak out against Hitler in the courts. This meant that as long as Hitler was able to find a number of his former comrades and officers who were willing to give testimony in his favour, the deceptive (and false) public image would be that the veterans of his regiment unanimously stood by him.

The people who provided affidavits for Hitler included the usual suspects such as Ernst Schmidt, whom Hitler still saw occasionally over meals with Eva Braun in his favourite Italian restaurant in Munich. However, Hitler's real coup was that he had managed to persuade Michael Schlehuber, Hitler's comrade from regimental HQ with Social Democratic leanings, to give testimony on his behalf, as we have seen earlier.[112] It is also important to bear in mind that Hitler and his comrades from the support staff of regimental HQ, irrespective of their political backgrounds, all sat in the same boat in that they all faced the criticism that they had been 'rear area pigs'. Even if they had not become Hitler's political disciples, they thus had no incentive to question his war service, as questioning his conduct in the war equalled questioning their own conduct.

The Nazi press, which put all its might into discrediting the *Echo der Woche* article, disseminated Hitler's clever defence all over Germany. *Die Volksgemeinschaft*, a Heidelberg-based Nazi newspaper, for instance, dedicated a full page to undermining the claim that Hitler had lied about his war service, claiming that 'superiors and comrades stand unanimously behind Adolf Hitler'. The message of the article is that all the List Regiment stood by Hitler and that the *Echo der Woche* article had merely been 'a dirty Marxist assassination attempt upon the honour of our Führer'.[113]

Even though a small number of the men of RIR 16 had come to Hitler's defence in 1932, the great majority of the men of the regiment publicly neither supported nor attacked him before 1933. Only two men sent letters of support to Hitler in 1932, which can hardly be taken as a ringing endorsement by the men of his regiment, especially since the article in the *Echo der Woche* had been penned by an officer of the List Regiment—who also was a former dispatch runner. The other letter was not even from a veteran of the List Regiment but merely from a veteran of a pioneer unit that had been stationed close to RIR 16 for a year during the war.[114]

In 1932, Hans Mend, who since writing his hagiographical account about Hitler's war years had parted company with Hitler, also joined in the attack on Hitler's war record. In a piece published by the Munich left-wing paper *Der Gerade Weg*, edited by Fritz Gerlich, who, once the Nazis came to power, had to pay dearly for this, Mend lashed out at Hitler: 'Had I mentioned all that I had consciously kept quiet about Hitler in my book, Hitler would not be the great hero he has been built up to be.'[115] The letter was reprinted by newspapers across Germany. Papers critical of Hitler had a field day using Mend's public letter to lay bare the 'fraud of the great hero Adolf'.[116]

Alexander Moritz Frey also clearly did not support Hitler's account of the List Regiment. Ever since the end of the war, he had continued to write pacifist anti-war stories about the mental and physical scars the war had left on veterans.[117] During occasional chance encounters with Hitler in his favourite café located in Munich's fashionable Hofgarten, Hitler—who tended to avoid personal confrontations—always greeted him fleetingly but quickly looked away. Amann, meanwhile, did not have any such qualms. When he ran into Frey, he told him, 'That Hitler, he will make it!', adding that it had been a mistake not to join the Nazis: 'You will become to regret that!'[118] Yet Frey had no intention of changing his mind.

In 1929, Frey published an autobiographical novel about his war experience as *Die Pflasterkästen*, telling the story of the List Regiment 'through the eyes of a stretcher bearer'.[119] The book was also published in Britain and America in 1930 and 1931 under the title *The Cross Bearers* and the Social Democratic newspaper *Vorwärts* and the *Daily Herald* in Britain also printed the novel in instalments.[120] The protagonist of the novel, based on Frey himself, declares in *Die Pflasterkästen*: 'I want, want, want to speak the truth—I want to say: the military and war are the most foolish, shameless, and ignorant vulgarities in the world.'[121] The novel soon became the target of bitter attacks by right-wing newspapers, upon which Frey restated his bitter criticism of the officers of the List Regiment:

> These things which I have written down, I have actually experienced—and experienced more horribly than I described them. These officers, who grew mushrooms for themselves instead of looking after the sick soldiers, who holed themselves up in a dugout when artillery fire came, who wanted to punish a medical orderly because he was not wearing the sanitary emblem that he did not even have to wear, who were drunk when they needed to be sober—I could name these officers and I have witnesses who could attest to the truth of these claims.[122]

Ultimately, Alexander Moritz Frey, Korbinian Rutz, and their comrades fought a losing battle, as masses of disenchanted voters moved towards supporting Hitler's party in the wake of the vast economic turmoil of the world economic crisis, ready to believe Hitler's promises to lead Germany out of the crisis and prepared to listen to Hitler's war stories about *Kameradschaft* as the source and inspiration of a new and united Germany. It was only now in a situation of extreme economic volatility that the NSDAP as 'a catch-all party of protest'[123] received wide-ranging support. Any argument that posits that the rise of the Nazi Party was not primarily a result of the economic and political crisis of the late 1920s and the early 1930s but that Germans wanted to become Nazis all along since they had dreamt ever since 1914 of unity and a national community of all Germans[124] ignores the fact that in the first national election after the world economic crisis 13.5 times more Germans voted for Hitler's party than in the election prior to the crisis. In the July 1932 German election, 32.9 per cent of Bavarians voted for Hitler's party. What is significant, however, is that non-Bavarians gave Hitler considerably more support (37.9 per cent of the German electorate had voted for him). Most of Hitler's support inside Bavaria came from Protestant northern Bavaria. In Upper Bavaria, where most of the men of the List Regiment came from, only 25.8 per cent of voters supported the National Socialists.[125] In other words, in no free election did more than one in four people in the core recruitment region of RIR 16 vote for Hitler.

By the second half of 1932, Hitler's popularity had already peaked. Hitler lost the 1932 presidential election by a wide margin to Hindenburg. Moreover, when, in November 1932, Germans had to go to the polls again as parliament had become ungovernable, the Nazi Party received huge losses. Private Hitler thought that all was lost, that he had lost momentum, and had no chance of ever becoming either Chancellor or President.

Hitler also had to fear that his war tales had finally been exposed as a fabrication, as General Kurt von Schleicher, the arch-conservative last Reich Chancellor before Hitler came to power, had heard rumours from journalists, while still Minister of Defence under Chancellor Franz von Papen, that the reality of Hitler's treatment at Pasewalk had been rather different from Hitler's own account. Realizing the value this information might have for his strategy to split the National Socialists and thus to prevent a Fascist dictatorship from coming to power, von Schleicher ordered military intelligence officers to confiscate Hitler's medical file from the files of the former army hospital at Pasewalk. Von Schleicher, however, tragically decided not to make immediate use of the file and kept it in a safe location.[126] His decision not to use the file immediately was a colossal mistake. In January 1933, at the urging of Conservatives who foolishly thought that they could control Adolf Hitler, von Schleicher was dismissed as Chancellor and replaced by Private Hitler in the greatest blunder and miscalculation of the twentieth century just over fourteen years after Hitler's first war had ended.

12

Private Hitler's Reich

1933–1939

O n the occasion of the twentieth anniversary of the outbreak of the war in 1934, newspapers, both in Germany and abroad, widely reprinted the photo depicting Hitler on Odeonsplatz in August 1914.[1] They thus disseminated the message that Hitler had been trying to convey for years: that he was a man of the people, that his volunteering in 1914 had been representative of the German people as a whole, and that the war had given birth to a new and more egalitarian Germany, to Private Hitler's Third Reich.

Two months later, the Nazi propaganda machine orchestrated a huge reunion of the List Regiment, an event full of pageantry displaying symbols of Germany's past and present, thus presenting the new state as the supposedly organic and natural product of Germany's history. Flags were hung all over Munich for the two-day event on 13 and 14 October 1914. The festivities featured a service in the courtyard of the barracks in which Ludwig III had inspected the men of RIR 16 in 1914 prior to their deployment to the front. Events also took place in City Hall in front of the commemorative window for the List Regiment as well as in one of Munich's beer halls. It also included a march through the streets of Munich which passed the Nazi Party headquarters and Odeonsplatz.

Only a relatively small number of the veterans of the List Regiment attended the reunion. Participants included non-Nazis such as Alois Schnelldorfer as well as committed Nazis such as Jackl Weiß and Ignaz Westenkirchner. List veterans such as Hans Ostermünchner—the sniper wartime acquaintance of Hitler and former local militia member, who had hidden machine guns on his farm throughout the years of the Weimar Republic before they were confiscated in 1933—stayed in their villages, feeling neither an affinity for Hitler's ideology nor particularly for the regiment at large. Anticipating this, Nazi organizers included in the celebrations large numbers of men from the SS, the SA Standarte List (the SA unit named after the List Regiment), the regular German Army, the German postal services, as well as a group of children, a deployment from the Hitler Youth, and representatives of the veterans' associations of various other regiments dressed in historic costumes. All these 'extras' ensured good photo opportunities in line with Hitler's claim that the veterans of RIR 16 almost unanimously supported him.[2]

The Nazi press made sure that Germans even in the remotest corners of Hitler's new Reich would be exposed to the reunion of the Führer's regiment and the symbolic significance that Nazi propaganda placed upon it. For instance, the *Illustrierter Beobachter*, the Third Reich's primary glossy magazine, published a photospread of the event. The *Völkischer Beobachter*, meanwhile, used the event once more to hammer the message home that Hitler had emerged as an unknown, ordinary soldier from the ranks of the men of the List Regiment to rescue Germany.[3]

Adolf Hitler himself, in fact, did not even attend the reunion, just as he came to Munich less and less frequently, preferring to spend his time in his alpine retreat close to Salzburg. From there he could fantasize about replacing the Munich that had often cold-shouldered him—a city of medieval, elegant nineteenth-century, as well as art deco buildings, and a city where as recently as 1927 the party had to amalgamate several local chapters for lack of members[4]—with a new Munich of his dreams, a city of cold, monumental buildings. Hitler's closest comrades were well aware of the reason why Hitler did not attend the reunion. It was because even in 1934 only a few of the veterans of RIR 16 supported him. The former dispatch runner of regimental HQ thus did not dare to meet the members of his regiment face to face. As the wife of one of Hitler and Jackl Weiß's wartime comrades wrote to Weiß the day after the reunion, 'I hope that the day will come soon when Hitler can stay with his loyal comrades. My heart is bleeding that there are still comrades who lack the holiest and inner conviction that the future lies with Hitler. This is why Hitler cannot attend [reunions of the List Regiment]. I understand this all even though I am just a woman.'[5]

Nazi propaganda, meanwhile, glossed over Hitler's absence by simply reproducing in the *Illustrierter Beobachter* photospread a photograph of Hitler from the 1922 reunion of the List Regiment.[6]

Hitler's decision to stay away from the event epitomizes why, a year after Hitler's seizure of power, Nazi propaganda still felt a need to put up a charade about the role of the List Regiment in the 'making' of Hitler. The reason for this was that even once Private Hitler had become Reich Chancellor in 1933, he still could not be sure of the support not only of his fellow soldiers from RIR 16 but also of Germans in general. Hitler's power, at least in the eyes of contemporaries, had indeed initially been seen as standing on shaky ground.

It was unclear whether the Germans who had voted for Hitler in the November 1932 national election would continue to support him. After all, only four years earlier, 97 out of 100 Germans had not voted for him. Even in the autumn 1932 election, 2 out of 3 Germans still had not given their support to the National Socialists.[7] Moreover, until Paul von Hindenburg's death in 1934, Hitler was not even formally Germany's leader and could, in theory, have been dismissed. In 1933, many Germans had not expected that the former dispatch runner from the List Regiment was there to stay. For instance, Victor Klemperer, a Jewish professor in Dresden, had noted in his diary in July 1933 that even though Hitler's position was strong for the moment, his political regime was 'absolutely un-German and consequently will not have any kind of long-term duration'. In the following month, he had noted: 'I simply cannot believe that the mood of the masses is really still behind Hitler. Too many signs of the opposite.'[8]

In order to consolidate his power, Hitler thus embarked on a triple strategy. It included the ruthless use of violence towards political opponents and even towards many of the Conservatives who had helped the Nazis come to power in the hope of using Hitler as a vehicle to further their own goals;[9] the pursuit of policies that had an appeal beyond the core Nazi constituency, focusing on fighting unemployment and on 'undoing' the Versailles settlement; and the continued propagation of *Kameradschaft*, sacrifice, and *Volksgemeinschaft*, in other words, concepts that appealed to a wide range of Germans from disparate political backgrounds. It was due to the last element of his strategy that Hitler's invented war experience in the List Regiment remained centrally important to Nazi policies and propaganda throughout the 1930s. It was deemed so important that every German student would be exposed to it in their history lessons.[10]

As Gunter d'Alquen, one of the Nazis' chief propagandists, wrote in an article about 'Front-line Soldier Hitler', published in the *Völkischer Beobachter*, 'the *Kameradschaft* [of the trenches] gave birth to the will for a

German Socialism, and with it to the firm belief in a new and great community. . . . For us class and origin did not count for anything [during the war]; all that mattered was achievement and sacrifice. This is how our storm troops became a living example of our will to create a new community; this is how the blood and the sacrificial death of our comrades became the proof of the sanctity of our convictions; only this allowed us to break the power of reactionary forces and of Marxism and thus to seize power in Germany.'[11]

In implementing Hitler's strategy to achieve greater public support for his movement and in thus presenting the Third Reich as a state of comrades based upon *Kameradschaft*,[12] Nazi propaganda cleverly focused on Hitler's wartime peers rather than on his own words.[13] For instance, in April 1933, a Nazi newspaper published a series of articles about Hitler's record in the war, based in large part on Hans Mend's recollections, glossing over the fact that Mend had recently turned against Hitler. The articles argued that an account of Hitler's war years, more than anything else, would allow people still unsure about Hitler's character to learn what Hitler was really like. This would show them that Germany was safe in Adolf Hitler's hands.[14]

Then, in 1934, Adolf Meyer's war memoirs were published under the title of *Mit Adolf Hitler im Bayerischen RIR 16 List*. The importance of the book for Nazi propaganda was underlined by the fact that Julius Streicher, the most infamous of all of Hitler's ideologues, wrote its preface. In his memoirs, Meyer claimed that Hitler's experience during the war had been typical of all ordinary men of his regiment and that it was that experience that had allowed him to become Germany's leader: 'Only from these fighters, who with their suffering and their lives had protected the homeland', wrote Meyer, 'could the man emerge, who would give form and expression to the longing of the best, and who would provide guidance for moving to a new age and who in this would be the uncontested and natural Leader.'[15]

Nazi propaganda also used the biography of Ignaz Westenkirchner to full effect. Hitler's fellow dispatch runner had emigrated to the United States in 1928. Following the Great Depression, Westenkirchner, a carpenter and wood carver, had become impoverished and felt increasingly ill at ease in his home in Reading, Pennsylvania. He thus approached Hitler, who offered to pay for his return ticket to Germany. Once back in Munich in the winter of 1933/4, he was given a job in the dispatch department of the *Völkischer Beobachter*. His return to Germany was a propaganda godsend, allowing the Third Reich to circulate the war myth of Hitler and the List Regiment in a subtle way. Photos of Hitler and Amann joking over coffee with Westenkirchner appeared in illustrated magazines and propaganda books. Furthermore, when the Nazi author Heinz A. Heinz wrote his pro-Hitler biography in 1934, which tells Hitler's life through the eyes of different people close to him, he chose to approach Westenkirchner to cover the war years of the new German leader. As we have seen, the story Westenkirchner and Heinz produced is full of verifiably wrong claims, all of which were aimed at backing up Hitler's invented war experience. In his interview with Heinz, Westenkirchner also made a direct connection between the war experience of the men of the List Regiment and the birth of the Nazi movement. He stated that after the war, he had met Hitler and the other veterans of RIR 16 in the Munich pub that was the spiritual home of the Nazi Party. 'We old comrades of the List Regiment', Westenkirchner posited, 'would meet at the Sterneckerbräu.'[16]

Nazi propaganda also disseminated the myth of Hitler's war experience through the story of Jackl Weiß, who became mayor of his village after Hitler's rise to power and who was extremely proud of being close to Hitler and of still occasionally meeting him.[17] Newspapers published articles about Hitler's visit to Weiß in late 1919, which Nazi propaganda used to present Hitler as the new messiah. The articles explicitly refer to Hitler as a 'prophet' to whom people initially had not listened. In their description of Hitler's visit they heavily borrowed from Christ's nativity story, telling a tale of Hitler arriving in Weiß's village at nighttime and being turned away by all inns in the region, as a result of which, just as Mary and Joseph, Hitler had to spend the night in the cold. The articles then proceed to tell the story of Hitler's rise to power through the eyes of Weiß, who presented Hitler as bringing salvation to Germany by basing the Third Reich on the ideals of *Kameradschaft*.[18]

The Nazi Party archive, meanwhile, vigorously attempted to get their hands on all documents—photographs, drawings, paintings, or letters—pertaining to Hitler's war years and to set up a central repository of material that could be used to tell the story Hitler wanted to put across. To the same end, the archive also sought to record as many glorifying reports about Hitler's war years as possible. Propaganda exhibitions throughout Germany displayed the documents showing his award of the Iron Cross 1st Class, while a bust of Hitler was put up in Hitler's former hospital in Pasewalk.[19]

The careers of two of Hitler's superiors from the List Regiment, Fritz Wiedemann and Max Amann, also reinforced the mythical public image of Hitler's and the men of the List Regiment's war experience.

In the year Hitler came to power, Amann became a Reichstag deputy, which was only of symbolic significance as the Reichstag had lost all its power in 1933—in other words, while keeping Amann, with his distinct lack of talent for politics, safely away from real political power, making him a Reichstag deputy nevertheless had huge propaganda value. It further underlined the message Hitler wanted to convey about the role of his military unit in forming him. More significantly, Amann was made President of the Reich Press Chamber, giving him control over the entire German press, a control which he exerted with an iron fist.[20] Even though Amann and Hitler were not friends in a social sense, their relationship was so close that, in 1943, the OSS, the American secret service, considered abducting or assassinating him and three other men close to Hitler, as 'the death of any of these close associates', as an OSS memorandum put it, 'can best be described as the most successful harpoons, except the death of Goebbels, to be directed at Hitler'.[21]

Unlike Amann, Wiedemann had not been close to Hitler during the years of the Weimar Republic. Since his refusal to join the Nazi movement during the 1922 List reunion, only a brief chance encounter in Hitler's favourite café in Munich in 1929 had brought Wiedemann and Hitler together again. However, the two met again after Hitler had come to power. Hitler now invited him to join him in the Reich Chancellory and to recreate the wartime regimental HQ under reversed roles. This time Wiedemann did not turn Hitler down.[22]

After a short stint in the office of Hitler's deputy, Rudolf Hess, Wiedemann became one of Hitler's personal adjutants. Only when he started to work for Hitler—but not before—did Wiedemann join the Nazi Party on 2 February 1934. He was now at the very heart of Hitler's empire. In Berlin and often also in Hitler's alpine retreat, Wiedemann, a tall, dark man, who, apart from his 'horrendous Prussian haircut', was handsome and well dressed, was at Hitler's side daily. Hitler, who could be quite charming, and Wiedemann clearly enjoyed each other's company, reminiscing about the old days in the war. He was present at Hitler's daily extensive luncheons, attended to Hitler's private correspondence, acted as go-between for people who wanted to approach Hitler, or accompanied him on his visit to Mussolini in Italy. In short, Wiedemann's task was, as it had been in regimental HQ during the war, to ensure the smooth running of Hitler's office rather than to formulate policy.[23] More than that, Wiedemann was the personification of the Nazi claim that the First World War and the List Regiment had 'made' Hitler.

Talking about the First World War was, of course, not just a propaganda tool for Hitler. At the height of his power, his war experience continued to be one of his favourite topics of conversation. After the daily screening of light entertainment movies in the Reich Chancellory or in Hitler's alpine retreat, nobody from his entourage in need of a full night's sleep dared to bring up the subject of the war. According to Fritz Wiedemann, when Hitler started to talk about the First World War following the screening of a film 'it might happen that we had to listen to him until 3 a.m., as we adjutants could not just get up and leave. As a result, we were ready to murder any guest who brought the conversation back to one of his infamous "favourite topics" after 11 p.m.'[24]

Others among Hitler's immediate comrades in regimental HQ may not have had quite as spectacular a career as Amann and Wiedemann. Yet in their small worlds, in the communities in which they lived, their careers mirrored those of the former adjutant and Staff Sergeant of regimental HQ and thus helped Hitler's attempt to boost public support for the Third Reich. Ernst Schmidt, for instance, who had been local party boss of the NSDAP in Garching an der Alz since 1926 as well as a local SA leader, became deputy mayor of Garching after his fellow dispatch runner had risen to power in 1933. Schmidt was also included in the official march on the tenth anniversary of Hitler's failed putsch in November 1933. The following year, he received the golden membership badge of the Nazi Party. On that occasion, photos of Hitler and Ernst Schmidt appeared in newspapers and magazines across Germany.[25]

How ruthlessly Nazi propaganda rewrote Hitler's war experience in order to help him widen his public appeal is nowhere more apparent than in Balthasar Brandmayer's war memoirs. First published on the eve of Hitler's ascension to power, it was in its ninth edition by 1940. All editions portrayed Hitler as a messianic prophet. However, over time, Nazi authorities made countless substantive changes to the book. They give firm evidence that all the memoirs of Hitler's comrades as well as his own wartime recollections in *Mein Kampf* are fairly useless in reconstructing Hitler's war experience.

For instance, Hans Mend was written out of Brandmayer's book after he turned against Hitler. Any characterizations of Hitler that ran against his public image, however well intended were also removed. For example, Brandmayer's original claim that, in 1915, Hitler had expected the war to be over within a year implicitly questioned Hitler's political judgement. In the 1940 edition of the book, Hitler's alleged claim was thus put into the mouth of one of the other dispatch runners. Other alterations were meant to embellish the accomplishments of the Germans. While, for instance, the 1933 edition of the book mentions Hitler and his comrades watching an enemy plane being forced down by the German air force, the number of neutralized enemy planes had miraculously increased by 1940.[26]

All of the more radical changes to the book were meant to increase the book's ability to advertise Hitler's regiment as the birthplace of a more egalitarian, National Socialist Germany. Any references that ran contrary to the claim that Hitler's regiment had been a role model of *Kameradschaft* (and had thus been the nucleus of the National Socialist *Volksgemeinschaft*) were either deleted or replaced with fictitious claims. The 1933 edition of the book, for instance, saw Brandmayer having to make his way back to German lines all on his own after being severely injured in the Battle of Neuve Chapelle. In the 1940 edition, 'merciful comrades' carry him back to safety.[27] Moreover, the 1933 edition includes a nineteen-page rant, not just against Jews but also against groups whose support Nazi authorities were trying to win—including traditional conservatives, aristocrats, and capitalists—yet which are portrayed by Brandmayer just as negatively as Jews. Meanwhile, he derided the Kaiser's government as having being run by freemasons. Nazis propagandists simply cut this entire section from the book.[28]

In the early editions of his book, Brandmayer also portrayed most of the officers of RIR 16 as incompetent, aloof, and selfish, and as having had no respect for the troops. He argued that Germany had lost the war in large part because the List Regiment and the German Army as a whole had had far too few good officers. The 1940 edition, meanwhile, turns Brandmayer's argument upside down, claiming that most of the officers of Hitler's regiment had been role models of exemplary behaviour towards ordinary soldiers. Similarly, Brandmayer originally described the officer in charge of the dispatch runners as having being hated by all his peers. He accused him of having continually bullied the dispatch runners of RIR 16 in petty ways.

By 1940, Brandmayer's complaint about Hitler's and his officer had been purged, as had the characterization of an NCO from RIR 16 as a 'bully' (i.e. as a *Leutschinder* and *Schikanierer*), and had been replaced with invocations of the *Kameradschaft* of the List Regiment: 'One day the time will come in which the song of songs of the comradeship of the trenches will be sung all over Germany. Everyone cared about the well-being of their fellow soldiers; everyone shared his joys and sorrows with their comrades; all felt like belonging to one big family.' Moreover, in stark contrast to the 1933 edition of his book, the claim of the 1940 edition was that almost all farmers in Brandmayer's village supported Hitler.[29] In short, neither Brandmayer's memoirs, nor any of the post-1933 publications about Hitler, his comrades, and the List Regiment were driven one iota by an attempt to give an accurate account of the war years of Hitler's military unit. They were motivated by one consideration only: to increase the popular support for Adolf Hitler and his regime.

When Hitler had come to power in 1933, many of his opponents had been well aware of the ruthlessness of Hitler and Nazi propagandists in inventing his war experience. They thus knew, as did Hitler himself, that his mythical story of his political coming of age was his Achilles heel. In other words, they sensed that persuading Germans that, in fact, Hitler's tale about his experiences during the war and the revolution had been made up out of thin air had the potential of undermining Hitler's attempt to widen his appeal. The Munich chapter of the Reichsbanner, for instance, thus embarked on one last-ditch attempt to attack Hitler on 26 February 1933. In a fully packed Zirkus Krone, Munich's largest venue for public functions, the event's main speaker asked: 'Where was Adolf Hitler when the fight against Bolshevism in Munich really was on?'[30]

Nazi authorities lost no time in putting down with an iron fist any such challenges to Hitler's legitimacy. They diligently and very successfully policed the carefully choreographed story of Hitler's experience in the war and the revolution. Anyone questioning Hitler's story about his First World War experience was immediately targeted and silenced, while the ranks of the police were once again augmented by thugs who had been fired during the years of the Weimar Republic, such as Karl Ostberg, the RIR 16 veteran and SS officer.[31]

Realizing the danger he was in as a Reichsbanner leader who previously had been Hitler's commanding officer, Major Karl Mayr feared for his life after the Nazis' rise to power. He thus fled to France in 1933.[32] Edmund Forster, the doctor who had treated Hitler in Pasewalk for psychosomatic hysteria, meanwhile, grew worried that Hitler would get his hands on his notes about Hitler's treatment in 1918. In the summer of 1933, he thus smuggled them out of the country, handing them over to Ernst Weiß, a German-Jewish émigré, medical doctor, and writer in Paris. Soon after returning to Germany, Forster committed suicide under circumstances that have remained unresolved to the present day. Hitler's official medical file, meanwhile, was still in the possession of either von Schleicher or one of his associates when Hitler came to power. Yet it did not remain there for long. In the wake of the Night of the Long Knives in 1934, the Nazis liquidated both von Schleicher and General Ferdinand von Bredow who had worked under von Schleicher. In the event, Hitler's medical file was taken from one of the two men and subsequently almost certainly locked away in Hitler's alpine retreat where it is believed to have been burnt during the final days of the Third Reich in 1945.[33]

Max Amann also did his best to silence critics of the myth that Hitler had created about himself. On 9 March 1933, just as the Nazis had taken control of Bavarian state institutions, Max Amann and a group of SA men burst into the offices of Der Gerade Weg, the weekly paper which had published Mend's article questioning Hitler's war record. They seized Fritz Gerlich, the paper's editor-in-chief, and pushed him into a dark room. Amann informed Gerlich—against whom Amann also held a personal grudge due to an article directed at him from 1931—that 'the time for revenge is now'. While SA men directed their pistol at Gerlich, Amann repeatedly punched him in the face. As Gerlich's face was bleeding, the former staff sergeant of RIR 16 decided that his deed had been done. As he left the office, his face was pale and trembling with excitement.[34]

Soon the Nazis turned their attention also to Alexander Moritz Frey. Since the publication of Die Pflasterkästen, of all the veterans of the List Regiment, Frey was arguably the most obvious target for the wrath of the Nazis. It came as no surprise to Frey that his autobiographical novel about Hitler's regiment was among the books burned in public squares all over Germany on 10 May 1933. Five days later, SA men turned up at his flat in Munich. They smashed his belongings to pieces. However, through a stroke of luck Frey visited a friend outside Munich that day. From there, Frey immediately fled the country. Hidden in the boot of a car, his friend drove him across the Austrian border, where he spent the next few years in exile just a short distance across the mountains from Hitler's alpine retreat.[35] In 1938, as Nazi Germany occupied Austria, it was time for Frey to flee again, ultimately settling in Basel in Switzerland. While in exile, his friends and acquaintances repeatedly asked Frey half-jokingly why he had not given Hitler rat poison during the war.[36]

Hans Mend was another obvious target. After he had turned against Hitler, claiming Hitler's account of his war years to be fraudulent, the Nazis cleverly started to discredit Mend. This was made all the easier by Mend's long criminal record which included convictions for fraud, embezzlement, and the forging of documents. In 1933, at a time when Nazi newspapers still made use of Mend's pro-Hitler war memoirs, Hitler's personal adjutant, Wilhelm Brückner, very swiftly issued an arrest warrant for Mend, as a result of which Mend spent more than a month in Dachau Concentration Camp in an attempt to intimidate him into keeping his mouth shut.[37] Curiously Hitler was hesitant to kill any of his immediate former comrades from the List Regiment. Nevertheless, the Nazi regime continued to target and sideline Mend, who spent much of 1937 and 1938 in custody. Then, in 1938, the Nazi regime decided to withdraw Mend's book, no longer considered 'the finest Christmas gift for any supporter of Hitler'.[38]

Moreover, soon after Hitler's rise to power, the former commander of 1st Company and author of the *Echo der Woche* article, Korbinian Rutz, a teacher in the foothills of the Alps, found himself interned in Dachau Concentration Camp, too. When a few days before Christmas 1933 Rutz was finally released from Dachau, he decided that his life and the well-being of his family was more important than exposing the truth about Hitler's war record. He signed a declaration in which he retracted his criticism of Hitler.[39]

A veteran who bravely did not agree to be silenced was Siegfried Heumann, the Jewish veteran who before 1933 had been a member of both the veterans' association of RIR 16 and of the Reichsbund jüdischer Frontkämpfer. In 1936, he anonymously sent copies of the official Reichsbund publication to approximately twenty officers based in Munich. He attached to the publications notes in which he complained about the treatment of Jewish veterans by Private Hitler's regime. One read: 'Léon Blum, the Frenchman and Jew, respects and venerates Adolf Hitler as a combatant— Adolf Hitler condemns, dishonours, and demeans Jewish combatants.' In the trial against him, Heumann declared that he had sent the notes to high-ranking officers in the hope of finding among them an understanding of the psyche of Jewish front-line soldiers'. Significantly, Heumann's superior from the List Regiment, Otto Rehm, an officer now working for the

Munich transport department, agreed to give testimony on Heumann's behalf and to defend him against the accusations levelled against his soldier by the regime of Private Hitler. Rehm declared that Heumann 'had proven his patriotic credentials in the field'. The testimony of the officer from RIR 16, however, did not sway the court. Heumann's bravery cost him the statutory prison term of three months as well as two other terms of 'protective custody' (*Schutzhaft*).[40]

Private Hitler had thus gone to great lengths to use (and police) the mythical account of his time in the List Regiment in his attempt to increase public support for National Socialism. Did his strategy work?

This question is extremely difficult to answer, as it is notoriously hard to measure the popularity of authoritarian states that do not hold free elections. It is equally tricky to attribute changes in Hitler's popularity to specific causes.

There is no doubt that support for Hitler grew considerably during his first six years in power. It is sometimes even argued that, by 1939, the German population supported Hitler almost universally, readily and knowingly giving consent even to the coercive elements of the Third Reich.[41] Even where as extreme a position as this is not accepted, the claim still is that the overwhelming majority of Germans backed Hitler by the late 1930s making him by far the most popular head of government in Europe. This was, the argument goes, because of the seductive nature of Hitler's charisma, a longing for 'heroic' leaders, and a *Volksgemeinschaft* among Germans as well as the personal cult that had been built around Hitler (and it is here where Hitler's war myth mattered so much), to foreign-policy successes, falling unemployment rates, and the championing of family and community values, generous new welfare programmes and other redistributive policies, and, more generally, to the 'seductive surface' of National Socialism with all its propaganda, architecture, and promises to make exotic travel and cars affordable for everyone.[42]

The behaviour of the veterans of Hitler's regiment and of the population of the recruitment regions of RIR 16, however, does not support the idea that, by the time he turned 50 in the spring of 1939, Hitler enjoyed the backing of an overwhelming majority. For instance, Ernst Schmidt's actions during the last election before the war in 1938, which were a sham event, indicate that the Nazis could not easily achieve overwhelming support even in staged and unfree elections. On the occasion, Hitler's closest comrade from the war drove from village to village close to his native Garching and manually turned all 'no' votes into 'yes' votes.[43]

The fate of the Jewish veterans of Hitler's regiment, too, suggests that at least in most of the recruitment areas of RIR 16, Hitler largely failed in his attempt to generate a huge increase in full-blown popular ideological support for his movement.

From the day that Hitler came to power, his former Jewish fellow soldiers had begun, of course, to suffer tremendously under Nazi persecution. For instance, Nazi authorities did not lose any time in instigating the dismissal of the Jewish veterans of the local veterans' association of Ichenhausen. Henceforth, the three veterans of the List Regiment living in Ichenhausen were only allowed to be members of the local chapter of the 'Reichsbund Jüdischer Frontsoldaten'. Then, on 1 April 1933, when the countrywide National Socialist boycott of Jewish businesses occurred, SA men stood guard outside the butcher's shop of Levi Erlanger and tried to prevent customers from entering. To add insult to injury, the street in which Erlanger's shop was located was renamed after his former comrade from the List Regiment, 'Adolf-Hitler-Strasse'.[44]

The 'half-Jewish' widow of Albert Weisgerber was also targeted. In November 1934, police appeared at her apartment and searched for 'immoral pictures' and confiscated a folder with ninety etchings by her deceased husband, the late commander of Hitler's 1st Company.[45] Hugo Gutmann, meanwhile, who ran a typewriter business in Nuremberg, was heavily hit by the boycott of Jewish businesses in 1933. Several companies producing typewriters revoked his licence and all municipal and state agencies with which he previously had done business cut ties with him.[46] Nuremberg was indeed one of Germany's foremost centres of anti-Semitic activity during the Third Reich. And it was particularly in Nuremberg's Protestant hinterland that the kind of anti-Jewish actions to which the Jewish veterans of Hitler's regiment were subjected were popular.[47]

Gutmann was in danger not just because he was a Jew. His personal safety was also in jeopardy because of his role in the award of Hitler's Iron Cross with its potential to expose the carefully created myth of Hitler's past as a lie. Gutmann also had contacts with Ernst Niekisch, Bavaria's revolutionary leader in the wake of Eisner's assassination, who had set up a resistance group to Hitler in the 1930s.[48] It was thus little surprise that in July 1937 the Gestapo arrested Gutmann, upon which he was interrogated and incarcerated in a Nuremberg prison for more than two months. During the interrogations, a Gestapo officer told him that Heinrich Himmler himself wanted to know everything Gutmann knew about the award of Hitler's Iron Cross 1st Class. Gutmann was charged with having made 'contemptuous, derogatory and untrue comments about the "Führer"'. To his great surprise, Gutmann was released in September.[49]

The reason why Gutmann and his fellow Jewish veterans from Hitler's regiment could cope at all during the dark days of the Third Reich prior to the outbreak of the Second World War was that many of their brothers-in-arms from the war, and many people in the communities in which they lived, never fully bought into Nazi ideology and its radical form of anti-Semitism.

After the Second World War, Gutmann was to write to a friend that he had been able to cope while being in prison because its prison guards, unlike the Gestapo officers, had treated him well:

> I was lucky that a few of the men in the Deutschhaus barracks had been in my regiment. Particularly decent was a policeman who was a guard in the prison. He often came to me and told me that as a good Catholic he despised the Nazis. He said he was there against his will. He got me all the food I required; he was even courageous enough to go at night into the Gestapo room where my files were kept. He informed me that they had nothing concrete, I mean no evidence, against me. Furthermore, through him I could keep up contact with my wife. . . . Later after my release, he visited me with his wife in my apartment under great danger to himself.[50]

Gutmann's treatment by the veterans of his regiment among the prison guards during his incarceration in 1937 thus further undermines the idea that Gutmann had been universally hated in the regiment, that RIR 16 had been a deeply, existentially and universally anti-Semitic band of brothers, and that Hitler enjoyed near-universal support in the second half of the 1930s.

We do not know for certain why Gutmann was released in September 1937. However, we do know that one of Gutmann's friends from the List Regiment, Mathias Mayrhofer—a Catholic bank clerk from Lower Bavaria, who in 1918 had been the officer in charge of RIR 16's dispatch runners and whom Gutmann described as 'a fearless friend'—went to see Fritz Wiedemann, Hitler's adjutant, to ask him if he could provide assistance in getting Gutmann out of prison. Gutmann later was to write that 'Wiedemann asked him not to speak but briefly to write down what he had to say because the walls of his room were bugged with microphones.'[51] Mayrhofer, the officer in charge of Hitler in 1918, thus chose to side with Hitler's enemies rather than with the dispatch-runner-turned-dictator. The role Wiedemann, meanwhile, played in getting Gutmann out of prison might appear as very odd at first hand but the motivations of Hitler's adjutant were only to be revealed by Wiedemann's actions during the Second World War.

The behaviour of the Catholic prison guard who had helped Gutmann, was unusual only for its bravery in actively helping a Jew targeted by the Nazis. The underlying political outlook—a lack of racial anti-Semitism and of Nazi ideology—was still reigning supreme in the Catholic recruitment regions of the List Regiment. In the Catholic regions of Bavaria, communal relations between Jews and non-Jews remained much more stable after 1933 than in Protestant regions. For instance, with few exceptions the population of Ichenhausen ignored Nazi calls for an anti-Jewish boycott for the first few years of the Third Reich.[52] Moreover, many farmers across Bavaria were reluctant to stop doing business with Jewish livestock traders. The farmers did not act in this way because they lived in a Catholic–Jewish utopia. On the contrary, many of them were not free of traditional Catholic anti-Semitism and their behaviour was often partly driven by economic concerns as Jewish traders tended to offer them better terms than agricultural cooperatives which outweighed any other concerns. In other words, while elsewhere the economic crisis following the Wall Street crash had spectacularly increased support for Hitler, the economic interests of many farmers, as well as their Catholicism, actively kept the Catholic rural population away from National Socialism.

By 1937, the Gestapo had still failed to stop the farmers of Nördlingen and Ichenhausen from continuing to do business with Jewish livestock traders, which included Nathan Winschbacher from Ichenhausen, who had served in one of the machine-gun units of RIR 16.[53] Moreover, in 1935, several signs that had been put up in streets in Memmingen, home to three of the List Regiment's Jewish soldiers, were secretly changed from 'Juden sind hier unerwünscht' ('Jews are not welcome here') to 'Juden hier erwünscht' ('Jews are welcome here'). In the same year, a 'Jews are not welcome here' sign was secretly removed in the Franconian town of Forchheim, where another Jewish veteran of the List Regiment lived. A similar incident is recorded from Ichenhausen. In the following year, Nazi authorities complained that trade between Jews and gentiles in Forchheim, far from dying down, was actually on the increase.[54]

The Nazis' failure to make serious inroads into the Catholic Bavarian population, it needs to be stressed, was less driven by economic concerns than by a relative lack of racial anti-Semitism in Catholic regions of Bavaria, about which Nazi authorities repeatedly complained after 1933. The anti-Jewish policy in the core recruitment region of the List Regiment was generally very much a top-down, rather than a bottom-up affair.

On many an occasion, Nazi authorities expressed in internal memoranda their concern that in the Catholic regions of Bavaria, both the local population and the Catholic Church were far too philo-Semitic.[55] One of the complaints was that 'reports of cooperation between Catholic circles and Jews are being reported repeatedly, particularly from Munich'.[56] Another one was that many Catholic priests told their parishes that the Jews were God's 'chosen people' and urged them to continue buying in Jewish shops.[57] Furthermore, Cardinal Faulhaber of Munich used a sermon in late 1933 to point out that Jesus had been a Jew.[58] According to a report from spring 1937, Jews were 'widely supported by the rural population [of Catholic regions of Bavaria] which opposed National Socialism'.[59] In August 1937, the Gestapo bitterly complained that the Bavarian Catholic rural population was still totally immune to Nazi racism and ideology. It concluded 'that particularly in the regions in which political Catholicism still exerts it pull, the farmers are so infected with the teachings of militant political Catholicism that they are deaf to all discussion of the racial problem. Furthermore, this fact shows that the majority of the farmers are completely unreceptive to the ideological teachings of National Socialism.'[60]

On the evening of 9 November 1938, in part out of frustration with the failure to effect a serious rise of popular support for Nazi racial ideology, the Nazis unleashed a pogrom that brought on that night—soon to be known as *Kristallnacht* or the Night of Broken Glass—and the following day the worst anti-Jewish violence in Germany for hundreds of years.

Being tipped off minutes before Nazi personnel arrived at his apartment on *Kristallnacht*, Gutmann managed to make an escape with his young family. They were first hidden by nuns in a Catholic hospital and then by relatives.[61] Most German Jews had been less lucky. In Munich, for instance, Nazis broke into the apartment of a Jewish doctor and veteran from RIR 16, searching and looting his property.[62] *Kristallnacht* was also driven to a large extent by a frustration among Nazi leaders that despite all the anti-Jewish measures of the previous years the great majority of Jews had remained in Germany[63] and that, by National Socialist standards, the German population

had hitherto acted in an insufficiently anti-Semitic manner; this was particularly true of places like Ichenhausen.

As communal relations in the small Swabian town had continued to be
fairly good until 1938, SS men and members of the Hitler Youth from
nearby towns were sent to Levi Erlanger and Nathan Winschbacher's home
town on 10 November 1938. Together with local collaborators, they laid
waste to the synagogue's interior, desecrated the Jewish graveyard, and
threw the books of Ichenhausen's Jewish teacher into the local river.
Boys, who had been instructed to shout 'Today we go against the Jews'
during the pogrom, chased old Jewish men—among them Levi Erlanger—
along the streets of the town while spitting at them. As many as twenty
Jewish men were taken to the concentration camp at Dachau that day. The
great majority of the non-Jewish population of Ichenhausen, however, did
not join in the pogrom. Jews and many non-Jews alike cried as they saw
how the pogrom brought an end to hundreds of years of Jewish–Christian
peaceful coexistence in Ichenhausen.[64] The Nazi district governor, meanwhile, was outraged by the behaviour of the non-Jewish population of
Ichenhausen declaring: 'I had to realize that parts of the Ichenhausen
population pity the "poor" Jews or even side with them.'[65] In the aftermath
of Kristallnacht, the Sicherheitsdienst (the intelligence service of the SS)
came to the conclusion that the anti-Jewish pogroms of 9 and 10 November
had backfired in Bavaria as the Bavarian population had been more prone to
believe foreign radio stations and the Catholic Church than the Nazi radio
station and Nazi propaganda in general and stood, as a result of Kristallnacht,
'almost in opposition' to Nazism. 'A majority of the population', the SD
concluded, was 'without any comprehension' of the 'Jewish question'.[66]

In one respect at least, Kristallnacht had worked from Private Hitler's
perspective. While in early 1938 the SS had complained that in the previous
year in Bavaria 'the emigration [had] practically [been] at a standstill',[67] Jews
were finally leaving Germany in droves, which, throughout the 1930s,
Hitler saw as the 'final solution' to the 'Jewish question'.

Even though Arthur Wechsler, an Orthodox Jew from Munich and a
former staff sergeant from 1st Company, had emigrated to Britain as early as
1933, most German Jews thought that they could wait out Private Hitler's
regime. As Wechsler later declared, he too had not imagined that the leaders
of the Third Reich would try to exterminate the Jews of Europe.[68] While by
the end of 1937, approximately 70 per cent of German Jews thus still
remained in the country of their birth, between 50 and 60 per cent had

emigrated by the outbreak of the Second World War—figures well in line
with those for the communities in which the Jewish veterans of RIR 16
lived.[69] In short, as after five years of life under the Third Reich, still no
popular large-scale grass-root National Socialist movement aimed at driving
Jews out of Germany had taken root, Hitler's regime had to revert to a top-
down demonstration of violence and intimidation to move forward Private
Hitler's anti-Semitic crusade.

Among the émigrés who left Germany as a result of the new top-
down anti-Semitism was Justin Fleischmann, who until then had continued
to live in his apartment just to the west of Munich's city centre. Deciding in
1939 that his life in Germany had become untenable, he made his way,
together with his family, to America, where he ultimately settled in Pittsburgh.[70] Similarly, in the summer of 1939, Alexander Wormser and Ernst
Dispecker, both recipients of Iron Crosses, decided that the country which
had once decorated them was no longer a place for them. Wormser set sail
for America, where he arrived in New York City on 17 August 1939. The
former Jewish war volunteer from RIR 16 ultimately settled with his family
in Buffalo in upstate New York, whereas Dispecker, who had been an
officer in the List Regiment, found a new home in New York City in
Manhattan. Later that year, Leo Sichel, a dentist who had served with 9th
Company, emigrated to the US too, while Hugo Neumann, a veteran from
the same company and living in Munich, emigrated to Spain.[71] Moreover,
Georg Dehn, the officer and archaeologist who had been close to Albert
Weisgerber and who had been one of the authors of the official regimental
history and who like Hitler had earned the Iron Cross 1st Class during the
war,[72] emigrated to South America. In Quito he became very active in the
local Lutheran parish.[73] The background behind the emigration of Weisgerber's friend remains unclear. However, Fritz Wiedemann, who knew
him very well, described him as Jewish[74] which suggests that one or both of
Dehn's parents were Jewish and that hence Dehn is likely to have fled racial
persecution.

After *Kristallnacht*, Hugo Gutmann had realized that he too had to get out
of the country with his family before it was too late. After a friend of
Gutmann's in Nuremberg's municipal offices had illegally issued him with
a passport, he managed to leave Germany in late February 1939 with the
help of the Belgian consul general in Cologne, another one of Gutmann's
friends. He then settled with his family in Brussels.[75] According to an
unconfirmed 1941 newspaper report from an American newspaper, it was

again Fritz Wiedemann who had helped him and, ostensibly rather strangely, had been instrumental in getting Gutmann out of the country.[76]

Both the fate of the Jewish veterans of the List Regiment and the complaints about the relative lack of racial anti-Semitism in the communities of Hitler's former Jewish comrades thus strongly suggest that Private Hitler's core ideology did not really resonate with the majority of the men of his regiment and that Hitler's attempt to widen his popular appeal after 1933 had not really worked. In relative terms, however, there was, of course, growing support for Hitler among the men of RIR 16 after 1933. Whereas prior to Hitler's rise to power, only a tiny number of veterans had fully supported the Nazi Party by joining it, a significant minority of veterans joined the party of their former wartime brother-in-arms after 1933.

While, as we have seen, only 2 per cent of the List veterans had joined Hitler's party by 1933, an additional 12.2 per cent entered the NSDAP between 1933 and the outbreak of the Second World War.[77] Those of the veterans who joined the party of their former comrade after 1933 did so for a variety of reasons, ranging from genuine ideological conviction in Hitler's cause to opportunism. One of the opportunists was Dr Albert Huth, a List veteran, careerist, and civil servant in the Bavarian employment agency. Having joined the SA in the second half of 1933 in order not to have to become a member of the Nazi Party, he became a member of the NSDAP anyway when SA members were automatically signed up for Hitler's party in 1937.[78] Two of the other new recruits to Hitler's cause were Ernst Tegethoff and Franz Aigner. The former had been an interpreter with regimental HQ during the war, while the latter, a Catholic, was a veteran of 1st Company and a policeman from Munich. Both joined the NSDAP in 1933, while Aigner also became a member of the National Socialist veterans' association and the NS-Reichskriegerbund. However, Aigner did not stop there. In order to be able to join the criminal investigation department of the Munich police, he joined the Gestapo in 1938.[79]

While support for Hitler had thus grown among the List veterans by the time the Second World War broke out, the levels of growth had been pitiful compared with Hitler's megalomaniac claims. The continued low levels of outright and unqualified support for their former comrade from the Great War among the men of RIR 16 was not as unusual as one might think. If an anonymous postal survey of their political attitudes during the Third Reich among 715 randomly selected Germans, conducted in 1985, is reliable, only

18 per cent of Germans had held an unqualified 'positive' view of National Socialism,[80] a figure almost exactly the same as the percentage of RIR 16 veterans who joined the Nazi Party.

If so few veterans from the List Regiment, so few people in the recruitment regions of RIR 16, and so few Germans in general fully supported Hitler, how, then, did he manage to stay in power for more than twelve years, unleashing war and genocide at an unprecedented level? Part of the answer is that Hitler's regime thrived to a large degree on partial support.[81] Even though only a minority of RIR 16 veterans wholeheartedly embraced all aspects of Nazi ideology, a far larger number of them gave partial support to Hitler.

A good example of such support is the qualified backing Anton von Tubeuf gave to Hitler. While in power, Hitler continued to adore von Tubeuf. In 1935, he even promoted him retrospectively to colonel.[82] Yet von Tubeuf doggedly refused to join the Nazi Party. Little is known about von Tubeuf's own political convictions but most signs suggest that he was the kind of German conservative who would never have voted for the Nazi Party yet who nevertheless saw the National Socialists as useful political allies. Some of Tubeuf's family members had actively supported Hitler's party from early on. His family indeed included members of the SS and veterans of Hitler's failed 1923 *coup d'état*. However, Tubeuf's brother, a professor at Munich University, had protested against the dismissal of Jewish academics in 1933. Tubeuf's niece, meanwhile, married a Jew. In November 1944 both she and her husband were arrested. While she survived the war, her husband fell victim to the Holocaust. Both Tubeuf's sister and her children ended up in internment camps.[83] Whatever von Tubeuf's exact political beliefs, he neither joined the Nazi Party, nor actively resisted Hitler. Because of the existence of a large number of Germans like von Tubeuf, it was easy for the Nazi regime to stay in power, even without unqualified majority support.

Even Franz Aigner's behaviour during the Third Reich was far more ambiguous than his Gestapo membership would suggest, as the denazification tribunal he had to face after the war recognized. Initially he received a sentence of two years and four months in a labour camp for his involvement with the Third Reich. However, his appeal tribunal decided that his actions during the Third Reich only warranted a classification of him as an opportunist, or *Mitläufer*. In their decision, the tribunal took into account the testimony, for instance, of a neighbour of the Gestapo man who was married to a Jew. She stated that Aigner had always been kind to them and had helped to rescind an evacuation order that would have thrown them out of their apartment in 1938, the year of *Kristallnacht*. Then in 1942, he tipped off an acquaintance who secretly corresponded with a Jewish relative of an imminent search of her apartment by the Gestapo. Similarly, during the Second World War the RIR 16 veteran was briefly arrested himself while serving on the French–German border for sending a hearing- and speech-impaired Jew who accidentally had crossed the border into Germany back into France. According to credible testimony provided by several witnesses, Aigner declared after his own arrest that he wanted to leave the Nazi Party. However, after he was threatened with being sent either to a concentration camp or to the Eastern Front, he decided to continue to stay in the party and to serve in the police.[84]

Tegethoff's denazification panel, meanwhile, decided that he also had been an opportunist. However, Tegethoff's opportunism had not been particularly selfish. When Hitler came to power, he taught at a Catholic school in the Bavarian countryside. He only joined the Nazi Party and the National Socialist Teachers' Association after his director had told him that doing so would help to prevent the closure of the school by Nazi authorities. Unlike many other members of regimental HQ he never met Hitler again after the war. When Nazi authorities tried to persuade him to act as an interpreter for a propaganda tour of the veterans' of RIR 16 to France that took place in 1938, he declined the offer. More than that, in the staunchly Catholic milieu of his students, the former NCO from regimental HQ and editor of collections of French fairy tales was brave enough, as one of his students from the early 1940s recalled, to poke fun at the stupidity of Nazi functionaries and to tell his students that Hitler had been known as the 'mad Austrian' in regimental HQ. In his classroom, Tegethoff was also said to have removed his Nazi Party lapel from his jacket, only putting it on again as he left his students at the end of each lesson. According to his students, Tegethoff also hid a 'half-Jewish' woman in his apartment for a while.[85]

While never joining the Nazi Party, Alois Schnelldorfer, like millions of other Germans, meanwhile, initially hoped that the new regime would deliver on its promise to bring economic recovery. Like many of his countrymen, he divorced the violence of the Third Reich from Hitler, blaming the SA for it and believing that his former comrade from the regimental HQ could not possibly condone mass violence.[86]

Why Hitler's regime could blossom for more than a decade also becomes apparent in the behaviour of three of the Protestant chaplains of RD 6. Epitomizing the problematic relationship between the Protestant Church and the National Socialists, at least two of them gravitated between support of and outright opposition to the Third Reich.

Oscar Daumiller's career really took off during the years of the Third Reich. In 1934, he became Kreisdekan, or head, of the Protestant Church in southern Bavaria. While many Protestants in Germany were in exuberant mood once Hitler came to power and while Daumiller had publicly shown support for Hitler in 1932,[87] Daumiller's career was not a result of Hitler's ascent to power. Once Hitler had been appointed Reich Chancellor, Daumiller immediately saw what Hitler's true colours were and realized that the advice he had given to voters to use support for Hitler as a vehicle to set up a more nationalist conservative state had been foolhardy. When the Protestant Church essentially split into two, with the 'German Christians' supporting the Third Reich and those supporting the 'Confessing Church' being critical of Hitler, Daumiller joined forces with the 'Confessing Church', as did Friedrich Käppel, who had also served as a divisional chaplain under Daumiller for a while. In 1933, Daumiller also resigned his membership in the Kriegerverein when it was incorporated into the NS-Reichskriegerbund. In 1934, the Protestant Bishop of Bavaria, Hans Meiser, sent him to Nuremberg to support the Confessing Church in Nuremberg against the 'German Christians'. As a result of his actions in Nuremberg, the 'German Christians' tried to force Daumiller out of office, temporarily suspending him from his post and banning him from public speaking. The 'German Christians' ultimately did not prevail in this. However, the Nazi regime did everything it could to intimidate people like Daumiller. The Gestapo repeatedly called him in and threatened him with arrest. They also appeared at Käppel's residence in 1939 to conduct a search of his house.[88]

By contrast, Hermann Kornacher, one of the former divisional Protestant ministers under Oscar Daumiller, who was physically almost a spitting image of Daumiller, moved from a critical distance to Hitler to being a supporter of the Third Reich. Initially, little love had been lost between Kornacher and Nazi authorities. After 1933, he was a member of the Confessing Church. In 1934, when Kornacher, a pastor in a Protestant parish in Erlangen in Franconia, who was about to take up a new post in Kempten in southern Bavaria, openly criticized the Nazi regime in his final sermon in his old parish, the local Nazi authorities were not amused.[89] They thus cancelled a farewell meeting with the members of his parish and placed an article critical of him in the local newspaper:

> Ministers of the kind we do not desire! Away with the Ministers Kornacher and Baum.
>
> Last night Ministers Kornacher and Baum wanted to bid their farewell to the parish in the Colloseum Hall. The planned event was, however, banned by the Political Police at the instigation of the NSDAP district headquarters, as the two ministers agitated in the most inflammatory manner in church yesterday morning, as a result of which serious disturbances were feared. The uproar among all classes is so intense that only a swift removal of the two ministers from Erlangen will save them from the justice of the mob.[90]

While in Kempten, Kornacher initially continued his critical stance towards the regime of Private Hitler. However, by 1936, Kornacher, believed that the Third Reich and Hitler were becoming more moderate, as did many other Germans.[91] The hope was that the violence and political extremism of the early period of the Third Reich had just been the unwelcome symptoms of a revolution and that Hitler had calmed down, ready to institute a conservative regime in a more traditional mould. In 1936, after the Rhineland had been returned to full German sovereignty, and men close to the Confessing Church had been appointed to senior positions in the church hierarchy, and after Hitler had given a speech in which he appeared conciliatory towards the Christian Churches, Kornacher decided that it was time to abandon his opposition to the Third Reich. On 28 March, the day prior to the 1936 sham plebiscite, the local newspaper in Kempten published a public appeal under the title, 'Why I will give my vote to the Führer on 29 March'. In the appeal, Kornacher and three other Protestant ministers in Kempten called on the population to vote for Hitler 'because they [i.e. the four Protestant ministers] had suffered, together with all Volksgenossen [compatriots], under the dishonour and lies of Versailles, they support with a clear conscience the will to liberate and to triumph of the man, to whom leadership of our people is entrusted and who, if any time, needs our prayers, our devotion and our loyalty.'[92] Kornacher, however, realized soon that his hopes that Private Hitler and the Third Reich had changed had merely been an illusion. Soon he was back criticizing the Third Reich as well as anti-Jewish pogroms and euthanasia. When, for instance, pro-Nazi posters were put up on his church doors after the 'Anschluss' of Austria, he removed them.[93]

How widespread partial support for Hitler exactly was among the veterans of his regiment is impossible to quantify. However, the small number of veterans who fully supported Hitler, as well as the motivation of the partial support of some of the veterans whom we have come across, suggest that the number of veterans who gave partial support to Hitler out of ideological conviction was limited. In other words, it is likely that no overwhelming majority among the veterans of RIR 16 existed that gave either full or partial support, that was driven primarily by conviction, to National Socialism. This finding is well in line with survey results about the behaviour of the German population at large, carried out in the 1980s and 1990s. The 1985 survey of 715 Germans suggests that in addition to the 18 per cent of Germans during the years of the Third Reich who had a 'positive' view of National Socialism, another 31 per cent had 'mostly positive' views, while 9 per cent had either ambivalent or neutral views and 43 per cent had 'mostly negative' or 'negative' views of National Socialism.[94] This would indicate that half the adult German population had sympathy for Hitler's regime at some point between 1933 and 1945. It is likely that the figures among the veterans of the List Regiment and the population of the main recruitment regions of RIR 16 were even lower than that.

A series of surveys from the 1990s, similar to the one from 1985, suggest that in predominantly Catholic regions support for Hitler remained much lower than in Protestant regions throughout the years of the Third Reich. For instance, only 31 per cent of the population of Cologne and 39 per cent of the inhabitants of Krefeld are believed to have harboured 'positive' or 'mostly positive' views of National Socialism.[95] Support among Catholics of the generation that had fought in the First World War was even lower than that. Of those surveyed in Cologne who had been born prior to 1910, only 23 per cent had sympathy with National Socialism.[96] The question, of course, remains how reliable surveys carried out in the 1980s and 1990s are in unearthing the political attitudes of Germans during the Third Reich. However, the fact that, for instance, 80 per cent of the people surveyed in Dresden, with a high-school education, admitted to having held sympathies with the Nazis[97] indicates that the survey results are almost certainly fairly trustworthy. In other words, the fact that people from a social, religious, and regional background, among whom we would expect high levels of support for National Socialism, had no problems admitting to their past support for Hitler in an anonymous survey, indicates that the surveys from the 1980s and 1990s about attitudes towards National Socialism prior to 1945 are fairly reliable.

If only half the German population is likely to have held positive or mostly positive views of National Socialism, where then does the claim come from that most Germans supported Hitler by the late 1930s? In the absence of democratic elections or reliable contemporaneous polling data, this view is essentially based on the results of the elections and plebiscites that the Nazis staged in 1934, 1936, and 1938; photos depicting crowds ecstatically cheering Hitler and other Nazi leaders or crowds attending public executions;[98] internal Nazi reports and intelligence gathered by Social Democrats who had gone into exile; and letters, diaries, and other sources relating to a selected number of individuals.

All these sources, however, are likely to overestimate the support Hitler received, as they tend to take public (and often staged) expressions of support as representative of society at large. Ultimately, of course, any statement made about the political attitudes of those large numbers of Germans who neither publicly supported, nor openly resisted, the regime is little more than an unfalsifiable hypothesis. However, it is safe to say that the problem with taking expressions of support, in the absence of widespread protest, as representative of the population at large is that in repressive dictatorships the default behaviour of people in disagreement with the status quo is to keep their heads down, rather than openly to speak up, due to the prohibitively high cost of protest. While the Third Reich accepted occasional semi-private expressions of disgruntlement, it struck down uncompromisingly with an iron fist both public expressions of dissent and attempts at dissenting collective action. Yet in dictatorships in which even loyalists have no vehicle to voice their dissent, no dissenting collective action is likely to occur without outside triggers. Where such a trigger does not emerge, simulated compliance—in the form of passive and opportunistic conformity (by publicly lying about one's own political preferences and by putting on false appearances) is the order of the day. Political privatism, rather than open expressions of political opposition, is the most common behaviour for dissenting people in authoritarian states. This all creates the potentially deceptive image of a stable regime with widespread popular support. Worse still, authoritarian regimes are provided with an extra lifeline through the public lies of members of the public about their real political preference.[99] We should not, then, be satisfied to interpret the absence of widespread protest in authoritarian states and the existence of some impressionistic reports as well as of photos depicting people cheering on the leaders of a regime as necessarily equating with almost universal support.

Particularly problematic has been the use of photographic evidence in publications which argue that, by 1939, the overwhelming majority of Germans backed Hitler. How do we know, for instance, that the people attending public executions[100] did so as an expression of support for the Third Reich, rather than out of sympathy with the condemned prisoners or for apolitical reasons? Similarly images depicting cheering and Nazi flag-waving Germans tell us nothing about how widespread support for Hitler was, in the same way that, for instance, a photo of a cheering sea of children from the fortieth anniversary of the German Democratic Republic, taken weeks before the fall of the Berlin Wall, would not be able to prove the popularity of Socialism among East Germans in 1989.

The fact that many of those disagreeing with Hitler kept their heads down did not constitute any problem for the Third Reich. In fact, wide-spread partial support for a regime, in combination with non-action among those partially or fully disagreeing with the status quo, allows authoritarian regimes, if necessary, to sustain themselves on relatively little core support. It even allows them to carry out unspeakable crimes. For instance, in a study of the involvement of the members of two police units in the Holocaust who, in effectively carrying out orders, became grass-root perpetrators of genocide, it was found that only between 24 and 31 per cent of the members of the unit were eager and ideologically motivated killers.[101]

Authoritarian regimes in Europe throughout the twentieth century— irrespective of whether they legitimately came to power, used *coups d'état*, or were forced upon one state by a more powerful one; irrespective of the prior histories of the states in which they were instituted; and irrespective of their political ideology—all survived for years, many for decades. Even if many authoritarian regimes might well have carried the ultimate seed of their own destruction in their fabric from inception, the short- and medium-term default position of all authoritarian regimes was their stability, which is why there is no easy equation between a regime's stability and its popularity.

The cases of men like Fridolin Solleder reveal why it has been so easy throughout the twentieth century for authoritarian states and dictatorships around the world to stay in power as long as they managed to seize control of central state institutions in the first place. The former vice-chairman of the veterans' association of the List Regiment and member of the most pro-Weimar party bravely wrote an article in early 1934 against one of the central tenets of Nazi ideology, the ideal of racial purity. He argued that Albrecht Dürer, the famous Renaissance artist and icon of the German nationalist Right, was of mixed ethnic heritage and that his case thus, in fact, showed that the mixing of the blood of peoples and tribes was more likely to create genius than racial purity. However, once he had been reprimanded for his article, Solleder decided that he did not want to compromise his career and his personal well-being, henceforth abstaining from any open criticism of National Socialism and keeping his head down, and subsequently making the most of the fact that he had edited the regimental history of Hitler's regiment. Solleder thus managed to be appointed the Director of the Bavarian State Archive in Nuremberg in 1940. While he was never to join the NSDAP and while the appraisals he received throughout the years of the Third Reich make it patently clear that his superiors were perfectly aware that Solleder did not believe in Nazi ideology, it was men like Solleder who through their service kept the Third Reich alive arguably more than anyone else.[102]

Authoritarian regimes such as the Third Reich thus managed to enforce cooperation even of those who had been full of disdain for Hitler's ideology but who had decided that the cost of protest was too high and its likely benefits too low—in other words, that individual acts of protest were unlikely to bring the regime down but were highly likely to have an immediate negative effect on the well-being and the careers of their families. The full and partial support afforded to Hitler by up to half the German population, in combination with the conformity of the great majority of those Germans who did not agree with Hitler, thus allowed Private Hitler progressively to radicalize his policies. These popular attitudes ultimately made it possible for him to lift the smokescreen from his real motives and to start his second war, a war that was meant to avoid the mistakes he thought had been made during his First War.

13

Hitler's Second War

1939–1945

Throughout the 1930s, Hans Ostermünchner, Alois Schnelldorfer, and many of their fellow veterans from the List Regiment were far from being alone in their hope and desire that the Great War would be the only war they would have to experience in their lifetimes.[1] The majority of Germans had no taste for a new war. Hitler was popular not because he was seen to plan for war but because he had undone the Versailles Treaty without war, thus being viewed as 'General Bloodless'.[2] Moreover, many Germans, including Alois Schnelldorfer,[3] divorced the violence of the Third Reich from Hitler, assuming that it was rogue elements, particularly in the SA, rather than Hitler, who were behind the regime's terror. A postcard personally signed by Hitler that Jackl Weiß kept among his most treasured possessions—depicting Hitler feeding two fawns and bearing the caption 'The Führer as a friend of animals' (see Plate 22)—gives us a good indication that even Hitler's closest comrades from the war did not associate aggressive warmongering activity with their former comrade. Private Hitler, meanwhile, had been busily building up Germany's military capability ever since coming to power, using his own war experience in RIR 16 as a clever smokescreen for his real plans for aggression, the goal of which he had defined in 1933, in the presence of several generals, as 'expanding the living space of the German people . . . with arms'.[4]

Hitler ruthlessly told people both at home and abroad to rest assured that he would do everything in his power to prevent a new war, as he had experienced the horrors of war himself. However, to avoid war, Hitler reasoned, Germany had to rearm in order to be taken seriously, thus making possible a peaceful resettlement of the Versailles Treaty that would bring long-term peace and stability to Europe. As early as in December 1933,

Hitler wrote to Lord Rothermere, the British newspaper tycoon and Nazi sympathizer: 'As an old soldier of the world war—I was myself in the front line for four and a half years facing British and French soldiers—we have all of us a very personal experience of the terrors of European war. Refusing my community with cowards and deserters we freely accept the idea of duty before God and our own nation to prevent with all possible means the recurrence of such a disaster.'[5] Hitler also used his own war experience to persuade Neville Chamberlain, the chief architect of British appeasement towards Germany, that all Germany wanted was to undo peacefully the injustices of the Versailles Treaty. Standing in front of a copy of a painting depicting Private Henry Tandey, one of the most decorated British soldiers from the Great War, which hung in Hitler's alpine retreat, he told Chamberlain an unlikely story of how Private Tandey had encountered him personally during the war and how Tandey could have shot him dead but had refused to do so.[6]

As part of Hitler's decoy for his real plans, in 1938, he sponsored a trip of approximately 200 List veterans to the places where the regiment had been deployed during the war. The *Völkischer Beobachter* used the occasion to claim, only thirteen months before Hitler's troops were to start overrunning Europe, 'that neither a feeling of hatred nor of revenge existed between the German and French front-line combatants but that a pure and honest front-line and warrior *Kameradschaft* was shared by everyone'.[7] This was indeed the sentiment felt during the trip. Among the veterans travelling to France was Alois Schnelldorfer, who recalled that everywhere the veterans of Hitler's regiment went, French hosts and German guests alike expressed the hope that war would never return.[8] Private Hitler, however, had fooled them all, as he readily admitted in late 1938 to Nazi journalists and publishers: 'It was only out of necessity that for years I talked of peace.'[9]

Twenty years and ten months after the end of his first war, the former dispatch runner from RIR 16 unleashed a new war—a conflict that would leave an estimated 60 million people dead. On the day war broke out, the mood of most Germans was sombre. While in 1914 sufficient numbers of Germans had assembled in Odeonsplatz and in public squares all over Germany at least superficially to give the appearance of enthusiasm for the war, even that did not happen on the day that Hitler's second war started. In response, Hitler made one of his rare appearances in parliament. As Germany's troops overran Poland on 1 September 1939, he tried everything he could to sell the conflict as a defensive war that had been forced upon Germany, just as the Great War supposedly had been. Huddled around radio transmitters in their living rooms across Bavaria, the veterans of the List Regiment could hear their former comrade tell the German people now that they all had to follow the example he had set as an ordinary soldier in the last war and uncompromisingly defend their country:

> This night for the first time Polish regular soldiers fired on our own territory. Since 5.45 a.m. we have been returning the fire, and from now on bombs will be met with bombs. . . . I will continue this struggle, no matter against whom, until the safety of the Reich and its rights are secured. . . . I am asking of no German man more than I myself was ready throughout four years at any time to do. There will be no hardships for Germans to which I myself will not submit. . . . I am from now on just first soldier of the German Reich. I have once more put on that coat that was the most sacred and dear to me. I will not take it off again until victory is secured, or I will not survive the outcome.[10]

The youngest ones among the RIR 16 veterans were still young enough initially to be asked to put on again, like Hitler, their 'sacred coats' and fight for Germany. Alois Schnelldorfer, for instance, had to report for duty after the outbreak of war. However, soon army authorities realized that the army had little use for men in their forties. As Schnelldorfer was sent home again,[11] it was thus the generation of those who had been too young to fight in Hitler's first war who defeated Poland within six weeks and who in the spring conquered with lightning speed Denmark, Norway, the Netherlands, Belgium, and France. It was a considerable personal triumph for Hitler that in as little as forty-four days Germany managed to defeat the two countries in which he had spent more than four unsuccessful years between 1914 and 1918.

After the fall of France, a triumphant Hitler, in the company of Ernst Schmidt and Max Amann, thus returned to the places which had been his home between 1914 and 1918. For two days, the three veterans of the List Regiment visited the places of Hitler's first war, stopping amongst other places in Gheluvelt, Wytschaete, Messines, Comines, Fournes, Fromelles, and Vimy,[12] where subsequently signs were put up to remind passing German soldiers that 'In 1916, our Führer Adolf Hitler lay in these quarters as a soldier of the Bavarian Inf. Rgt. List'.[13] During the trip, Hitler also visited Ypres and the German military cemetery to capitalize on the Langemarck myth and thus remind a generation of new young Germans that it should be their duty and their honour enthusiastically and unreservedly to fight for Germany.[14]

During the war, the Nazi propaganda machine continued to make the most of Hitler's war experience in its attempt to rally the German people behind Hitler. It tried its utmost to capitalize on Hitler's visit to the places at which the List Regiment had been deployed in the Great War. To that end, Heinrich Hoffmann, Hitler's photographer, accompanied him to Belgium and France. Soon after the visit, Hoffmann brought out *Mit Hitler im Westen*, a beautifully produced book with a print-run in the hundred of thousands, which showed Hitler, for instance, in the company of Schmidt and Amann (see Plate 8) in the garden of the former regimental HQ in Fournes and at the Canadian war memorial at Vimy Ridge.[15]

Hitler's regime also tried to benefit from the myth surrounding his First World War regiment by naming a new unit after RIR 16, which, as we have seen, ceased to exist at the end of the Great War. The Grenadier Regiment 19 was thus redesignated as 'List Regiment' in 1942.[16]

While most Germans would have preferred to have avoided a new war in 1939, the phenomenal successes of 1939 and 1940 and the early successes in the Balkans and the Soviet Union let most Germans forget their qualms about a new war, which helped to sustain Hitler's popularity. It is, however, doubtful whether Hitler's popular support really was, as conventionally believed,[17] on a meteoric upward swing from the moment Poland was defeated until Germany's 6th Army was obliterated in Stalingrad in late 1942 and early 1943.

A good indicator of how the popularity of Hitler and his regime changed during the war is to look at the changing popularity of the name 'Adolf' and 'Horst' (after Horst Wessels, a Nazi activist killed by Communists in 1930 and lionized by the Nazis after his death) for new babies. The popularity of baby names cannot, of course, measure the absolute percentage of Germans supporting Hitler but gives a good indication of changes in public opinion. The popularity of the name 'Adolf' decreased steadily from the moment Hitler embarked on war, while the popularity of the name 'Horst' only grew marginally between 1939 and 1940 and then plunged dramatically.[18] This would suggest that Germany's early successes in the war did not translate into a phenomenal rise in the Nazis' popularity. Furthermore, the men of the new List Regiment, who were fighting on the Eastern Front, were less proud to serve in a unit named after the Führer's First World War regiment than they worried about the impact on their safety that the new name tag added to their uniforms would have if they fell into the hands of Russians. As a soldier serving in the new List Regiment was to recall: 'We were now even more afraid to become prisoners of the Russians because [we were worried that] they would see us as a Nazi elite [unit].'[19] The very small number of RIR 16 veterans who joined the Nazi Party during the war also suggests that the war did not suddenly became hugely and overwhelmingly popular after it had turned out victorious. During the entire war only 1.6 per cent of the veterans of Hitler's regiment became new members of his party.[20]

It would, of course, be wrong to suggest that Hitler's second war was hugely unpopular. Among wide sections of society, particularly among young Germans, it was indeed very popular. Men like my own grandfather—who was accepted into the Luftwaffe as a volunteer in 1943 at the age of 17—were extremely proud to be admitted into the German armed forces. However, the argument here is that while the war was not hugely unpopular, it was not overwhelmingly popular either. Even prior to the invasion of the Soviet Union—at a time when Nazi Germany was still unbeaten on the European continent—secret reports from the southern Bavarian countryside suggested, in language reminiscent of similar reports from the First World War, that the mood was 'bad and tired of war'.[21] As we have seen while encountering the reasons why the men of the List Regiment continued to fight in the First World War for more than four years, a willingness to fight should not necessarily be equated with an enthusiasm to fight. Once a nation is embroiled in war, the default position for men is to continue fighting for a host of reasons. Moreover, while the cost of protest in authoritarian states is already prohibitively high during peacetime, it becomes unacceptably high during a war as acts of protest or other acts of resistance are now seen as treason in a situation where the nation is under siege. Moreover, many members of the German resistance thought that they had to wait for the right moment to attack Hitler, in order to avoid creating a renewed 'stab-in-back' legend that would undermine their legitimacy.[22] These facts arguably help to explain why so few Germans ever openly resisted Hitler during the war and why it took those conservatives who ultimately tried to assassinate Hitler so long to take action. The threshold to engage in acts of collective resistance[23] was thus only lowered sufficiently for a critical mass of Germans in the second half of the Second World War, culminating in the attempt on Hitler's life on 20 July 1944. However, much earlier on a number of men from the List Regiment and its brigade had already crossed the line from support, collaboration, or cooperation with Hitler to resistance. Among them were Wilhelm Diess, Ludwig von Vallade, and Friedrich Wiedemann, Hitler's adjutant.

During the war, Ludwig von Vallade, the former commander of RIB 12, formed a resistance group which included Wilhelm Diess, with whom he had occasionally played the piano during the First World War; as we have seen, Diess had given the main address at the List reunion at which Hitler had been shunned. It also included a number of former high-ranking officers as well as the closest aide to Rupprecht von Bayern. They met regularly to discuss their stand towards Hitler as well as steps that should be taken to bring him down. Towards the end of his life, von Vallade was to state that the greatest regret of his life was that their discussions had not been translated into an attempt on Hitler's life.[24]

Rupprecht himself travelled to Italy in late 1939 and was not allowed to re-enter Germany for the entire course of the Second World War. While in Florence, he was put up for a while and helped by the Franchetti family, an aristocratic Jewish family related to the Rothschilds.[25] When his wife and children followed him to Italy in early 1940, SS men shouted at Rupprecht's children: 'You all should have been shot a long time ago.'[26]

Realizing that Hitler's myth about his First World War years continued to be his Achilles heel, the Conservative resistance to Hitler tried to find out the truth behind Hitler's war service. Rather unfortunately, they made contact with Hans Mend, who was not the most reliable of sources, as we have seen.

Early in the Second World War, Hans Mend was interviewed by Friedrich Schmid Noerr, who probably knew Mend because they both lived on Lake Starnberg south of Munich, where Mend worked as a riding instructor at Eltzholz Castle. In an honest attempt to dig up murky aspects of Hitler's past for a resistance group that had been formed in the German Military Intelligence Service, Schmid Noerr interviewed Mend for several hours. It was now that Mend told the tale of Hitler's homosexual activities as well as a lot of other equally unlikely yarns. Schmid Noerr subsequently passed on the summary of his interview to Wilhelm Canaris, the chief of the Military Intelligence Service, and to General Ludwig Beck, the general who had broken with Hitler in 1938, as well as to a number of foreign diplomats.[27] We do not know how they responded to Mend's account. However, it is not too difficult to imagine that Mend did not help his own cause. His testimony would no doubt have had a greater impact had he stuck to the facts rather than tell Schmid Noerr whatever he thought the philosopher wanted to hear.

Soon Mend, who had been in and out of prison since his release from Dachau, was again in prison. In March 1941, he was sentenced to another two years. In attempts to strike up extramarital affairs, he had boasted about his personal encounters with Hitler, telling young women he encountered on Lake Starnberg of Hitler's homosexuality. He claimed 'that he knew the Führer well and knew exactly why the Führer was not getting married,' adding that 'the Führer had lived with him for weeks on end and had often stood in front of him with his dressing gown open.' Mend told the young women, between claiming that he would fulfil their wildest wishes and fantasies, that Hitler had had 'the others who were like that shot and [Hitler] himself was also that way'. Once jailed, this time, Mend was not to leave prison again. The former cavalry dispatch rider and author of one of the most hagiographical accounts of Hitler's years in the List Regiment finally died in prison in 1942 almost certainly of natural causes.[28]

Oscar Daumiller, meanwhile, who had long realized his misjudgement of Hitler in 1932, was in contact with one of the leading members of the White Rose resistance group. Soon after Sophie and Hans Scholl, two university students and today the most famous members of the group, had been arrested following their failed attempt to distribute their anti-Hitler flyers at Munich University, Professor Kurt Huber, one of their co-conspirators, was also apprehended. When the Gestapo interrogated Huber, they tried to implicate Oscar Daumiller, showing him incriminating documents against Daumiller and trying to force Huber to tell them about the degree to which Daumiller was involved in the resistance to Hitler. Huber bravely resisted these pressures and through a Protestant minister he was allowed to see in prison prior to his execution, he warned Daumiller that the Nazi regime was targeting him too.[29]

The most astonishing change of heart towards Hitler, however, did not occur with Daumiller but with Fritz Wiedemann. No man from the List Regiment had been as close to Hitler as Wiedemann after 1934. Few men in general had indeed been as close to Hitler, since Wiedemann was one of his personal adjutants.

At the height of his power in the summer of 1938, when Goering was about to send Wiedemann to London on a precarious mission, no one could have foreseen Wiedemann's actions during the Second World War. At the time, Wiedemann's task in London was to find out whether Goering could be invited to England. Goering thought that an understanding between Germany and Britain could be reached but the new German foreign secretary, Joachim von Ribbentrop, whom Goering thought incompetent and stupid, stood in the way of any deal with Britain. Hitler had given approval for the visit, during which Wiedemann met Lord Halifax, the British foreign secretary. With the news in his pocket that the British were in principle prepared to invite Goering (which is not quite what Halifax had said but was what Wiedemann had heard) and that one day they would like to invite Hitler to London, he travelled back to Germany. However, by the time Wiedemann arrived back in Berlin, Hitler had lost interest in the endeavour, while Ribbentrop was furious that Wiedemann had gone behind his back. From that point on, Wiedemann's position was weakened. When it then became known that Wiedemann thought that Hitler should make a compromise on his territorial demands against Czechoslovakia in order to avoid war, Hitler dismissed Wiedemann in January 1939.[30] After the war, while giving testimony in the run-up to the Nuremberg Trials, Wiedemann claimed, maybe somewhat self-servingly, that Hitler had told him on dismissing him: 'I have no use for people in my entourage who do not support my policies with their full heart.'[31]

In early 1939, Hitler decided that he wanted to get the former adjutant of his regiment out of his sight, yet he still felt obliged to him and remained courteous towards him even then. Hitler thus appointed Wiedemann as German Consul General in San Francisco, the city that Wiedemann had loved since his 1937 holidays in America.[32] As a US interrogator put it in 1945, Wiedemann had 'showed [his] dissatisfaction and [was] put in the doghouse'.[33]

On arrival on the West Coast of America, Wiedemann set up residence in the affluent suburb of Hillsborough between the San Francisco Bay and the Pacific Ocean and contemplated his next move. US authorities were rather nervous about his arrival, suspecting that a former top aide to Hitler on a third-rate diplomatic posting could only mean that Wiedemann was on a secret mission to set up and run a Japanese–American spy ring out of San Francisco. An American illustrated magazine covering his arrival in the Bay area was clearly confused about Wiedemann: 'The Captain's arrival was somewhat of an anticlimax. Instead of a shorn-haired, gimlet-eyed officer of the Prussian type, the reporters found a friendly and very courteous man with a quick smile and pleasant manners.' According to the magazine, Wiedemann's 'appearance was attractive. Tall, dark, and immaculate, he looks ten years younger than his age of 48. He dresses informally but well. The pugnaciousness in his face with his massive jaw and low, receding forehead disappears when he grins—and he grins frequently.' With his 'disarming way', the former regimental adjutant of RIR 16 was 'to the newspapermen . . . a surprise and a disappointment'. The article also noted that he had acted in a most reserved manner towards local Nazis and that in a speech he had told 'West-coast Germans that they are not Germans but Americans and should act as such'. Wiedemann even mentioned at parties, to the surprise of the magazine, that he was 'really in disfavour with the Fuehrer'. However, the magazine as well as the FBI, acting on intelligence received from the State Department, concluded that Wiedemann's behaviour was just a smokescreen for his spy activities.[34]

When shortly after Wiedemann, Princess Stephanie von Hohenlohe Waldenburg Schillingfürst—a colourful Hungarian socialite and divorcee in her mid-forties, daughter of a Jewish convert to Catholicism, occasional guest of Hitler's, rumoured lover of Wiedemann, and suspected spy-master—also arrived in San Francisco, the suspicions of the FBI were seemingly confirmed. US authorities speculated that Hitler had sent Stephanie von Hohenlohe, whom the bureau 'characterized as being extremely intelligent, dangerous and clever, and as an espionage agent worse than ten thousand men', to teach Wiedemann how to set up a spy network.[35] It was only during the Second World War that US authorities realized that they had been very much mistaken about the plans of both the former regimental adjutant of RIR 16 and the red-haired Hungarian aristocrat.

Out of genuine disgust with Hitler's policies, disillusionment, or resentment following his demotion, Wiedemann continued to distance himself from Hitler after the outbreak of war.

His distancing started with small things, such as not sending a birthday telegram to Hitler for his birthday in April 1940. Yet he did not leave things there, deciding to make himself available to British intelligence. Using her British contacts, Stephanie von Hohenlohe arranged two meetings with Sir William Wiseman, a New York City-based banker in his mid-fifties, who worked for British intelligence. The second and more crucial of the meetings took place in the presence of Hohenlohe on 27 November 1940 in Wiseman's room in the Mark Hopkins Hotel in San Francisco, lasting from 7.30 p.m. until the early hours of the following morning. After exchanging a few pleasantries, they quickly settled down to business, discussing how the war could be brought to an end and how a lasting peace could be established. There was no beating about the bush. Wiseman flatly stated that 'this peace, to be lasting, cannot and will not be made with Chancellor Adolf Hitler'. Wiedemann immediately agreed, stating that only a constitutional monarchy would have both the legitimacy and stability to secure a lasting, stable, and sustainable peace, arguing that he 'believes that a lasting peace can be made' but 'that this peace must be made with a strong political party, possibly a monarchy headed by the German Crown Prince, and to accomplish this the present Hitler [regime] must be destroyed. In this connection, he stated that Germany should return to the monarchical [system] because the present system has no constitutional rights. . . . it will be necessary to go back and establish some form of government based upon a constitution.' Wiedemann had lost all faith in the former dispatch runner of his regiment, replying to Hohenlohe's question about whether he thought that it would make all the difference if Hitler were removed: 'All the difference'.[36] Hohenlohe also speculated that 'the Jew banker, who is a friend of [Wiedemann's] might be able to help them in their endeavour'.[37]

For very much the same reason that Wiedemann had joined a *Freikorps* in 1919, namely to prevent a Bolshevik takeover of Bavaria, he now opposed Hitler and discussed the best methods of removing him from power. Bolshevism and Hitler's National Socialism, Wiedemann argued, were but two sides of the same coin. He 'commented that besides the great struggle between England and Germany, there was a terrific struggle between Bolshevism and National Socialism on one hand and Capitalism on the other. . . . the only difference between Russian Bolshevism and German Socialism is that Russian Bolshevism has an international aspect and on the other hand, German Socialism is only national. Otherwise . . . the two are identical.'[38] According to the secret FBI recording of their conversation, Hohenlohe, who acted as an interpreter when Wiedemann had difficulty in expressing his thoughts adequately in English, told Wiseman: '[Wiedemann] says that irony of fate consisted in that Hitler, who has had so many people drawn to him and he has gotten them to vote (phonetic) and to pauper (phonetic) by fighting Bolshevism in Germany, who was in truth the person who created Bolshevism in Germany.'[39]

Even though Wiseman flew straight to Washington DC to see his contacts in the British Embassy and to notify Lord Halifax, Wiedemann and Wiseman's initiative came to nothing, in spite of the US President, Franklin D. Roosevelt being briefed.[40] However, the political evolution of Wiedemann provides us with a fascinating insight into how the attitudes of veterans of the regiment towards Hitler were not fixed and unchanging but determined by changing perceptions of who Hitler was and what he stood for.

Half a year after the meeting with Wiseman, Wiedemann again decided that he had to do something against Hitler. He volunteered to provide everything he knew about the Nazi regime to one of the magazines of the publishing empire of William Randolph Hearst, America's most successful and famed media tycoon. However, Wiedemann's offer was vetoed by the US State Department, as the Under-Secretary of State, Sumner Welles, was opposed to bargaining with Wiedemann and, more importantly, was worried about endangering the position of US representatives in Germany, if a German diplomat and former top aide to Hitler was allowed to speak out against him.[41]

After all the German consulates in the US were ordered to close in July 1941, Wiedemann sailed back to Germany, where he had an uncomfortable twenty-minute meeting with Joachim von Ribbentrop, Hitler's foreign minister, who, as we have seen, intensely disliked Wiedemann. Without having seen Hitler, Wiedemann was sent off to a posting in the German consulate in Tientsin, approximately 150 kilometres to the south-east of Beijing—as far out of the sight of Hitler as possible. According to intelligence obtained by the OSS, Wiedemann had been told by army officers while in Germany that they were disgusted at the senseless killing of civilians in the East and had noticed a growing resentment in Bavaria towards northern Germany and the anti-Catholicism of the Nazi regime. While Wiedemann was on the way to his new posting, the director of the OSS, William J. Donovan, asked Roosevelt if he thought it 'desirable, in view of the present situation, to see if Wiedemann would repudiate his party'. In the event, however, the White House and the OSS decided not to pursue the matter further.[42]

While in Tientsin, sensing that he had to jump a sinking ship soon, Wiedemann already prepared notes about his time as Hitler's adjutant, collecting incriminating facts about Hitler and other top Nazis.[43]

What do we make of the behaviour of people like Wiedemann or of others on the Conservative political spectrum such as Oscar Daumiller or Hermann Kornacher, who at some point had supported Hitler but then distanced themselves from him again? For a long time, this question was hopelessly politicized as the generation that had lived through the Third Reich retrospectively constructed a version of their own involvement with the Nazi regime that overemphasized resistance. It continued to be politicized heavily as the children of those implicated with Nazi Germany tried to persuade them to live up to their involvement. However, as the conflict between the generations of 1933 and of 1968 no longer dominates public debate, it has become much easier to explain in non-moralistic terms the collaboration of Germans with Hitler's regime—whether conscious or unconscious, voluntary or involuntary, informed or uninformed, ideological or opportunistic, collusive or combative.

While for a long time there was a tendency to portray the Catholic milieu from which most of the men of the List Regiment came as not fundamentally different from the Nazis for its lack of collective action against crimes committed under Hitler's regime, and to view Conservatives as essentially the same as National Socialists due to their role in bringing Hitler to power, these views have lost much of their persuasive power. We now know, for instance, that, even though the key responsibility for Hitler's rise to power lies with Hitler's voters and with the Conservative establishment, the reason why there was so little Conservative resistance to Hitler until well into the war was to a large extent a result of the coercive measures and the violence against key Conservative figures in 1933, thus rendering Conservative institutions impotent.[44]

The initial ideological distance between men such as Wiedemann and Daumiller on the one hand and Hitler on the other, followed by support for Hitler, and eventual resistance to him suggests that there never was a near congruence between their ideologies. Rather it indicates that they always saw support for Hitler as 'merely' a vehicle to further their own political convictions which, needless to say, does not take away any of their responsibility for the crimes committed under Hitler. Even though the actions of German Conservatives were pivotal in Hilter's rise to power, the Third Reich was not necessarily the sum of the individual intentions and preferences of all the Germans who directly or indirectly had contributed to Hitler's appointment as German Chancellor; political actors regularly behave in ways contingent on one another, frequently creating new political regimes and institutions that are only distantly related to the expected outcomes of most of the actors involved.[45]

The beliefs of the many Germans who were at least temporarily drawn to National Socialism were often different from the ideological core of Hitler's own beliefs, such as, for instance, redemptive anti-Semitism or the belief in an imminent social Darwinian showdown. They were drawn to Hitler's regime for the same reason that Europeans across the continent were drawn to authoritarian, collectivist regimes: for instance, a disillusionment with liberal democracy in the aftermath of the world economic crisis, the growth of leadership cults, anti-Bolshevism, integral nationalism, anti-minority movements, and fear of Russia.[46]

The emergence of the Third Reich was thus a result of two sets of contingent factors, both of which are only marginally linked to the First World War: the first was that a situation arose in the late 1920s and early 1930s that was conducive to the rise of authoritarian, collectivist political movements. The second one was closely related to Hitler. It was that in the German case Hitler, together with other Nazi leaders similar to him—in other words a leader who was often not perceived as, but would ultimately turn out, far more radical than his counterparts in the rest of Europe—was the only viable person on the Right to exploit the opening created by the crisis of the late 1920s and early 1930s for a collectivist, authoritarian movement. This was the case because other right-wing authoritarian, collectivist groups and different (more moderate) factions within the NSDAP had been sidelined for a host of other contingent factors.

As a result of this constellation, many of those who helped Hitler come to power ignored, or were blind to, Hitler's more radical ideas, thinking that he and his party could be used as a tool, for instance, to combat the economic consequences of the Depression, to fight Bolshevism, to 'undo' the Versailles Treaty, or to set up a more conservative state. They did not realize either that Hitler's core beliefs went well beyond their own (in other words, they assumed that Hitler's more radical goals had to be understood metaphorically) or they underestimated the fact that Hitler, once in power, would not treat them as equal partners but sideline, and sometimes even target them, and thus use them as a tool to further his own core beliefs (i.e. they assumed that Hitler would be in no position to carry out his more radical goals).

Hitler's rise to power and the support he at least temporarily received from wide sections of the conservative milieu were thus a result of a whole series of contingent factors. Yet the process we have seen here is common to the rise of charismatic leaders who tend to gain control of the society they wish to destroy by sharing certain traditional features of the society they wish to transform which they exploit at a time of serious disruptions and crises. It is these features that allow them to garner widespread support. Hitler's invocation both of goals that were formally congruent with the goals of many German Conservatives and of the ideals of *Kameradschaft* based on his mythical war experience in the List Regiment thus made it tempting for so many Germans to help Hitler into power; yet it also allowed Hitler, once in power, to pursue policies that many a German who had initially colluded with Hitler, including men like Wiedemann and Daumil-ler, came to rue.[47]

For Hitler himself, his First World War experience in the List Regiment was pivotal for the way he fought the Second World War.

Hitler had not been 'made' by the Great War, as we have seen. Nor did he see his second war as a rerun of his first one. Yet, there is a very direct connection between the two world wars, as far as Hitler was concerned. The link is the way in which Private Hitler tried to put the lessons of the First World War into practice as he saw them from the vantage point of the post-1918 war world (as opposed to the time of the Great War itself). And this is why the Second World War was 'a very, very different war indeed' from Hitler's first war.[48] However, Hitler drew the most import-ant lesson for fighting his second war less from the First World War itself than from history in general (in the form that had filtered through into Hitler's mind in the aftermath of the Great War). The lesson was that nations and states were locked in a Darwinian struggle for survival, which depended on sufficient Lebensraum, or living space, for its people; nations also had to eradicate any influences on them which would weaken them in their epic struggle for survival. A new war thus had to have two goals: to create new Lebensraum and to 'cleanse' the German people of any negative influence. And it was here—in solving the question of how such a war could be won and in identifying supposedly poisonous influences on the nation—that Hitler turned to his First World War experience for inspiration.

The scrupulous German propaganda colossus that was at work during the Second World War, aimed at rallying the German people behind the war and at wooing foreign collaborators, was thus driven by Hitler's belief, as expressed in Mein Kampf, that Germany's allegedly inferior propaganda between 1914 and 1918 had been one of the main causes of Germany's defeat. Another lesson Hitler drew from his first war was that the compara-tively benign and lenient approach towards military justice in his regiment and in the German armed forces as a whole had undermined the German war effort. As a result, between 20,000 and 22,000 German soldiers were executed during the Second World War.[49]

Hitler also claimed that seeing the waste of resources during the First World War at first hand, when soldiers were sent, 'for instance, from Messines to Fournes to take a pound of butter there',[50] taught him to cut waste and use resources more efficiently both in running the German economy and the war effort.

Hitler's own experience in the war almost certainly heavily contributed to the fact that he remained impressed with the fighting power of Britain and of Dominion troops throughout the Second World War, while he never took the French armed forces too seriously. In 1940, Hitler humiliated the French by making them sign the official declaration of surrender in the forest of Compiègne, on the very spot the Germans had to sign the armistice in 1918. He also had the French memorial in the forest blown up. By contrast, shortly after he had had that memorial obliterated, Hitler visited the Canadian war memorial at Vimy Ridge—a stunning and solemn modernist sculpture in which two grieving figures are set against two pylons of sandstone—to pay respect to the almost 60,000 fallen Canadian soldiers of the Great War.[51] Furthermore, Hitler told Wiedemann in 1936 when discussing the Abyssinian question: 'If I had a choice between the Italians and the English, then I would naturally go with the English. Mussolini is closer to me but I know the Englishmen from the last war, I know they are hard fellows.'[52]

Hitler also drew what he thought were positive lessons from the Great War. In 1941, for instance, he used the memory of the perceived partisan attacks in Belgium in 1914 to justify brutal conduct against civilians in the Soviet Union: 'The old Reich already knew how to act with firmness in the occupied areas. That's how attempts at sabotaging the railways in Belgium were punished by Count von der Goltz. He had all the villages burnt within a radius of several kilometres, after having had all the mayors shot, the men imprisoned, and the women and children evacuated. There were three or four acts of violence in all, then nothing more happened.'[53]

As Hitler listened less and less to his own generals after the German war effort had started to turn sour, he increasingly turned to his own war experience for inspiration in deciding how to direct the war. For example, he overruled Heinz Guderian, the commander of the 2nd Panzer Army during the invasion of the Soviet Union, when Guderian advised Hitler to retreat in December 1941. Hitler instructed him that his troops should blast craters in the ground with howitzers, as had been done in Flanders during the First World War, and dig themselves in for the winter, ignoring Guderian's plea that mid-winter conditions in Flanders were hardly comparable to the Russian winter.[54]

Hitler increasingly became prisoner of his own lies which he had internalized. For instance, on 18 June 1944, less than two weeks after the Allied forces had landed in Normandy on D-Day, forgetting that towards the end of the 1918 spring offensive, he and the men of his regiment had had to run for their lives, Hitler, full of megalomania, told his generals that all they had to do was what the Germans had done in early 1918, when 'during our offensive during the Great Battle of France, we chased the Englishmen out of the area completely'.[55] On another occasion, Hitler dismissed advice from his officers because, as Fritz Wiedemann put it, he thought that he knew much more about how to build new positions than his generals 'because he himself as a simple soldier had sat in dugouts', while his generals had seen nothing but drawing boards far behind the front during the Great War.[56]

The longer Hitler directed the Second World War, the more he looked back at, and romanticized, his own experiences as a private in the Great War. In the summer of 1941, for instance, as his soldiers overran the Soviet Union, Hitler declared during one of his infamous monologues that during the Great War, he had been 'passionately glad to be a soldier'.[57] Then in October 1941, he reminisced about his time in the List Regiment as 'the one time' when he had 'had no worries' as food, clothing, and accommodation were all provided for him.[58] Hearing about former comrades from the List Regiment thus provided Hitler with one of the few joys he had after the fall of Stalingrad. For example, when, in 1944, he happened to read an article in a Munich newspaper about the Liebhardt brothers, who had served with him in 1st Company at the beginning of the war, he instructed Max Amann to find out more about the life story of the brothers since 1914.[59]

Those groups that Hitler had retrospectively identified as having had the most negative influence on Germany during the First World War—primarily Jews and Socialists—were sidelined from the day Hitler came to power, as Hitler believed that Germany could only survive the Darwinian showdown that lay ahead, if Germany 'cleansed' herself of Jews and Socialists. Until the end of the 1930s, Hitler's preferred solution to ridding his Third Reich of Jews and Socialists was almost certainly non-genocidal. For the first two years of the war, too, ethnic cleansing, rather than genocide, was meant to free Germany of Jews and to liberate the new *Lebensraum* in the East for German colonization. However, as the Jews whom German forces had rounded up in the occupied territories in the East since 1939 could not be moved anywhere else during wartime and as they were deemed as unnecessary consumers in a time of a worsening shortages, sometime in 1941, Hitler and his regime embarked on genocide as the preferred option. In justifying the physical extermination of the Jews of Europe to himself and to his inner circle, Hitler obsessively repeated his idea that the Jews were the chief culprits of Germany's defeat in his first war. On 25 October 1941, in a disjointed fashion, he told the leader of the SS and his deputy, Heinrich Himmler and Reinhard Heydrich: 'This criminal race has the two million dead of the World War on its conscience, now again hundred of thousands. Don't anyone tell me we can't send them into the marches [*Morast*]! Who bothers, then, about our people? It's good when the horror [*der Schrecken*] precedes us that we are exterminating Jewry.'[60]

By the end of the Holocaust between five and six million Jews had been killed at the hands of a large number of Germans and their local collaborators. Among the victims were at least twelve of the forty-nine Jewish soldiers in RIR 16 who had survived the First World War.[61] Arthur Rödl, meanwhile, was one of the leading perpetrators of the Holocaust. After 1933, the RIR 16 veteran had served in the concentration camps at Lichtenburg, Sachsenburg, and Buchenwald. In 1941, he became the Commander of the Groß-Rosen Concentration Camp, which was at the time primarily a slave labour camp. Under his command, thousands of Soviet POWs were shot dead. From 1943, he served as a Standartenführer (the SS equivalent of a colonel) with the SS in Ukraine and later in Croatia.[62]

The only reason for the survival of a significant number of the Jewish veterans from RIR 16 was the rather reluctant embrace that the democracies of the New World, as well as Britain and her authorities in Palestine, afforded to those who had decided to emigrate from Germany. One of the émigrés was Justin Fleischmann. He and his brothers put all their energy into defeating Private Hitler's regime from the shores of America, just as they had put their whole heart into fighting for Germany during the First World War. While one of Justin's brothers developed and patented high-quality bullets, his other brother was to experience the invasion of Germany as a colonel in the Combined Intelligence Ordnance Section of the US Army.[63]

America also saved the life of Hugo Gutmann. When Hitler's army overran western Europe in 1940, Gutmann and his family managed to flee to Lisbon, from where they set sail for New York on 28 August. Six weeks after arriving in New York City, Gutmann and his family moved on to St Louis. Along with Wiedemann, two of the former regimental adjutants of RIR 16 were now in the United States. Once in Missouri, the officer who had facilitated the Iron Cross 1st Class for the private who was now driving Germany's Jewry out of the country, broke with his past. Gutmann renamed himself, transforming himself from Hugo Gutmann into Henry G. Grant. He declared in court that due to 'many harrowing experiences at the hands of the German Government and its people' he and his family wished to 'dissociate themselves from anything German, including the names they bear'. Living with his wife and two children in an old apartment building on Clara Avenue, a high-rent area of the city close to the fashionable Forest Park, he now worked for the Underwood Elliott Fisher typewriter company in downtown St Louis, telling a local newspaper: 'My past is entirely forgotten and all I want to do now is live peaceably and sell some typewriters.' Two years after their arrival in America, Gutmann/Grant's son Howard Charles (Heinz Werner) joined the US Army, enlisting at Jefferson Barracks in South St Louis County. He was deployed in the European war theatre. Later the son of RIR 16's former regimental adjutant was to join the US civil occupation force of Germany that was to try to extinguish any traces of Private Hitler in the minds of Germans.[64]

Ernst Weiß, the physician and writer to whom Hitler's doctor from Pasewalk had handed over his notes in 1933, was less lucky than Hugo Gutmann. Weiß desperately tried to get out of France after the German invasion of 1940. Not knowing that his visa and transatlantic ticket were already ready and waiting at the American Embassy, he gave up all hope on 14 June 1940 and went to the bathroom attached to his room in Paris, ran a bath, took sleeping pills, and slashed open his wrists, thus taking his life. Another émigré who knew of Hitler's medical history and who had been more fortunate with the destination of his emigration than Weiß was Karl Kroner, a Jewish doctor who had worked with Edmund Forster at Pasewalk and who had emigrated to Iceland. US Naval Intelligence located him there and used his testimony as the core for a report about Hitler that they produced for the Office of Strategic Services.[65] Like Weiß, Karl Mayr found himself stranded in France after the German invasion of 1940. Hitler's former political mentor, who unlike Hitler had ended up a defender of the Weimar Republic and a Social Democrat, was now arrested and taken back to Germany. He died or was killed in Buchenwald Concentration Camp in early 1945.[66]

The widow of Albert Weisgerber—the celebrated officer of the List Regiment—also survived the Holocaust in exile. While she spent the war in London, her family was less fortunate. Weisgerber's brother-in-law pre-empted his own death at the hands of the Nazis by committing suicide, while other members of the family were killed in Nazi camps.[67]

The great tragedy of those Jewish veterans who perished in the Holocaust is that because of their service in the war and the relatively good relations in their communities they remained in Germany,[68] when other German Jews, particularly the young ones, had chosen to leave. For instance, Levi Erlanger's sons, Arnold and Gustav, emigrated to the Netherlands in February 1939 and the daughter of Julius Mannheimer, a veteran of 4th Company, moved to Britain with the financial help of non-Jewish friends of her parents, while their fathers stayed behind. Even fifty years later, the daughter 'still remember[ed] the despair in their eyes when (prior to a rigorous body search) on Munich airport, [she] embraced and kissed them for the last time.'[69]

As the tragic and inadvertent effect of the relatively low levels of anti-Semitism in many of the communities in which RIR 16 veterans lived, many veterans of the List Regiment thus found themselves trapped in Second World War Germany.[70] At the beginning of the war, many of them were forced to carry out slave labour, among them Levi Erlanger and Josef Heller, one of the two other Jewish RIR 16 veterans from Ichenhausen, who were forced to work in a brickworks factory. Julius Mannheimer, meanwhile, had to work in a stone quarry. The material conditions of Erlanger, Heller, Nathan Winschbacher, and their fellow Jews in Ichenhausen also grew progressively worse, as Hitler's regime took the inherent logic of total war, already visible during the Great War, to its extreme, allocating only very meagre food rations to anyone deemed not to be contributing to victory in a total war.

There was, however, a crucial difference between Germany's totalizing war effort in Hitler's first and second wars. This difference was not that only now did the Germans, as did the other warring nations, try to fulfil the full potential of fighting a total war. The fundamental difference was that Private Hitler's policy makers had mixed the concept of total war with that of a racial war, thus allocating resources not according to the ability of individuals to contribute to the war effort, but according to their (per-ceived) ethnic background. This was not an extreme form of the kind of total war fought by the List Regiment in the First World War, but it was its counter-productive perversion. Or differently put, it diverted resources away from the real military conflict in order to fight an imaginary enemy, namely international Judaism. The material conditions of Jewish veterans in Ichenhausen and in other communities was only slightly alleviated by acts of kindness of local non-Jews, who secretly passed them food across the fences of their back gardens.[71]

The first Jewish veteran of RIR 16 had already been killed before the Holocaust started. The veteran was Siegfried Schönfeld from 11th Company who died in Buchenwald Concentration Camp on 20 March 1941.[72] The earliest Jewish veterans to die in the Holocaust were those from Munich. Julius Mannheimer, who had joined the List Regiment on the eve of the Battle of the Somme, decided that, rather than be deported to the East, he would take his own life. On 12 November 1941, eight days before he was to be deported, the recipient of an Iron Cross in the List Regiment threw himself, together with his wife, at 9.27 a.m. in front of a moving train on a suburban railway track.[73] A day and a week later, Karl Goldschmidt, a merchant and former NCO in 9th Company, was deported on a transport that took 999 Jews to the Baltic. On their arrival in Kowno (Kovno) in Lithuania, members of the German Police Battalion 11 and local collaborators took them out of the train and started to march them in the direction of the ghetto. Goldschmidt did not know what awaited him. As the people on his transport were led along the street that cuts through the Kowno ghetto, they asked Jews behind the fences: 'Is the Camp still far away?' They were, however, led straight to Fort IX, a fortification built during tsarist times, where pits had already been dug for their bodies. Once there, Goldschmidt had to climb into the pit. Then the SS Einsatzkommando 3 opened their machine guns on Hitler's fellow soldier from the List Regiment, while they ran the engines of all their trucks continuously, to prevent the gunfire and screaming from being heard. Subsequently they threw hand grenades into the pit full of dying Jews, and ordered the pits to be filled with earth, without first checking if all victims were already dead.[74]

The next Jewish veteran to be murdered was Michael Früh. A veteran of 7th Company and a recipient of an Iron Cross, he had returned after the First World War to his native Fürth, known due to its thriving Jewish community as 'the Bavarian Jerusalem'. Unlike other Jews from his home town, such as young Henry Kissinger, he had decided against emigration. On 24 March 1942, he was taken to the grounds of the monumental Nazi Party rallies in Nuremberg. Together with another 431 Jews, he boarded a train, which took him to the Jewish ghetto of Izbica in Central Poland. In Izbica, he might have met Julius Lindauer, a veteran of 5th Company, who, like Früh, had been the recipient of an Iron Cross. None of the 432 Jews on Früh's train, including Lindauer, survived the Holocaust.[75]

Soon after Früh's and Lindauer's deportation, Nathan Winschbacher and Josef Heller from Ichenhausen and Karl Leiter from Augsburg, who had served in 2nd Company, were taken to Piaski, another ghetto in central Poland. Prior to their departure, they had been told that they were to carry out forced labour in Poland. However, all three veterans of Hitler's regiment were killed either straightaway in Piaski, or subsequently in the death camps of Trawniki (Travniki), Sobibor, or Belzec. Meanwhile, in Ichenhausen, the belongings of Heller, Winschbacher, and their fellow evacuees were sold off in a street auction carried out by the SS and the SA, which attracted a despicable crowd of greedy people from the entire region out for a 'good' bargain.[76]

The deportation and killing of the Jewish veterans still in Germany continued without mercy: in the summer of 1942, Arthur Dreyer, one of the regimental physicians of RIR 16, and Gabriel Steiner, a veteran from 8th Company, were deported on two separate transports to Theresienstadt Concentration Camp. The camp had been set up on the site of a former Habsburg fortress as a 'model' concentration camp for Jewish war veterans with decorations or who had been injured during the war, as well as for other 'privileged' Jews. One of the goals of the establishment of the camp was to deceive the Red Cross and international opinion about the real character of Nazi concentration camps. However, with the exception of a few apartments for prominent Jews at the centre of the camp that took the character of a Potemkian village, conditions were dire in the camp. Shortly after Steiner's and Dreyer's arrival in Theresienstadt, the aunt of Wiedemann's co-conspirator Stephanie von Hohenlohe died there. Dreyer and Steiner did not survive the Holocaust either. Dreyer died in February 1943, whether from the typhus epidemic that was running riot in the camp that winter we cannot know, while Steiner was sent to Auschwitz in January 1943 and killed there, after the Nazis had decided to reduce the number of Jews in Theresienstadt in preparation for an inspection by the International Red Cross and a number of international guests.[77] Auschwitz was also where Levi Erlanger was taken, as was Siegfried Heumann, the veteran who had been a member of the regimental veterans' association and who had bravely protested against the marginalization of Jewish veterans in 1936. Within a few months of each other the two veterans from Hitler's regiment were killed in Auschwitz.[78]

After March 1943, at most a handful of Jewish veterans from the List Regiment were still left in Germany. They were most likely 'protected' Jews; in other words, Jews with non-Jewish wives. Jakob Rafael, from 6th Company, who had been severely injured on the Somme and who had been awarded an Iron Cross, for instance, continued to live in Augsburg, together with his wife, until 22 February 1945. By the time 'protected' Jews were also deported, only forty-four Jews out of more than 1,200 were left in Rafael's home town of Augsburg. Rafael was taken to Theresienstadt concentration camp on the second last deportation from Munich. On the same transport was Hugo Günzburger, the RIR 16 veteran from Memmingen.[79]

It has been suggested that it was a result of the First World War that a crime as heinous as the Holocaust could occur: 'What the 1914–18 war did was to make those crimes possible. The war opened a doorway to brutality through which [the perpetrators of the Holocaust] willingly passed. To them, the war and the revolutionary upheaval that followed it were a training course in mass violence and male comradeship.'[80]

It is perfectly true that the Second World War and the Holocaust grew out of a political situation that would not have existed without the First World War. It is also true that the emergence of total and industrialized war made Nazi genocide possible. However, the supposition that the brutalization that the First World War is said to have brought made the Holocaust possible is rather dubious. First, the overwhelming majority of the men who carried out the mass killing on the ground were SS men who had been too young to fight (and thus experience brutalization) in the First World War.[81] Moreover, none of the four main architects of the Holocaust within the SS—Heinrich Himmler, Reinhard Heydrich, Adolf Eichmann, and Ernst Kaltenbrunner—had seen active service in the First World War either. When the Great War broke out in 1914, Josef Mengele, the chief doctor of Auschwitz, who grew up a mere 10 kilometres from Ichenhausen, was barely old enough to walk. Secondly, if it is true that the Holocaust became possible through the brutalization which its perpetrators had experienced in the First World War, the obvious question arises about where the perpetrators of a great number of other instances of modern genocide and ethnic cleansing—in which no wars took place in their countries during their lifetimes (e.g. Cambodia in the 1970s or Yugoslavia in the 1990s)—received their training course in mass violence.

It also unconvincing to claim a direct causal link between colonial violence and the Holocaust. It is, of course, true that the father of Hermann

Goering had been Reich Commissioner of German South West Africa in the late 1880s and that Franz Ritter von Epp, who was Nazi governor of Bavaria, had served in German South West Africa during the time of the massacres against the Herero and Nama. It is also true that German advisers to the Ottoman rulers were implicated in the ethnic cleansing of the Armenians during the First World War.[82] However, what do these links reveal? They are at best tenuous. The majority of men who had served in the colonies did not become involved in genocide. At any rate, Goering had been a colonial official in German South West Africa well before the massacres against the Herero and Nama took place. Moreover, the massacres in the colonial empires of other European powers did not translate into genocide, nor did the ethnic cleansing and mass killings of the Armenians in the First World War turn the sons of wartime leaders of the Ottoman Empire into perpetrators of genocide in the 1940s.

A far more convincing answer to the question of what made possible the killing of at least twelve Jewish veterans from the List Regiment as well as another five to six million other Jews, rather than focusing on First World War brutalization, colonial violence, or a claimed loss of human solidarity in nineteenth century Germany,[83] is to point towards the lethal cocktail of ethnic conflict, extreme economic volatility, and empires in decline;[84] as well as the transformation of a European state system of multi-ethnic empires to modern ethnically defined nation states and an obsessive fear of Bolshevism in general, and Hitler's paranoid anti-Semitism in particular.

The transformation process from the multi-ethnic, multi-religious dynastic world of Central, Eastern, and South-Eastern Europe into a world of modern nation states was, in large part, so very bloody because the ethnically mixed character of the region made the seamless creation of new nation states with clear ethnically defined borders well nigh impossible. It is of note in this context that men from ethnically mixed areas abroad and German territories lost after 1918 were heavily overrepresented among Nazi war criminals.[85] It is probably no exaggeration to say that the Holocaust is unlikely to have happened, or at least to have occurred on the same scale, had it not been for Nazi war criminals from multi-ethnic borderlands.

Similarly, as we have seen earlier, the dropping of the atomic bomb on Hiroshima and Nagasaki and the bombing of British and German cities, rather than the Holocaust, stand in the tradition of the German massacres of 1914 and of the harsh policies of Operation Alberich. Hitler's second war was at its core, not just a total war, but a racial war and a war for *Lebensraum*; his first war had been neither.[86]

In the spring of 1944 when bad news continued to arrive in Berlin from all fronts, Hitler became increasingly worried that the Second World War was to become a rerun of the final stages of his first war. In a conversation with Albert Speer, Hitler's architect and confidante turned minister for munitions, Private Hitler even indirectly acknowledged that his blindness at the end of the First World War had been a result of psychosomatic hysteria. He told Speer that he was worried that as in 1918 he would again go blind.[87]

As American, British, Dominion, and Soviet troops made their way into Germany in late 1944 and early 1945 and as Jakob Rafael and Hugo Günzburger were liberated by the Red Army in Theresienstadt,[88] Hitler did not understand why 'his' Germans had 'betrayed' him and refused to stage large-scale partisan warfare against the forces of the democracies of the West. Hitler's myopia was in part a result of his flawed analysis of what had gone wrong in the List Regiment and in the German armed forces at large in the First World War. In an attempt to maintain morale among Germans and to trigger a 'stab-in-the-back' in the armies of Germany's enemies, the Nazi regime tried in 1944/5 to recreate with reverse roles the conditions Hitler believed had existed in 1917/18: the Nazi leadership thought that its superior propaganda would allow it to create an ideologically and committed home guard (*Volkssturm*) that would draw out the war long enough and inflict casualties high enough for the American and British home front to waver and stab their victorious armies in the back. The result would be German victory supposedly in the same way the Allies had won the war in 1918.[89] In short, Hitler's post-war delusions about the war experience of the List Regiment fed his delusions at the end of the Second World War, which in turn determined Germany's fate during the twilight of the Third Reich.

Right until his suicide in the ruins of Berlin in the final days of the war, his war service in the List Regiment remained the focal point of Hitler's self-identity and the propagandistic staging of his life story. During the night of 28 and 29 April, with Russian tanks only blocks away from Hitler's bunker, Private Hitler dictated his political testament, reminiscing in his darkest hours about his days in the First World War in the List Regiment. The opening sentence of his testament makes clear how he wanted to be remembered: as an ordinary man who hade been 'made' by his experiences in the First World War and who courageously tried to lead Germany back to greatness: 'Since 1914, when as a volunteer, I made my modest contribution to the World War that was forced upon the Reich. . . . '[90]

Around the same time that Hitler contemplated how he wanted to be remembered, and that members of the Hitler Youth put death threats bearing a skull and crossbones into the letter box of the List veteran who had disrupted a Pan-German meeting at the end of the First World War,[91] many Nazis tried to take as many of their declared enemies down with them as possible, taking concentration camp prisoners on death marches away from advancing Allied troops. When in late April Oscar Daumiller heard that Dachau Concentration Camp had begun to be evacuated, he courageously tried to foil the plans of the Nazis behind the Dachau death march. Together with a Catholic priest, he told local farmers along the path of the death march to go out into the street with their dogs in order to intimidate the guards leading the marches.[92]

The wife and daughters of Rupprecht von Bayern were now also liberated. They had been arrested in Italy in the aftermath of the attempt on Hitler's life, whereas the would-be heir to the Bavarian throne having managed to flee to the unoccupied part of Italy. Since then, his wife and daughters had been taken to the concentration camps at Sachsenhausen, Dachau, and Flossenbürg, where they were liberated by US forces.[93]

A day and a half after he had looked back at his first war while dictating his testament, Adolf Hitler, newly wedded to Eva Braun, retired with his bride to his study. He put a cyanide capsule into his mouth and at the same time as biting it, he put his 7.65 mm Walther pistol to his right temple and pulled the trigger.[94] His second war was over. Private Hitler was dead.

Epilogue

The interrogators of the 7th US Army had questioned Max Amann for a while on 26 May 1945, when Amann saw Goering being marched past the interrogation room. The former staff sergeant of the List Regiment, whose eldest son had died during the invasion of the Soviet Union, jumped up from his seat, excitedly pointing at Goering and saying: 'This fat slob here, you should hang him. He is responsible for the war and the death of my son. It is him, not we small people.' Neither then nor during any of his subsequent interrogations in Nuremberg later that year, did Amann show any remorse. All he could think of was to blame Goering. Amann, who was described by his interrogators as 'homely' in appearance and 'coarse by nature', did not show any sign that he thought that there was anything wrong with National Socialism as such or with own deeds, often giving defiant and snappy answers in his thick Bavarian accent to his interrogators.[1]

Rather ludicrously, Amann was trying to present himself as only having had a business relationship with Hitler. More preposterously still, he described himself as a philanthropist who had saved confiscated non-National Socialist publishing houses from ruin.[2] During an interrogation in 1947, he was trying to convince his interrogators that he had only served Hitler out of loyalty to him as an old war comrade, with no eyes for politics: 'That's how one can get caught up in things if one is loyal to others...I would never have thought that this man would start a war because he had served in a war as a simple soldier himself.' Amann tried to blame Himmler for having corrupted Hitler, conveniently not mentioning that Himmler had been his neighbour on Tegernsee.[3] Amann was eventually tried by a denazification tribunal for his political involvement with National Socialism, for which he received a sentence of ten years' imprisonment in a labour camp. He was also tried by a regular court for his 1933 assault against the editor of the Munich weekly that had questioned Hitler's war record, for which he was condemned to a prison term of two and a half years. The public prosecutor declared in his final statement during his denazification hearing: 'Amann has remained all his life nothing other than a brutal sergeant'.[4] Amann was released from prison in 1953 and lived another four years before dying in 1957.[5]

Fritz Wiedemann, who despite all his defects, had let his disagreement with Hitler's Czechoslovakia policy be known when it would have been easier to keep quiet and who had discussed possible ways of removing Hitler with British intelligence when he could have just kept his head down, took a rather different line of action. The former regimental adjutant decided that his best course of action in order to save his neck was to cooperate fully with the Allies. Having weathered the summer of 1945 in Tientsin, he contacted the Swiss consul in the city in mid-September asking him to convey a message to the Allies that he desired to place himself in their hands and that he wished to contact Lord Halifax, the former British foreign secretary who was by now British ambassador to the United States. Within days, he was in the custody of the OSS. After being flown to the Chinese headquarters of the OSS in Kunming in south-west China on 18 September, Wiedemann gave testimony to four OSS counter-intelligence officials for several days, willingly detailing German Gestapo and intelligence activities in China and the United States. If Wiedemann was frightened, he did not show it, rather repeatedly joking and laughing during his testimony.[6] Realizing the intelligence value of Wiedemann, who was 'believed reliable', within days the Military Intelligence Service flew him to Washington DC, where he was interrogated between 29 September and 3 October 1945.[7]

His Washington interrogators detected behind Wiedemann's desire 'of being most cooperative' and his 'ingratiating and talkative attitude' a fear that Wiedemann 'himself may be considered a war criminal'. They concluded that 'this threat used at the proper time should not only bring results but be most helpful in using subject as an informer for more incriminating details on the lives of the Nazi War Criminals'. He volunteered his recollections of how the former dispatch runner from his regiment had actively planned for war. He also offered character analyses of Nazi leaders and advocated the death penalty for most former Nazi leaders still alive, including Goering, Ribbentrop, Ley, Keitel, Kaltenbrunner, Rosenberg, Frank, Frick, Streicher, Dönitz, Rader, von Schirach, Jodl, Bormann, von Papen, Seyss-Inquart, and Neurath. Wiedemann tried to talk US authorities out of using him as an official witness in Nuremberg, rather suggesting that he would check statements made by Nazi war criminals instead. His request was not granted.[8] Wiedemann was hurried via Paris to Nuremberg, where he would repeatedly give testimony to US authorities. He continued his policy of full cooperation, detailing the inner workings of Hitler's Chancellery in the 1930s and explaining why any protestations by German leaders and their underlings not to have known what had been going on in the concentration camps were implausible. Unlike his interrogators in Washington, the ones in Nuremberg did not think that Wiedemann's forthrightness in giving testimony was driven by fear of being tried himself, concluding: 'The witness is cooperative and since he feels that he is far removed from being charged as a war criminal he is disposed to be helpful.' Wiedemann agreed with his interrogators that 'a number of unspeakable crimes had been committed under the Nazi regime'.[9] For the rest of his life Wiedemann led a quiet existence on his son's farm in a Lower Bavarian village upon his release from US custody in May 1948. In 1964, he published his memoirs with the help of Stephanie von Hohenlohe, with whom he had reconnected after the war. He died in January 1970 at the age of 78.[10]

Unlike Wiedemann, Ernst Schmidt never broke with Hitler. US forces apprehended him in late May 1945. A week later he was transferred to the labour and internment camp that had been set up on the site of the former concentration camp at Dachau. He remained in internment camps for three years. Unlike all the other Nazis who now claimed to have never really supported Hitler fully, Schmidt remained steadfast to his dying day in his support of Hitler, telling American interrogators that he had already recognized Hitler's 'genius' in 1914 and that he had been a great man both in public and in private.[11] According to friends, even towards the end of his life, Schmidt never said 'anything about Hitler that might have changed his reputation'.[12]

Oscar Daumiller, meanwhile, encountered many Nazi criminals after the war. His job as head of the Protestant Church in southern Bavaria included providing pastoral care for suspected Nazi criminals. His task often took him to Landsberg prison, where many of the death sentences against Nazis were carried out. As Daumiller recalled, 'they were hung with a view of the cell in which Adolf Hitler had been interned.'[13]

Alexander Moritz Frey survived the war in exile. In 1945, Frey published *Hölle und Himmel*, his autobiographical novel about his encounter with Hitler. He briefly contemplated returning to Germany but then decided against it. He had grown too embittered with his compatriots while in exile.

In a letter to the editor of the Zurich periodical *Tat*, he wrote in 1946: 'This is how I recognize my Germans, [or] a particular kind of them. . . . When they got themselves into a mess, they start to waffle in arrogant grandeur rather than objectively and without remorse face the new conditions, which has nothing in common with masochism.'[14] With a singled-minded vigour and tenacity, he now embarked on a crusade against writers who had lent their support to Hitler's regime, naming and shaming them wherever he could. He died of a stroke in early 1957 in Switzerland without ever having set foot in Germany again.[15] Others from Hitler's regiment or from among the officers in charge of Hitler, however, contributed to the rebuilding of a new democratic Germany. Albert Weisgerber's friend Theodor Heuss became West Germany's first president. Moreover, Michael von Godin, the commander of the brigade that had shot at Hitler and put down his *coup d'etat* in 1923 and also the brother of Hitler's wartime regimental commander, was appointed chief of the Bavarian police in 1945.[16] Fridolin Solleder, meanwhile, became the director of the state archives of Bavaria.[17]

After the war, Wilhelm Diess was asked to rebuild and purge Nazi ideology from both the Bavarian legal system and the arts scene. The former officer in charge of Hitler and the other dispatch runners of RIB 12, worked tirelessly towards this goal as a high-ranking civil servant in the Bavarian Ministry of Justice, as an adjunct professor of law at Munich University, as Director General of the State Theatre of Bavaria, and as director of the literature section of the Bayerische Akademie der Schönen Künste, before dying in 1957.[18]

Ludwig von Vallade remained a monarchist all his life, moving in with two of the daughters of his friend Rupprecht von Bayern, Hildegard and Helmtrud von Bayern. He put a lot of his energy in his remaining years into preventing functionaries of the Third Reich from regaining influence in post-war Germany. For instance, Hitler's former superior tried to prevent the publication of a book by Werner Naumann, the former deputy of Joseph Goebbels. A few months before his death, von Vallade noted down his views about the state of the world, concluding that despite being a monarchist at heart himself, Germans should show their full support for Konrad Adenauer's republicanism and Western orientation. The future of Germany, von Vallade wrote in mid-1955, lay in a 'United States of Europe'.[19] The case of the former commander of Hitler's brigade was thus the personification of an alternative vision of Germany that was killed by the combined onslaught of the First World War, Woodrow Wilson's demand for an abolition of the monarchy, and subsequent events: a reformist constitutional monarchy transforming Germany into a modern progressive Western state without the horrors of the period from 1914 to 1945.

Hugo Gutmann/Henry G. Grant never told his story. As we have seen, he had already told a St Louis newspaper shortly after his arrival in the Mid-West that his 'past is entirely forgotten' and that he wanted to move on.[20] Attempts to locate his family were unsuccessful: he lived until the early 1960s in his apartment on Clara Avenue but there is no trace of his later life; his daughter Helen Mary (Hella Maria) Grant, was a commercial artist; his son's army records were destroyed in a fire.[21] Justin Fleischmann (see Plate 15), meanwhile, lived a fulfilled life as a photographer in Pittsburgh and died at the biblical age of 95 in 1993. It was my good fortune that a student of mine from the University of Pennsylvania, Marvin Verman, had known Fleischmann while growing up in Pittsburgh, which allowed me to locate Justin Fleischmann's son and thus his remarkable war diary.[22]

Hugo Günzburger was one of the few Jewish veterans of Hitler's regiment who remained in Germany after the war. After his liberation in Theresienstadt he returned to Memmingen, where he died in 1977.[23]

Very few visible traces are still left of the List Regiment on the Western Front. Outside Fournes, one of the German concrete bunkers that formed part of the German third trench line still survives. In Fournes itself, the most obvious sign of the presence of Hitler's regiment in the village for a year and a half is the German military cemetery in which so many of Hitler's comrades still lie buried. However, unlike the beautifully maintained and dignified British and French cemeteries, Fournes' German military cemetery has disgracefully but understandably been tucked away behind mountains of sand and the factory workshop of a local company. Understandably, there are no references to Hitler's presence in wartime Fournes anywhere in today's sleepy but friendly village. Today the most visible reference to Bavaria in Fournes are the huge logos of Paulaner beer from Munich—which includes the profile of a Bavarian monk who is almost a spitting image of Father Norbert—in the windows of the local sports bar on the village's main street.

The scarcity of surviving visible traces of the List Regiment's more than four years on the Western Front is matched by the paucity of surviving records about Hitler's time between 1914 and 1919, which explains why the myth that Hitler created about his own war experience has proved so very resilient. As we have seen, Hitler treated his war experience as a palimpsest from which he erased, as he felt fit, his real war experience and replaced it with one that suited his political needs. Yet, despite all his attempts to destroy any incriminating evidence, Hitler did not cover his traces diligently enough. The letters, diaries, and other pieces of evidence pertaining to the men of RIR 16, scattered in archives and private homes around the world, have allowed us to reconstruct with a high degree of probability what Hitler did not want us to see. We thus no longer have to rely either on Hitler's lies or on an understanding of his war years that matches the blurry, out-of-focus image of Private Hitler from the regimental history, depicting him in Fournes in 1915.

Piece by piece, the picture that has conclusively emerged by putting all the surviving pieces of evidence together is the image of a Private Hitler who was shunned by most of the front-line soldiers as a 'rear area pig', and who was still unsure of his political ideology at the end of the war in 1918. The view of the List Regiment as a band of brothers, with Hitler a hero at its heart, has its origins in Nazi propaganda, not in reality. The First World War did not 'make' Hitler. Even the revolutionary period seems to have had a far less immediate impact on Hitler's politicization than hitherto assumed. Central for Hitler's radicalization was thus the post-revolutionary period, a time when he was still surrounded by people like Ernst Schmidt and Karl Mayr, who like him possessed fluctuating political attitudes. This period of Hitler's life is still clouded in much secrecy.

His invented First World War (and his made-up revolutionary) experience was nevertheless of the utmost importance for Adolf Hitler. It became the focal point of his self-identity and for the propagandistic staging of his life story. Throughout the years of the Weimar Republic and the Third Reich, Hitler continued to reconfigure his war experience for political ends. Retrospectively, his war experience in the List Regiment thus mattered greatly. Hitler's tactical conscious reinvention of his war experience thus lies at the heart of the story of how he rose to power.

Hitler also used the war retrospectively to rationalize his own new world-view. For instance, with hindsight his war experience at the front seemed to support perfectly his view that force was not just the last, but the primary, resort of politics. The same is true of his virulent anti-Bolshevism and anti-Semitism. Retrospectively, the war was thus indeed a formative period in

Hitler's political coming of age. His 'near miss' experiences from the First World War might also have helped to convince Hitler that he was saved for great things in the future. Furthermore, it seems reasonable to argue that he used the organizational model of regimental HQ of RIR 16 when reorganizing the NSDAP and when remodelling the Reich Chancellery after 1933. Furthermore, during the Second World War, Hitler looked back to his war experience in the List Regiment (in its reformulated post-1919 form) for inspiration for how to fight his new war. However—not only because he turned to war experiences that had been reconfigured under the conditions of Weimar but also because Hitler tried to learn the lessons from the Great War, rather than to refight it—his second war turned out to be a very different war indeed from his first one.

The origins of Hitler's radicalization hence lie in the post-war period, not in the First World War. As far as Hitler is concerned, the First World War was thus not the seminal catastrophe of the twentieth century. The same is true for the men of his regiment. The majority of them had not been brutalized, radicalized, and politicized by the war but had returned to their towns, villages, and hamlets with their pre-war political outlook more or less intact. The war for them had not caused—to use a term that has been applied to describe the situation in France—a 'great mutation' of their minds.[24] It has been the argument of this book that their political attitudes, as well as those of Bavarians and Germans in general, were not incompatible with a democratization of Germany.

The men of Hitler's regiment were a product of a conservative, reformist society that had gradually been moving towards more democracy. Popular attitudes had of course not always been actively pushing for more democracy and liberalism—far from it. However, despite or maybe because of traditions of confessional politics and apolitical deference, by voting in overwhelming numbers for the parties of the Reichstag Peace Initiative and of the Weimar Coalition, the people from the recruitment regions of the List Regiment had proved compatible both with the gradual democratization of the pre-1914 period and with post-war democratization. Post-1918 democratization, of course, ultimately failed spectacularly. Yet neither the experience of an extremely violent war—as the case of the post-Civil War United States indicates[25]—nor concessions to pre-democratic elites as such necessarily derail democratization. Quite to the contrary, they can even foster democratization. In the nineteenth and early twentieth centuries, democratization was a far more turbulent and muddled process than long believed. It neither tends to occur in a linear and gradual way, nor in a clear-cut revolutionary fashion,[26] which means that both the pre-1914 and post-First World War processes of democratization in Germany were far less unusual than commonly assumed.

Yet because of its turbulent character, democratization is also far more volatile and more exposed to contingencies than was traditionally thought, and therefore also open to failure and spectacular episodes of de-democratization. From the perspective of early 1919, the chances that Bavaria's and Germany's democratization would prove sustainable and that Private Hitler would have to return to drawing postcards were reasonably high. The story of how Private Hitler managed to transform himself from a 'rear area pig', shunned by the men of his regiment, to the most powerful right-wing dictator of the twentieth century is thus a cautionary tale for all democratizing and democratized countries. If de-democratization could happen in interwar Germany, it can arguably occur anywhere.[27]

Postscript
Hugo Gutmann's Story

One day in the spring of 2010, Andrés and Carolina Strauss, from Buenos Aires, visited the villa on Lake Wannsee in which top Nazi bureaucrats had plotted the implementation of the Holocaust in early 1942. To my great good fortune, the Argentinean couple struck up a conversation with Veronika Springmann, a friend of mine who was working at the museum housed in the villa, who put them in touch with me; for Andrés's grandmother was Hugo Gutmann's sister.

Neither Hugo Gutmann nor his son ever wanted to talk about their experiences in Germany, especially not to journalists and historians. However, after the recent death of Gutmann's son, Howard Charles, in February 2010, his family decided that it now was the time to tell the amazing life stories of Hugo/Henry and Heinz/Howard. Andrés Strauss, as well as his family across three continents, were thus happy to help me, not least because they were eager to find out more about the early lives of Hugo and Heinz Gutmann themselves. As Gutmann's grandson Rohn Grant put it, 'probably one of the reasons my hunger is so great is that my family's history was often shrouded in a mysterious veil. My father never spoke more than a few words about his complete past, and never set foot in Germany again after the war. . . . When I was a small child [my grandfather] would take us to the Zoo in St. Louis, or join our family vacation in Florida. He did not talk about the past to us, even in a story telling manner.'[1]

As it turned out, Hugo Gutmann's son had lived just a few miles north of where I myself had stayed when I had first tried to locate him, close to Chicago's O'Hare International Airport. This is the story of the highest-serving Jewish officer in Hitler's regiment as it emerged from the recollections of Hugo Gutmann's family, and especially from the documents and stories that Howard's wife, Beverly—the epitome of a warm-hearted Jewish grandmother—shared with me over bagels and cakes on my visit to her house:[2]

Howard barely spoke about the war even to his wife. It was only after his death that she found out that Hugo Gutmann's son had been decorated several times while serving in the US Army. One reason for the silence of both father and son was, as Rohn Grant put it, that they 'wanted very much fully to assimilate and disappear into the conformity of middle America'. Howard would regularly tell his family and friends: 'we look forward; you don't look back.' Yet there was more to their silence than a wish fully to embrace their new American identity. For Howard it was his service in US intelligence in the aftermath of the Second World War (and possibly during the war too). However, the most immediate reason for Hugo Gutmann to keep his head down and to change his name was fear. Following his interrogation by the Gestapo about Hitler's Iron Cross, Gutmann was worried that Nazi agents would track him down in America and liquidate him. So when Hugo walked past a [branch] of the W. T. Grant dime store chain shortly after his arrival in New York City, he decided that the store's name would provide the perfect cover against being hunted down by Hitler's agents.

For the next twenty years, Hugo Gutmann lived a quiet life centred in St Louis; his work as a salesman took him to the Midwest and the West where he sold typewriters and later furniture, never speaking German in the presence of his daughter-in-law, and spending his holidays hiking through the mountains of Colorado. When in 1961 the former officer from Hitler's regiment and his wife retired to San Diego in California, he could look back on a full and rich life, unlike so many of his Jewish peers from the List Regiment who were murdered in the Holocaust. A few months before his death from cancer in early summer 1962, he wrote to his son: 'I enjoyed a wonderful life and with 81 you have to know that you cannot live for ever.'[3]

After Hugo Gutmann's death, his wife started to talk more about their lives in Germany, telling her grandson 'incredible stories over dinner about her life with [his] grandfather, and in particular why they stayed so long, and then how fast they had to leave Germany'. To a post-war generation of American Jews, it seemed incomprehensible why most German Jews had emigrated only in the late 1930s, but Hugo's wife would remind them that Germany had been their home in every sense of the word and that they had thought that they could weather the storm, expecting Hitler's rule to pass.

Whereas Hugo Gutmann never talked about his experiences with Hitler during the First World War once he had arrived in the New World, his sister Klara did. Andrés Strauss recalls how as a little boy his grandmother told him how his great-uncle had been involved in the award of Hitler's Iron Cross 1st Class. Her story is almost certainly historically inaccurate. Yet it provides us with a fascinating insight either into how Hugo himself had tried to find a way of relating his story to his immediate family or how his sister had struggled to find a way in which she could tell arguably the most painful episode of her brother's life to her own family:

> Adolf Hitler was one day sent to the front with some other soldiers, and from this mission the only one who came back alive was Adolf Hitler. Of course, then people said that Adolf Hitler was a coward, never went to the front to this mission and hid behind a tree, so when all other soldiers died (or most of that patrol died), Adolf Hitler did not . . . So when World War One finished there was a whole discussion if the soldier Adolf Hitler should get the Iron Cross 1st Class or 2nd Class. Of course, my great uncle Hugo did not want to give him the 1st Class Cross (he knew that Adolf Hitler never went to the mission) and only the 2nd Class Cross. But then some kind of discussion went on with other officers and Adolf Hitler got the 1st Class Cross! You can imagine that for Adolf Hitler it was not good to say that a Jew gave him the Iron Cross, so my great-uncle had to escape in one way or another from Germany because Adolf Hitler was looking for him to eliminate him.

Even though Hugo Gutmann and his son had never disclosed anything about their past in Germany other than occasional passing remarks, the letters, notes, and other documents that they kept all their lives and that have surfaced in recent months in Howard's house finally allow us to shed light on some of the mysteries surrounding Hugo Gutmann, the List Regiment, and the 'making' of Adolf Hitler.

As we have seen, while still in Germany, Hugo Gutmann had talked about his role in the award of Hitler's Iron Cross not just with his sister but also with Ernst Niekisch. It was the conversation with Niekisch, and the notes Niekisch took of it, that landed Gutmann in the hands of the Gestapo in 1937. Hugo Gutmann had also shared his story with others. One of them recounted the story (but with some inaccuracies) to *Aufbau*, the newspaper of the German Jewish community in New York City, which printed the account during the early days of the Second World War. Without identifying how exactly Hitler had earned his Iron Cross, the article gave an account of how Gutmann had awarded it to him. The article also claims that after the war, Gutmann had been on the executive committee of the Nuremberg chapter of the Reichsbund jüdischer Frontsoldaten.[4]

From Hugo Gutmann's private papers, we also learn how close he came himself to becoming a victim of the Holocaust. On 14 May 1940, Hugo Gutmann, his wife, daughter, and mother-in-law managed to get out of Brussels on the last train before German troops moved in. Their escape was so close that the German Air Force attempted to bomb their train. After an odyssey through France, during which they passed the area close to Lille where Private Hitler and Gutmann had served together in their first war, the Gutmanns arrived in Perpignan, close to the Spanish border.

Gutmann's son, who had been a classmate of Henry Kissinger in Nuremberg, had been less lucky. Together with his uncle and scores of other German Jewish refugees, he was arrested after the German occupation of Brussels. He was deported by rail to the Saint Cyprien Internment Camp, just miles from Perpignan. Soon Hugo Gutmann had to join his son and brother-in-law in the camp that lay on the shores of the Mediterranean and that was run by the Vichy government. For now, the camp was 'just' an internment camp. However, had Hugo Gutmannn, his son, and brother-in-law not managed to get out the camp, they would have been transferred to Gurs Internment Camp in the autumn in 1940 and from there to Auschwitz in 1942. Yet Gutmann's ability to make friends and the crucial and unwavering support of a distant relative in the United States, Leo F. Keiler, saved them. The letters that Gutmann had received from Keiler's friends—among them Alben W. Barkley, the majority leader of the US Senate—and, maybe, more importantly, the 'tips' that Gutmann was able to pay due to Keiler's help, immensely impressed the officials and thus opened the gates of Saint Cyprien Internment Camp and allowed them legally to cross into Spain.

Hugo Gutmann sighed with relief once he had boarded the *Excalibur*, the ship that took the Gutmanns from Lisbon to New York City, on 28 August 1940: 'We were now on American, free territory.... Dusk was breaking, the lights of Lisbon and the search lights of the light house flashed.... strife-torn Europe disappeared from our sight.... The stars began to glisten; now we were hopefully steering towards our new home, the United States of America, the country of freedom and happiness.'[5]

Although Hugo broke with his German past the moment he stepped onto American soil in New York City harbour, he nevertheless had with him a number of photos from his service in the List Regiment, including one that depicts him sitting on an artillery gun. He even had a private photo of Adolf Hitler and a number of his fellow dispatch runners taken in 1916

(Plate 28). He presented the photo to his old friend Berthold Kaufmann, who hosted the Gutmanns for their first six weeks in America. We can only speculate about the exact reasons why Gutmann kept the photo between 1916 and 1918 (at a time when Hitler was a nobody) and took the photo home with him at the end of the First World War. The most likely explanation is that he felt that he had a good relationship with the dispatch runners of regimental HQ and had thus kept the photo of Hitler and his peers as a memory of the war, in the same way that employers keep photos of some of their former loyal employees.

Although he gave away his photo of Hitler, Gutmann kept his other photos from the war. Despite outward appearances, Hugo, his wife, and children never quite managed to break with their past. When in 1958 Ernst Niekisch published his memoirs, which included the account Hugo Gutmann had given to him about Hitler's Iron Cross, either Hugo or his son cut out a newspaper article that published excerpts of the story.[6] It should be added for the record that outlandish stories that populate the internet claiming that Niekisch and Gutmann met after the war, that Hitler and Gutmann secretly met in 1936, or that Gutmann continued to receive a pension from Hitler until 1945[7] are without foundation. For the rest of his life, Gutmann continued to correspond with a number of old friends and acquaintances in Germany. Sometimes in these letters he enquired about the state of anti-Semitism in Germany, about which he remained worried until his death.[8]

From Gutmann's private papers we also learn that after the Great War he had served in a Freikorps,[9] a fact that supports the argument advanced in this book about the political character of post-First World War Germany. Gutmann's papers also confirm how well integrated he was in Hitler's regiment. In the letter Gutmann wrote after the war, in which he detailed how men from his regiment among the prison guards had helped him while he was incarcerated in 1937, he also singled out his old friend Franz Christ for having helped him 'under great danger to his own safety' when he was targeted by the Gestapo.[10] A letter Christ wrote to Gutmann's widow in early 1982 identifies Gutmann's close friend as an officer from the List Regiment. After Gutmann's death, Christ and Gutmann's wife stayed in touch over the years, from time to time exchanging news about their families. In his letter from 1982, Christ—old, frail, and almost blind—told Gutmann's wife that he was one of only two officers from the List Regiment still alive. He also recalled how Gutmann had travelled to visit him briefly before fleeing Germany.[11] As Gutmann's letter from 1946 testifies, Franz Christ stood by him at a time when it was very dangerous for him to do so. As revealed by the behaviour of Gutmann's fellow members of the List Regiment towards him both during and after the First World War, the highest-ranking Jew in Hitler's regiment was respected and integrated among the men of RIR 16 in a way that Hitler never was.

Notes

PRELUDE

1. Solleder, *Westfront*, 168.
2. Solleder, 'Geleit', p. ix.
3. Hamann, *Hitlers Wien*.
4. Overy, *Dictators*, 15. Norman Davies, meanwhile, argues in his *Europe*, 904, that Hitler's war experience 'undoubtedly fired the pathological drive of his subsequent career' and that the war experience of the men who fought together with him at Langemarck symbolizes the psychological link 'between the slaughter of Ypres and Verdun, and that of the London Blitz, Warsaw, and Stalingrad'.
5. Wasserstein, *Barbarism*, 174.
6. Fest, *Hitler*, 116.
7. Bullock, *Hitler*, 53.
8. Keegan, *Mask of Command*, 237.
9. Williams, *Corporal Hitler*, 3. In 2006, another book on Hitler's wartime years appeared, brought out by a publishing house which specializes in right-wing nationalist publications. The book, Russell's *Hitler*, provides very basic information on Hitler's wartime years as well as a remarkable photo documentary of the places Hitler frequented during the war. Rather absurdly, it attempts to prove that the historical profession, out of political correctness, has shied away from admitting that Hitler was 'emotionally and mentally sound' ('seelisch-geistig gesund') (p. 4) during the First World War. The year 2008 saw the publication of Grebner, *Hitler*, which limited itself to extracting and compiling very basic biographical information from Solleder, *Westfront*, and Joachimsthaler, *Hitlers Weg*.
10. See Fest, *Hitler*, 104.
11. Hitler made this claim in a speech in Hamburg in 1934; see Bullock, *Hitler*, 52.
12. Williams, *Corporal Hitler*; Bullock, *Hitler*, 50. Cobb, *Fromelles*, 231, also claims that Hess was in Hitler's regiment. See also Koch-Hillebrecht, *Hitler*, for a claim that the war 'made' Hitler.
13. Kershaw, *Hitler*, i. 87.
14. Ibid., ii. 403.
15. Ibid., i. 87. Kershaw's treatment of Hitler's war years in *Hitler*, i, is based to a large degree on Joachimsthaler's *Hitlers Weg*. Joachimsthaler has done a brilliant

job at correcting numerous details about Hitler's early life but has not seen it as his task to reinterpret Hitler's life in a cohesive manner.

16. Kershaw, *Hitler*, i. 92.

17. Hitler, *MK*.

18. See e.g. Brandmayer, *Meldegänger Hitler* (1933); Meyer, *Hitler*; Mend, *Hitler*. One of Hitler's other close comrades, Jakob Weiß, embarked on writing his war memoirs of his time with Hitler during the years of the Third Reich. Yet by the time of his death, we had not advanced beyond completing a few fragments of his memoirs; see Nachlaß Jakob Weiß.

19. Thomas Weber, review of John F. Williams's *Corporal Hitler and the Great War*, *Times Literary Supplement*, 7 October 2005. Russell's *Hitler* is written in a similar mode as Williams's book.

20. See Thomas Weber, review of John F. Williams's *Copporal Hitler and the Great War*, *Times Literary Supplement*, 7 October 2005.

21. Reimann, 'Soldaten', has argued that letters written by soldiers do not report what really happened at the front, just as, for instance, they do not tend to describe the act of killing. They supposedly thus only provide glimpses of how soldiers attempted give meaning to the war and how they tried to stay in touch with their families. This argument clearly goes too far. As long as we read letters written by soldiers critically, they provide as good as source as any about life at the front.

22. Kennan, *Decline*, 3.

23. Of course, no *Sonderweg* (Special Path) historian has ignored the importance of inter-war events. Yet *Sonderweg* historians have tended to see purported long-term structural deficiencies in German history as the key determining factors in Germany's development towards the Third Reich.

24. Fry, *Making History*.

25. Margalit, 'Sectarianism'.

26. Sternhell, *Neither Right*.

1. A CROWD IN ODEONSPLATZ

1. Sauder, *Wilder*; Hausenstein, *Weisgerber*; Dehn, 'Weisgerber', 148–9.

2. See e.g. Maser, *Letters*, 49.

3. See e.g. Joachimsthaler, *Hitlers Weg*, 98 ff.; Fest, *Hitler*, 98; Maser, *Legende*, 128; Large, *München*, 84.

4. See e.g. Rürup, 'Geist'; Joachimsthaler, *Hitlers Weg*, 98.

5. Solleder, 'Vaterland', 2.

6. Hitler, *MK*, 99.

7. Ibid. 98–9.

8. Kershaw, *Hitler*, i. 81, 85–6.

9. Hitler, *MK*, 100. The claim was repeated by Mend, *Hitler*, 17, and by Bullock, *Hitler*, 50.

10. Joachimsthaler, *Hitlers Weg*, 105–11.

11. Hitler, *MK*, 99.

12. Solleder, 'Vaterland', 2.

13. NARA, BDC/A3343/SSO/Arthur Rödl.

14. See e.g. Bullock, *Hitler*, 50; Kershaw, *Hitler*, i. 89–90; Solleder, *Westfront*; Mend, *Hitler*, 14; *List Regiment*; Daumiller, *Schatten*, 26.

15. Meyer, *Hitler*, 17.

16. Solleder, 'Neues Jahr', 98. The poem is also reproduced in *List Regiment*, 3. For the postcard versions of the poem, see also postcards written on 14 June 1915 (Alfons Erlacher to M. Mayer) and on 7 May 1916 (Ferdinand to Johannes Pösl) by members of RIR 16 and RIR 21; in the possession of the author.

17. Witt, 'Einstellung', 5.

18. Mend, *Hitler*, 14–15; Joachimsthaler, *Hitlers Weg*, 111.

19. Keegan, *Mask of Command*.

20. Witt, 'Einstellung', 6.

21. See e.g. Joachimsthaler, *Hitlers Weg*, 101 ff.; Bullock, *Hitler*, 50; Kershaw, *Hitler*, i. 89.

22. Meyer, *Hitler*, 58.

23. Joachimsthaler, *Hitlers Weg*, 99.

24. Verhey, *Spirit of 1914*.

25. Ziemann, *Heimat*, 39; Longerich, *Himmler*, 27.

26. Stürmer, *Reich*, 53.

27. Knopp and Remy, 'Hitler', episode 1.

28. BHStA/IV, MG/RD6, Eduard Abtmayr.

29. BHStA/IV, MG/RD6, Georg Ferchl.

30. German war volunteers often became disillusioned about the war when they had to experience the drill and perceived brutality of the initial training period; see Ulrich, 'Desillusionierung', 116.

31. Solleder, *Westfront*, 5.

32. BHStA/IV, KSR/3039.

33. BHStA/IV, RIR16/Bd.12, I Batl./diary, 1 September 1914. 32 out of 216 men were volunteers.

34. Reichsbund Jüdischer Frontsoldaten, *Kameraden*, 27; BHStA/IV, KSR/3038–9, 3067, 3070, 3073, 3077–8, 3081–2, 3084. The figure is based on the data of the 2,515 soldiers from 1st, 4th, and 7th–12th Companies who joined up in 1914. 78.8 per cent of Catholic students were volunteers. The figure for Protestant students is 57.1 per cent, and for Jewish ones 66.7 per cent. (The figures for the religious background of soldiers excludes the data of 1st Company.) For the claim that RIR 16 was full of academics, see Maser, *Legende*, 129.

35. BHStA/IV, KSR/3039. (Based on a sample of 494 soldiers all of whom joined the regiment before the end of 1914.) The figure is 17.6 per cent.

36. Ingenlath, *Aufrüstung*, 389.

37. Scheibert, *Militär-Lexikon*, s.v. 'Ersatzreserve'.
38. BHStA/IV, RIR16/Bd.12, I Batl./diary, 8 September 1914.
39. Stark, 'All Quiet', 62.
40. Joachimsthaler, *Hitler Weg*, 108.
41. Solleder, '12. Kompanie', 53; Kraus, *Deutsche Armee, passim*.
42. US General Staff, *Divisions*, 138–9; Cron, *Organisation*, 1; Cron, *Geschichte*, 119. BHStA/IV, KSR/3038–40; BHStA/IV, RIR17/Bd.1, war diary, introductory notes and entries for 5–8 September 1914.
43. BHStA/IV, KSR/3038–40. A total of approximately 1,600 men served in 1st Company during the war.
44. Solleder, 'Führerliste', 369 ff.; Schnee, *Kolonial-Lexikon*, iii, s.v. 'Zech, Julius Graf von'.
45. BHStA/IV, RIR16/Bd.12, I Batl./diary, 3 September–10 October 1914.
46. BHStA/IV, RIR16/Bd.3,4/diary, Waldbott von Bassenheim, 26 October 1914; IFZ, F 19/6, No. 2, 'Militärpaß des Gefreiten Hitler'.
47. BHStA/IV, KSR/3039–41. The figures are based on a random sample of 623 soldiers who served in 1st Company: 46.6 per cent of soldiers were born later than 1889; 59.2 per cent of RIR 16 members were born between 1885 and 1894. The occupation of thirteen soldiers could not be established. The exact figure for farmers is 16.1 per cent and 14.3 per cent for agricultural workers.
48. BHStA/IV, KSR/3039–41. The figure for Upper Bavaria is 51.7 per cent, for Lower Bavaria 14.1 per cent, and for Swabia 14.2 per cent. 4.2 per cent of soldiers came from the Oberpfalz, 8.3 per cent were Franconian, 3.2 per cent came from the Palatinate, and another 4.4 per cent from regions outside Bavaria. The figures are based on a sample of 623 soldiers from 1st Company of RIR 16.
49. BHStA/IV, KSR/3039–41. 56.8 per cent of soldiers came from rural communities, and 21.7 per cent lived in Munich. Towns of small to medium size were defined as having between 2,000 and 20,000 inhabitants. The figures are based on the 584 soldiers within a random sample of 623 soldiers from 1st Company who lived in Bavaria.
50. Ziemann, *Heimat*, 34 ff.
51. Ibid. 37–8; http://wahlen-in-deutschland.de/kuRbbNiederbayern.htm; http://wahlen-in-deutschland.de/kuRbbOberbayern.htm; http://wahlen-in-deutschland.de/kuRbbOberpfalz.htm, all accessed 9 June 2009.
52. Brandmayer, *Hitler* (1940), 14.
53. Ziemann, *Heimat*, 33–54.
54. http://wahlen-in-deutschland.de/kuRbbOberbayern.htm, accessed 9 June 2009; Neumann-Adrian, *Lust*. See also Thomas Mann's 'Gladius Dei', published in Mann, *Tristan*.
55. BHStA/IV, KSR/3077 (No. 288), 3078 (No. 592), 3084 (No. 513).
56. BHStA/IV, KSR/3038–9, 3067, 3070, 3073, 3077–8, 3081–2, 3084. The figure is based on the data of the 2,515 soldiers from 1st, 4th, and 7th–12th Companies who joined up in 1914.

57. BHStA/IV, KSR/3039.
58. BHStA/IV, KSR/3077–89.
59. Messerschmidt, *Soldaten*, 105–6; Hoffmann, 'Integration', 92.
60. Kershaw, 'Antisemitismus', 289.
61. Solleder, 'Judenschutzherrlichkeit', quotes at 261, 263, 283, 297, 298, 302.
62. Neumann-Adrian, *Lust*, 14.
63. Weber, 'Anti-Semitism', 86–119.
64. Messerschmidt, *Soldaten*, 103–5; *Jewish Year Book*, 1911.
65. Haus der Bayerischen Geschichte, *Ichenhausen*, 18–27, 84–5; Wasserstein, *Jerusalem*, 46; Gilbert, *Atlas of Jewish History*; US Bureau of the Census, *Population*. For the communal life in the communities from which the Jewish soldiers in RIR 16 came, see Ophir and Wiesemann, *Gemeinden*, *passim*; Flade, 'Judentum', 47–50; Arnsberg, *Gemeinden*, i.274–5, and ii.246–9.
66. BHStA/IV, RIR16/Bd.12, I Batl./diary, 8 October.
67. LAELKB, OKM/2340, Oscar Daumiller's report, 20 October 1914.
68. Maser, *Letters*, 45–9, Hitler to Anna Popp, 20 October 1914.
69. Ibid.
70. BHStA/IV, RIR16/Bd.3,4, Count Bassenheim's diary, 20 October 1914.
71. BHStA/IV, RIR16/Bd.3,4, Count Bassenheim's diary, 26 October 1914.
72. Maser, *Letters*, 45–7, Hitler to Anna Popp, 20 October 1914.
73. Rubenbauer, 'Ypern', 9.
74. BHStA/IV, RIR16/Bd.3,4, Count Bassenheim's diary, 11 and 12 October 1914.
75. BHStA/IV, RIR16/Bd.3,4, Count Bassenheim's diary, 11 and 17 October 1914.

2. BAPTISM OF FIRE

 1. PBK, II/9/Facs.3m/Stumpf/diary, 21 October 1914; BHStA/IV, RIR16/Bd.12, I Batl./diary, 21 October 1914; BHStA/IV, MG/RD6/Friedrich Neuner, letter, Albert Geiger to Lieutenant Schlamp, 24 August 1915.
 2. Maser, *Letters*, 45–9, Hitler to Anna Popp, 20 October 1914.
 3. Witt, 'Ausmarsch', 7.
 4. Maser, *Letters*, 45–9, Hitler to Anna Popp, 20 October 1914.
 5. Sauder, *Wilder*, 186, Weisgerber to his wife, 17 October 1914.
 6. Ibid. 186, Weisgerber to his wife, 17 October 1914.
 7. PBK, II/9/Facs.3m/Stumpf/diary, 21 and 22 October 1914; LAELKB, OKM/2340, Oscar Daumiller's report, 2 November 1914.
 8. Maser, *Letters*, 49, postcard, Hitler to Joseph Popp, 21 October 1914.
 9. Ibid. 50, letter, Hitler to Joseph Popp, 3 December 1914.
10. BHStA/IV, HS 2550/diary, Max von Speidel, the commander of RD 6, 21 October 1914. See also Rubenbauer, 'Ypern', 10.

11. Reichert and Wolgast, *Hampe*, 101, entry for 5 August.
12. BHStA/IV, RIR16/Bd.3,4, Count Bassenheim's diary, 21 October 1914; Hitler, *MK*, 100; Rubenbauer, 'Ypern', 10–11.
13. Hewett, *Reader*, 90–1.
14. Weber, *Friend*, ch. 3 and 'Conclusion'.
15. For an argument to the contrary, see Jeismann, *Vaterland*.
16. Weber, *Friend*.
17. Sauder, *Wilder*, 185, Weisgerber to Fritz Burger, 13 September 1914.
18. Jones, 'Enemy', 145–6.
19. BHStA/IV, RIR16/Bd.3,4, Count Bassenheim's diary, 23 October 1914.
20. BHStA/IV, RIR16/Bd.3,4, Count Bassenheim's diary, 23 and 24 October 1914; PBK, II/9/Facs.3m/Stumpf/diary, 22 October 1914.
21. Quoted in Heinz, *Hitler*, 72.
22. Maser, *Letters*, 50, Hitler to Joseph Popp, 3 December 1914.
23. Ibid. 68, 71, Hitler to Ernst Hepp, 5 February 1915.
24. PBK, II/9/Facs.3m/Stumpf/diary, 23 October 1914.
25. Rupprecht, *Kriegstagebuch*, i. 203, 13 October 1914.
26. Maser, *Letters*, 50, Hitler to Joseph Popp, 3 December 1914.
27. *Toronto Globe*, 'Women Spies Shot; A Terrible Task', 24 October 1914, quoted in Young, *Siege*, 21–2.
28. PBK, II/9/Facs.3m/Stumpf/diary, 23 October 1914.
29. Sauder, *Wilder*, 187, Weisgerber to his wife, 26 October 1914.
30. Maser, *Letters*, 71–2, Hitler to Joseph Popp, 5 February 1915.
31. Maser, *Letters*, 72, Hitler to Joseph Popp, 5 February 1915.
32. Ibid. 72, Hitler to Joseph Popp, 5 February 1915.
33. Ibid. 71, Hitler to Ernst Hepp, 5 February 1915; PBK, II/9/Facs.3m/Stumpf/diary, 27 October 1914; Rubenbauer, 'Ypern', 15.
34. Quoted in Stibbe, *Anglophobia*, 21.
35. Pollard, *Ypres*, 14–15.
36. Strachan, *To Arms*, 265.
37. Ibid. 276.
38. Maser, *Letters*, 72, 75, Hitler to Ernst Hepp, 5 February 1915.
39. See Rubenbauer, 'Ypern', 12.
40. BHStA/IV, RIR16/Bd.3,4, Count Bassenheim's diary, 27 October 1914.
41. BHStA/IV, RIR16/Bd.3,4, Count Bassenheim's diary, 27 October 1914.
42. BHStA/IV, RIR16/Bd.3,4, Count Bassenheim's diary, 29 October 1914.
43. Horne and Kramer, 'War', 153–68; Horne and Kramer, *Atrocities*. See also Kramer, *Destruction*. Horne and Kramer play down the significance of the Garde Civique in their otherwise magnificent *Atrocities*, 419–20, arguing that members of the Garde Civique had been present in only a minority of cases of German atrocities and positing that Belgium had every right to set up a Garde Civique dressed in makeshift uniforms. This may be true but misses the point that, immediately prior to their eleven-day killing spree, German troops

encountered tens of thousands, possibly more, of Belgians in garments that deceptively looked like those of guerrilla fighters. This does not legally or morally justify German behaviour. However, our primary task is to explain rather than morally judge the behaviour of German troops: The fact remains that the Germans encountered combatants that ostensibly looked like guerrilla fighters which seemingly confirmed the expectation of German soldiers that they would encounter partisans and therefore increased the likelihood that the German soldiers would see behind every unaccounted shot a *franc-tireur*.

44. Horne and Kramer, 'War', 161 ff. Larry Zuckerman's *Rape* is more interested in recording German atrocities and linking them to Nazi atrocities than in explaining why they happened. Jeff Lipkes's *Rehearsals* takes his case even further than either Horne and Kramer or Zuckerman, invoking a version of a German *Sonderweg* reminiscent of the 1940s. According to Lipkes, German officers (in full knowledge that no cases of *francs-tireurs* terror had taken place), in an intentional and premeditated fashion, terrorized the Belgian population to ensure speedy passage of their troops. The problem with this argument is that it does not go beyond the level of an assertion as it is based exclusively on Belgian sources. Moreover, it is difficult to see why German officers would have thought that the atrocities would speed up the German advance if they had not expected trouble in the form of *francs-tireurs* attacks in the first place.

45. Horne and Kramer, *Atrocities*, 106, refer to the involvement of Catholic German soldiers primarily in the case of Alsace and Lorraine, arguing that they participated in the killing of Catholic priests as suspected *francs-tireurs* out of 'feelings of national betrayal' that was deemed as more important than 'confessional solidarity'. However, this argument does not help their case. If it were true that a 'feeling of national betrayal' outweighed 'confessional solidarity', the cases under discussion by Horne and Kramer would suggest that considerations other than anti-Catholicism drove German soldiers.

46. Ibid. 104 ff.

47. Statistisches Reichsamt, *Jahrbuch, 1914*, 9. Of course, I do not question the fact that cases existed in which anti-Catholicism had an amplifying effect but I do question anti-Catholicism as a central motivation behind German atrocities in 1914.

48. Engelstein, 'Kalisz'.

49. Hull, *Destruction*. See also Roger Chickering, review of *Absolute Destruction*, in *German History*, 24/1 (2006), 138–9.

50. Hull, *Destruction*, 182–96.

51. A better point of comparison would have been the British treatment of the Zulu or of the Mahdi Army. An Anglo-German comparison of colonial counter-insurgency measures would also have to take into account the relative

German lack of experience in asymmetric warfare, compared to the long experience of British and French forces in facing counter-insurgencies.

52. In order to understand why so many German soldiers got involved, and the men of the List Regiment nearly got involved, in atrocities in 1914, we have to travel a decade and a half back in time to Africa to see what really set German colonial warfare apart from the British variant: The (Second) Boer War lasted slightly longer than two and a half years. It had broken out in October 1899. By September 1900, the Boers turned the war against the British into a guerrilla war. By late November, the British were employing what is widely seen as disproportionate force as part of their counter-insurgency strategy. By February, criticism over the policies erupted in earnest back in Britain. However, it took another seven months before British policies in South Africa were reversed. It thus took three months for criticism to be prominently voiced and twelve months for policy to change. The Herero rebellion against German colonial rule, meanwhile, broke out in January 1904. In mid-August, German colonial troops tried to defeat the Herero in the Battle of Waterberg. They drove the survivors of the battle, together with their families, into the desert and left them there to die. Just as in the Boer War, there was a delay before criticism about German conduct was voiced in earnest in Germany. This was largely due to slow communication lines between a colony that lay weeks of travel away and Germany. Even when Social Democrats started to voice criticism, *The Times* (of London)—the ultimate place from which we would have expected criticism of military policies of 'absolute destruction' if the 'absolute destruction' theory were correct—did not criticize the German military but in fact the Social Democrats as late as 10 October. After scolding the Social Democrats for their 'ill-disguised elation' at the difficulties Trotha and his troops were encountering, *The Times* encouraged Trotha 'immediately' to take 'energetic measures ... to put a speedy end' to the rebellion of the Herero and the Nama; *The Times*, 10 October 1904, 'The Troubles in German South-West Africa', 3. Only once news broke of a letter Trotha had sent to the Herero on 2 October, calling for the annihilation of all Herero who did not immediately leave the German colony, did all hell break loose in Europe. After a brief power struggle between the political and military leadership of Germany, Kaiser Wilhelm countermanded Trotha's policies on 8 December; see Clark, *Prussia*, 605 ff. (For the Boer War, see Saunders and Smith, 'Southern Africa', 597–623.) The period it took for criticism to erupt and for policy to be reversed was thus actually shorter in the German case than in the British one.

53. Citino, *Way*; on the Clausewitzian concept of a war of annihilation as the disarmament of the enemy, see Paret, *Clausewitz*, 384 ff.

54. Ferguson, 'Finance', 141–68.

55. Germany and her enemies agreed that this kind of warfare was barbarian. However, while the Germans argued that the use of civilians as combatants

creates barbarian warfare and necessitates an extreme response, her opponents argued that only the use of such an extreme response was barbarian.

56. BHStA/IV, RIR16/Bd.3,4/diary, Waldbott Graf von Bassenheim, 28 October 1914.
57. PBK, II/9/Facs.3m/Stumpf/diary, 28 October 1914.
58. BHStA/IV, RIR16/Bd.3,4/diary, Waldbott Graf von Bassenheim, 27 October 1914.
59. W[itt], 'Gefechte', 15; Roth, 'Feuertaufe', 19.
60. Rubenbauer, 'Ypern', 17; BHStA/IV, RIR16/Bd.3,4, Count Bassenheim's diary, 29 October 1914.
61. BHStA/IV, RIR16/Bd.3,4, Count Bassenheim's diary, 26 October 1914.
62. Solleder, '12. Kompanie', 49–50; Haugg, 'Feuertaufe', 55; Rubenbauer, 'Ypern', 18–19.
63. 'Kaisers Dank', in List Regiment, 47.
64. 'Brief eines Kriegsfreiwilligen', 68.
65. BHStA/IV, RIR16/Bd.3,4, Count Bassenheim's diary, 29 October 1914.
66. Weisgerber, 'Gheluvelt', 18.
67. Meyer, Hitler, 18.
68. BHStA/IV, RIR16/Bd.3,4, Count Bassenheim's diary, 29 October 1914.
69. Beckett, Ypres, 114.
70. Rubenbauer, 'Ypern', 20–1.
71. BHStA/IV, HS,1928(4), Ludwig Klein, letter written after the battle. Klein wrote: 'I had high spirits.'
72. Hitler, MK, 100.
73. Weisgerber, 'Gheluvelt', 18.
74. BHStA/IV, RIR16/Bd.3,4, Count Bassenheim's diary, 29 October 1914. See also Rubenbauer, 'Ypern', 21.
75. BHStA/IV, RIR17/Bd.1/diary, 31 October 1914.
76. Rubenbauer, 'Ypern', 24.
77. BHStA/IV, HS,1928(4), letter from Ludwig Klein.
78. Weisgerber, 'Gheluvelt', 18.
79. Sauder, Wilder, 204, Weisgerber to his sister, 1 January 1915.
80. Hitler, MK, 100.
81. Ibid. 118.
82. Schuhmacher, Leben, 1–183.
83. See e.g. BHStA/IV, RIR16/Bd.3,4, Count Bassenheim's diary, 29 October 1914; HS,1928(4), Ludwig Klein; List Regiment.
84. Maser, Letters, 53–4, Hitler to Joseph Popp, 3 December 1914 and 77–86, Hitler to Ernst Hepp, 5 February 1915.
85. Solleder, '12. Kompanie', 51.
86. BHStA/IV, RIR17/Bd.1/diary, 1 November 1914.
87. 'Die ersten Auszeichnungen', in List Regiment, 48.
88. Rubenbauer, 'Ruhe', 64.

89. Unruh, *Langemarck*; see e.g. Beumelburg, *Ypern*, 9–11.

90. BHStA/IV, RIR16/Bd.3,4, Count Bassenheim's diary, 29 October 1914.

91. BHStA/IV, HS,1928(4), letter from Ludwig Klein.

92. Beckett, *Ypres*.

93. Maser, *Letters*, 78, Hitler to Ernst Hepp, 5 February 1915.

94. Beckett, *Ypres*, 114–19.

95. Maser, *Letters*, 82, 85, Hitler to Ernst Hepp, 5 February 1915.

96. Evans, *Battles*, 16–17; Beckett, *Ypres*, 114–19. North of the Menin Road lay two companies of the 1st Coldstream Guards and one of the 1st Black Watch (Royal Highlanders), all of which belonged to the 1st (guards) Brigade, 1st Division (Lomax), I Corps (Haig), BEF. South of the street, lay the 1st Grenadier Guards and the 2nd Gordon Highlanders both of which belonged to the 20th Brigade, 7th Division (Capper), IV Corps (Rawlinson), BEF.

97. Maser, *Letters*, 53, Hitler to Joseph Popp, 3 December 1914.

98. Jäckel and Kuhn, *Hitler*, 68, Hitler to Ernst Hepp, 5 February 1915.

99. Stöhr, 'Verluste', 389.

100. Rubenhauer, 'Ypern', 22, 25.

101. Maser, *Letters*, 85, Hitler to Ernst Hepp, 5 February 1915.

102. Roth, 'Feuertaufe', 23.

103. BHStA/IV, RIR16/Bd.3,4, Count Bassenheim's diary, 29 October 1914.

104. BHStA/IV, RIR16/Bd.12, I Batl./diary, 6 November 1914.

105. BHStA/IV, RIR16/Bd.3,4, Count Bassenheim's diary, 29 October 1914; Rubenbauer, 'Ypern', 27; Solleder, '12. Kompanie', 51; W[itt], 'Gefechte', 16.

106. IFZ, MA-732, NSDAP/Hauptarchiv, Hans Raab to the NSDAP party archive, 5 August 1939; see also BHStA/IV, HS,1928(4), Ludwig Klein, letter written after the battle.

107. Beckett, *Ypres*, 114–19.

108. Weisgerber, 'Gheluvelt', 18.

109. Rubenbauer, 'Ypern', 32–3; PBK, II/9/Facs.3m/Stumpf/diary, 30 October 1914.

110. Beckett, *Ypres*, 142.

111. Ibid. 130 ff.; von Dellmensingen and Feeser, *Bayernbuch*, 185.

112. Rubenbauer, 'Ypern', 36–9; Solleder, '12. Kompanie', 54–5.

113. Pollard, *Ypres*, 20, 29.

114. LAELKB, OKM/2340, Oscar Daumiller's report, 2 November 1914.

115. PBK, II/9/Facs.3m/Stumpf/diary, 1 and 3 November.

116. Maser, *Letters*, 50, Hitler to Joseph Popp, 3 December 1914.

117. Quoted in Rubenbauer, 'Ypern', 28.

118. Sauder, *Wilder*, 190, Weisgerber to his wife, 8 November 1914.

119. Maser, *Letters*, 50, Hitler to Joseph Popp, 3 December 1914.

120. Rubenbauer, 'Ruhe', 62.

121. Meyer, *Hitler*, 20.

122. Sauder, *Wilder*, 189, Weisgerber to E. Ebers, 2 November 1914.

123. Sauder, *Wilder*, 190, Weisgerber to his wife, 8 November 1914.

124. Ibid. 188, Weisgerber to Ludwig Prager, 2 November 1914.

125. Ibid. 189, Weisgerber to E. Ebers, 2 November 1914.

126. Solleder, '12. Kompanie', 53; IFZ, MA-732, NSDAP/Hauptarchiv, Hans Raab to the NSDAP party archive, 5 August 1939; NARA, BDC/A3343/SSO/Arthur Rödl; Rubenbauer, 'Ypern', 28; BHStA, HS,1928(4), Ludwig Klein's letter; PBK, II/9/Facs.3m/Stumpf/diary, 3 November.

127. Evans, *Battles*, 18.

128. Stöhr, 'Verluste', 381 ff.

129. Quoted in Kershaw, *Hitler*, i. 91.

3. TWO TALES OF ONE CHRISTMAS

1. Rubenbauer, 'Messines', 65; Maser, *Letters*, 60, Hitler to Joseph Popp, 26 January 1915.

2. Information obtained during visit to Mesen in August 2008.

3. Maser, *Letters*, 63, Hitler to Joseph Popp, 26 January 1915.

4. PBK, II/9/Facs.3m/Stumpf/diary, 21 February 1915.

5. Solleder, 'Verbrüderung', 89–90; Frey, 'Weihnachten', 94–5; BHStA/IV, RIR16/Bd.1/diary, 23–6 December 1914; LAELKB, OKM/2340, programme for the 'Weihnachtsfeier im Felde 1914' for the troops of RD 6.

6. Sauder, *Wilder,* 199, Weisgerber to the wife of Commerzienrat Freundlich, 25 December 1914.

7. Solleder, 'Verbrüderung', 89–90.

8. Joachimsthaler, *Hitlers Weg*, 131.

9. The only surviving wartime correspondence of Hitler with people he had known before the war was with the family of his landlord in Munich and an acquaintance (Ernst Hepp), who was a law trainee and with whom Hitler was not on a first-name basis; see Maser, *Letters* and Jäckel and Kuhn, *Hitler*.

10. For an argument to the contrary, see Weintraub, *Silent Night*, 71.

11. PBK, II/9/Facs.3m/Stumpf/diary, 17 December 1914.

12. EPF, Georg Arneth to Karl Crämer, 16 November 1914.

13. Maser, *Letters*, 50, Hitler to Joseph Popp, 3 December 1914; Rubenbauer, 'Ruhe', 62; Sauder, *Wilder*, 190, 195, letters, Weisgerber to his wife, 8 November 1914, and to his brother, 6 December 1914.

14. NATO Standardization Agreement 2116.

15. See e.g. Williams, *Corporal Hitler*; Kershaw, *Hitler*, i. 91; Bullock, *Hitler*, 52; Toland, *Hitler*, 60; Stone, *Hitler*, 7; McClelland, *Political Thought*, 712; Sayer and Botting, *Hitler*, 21 ff. Lindsay, *Fromelles*, 48, even makes Hitler an NCO.

16. Kershaw, *Hitler*, i. 91.

17. Eichelsdörfer, 'Sturm', 75–6.

18. W[itt], 'Oostaverne', 36.

19. Maser, *Letters*, 89, Hitler to Ernst Hepp, 5 February 1915.

20. Eichelsdörfer, 'Sturm', 77-8; Kershaw, *Hitler*, i. 91; Maser, *Letters*, 50, Hitler to Joseph Popp, 3 December 1914, and 68-90, Hitler to Ernst Hepp, 5 February 1915.

21. BHStA/IV, RIR16/Bd.1/diary, 2 December 1914; KSR/3046, No. 1062; W[itt], 'Oostaverne', 37. Twenty-five members of RIR 16 had already received Iron Crosses on 8 November; see 'Auszeichnungen', in *List Regiment*, 47; Kershaw, *Hitler*, i. 92; Sauder, *Wilder*, 193, Weisgerber to Ludwig Prager, 2 December 1914. Reports according to which Kaiser Wilhelm II personally awarded Hitler the Iron Cross are unfounded; see e.g. Weintraub, *Silent Night*, 70.

22. Maser, *Letters*, 50, 57, Hitler to Joseph Popp, 3 December 1914.

23. Solleder, 'Winter', 84-5; Wakefield, *Christmas*, 2; Atkinson, *Devonshire Regiment*, 31; Aggett, *Bloody Eleventh*, ii. 444; Strachan, *To Arms*, 993-4.

24. Quoted in Joachimsthaler, *Hitlers Weg*, 132.

25. Nießl, Prägner, and Stöhr, 'Ehrentafel', 409-11.

26. PBK, II/9/Facs.3m/Stumpf/diary, 18 November 1914.

27. Solleder, '12. Kompanie', 55.

28. Solleder, 'Winter', 80-1.

29. PBK, II/9/Facs.3m/Stumpf/diary, 7 December 1914.

30. EPF, Robert Hell to Karl Crämer.

31. Sauder, *Wilder*, 196, Weisgerber to his wife, 12 December 1914.

32. 'Flanders', *Encyclopædia Britannica Online*, accessed 10 October 2008.

33. BHStA/IV, RIR16/Bd.1 and RIR17/Bd.1, diaries, November and December 1914; BHStA/IV, RIR17/Bd.2, Kriegserfahrungen des I. Batls-RIR 17, December 1914; Atkinson, *Devonshire Regiment*, 30-5; Solleder, 'Winter', 79-89.

34. Solleder, 'Winter', 82-3; PBK, II/9/Facs.3m/Stumpf/diary, entries for winter 1914/15.

35. Sauder, *Wilder*, 191, Weisgerber to the wife of Commerzienrat Freundlich, 22 November 1914.

36. Ibid., 196, Weisgerber to his wife, 12 December 1914.

37. ADN, 9R/505, Comines, occupation report.

38. Sauder, *Wilder*, 197, Weisgerber to Ludwig Prager, 18 December 1914.

39. PBK, II/9/Facs.3m/Stumpf/diary, 4 December 1914.

40. Rubenbauer, 'Messines', 65.

41. BHStA/IV, RIR17/Bd.2, Kriegserfahrungen des I. Batls-RIR 17, December 1914.

42. BHStA/IV, RIB12/Bd.1/diary, 22 November 1914. See also BHStA/IV, RIR17/Bd.1/diary, 22 November 1914.

43. PBK, II/9/Facs.3m/Stumpf/diary, 21 November 1914.

44. PBK, II/9/Facs.3m/Stumpf/diary, 18 November 1914.

45. PBK, II/9/Facs.3m/Stumpf/diary, 7 December 1914.

46. Quoted in Kramer, *Destruction*, 36-7.

47. Sauder, *Wilder*, 195, Weisgerber to his brother Fritz, 6 December 1914.
48. Ibid. 198, Weisgerber to his wife, 18 December 1914.
49. Ibid. 199, Weisgerber to the wife of Commerzienrat Freundlich, Christmas 1914.
50. Watson, *Enduring*, ch. 5.
51. LAELKB, OKM/2340/Oscar Daumiller's report, 30 November 1914.
52. 'Brief eines Kriegsfreiwilligen', 70.
53. Ziemann, *Heimat*, 246–65; Becker, *Faith*.
54. PBK, II/9/Facs.3m/Stumpf/diary, November–December 1914; LAELKB, OKM/2340/Oscar Daumiller's report, 20 January 1915.
55. PBK, II/9/Facs.3m/Stumpf/diary, 21 November 1914.
56. PBK, II/9/Facs.3m/Stumpf/diary, 22 November (quote) and 29 November 1914; ADN, 9R/505, Comines, occupation report; ADN, 9R/1229, investigation against Paul Le Safre.
57. 'Brief eines Kriegsfreiwilligen', 67.
58. BHStA/IV, HS/1952, war diary of an unidentified French physician, entries for 18 and 22 October 1914.
59. ADN, 9R/505, Comines, occupation report.
60. PBK, II/9/Facs.3m/Stumpf/diary, 27 November 1914.
61. PBK, II/9/Facs.3m/Stumpf/diary, 3 December 1914.
62. PBK, II/9/Facs.3m/Stumpf/diary, 6 December 1914.
63. Devon County Council Library, *Western Times*, 2 January 1915, 'Christmas Eve at the Front'; Solleder, 'Verbrüderung', 90; PBK, II/9/Facs.3m/Stumpf/diary, 24 December 1914; Aggett, *Bloody Eleventh*, 444–7; Jürgs, *Frieden*, 52–3, 99.
64. Royal Norfolk Regimental Museum, 15th Brigade, War Diary, 25 December 1914.
65. Letter from Josef Wenzl, dated 28 December 1914, quoted in Solleder, 'Verbrüderung', 91–2.
66. Sauder, *Wilder*, 200, Weisgerber to his brother, 26 December 1914.
67. Solleder, 'Verbrüderung', 90.
68. Brown and Seaton, *Christmas*, 110.
69. Weintraub, *Silent Night*, 50; Brown and Seaton, *Christmas*.
70. Quoted in Wakefield, *Christmas*, 8.
71. Quoted ibid. 12.
72. Brown and Seaton, *Christmas*.
73. BHStA/IV, RIR16/Bd.12, I Batl., 26 December 1914.
74. Crofton, *Massacre*, 101.
75. BHStA/IV, RIR16/Bd.1/diary, 28 December 1914.
76. Brown and Seaton, *Christmas*, 155, 169; Crofton, *Massacre*, 108–9.
77. Williamson, *Goodbye*, 9, 22–3, 161–3, 228; Lamplugh, *Shadowed Man*, 101, 142.
78. IFZ, MA-732, NSDAP/Hauptarchiv, report by Heinrich Lugauer, 5 February 1940.

79. Brown and Seaton, *Christmas*, p. xii.
80. Brown, 'Introduction', 7–8. See also Brown and Seaton, *Christmas*, 192.
81. 'Joyeux Noël', directed by Christian Carion, 2005.
82. Wakefield, *Christmas*, 17.
83. Brown and Seaton, *Christmas*, 79.
84. See e.g. Eksteins, *Rites*, 127, 133. Eksteins claims that Prussia's modernism stood in the way of more widespread Prussian participation in the Truce.
85. Brown and Seaton, *Christmas*, 36, 80–6, 149–53; Weintraub, *Silent Night*, 25–6, 66; Eksteins, *Rites*, 113–14; French, *Identities*, 111, 131. Cultural factors, including a British sporting culture and a tradition within British units to bury all feuds during Christmas, might have also played a role; see Snape, *God*, 188; Eksteins, *Rites*, 119 ff.
86. BHStA/IV, RIR16/Bd.3,2, Meldung by RIR 16, I. Battalion.
87. Berghahn, *Europe*, 1–32.
88. Fromkin, *Summer*, 337.
89. See e.g. Kennedy, *Antagonism*.
90. Stibbe, *Anglophobia*, 207.
91. See on this point Weber, *Friend*, ch. 2 and 'Conclusion'.
92. Stibbe, *Anglophobia*, describes these activities in great detail but asserts rather than proves how widespread extreme forms of Anglophobia really were in wartime Germany.
93. Strachan, *To Arms*, 10, 1138–9. See also Jeismann, *Vaterland*, 379 ff.
94. Strachan, *To Arms*, 1138, refers to Philipp Witkop's *Kriegsbriefe gefallener Studenten*.
95. Quoted in Hettling and Jeismann, 'Epos', 178; see also Ulrich, *Augenzeugen*, chs. 3 and 4; Natter, *Literature*, 94–5; Lipp, *Meinungslenkung*, 62 ff.
96. Brocks, *Welt*, 238–9; EPF, see the twenty-five postcards sent by different members of RIR 16 and of divisional HQ of RD 6 to the Protestant pastor of Feldkirchen.
97. See ch. 2.
98. Stevenson, *Cataclysm*, 75.

4. DREAMS OF A NEW WORLD

1. Maser, *Letters*, 57, Hitler to Joseph Popp, 3 December 1914.
2. Ibid. 58, Hitler to Joseph Popp, 22 January 1915.
3. Ibid. 59, Hitler to Ernst Hepp, 22 January 1915.
4. Ibid. 60, Hitler to Joseph Popp, 26 January 1915.
5. PBK, II/9/Facs.3m/Stumpf/diary, 18 February 1915.
6. Solleder, 'Neues Jahr', 99.
7. Maser, *Letters*, 89, Hitler to Ernst Hepp, 5 February 1915.
8. EPF, Georg Arneth to Karl Crämer, 12 January 1915.

9. Solleder, 'Neues Jahr', 97–100; BHStA/IV, RD6/Bd.147,6, Sitzungsbericht, undated; BHStA/IV, RIR17/Bd.1/diary, January–March 1915; BHStA/IV, RIR17/Bd.1/diary, 6 and 18 January 1915; BHStA/IV, RD6/Bd.147,2, decree/3803, 14 February 1915; Solleder, 'Neues Jahr', 99.

10. BHStA/IV, RD6/Bd.147,6, letter written by Gustav von Scanzoni, 3 February 1915.

11. BHStA/IV, RIR17/Bd.3, RD 6 to RIB 12, 20 February 1915.

12. Solleder, 'Neues Jahr', 99; BHStA/IV, RD6/Bd.147,11, RIR 16 to RIB 12, 4 March 1915.

13. Maser, *Letters*, 64, Hitler to Joseph Popp, 26 January 1915.

14. Solleder, 'Neues Jahr', 97–100.

15. Maser, *Letters*, 64, 67, Hitler to Joseph Popp, 26 January 1915.

16. Ibid. 89, and Jäckel and Kuhn, *Hitler*, 69, Hitler to Ernst Hepp, 5 February 1915.

17. BHStA/IV, RIB12/Bd.1/diary, 6–28 February 1915.

18. PBK, II/9/Facs.3m/Stumpf/diary, 3 March 1915.

19. Solleder, 'Neues Jahr', 104.

20. BHStA/IV, RD6/Bd.147,7, K.H.Qu. to Generalkommando II.B., 19 January 1915; Generalquartiermeister of the Gr.H.Qu., 19 February 1915; Divisions-stabsquartier to AOK 6, 7 March 1915.

21. PBK, II/9/Facs.3m/Stumpf/diary, 3 March 1915.

22. Wilcox, 'Discipline', 80–1; Jahr, *Soldaten, passim*.

23. PBK, II/9/Facs.3m/Stumpf/diary, 6–7 January, 5 February 1915; Solleder, 'Neues Jahr', 98–101.

24. Rupprecht, *Kriegstagebuch*, i. 296, entry for 5 February 1916.

25. BHStA/IV, RIB12/Bd.1, August–September 1915.

26. PBK, II/9/Facs.3m/Stumpf/diary, 28 January 1915. See also the entries for 2 and 3 February, and LAELKB, OKM/2340/Oscar Daumiller's report, 4 March 1915.

27. Watson, *Enduring*, 90.

28. PBK, II/9/Facs.3m/Stumpf/diary, 9 February 1915.

29. PBK, II/9/Facs.3m/Stumpf/diary, 93 ff.

30. PBK, II/9/Facs.3m/Stumpf/diary, 15 January 1915.

31. SP, Schnelldorfer to his parents, 7 March 1915.

32. PBK, II/9/Facs.3m/Stumpf/diary, 1 January–7 March 1915; Ziemann, *Heimat*, 51; Becker, *Faith*, 42; Solleder, 'Neues Jahr', 98–101.

33. Bruner, *Matthew*, 101–2.

34. EPF, Robert Hell to Crämer, 22 April 1915.

35. EPF, Robert Hell to Crämer, 7 December 1915.

36. Porter, 'Jerusalems', 119.

37. Ibid. 101–32.

38. Ibid.

39. LAELKB, OKM/2340, Oscar Daumiller's report, 1 May 1915.

40. LAELKB, OKM/2340, Wilhelm Stählin's report for the period of 21 November 1914 to 31 December 1915.

41. PBK, II/9/Facs.3m/Stumpf/diary, 6 January and 17 February 1915; EPF, Robert Hell to Karl Crämer, 4 May 1915; Solleder, 'Neues Jahr', 102.

42. SP, Schnelldorfer to his parents, 2 March 1915.

43. Solleder, 'Neues Jahr', 97.

44. PBK, II/9/Facs.3m/Stumpf/diary, 8 March 1915.

45. PBK, II/9/Facs.3m/Stumpf/diary, 9 March 1915.

46. PBK, II/9/Facs.3m/Stumpf/diary, 10 March 1915; LAELKB, OKM/2340, Oscar Daumiller's report, 1 May 1915.

47. Solleder, 'Neues Jahr', 103–4; Stiegler, 'Tagebuch', 113.

48. Gilbert, First World War, 132; Prior and Wilson, Command, 23, 84.

49. BHStA/IV, MG/RD6/Jakob Schäfer.

50. BHStA/IV, MG/RD6/Friedrich Neuner, Albert Geiger to Lieutenant Schlamp, 7 August 1915.

51. See e.g. Stiegler, 'Tagebuch', 113.

52. BHStA/IV, RIB12/Bd.1 and RIR16/Bd.1, diaries, 10–12 March 1915; Eichelsdörfer, 'Neuve Chapelle', 106–13.

53. Sauder, Wilder, 208, Weisgerber to his wife, 15 March 1915.

54. Eichelsdörfer, 'Neuve Chapelle', 106–13; Stiegler, 'Tagebuch', 114–16; Wenzl, 'Feldpostbrief', 118–19; Solleder, 'Gefechten', 120; Stöhr, 'Verluste', 382; Bridger, Neuve Chapelle, 24, 87, quote at 82; BHStA/IV, MG/RD6/Jakob Schäfer; BHStA/IV, RIR17/Bd.1/diary, 12 March 1915.

55. SP, Schnelldorfer to his parents, 18 March 1915.

56. BHStA/IV, RD6/Bd.110,4, RD 6 to A.O.K. 6, 23 March 1915.

57. Watson, Enduring, 69.

58. Eichelsdörfer, 'Neuve Chapelle', 110; Bridger, Neuve Chapelle, quote at 88.

59. Brandmayer, Meldegänger Hitler (1933), 22.

60. Gilbert, First World War, 133; Keegan, First World War, 212.

61. BHStA/IV, RIR16/Bd.1/diary, 13–16 March 1915; PBK, II/9/Facs.3m/ Stumpf/diary, 13–16 March 1915.

62. SP, Schnelldorfer to his parents, 16 March 1915.

63. Solleder, 'Gefechten', 120; PBK, II/9/Facs.3m/Stumpf/diary, 18 March 1915.

64. Solleder, 'Gefechten', 120–1; Wiedemann, 'Kriegswinter', 189.

65. SP, Schnelldorfer to his parents, 25 March 1915.

66. Solleder, 'Gefechten', 120–1.

67. Maser, Letters, 89, Hitler to Ernst Hepp, 5 February 1915.

68. Solleder, 'Gefechten', 120–1.

69. PBK, II/9/Facs.3m/Stumpf/diary, 20 March 1915.

70. See Solleder, 'Gefechten', 122; Wiedemann, 'Stellung', 205; Solleder, Westfront, illustrations on 133, 187, 197, 231; Meyer, Hitler, 31–2.

71. BHStA/IV, RIR16/Bd.1 and RIR17/Bd.1, diaries, 17 March–8 May 1915; Nießl, Prägner, and Stöhr, 'Ehrentafel', 419–21.

72. BHStA/IV, RIR17/Bd.2, RD 6, divisional order, 14 April 1915.

73. Twenty-seven members of RIR 16 were killed in January, while overall membership in the regiment stood at 1,794 in early January; see Nießl, Prägner, and Stöhr, 'Ehrentafel', 411–13; Solleder, 'Neues Jahr', 97.

74. BHStA/IV, RIR16/Bd.12, I Batl./diary, 23 April 1916.

75. Solleder, 'Gefechten', 124 ff.; Sauder, Wilder, 211, Weisgerber to his wife, 28 March 1915.

76. Sauder, Wilder, 213, Weisgerber to his wife, 4 April 1915.

77. Solleder, 'Gefechten', 120 ff.; BHStA/IV, RIR16/Bd.1/diary, 17 March–8 May 1915; BHStA/IV, RIR17/Bd.1/diary, 29 March–8 May 1915.

78. EPF, Georg Arneth to Karl Crämer, 23 April 1915.

79. SP, Schnelldorfer to his parents, 25 March 1915.

80. Alexander, Weiß, 'Bei Fromelles, März 1915 bis Sept. 1916', quoted in Solleder, 'Gefechten', 122. See also Wiedemann, 'Kriegswinter', 189.

81. BHStA/IV, HS/1952, war diary of an unidentified French physician, 17 December 1914.

82. BHStA/IV, RIR17/Bd.2, RD 6, divisional order, 5 May 1915.

83. Ziemann, Heimat, 272 ff.; Ay, Entstehung, 134 ff.

84. Hitler, MK, 112.

85. SP, Schnelldorfer to his parents, 26 April 1915.

86. BHStA/IV, MG/RD6, Wilhelm von Lüneschloß.

87. Ziemann, Heimat, 140 ff.

88. SB, Z2, Volksfreund, 3 March 1932, 'Ein Kriegskamerad erzählt: Mit Adolf im Felde, von Josef Stettner'.

89. Axelrod, Cooperation, pp. vii–viii, 73–87; Ashworth, Warfare.

90. Solleder, 'Gefechten', 124.

91. Nießl, Prägner, and Stöhr, 'Ehrentafel', 387–502.

92. Sauder, Wilder, 216, Weisgerber to his wife, 17 April 1915.

93. Solleder, 'Gefechten', 126.

94. PBK, II/9/Facs.3m/Stumpf/diary, 6 May 1915.

95. Eichelsdörfer, 'Fromelles', 130–4; Bestle, 'Engländer', 142–3; Dehn, 'Weisgerber', 148–9; PBK, II/9/Facs.3m/Stumpf/diary, 9 May 1915.

96. Eichelsdörfer, 'Fromelles', 132–6; Meyer, 'Härtester Tag', 141–2; Meyer, Hitler, 23 ff.; Bestle, 'Engländer', 144–5; Solleder, 'Einbruch', 92; BHStA/ IV, RIB12/Bd.17,7, 'Übersetzung eines englischen Angriffsentwurfes', 7 May 1915.

97. BHStA/IV, RD6/Bd.110,4, Engelbert Niederhofer's testimony, 19 May 1915.

98. BHStA/IV, RIR17/Bd.1/diary, 9–10 May 1915; PBK, II/9/Facs.3m/Stumpf/ diary, 10 May 1915; Eichelsdörfer, 'Fromelles', 132–41; Bestle, 'Engländer', 143–5; Dieß, 'Geiger', 145–8; Dehn, 'Weisgerber', 148–9; Sauder, Wilder, 240, Dr Arnold to Grete Weisgerber; Solleder, 'Einbruch', 92; Solleder, 'Fromelles', 153; Nießl, Prägner, and Stöhr, 'Ehrentafel', 421–9.

99. Solleder, 'Einbruch', 92. The wartime pamphlet about the war effort of RIR 16, published probably in late 1915, includes a piece written by Weisgerber; see Weisgerber, 'Gheluvelt', 18.

100. Sauder, *Wilder*, 235, 359.

101. Ibid., 229, 'Die Beisetzung Albert Weisgerbers', article from unidentified newspaper; for similar articles from various Bavarian newspapers, see ibid. 231–56.

102. For Weisgerber, see Solleder, 'Gefechten', 128; Solleder, 'Fromelles', 154–6; Eichelsdörfer, 'Fromelles', 138; Dehn, 'Weisgerber', 148–9. The regimental history also reproduces three photographs depicting Weisgerber; see Solleder, *Westfront*, 103, 105, 139. By contrast, it includes one perfunctory reference to Hitler in Solleder, 'Geleit', p. ix, one other mentioning him, Eichelsdörfer, 'Sturm', 75–6, as well as one blurred image of Hitler with a caption that includes a spelling mistake; see Solleder, *Westfront*, 168.

103. BHStA/IV, RD6/Bd.110,4, OL Eichelsdörfer to RD 6, 12 May 1915.

104. Wilke, 'Schiedsgericht', 105.

105. BHStA/IV, RIR17/Bd.3, 6/RIR 17, battle report, 17–20 May 1915.

106. BHStA/IV, RIR16/Bd.1/diary, 9 February 1915.

107. Sauder, *Wilder*, 218, Weisgerber to his wife, 6 May 1915.

108. Ferguson, *War of the World*, 123–30; Ferguson, 'Prisoner Taking', 34–78; Ferguson, *Pity*, ch. 13; Smith, Audoin-Rouzeau, and Becker, *France*, 91; Eksteins, *Rites*, 109.

109. PBK, II/9/Facs.3m/Stumpf/diary, 10 May 1915.

110. BHStA/IV, RIR17/Bd.2, RD 6, divisional order, 16 May 1917.

5. OF FRONT-LINE SOLDIERS AND 'REAR AREA PIGS'

1. SP, Schnelldorfer to his parents, 2 June 1915.

2. PBK, II/9/Facs.3m/Stumpf/diary, 10 May and 17 June (quote) 1915; Solleder, 'Fromelles', 152–8; Roach, *Stiff*, ch. 3.

3. Roach, *Stiff*, 70–1.

4. Solleder, 'Fromelles', 152–8.

5. W[itt], 'Messiners-Betlehem-Ferme', 28; Rubenbauer, 'Messines', 66.

6. Maser, *Letters*, 54, Hitler to Joseph Popp, 3 December 1914.

7. Ibid. 88, Hitler to Ernst Hepp, 5 February 1915.

8. Ibid. 63, Hitler to Joseph Popp, 26 January 1915.

9. Stiehler, *Hitler*, 28. A similar account was given by one of the standard history school textbooks in the Third Reich, see Kumsteller *et al.*, *Geschichtsbuch*, 6–8.

10. Stiehler, *Hitler*, 33.

11. IFZ, MA-732, NSDAP/Hauptarchiv, note by Karl Lippert, 28 March 1940.

12. IFZ, MA-732, NSDAP/Hauptarchiv, report by Heinrich Lugauer to the NSDAP Hauptarchiv, 5 February 1940.

13. Quoted in Heinz, *Hitler*, 75–6.

14. Mend, *Hitler*, 10.
15. Brandmayer, *Meldegänger Hitler* (1933), 68 and *passim*. Private papers of Jakob Weiß, newspaper cutting from the *Süddeutsche Sonntagspost*, 2 April 1933, 'Jakob Weiß'.
16. NARA, M1270-Roll1, interrogation file on Amann.
17. Winter and Baggett, *Great War*, 188–9. Similarly, David Jablonsky, described Hitler's job as 'particularly dangerous and thankless' and told his readers that 'runners would hunch forward in trenches and shell-holes and then spring up'; see Jablonsky, 'Paradox of Duality', 55. Kershaw, *Hitler*, i. 91, dismisses interwar 'attempts of [Hitler's] political enemies in the early 1930s to belittle the dangers' of Hitler's war service on account of the fact that Hitler had to carry 'messages to the front through the firing line'. Asprey, *Command*, 123, meanwhile, posited that Hitler was a battalion (rather than a regimental) dispatch runner who 'was almost constantly exposed to heavy fire' and 'would continue to fight bravely to the end of the war'.
18. Keegan, *First World War*, 211. Another historian even claims that 'Hitler saw the whole war out as a fighting soldier'; see McClelland, *Political Thought*, 712. According to Stone, *Hitler*, 7, Hitler 'fought fiercely'. For Davies, *Europe*, 904, Hitler was a 'courageous *Meldegänger*'. Lindsay, *Fromelles*, 51, meanwhile tells us that Hitler's job was one 'with a short life expectancy'.
19. Overy, *Dictators*, 13.
20. Fest, *Hitler*, 102–3.
21. The characterization was made by Robert Wohl in an interview for 'The Great War and the Shaping of the 20th Century'; see www.pbs.orf/historian/hist_wohl_06_hitler.html, accessed 11 March 2009.
22. Toland, *Hitler*, 60, 63–4.
23. Ibid. 61 (quote), 65.
24. Bullock, *Hitler*, 51–2. Bullock pointed out that Hitler was actually not in the trenches but maintains that he took messages from regimental HQ to the companies.
25. Kershaw, *Hitler*, i. 91; Solleder, 'Gefechten', 122 ff.
26. ADN, 9R/129, the Director of the Ecole Primaire Superieure in Fournes, J. Gombert, to the Rector of the Académie de Lille, 20 December 1914.
27. *Baedeker's Northern France*, p. xx.
28. The claim was made by Robert Wohl in an interview for 'The Great War and the Shaping of the 20th Century'; see www.pbs.org/historian/hist_wohl_06_hitler.html, accessed 11 March 2009.
29. Solleder, 'Fromelles', 172.
30. Mend, *Hitler*, 89, 91; Wiedemann, *Feldherr*, 23.
31. At best, only stray bullets could have flown all the way up to the crossroads at Messines. However, even this is highly unlikely. A standard maximum range for direct machine-gun fire in the First World War was about 1,000 yards. However, machine-gun fire was only effective at much shorter ranges,

400 yards in desert warfare but less than half of that distance in the Western European countryside. I am grateful to Simon Ball for this information.

32. Wiedemann, *Feldherr*, 20–50.

33. Toland, *Hitler*, 60, 63–4.

34. Solleder, 'Führerliste', 370.

35. See ch. 2.

36. See e.g. Bullock, *Hitler*, 52; Fest, *Hitler*, 103; Stone, *Hitler*, 7; Maser, *Legende*, 138; Steinert, *Hitler*, 89; Davidson, *Hitler*, 66; McClelland, *Political Thought*, 712.

37. Kershaw, *Hitler*, i. 96.

38. Toland, *Hitler*, 61. In fact, if Fritz Wiedemann's memoirs are reliable, Amann and Wiedemann unsuccessfully proposed Hitler for an Iron Cross 1st Class later in the war; see Wiedemann, *Feldherr*, 25.

39. Solleder, 'Führerliste', 370; NARA, M1270-Roll22, interrogation report of Fritz Wiedemann; Wiedemann, *Feldherr*, 23.

40. EPF, Georg Arneth to Karl Crämer, 25 December 1914; PBK, II/9/Facs.3m/ Stumpf/diary, 7 and 18 November 1914.

41. Solleder, 'Erster Winter', 86.

42. Hans Ostermünchner's copy of Solleder, *Westfront* is in the possession of his grandson Hans.

43. This claim has generally been accepted by historians as true; see e.g. Davidson, *Hitler*, 66; Bullock, *Hitler*, 52; Stone, *Hitler*, 7.

44. See NARA, RG242, T-581-52, testimony of Wihelm von Lüneschloß, 20 February 1922.

45. NARA, RG242, T-581-52, testimony of Friedrich Petz, 20 February 1922.

46. NARA, RG242, T-581-52, testimonies of Emil Spatny and Anton von Tubeuf, 20 March 1922. For Tubeuf's verdict, see Ch. 10.

47. Quoted in *Die Volksgemeinschaft*, 7 March 1932, 2, 'Marxistische Lügen über Adolf Hitlers Fronttätigkeit vor Gericht gebrandmarkt'. See also Meyer, *Hitler*, 35.

48. IFZ, MA-732, NSDAP/Hauptarchiv, Berichte und Aussagen ehemaliger Frontkameraden.

49. SB, Z2, *Volksfreund*, 3 March 1932, 'Ein Kriegskamerad erzählt'.

50. SB, Z2, *Volksfreund*, 3 March 1932, 'Ein Kriegskamerad erzählt'.

51. Solleder, 'Gefechten', 122 ff. They lay in Fromelles-Nord, in La Voirie, and to the south-east of the Deleval farm.

52. NARA, RG242, T-581/1A, newspaper cutting, *Fränkischer Volksfreund*, 12 March 1932, 'Kamerad Hitler'. This is a reprint of the *Echo der Woche* article.

53. BHStA/IV, officer files/Korbinian Rutz.

54. BHStA/IV, RIR16/Bd.12, I Batl./diary, 5 June 1916.

55. Alexander Moritz Frey, 'Der unbekannte Gefreite—persönliche Erinnerungen an Hitler' (1946), quoted in Ernsting, *Frey*, 49–55.

56. Quoted in Ernsting, *Frey*, 56–7.

57. Ibid. 55.

58. Ibid. 59–60. Frey's first novel, *Solnemann der Unsichtbare*, published in 1914, meanwhile, had made fun of a Bavarian officer.

59. Meyer, *Hitler*, 32 ff., 65–6.

60. SP, Schnelldorfer to his parents, 3 April 1915.

61. SP, Schnelldorfer to his parents, 10 April 1915.

62. SP, Schnelldorfer to his parents, 26 April 1915.

63. SP, Schnelldorfer to his parents, 4 July 1915.

64. SP, Schnelldorfer to his parents, 8 July 1915.

65. IFZ, MA-732, NSDAP/Hauptarchiv, Berichte und Aussagen ehemaliger Frontkameranden; see also NARA, T-581-47, Hitler als Soldat—Briefe ueber ihn—Frontkameraden.

66. NARA, T-581-1, letters sent to Hitler.

67. NARA, T-581-1, Ferdinand Widman to Hitler, 9 March 1932.

68. EPF, Georg Arneth to Karl Crämer, 29 August 1915.

69. BHStA/IV, RIR17/Bd.1/diary, 2–8 October 1915; BHStA/IV, RIR17/Bd.2, RD6, divisional order, 16 June 1915; BHStA/IV, RIR17/Bd.3, RIR 16, Gefechtsbericht vom 2. mit 8.10.15; Spatny, 'Kämpfe', 179–88.

70. EPF, Robert Hell to Crämer, 29 September 1915.

71. Spatny, 'Kämpfe', 179–88.

72. Channel 5, 'The Trench Detectives', Season 1, Episode 1: 'Loos'.

73. BHStA/IV, Offiziersakte Hugo Gutmann; RIR16, Bd.1/diary, 14 January 1915; Solleder, 'Neues Jahr', 99.

74. LAELKB, OKM/2340/Oscar Daumiller's report for 1915.

75. BHStA/IV, RIB12/Bd.1, RIR16/Bd.1, and RIR17/Bd.1, diaries, May–December 1915; PBK, II/9/Facs.3m/Stumpf/diary, 9 July 1915; Solleder, 'Fromelles', 158–77; Nießl, Prägner, and Stöhr, 'Ehrentafel', 429–40; Müller, 'Weapons', 98; Smith, Audoin-Rouzeau, and Becker, *France*, 88. The poisonous gas first used by the French was not lethal.

76. SP, Schnelldorfer to his parents, 10 June 1915.

77. SP, Schnelldorfer to his parents, 1 July 1915.

78. Becker, *Great War*, 195.

79. See Solleder, 'Fromelles', 163–4. See also Watson, *Enduring*, ch. 3.

80. SP, Schnelldorfer to his parents, 27 May 1915.

81. SP, Schnelldorfer to his parents, 22 June 1915.

82. SP, Schnelldorfer to his parents, 25 July 1915.

83. BHStA/IV, RIB12/Bd.1/diary, monthly summary for June 1915; EPF, Robert Hell to Crämer, 29 September 1915.

84. See for this theme, Bourke, *Fear*, 210.

85. BHStA/IV, RIB12/Bd.17,4, RIR 16, Erfahrungen, 16 October 1915.

86. Otto Bestle, 'Engländer', 144.

87. PBK, II/9/Facs.3m/Stumpf/diary, 9 July 1915; Solleder, 'Fromelles', 171.

88. BHStA/IV, RIR 16/Bd.3, Gefechtsbericht vom 2. mit 8.10.15.

89. SP, Schnelldorfer to his parents, 4 August 1915.

90. SP, Schnelldorfer to his parents, 26 September 1915.
91. Doughty, *Victory*, 509; Geyer, 'Tötungshandeln', 112; Ziemann, *Heimat*, 60.
92. Rupprecht, *Kriegstagebuch*, i. 227, entry for 22 October 1914.
93. Ibid. 33, entry for 21 August 1914. See also 190, 243, 244, entries for 8 October, 3 November, and 4 November 1914.
94. BHStA/IV, RIB12/Bd.25,1, Rittmeister Müller-Brand to Kronprinz Rupprecht, without date.
95. BHStA/IV, RIB12/Bd.25,1, instruction issued by Gustav von Scanzoni, 14 October 1915.
96. See Ch. 2, for a discussion of the idea that the German armed forces were supposedly always gravitating towards the most extreme of measures.
97. Solleder, 'Fromelles', 172.
98. BHStA/IV, RIR17/Bd.1/diary, 24 August and 7 September 1915; BHStA/IV, RIR16/Bd.1/diary, 26 November 1915; Solleder, 'Fromelles', 174.
99. BHStA/IV, RIR16/Bd.8, report by III Batl., 14 November 1915.
100. PBK, II/9/Facs.3m/Stumpf/diary, 16 and 20 July 1915.
101. Weber, *Friend*, 3.
102. PBK, II/9/Facs.3m/Stumpf/diary, 28 June 1915.
103. PBK, II/9/Facs.3m/Stumpf/diary.
104. PBK, II/9/Facs.3m/Stumpf/diary, entries for May–December 1915.
105. PBK, II/9/Facs.3m/Stumpf/diary, 13 June 1915.
106. PBK, II/9/Facs.3m/Stumpf/diary, 30 October–4 November 1915.
107. PBK, II/9/Facs.3m/Stumpf/diary, 13 May, 17 June, and 9 July 1915.
108. LAELKB, OKM/2340, Oscar Daumiller's report, 2 September 1915.
109. PBK, II/9/Facs.3m/Stumpf/diary, e.g. 9 April 1915.
110. PBK, II/9/Facs.3m/Stumpf/diary, 28 April 1915.
111. Hitler, *MK* 100–1.
112. AEM, NL Faulhaber, 6779/3, Norbert Stumpf to Faulhaber, 17 October 1915.
113. BHStA/IV, MG/RD6/Eduard Ziegler.
114. Meyer, *Hitler*.
115. BHStA/IV, RIR16/Bd.18, order by III. Batl., 12 November 1915.
116. Watson, *Enduring*, ch. 3.
117. BHStA/IV, MG/RD6, Hans Amnon.
118. Solleder, 'Gefechten', 126.
119. PBK, II/9/Facs.3m/Stumpf/diary, 9 April 1915.
120. PBK, II/9/Facs.3m/Stumpf/diary, 4 August 1915.
121. PBK, II/9/Facs.3m/Stumpf/diary, 2, 5, and 12 June 1915.
122. BHStA/IV, RIR17/Bd.1/diary, 19 September 1915.
123. PBK, 11/9/Facs.3m/Stumpf/diary, 28 June 1915.
124. BHStA/IV, RD6/Johan Dinkelmeier.
125. BHStA/IV, RD6/Bd.147,4, von Scanzoni to the regiments of RD6, 21 September 1915.

126. BHStA/IV, MG/RD6/Jakob Schäfer, letter to Marie Welsberger, 24 September 1915.

127. BHStA/IV, MG/RD6/Jakob Schäfer, Schäfer's testimony.

128. BHStA/IV, MG/RD6/Johann Dinkelmeier.

129. BHStA/IV, MG/RD6, Untersuchungsakten, No. 285.

130. SP, Schnelldorfer to his parents, 4 November 1915.

131. BHStA/IV, RIR16/Bd.1, RIB12/Bd.1, and RIR17/Bd.1, diaries, November–December 1915; Wiedemann, 'Kriegswinter', 191–6; BHStA/IV, RIR17/RD 6, divisional order, 11 December 1915.

132. EPF, Arneth to Karl Crämer, 13 December 1915. For Arneth's death, see telegram, Robert Hell to Karl Crämer, 13 January 1916.

133. Ryback, *Library*, 3 ff.

134. BHStA/IV, RIR17/Bd.1/diary, 8 December 1915.

135. BHStA/IV, RIR16/Bd.1 and RIR17/Bd.1, diaries, 25 December 1915.

136. BHStA/IV, RIR17/Bd.1/diary, 25 December 1915.

137. Quoted in Wakefield, *Christmas*, 44.

138. Quoted in ibid. 44.

139. BHStA/IV, RIR17/Bd.1/diary, 25 December 1915.

140. BHStA/IV, RIR16/Bd.12, I Batl/diary, 25 December 1915.

141. BHStA/IV, RIB12/Bd.1 diary, 24 December 1915.

142. 1/8th Londons, War Diary, quoted in Wakefield, *Christmas*, 41.

143. SP, Schnelldorfer to his parents, 25 December 1915.

144. BHStA/IV, RIB12/Bd.1/diary, monthly report for December 1915.

145. PBK, II/9/Facs.3m/Stumpf/diary, 24–30 December 1915.

146. See on this theme, Bourke, *Fear*, ch. 7; Bourke, *Intimate History*; Ferguson, *Pity*; Grossman, *Killing*, 111–12, 235–45; Kühne, 'Massen-Töten', 38 ff.; McCarthy, *Soldiers*, 240.

147. Nießl, Prägner, and Stöhr, 'Ehrentafel', 411–13; Doughty, *Victory*, 509.

6. OCCUPATION

1. Rupprecht, *Kriegstagebuch*, i. 415, entry for 15 January 1916.

2. BHStA/IV, RD6/Bd.38, Bierabteilungen.

3. BHStA/IV, MG/RD6/Georg Weiner.

4. IFZ, MA-732, NSDAP/Hauptarchiv, Karl Lippert's recollections, 28 March 1940; BHStA/IV, RD6/Bd.110,1, letter from the Gouvernement Lille, 23 August 1915; BHStA/IV, MG/RD6, Georg Ferchl; BHStA/IV, RIR16/Bd.12, I Batl./diary, 23 June 1916; Baumeister, *Kriegstheater*, 270–5; Lipp, *Meinungslenkung*, 83–4.

5. IFZ, MA-732, NSDAP/Hauptarchiv, note by Karl Lippert, 28 March 1940. A fair number of Hitler's artworks from the war years have survived, see Joachimsthaler, *Hitlers Weg*, 134–8; Englmann, 'Kriegsbild', 80–1. Price, *Hitler*, lists and reproduces many of Hitler's wartime drawings and pictures but

inadvertently also includes many forgeries, see IFZ, ED/147, photocopies of forged documents; see also Jäckel and Kuhn, 'Erkenntnisse'.

6. BHStA/IV, RD6/Bd.147,6, letter dated 20 June 1916; BHStA/IV, MG/RD6/ Georg Rutz, Josef Sieglbauer, Johann Altmann.

7. BHStA/IV, MG/RD6/Franz Geser.

8. Yerta, Marguerite, *Six Women and the Invasion* (London, 1917), 202–3, quoted in Grayzel, *Identities*, 41.

9. See e.g. Brandmayer, *Meldgänger Hitler* (1933), 105; Ziemann, *Heimat*, 245.

10. Mulders, *Sohn*. The claim had been made amongst others by Maser, 'Vater', 173–202, and de Launay, *Hitler*.

11. BHStA/IV, HS/1952, war diary of an unidentified French physician, 20 and 21 November 1914.

12. LAELKB, OKM/2340, Daumiller's report, 20 January 1915.

13. Natter, *Literature*, 162.

14. LAELKB, OKM 2340/Hermann Münderlein's report, 30 January 1916.

15. BHStA/IV, RD6/Bd.147,6, announcements by the Armee-Arzt 6, 12 March 1915, and 11 August 1915.

16. Quoted in ADN, J/1362.2, George Druelle's memoirs.

17. BHStA/IV, RD6/Bd.147,6, Sitzungsbericht, undated, and letter from Generalkommando X.A.K., 12 January 1917.

18. LAELKB, OKM/2340, Daumiller's report, 10 June 1916.

19. LAELKB, OKM/2340, Daumiller's report, 20 January 1915.

20. There is no quantitative evidence to support Audoin-Rouzeau's claim to the contrary; see his *L'Enfant de l'ennemi*.

21. Bourke, *Rape*, 359 ff.; Grossman, *Killing*, 210–11; Kramer, *Destruction*, 246 ff. The prevalence of wartime rape has, of course, varied greatly over time and across cultures.

22. BHStA/IV, MG/RD6, Kasimir Gerhard.

23. Beaumont, 'War', 9.

24. BHStA/IV, RD6/Bd.110,4, letter, 12 September 1916. See also Chickering, *Imperial Germany*, 83.

25. BHStA/IV, RD6/Bd.110,3, Meldung der Ortskommandantur Fournes, 20 November 1915.

26. BHStA/IV, HS/1952, war diary of an unidentified French physician, 3 December 1914.

27. BHStA/IV, RD6/Bd.110,3, list of deliverers of the *Gazettes des Ardennes*, 31 December 1915.

28. ADN, 9R/505, Comines, occupation report; ADN, 9R/1229, investigation against Paul Le Safre.

29. BHStA/IV, RIR17/Bd.2, RD 6, divisional policy announcement, 17 February 1915; BHStA/IV, MG/RD6, Robert Linder; PBK, II/9/Facs.3m/ Stumpf/diary, 9 and 17 February 1915; ADN, J/1362.2, George Druelle's memoirs.

30. ADN, 9R/129, J. Gombert to the Rector of the Académie de Lille, 20 December 1914.
31. BHStA/IV, MG/RD6/Josef Leclerq.
32. ADN, J/1362.2, George Druelle's memoirs; ADN, J/1386.3, Haubourdin, 1914–1918, Souvenirs de l'occupation allemande.
33. This is the argument of Smith, Audoin-Rouzeau, and Becker, *France*, 42–5. See also McPhail, *Silence*; Kramer, *Destruction*, 41 ff.; Geyer, 'Tötungshandeln', 122; Hull, *Destruction*, ch. 10; Audoin-Rouzeau and Becker, *14–18*, ch. 2; Becker, 'Occupied Zone'.
34. See Weber, *Lodz*; see also Föllmer, 'Feind'.
35. Grayzel, *Identities*, 42, 50–66.
36. ADN, 9R/1229, investigation against Paul Le Safre.
37. BHStA/IV, MG/RD6/Sammelakten, Karolina Burie.
38. Gildea, *Marianne*, 1.
39. Cobb, *French*, 1–31.
40. See also de Schaepdrijver, *La Belgique*, 106 ff.
41. BHStA/IV, HS/1952, war diary of an unidentified French physician, 10 February 1915.
42. PBK, II/9/Facs.3m/Stumpf/diary, 7 February 1915.
43. BHStA/IV, RIR17/Bd.2, RD 6, divisional order, 13 February 1915.
44. PBK, II/9/Facs.3m/Stumpf/diary, 14–19 December 1915.
45. Bourke, *Rape*, ch. 13.
46. Horne and Kramer, *Atrocities*, 197.
47. Smith, Audoin-Rouseau, and Becker, *France*, 49.
48. BHStA/IV, MG/RD6/Kasimir Gerhard.
49. ADN, J/1362.2, George Druelle's memoirs.
50. Cobb, *French*, 10.
51. BHStA/IV, RIR17/Bd.2, RD 6, divisional order, 23 February 1915.
52. BHStA/IV, RIR17/Bd.2, RD 6, divisional order, 13 May 1915.
53. BHStA/IV, MG/RD6/Robert Weber.
54. BHStA/IV, RIR17/Bd.2, RD 6, divisional order, 24 June 1915.
55. PBK, II/9/Facs.3m/Stumpf/diary, 13 January 1915.
56. BHStA/IV, RIB12/Bd.17,8, 'Urteile über das Verhalten der Deutschen'.
57. BHStA/IV, MG/RD6/Sammelakten, investigative files of the Ortskommandantur Haubordin, February 1916.
58. SP, Schnelldorfer to his parents, 5 April 1916.
59. Ziemann, *Heimat*, 125.
60. Deist, *Militär*, i.300, Erlaß des bayerischen Kriegsministeriums, 1 February 1916.
61. BHStA/IV, MG/RD6/Friedrich Strasser.
62. BHStA/IV, RIR17/Bd.1/diary, 30 April 1916.
63. BHStA/IV, MG/RD6/Ludwig Carus.
64. BHStA/IV, MG/RD6/Dominikus Dauner.

65. Pedersen, *Fromelles*, 29.

66. Ferguson, *War of the World*, 120–1; Ziemann, *Heimat*, 76 ff.

67. Bourke, *Intimate History*, 1.

68. See BHStA/IV, RD6/Bd.110,1, letter from the War Ministry, Berlin, 22 March 1916; letter from the War Ministry, Berlin, 25 November 1916.

69. BHStA/IV, RD6/Bd.110,1, letter dated mid-March 1916.

70. Natter, *Literature*, 154–7.

71. AEM, Ordinariat, DK Buchberger (ungeordent), Norbert Stumpf to the archdiocese of Munich and Freising, Seelsorgebericht and diary, 1 July–31 December 1916.

72. See LAELKB, OKM/2340/Oscar Daumiller's report, 30 November 1914; see also Ziemann, *Heimat*, 250–65.

73. Ziemann, *Heimat*, 250 ff.; LAELKB, OKM/2340, Körnacher's report, 25 January 1916; and OKM 2340, Münderlein's report, 30 January 1916.

74. LAELKB, OKM, 2340, Daumiller's report for 1916.

75. LAELKB, OKM, 2340, Körnacher's report, 25 January 1917. Similar arguments were made by Wilhelm Stählin and Oscar Daumiller; see LAELKB, OKM/2340, Stählin's report for 1914 and 1915, and OKM/2340, Daumiller's report, 30 June 1917.

76. Wiedemann, *Feldherr*, 27.

77. NARA, M1270-Roll1, interrogation file on Amann.

78. SP, Schnelldorfer to his parents, 3 April 1916.

79. SP, Schnelldorfer to his parents, 29 April 1916.

80. SP, Schnelldorfer to his parents, 30 April 1916.

81. Frey, Alexander Moritz, 'Der unbekannte Gefreite – persönliche Erinnerungen an Hitler' (1946), quoted in Ernsting, *Frey*, 49.

82. Cron, *Geschichte*, 116.

83. Kershaw, *Hitler*, i. 93.

84. Bullock, *Hitler*, 51; Machtan, *Hitler*, 90.

85. See the two postcards Hitler sent Mayer in 1916, Jäckel and Kuhn, *Hitler*, 75, 77.

86. Quoted in Machtan, *Hitler*, 68.

87. SAM, StanW/9959, Auszug aus dem Strafregister, Hans Mend.

88. Mend, *Hitler*.

89. BHStA/IV, HS/3231, Mend Protokoll.

90. Quoted in Machtan, *Hitler*, 68.

91. Mend, *Hitler*, 19.

92. Ibid. 24, 27.

93. All six photos are reproduced in Brandmayer, *Meldgänger Hitler* (1933) and Mend, *Hitler*.

94. NARA, RG242, T-581-3, investigation by the NSDAP party archive, 1938–9; IFZ, MA-732, NSDAP/Hauptarchiv, note by Karl Lippert, 28 March 1940; Englmann, 'Kriegsbild', 80–1.

95. SP. Unpublished account of Schnelldorfer's life by his wife.
96. IFZ, MA-732, NSDAP/Hauptarchiv, report by Heinrich Lugauer to the NSDAP Hauptarchiv, 5 February 1940.
97. IFZ, MA-732, NSDAP/Hauptarchiv, note by Karl Lippert, 28 March 1940.
98. IFZ, MA-732, NSDAP/Hauptarchiv, recollection of Hans Bauer, 15 May 1940.
99. Böhm, 'Tegethoff', 317, which refers to the recollections of Ernst Tegethoff, an NCO and interpreter for regimental HQ.
100. Private papers of Jakob Weiß, newspaper cutting from the *Freisinnenger Tagblatt*, 26 March 1933, 'Reichkanzler Adolf Hittler'.
101. Quoted in Heinz, *Hitler*, 67, 85.
102. Mend's accounts have been used extensively by some of the greatest Hitler biographies, see e.g. Bullock, *Hitler*, 53. However, as we have seen, Mend's accounts are so unreliable as to render them useless.
103. SP, Schnelldorfer to his parents, 20 April 1916.
104. NARA, RG226, M-1642-Roll109, 'Report on four close associates of Hitler', 1943.
105. Alexander Moritz Frey, 'Der unbekannte Gefreite—persönliche Erinnerungen an Hitler' (1946), quoted in Ernsting, *Frey*, 49.
106. Meyer, *Hitler*; Wiedemann, *Feldherr*, 23–50, quotes at 25, 27, 28.
107. NARA-RG238-M1019-2, interrogation, 5 November 1947. He gave a similar characterization during an interrogation in 1951, see StanW/I, 28791/31/ Amann.
108. BHStA/IV, KSR/3039, No. 166 and KSR/3046, No. 1062; IFZ, F/19/6/2, military ID, Adolf Hitler, 1 March 1917.
109. Ryback, *Library*, 3–27; Kershaw, *Hitler*, i. 191; Wiedemann, *Feldherr*, 29.
110. NARA-RG238-M1019-2, interrogation, 5 November 1947.
111. NARA-RG238-M1019-2, interrogation, 5 November 1947.
112. NARA, M1270-Roll1, interrogation file on Amann.
113. *Die Volksgemeinschaft*, 7 March 1932, 2, 'Marxistische Lügen' (quote); BHStA/IV, officer files, Bruno Horn.
114. Kershaw, *Hitler*, i. 87.
115. NARA-RG238-M1019-2, interrogation, 5 November 1947. Wiedemann's account is less dramatic but makes much the same point, namely that Hitler did not want to be promoted, see Wiedemann, *Feldherr*, 26.
116. Stone, *Hitler*, 7.
117. Bullock, *Hitler*, 52; Fest, *Hitler*, 104.
118. Information provided by Ernst Richter, who was one of Wilhelm Diess's Ph.D. students.
119. Wiedemann, *Feldherr*, 26.
120. Hitler, *MK*, 101.
121. Ibid. 103 ff.
122. Ibid. 105.

123. Quoted in Wiedemann, *Feldherr*, 24.
124. Machtan, *Hitler*, 93
125. NARA-RG238-M1019-2, interrogation, 5 November 1947.
126. See e.g. Mend, *Hitler*, 59–60, 100, 139.
127. Alexander Moritz Frey, 'Der unbekannte Gefreite—persönliche Erinnerungen an Hitler' (1946), quoted in Ernsting, *Frey*, 50–1.

7. COLLAPSE

1. BHStA/IV, RIB12/Bd.1/diary, 4 June 1916; Wiedemann, 'Gesundheitszustand', 202.
2. Wiedemann, 'Kriegswinter', 196–7.
3. BHStA/IV, RIB12/Bd.2,4, Gefechtsbericht, dated 22 July 1916; Wiedemann, 'Gefecht', 214–27; Pedersen, *Fromelles*, 33; Cobb, *Fromelles*.
4. Wiedemann, 'Gefecht', 214–27.
5. BHStA/IV, RIB12/Bd.2, 4, A.O.K.6, 'Der Angriff', B.No.6179, and Gefechtsbericht, dated 22 July 1916; Wiedemann, 'Gefecht', 214–27; Cobb, *Fromelles*; LMU, Stud.-Kart., Georg Dehn; Meyer, *Hitler*, 39.
6. Quoted Meyer, *Hitler*, 103.
7. BHStA/IV, RIB12/Bd.2,4, A.O.K.6, 'Der Angriff'; Wiedemann, 'Gefecht', 214–27; Cobb, *Fromelles*; Stöhr, 'Verluste', 383.
8. Wiedemann, 'Gefecht', 214–27; Cobb, *Fromelles*, 109; Lindsay, *Fromelles*, 5, 142.
9. Cobb, *Fromelles*, 101, 122.
10. Pedersen, *Fromelles*, 104.
11. BHStA/IV, RIR16/Bd.12, I. Batl./diary, Gefechtsbericht für 19/20 July 1916.
12. SP, Schnelldorfer to his parents, 14 July 1916.
13. Cobb, *Fromelles*, 101, 122.
14. Pedersen, *Fromelles*, 104.
15. Ibid. 119.
16. Wiedemann, 'Gefecht', 226; BHStA/IV, RIB12/Bd.17,5, RIR16, 'Erfahrungen', dated 2 August 1916; BHStA/IV, RIB12/Bd.1/diary, 2 August 1916; Cobb, *Fromelles*, 122–3.
17. Wiedemann, 'Atempause', 231–6.
18. BHStA/IV, RIR17/Bd.1/diary, 28 August 1916.
19. BHStA/IV, MG/RD6/Josef Bauer and Max Herz.
20. SP, Schnelldorfer to his parents, 5 April 1916.
21. BHStA/IV, MG/RD6/Heinrich Munzer and Xaver Christl.
22. BHStA/IV, MG/RD6/Alois Baumgartner.
23. SP, Schnelldorfer to his parents, 19 September 1916.
24. Wiedemann, 'Sommeschlacht', 237; Duffy, *German Eyes*, 208–48; Cowley, 'Somme', 344, 355; Gilbert, *Somme*, pp. xvii, xix, 111, 181 ff., 197, 202; Winter and Baggett, *Great War*, 188.
25. Quoted in Schramm, *Deutschlandbild*, 454.

26. Wiedemann, 'Sommeschlacht', 237.

27. BHStA/IV, RIB12/Bd.25,1, RD 6, order, 26 August 1916.

28. BHStA/IV, MG/RD6/Jakob Reindl and Ludwig Reininger.

29. BHStA/IV, MG/RD6/Johann Altmann, Wolfgang Berghammer, Kaspar Bretzger, Xaver Christl Andreas Eglseer, Edwin Friesecke, Karl Gutermann, Anton Haimbacher, Michael Kellner, Karl Lederstetter, Heinrich Munzer, Josef Moosburger, Karl Pfeiffer, Jakob Reindl, Ludwig Reininger, Ludwig Schuster, Johann Wandinger, Simon Weiss, and Johann Weissmantel.

30. BHStA/IV, MG/RD6/Anton Haimbacher.

31. Weber, *Peasants*.

32. Quoted in Ziemann, *Heimat*, 136 n. 458.

33. Ibid. 286–7. There is scant evidence for Ziemann's claim that the second half of the war witnessed a widespread rejection of the Bavarian monarchy.

34. BHStA/IV, RIR16/Bd.12, I Batl./diary, September 1916.

35. See Bourke, *Fear*, ch. 7.

36. Rupprecht, *Kriegstagebuch*, i. 10, entry for 4 September 1916.

37. BHStA/IV, RIB12/Bd.1/diary, 25–8 September 1916; Wiedemann, 'Sommeschlacht', 238.

38. Alexander Moritz Frey, 'Der unbekannte Gefreite' (1946), quoted in Ernsting, *Frey*, 52; Wiedemann, 'Sommeschlacht', 238.

39. BHStA/IV, RIB12/Bd.1/diary, 28 September 1916, and Bd.17,5, letter by the commander of the Pioneer units of RD 6, 12 August 1916; Wiedemann, 'Sommeschlacht', 238–9; Blersch, 'Großkampftage', 256.

40. Wiedemann, 'Sommeschlacht', 238–9.

41. Ibid. 239–43; Blersch, 'Großkampftage', 256–8; BHStA/IV, RIB12/Bd.1/diary, 3 October 1916.

42. IFZ, F 19/6/2 Hitler's military ID; BHStA/IV, RIR16/Bd.12, I. Batl., Verlustliste, Oktober 1916; IFZ, MA-732, NSDAP/Hauptarchiv, Hans Bauer's recollection, 15 May 1940; Machtan, *Hitler*, 90.

43. Gruchmann/Weber, *Hitler-Prozess*, i. 19; Wiedemann, *Feldherr*, 28–9; Meyer, *Hitler*, 57; NARA, RG242/T-581/1A, documents pertaining to Hitler's injury.

44. See e.g. Winter and Baggett, *Great War*, 189.

45. *Bild*, 19 November 2008, 'Wie Hitler seinen Hoden verlor', www.bild.de/Bild/news/vermischtes/2008/11/19/adolf-hitler-hoden/sanitaeter-bestaetigung-aussage.html, accessed 19 November 2008; *The Sun*, 19 November 2008, 'Hitler only had one ball'.

46. See also Andrew Roberts, 'Did Hitler really only have ONE testicle?', *Daily Mail Online*, www.dailymail.co.uk/news/worldnews/article-1087380/Did-Hitler-really-ONE-testicle-A-historian-sorts-extraordinary-truth-far-flung-myths-Fuhrer.html, accessed 20 November 2008.

47. Quoted in Wiedemann, *Feldherr*, 29.

48. IFZ, MA-732, NSDAP/Hauptarchiv, Verlustliste Nr. 320, 2 December 1916. Wiedemann, *Feldherr*, 29.

49. Hitler, *MK*, 113; BHStA/IV, RIR16/Bd.12, I. Batl., Verlustliste, Oktober 1916.

50. Quoted in Heinz, *Hitler*, 81–2.

51. Brandmayer, *Meldegänger Hitler* (1933), 81–9.

52. IFZ, F/19/6/2 Hitler's military ID; BHStA/IV, RIR16/Bd.12, I. Batl., Verlustliste, Oktober 1916. According to both his military ID and the casualty list of his battalion, he was wounded on 5 October 1916 and not on 7 October as Hitler had stated in *Mein Kampf*, 113.

53. Prior and Wilson, *Somme*, 266 ff.; Sheffield, *Somme*, 136–7; Gilbert, *Somme*, 206–7; Wiedemann, 'Sommeschlacht', 245–52; Nießl, Prägner, and Stöhr, 'Ehrentafel', 451–9; Hitler, *MK*, 113; BHStA/IV, MG/RD6, Friesecke, Edwin; Reichsbund Jüdischer Frontsoldaten, *Gefallenen*, 114.

54. BHStA/IV, RIR16/Bd.12, 3rd Company, 'Erfahrungen an der Somme'.

55. Hirschfeld, 'Somme-Schlacht', 85.

56. Quoted in Kramer, *Destruction*, 215.

57. Roach, *Stiff*, 149.

58. BHStA/IV, RIR16/Bd.12, I Batl., 'Gefechtsbericht über die Sommeschlacht'.

59. Wiedemann, *Feldherr*, 30–1.

60. LAELKB, OKM/2340, Daumiller's report for 1916, 1917.

61. LAELKB, OKM/2340, sermon manuscript, 27 November 1916.

62. BHStA/IV, RIR20/Bd.1, Erfahrungsbericht der Sommeschlacht.

63. BHStA/IV, RIR16/Bd.12, I Batl./diary, October 1916.

64. Nießl, Prägner, and Stöhr, 'Ehrentafel', 451–9; BHStA/IV, RIR16/Bd.1/diary, '1.7.1916 bis 21.12.1916', page 37, Verlustliste; BHStA/IV, KSR/3038, No. 89.

8. IN THE SHADOW OF THE SOMME

1. Hitler, *MK*, 113–14.

2. Jäckel and Kuhn, *Hitler*, 77, Hitler to Franz Mayer, 4 November 1916.

3. Hitler, *MK*, 113.

4. BHStA/IV, MG/RD6/Friedrich Hofbauer.

5. BHStA/IV, RIB12/Bd.17,2, Verteidigungsplan, February 1917; Wiedemann, 'Vimyhöhen', 261–6; Meyer, *Hitler*, 46 ff.; Breton, *Vimy*, 74–5.

6. Wiedemann, 'Vimyhöhen', 261–6; BHStA/IV, RIR16/Bd.1/diary, October–December 1916.

7. BHStA/IV, MG/RD6/Friedrich Hofbauer.

8. BHStA/IV, MG/RD6/Josef Leicher.

9. BHStA/IV, MG/RD6/Alois Müller.

10. BHStA/IV, MG/RD6/Max Bentenrieder, Bentenrieder's brother to Bentenrieder, 9 February 1917.

11. BHStA/IV, MG/RD6/Johann Wandinger.

12. SP, Schnelldorfer to his parents, 12 and 14 November 1916.

13. Wiedemann, 'Vimyhöhen', 261–6; BHStA/IV, RIR16/Bd.1, RIR17/Bd.1, and RIB12/Bd.1, diaries, October–December 1916.

14. Wiedemann, 'Vimyhöhen', 265; Berton, *Vimy*, 85; Zuehlke, *Battalion*, 144–55; Meyer, *Hitler*, 48; BHStA/IV, RIB12/Bd.1 and RIR17/Bd.1, diaries, October–December 1916; BHStA/IV, RIB12/Bd.17,2, 'Verteidigungsplan', February 1917.

15. BHStA/IV, MG/RD6/Karl Hackspacher, letter to his parents, 2 January 1917.

16. BHStA/IV, MG/RD6/Josef Daxberger.

17. BHStA/IV, MG/RD6/Josef Ackermann and Jakob Lindauer.

18. BHStA/IV, MG/RD6/Untersuchungsakten.

19. Watson, *Enduring*, ch. 4.

20. See e.g. Strachan, 'Morale', 387.

21. See Costa and Kahn, 'Deserters', 323.

22. BHStA/IV, RIR 16/Bd.12/I Batl./diary, 26 December 1914.

23. Jahr, *Soldaten*, 81, 290–300.

24. See Ziemann, *Heimat*, 106–20.

25. Duménil, 'Suffering', 50; Jahr, *Soldaten*, 30.

26. Meyer, *Hitler*, 13.

27. Watson, *Enduring*, 87–8.

28. BHStA/IV, MG/RD6 Jakob Schäfer, Schäfer's testimony.

29. Jahr, *Soldaten*, 131, 134–5.

30. Hitler, *MK*, 114.

31. Davis, *Home Fires*; Kramer, *Destruction*, 154; Bessel, *Germany*, 39; Neitzel, *Weltkrieg*, 136. There has been considerable debate about how many Germans really died of malnutrition. Avner Offer, see e.g. his 'Blockade', has expressed doubts about the figures normally quoted as well as about the reasons behind the wartime excess mortality. The supposedly inferior organization of the war economy has also been blamed for Germany's worsening situation; see Winter and Robert, *Cities*. However, in terms of how Germany translated her limited resources into success on the battlefield, the Germans used their resources, in fact, more effectively than the Allies to fight the war; see Ferguson, *Pity*.

32. Kennedy, *Rise and Fall*; Wasserstein, *Barbarism*, 68.

33. Jäckel and Kuhn, *Hitler*, postcard, Hitler to Brandmayer, 21 December 1916.

34. Machtan, *Hitler*, 90.

35. Berton, *Vimy*, 79.

36. Ibid. 78, 80.

37. Nießl, Prägner, and Stöhr, 'Ehrentafel', 387–502. Excluding the months in which the battles of Neuve Chapelle, Aubers Ridge, Loos, Fromelles, and the Somme took place, on average 30.6 members from RIR 16 were killed a day in 1916, while the figure for 1915 is 31.1. In December 1918, 18 men were killed.

38. LAELKB, OKM/2340/Daumiller's report for 1916.

39. BHStA/IV, RIR17/Bd.1 and RIB12/Bd.1, diaries, 24–5 December 1916; Berton, *Vimy*, 80–1.

40. Geyer, *Verkehrte Welt*; BHStA/IV, RIB12/Bd.25,1, letter from the Stellvetretende Generalkommando I.b.AK, 25 February 1916; Bauer, Gerstenberg, and Peschel, *Dunst*, 140–3.

41. Hitler, *MK*, 114.

42. Jaeckel and Kuhn, *Hitler*, 78–9, postcard, Hitler to Brandmayer, 21 December 1916.

43. BHStA/IV, MG/RD6/Heinrich Bachfisch, Josef Eder, Josef Hössl, Josef Hofbauer, Wolfgang Hoffmann, Ignaz Prieller, Georg Rassbichler, Anton Schäfler, Georg Weiss, and Heinrich Zettmeisl.

44. BHStA/IV, MG/RD6/Martin Bader, Johann Berchtold, Josef Leicher, Mathias Oexler, Leonhard Steinbeiss, Max Bentenrieder, Johann Lengmüller, and Josef Nagl.

45. Hitler, *MK*, 114.

46. Ibid. 114.

47. Ibid. 114–15.

48. Bullock, *Hitler*, 52. Fest, *Hitler*, 107, expresses a similar idea but Reuth, *Judenhass*, recently challenged the idea that Hitler's anti-Semitism had already been fully developed during the First World War.

49. Kershaw, *Hitler*, i. 636–7, n. 150.

50. Kershaw, *Hitler*, i. 95.

51. Davis, *Home Fires*, 132 ff.; Hoffmann, 'Integration', 97–8; Messerschmidt, *Soldaten*, 106–7; Bergmann and Wetzel, 'Antisemitismus', 437–48.

52. BHStA/IV, RIB12/Bd.25, 1, letter from the Prussian Ministry of War, 11 October 1916. Messerschmidt, *Soldaten*, 107–8; Rosenthal, *Ehre*, 12; Bergmann and Wetzel, 'Antisemitismus', 441–4.

53. BHStA/IV, RD6/Bd.125,8, 'Nachweisung', 15 November 1916; BHStA/IV, KSR/3038-92.

54. BHStA/IV, KSR/3038-92.

55. Vogel, *Stück*, 141–8.

56. Gregory, *War*, 240.

57. The claim by Kershaw, *Hitler*, i. 95, that the streets of Munich were rife with anti-Semitic agitation is largely based on Ay, *Entstehung*. There is, however, only one single reference to anti-Semitism in Ay's book, see *Entstehung*, 32, and the reference concerns the summer of 1918, and not the year of the Jewish census. There is also no evidence for assertions, such as the one by Hoffmann, 'Integration', 95 ff., that most members of the German elite were gravitating more and more towards *völkisch* anti-Semitism during the war.

58. Ziemann, *Heimat*, 335.

59. Quoted in Hoffmann, 'Integration', 97.

60. Davis, *Home Fires*, 133.

61. EPF, Mrs Eberlein to Karl Crämer, 29 October 1916.

62. Hank and Simon, *Feldpostbriefe*, 21. For the letter recording anti-Semitism, see vol. i. 164.
63. See e.g. BMF, PH/3/534, Armeeoberkommando 2, decree, 14 August 1915; BMF, PH/7/27, Stellvertretendes Generalkommando des Gardekorps to the jüdische Gemeinde of Berlin, 19 March 1915; BHStA/IV, RIB12/Bd.25,1, letters by the Kriegsministerium, 20 March and 21 June 1916.
64. Kramer, *Destruction*, 49.
65. Wasserstein, *Barbarism*, 75.
66. Freund, *Aufsätze*, 1, 13, 16.
67. BHStA/IV, KSR/3038-92.
68. BHStA/IV, KSR/3038/No. 89; BHStA/IV, Offiziersakte/Hugo Gutmann; RD6/Bd.112,1, Vorschläge und Verleihungen.
69. SAM, StanW/8544, Siegfried Heumann.
70. Mend, *Hitler*, 17, 60–2, 115; Brandmayer, *Meldgänger Hitler* (1933), 55, 115; Kershaw, *Hitler*, i. 95. Significantly, Westenkirchner would claim after 1945 that his 1930s account of Hitler's First World War anti-Semitism was a fabrication, see ibid. 94 n. 133, even though that account, of course, also needs to be treated with a grain of salt.
71. Quoted in Heinz, *Hitler*, 74.
72. Brandmayer, *Meldegänger Hitler* (1933), 55, 115.
73. Wiedemann, *Feldherr*, 33–4.
74. BHStA/IV, RIB12/Bd.17,2, 'Verteidigungsplan', February 1917; BHStA/IV, RIR17/Bd.1/diary, January–February 1917; BHStA/IV, RIR16/Bd.2/diary, January–February 1917; Wiedemann, 'Vimyhöhen', 265–6.
75. BHStA/IV, RIB12/Bd.17,2, 'Verteidigungsplan', February 1917.
76. BHStA/IV, RIR16/Bd.8,40, III Batl., report for the period of 28 April to 17 May 1917.
77. Kitchen, *Silent Dictatorship*. Kitchen's assertion that Hindenburg and Ludendorff's rule amounted to a 'silent dictatorship' grossly overstates its case.
78. De Schaepdrijver, *La Belgique*, ch. 7; Foley, *Strategy*.
79. Erhard, *Städten*, 49–81; Hull, *Destruction*, 256 ff.; Geyer, 'Rückzug', 172–8; Holmes, *Front*, 145–6.
80. BHStA/IV, RIB12/Bd.17,2/RD6, Zerstörungsplan, 9 January 1917.
81. Geyer, 'Rückzug', 171, 173; Geyer, 'Tötungshandeln'.
82. Kramer, *Destruction*, 151.
83. Hull, *Destruction*, part III, quotes at 206, 207.
84. Kramer, *Destruction*, ch. 4.
85. Whether the Shoah is the end point of the inherent logic of total war in an industrial age is dependent on whether the perpetrators of the Holocaust saw the killing of Jews primarily as a means of winning the Second World War or as a competing goal to militarily defeating the enemy. In the latter case, the Holocaust would not follow from the inherent logic to employ any means necessary to win a total war.

86. Wiedemann, 'Somain', 266–8.
87. Jaeckel and Kuhn, *Hitler*, 80, Hitler to Wiedemann, undated.
88. BHStA/IV, RIB12/Bd.1/diary, March–April 1917; BHStA/IV, RIR17/ Bd.1/diary, 23 March 1917; Wiedemann, 'Somain', 268–73.
89. Keegan, *First World War*, 200.
90. Tubeuf, 'Tubeuf', 275–80; Wiedemann, 'Somain', 273; BHStA/IV, RIB12/ Bd.1/diary, April–May 1917.
91. EPF, Pfaffmann to Karl Crämer, 19 May 1917.
92. Stöhr, 'Verluste', 381 ff.
93. Tubeuf, 'Tubeuf', 280; Wiedemann, *Feldherr*, 31.
94. BHStA/IV, RD6/Bd.45,2,5a, report, 17 May 1917.
95. Quoted in Maser, *Legende*, 145.
96. See Freeman and Nielsen, *Home*, 113. See also Christie, *King*.
97. Wilson, *Faces*, 455–6; Evans, *Battles*, i. 34–5.
98. Jahr, *Soldaten*, 150–1; Ziemann, *Heimat*, 209, 214.
99. BHStA/IV, RIB12/Bd.17,6, I Batl., Kampferfahrungen, 21 May 1917.
100. BHStA/IV, MG/RD6/Georg Dankert.
101. BHStA/IV, MG/RD6/Alexus Blank.
102. BHStA/IV, MG/RD6/Ludwig Hartl.
103. Kühne, *Kameradschaft*; Ziemann, *Heimat*, 230.
104. Ziemann, *Heimat*, 61, 230 ff.
105. Rupprecht, *Kriegstagebuch*, i. 461, entry for 7 May 1916.
106. Quoted Ibid. 235.
107. LBI, AR/25349/359197/diary, entries for 25 and 26 October 1917 and 11 April 1918.
108. See e.g. McCarthy, *Soldiers*, 130–2.
109. Ziemann, *Heimat*, 232–4.
110. Quoted Ibid. 234.
111. BHStA/IV, MG/RD6/Josef Münsterer.
112. Ziemann, *Heimat*, 235–6; Smith, Audoin-Rouzeau, and Becker, *France*, 98.
113. Tubeuf, 'Tubeuf', 280–1; BHStA/IV, RIB12/Bd.1/diary, 19–31 May 1917; LAELKB, OKM/2340, Daumiller's report, 30 June 1917 (quote).
114. US General Staff, *Divisions*, 140.
115. Tubeuf, 'Tubeuf', 280–1.
116. BHStA/IV, MG/RD6/Anton Haimbacher.
117. Showalter, 'Approaches', 39.
118. BHStA/IV, RIB12/Bd.1/diary, June 1917; Tubeuf, 'Tubeuf', 281–2.
119. See e.g. BHStA/IV, MG/RD6/Friedrich Frankl and Hermann Schnell.
120. BHStA/IV, RD6/Bd.44,24a, letter from AOK 4, 14 June 1917.
121. LAELKB, OKM/2340, Daumiller's report, 30 June 1917.
122. BHStA/IV, MG/RD6/Josef Asanger.
123. Tubeuf, 'Tubeuf', 280.
124. BHStA/IV, RD6/Bd.44,5a, RIR 16 to RIB 12, 10 July 1917.

125. BHStA/IV, RIR16/Bd.13, I Batl./diary, June 1917; Tubeuf, 'Tubeuf', 281–2.
126. EPF, Pfaffmann to Karl Crämer, 29 June 1917.
127. BHStA/IV, RIB12/Bd.1/diary, June–July 1917; BHStA/IV, RIR16/Bd.17, III Batl., Sportsfest, 26 June 1918; Tubeuf, 'Tubeuf', 282–3.
128. BHStA/IV, RD6/Bd.44, Anordnung, 26 June 1917.
129. BHStA/IV, RD6/Bd.44, divisional orders, 27 and 30 June 1917.
130. Kramer, Destruction, 68.
131. BHStA/IV, RIB12/Bd.25,1, letter from the Generalquartiermeister, Gr.H.Qu., 14 March 1918.
132. See Watson, 'Culture'; Watson, Enduring; Weber, Friend.
133. Kitchen, Offensives, 10.
134. LAELKB, Personen/XVIII/43a/Stählin/diary, Wilhelm Stählin, 9 September 1917.
135. LAELKB, Personen/XVIII/43a/Stählin/diary, Wilhelm Stählin, 3 July 1917.
136. Chickering, Imperial Germany, 161.
137. www.lib.byu.edu/~rdh/wwi/1917/reichpeace.html, accessed, 15 July 2005.
138. Ziemann, Heimat, 282 ff.
139. http://wahlen-in-deutschland.de/kuBayern.htm; http://wahlen-in-deutschland.de/kuRbbOberbayern.htm; http://wahlen-in-deutschland.de/kuRbbOberpfalz.htm, all accessed 9 June 2009.
140. Geyer, 'Rückzug', 173.
141. Rupprecht, Kriegstagebuch, ii. 98, 13 February 1917.
142. Ibid., i. 332, 3 May 1915.
143. Quoted in Geyer, 'Rückzug', 174.
144. Deist, Militär, ii. 662 n. 2.
145. Tapken, Reichswehr, 55.
146. Meyer, Hitler, 71.
147. Tubeuf, 'Tubeuf', 283–4; Meyer, Hitler, 72; BHStA/IV, RIR16/Bd.2 and RIB12/Bd.1, diaries, 13–22 July 1917; Sheldon, Passchendaele, pp. xi–xii, chs. 1–2; Prior and Wilson, Passchendaele, 86; Wilson, Faces, 449; Palazzo, Victory, 119.
148. BHStA/IV, RIR16/Bd.8,35, report, 24 July 1917.
149. BHStA/IV, RIR16/Bd.8,35, report, 24 July 1917.
150. BHStA/IV, MG/RD6/Anton Markl.
151. Tubeuf, 'Tubeuf', 283–4; Sinz, Ichenhausen, photo page between pages 18 and 19.
152. BHStA/IV, RIB12/Bd.1/diary, 23–30 July 1917; Tubeuf, 'Tubeuf', 284–7; Beumelburg, Flandern, 29; Meyer, Hitler, 72.
153. Meyer, Hitler, 74.
154. BHStA/IV, RIR16/Bd.9, RD 6, battle report, 31 July and 1 August 1917; Tubeuf, 'Tubeuf', 284–7; Prior and Wilson, Passchendaele, 195.
155. Quoted in Kershaw, Hitler, i. 93.

9. BLINDED

1. EPF, Pfaffmann to Karl Crämer, 7 August 1917.
2. BHStA/IV, RD6/Bd.45,2,5a, report by the Generalkommando X. Armee-korps, 31 August 1917, reports by RD 6, RIB 12, and RIR 16, September–October 1917; BHStA/IV, RIR16/Bd.16, II Batl., minutes of regimental meeting, 10 August 1917; BHStA/IV, RIB12/diary, August–October 1917; Meyer, *Hitler*, 75–6; Tubeuf, 'Tubeuf', 287–8. Only seven cases of insubordination from the almost two and a half months RIR 16 spent in Alsace made it to the divisional court of RD 6, see BHStA/IV, MG/RD6.
3. BHStA, KSR/3067/No. 1082.
4. Weber, *Friend*; Weber, 'Studenten'.
5. LBI, AR/25349/359197, file on Ernst and Martin Fleischmann.
6. LBI, AR/25349/359197/diary, 4 August–12 October 1917.
7. LBI, AR/25349/359197/diary, entries for 17 and 25–6 September 1917.
8. Hitler, *MK* 115 ff.
9. BHStA/IV, RD6/Bd.45,2,5a, RIR 16, report, 3 September 1917.
10. BHStA/IV, RD6/Bd.45,2,5a, RD 6 and RIR 16, reports, August–September 1917.
11. LBI, AR/25349/359197/diary, entries for 16 August and 8 October 1917.
12. BHStA/IV, RD6/Bd.21,1,1, note, 31 August 1917; Bd.45,2,5a, RIB12, report, 19 September 1917.
13. BHStA/IV, RIB12/Bd.25,1, letter by RIR 20, 2 October 1917.
14. BHStA/IV, KSR/3046/No. 1062. Kershaw, *Hitler*, i. 95, 101; Joachimsthaler, *Hitlers Weg*, 169; Machtan, *Hitler*, 92. Hitler did not visit his family, as claimed by Fest, *Hitler*, 105, and Maser, *Legende*, 144.
15. Kitchen, *Offensives*, 10–11.
16. Chickering, *Freiburg*, 278–89, 519–31; Chickering, *Imperial Germany*, ch. 5.
17. Maser, *Letters*, 96, postcard, Hitler to Schmidt, 6 October 1917.
18. Jaeckel and Kuhn, *Hitler*, 82, postcards, Hitler to Max Amann, 8 October, 11 October, and 12 October 1917.
19. The claim made by Nazi propaganda has generally been uncritically accepted; see e.g. Fest, *Hitler*, 96.
20. Quoted in Large, *München*, 75.
21. BHStA/IV, RD6/Bd.45,2,5a, reports by RD 6, 10 October and 17 October 1917; report by RIR 16, 9 October 1917.
22. LBI, AR/25349/359197/diary, entries for 12, 13, and 15 October 1917.
23. BHStA/IV, RD6/Bd.45,2,5a, RIR16, report, 23 October 1917; RD6, reports, 24 and 31 October 1917; Tubeuf, 'Tubeuf', 288, 292.
24. LBI, AR/25349/359197/diary, entry for 25 October 1917.
25. LBI, AR/25349/359197/diary, entry for 2 December 1917.
26. LBI, AR/25349/359197/diary, entry for 25 October–3 November 1917.
27. Tubeuf, 'Tubeuf', 292–3; Meyer, *Hitler*, 77; BHStA/IV, RIB12/Bd.1 and RIR16/Bd.2, diaries, October 1917–March 1918; Wiedemann, *Feldherr*, 31–2.

28. LBI, AR/25349/359197/diary, entries for 5–9 December 1917; BHStA, KSR/ 3067/No. 1082.

29. Meyer, *Hitler*, 80.

30. Hitler, *MK*, 115.

31. BHStA/IV, RD6/Bd.50,5, report, 31 October 1917.

32. Tubeuf, 'Tubeuf', 294; BHStA/IV, RIR16/Bd.2/diary, October 1917–February 1918.

33. BHStA/IV, RD6/Bd.50,5, weekly reports, November 1917–January 1918; weekly reports of the Front-Division Lanisberg, January–March 1918; Stöhr, 'Verluste', 381 ff.

34. Hitler, *MK*, 115.

35. BHStA/IV, MG/RD6; see e.g. Sebastian Rieder, Johann Geiger, and Josef Ruhland.

36. Lipp, *Meinungslenkung* 177.

37. Deist, *Militär*, ii. 1145, War Ministry, memorandum draft, 30 January 1918.

38. BHStA/IV, HS928, Speidel's recollections of the revolution.

39. BHStA/IV, RD6/Bd.45, RIR 16, weekly report, 30 October 1917; RD6, Bd.50,5, weekly reports of RD 6 and of the Front-Division Lanisberg, November 1917–March 1918; RD6, Bd.50,7, RIR 16, report, 9 March 1918.

40. Kitchen, *Offensives*, 22–43.

41. Keegan, *First World War*, 404 ff., 421–39; Gudmundsson, *Stormtroop Tactics*; Kitchen, *Offensives*, 16; Kramer, *Destruction*, 270 ff.

42. Tubeuf, 'Tubeuf', 295–9.

43. EPF, Pfaffmann to Karl Crämer, 9 April 1918.

44. BHStA/IV, HS928, Max von Speidel's recollections.

45. BHStA/IV, MG/RD6/[Russo] Leitenstorfer.

46. SAM, Sprachkammerakten, Streicher, August.

47. BHStA/IV, RIR16/Bd.2 and RIB12/Bd.1, diaries, March–May 1918; Tubeuf, 'Tubeuf', 295–9; Meyer, *Hitler*, 84.

48. LBI, AR/25349/359197/diary, entry for 16 April.

49. BHStA/IV, RIR16/Bd.2 and RIB12/Bd.1, diaries, March–May 1918; Tubeuf, 'Tubeuf', 295–9; Meyer, *Hitler*, 84; Kitchen, *Offensives*, 122; LBI, AR/25349/ 359197/diary, entry for 18 April.

50. Tubeuf, 'Tubeuf', 299–308; LBI, AR/25349/359197/diary, entries for late May 1918.

51. Quoted in Maser, *Legende*, 146. Hitler, living in a delusional world, did not see this as a problem.

52. Tubeuf, 'Tubeuf', 299–308; Kitchen, *Offensives*, 204.

53. EPF, Pfaffmann to Karl Crämer, 11 June 1918.

54. Tubeuf, 'Tubeuf', 299–308.

55. Kitchen, *Operations*, 205–8; BHStA/IV, RIB12/Bd.1/diary, June 1918.

56. LBI, AR/25349/359197/diary, entries for 19 June, and 27 June–19 October 1918.

57. BHStA/IV, MG/RD6, Karl Koch.

58. BHStA/IV, HS928, Max von Speidel's recollections; Tubeuf, 'Tubeuf', 308–10.

59. Tubeuf, 'Tubeuf', 308–10; Gehring, 'Schicksalstrom', 316–25; Bernreuther, 'Patrouille', 325–7; Keegan, *First World War*, 438–9; SP, unpublished account of Alois Schnelldorfer's life by his wife.

60. NARA, RG165, RD6/diary, July 1918; Stöhr, 'Verluste', 381 ff.; Kitchen, *Offensives*, 234.

61. Hitler, *MK*, 117.

62. Quoted in Keegan, *First World War*, 435.

63. Ibid. 437–9.

64. Kitchen, *Offensives*, 14.

65. NARA, RG165/Box 35/a, Heeresgruppe Kronprinz Rupprecht/diary, 10 January 1918.

66. Hitler, *MK*, 111 ff.

67. Quoted in Bauer, Gerstenberg, and Peschel, *Dunst*, 143.

68. Deist, *Militär*, ii. 855, bayerisches Kriegsministerium, decree, 11 August 1918.

69. NARA, RG165, RD6/diary, July–August 1918; Tubeuf, 'Tubeuf', 310; Baligand, 'Ende', 328; Kitchen, *Offensives*, 210.

70. Cron, *Geschichte*, 26–7.

71. Bullock, *Hitler*, 52; Fest, *Hitler*, 103; Stone, *Hitler*, 7; Maser, *Legende*, 138; Steinert, *Hitler*, 89; Davidson, *Hitler*, 66; McClelland, *Political Thought*, 712.

72. BHStA/IV, RD6/Bd.114, E.K.II, April–December. 1916; BHStA/IV, RD6/Bd.112,1, A.Z.28, K.I., Nachweisungen, November 1914–May 1918; Kitchen, *Offensives*, 219.

73. SB, Z2, Volksfreund, 3 March 1932, 'Ein Kriegskamerad erzählt'.

74. BHStA/IV, RD6/Bd.112,1, K.I.–Vorschläge.

75. Wiedemann, *Feldherr*, 25. Wiedemann provides no date for this incident.

76. IFZ, ZS/1751, Eugen Tannhauser to Nürnberger Nachrichten, 4 August 1961. Tannhauser's letter is based on his recollections about a conversation he had had with Gutmann. See also Wiedemann, *Feldherr*, 25–6.

77. IFZ, MA-732, NSDAP/Hauptarchiv, Vorschlag Hitlers durch Godin, 31 July 1918.

78. BHStA/IV, RD6/Bd.118, 2, letter from AOK 4 to RD 6, 24 October 1918.

79. Brandmayer, *Meldegänger Hitler* (1933), 55.

80. Mend, *Hitler*, 161.

81. See e.g. Kershaw, *Hitler*, i. 96.

82. BHStA/IV, Offiziersakte Hugo Gutmann, Beurteilung by Wilhelm von Lüneschloß, 1 May 1917.

83. *Die Volksgemeinschaft*, 7 March 1932, 2, 'Marxistische Lügen'.

84. Kershaw, *Hitler*, i. 96; Fest, *Hitler*, 102; Bullock, *Hitler*, 51–2; Steinert, *Hitler*, 95. This version of the incident for which Hitler supposedly earned his Iron Cross 1st Class was also told by Mend, *Hitler*, 190.

85. Heinz, *Hitler*, 92.
86. BHStA/IV, Offiziersakte Hugo Gutmann, letter dated 4 August 1918.
87. Baligand, 'Ende', 328–33; BHStA/IV, RIR16/Bd.2/diary, 20–6 August 1918; BHStA/IV, KSR/3046/No. 1062; Kershaw, *Hitler*, i. 96.
88. Baligand, 'Ende', 328–33.
89. Weber, *Friend*, ch. 2.
90. Baligand, 'Ende', 331–2.
91. BHStA/IV Offiziersakten Otto Rosenkranz, Rosenkranz to Abwicklungstelle of IR 2, 17 April 1920.
92. BHStA/IV, MG/RD6/Wilhelm Grillenberger.
93. Deist, 'Militärstreik'.
94. Kitchen, *Offensives*, 217–30; Ziemann, *Heimat*, 124–5, 131, 373.
95. Hitler, *MK*, 118.
96. Ibid. 117 ff. See also Kershaw, *Hitler*, i. 102.
97. BHStA/IV, KSR/3046, No. 1062; Kershaw, *Hitler*, i. 96. The claim made by Fest, *Hitler*, 105, that Hitler visited his family in Austria is incorrect.
98. Hitler, *MK*, 117 ff.
99. BHStA/IV, MG/RD6, Sammelakten, investigation against Friedrich Fetzer.
100. Baligand, 'Ende', 333–6.
101. BHStA/IV, RIR16/Bd.2/diary, 13 October 1918.
102. IFZ, MA-732, NSDAP/Hauptarchiv, Heinrich Lugauer's report, 5 February 1940.
103. Baligand, 'Ende', 336.
104. Gruchmann and Weber, *Hitler-Prozess*, i. 19. Even the men gassed together with him, who both later became his followers (Heinrich Lugauer and Hans Bauer), did not claim that any of Hitler's comrades were either killed or blinded for life; see IFZ, MA-732, NSDAP/Hauptarchiv.
105. IFZ, MA-732, NSDAP/Hauptarchiv, Heinrich Lugauer's report, 5 February 1940; and Hans Bauer's recollection, 15 May 1940. See also Kershaw, *Hitler*, i. 96.
106. BHStA/IV, RD6/Bd.126,3, Übersicht der Gasmunition, 10 July 1917.
107. Hitler, *MK*, 118–19.
108. Köpf, 'Erblindung'. According to the casualty lists of the Bavarian Army, Hitler had indeed only been 'l[ightly] wounded'. See NARA, RG242, T-581/1A, documents pertaining to Hitler's second injury.
109. Köpf, 'Erblindung'.
110. Horstmann, *Pasewalk*, 28.
111. Ibid., *passim*; see also Lewis, *Men*, ch. 13.
112. BHStA/IV, KSR/3044/No. 1605, adjoining testimony by Eugen Schneider, 14 December 1920.
113. Baligand, 'Ende', 336–8; BHStA/IV, RIR16/Bd.17, II Batl./diary, 11 November 1918.

114. Quoted in Fest, *Hitler*, 114.

115. The average time RIR 16 soldiers served is difficult to compute. The average period Munich-based veterans of all Bavarian units, who applied for a pension after the war because they were suffering from a long-term damage of their nervous system, was fourteen months; see Ziemann, *Heimat*, 59. However, this figure inevitably lies below the Bavarian average as it provides a figure for a sub-section of soldiers who became casualties of the war.

116. Stöhr, 'Verluste', 381 ff.

117. The figures for the List Regiment are based on the assumption that approximately 16,000 men served in RIR 16 during the war. For national figures, see Geyer, 'Tötungshandeln', 110–11.

118. Ziemann, *Heimat*, 59 n. 23.

119. Ibid. 58.

120. IFZ, MA-732, NSDAP/Hauptarchiv, letter by Hans Raab, 5 August 1939, and Raab's report, 15 May 1940; report by Heinrich Lugauer, 5 February 1940, and note by Karl Lippert, 28 March 1940; Mend, *Hitler*; Heinz, *Hitler*, 64–96; Brandmayer, *Meldegänger Hitler* (1933); Joachimsthaler, *Hitlers Weg*, 341 n. 380, 381, 384; Bullock, *Hitler*, 51.

10. REVOLUTION

1. See e.g. Mitchell, *Revolution*, 27, 73, 90; Winkler, *Weg*, 368.

2. Winkler, *Weg*, 368, 371.

3. Mitchell, *Revolution*. Eisner's revolutionary regime was, however, also backed by the Social Democrats.

4. Hitler, *MK*, 120.

5. See e.g. Bessel, *Nazism*; Kershaw, *Hitler*, i. 101. Kershaw, however, allows that the men of the regiment did not 'form a unified "front generation"'.

6. BHStA/IV, RD6/Bd.72,4, decree, No. 36550/II 6. The demobilization unit of RIR 16 was the Reserve Battalion of the 2nd Infantry Regiment, see BHStA/IV, RD6/Bd.72,4, decree, No. 21320, 21 November 1918. Hitler initially joined the 7th Company of the 1st Reserve Battalion of the regiment and on 12 February he was assigned to the 2nd Demobilization Company; see Kershaw, *Hitler*, i. 116–17.

7. Machtan, *Hitler*, 340.

8. Information provided by Max Mund's nephew, Johann Benkner.

9. Kershaw, *Hitler*, i. 116 ff.; Machtan, *Hitler*, 93; Heinz, *Hitler*, 102–3.

10. Baligand, 'Heimwärts', 344–5; BHStA/IV, RIR16/Bd.2/diary, 14–17 November 1918.

11. Baligand, 'Heimwärts', 344–5.

12. BHStA/IV, RD6/Bd.72,3, AOK 6, memorandum, 12 November 1918.

13. Baligand, 'Heimwärts', 345; Meyer, *Hitler*, 108. Meyer's account of this period is based on hearsay, as, following an injury, he was no longer with the regiment.

14. BHStA/IV, RD6/Bd.72,3, RIR 16 to RD 6, 22 November 1918.
15. Quoted in Schmolze, *Revolution*, 150.
16. BHStA/IV, RD6/Bd.72,3, von Baligand to RD6, 28 November 1918.
17. BHStA/IV, RIR16/Bd.2/diary, 3–9 December 1918, and 8th Bavarian Infantry Brigade, Brigade-Befehl, 2 December 1918; BHStA/IV, RD6/Bd.72,3, Generalkommando of 1st Bavarian Reserve Corps to 8th Bavarian Infantry Brigade, 5 December 1918; Baligand, 'Heimwärts', 345; Knies, 'Wuppertal', 83–119; see *General-Anzeiger für Elberfeld-Barmen* and *Barmer Zeitung*, coverage of local affairs, 18 November–14 December 1918.
18. See e.g. Large, *München*, 124 ff.; Kramer, *Destruction*, 310; Kolb, *Republik*, 160 ff.; Weitz, *Germany*, 28.
19. Even once the Munich Soviet Republic had been defeated, many locals did not rule out the possibility of a reappearance of a Communist regime. In the words of an army report from mid-May 1919 about the situation in Munich, 'many people from all walks of life still fear the return of the Communist regime and thus carry out their duties half-heartedly. In the depths of their souls, they don't want to get on the bad side of anyone'. See BHStA/IV, RWGr.Kdo 4, Nr. 252, 'Die Lage in München', 18 May 1919.
20. Figes, *Tragedy*.
21. BHStA/IV, RIR16/Bd.2/diary, 9–15 December 1918.
22. BHStA/IV, RIR16/Bd.11,78, regimental order, 12 December 1918.
23. BHStA/IV, RD6/Bd.72,3, RIB 16 to RIB 12, 3 December 1918; Verfügung of the Oberkommando der 6. Armee, Ia/Ib Nr. 6452, 15 December 1918.
24. Ziemann, *Heimat*, 372 ff.
25. NARA-RG238-M1019-2, interrogation, 5 November 1947.
26. IFZ, MA-732, NSDAP/Hauptarchiv, recollection of Hans Bauer, 15 May 1940.
27. NARA, M1270-Roll22, testimony of Wiedemann.
28. This is the claim of the *Sonderweg* historians.
29. Hans Ostermünchner's copy of Solleder, *Westfront*, in the possession of his grandson Hans.
30. Mitchell, *Revolution*, 27, 73, 90; Hennig, *Hoffmann*, 85, 90–1; Albrecht, *Landtag*; Ay, *Entstehung*, 50–1; Weitz, *Weimar*, 19; Ziemann, *Heimat*, 267. The often articulated claim that the Bavarian monarchy, as well as the Imperial political system, was bankrupt and had lost all its legitimacy by the end of the war is thus not supported by the facts; see e.g. Karl, *Räterepublik*, 8–9; Mehringer, 'KPD', 5; Kluge, *Republik*, 28; Bessel, *Germany*, 48; and Horne, 'Remobilizing', 211.
31. Rupprecht, *Kriegstagebuch*, i. 470, 22 May 1916.
32. Deist, 'Army', 167; Fischer, *Zensurstelle*.
33. BHStA/IV, HS928, Speidel's recollections of the revolution.
34. Birnbaum, *Juden*, 303.

35. Albrecht, *Landtag*, 27; Volkert, *Geschichte*, 75–6; Chickering, *Imperial Germany*, 163.

36. Fischer, 'Revolution'; Mulligan, Reichswehr.

37. Deist, 'Army', 167.

38. Schulze, *Weimar*, 215–19; Schumann, 'Einheitssehnsucht', 93; Wasserstein, *Barbarism*, 148.

39. Ziemann, 'Erwartungen', 181; Watson, *Enduring*, chs. 5 and 6.

40. Thus the claim by Smith, *People's War*.

41. See Ziblatt, *State*, preface.

42. Weitz, *Germany*, 83.

43. Neiberg, *Great War*, 364.

44. www.wahlen-in-deutschland.de/wlBayern.htm; Mitchell, *Revolution*, 186–8; SPD Ortsverein Ichenhausen, *Festschrift*, 14.

45. Brandmayer, *Meldegänger Hitler* (1933), 114.

46. Kennan, *Decline*, 3.

47. Mitchell, *Revolution*, 237–53.

48. Hennig, *Hoffmannn*, 186.

49. Wasserstein, *Barbarism*, 96 ff.

50. Hennig, *Hoffmann*, 14–15, 267 ff.; Winkler, *Weg*, 397.

51. BHStA/IV, HS2421, Ministerium für militärische Angelegenheiten to Generalkommando II.&III.A.K., 14 April 1919.

52. Mitchell, *Revolution*, 266 ff.; Mehringer, 'KPD', 7; Ziemann, *Heimat*, 330.

53. NARA, M1270-Roll1, interrogation file on Amann. It is rather unlikely that Amann really witnessed the shooting of hostages.

54. BHStA/IV, HS2421, 'Aufruf', 17 April 1919.

55. BHStA/IV, HS2421, 'Aufruf'.

56. Quoted in Ziemann, *Heimat*, 397.

57. Ibid. 398.

58. NARA, BDC/A3343/SSO, Arthur Rödl.

59. NARA, M1270-Roll22, Wiedemann's testimony; Wiedemann, *Feldherr*, 53; Ziemann, *Heimat*, 398.

60. BHStA/I, Generaldirektion der Bayerischen Archive, 3152, information regarding Solleder's time during the revolution.

61. LAELKB, LKR/50001/Personalakte, Karl Frobenius; Karl, *Räterepublik*, 246.

62. SM, ZAP/Philipp Engelhardt.

63. BHStA/IV, HS/2727/Ludwig von Vallade.

64. See e.g. BHStA/IV, KSR/22675–7, Freikorps Oberland.

65. Bauer *et al.*, *Bewegung*, 47–9; information provided by Hans Ostermünchner's grandson Hans.

66. Schumann, 'Einheitssehnsucht'.

67. See, on the dynamics of violence in civil wars, Kalyvas, *Logic*.

68. Audoin-Rouzeau and Becker, *14–18*, 169.

69. Weitz, *Weimar*, 97.

70. Ibid. 97.

71. BHStA/IV, KSR, 22646, 22654, 22657, 22675, 22676, 22677 (selected muster rolls of the Freikorps Oberland, Freikorps Hübner, and the Zeitfreiwilligen unit Rauscher); Longerich, *Himmler*, 33–4, 66–73.

72. Mitchell, *Revolution*, 288–9.

73. See LAELKB, LKR/50088, Amtsgericht München, Urteil, 17 June 1927, Robert Hell against Hermann Schützinger *et al.* See also Wiegand, *Verraten*, 183.

74. Mitchell, *Revolution*, 288–9; Hennig, *Hoffmann*, 315–19; Winkler, *Weg*, 397.

75. LAELKB, LKR/50088, Amtsgericht München, Urteil, 17 June 1927, Robert Hell against Hermann Schützinger; *Münchener Zeitung*, 13 January 1926, 'Unter der Anklage'.

76. LAELKB, LKR/50088, Amtsgericht München, Urteil, 17 June 1927, Robert Hell against Hermann Schützinger. The article was published on 16 January 1926.

77. Sternhell, 'Counter-Enlightenment', 3–18.

78. BHStA/IV, RWGr.Kdo 4/Nr. 204, Judenhetze.

79. Kramer, *Destruction*, 292.

80. Walter, *Kriminalität*; Hoffmann, 'Verfolgung', 376–7.

81. Ziemann, *Heimat*, 336–9, 376.

82. Information provided by Hans Ostermünchner's grandson Hans.

83. Erlanger, *Schwabe*, 19.

84. BHStA/IV, RWGr.Kdo 4/Nr. 204, Judenhetze.

85. Longerich, *Himmler*, 39.

86. Knopp and Remy, *Hitler*, Episode 1.

87. Historisches Lexikon Bayern, s.v. 'Beisetzung Kurt Eisners', www.historisches-lexikon-bayerns.de/document/artikel_44676_6_beisetzung-eisners3.jpg, accessed 25 February 2009.

88. Quoted in Karl, *Räterepublik*, 39.

89. Kershaw, *Hitler*, i. 116 ff.; Machtan, *Hitler*, 93. For the footage of Eisner's funeral procession, see Knopp and Remy, *The Rise and Fall of Adolf Hitler*.

90. Thus Ian Kershaw's interpretation in his *Hitler*, i. 119–20.

91. Heinz, *Hitler*, 106.

92. Quoted in Fest, *Hitler*, 123.

93. For instance, Kershaw, *Hitler*, i. 94, argues that Hitler must have become increasingly anti-social democratic during the war and 'it indeed does seem very likely . . . that Hitler's political prejudices sharpened in the latter part of the war, during and after his first period of leave in Germany in 1916'.

94. For Niekisch's ideology, see Rätsch-Langejürgen, *Widerstand*, 358–9; Karl, *Räterepublik*, 105–27.

95. Vogt, *Sozialismus*.

96. Sternhell, *Birth*; Sternhell, *Neither Right*.

97. Machtan, *Hitler*, 96.

98. Kershaw, *Hitler*, i. introduction.

11. HITLER'S *KAMPF* AGAINST THE LIST VETERANS

1. BHStA/IV, RWGrKdo 4/Nr. 314, Propagandakurse/Teilnehmer/G-Z, letters, Adolf Gemlich to Mayr, 4 September 1919, Mayr to Hitler, 10 September 1919.

2. BHStA/IV, RWGrKdo 4/Nr. 314, Propagandakurse/Teilnehmer/G-Z, letters, Hitler to Gemlich, 16 September 1919.

3. NARA, RG238, M-1019-2, interrogations of Max Amann.

4. Fest, *Hitler*, 123; NARA-RG238-M1019-2, Amann's interrogation, 5 November 1947.

5. Ziemann, *Heimat*, 382.

6. NARA-RG238-M1019-2, interrogation, 5 November 1947.

7. Joachimsthaler, *Hitlers Weg*, 252 ff.

8. SAM, StanW/9959, Sondergericht 1, Urteil, 15 March 1941; NARA, RG242, T-581-3, investigation by the NSDAP party archive, 1938–9; NARA, RG242, T-581-3, investigation by the NSDAP party archive, 1938–9; Englmann, 'Kriegsbild', 81. Hitler had given photographs, drawings, paintings, or other presents *inter alia* to Josef Inkofer, Max Mund, Balthasar Brandmayer, Franz Küspert, and Hans Mend.

9. Kershaw, *Hitler*, i. 105.

10. Joachimsthaler, *Hitlers Weg*, 337; Machtan, *Hitler*, 95–6.

11. Private papers of Jakob Weiß, newspaper cutting from the *Freisinninger Tagblatt*, 26 March 1933, 'Reichskanzler Adolf Hitler'.

12. NARA, M1270-Roll1, interrogation file on Amann; StanW/I, 28791/31/ Amann; Hale, *Press*, *passim*.

13. NARA, BDC/A3343/SSO, Arthur Rödl.

14. For this stereotype, see Mosse, *Gefallen*, chs. 8–9.

15. NARA, BDC/A3343/SSO, Karl Ostberg; Rogge, *Opern*, 65–6; McKale, *Courts*, 20–8; Rösch, *NSDAP*, 70, 74.

16. Ernsting, *Frey*, 68.

17. Brandmayer, *Meldegänger Hitler* (1933), 116.

18. NARA, M1270-Roll22, interrogation file on Wiedemann; NARA, RG65-Box105-108, Memorandum, 21 April 1941; Wiedemann, *Feldherr*, 54.

19. Information provided by Manfred von Tubeuf.

20. BHStA/IV, officer files/Anton von Tubeuf, Begutachtung, 14 June 1918. For the troops' dislike of Tubeuf, see Wiedemann, *Feldherr*, 31.

21. Information provided by Manfred von Tubeuf.

22. Quoted in Maser, *Legende*, 146.

23. Meyer, *Hitler*, 70.

24. NARA, RG242, T-581-52, testimony of Anton von Tubeuf, 20 March 1922.

25. Information provided by Manfred von Tubeuf.

26. See NARA, RG242, T-581-52, Landgericht Hamburg, Urteil, Hitler gegen Echo der Woche, 9 March 1932; Wiedemann, *Feldherr*, 55; BHStA/IV, officer files, Nr. 6115/Wilhelm Diess.

27. *Erinnerungen an das List Regiment 1914–1918 (Sonderabdruck aus 'Das Bayernland')* (Munich, 1920), available at BHStA/IV, Amtsbücherei, No. 3653. The articles were by Rupert Frey, Carl Stiegler, Adolf Meyer, Adam Blersch, Valentin Mayer, Wilhelm Diess, Anton von Tubeuf, and Georg Dehn; BHStA/I, MK/45448/Solleder, arischer Nachweis, Formblatt 1; www.iglesialuterana.ec/historica.htm, accessed 26 August 2009.

28. Kershaw, *Hitler*, i. 92.

29. Schwarzwäller, *Stellvertreter*, 3.

30. Winter and Baggett, *Great War*, 394–8.

31. Herbert, *Best*.

32. See Mosse, *Gefallen*, chs. 8–9.

33. SAM, PDM/10003/Reichsbanner, police reports, 22 and 23 February 1931.

34. NARA, BDC files. The figure is based on the NSDAP Ortsgruppenkartei and the NSDAP Zentralkartei in the US National Archives in College Park, MD. The names that appear in these membership files account for approximately 85–90 per cent of all members of the Nazi Party. In order to test if a large number of NSDAP membership files of RIR 16 veterans might have been among the NSDAP membership files that have not survived, I ran the entire sample of soldiers under investigation against the denazification files of the Spruchkammer Munich (located in the Staatsarchiv München). These files include the files of all residents of Munich implicated with the Nazi regime, as well as the files of residents of all other Upper Bavarian Spruchkammer districts who appealed against the initial ruling of their Spruchkammer. Not a single veteran of RIR 16 had an entry among the files of the Spruchkammer Munich who was not also listed among the Nazi Party membership files in the US National Archives. We can thus confidently conclude that the fact that between 10 to 15 per cent of membership files of the NSDAP are no longer available has no significant impact on the survey of Nazi Party membership among the veterans of RIR 16.

35. Overy, *Dictators*, 139–44.

36. NARA, BDC files, alphabetic list of SS officers and enlisted men (available in the Microfilm Reading Room).

37. NARA, BDC/A3343/SSO, Arthur Rödl and Karl Ostberg.

38. Unlike for the SS, no full SA membership have survived.

39. Hitler's immediate comrades from amongst the dispatch runners of regimental HQ tended ultimately to join Hitler in his party. It seems that other soldiers who had served with the support staff of either the regiment or one of the battalions in Fournes were also more likely to join the Nazi Party than the men who were in the trenches. Of the 9 soldiers from the sample of 623 soldiers from 1st Company who, in addition to Hitler, served in Fournes in mid-1915, 3 joined the Nazi Party; see BHStA/IV, RIB12/25/1, Verzeichnis über die in Fournes untergebrachten Offiziere, Unteroffiziere und Mannschaften.

40. 16.8 per cent of privates (including infantrymen, *Ersatzreservist*, Gefreite, etc.) joined the Nazi Party; the figure for Gefreite is 20.5 per cent, for NCOs 18.4 per cent and for war volunteers 15.4 per cent.

41. 13.7 per cent of veterans of the 1875–9 age cohort joined the NSDAP. The corresponding figure for the 1889–4 cohort is 11.8 per cent, for the 1885–9 cohort (i.e. Hitler's age cohort) 17.5 per cent, for the 1890–4 cohort 22.3 per cent, and for the 1895–9 cohort 15.7 per cent.

42. 28.0 per cent of the Protestant veterans joined the NSDAP, compared to 14.7 per cent of Catholic veterans. The overall figure of Upper Bavaria was 16.9 per cent, for Lower Franconia 16.7 per cent, for the Rheinpfalz 25 per cent, for German regions outside Bavaria 14.3 per cent, and for soldiers resident abroad 15.4 per cent.

43. The figures are based on the 584 soldiers of the random sample of 623 soldiers from 1st Company who lived in Bavaria. The classification of community sizes follows the convention of the Statistisches Reichsamt (ed.), *Statistisches Jahrbuch für das Deutsche Reich*, Band 113 (Berlin, 1914), 4–5.

44. BHStA/IV, KSR/3039–41; NARA, BDC, NSDAD membership files. The figures are based on a random sample of 623 soldiers who served in 1st Company. The occupation of thirteen soldiers could not be established.

45. See e.g. Childers, *Nazi Voter*.

46. Brutscher, *Weltreiseziel*, 28.

47. NARA, T-581-13, [Wackerl] to Hitler, 19 April 1923.

48. SP, unpublished account of Alois Schnelldorfer's life by his wife.

49. Large, *München*, 240.

50. Gruchmann and Weber, *Hitler-Prozess*.

51. SAM, PDM/10003/Amann; Hale, *Press*, 23–4.

52. NARA, BDC/A3343/SSO, Arthur Rödl and Karl Ostberg; Schönhoven, 'Katholizismus', 542–5; Schulze, *Weimar*, 268; Wasserstein, *Barbarism*, 149; Pridham, *Rise*, 42–64.

53. This is Eberhard Kolb's claim in his *Republik*, 40–1.

54. Machtan, *Hitler*, 96.

55. Hitler, *MK*, 101.

56. Ibid., all quotes from 101–5.

57. Ibid., all quotes from 101–6.

58. Ibid. 102.

59. Ibid. 121.

60. See Ibid.

61. See e.g. Ibid.

62. SM, ZAP/Hitler, *Völkischer Kurier*, 18 October 1924, 'Adolf Hitlers Staatsangehörigkeit'.

63. Fest, *Hitler*, 103; SM, ZAP/Hitler, *Völkicher Kurier*, 19 October 1924, 'Geistige und politische Wahlverwandtschaft', and *Vaterland*, 15 October 1924, 'Spaß beiseite'.

64. Quoted in James, *Europe*, 113.

65. Weinberg, *Zweites Buch*.

66. Weinberg, 'Einleitung', 15–39.
67. Kühne, *Kameradschaft*.
68. Ibid., 42 ff.
69. Ibid.; Ziemann, *Heimat*, 230; Natter, *Literature*, 149.
70. Sternhell, 'Counter-Enlightenment', 4–5.
71. For the sectarian mode of politics, see Margalit, 'Sectarianism'.
72. Quoted in Linder, *Princes*, 111. The book was Hans Zöberlein's *Der Glaube an Deutschland*.
73. *Die Volksgemeinschaft*, 7 March 1932, 2, 'Marxistische Lügen'. *Die Volksgemeinschaft* is available in the University Library of Heidelberg University.
74. Harari, *Experience*.
75. Mend, *Hitler*.
76. Quoted in Machtan, *Hitler*, 78.
77. NARA, RG242, T-581-13, *Fränkische Tagespost*, 24 October 1932, 'Adolf Hitler im Felde'.
78. Mend, *Hitler*, 9.
79. NARA, M1270-Roll1, interrogation file on Amann.
80. Quoted in Hale, *Press*, 48.
81. BHStA/I, Sig/Personen, 3919/Amann, newspaper cuttings, *Neue Zeitung*, 9 April 1929, 'Theorie und Praxis', *Münchner Post*, 13/14 April 1929, 'Nationalsozialistische Geschäftspraktiken'; *Münchner Post*, 28 September 1931, 'Feine Manieren' (quote); SAM, StanW/I, 19038/1/Amann; SAM, AG/114, Amann against Johann Jacob; StanW/I, PDM/10003/Amann; Hale, *Press*, 24–32.
82. SM, ZAP/Fridolin Solleder, *München-Augsburger Abendzeitung*, 31 January 1919.
83. SAM, StanW/8544, Siegfried Heumann; Stadtarchiv München, *Gedenkbuch*, i. 582; Dunker, *Reichsbund*.
84. Römer, *Leidensweg*, 74; Lechner, *Synagoge*, 23. In Ichenhausen, there had been some opposition to the admittance of Jews to the local veterans' association. However, opponents lost out against those who had no problem admitting Jews.
85. Hoffmann, 'Verfolgung', 374–5.
86. Email of Stadtarchiv Memmingen to the author, 19 June 2008; BHStA/IV, KSR/3039, Nr. 17.
87. Only Valentin Mayer's *Bayerland* contribution was not included.
88. SM, Kulturant, 837, 'Kriegsteilnehmer' to Munich city council, 6 April 1917, and Eugen Roth to the Lord Mayor of Munich, 12 April 19.
89. Solleder, *Westfront*. The references to Gutmann are in Spatny, 'Kämpfe', 180, 184; NARA, RG238, M-1019-79, Wiedemann's interrogations, 1946–1947. SAM, NSDAP, 8, Hitler gegen Max Wutz. Hitler's own personal copy of the regimental history bears witness of his continued good relationship with the last commander of the List Regiment, Maximilian von Baligand. It was a present by the former commander to Hitler. It bears the inscription: 'To his brave message runner, the highly decorated former [Private] Mr Adolf Hitler in memory of serious but great times, with thanks.' See Ryback, *Library*, 14.

90. Haugg, *Deutsche Heraus!*

91. See Prost, *Wake*.

92. Berman, 'Civil Society', quotes at 402 and 425.

93. Schönhoven, 'Katholizismus', 547.

94. SAM, PDM/6886/Reichsbanner, police report, 9 July 1924; SAM, PDM/6887/Reichsbanner, police report, 12 March 1931 (quote), and police report, P.N.D./767; SAM, PDM/6892/Reichsbanner; Vogt, *Sozialismus*, 120; Kühne, *Kameradschaft*, 34–41; Fischer, *Stormtroopers*, 26–8.

95. See e.g. Joachimsthaler, *Hitlers Weg*, 255.

96. Rohe, *Reichsbanner*, *passim*; Vogt, *Sozialismus*, 120.

97. See Rohe, *Reichsbanner*, 150. Mayr saw himself as a 'nationaler Sozialist', rather than a 'Nationalsozialist'.

98. For the ideological strands that some Fascists and some Socialists shared and for more examples of intellectuals who moved between Fascism and Socialism, see also Berman, *Primacy*.

99. Schüddekopf, *Linke Leute*.

100. SAM, PDM/6886/Reichsbanner, police reports, 22 and 23 February 1931.

101. Kühne, *Kameradschaft*, 38 ff., sees such a binary opposition.

102. Bessel, *Germany*; Kershaw, *Hitler*, i. 98; BSAM Spruchkammerakten, Streicher, August.

103. NARA, T-581-1, Ferdinand Widman to Hitler, 9 March 1932.

104. IFZ, MA-732, NSDAP/Hauptarchiv, Georg Hammerl to Gauleitung München-Oberbayern der NSDAP, 25 January 1932.

105. Brandmayer, *Meldegänger Hitler* (1933), 116.

106. Daumiller, *Schatten*, 25.

107. Krumeich, 'Erinnerung', 239.

108. See e.g. SM, ZAP/Hitler, *Münchener Post*, 30 April 1926, 'Hitler, der Held des Weltkrieges'.

109. *Die Volksgemeinschaft*, 7 March 1932, 2, 'Marxistische Lügen über Adolf Hitlers Fronttätigkeit vor Gericht gebrandmarkt'; NARA, RG242, T-581, Landgericht Hamburg, Urteil, Hitler gegen Echo der Woche, 9 March 1932.

110. *Die Volksgemeinschaft*, 7 March 1932, 2, 'Marxistische Lügen über Adolf Hitlers Fronttätigkeit vor Gericht gebrandmarkt'; NARA, RG242, T-581, Landgericht Hamburg, Urteil, Hitler gegen Echo der Woche, 9 March 1932.

111. NARA, RG242, T-581-13, newspaper cutting, *Münchner Post*, 'Held Hitler', *c*.March 1922 (date missing).

112. *Die Volksgemeinschaft*, 7 March 1932, 2, 'Marxistische Lügen über Adolf Hitlers Fronttätigkeit vor Gericht gebrandmarkt'; Machtan, *Hitler*, 96; Fest, *Hitler*, 94.

113. *Die Volksgemeinschaft*, 7 March 1932, 2, 'Marxistische Lügen über Adolf Hitlers Fronttätigkeit vor Gericht gebrandmarkt'.

114. IFZ, MA-732, NSDAP/Hauptarchiv, Paul Müller to Hitler, 3 March 1932; Max Störkl to the NSDAP, 4 March 1932 (Störkl equally was not a veteran of the List Regiment but wrote that his friend Josef Pledel, who was a List Regiment veteran, would be prepared to defend Hitler). While Rutz's identity as the author of the *Echo der Woche* article was not disclosed at the time, Rutz, however, did agree elsewhere to put his name to the criticism of Hitler's fictional war record. He penned another article, published in a number of newspapers, to a similar effect as the *Echo der Woche* article; see Joachimsthaler, *Hitlers Weg*, 150–1, 344. In 1932, a Franconian newspaper also printed a letter by Rutz, in which the former Commander of 1st Company, pointed out that neither Hitler nor Amann had served in the trenches; see NARA, RG242, T-581-13, *Fränkische Tagespost*, 8 April 1932, 'Wo war Hitler Frontsoldat'.

115. BHStA/IV, HS 3231, *Der Gerade Weg*, 9 October 1932, 'Der Schimmelreiter meldet'.

116. NARA, RG242, T-581-13, *Fränkische Tagespost*, 24 October 1932, 'Adolf Hitler im Felde'. The letter was also published by the *Münchner Post*.

117. Ernsting, *Frey*, 74.

118. BHStA/I, Sig/Personen, 4924/Frey, *Luzerner Neueste Nachrichten*, 28 March 1951, 'Spuk, Satire und Humanismus: Zum 70. Geburtstag von Alexander M. Frey'.

119. Alexander Moritz Frey, 'Der unbekannte Gefreite—persönliche Erinnerungen an Hitler' (1946), quoted in Ernsting, *Frey*, 55.

120. Ernsting, *Frey*, 91.

121. Quoted in Ibid.

122. Quoted in Ibid. 90.

123. Fischer, *Stormtroopers*, 2.

124. Fritzsche, *Nazis*, 18.

125. Pridham, *Hitler's Rise*, 322.

126. Horstmann, *Pasewalk*, 16–21.

12. PRIVATE HITLER'S REICH

1. For instance, the *Daily Telegraph* reprinted the photo on 3 August 1934, see Kershaw, *Hitler*, i. 633 n. 90.

2. The previous two paragraphs are based on SM, Bürgermeister/Rat, 1108/1/Militärvereine, letters and newspaper cuttings pertaining to the 1934 reunion of RIR 16, and Historische Bildarchiv, Valérien, 82/3/23–8, 82/4/7–18, and Huhle, 2219–22; private papers of Jakob Weiß, photos from the 1934 reunion; SP, programme of the RIR 16 reunion, 13/14 October 1934; and unpublished account of Alois Schnelldorfer's life by his wife; interview with Hans Ostermünchner's grandson Hans, April 2009.

3. *Illustrierter Beobachter*, 27 October 1934, 1747, photospread; SM, Bürgermeister/Rat, 1108/1/Militärvereine, cutting from the *Völkischer Beobachter*, 13 October 1934.

4. Rösch, *NSDAP*, 209.

5. Private papers of Jakob Weiß, Beatrix Weichenrieder to Jakob Weiß, 15 October 1934.

6. *Illustrierter Beobachter*, 27 October 1934, 1747, photospread.

7. http://wahlen-in-deutschland.de/wrtw.htm, accessed 1 July 2009.

8. Klemperer, *Witness*, 30, 37, entries for 13 July and 19 August 1933.

9. Beck, *Alliance*.

10. Bendick, *Kriegserfahrung*.

11. *Völkischer Beobachter*, 14 August 1934, p. 3, 'Frontsoldat Hitler'.

12. Kühne, *Kameradschaft*, part II.

13. Hitler, however, frequently invoked the war in speeches either by pointing out that the First World War had given birth to National Socialism or by presenting his foreign policy successes as having finally repaired the damage that traitors on the home front had inflicted on Germany; see Hirschfeld, 'Führer'.

14. BHStA/IV, HS/3466, newspaper cuttings from *Aufwärts*, 4–7 April 1933.

15. Meyer, *Hitler*, 109. Amann, *Leben*, without pages, uses a very similar formula to Meyey's in describing the role of RIR 16 in producing Hitler.

16. Heinz, *Hitler*, 65 (quote); *New York Times*, 21 December 1933, 22, 'Hitler Pays Fare'; Amann, *Leben*.

17. Private papers of Jakob Weiß, see the draft of his war memoirs.

18. Private papers of Jakob Weiß, newspaper cuttings from the *Freisinninger Tagblatt*, 26 March 1933, 'Reichskanzler Adolf Hitler', and from the *Süddeutsche Sonntagspost*, 2 April 1933, 'Jakob Weiß, des Kanzlers Kriegskamerad'.

19. NARA, RG242, T-581-3, investigation by the NSDAP party archive, 1938–9; IFZ, MA-732, NSDAP/Hauptarchiv, report by Heinrich Lugauer, 5 February 1940, note by Karl Lippert, 28 March 1940, and recollection of Hans Bauer, 15 May 1940; BHStA/IV, Offiziersakte/Hugo Gutmann; RD6, Bd.112,1, A.Z. 28, note dated 10 March 1937; Steinert, *Hitler*, 96. As we have seen, it was the reports submitted to the Nazi Party archive which many historians have taken as evidence that Hitler's own version of his war service were not mythical but more or less accurate.

20. NARA, M1270-Roll1, interrogation file on Amann; Hale, *Press*, passim.

21. NARA, RG226, M-1642-Roll109, 'Report on four close associates of Hitler', 1943.

22. NARA, M1270-Roll22, interrogation file on Wiedemann; Schad, *Spionin*, 54; Wiedemann, *Feldherr*, 57–8.

23. NARA, M1642-Roll 120, Frames 264–506, OSS file on Wiedemann's arrest; NARA, RG238, M-1019-79, Wiedemann's interrogations, 1946–7; NARA, M1270-Roll22, interrogation file on Wiedemann. For Wiedemann's appearance, see Hohenlohe, *Stephanie*, 158.

24. Wiedemann, *Feldherr*, 78.

25. Machtan, *Hitler*, 89, 97.

26. Brandmayer, *Meldegänger Hitler* (1933), 57, 71, 79; Brandmayer, *Mit Hitler* (1940), 39, 51, 57.

27. Brandmayer, *Meldegänger Hitler* (1933), 22–3.; Brandmayer, *Mit Hitler* (1940), 24.

28. Brandmayer, *Meldegänger Hitler* (1933), 35–48.

29. Ibid. 20, 66, 72–3; Brandmayer, *Mit Hitler* (1940), 46, 53, 91.

30. SAM, PDM/6886/Reichsbanner, police report, 14 March 1933.

31. NARA, BDC/A3343/SSO, Karl Ostberg.

32. Joachimsthaler, *Hitlers Weg*, 348 n. 539.

33. Köpf, 'Erblindung'; Horstmann, *Pasewalk*, 7–21, 65–6, 169, 182–90; Lewis, *Men*, 218. Ernst Weiß used Forster's notes for a novel he wrote in the 1930s. *Der Augenzeuge*, the novel, which was not published until 1963, provides a semi-fictional account of Hitler's time at Pasewalk.

34. SAM, StanW/I, 19038/1/Amann; BSAM, StanW/I, 19038/2/Amann; SAM, PDM/10003/Amann.

35. Ernsting, *Frey*.

36. Ibid. 51, 56–7, 84, 105, 113–20, 137–64.

37. SAM, StanW/9959, Sondergericht 1, Urteil, 15 March 1941, Auszug aus dem Srafregister, Hans Mend, and Gestapo Munich to Sondergericht 1, 31 December 1940; Joachimsthaler, *Hitlers Weg*, 333–4.

38. NARA, RG242, T-581-3, investigation by the NSDAP archive, 1938–9; SAM, StanW/9959, Sondergericht 1, Urteil, 15 March 1941.

39. Joachimsthaler, *Hitlers Weg*, 153.

40. Ibid., Gruppe IIb/1976, Stapoleitstelle München I/1/A, report, 1 November 1936; SAM, StanW/8544, Siegfried Heumann; Stadtarchiv München, *Gedenkbuch*, i. 582.

41. Gellately, *Backing Hitler*.

42. Kershaw, *Hitler*, ii. 184–5; Stern, *Dreams*, 147–91; Fritzsche, *Life*; Frei, 'People's Community'; Benz, 'Konsilidierung'; Thamer, *Verführung*; Gregor, *Nazism*, 211; Johnson and Reuband, *What We Knew*, 341, 344; Aly, *Beneficiaries*, 2–7; Overy, *Dictators*, 640.

43. SAM, Spruchkammern/Karton 1643/Ernst Schmidt/16.12.1889, testimony based on a statement by the mayor of Oberburgkirchen.

44. Lechner, *Synagoge*, 23; Haus der Bayerischen Geschichte, *Ichenhausen*, 111; Sinz, 'Vierzig Jahre', 54, 75–77; BHStA, KSR/3063, Nr. 708.

45. Sauder, *Wilder*, 269–70, 382–3.

46. Müller, *Nürnberg*, 219.

47. Hoffmann, 'Verfolgung', 373–98; Kershaw, 'Antisemitismus', 294 ff.

48. BHStA/IV, Offiziersakte/Hugo Gutmann, Gutmann (Henry G. Grant) to Joseph Drexel, 6 November 1946; Drexel, *Mauthausen*; Rätsch-Langejürgen, *Widerstand*.

49. BHStA/IV, Offiziersakte/Hugo Gutmann, Gutmann to Joseph Drexel, 6 November 1946.

50. BHStA/IV, Offiziersakte/Hugo Gutmann, Gutmann to Joseph Drexel, 6 November 1946 (quote); BHStA/IV, officer files/Mathias Mayrhofer.

51. BHStA/IV, Offiziersakte/Hugo Gutmann, Gutmann to Joseph Drexel, 6 November 1946.

52. Haus der Bayerischen Geschichte, *Ichenhausen*, 29–33, 106; Erlanger, *Schwabe*, 25.

53. Hoffmann, 'Verfolgung', 381 ff.; Ophir and Wiesemann, *Gemeinden*, 486–8; Haus der Bayerischen Geschichte, *Ichenhausen*, 29–33; BHStA, KSR/3088-9.

54. Römer, *Leidensweg*, 96; Kulka and Jäckel, *Juden/CD-ROM*, Gruppe IVb/1150, Gendarmerie Baiersdorf, report, 6 August 1935, Gruppe III/1459, Regierungspräsident Schwaben/Neuburg, report, 7 December 1935, and Gruppe IVb/2038, Gendarmeriebezirk Ebermannstadt, report, 5 December 1936.

55. Kulka and Jäckel, *Juden/CD-ROM*, Gruppe Ia/2118, SD-Hauptamt/II/112, report, 8 April 1937, and Gruppe Ia/2117, SD-Hauptamt/II/112, report, 18 March 1937.

56. Ibid., Gruppe Ia/1860, SD-Hauptamt/II/112, report, 25 June 1936.

57. Ibid., Gruppe IIb/2193, Stapoleitstelle München, report, 1 January 1937.

58. Jesse, *Kirchengemeinden*, 276.

59. Kulka and Jäckel, *Juden/CD-ROM*, Gruppe Ia/2118, SD-Hauptamt/II/12, report, 8 April 1937.

60. Ibid., Gruppe IIb/2213, Stapoleitstelle München/II/2/A, report, 7 August 1937.

61. BHStA/IV, Offiziersakte/Hugo Gutmann, Gutmann to Joseph, 6 November 1946.

62. SAM, Wiedergutmachungsakten/Antrag/WB/Ia/3873.

63. By the end of 1937, 'only' approximately 30 per cent of German Jews had emigrated; see Evans, *Drittes Reich*, ii. 2, 673.

64. Sinz, 'Vierzig Jahre', 70–2; Haus der Bayerischen Geschichte, *Ichenhausen*, 40–3, 112–13; Ophir and Wiesemann, *Gemeinden*, 472–3.

65. Quoted in Römer, *Leidensweg*, 77–9.

66. Kulka and Jäckel, *Juden/CD-ROM*, Gruppe Ib/2774, SD–Oberabschnitt Süd/II/112, annual report, 1938.

67. Ibid., Gruppe Ib/2331, SD-Oberabschnitt Süd/II/112, Bericht für 1937.

68. BHStA/IV, KSR/3039, Nr. 450; Yad Vashem, Documents Archive/3548104, Arthur Wechsler, 'Conditions in Munich', 1954; Stadtarchiv München, *Gedenkbuch*, ii. 699.

69. Evans, *Drittes Reich*, ii. 2, 673, 725; Römer, *Leidensweg*, 27, 90, 101; Ophir and Wiesemann, *Gemeinden*, 453, 473, 480, 486–8; Haus der Bayerischen Geschichte, *Ichenhausen*, 106; Diefenbacher and Fischer-Pache, *Gedenkbuch*, 441–3.

70. SAM, Wiedergutmachungsakten/Antrag, I N/387/Antragstellung.

71. Römer, *Leidensweg*, 42; www.ancestry.com, entries for Alexander Wormser, Ernst Dispecker, and Leo Sichel; Stadtarchiv Augsburg, Städtische Polizei/ Familienbögen/Meldekarten/1–3: Alexander Wormser; BHStA/IV, KSR/ 3038, Nr. 334, KSR/3073, Nr. 157 and KSR/3074, Nr. 160, and KSR/3078, Nr. 580; Hepp, *Ausbürgerung*, i. 290.

72. BHStA/IV, RIR16/Bd.12, I Batl./diary, 12 October 1916.

73. www.iglesialuterana.ec/historica.htm, accessed 26 August 2009.

74. Wiedemann, *Feldherr*, 56.

75. BHStA/IV, Offiziersakte/Hugo Gutmann, Gutmann to Joseph Drexel, 6 November 1946.

76. *St Louis Post-Dispatch*, 4 August 1941, 5A, 'Refugee, Once in Hitler's Regiment, Now Living Here'.

77. NARA, BDC files.

78. SAM, Spruchkammerakten, Albert Huth/9.10.1892.

79. SAM, Spruchkammerakten, Karton 9/Franz Aigner/7.7.1891; Böhm, 'Tegethoff', 313.

80. Johnson and Reuband, *What We Knew*, 331.

81. Fritzsche, *Life*; Mommsen, *Alternative*, 9; Kurlander, *Hitler*.

82. Joachimsthaler, *Hitlers Weg*, 167 f.; NARA-RG238-M1019-2, interrogation, 5 November 1947.

83. Information provided by Manfred von Tubeuf, Wolo von Tubeuf, and Ekkehard Müller.

84. SAM, Spruchkammerakten, Karton 9/Franz Aigner/7.7.1891.

85. Böhm, 'Tegethoff', 311–17.

86. SP, unpublished account of Alois Schnelldorfer's life by his wife.

87. Jesse, *Kirchengemeinden*, 242.

88. LAELKB, PA/Theol/1327, Daumiller, Daumiller's denazification file, and letter, Rechtsverwalter der Deutschen Evangelischen Kirche to Daumiller, 11 October 1934, and Gestapo Personalakte II/1/B/1; Daumiller, *Schatten*, 62–79; LAELKB, LKR/50403, Friedrich Käppel, and PA/Theol/461, Friedrich Käppel.

89. LAELKB, LKR/50118, Spruchkammer file, Hermann Kornacher.

90. Quoted in LAELKB, LKR/50118, Spruchkammer file, Hermann Kornacher.

91. LAELKB, LKR/50118, Spruchkammer file, Hermann Kornacher.

92. See LAELKB, LKR/50118, Spruchkammer file, Hermann Kornacher.

93. LAELKB, LKR/50118, Spruchkammer file, Hermann Kornacher.

94. Johnson and Reuband, *What We Knew*, 331.

95. Ibid. 333.

96. Ibid. 335.

97. Ibid.

98. Gellately, *Backing Hitler*, images 1, 3 8, 38; Aly, *Beneficiaries*, cover image.

99. Pfaft, *Dynamics*, 9–10, 259–60; Kuran, *Truths*, chs. 6–7; Jowitt, *Disorder*, 80, 288, 310.

100. See e.g. Gellately, *Backing Hitler*, image 38.

101. Browning, 'Killers', 142–69.

102. BHStA/I, MK/45448/Solleder, article in *Der Heimgarten*, 27 January 1934, 'Handwerkerblut und deutsche Kultur'; letter, Ministerialdirektor Fischer to Solleder, 2 February 1934; letter Solleder to the Bavarian Ministry of Education, 18 October 1938; BHStA/I, Generaldirektion, 3152, Personalakte Solleder.

13. HITLER'S SECOND WAR

1. Interviews with Hans Ostermünchner's grandson Hans, April 2009 and with Alois Schnelldorfer's daughter, Marie Anna Ekert, April 2009.

2. Frei, 'People's Community', 66.

3. SP, unpublished account of Alois Schnelldorfer's life by his wife.

4. Quoted in Bessel, *Nazism*, 33.

5. NARA, RG65-Box105-108, letter from Hitler to Rothermere, 1 Dec. 1933.

6. *Berliner Zeitung*, 31 July 1997, 'Wie Adolf Hitler das Leben geschenkt wurde'.

7. SM, Bürgermeister/Rat, 1108/1/Militärvereine, cutting from the *Völkischer Beobachter*, 2 August 1938.

8. SP, unpublished account of Alois Schnelldorfer's life by his wife.

9. Quoted in Bessel, *Nazism*, 73.

10. Yale Law School, Avalon Project, speech by Hitler to the Reichstag, 1 September 1939; http://avalon.law.yale.edu/wwii/blbk106.asp, accessed 23 May 2009.

11. SP, unpublished account of Alois Schnelldorfer's life by his wife.

12. Hoffmann, *Westen*, photo of Hitler, Amann, and Schmidt; NARA, RG242, T-581-16, Daten aus alten Notizbüchern; Mathot, *Ravin du Loup*.

13. ADN, 8/Fi/26/13, Expo 13, photo of sign put up by German troops in 1942.

14. Beckett, *Ypres*, 187.

15. Hoffmann, *Westen*.

16. War memoirs of Ernst Cambensy, in the possession of his son Martin.

17. Bessel, *Nazism*, 90; Evans, *Third Reich at War*, 133–6, 450.

18. Wolffsohn and Brechenmacher, *Vornamen*, 27.

19. War memoirs of Ernst Cambensy, in the possession of his son Martin.

20. NARA, BDC files. The year of entry of 1.1 per cent of veterans from the sample of 623 veterans from 1st Company who joined the Nazi Party could not be established. It is a safe assumption that the majority of them are likely to have joined the NSDAP between 1933 and 1939.

21. Quoted in Kershaw, *Hitler*, ii. 424. The quotation is from a report from the Gendarmerie-Posten Mittenwald of 24 May 1941.

22. Kershaw, *Hitler*, ii. 657.

23. See Granovetter, 'Threshold Models'.

24. BHStA/IV, HS/2729 and HS/2731/Ludwig von Vallade.

25. Information provided by Prince Leopold d'Arenberg.

26. Weiß, *Rupprecht*, 304.

27. BHStA/IV, HS/3231, Mend Protokoll.

28. SAM, StanW/9959, Sondergericht 1, Urteil, 15 March 1941.

29. LAELKB, PA/Theol/1327, Daumiller, testimony of Dr Alt, 7 November 1945.

30. NARA, M1270-Roll22, interrogation file on Wiedemann; Schad, *Spionin*, 98.

31. NARA, RG238-M-1019-79, Wiedemann's interrogations, 1946-7. The claim that the meeting with Lord Halifax prepared the Munich Conference, see Whitehead, *FBI*, 224 ff., is without foundation.

32. NARA, M1642-Roll120, Frames 264-506, OSS file on Wiedemann's arrest; NARA, M1270-Roll22, interrogation file on Wiedemann.

33. NARA, M1270-Roll22, interrogation file on Wiedemann.

34. NARA, RG65-Box99, 'Captain Fritz: Consul Wiedemann, Hitler's Old Superior Officer, Runs into Trouble Selling Nazism to West', article from unidentified magazine (quote); NARA, RG65-Box105-108, Memorandum, 21 April 1941; Whitehead, *FBI*, 227; Hohenlohe, *Stephanie*, 190.

35. NARA, RG65-Box105-108, Memorandum, 21 April 1941.

36. NARA, RG65-Box105-108, Memorandum, 21 April 1941.

37. NARA, RG65-Box99, transcript of Wiedemann and Wiseman's meeting.

38. NARA, RG65-Box105-108, Memorandum, 21 April 1941.

39. NARA, RG65-Box99, transcript of Wiedemann and Wiseman's meeting.

40. NARA, RG65-Box104, File on Steffi Richter *et al.*

41. NARA, RG65-Box105-108, Memorandum for the FBI Director, 10 July 1941.

42. NARA, M1642-Roll120, Frames 264-506, OSS file on Wiedemann's arrest; NARA, RG226-M1642-Roll123, W. J. Donovan to Franklin D. Roosevelt, 15 September 1941 and OSS intelligence report.

43. NARA, M1642-Roll 120, Frames 264-506, OSS file on Wiedemann's arrest.

44. Beck, *Alliance*.

45. See Granovetter, 'Threshold Models', 1441-2; Ziblatt, *State*.

46. Pulzer, 'Holocaust'.

47. See Jowitt, *Disorder*, 14.

48. See www.pbs.org/greatwar/interviews/fergus2.html, interview with Niall Ferguson, accessed 11 November 1997.

49. Messerschmidt and Wüllner, *Wehrmachtjustiz*, 63-91.

50. Quoted in Maser, *Legende*, 146.

51. Hoffmann, *Hitler im Westen*, photo of Hitler at the Canadian memorial at Vimy Ridge.

52. NARA, M1270-Roll22, interrogation file on Wiedemann.

53. Quoted in Horne and Kramer, *Atrocities*, 407.

54. Kershaw, *Hitler*, ii. 454.

55. Quoted in Maser, *Legende*, 145.

56. Wiedemann, *Feldherr*, 104.
57. Quoted in Kershaw, *Hitler*, i. 88.
58. Quoted ibid.
59. IFZ, MA-732, NSDAP/Hauptarchiv, Max Amann to Martin Bormann, 16 February 1944.
60. Quoted in Kershaw, *Hitler*, ii. 488.
61. BHStA/IV, KSR/3038-92; YVD (The Central Database of Shoah Victims' Names); www.ancestry.com; Stadtarchiv München, *Gedenkbuch*, 2 vols.; Diefenbacher and Fischer-Pache, *Gedenkbuch*; Institut Theresienstädter Initiative, *Gedenkbuch*; Hepp, *Ausbürgerung*, 2 vols.; Röder/Strauss, *Handbuch*, 2 vols.; State Museum of Auschwitz-Birkenau, *Death Books*.
62. NARA, BDC/A3343/SSO, Arthur Rödl.
63. LBI, AR/25349/359197, files on Justin, Ernst, and Martin Fleischmann.
64. BHStA/IV, Offiziersakte/Hugo Gutmann, Gutmann to Joseph Drexel, 6 November 1946; *St Louis Post-Dispatch*, 4 August 1941, 5A, 'Refugee, Once in Hitler's Regiment, Now Living Here'(quotes); *St Louis Star-Times*, 6 August 1941, 3, 'Man Who Served With Hitler Has His Name Changed'; information provided by Linda Hagen, St. Louis.
65. Horstmann, *Pasewalk*, 24–31; Köpf, 'Erblindung', 790.
66. Joachimsthaler, *Hitlers Weg*, 360.
67. Sauder, *Wilder*, 269 f., 382 f.
68. Life in places such as Ichenhausen had remained tolerant towards Jews and many Jews did not expect that the Nazis were there to stay. By the end of 1938, only one out of six Jews in Ichenhausen had emigrated abroad, less than half the national figure; see Haus der Bayerischen Geschichte, *Ichenhausen*, 29–33.
69. Sinz, 'Vierzig Jahre' 58; Evans, *Drittes Reich*, ii.2, 684; BHStA/IV, KSR/3051, Nr. 1086; YVD, entry for Julius Mannheimer; LBI, AR/ME 269, MS/Stoppleman.
70. See on this problem, Hoffmann, 'Verfolgung', 398.
71. Sinz, 'Vierzig Jahre', 69.; BHStA/IV, KSR/3063, Nr. 569; Haus der Bayerischen Geschichte, *Ichenhausen*, 116; Erlanger, *Schwabe*, 79; Römer, *Leidensweg*, 79; LBI, AR/ME 269, MS/Stoppleman.
72. BHStA/IV, KSR/3083, Nr. 761; YVD, entry for Siegfried Schönfeld; Stadtarchiv München, *Gedenkbuch*, i. 475, and ii. 457–8.
73. LBI, AR/ME 269, MS/Stoppleman; BHStA/IV, KSR/3051, Nr. 1086; YVD, entry for Julius Mannheimer; Stadtarchiv München, *Gedenkbuch*, ii. 41.
74. BHStA/IV, KSR/3074, Nr. 300; YVD, entry for Karl Goldschmidt; Scheffler and Schulle, *Erinnerung*, i, 83–7, 111, 115 (quote); United States Holocaust Memorial Museum, *Kovno*, 19, 70.
75. BHStA, KSR/3068, Nr. 1253, and KSR/3059, Nr. 1091; YVD, entries for Michael Früh and Julius Lindauer; Diefenbacher and Fischer-Pache, *Gedenkbuch*, 457 f.; Kuwalek, 'Station', 157–73.

76. BHStA/IV, KSR/3044, Nr. 1724, YVD, entries for Karl Leiter, Nathan Winschbacher, and Josef Heller; Diefenbacher/Fischer-Pache, *Gedenkbuch*, 460 f.; Haus der Bayerischen Geschichte, *Ichenhausen*, 33–4, 142.

77. YVD, entry for Arthur Dreyer and Gabriel Steiner; BHStA/IV, KSR/3038, Nr. 281 and KSR/3071, Nr. 1059; Kárný, 'Theresienstadt', 17–31; Schad, *Spionin*, 127.

78. Haus der Bayerischen Geschichte, *Ichenhausen*, 130–3; Sinz, 'Vierzig Jahre', 82–4; Stadtarchiv München, *Gedenkbuch*, i. 582; YVD, entry for Siegfried Heumann.

79. BHStA/IV, KSR/3063, Nr. 700; Institut Theresienstädter Initiative, *Gedenkbuch*, 61, 321–3; Stadtarchiv Augsburg, Städtische Polizei/Familienbögen/Meldekarten/1-3, Jakob Rafael; Ophir/Wiesemann, *Gemeinden*, 453.

80. Winter and Baggett, *Great War*, 399. For similar arguments, see the literature discussed in Smith, 'Culture de guerre'.

81. The argument advanced in Audoin-Rouzeau and Becker, *14–18*, 169 f. that the grassroot perpetrators of the Holocaust are likely to have been disproportionately old men who had seen service in the First World War is thus unlikely to be accurate.

82. Kiernan, *Blood*, 35 f.

83. See Smith, *Continuities*.

84. Ferguson, *War of the World*. See also Lieberman, *Fate*.

85. Mann, *Dark Side*, 221–8.

86. Neither the fact that some planners in Ober Ost thought about Central and Eastern Europe in racial terms (see Liulevicius, *War Land*) makes the German war at large into a racial war, nor did the plans of mainstream thinkers for a German controlled *Mitteleuropa* propose German settlement of the East at the cost of ethnic cleansing.

87. Fest, *Hitler*, 115.

88. Institut Theresienstädter Initiative, *Gedenkbuch*, 321–3.

89. Yelton, *Volkssturm*.

90. Quoted in Keegan, *Mask of Command*, 235.

91. SAM, Spruchkammerakten, Streicher, August.

92. Daumiller, *Schatten*, 82.

93. Information provided by Prince Leopold d'Arenberg.

94. Kershaw, *Hitler*, ii. 828.

EPILOGUE

1. NARA, M1270-Roll1, interrogation file on Amann.

2. Hale, *Press*, 123, 134.

3. NARA-RG238-M1019-2, interrogation, 5 November 1947.

4. SAM, StanW/I, 19038/1/Amann; PDM/10003/Amann, *Süddeutsche Zeitung*, 7 December 1948, 'Der Herr der Presse'.

5. SAM, StanW/I, 19038/1/Amann.
6. NARA, M1642-Roll 120, Frames 264–506, OSS file on Wiedemann's arrest.
7. NARA, M1270-Roll22, interrogation file on Wiedeman; NARA, RG65-Box105, note sent to the FBI Director, 28 September 1945.
8. NARA, M1270-Roll22, interrogation file on Wiedeman.
9. NARA, RG238-M-1019-79, Wiedemann's interrogations, 1946–7; NARA, M1270-Roll22, interrogation file on Wiedemann.
10. NARA, RG65-Box104, note sent to the FBI Director, July 1956; Schad, *Spionin*, 261 n. 252.
11. Machtan, *Hitler*, 98.
12. Quoted in Machtan, *Hitler*, 98.
13. Daumiller, *Schatten*, 94.
14. Quoted in Ernsting, *Frey*, 171.
15. Ibid. 177–88.
16. Large, *München*, 439.
17. BHStA/I, MK/45448/Solleder.
18. BHStA/IV, officer files, Nr. 6115/Wilhelm Diess, newspaper cuttings.
19. BHStA/IV, HS/2729 and HS/2731/Ludwig von Vallade.
20. *St Louis Post-Dispatch*, 4 August 1941, 5A, 'Refugee, Once in Hitler's Regiment, Now Living Here'.
21. *St Louis Post-Dispatch*, 8 June 2005, 'Looking for Gutmann'; information provided by Linda Hagen.
22. Information provided by James Fleischmann and Marvin Verman.
23. Email of Stadtarchiv Memmingen to the author, 19 June 2008.
24. Becher, *Mutation*.
25. Berman, 'Lessons', 38.
26. Ziblatt, 'Europe'.
27. See also Stern, 'Fear'; Stern, 'Lessons'.

POSTSCRIPT: HUGO GUTMANN'S STORY

1. Email from Rohn Grant.
2. This account of Gutmann's life is based on my interview with Beverly Grant, emails from Rohn and Karen Grant and Andrés Strauss, as well as hundreds of documents the Grants made available to me.
3. Letter, Henry to Howard and Beverly Grant, 11 June 1961.
4. Newspaper cutting from *Aufbau*, 22 December 1939, in the possession of Andrés Strauss.
5. Written account by Hugo Gutmann on his escape from Germany, October 1940.
6. Newspaper cutting from *Deutsche Zeitung*, 23 August 1958; Niekisch's recollection of the incident was published in Ernst Niekisch, *Gewagtes Leben* (Cologne, 1958), 282–3.

7. See e.g. http://h-net.msu.edu/cgi-bin/logbrowse.pl?trx=vx&list=h-holocaust&
   month=9805&week=c&msg=77Xx4NXhjKlaovs3uzLxIg&user=&pw=.
8. Letter, Arthur Langer to Henry G. Grant, 4 February 1960.
9. Undated account of Gutmann's life in Nazi Germany, written shortly after his
   arrival in Belgium.
10. Letter, Henry G. Grant to Joseph Drexel, 6 November 1946.
11. Letter, Franz Christ to Mary Tedi Grant, 21 January 1982.

Bibliography

Archives

Archiv der Ludwig-Maximilians-Universität, Munich (LMU)
   Studierendenkartei (Stud.-Kart.)
Archiv des Erzbistums München und Freising, Munich (AEM)
   Ordinariat, DK Buchberger
   Nachlass Faulhaber (=NL Faulhaber)
Archives Départementale du Nord, Lille (ADN)
   9R/129, 9R/505, 9R/515, 9R/1229: Affaires militaires, 1914–18
   8/Fi/26/13, Expo 13: Le Nord en guerre
   J/1362.2, J/1386.3: Documents entres par voie extraordinaire, 1914–18
Bayerische Staatsbibliothek, Munich
   Bildarchiv Hoffmann
Bayerisches Hauptstaatsarchiv, Abt. I, Munich (BHStA/I)
   Generaldirektion der Bayerischen Archive
   MK, files of the Bavarian Ministry of Cultural Affairs
   Sig/Personen
Bayerisches Haupstaatsarchiv, Abt. IV, Kriegsarchiv, Munich (BHStA/IV)
   Amtsbücherei, collections of the
   HS, personal papers (Handschriften)
   KSR, muster rolls (Kriegsstammrollen)
   MG/RD6, investigation files of the court martial of the 6th Bavarian Reserve
      Division (Militärgerichte, Gericht bei der 6. Reserve Division,
      Untersuchungsakten), uncatalogued
   Offiziersakten (officer files)
   RD6, files of the 6th Bavarian Reserve Division
   RIB12, files of the 12th Bavarian Infantry Brigade
   RIR16, files of the 16th Bavarian Reserve Infantry Regiment
   RIR17, files of the 17th Bavarian Reserve Infantry Regiment
   RIR20, files of the 20th Bavarian Reserve Infantry Regiment
   RWGrKdo 4, files of the Reichswehrgruppenkommando 4
Bundesarchiv Militärachiv, Freiburg (BMF)
   PH/3/534, files of the Armeeoberkommando 2
   PH/7/27, files of the Stellvertretendes Generalkommando des Gardekorps
Devon County Council Library, *The Western Times*

Evangelisches Pfarramt Feldkirchen, Feldkirchen (EPF)
    Collection of letters from the front
Institut für Zeitgeschichte, Munich (IFZ)
    ED147, Sammlung Jäckel/Kühn
    F/19/6, Hitlers Militärpapiere
    MA-732, NSDAP/Hauptarchiv, Hitler als Soldat
    ZS/1751
Landeskirchliches Archiv der Evangelischen Landeskirche von Bayern, Nuremberg
    (LAELKB)
    OKM/2340, Berichte der Feldgeistlichen, 1. Weltkrieg
    LKR/50001, Karl Frobenius.
    LKR/50118, Hermann Kornacher
    LKR/50088, Robert Hell
    LKR, files of the Landeskirchenrat
    PA/Theol/1327, Daumiller
    PA/Theol, Personalakten, Theologen
    Personen/XVIII, 43a, Wilhelm Stählin
Leo Baeck Institute, New York City (LBI)
    AR/25349/359197, war diary of Justin Fleischmann
    AR/ME 269, typscript MS, Gerdy Stoppleman, 'Lest You Forget'
National Archives of the United States of America, College Park, Md. (NARA),
    BDC, A3343/SSO, Berlin Document Center, Microfilm, SS Officers' Service
    Records
    BDC, NSDAP membership files
    RG65, Records of the Federal Bureau of Investigation, World War II, FBI
        Headquarters
    RG165, Records of the War Department, General and Special Staffs (War
        College Division and War Plans Division—Army War College Historical
        Section),German Military Records Relating to World War I
    RG226, M-1642, Records of the OSS Washington Director's Office, Roll123
    RG238, War Crimes Record Collection, Record of the US Nuremberg War
        Crimes Trials Interrogations, 1946-9, M-1019-2, M-1019-79
    RG242, Foreign Records Seized Collection: Captured German Records filmed
        at Berlin (Hoover), T-581-1A, T-581-3, T-581-52
    M1270, Interrogation records prepared for war crimes proceedings at
        Nuremberg
    M1642, Records of the Office of Strategic Services (OSS) Washington,
        Director's Office
Provinzarchiv der Bayerischen Kapuziner, Munich (PBK)
    II/9/Facs.3m, Kriegsberichte von Pater Norbert Stumpf
    X/151/113-855, Personalakt, Norbert Stumpf
Royal Norfolk Regimental Museum, Norwich
    15th Brigade, War Diary

Staatsarchiv München (SAM)
  AG, files of the Amtsgericht München
  NSDAP, files of the NSDAP
  PDM, files of the Polizeidirektion München
  StanW, files of the Staatsanwaltschaften München I and II
  Wiedergutmachungsakten, Anträge
Stadtarchiv Augsburg, Städtische Polizei/Familienbögen/Meldekarten
Stadtarchiv Braunschweig (SB)
  Z2, *Volksfreund*
Stadtarchiv München (SM)
  Bürgermeister/Rat
  Historisches Bildarchiv
  Kulturamt
  Zeitungsausschnittssammlung-Personen (ZAP)
Yad Vashem, Jerusalem
  The Central Database of Shoah Victims' Names (YVD)
  Documents Archive

In the possession of the author
  postcards sent by members of RIR 16 (Alfons Erlacher, Ferdinand Pösl)
Private papers of Ernst Cambensy, Justin Fleischmann, Hugo Gutmann, Hans
  Ostermünchner, Alois Schnelldorfer, and Jakob Weiß, in the possession of
  their families
Interviews/information provided by: Prince Leopold d'Arenberg, Ekkehard
  Müller (Anton von Tubeuf), Ursula Paszkowski (Wiedemann), Manfred von
  Tubeuf, Wolo von Tubeuf, Katharina Weiß, Linda Hagen (Gutmann), James
  Fleischmann, Hans (grandson of Hans Ostermünchner), Marvin Verman
  (Fleischmann) Beverley, Karen, and Rohn Grant (Gutmann), Ernst Richter
  (Diess), and Andre's Strauss (Gutmann)
Email of Stadtarchiv Memmingen to the author.

Published Material
Aggett, W. J. P., *The Bloody Eleventh: History of The Devonshire Regiment*; vol. ii:
  1815–1914 (Exeter, 1994).
Albrecht, Willy, *Landtag und Regierung in Bayern am Vorabend der Revolution von
  1918* (Berlin, 1968).
Aly, Götz, *Hitler's Beneficiaries: Plunder, Racial War, and the Nazi Welfare State*
  (New York, 2005).
Amann, Max, *Ein Leben für Führer und Volk* (Berlin, 1941).
Angermair, Elisabeth, 'Eine selbstbewußte Minderheit', in Richard Bauer and
  Michael Brenner (eds), *Jüdisches München: Vom Mittelalter bis zur Gegenwart*
  (Munich, 2006), 110–36.

Armin, Otto, *Die Juden im Heer: Eine statistische Untersuchung nach amtlichen Quellen* (Munich, 1919).

Arnsberg, Paul, *Die jüdischen Gemeinden in Hessen: Anfang, Untergang, Neubeginn*, 2 vols (Darmstadt, 1971).

Ashworth, Tony, *Trench Warfare 1914–1918: The Live and Let Live System* (London, 1980).

Asprey, Robert, *The German High Command at War: Hindenburg and Ludendorff Conduct World War I* (New York, 1991).

Atkinson, C. T., *The Devonshire Regiment, 1914–1918* (London, 1926).

Atrocités allemandes à Lille: Trois témoignages de députés socialistes, Les (Paris, 1919).

Audoin-Rouzeau, Stéphane, *L'Enfant de l'ennemi 1914–1918: Violence, avortement, infanticide pendant la grande guerre* (Paris, 1995).

—— *La guerre des enfants 1914–1918: Essai d'histoire culturelle* (Paris, 1993).

—— and Becker, Ammette, *14–18: Understanding the Great War* (New York, 2003).

Axelrod, Robert, *The Evolution of Cooperation* (New York, 1984).

Ay, Karl-Ludwig, *Die Entstehung einer Revolution: Die Volksstimmung in Bayern während des Ersten Weltkrieges* (Berlin, 1968).

Badisches Ministerium des Kultus und Unterrichts (ed.), *Badische Schulstatistik: Die Hochschulen*, 2 vols (Karlsruhe, 1912).

Baedeker's Northern France from Belgium and the English Channel to the Loire Excluding Paris and its Environs: Handbook for Travellers, 5th edn (Leipzig, 1909).

Baligand, Maximilian von, 'Ende wie Anfang: "Regiment List"', in Solleder, *Westfront*, 328–38.

—— 'Heimwärts', in Solleder, *Westfront*, 344–6.

Bauer, Reinhard, Gerstenberg, Günther, and Peschel, Wolfgang (eds), *Im Dunst aus Bier, Rauch und Volk: Arbeit und Volk in München von 1840 bis 1945* (Munich, 1989).

Bauer, Richard *et al.*, 'Einführung', in Bauer *et al.* (eds), *München—'Haupstadt der Bewegung': Bayerns Metropole und der Nationalsozialismus* (Munich, 2002), 11–14.

—— *et al.* (eds), *München—'Haupstadt der Bewegung': Bayerns Metropole und der Nationalsozialismus* (Munich, 2002).

Baumeister, Martin, *Kriegstheater: Großstadt, Front und Massenkultur 1914–1918* (Essen, 2005).

Beaumont, Joan, 'Australia's War', in Beaumont (ed.), *Australia's War, 1914–18* (St Leonards, NSW, 1995), 1–34.

Beck, Hermann, *The Fateful Alliance: German Conservatives and Nazis in 1933* (New York, 2008).

Becker, Annette, *Oubliés de la Grande Guerre: Humanitaire et culture de guerre* (Paris, 1995).

—— 'Life in an Occupied Zone: Lille, Roubaix, Tourcoing', in Cecil and Liddle, *Armageddon*, 630–41.

—— *War and Faith: The Religious Imagination in France 1914–1930* (Oxford, 1998 (1994)).

Becker, Jean-Jacques, *The Great War and the French People* (Leamington Spa, 1985).

—— *La France en guerre, 1914–1918: la grande mutation* (Brussels, 1988).

Beckett, Ian, *Ypres: The First Battle, 1914* (Harlow, 2004).

Bendick, Rainer, *Kriegserwartung und Kriegserfahrung: Der Erste Weltkrieg in deutschen und französischen Schulgeschichtsbüchern (1900–1939/45)* (Pfaffenweiler, 1999).

Benz, Wolfgang, 'Konsilidierung und Konsenz 1934–1939', in Martin Broszat and Norbert Frei (eds), *Das Dritte Reich im Überblick* (Munich, 1999), 48–64.

Berghahn, Volker, *Europe in the Era of Two World Wars: From Militarism and Genocide to Civil Society, 1900–1950* (Princeton, 2006).

Bergmann, Werner, and Wetzel, Juliane, 'Antisemitismus im Ersten und Zweiten Weltkrieg: Ein Forschungsüberblick', in Bruno Thoß and Hans-Erich Volkmann (eds), *Erster Weltkrieg. Zweiter Weltkrieg: Ein Vergleich* (Paderborn, 2002), 437–69.

Berman, Sheri, 'Civil Society and the Collapse of the Weimar Republic', *World Politics* 49/3 (1997), 401–29.

—— *The Primacy of Politics: Social Democracy and the Making of Europe's Twentieth Century* (New York, 2006).

—— 'How Democracies Emerge: Lessons from Europe', *Journal of Democracy*, 18/1 (2007), 28–41.

Berneuther, August, 'Die letzte Patrouille an der Marne', in Solleder, *Westfront*, 325–7.

Berton, Pierre, *Vimy* (Toronto, 1987).

Bessel, Richard, *Germany after the First World War* (Oxford, 1993).

—— *Nazism and War* (London, 2004).

Bestle, Otto, 'Die Engländer sind im Graben', in Solleder, *Westfront*, 142–5.

Beumelburg, Werner, *Flandern 1917* (Oldenburg, 1928).

—— *Ypern 1914* (Oldenburg, 1925).

Birnbaum, Immanuel, 'Juden in der Münchener Räterepublik', in Hans Lamm, *Vergangene Tage: Jüdische Kultur in München* (Munich, 1982), 301–3.

Blersch, Adam, 'Großkampftage der 2. Kompanie an der Somme', in Solleder, *Westfront*, 256–60.

Böhm, Anton, 'Erinnerungen an einen beliebten Gymnasiallehrer: Dr. Ernst Tegethoff', *Die Oberpfalz*, 96/5 (2008), 311–18.

Bourke, Joanna, *An Intimate History of Killing: Face-to-Face Killing in Twentieth Century Warfare* (London, 1999).

—— *Fear: A Cultural History* (London, 2005).

—— *Rape: Sex, Violence, History* (London, 2007).

Brandmayer, Balthasar, *Meldegänger Hitler 1914–18*, 2nd edn (Munich, 1933).

—— *Mit Hitler: Meldegänger 1914–18*, 9th edn (Ueberlingen, 1940).

Bridger, Geoff, *The Battle of Neuve Chapelle* (Barnsley, 2000).

'Brief eines Kriegsfreiwilligen vom Regiment List', in Siegfried Radner (ed.), *Jahrbuch für die evangelisch-lutherische Landeskirche Bayerns, 1915* (Munich, 1915), 67–73.

Brocks, Christine, *Die bunte Welt des Krieges: Bildpostkarten aus dem Ersten Weltkrieg 1914–1918* (Essen, 2008).

Brown, Malcolm, 'Introduction', in Marc Ferro *et al.*, *Meeting in No Man's Land: Christmas 1914 and Fraternization in the Great War* (London, 2007; French edn 2005), 1–8.

—— , and Seaton, Shirley, *Christmas Truce* (New York, 1984).

Browning, Christopher, 'German Killers: Behavior and Motivation in the Light of New Evidence', in Browning, *Nazi Policy, Jewish Workers, German Killers* (Cambridge, 2000), 142–69.

Bruner, Fredrick Dale, *Matthew: A Commentary* (Grand Rapids, Mich., 2004).

Brutscher, H., *München Weltreiseziel* (Munich, 1936).

Bucholz, Arden, review of Isabel Hull's *Absolute Destruction*, *Journal of Modern History*, 79 (2007), 208–10.

Bullock, Alan, *Hitler: A Study in Tyranny* (New York, 1962).

Cecil, Hugh, and Liddle, Peter (eds), *Facing Armageddon: The First World War Experienced* (London, 1996).

Chickering, Roger, *Imperial Germany and the Great War, 1914–1918* (Cambridge, 2nd edn, 2004).

—— review of *Absolute Destruction*, in *German History*, 24/1 (2006), 138–9.

—— *The Great War and Urban Life in Germany: Freiburg, 1914–1918* (Cambridge, 2007).

—— and Förster, Stig (eds), *Great War, Total War: Combat and Mobilization on the Western Front, 1914–1918* (Cambridge, 2000).

Childers, Thomas, *The Nazi Voter: The Social Foundations of Fascism in Germany, 1919–1933* (Chapel Hill, NC, 1983).

Christie, N. M., *For King & Empire: The Canadians at Vimy, April 1917* (Ottawa, 2002).

Citino, Robert, *The German Way of War: From the Thirty Years' War to the Third Reich* (Lawrence, Kan., 2005).

Clark, Christopher, *Iron Kingdom: The Rise and Downfall of Prussia, 1600–1947* (Cambridge, Mass., 2006).

Cobb, Paul, *Fromelles 1916* (Stroud, 2007).

Cobb, Richard, *French and Germans, Germans and French: A Personal Interpretation of France under Two Occupations* (Hanover, NH, 1983).

Commonwealth War Graves Commission, The, *The War Dead of the Commonwealth: Aubers Ridge British Cemetery* (London, repr., 2002).

Costa, Dora, and Kahn, Matthew, 'Deserters, Social Norms, and Migration', *Journal of Law and Economics*, 50 (May 2007), 323–53.

Cowley, Robert, 'The Somme: The last 140 Days', in Cowley (ed.), *The Great War: Perspectives on the First World War* (New York, 1994), 339–62.

Crofton, Morgan, *Massacre of the Innocents: The Crofton Diaries, Ypres 1914–1915* (Thrupp, 2004).

Cron, Hermann, *Die Organisation des deutschen Heeres im Weltkriege* (Berlin, 1923).

—— *Geschichte des deutschen Heeres im Weltkrieges, 1914–1918* (Osnabrück, 1990 (1937)).

Daumiller, Oscar, *Geführt im Schatten Zweier Kriege* (Munich, 1961).

Davidson, Eugene, *The Making of Adolf Hitler* (New York, 1977).

Davies, Norman, *Europe: A History* (New York, 1998 (1996)).

Davis, Belinda, *Home Fires Burning: Food, Politics, and Everyday Life in World War I: Berlin* (Chapel Hill, NC, 2000).

Dehn, Georg, 'Albert Weisgerber', in Solleder, *Westfront*, 148–9.

Deist, Wilhelm, 'Verdeckter Militärstreik im Kriegsjahr 1918?', in Wolfram Wette (ed.), *Der Krieg des kleinen Mannes: Eine Militärgeschichte von unten* (Munich, 1992), 146–67.

—— (comp.), *Militär und Innenpolitik im Weltkrieg, 1914–1918*, 2 vols (Düsseldorf, 1970).

—— 'The German Army, the Authoritarian Nation-State and Total War', in Horne, *State*, 160–72.

Dellmensingen, Konrad Krafft von, and Feeser, Friedrichfranz, *Das Bayernbuch vom Weltkriege 1914–1918: Ein Volksbuch*, vol. i (Stuttgart, 1930).

Diefenbacher, Michael, and Fischer-Pache, Wiltrud (eds), *Gedenkbuch für die Nürnberger Opfer der Schoa* (Nuremberg, 1998).

Dieß, Wilhelm, 'Unteroffizier Geiger', in Solleder, *Westfront*, 145–8.

Doughty, Robert, *Pyrrhic Victory: French Strategy and Operations in the Great War* (Cambridge, Mass., 2005).

Drexel, Joseph, *Die Reise nach Mauthausen: Ein Bericht* (Nuremberg, 1961).

Duffy, Christopher, *Through German Eyes: The British and the Somme 1916* (London, 2006).

Duménil, Anne, 'Soldier's Suffering and Military Justice in the German Army of the Great War', in Jenny Macleod and Pierre Purseigle (eds), *Uncovered Fields: Perspectives in First World War Studies* (Leiden, 2004), 43–60.

Dunker, Ulrich, *Der Reichsbund jüdischer Frontsoldaten, 1919–1938: Geschichte eines jüdischen Abwehrvereins* (Düsseldorf, 1977).

Eichelsdörfer, Georg, 'Das Gefecht bei Fromelles', in Solleder, *Westfront*, 130–41.

—— 'Sturm auf das beilförmige Waldstück', in Solleder, *Westfront*, 73–6.

—— 'Die Schlacht bei Neuve Chapelle', in Solleder, *Westfront*, 106–13.

Eksteins, Modris, *Rites of Spring: The Great War and the Birth of the Modern Age* (Toronto, 1989).

Encyclopædia Britannica Online

Engelstein, Laura, ' "A Belgium of Our Own"—The Sack of Russian Kalisz, August 1914' (forthcoming, *Kritika*, 2009).

Englmann, Felicia, 'Adolf Hitlers Kriegsbild', *P.M. History Spezial: 850 Jahre München* (2008), 80–1.

Erhard, H., *Aus Städten und Schlössern Nordfrankreichs* (Bapaume, 1915).

Erinnerungen an das List Regiment 1914–1918 (Sonderabdruck aus 'Das Bayernland') (Munich, 1920) (BHStA/IV, Amtsbücherei, Nr. 3653).

Erlanger, Arnold, *Ein Schwabe überlebt Auschwitz* (Augsburger, 2002).

Ernsting, Stefan, *Der phantastische Rebell Alexander Moritz Frey oder Hitler schießt dramatisch in die Luft* (Zurich, 2007).

'Ersten Auszeichnungen, Die', in *List Regiment*, 47–8.

Evans, Martin Marix, *Battles of World War I* (Ramsbury, 2004).

Evans, Richard, *Das Dritte Reich*, 3 vols (Munich, 2004–9).

—— *The Third Reich at War, 1939–1945* (London, 2008).

Fabian, Gary, 'Vale Volunteer Arnold Erlanger, 22/7/1916–11/2/2007', *Centre News* [*of the Jewish Holocaust Centre, Elsternwick, Victoria, Australia*], 29/1 (April 2007), 19.

Ferguson, Niall, 'Public Finance and National Security: The Domestic Origins of the First World War Revisited', *Past and Present*, 142 (1994), 141–68.

—— *The Pity of War* (London, 1998).

—— 'Prisoner Taking and Prisoner Killing in the Age of Total War: Towards a Political Economy of Military Defeat', *War in History*, 11/1 (2004), 34–78.

—— *The War of the World: Twentieth-Century Conflict and the Descent of the West* (New York, 2006).

Fest, Joachim, *Hitler* (Berlin, 1973).

Figes, Orlando, *A People's Tragedy: The Russian Revolution, 1891–1924* (London, 1996).

Fischer, Conan, *Stormtroopers: A Social, Economic and Ideological Analysis, 1929–35* (London, 1983).

—— ' "A Very German Revolution"? The Post-1918 Settlement Re-Evaluated', *German Historical Institute London Bulletin*, 27/2 (November 2006), 6–32.

Fischer, Doris, *Die Münchner Zensurstelle während des Ersten Weltkrieges: Alfons Falkner von Sonnenburg als Pressereferent im Bayerischen Kriegsministerium in den Jahren 1914 bis 1918/19* (Munich, 1973).

Flade, Roland, 'Ländliches Judentum in Unterfranken im 20. Jahrhundert', in Zweckverband Fränkische-Schweiz-Museum (ed.), *Jüdische Landgemeinden in Franken* (Bayreuth, 1987), 47–50.

'Flanders', *Encyclopædia Britannica Online*, accessed 10 October 2008.

Foerster, F. W., 'Der Krieg und die sexuelle Frage', in *Deutscher März: Zweite Liebesgabe deutscher Hochschüler* (Kassel, 1915), 114–19.

Foley, Robert, *German Strategy and the Path to Verdun: Erich von Falkenhayn and the Development of Attrition, 1870–1916* (Cambridge, 2005).

Föllmer, Moritz, 'Der Feind im Salon: Eliten, Besatzung und nationale Identität in Nordfrankreich und Westdeutschland 1914–1930', *Militärgeschichtliche Zeitschrift*, 61 (2002), 1–14.

—— and Graf, Rüdiger (eds), *Die 'Krise' der Weimarer Republik: Zur Kritik eines Deutungsmusters* (Frankfurt, 2005).

Freeman, Bill, and Nielsen, Richard, *Far From Home: Canadians in the First World War* (Whitby, Ont., n.d.).

Frei, Norbert, 'People's Community and War: Hitler's Popular Support', in Hans Mommsen (ed.), *The Third Reich between Vision and Reality* (Oxford, 2001), 59–77.

French, David, *Military Identities: The Regimental System, the British Army, and the British People, c.1870–2000* (Oxford, 2005).

Freund, Ismar, *Zwei Aufsätze über die Ostjuden; Sonderabdruck aus der Zeitung der 10. Armee (Wilna), Nr. 23 u. 25* (Berlin, 1916).

Frey, Rupert, 'Weihnachten im Felde', in Solleder, *Westfront*, 94–6.

Fritzsche, Peter, *Germans into Nazis* (Cambridge, Mass., 1998).

—— *Wie aus Deutschen Nazis wurden* (Zurich, 1999).

—— *Life and Death in the Third Reich* (Cambridge, Mass., 2008).

Fromkin, David, *Europe's Last Summer: Who Started the Great War in 1914?* (New York, 2005 (2004)).

Fry, Stephen, *Making History: A Novel* (New York, 1997).

Gehring, Egid, 'Am Schicksalsstrom Deutschlands', in Solleder, *Westfront*, 316–25.

Gellately, Robert, *Backing Hitler: Consent and Coercion in Nazi Germany* (Oxford, 2001).

Geyer, Martin, *Verkehrte Welt: Revolution, Inflation und Moderne, München 1914–1924* (Göttingen, 1998).

Geyer, Michael, 'Vom massenhaften Tötungshandeln, oder: Wie die Deutschen das Krieg-Machen lernten', in Gleichmann and Kühne, *Massenhaftes Töten*, 105–42.

—— 'Rückzug und Zerstörung 1917', in Gerhard Hirschfeld, Gerd Krumeich, and Irina Renz (eds), *Die Deutschen an der Somme, 1914–1918: Krieg, Besatzung, Verbrannte Erde* (Essen, 2006), 163–79.

Gilbert, Martin, *The Routledge Atlas of Jewish History*, 5th edn (London, 1993 (1969)).

—— *The First World War: A Complete History* (London, 2004).

—— *The Somme: Heroism and Horror in the First World War* (New York, 2006).

Gildea, Robert, *Marianne in Chains: Daily Life in the Heart of France during the German Occupation* (New York, 2002).

Gleichmann, Peter, and Kühne, Thomas (eds), *Massenhaftes Töten: Kriege und Genozide im 20. Jahrhundert* (Essen, 2004).

Granovetter, Mark, 'Threshold Models of Collective Behavior', *American Journal of Sociology*, 83 (1978), 1420–2.

Grayzel, Susan, *Women's Identities at War: Gender, Motherhood, and Politics in Britain and France during the First World War* (Chapel Hill, NC, 1999).

—— ' "The Soul of Soldiers": Civilians under Fire in First World War France', *Journal of Modern History*, 78 (2006), 588–622.

Grebner, Werner, *Der Gefreite Adolf Hitler 1914–1920* (Graz, 2008).

Gregor, Neil, *Nazism* (Oxford, 2000).

Gregory, Adrian, *The Last Great War: British Society and the First World War* (Cambridge, 2008).

Grossman, Dave, *On Killing: The Psychological Cost of Learning to Kill in War and Society* (Boston, 1995).

Gruchmann, Lothar, and Weber, Reinhard (eds), *Der Hitler-Prozess: Wortlaut der Hauptverhandlung vor dem Volksgericht München*, i (Munich, 1997).

Gudmundsson, Bruce, *Stormtroop Tactics: Innovation in the Germany Army, 1914–1918* (New York, 1989).

Hale, Oron James, *The Captive Press in the Third Reich* (Princeton, 1964).

Hamann, Brigitte, *Hitlers Wien: Lehrjahre eines Diktators* (Munich, 1996).

Hank, Sabine, and Simon, Hermann (eds), *Feldpostbriefe Jüdischer Soldaten 1914–1918*, 2 vols (Teetz, 2002).

Harari, Yuval Noah, *The Ultimate Experience: Battlefield Revelations and the Making of Modern War Culture, 1450–2000* (New York, 2008).

Haugg, August, *Deutsche Heraus!* (Munich, 1924).

—— 'Die Feuertaufe der 2. Kompagnie', in Solleder, *Westfront*, 55–7.

Haus der Bayerischen Geschichte, *Juden auf dem Lande: Beispiel Ichenhausen* (Munich, 1991).

Hausenstein, Wilhelm, *Albert Weisgerber: Ein Gedenkbuch* (Munich, 1918).

Heinz, Heinz A., *Germany's Hitler* (London, 1934).

Hennig, Diethard, *Johannes Hoffmann: Sozialdemokrat und Bayerischer Ministerpräsident* (Munich, 1990).

Hepp, Michael (ed.), *Die Ausbürgerung deutscher Staatsangehöriger 1933-45 nach den im Reichsanzeiger veröffentlichten Listen*, 2 vols (Munich, 1985).

Herbert, Ulrich, *Best: Biographische Studien über Radikalismus, Weltanschauung und Vernunft, 1903–1989* (Bonn, 1996).

Hettling, Manfred, and Jeismann, Michael, 'Der Weltkrieg als Epos. Philipp Witkops "Kriegsbriefe gefallener Studenten"', in Gerhard Hirschfeld *et al.*, *Keiner fühlt sich mehr als Mensch: Erlebnis und Wirkung des Ersten Weltkrieges* (Essen, 1993), 175–98.

Hewett, Waterman (ed.), *A German Reader* (London, 1899).

Hirschfeld, Gerhard, 'Die Somme-Schlacht von 1916', in Gerhard Hirschfeld, Gerd Krumeich, and Irina Renz (eds), *Die Deutschen an der Somme, 1914–1918: Krieg, Besatzung, Verbrannte Erde* (Essen, 2006), 79–89.

—— 'Der Führer spricht vom Krieg—Der Erste Weltkrieg in den Reden Adolf Hitlers' (unpublished paper).

Historisches Lexikon Bayern, www.historisches-lexikon-bayerns.de

Hitler, Adolf, *Mein Kampf* (*MK*), trans. James Murphy (London, 1942).

Hoffmann, Christhard, 'Between Integration and Rejection: The Jewish Community in Germany, 1914–1918', in Horne, *State*, 89–104.

—— 'Verfolgung und Alltagsleben der Landjuden im nationalsozialistischen Deutschland', in Monika Richarz and Reinhard Rürup (eds), *Jüdisches Leben auf dem Lande* (Tübingen, 1997), 373–98.

Hoffmann, Heinrich, *Mit Hitler im Westen* (Munich, 1940).

Hohenlohe, Franz zu, *Stephanie: Das Leben meiner Mutter* (Vienna, 1991).

Holmes, Richard, *The Western Front* (London, 1999).

Horne, John, 'Remobilizing for "Total War": France and Britain, 1917–1918', in Horne, *State*, 195–2 11.

—— (ed.), *State, Society, and Mobilization in Europe during the First World War* (Cambridge, 1997).

—— 'War Between Soldiers and Enemy Civilians, 1914–1915', in Chickering and Förster, *Total War*, 153–68.

—— and Kramer, Alan, *German Atrocities, 1914: A History of Denial* (New Haven, 2001).

Horstmann, Bernhard, *Hitler in Pasewalk: Die Hypnose und ihre Folgen* (Düsseldorf, 2004).

Hull, Isabel, *Absolute Destruction: Military Culture and the Practices of War in Imperial Germany* (Ithaca, NY, 2005).

Ingenlath, Markus, *Mentale Aufrüstung in Frankreich und Deutschland vor dem Ersten Weltkrieg* (Frankfurt, 1998).

Institut Theresienstädter Initiative (ed.), *Theresienstädter Gedenkbuch: Die Opfer der Judentransporte aus Deutschland nach Theresienstadt* (Prague, 2000).

Jablonsky, David, 'The Paradox of Duality: Adolf Hitler and the Concept of Military Surprise', in Michael Handel (ed.), *Leaders and Intelligence* (London, 1989), 55–117.

Jäckel, Eberhard, and Kuhn, Axel (eds), *Hitler: Sämtliche Aufzeichnungen, 1905–1924* (Stuttgart, 1980).

—— 'Neue Erkenntnisse zur Fälschung von Hitler-Dokumenten', *Vierteljahrshefte für Zeitgeschichte*, 32 (1984), 163–4.

Jahr, Christoph, *Gewöhnliche Soldaten: Desertion und Deserteure im deutschen und britischen Heer 1914–1918* (Göttingen, 1998).

James, Harold, *Europe Reborn: A History, 1914–2000* (Harlow, 2003).

Jeismann, Michael, *Das Vaterland der Feinde: Studien zum nationalen Feindbegriff und Selbstverständnis in Deutschland und Frankreich, 1792–1918* (Stuttgart, 1992).

Jesse, Horst, *Die Geschichte der Evangelisch-Lutherischen Kirchengemeinden in München und Umgebung, 1510–1990* (Neuendettelsau, 1994).

Jewish Year Book, 1911 (London, 1912).

Joachimsthaler, Anton, *Hitlers Weg begann in München, 1913–1923* (Munich, 2000).

Johnson, Eric, and Reuband, Karl-Heinz, *What We Knew: Terror, Mass Murder, and Everyday Life in Nazi Germany* (Cambridge, Mass., 2006).

Jones, Heather, 'Encountering the "Enemy": Prisoner of War Transport and the Development of War Cultures in 1914', in Purseigle, *Warfare*, 133–62.

Jowitt, Ken, *New World Disorder: The Leninist Extinction* (Berkeley, 1993).

Jürgs, Michael, *Der kleine Frieden im Großen Krieg: Westfront 1914* (Munich, 2003).

'Kaisers Dank', in *List Regiment*, 46–7.

Kalyvas, Stathis, *The Logic of Violence in Civil War* (Cambridge, 2006).

Karl, Michaela, *Die Münchener Räterepublik: Porträts einer Revolution* (Düsseldorf, 2008).

Kárný, Miroslav, 'Theresienstadt 1941–1915', in Institut Theresienstädter Initiative, *Gedenkbuch*, 15–40.

Keegan, John, *The Mask of Command* (New York, 1987).

—— *The First World War* (London, 1998).

Kennan, George, *The Decline of Bismarck's European Order: Franco-Russian Relations, 1875–1890* (Princeton, 1979).

Kennedy, Paul, *The Rise of the Anglo-German Antagonism 1860–1914* (London, 1980).

—— *The Rise and Fall of the Great Powers, 1500–2000* (London, 1988).

Kershaw, Ian, 'Antisemitismus und Volksmeinung: Reaktionen auf die Judenverfolgung', in Martin Broszat and Elke Fröhlich (eds), *Bayern in der NS-Zeit*, ii (Munich, 1979).

Kershaw, Ian, *Hitler*, vol. i: *1889–1936: Hubris* (New York, 1999); vol. ii: *1936–1945, Nemesis* (London, 2000).

—— *The Nazi Dictatorship: Problems and Perspectives of Interpretation*, 4th edn (London, 2000).

Kiernan, Ben, *Blood and Soil: A World History of Genocide and Extermination* (New Haven, 2007).

Kitchen, Martin, *The Silent Dictatorship: The Politics of the German High Command under Hindenburg and Ludendorff* (London, 1976).

—— *The German Offensives of 1918* (Stroud, 2001).

Klemperer, Victor, *I Shall Bear Witness: The Diaries of Victor Klemperer 1933–41* (London, 1998).

Kluge, Ulrich, *Die Weimarer Republik* (Paderborn, 2006).

Knies, Hans-Ulrich, 'Arbeiterbewegung und Revolution im Wuppertal', in Reinhard Rürup (ed.), *Arbeiter- und Soldatenräte im rheinisch-westfälischen Industriegebiet: Studien zur Geschichte der Revolution 1918/19* (Wuppertal, 1975), 83–153.

Koch-Hillebrecht, Manfred, *Hitler—Ein Sohn des Krieges* (Munich, 2003).

Kolb, Eberhard, *Die Weimarer Republik*, 4th edn (Munich, 1998).

Köpf, Gerhard, 'Hitlers psychogene Erblindung: Geschichte einer Krankenakte', *Nervenheilkunde: Zeitschrift für interdisziplinäre Forschung*, 9 (2005), 783–90.

Kramer, Alan, *Dynamic of Destruction: Culture and Mass Killing in the First World War* (Oxford, 2007).

Kraus, Jürgen (ed.), *Die deutsche Armee im 1. Weltkrieg: Uniformierung und Ausrüstung—1914 bis 1918* (Vienna, 2004).

Krumeich, Gerd, 'Die deutsche Erinnerung an die Somme', in Gerhard Hirschfeld, Gerd Krumeich, and Irina Renz (eds), *Die Deutschen an der Somme, 1914–1918: Krieg, Besatzung, Verbrannte Erde* (Essen, 2006), 231–46.

Kühne, Thomas, 'Massen-Töten: Diskurse und Praktiken der kriegerischen und genozidalen Gewalt im 20. Jahrhundert', in Gleichmann and Kühne, *Massenhaftes Töten*, 11–52.

—— *Kameradschaft: Die Soldaten des nationalsozialistischen Krieges und das 20. Jahrhundert* (Göttingen, 2006).

Kulka, Otto Dov, and Jäckel, Eberhard (eds), *Die Juden in den geheimen NS-Stimmungsberichten 1933–1945* (Düsseldorf, 2004), supplementary CD-Rom.

Kumsteller, Bernhard, *et al.* (eds), *Geschichtsbuch für die deutsche Jugend, Klasse 1* (Leipzig, 1941).

Kuran, Timur, *Private Truth, Public Lies: The Social Consequences of Preference Falsification* (Cambridge, Mass., 1995).

Kurlander, Eric, *Living with Hitler: Liberal Democrats in the Third Reich* (New Haven, 2009).

Kuwalek, Robert, 'Die letzte Station vor der Vernichtung: Das Durchganslager in Izbica', in Andrea Löw *et al.* (eds), *Deutsche, Juden, Polen: Geschichte einer wechselvollen Beziehung im 20. Jahrhundert* (Frankfurt am Main, 2004), 157–73.

Lamplugh, Lois, *A Shadowed Man: Henry Williamson, 1895–1977* (Springside, 1990).

Large, David Clay, *Hitlers München: Aufstieg und Fall der Haupstadt der Bewegung* (Munich, 1998).

Launay, Jacques de, *Hitler en Flandres* (Strombeek, 1975).

Lechner, Silvester, *Synagoge Ichenhausen: Festschrift zur Eröffnung der ehemaligen Synagoge von Ichenhausen* (Günzburg, 1987).

Lewis, David, *The Men who Invented Hitler* (London, 2003).

Lieberman, Benjamin, *Terrible Fate: Ethnic Cleansing in the Making of Modern Europe* (Chicago, 2006).

Linder, Ann, *Princes of the Trenches: Narrating the German Experience of the First World War* (Columbia, SC, 1996).

Lindsay, Patrick, *Fromelles: The Story of Australia's Darkest Day* (Prahran, 2007).

Lipkes, Jeff, *Rehearsals: The German Army in Belgium, August 1914* (Leuven, 2007).

Lipp, Anne, *Meinungslenkung im Krieg: Kriegserfahrungen deutscher Soldaten und ihre Deutung, 1914–1918* (Göttingen, 2003).

List Regiment, no editor given (no place, *c*.1915) (= BHStA/IV, Amtsbücherei, Nr. 3651).

Liulevicius, Vejas Gabriel, *War Land on the Eastern Front: Culture, National Identity, and German Occupation in World War I* (Cambridge, 2000).

Longerich, Peter, *Heinrich Himmler: Biographie* (Munich, 2008).

McCarthy, Helen, *Citizen Soldiers: The Liverpool Territorials in the First World War* (Cambridge, 2005).

McClelland, J. S., *A History of Western Political Thought* (London, 1996).

Machtan, Lothar, *The Hidden Hitler* (New York, 2001).

McKale, Donald, *The Nazi Party Courts: Hitler's Management of Conflict in his Movement, 1921–1945* (Lawrence, Kan., 1974).

McPhail, Helen, *The Long Silence: Civilian Life under the German Occupation of Northern France 1914–1918* (London, 2001).

Mann, Michael, *The Dark Side of Democracy: Explaining Ethnic Cleansing* (Cambridge, 2004).

Mann, Thomas, *Tristan: Sechs Novellen* (Berlin, 1903).

Margalit, Avishai, 'Sectarianism', *Dissent* (Winter 2008) 37–46.

Maser, Werner, *Adolf Hitler: Legende, Mythos, Wirklichkeit* (Munich, 1971).

—— *Hitler's Letters and Notes* (New York, 1974).

—— 'Adolf Hitler: Vater eines Sohnes', in *Zeitgeschichte*, 5 (1977/8), 173–202.

Mathot, René, *Au Ravin du Loup: Hitler en Belgique et en France, Mai–Juin 1940* (Brussels, 2000).

Mehringer, Hartmut, 'Die KPD in Bayern, 1919–1945', in Martin Broszat and Hartmut Mehringer (eds), *Bayern in der NS-Zeit*, v (Munich, 1983), 1–286.

Mend, Hans, *Adolf Hitler im Felde, 1914–1918* (Diessen, 1931).

Messerschmidt, Manfred, 'Juden im preußischen-deutschen Heer', in Militärgeschichtliches Forschungsamt (ed.), *Deutsche jüdische Soldaten 1914–1945* (Herford, n.d.), 96–127.

Messerschmidt, Manfred, and Wüllner, Fritz, *Die Wehrmachtjustiz: Zerstörung einer Legende* (Baden-Baden, 1987).

Meyer, Adolf, 'Der härteste Tag der 10. Kompanie', in Solleder, *Westfront*, 141–2.

Meyer, Adolf, *Mit Adolf Hitler im Bayerischen Reserve-Infanterie-Regiment 16 List* (Neustadt/Aisch, 1934).

Mitchell, Allan, *Revolution in Bayern 1918/1919: Die Eisner-Regierung und die Räterepublik* (Munich, 1967).

Mommsen, Hans, *Alternative zu Hitler: Studien zur Geschichte des deutschen Widerstandes* (Munich, 2000).

Mosse, George, *Gefallen für das Vaterland: Nationales Heldentum und namenloses Sterben* (Stuttgart, 1990).

Mulders, Jean-Paul, *Auf der Suche nach Hitlers Sohn: Eine Beweisaufnahme* (Munich, 2009).

Müller, Arndt, *Geschichte der Juden in Nürnberg 1146–1945* (Nuremberg, 1968).

Müller, Rolf-Dieter, 'Total War as a Result of New Weapons? The Use of Chemical Agents in World War I', in Chickering and Förster, *Total War*, 95–111.

Mulligan, William, 'The Reichswehr and the Weimar Republic', in Anthony McElligott (ed.), *Weimar Germany: The Short Oxford History of Germany* (Oxford, 2009), 78–101.

NATO Standardization Agreement 2116, NATO codes for grades of military personnel.

Natter, Wolfgang, *Literature at War, 1914–1940: Representing 'The Time of Greatness' in Germany* (New Haven, 1999).

Neiberg, Michael S., *Fighting the Great War: A Global History* (Cambridge, Mass., 2005).

Neitzel, Sönke, *Weltkrieg und Revolution, 1914–1918/19* (Berlin, 2008).

Neumann-Adrian, Edda and Michael, *Münchens Lust am Jugenstil: Häuser und Menschen um 1900*, 2nd edn (Munich, 2006).

Nießl, Jost, Prägner, Erhard, and Stöhr, Fritz, 'Ehrentafel', in Solleder, *Westfront*, 387–502.

Offer, Avner, 'The Blockade of Germany and the Strategy of Starvation, 1914–1918: An Agency Perspective', in Chickering and Förster, *Total War*, 169–88.

Ophir, Baruch, and Wiesemann, Falk (eds), *Die jüdischen Gemeinden in Bayern 1918–1945* (Munich, 1979).

Overy, Richard, *The Dictators: Hitler's Germany and Stalin's Russia* (London, 2004).

Palazzo, Albert, *Seeking Victory on the Western Front: The British Army and Chemical Warfare in World War I* (Lincoln, Nebr., 2000).

Paret, Peter, *Clausewitz and the State: The Man, his Theories, and his Times* (Princeton, 1985 (1976)).

Pedersen, Peter, *Fromelles* (Barnsley, 2004).

Pfaff, Steven, *Exit-Voice Dynamics and the Collapse of East Germany: The Crisis of Leninism and the Revolution of 1989* (Durham, NC, 2006).

Pollard, Hugh, *The Story of Ypres* (New York, 1917).

Porter, Patrick, 'New Jerusalems: Sacrifice and Redemption in the War Experiences of English and German Military Military Chaplains', in Purseigle, *Warfare*, 101–32.

Price, Billy, *Adolf Hitler: The Unknown Artist* (Houston, Tex., 1984).

Pridham, Geoffrey, *Hitler's Rise to Power: The Nazi Movement in Bavaria, 1923–1933* (New York, 1974).

Prior, Robin, and Wilson, Trevor, *Command on the Western Front: The Military Career of Sir Henry Rawlinson, 1914–1918* (Oxford, 1991).

—— *Passchendaele: The Untold Story*, 2nd edn (New Haven, 2002).

—— *The Somme* (New Haven, 2005).

Prost, Antoine, *In the Wake of War: Les Anciens Combattants and French Society* (Oxford, 1992).

Pulzer, Peter, 'How the Holocaust Happened', *Times Literary Supplement*, 2 January 2008, http://entertainment.timesonline.co.uk/tol/arts_and_entertainment/the_tls/article3121515.ece, accessed 11 February 2008

Purseigle, Pierre (ed.), *Warfare and Belligerence: Perspectives in First World War Studies* (Leiden, 2005).

Rätsch-Langejürgen, Birgit, *Das Prinzip Widerstand: Leben und Wirken von Ernst Niekisch* (Bonn, 1997).

Reichert, Folker, and Wolgast, Eike (eds), *Karl Hampe: Kriegstagebuch 1914–1919* (Munich, 2004).

Reichsbund Jüdischer Frontsoldaten, Ortsgruppe München (ed.), *Unseren Gefallenen Kameraden: Gedenkbuch für die im Weltkrieg Gefallenen Münchener Juden* (Munich, 1929).

Reimann, Aribert, 'Wenn Soldaten vom Töten schreiben—Zur soldatischen Semantik in Deutschland und England, 1914–1918', in Gleichmann and Kühne, *Massenhaftes Töten*, 307–19.

Reuth, Ralf Georg, *Hitlers Judenhass* (Munich, 2009).

Rieker, Heinrich, *Nicht schießen, wir schießen auch nicht! Versöhnung von Kriegsgegners im Niemandsland 1914–1918 und 1939–1945* (Bremen, 2007).

Roach, Mary, *Stiff: The Curious Lives of Human Cadavers* (New York, 2004).

Roberts, Andrew, 'Did Hitler really only have ONE testicle?', *Daily Mail Online*, www.dailymail.co.uk/news/worldnews/article-1087380/Did-Hitler-really-ONE-testicle-A-historian-sorts-extraordinary-truth-far-flung-myths-Fuhrer.html, accessed 20 November 2008.

Röder, Werner, and Strauss, Herbert (eds), *Biographisches Handbuch der deutschsprachigen Emigration nach 1933*, 2 vols (Munich, 1980–3).

Rogge, Wolfgang, *Ernst Kreneks Opern: Spiegel der zwanziger Jahre* (Wolfenbüttel, 1970).

Rohe, Karl, *Das Reichsbanner Schwarz Rot Gold, Ein Beitrag zur Geschichte und Struktur der politischen Kampfverbände zur Zeit der Weimarer Republik* (Düsseldorf, 1966).

Römer, Gernot, *Der Leidensweg der Juden in Schwaben: Schicksale von 1933 bis 1945 in Berichten, Dokumenten und Zahlen* (Augsburg, 1983).

Rösch, Mathias, *Die Münchner NSDAP, 1925–1933* (Munich, 2002).

Rosenthal, Jacob, *'Die Ehre des jüdischen Soldaten': Die Judenzählung im Ersten Weltkrieg und ihre Folgen* (Frankfurt, 2007).

Roth, Eugen, 'Feuertaufe', in *List Regiment*, 19–23.

Rubenbauer, Franz, 'Im Schützengraben vor Messines', in Solleder, *Westfront*, 65–6.

—— 'Sturm auf Ypern: Freiwillige vor!', in Solleder, *Westfront*, 3–46.

—— 'Tage der Ruhe in Werwick-Comines', in Solleder, *Westfront*, 59–64.

Rupprecht von Bayern, *Mein Kriegstagebuch*, 2 vols (Berlin, 1929).

Rürup, Reinhard, 'Der "Geist von 1914" in Deutschland: Kriegsbegeisterung und Ideologisierung des Krieges im Ersten Weltkrieg', in Bernd Hüppauf (ed.), *Ansichten vom Krieg: Vergleichende Studien zum Ersten Weltkrieg in Literatur und Gesellschaft* (Königstein, 1984), 1–30.

Russell, Stuart, *Frontsoldat Hitler: Der Freiwillige des Ersten Weltkrieges—Zeitgeschichte in Bildern* (Kiel, 2006).

Ryback, Timothy, *Hitler's Private Library: The Books that Shaped his Life* (New York, 2008).

Sauder, Gerhard (ed.), *'Ich male wie ein Wilder': Albert Weisgerber in Briefen und Dokumenten* (Blieskastel, 2006).

Saunders, Christopher, and Smith, Iain, 'Southern Africa, 1795–1910', in Andrew Porter, *The History of the British Empire*, iii (Oxford, 1999), 597–623.

Sayer, Jan, and Botting, Douglas, *The Women who Knew Hitler: The Private Life of Adolf Hitler* (London, 2004).

Schad, Martha, *Hitlers Spionin: Das Leben der Stephanie von Hohenlohe* (Munich, 2002).

Schaepdrijver, Sophie de, *La Belgique et la Première Guerre Mondiale* (Brussels, 2004).

Scheffler, Wolfgang, and Schulle, Diana, *Buch der Erinnerung: Die ins Baltikum deportierten deutschen, östereichischen und tschechoslowakischen Juden*, 2 vols (Munich, 2003).

Scheibert, J., *Illustriertes Deutsches Militär-Lexikon* (Berlin, 1897).

Schmolze, Gerhard (ed.), *Revolution und Räterepublik in München 1918/19 in Augenzeugenberichten* (Düsseldorf, 1969).

Schnee, Heinrich, *Deutsches Kolonial-Lexikon, III. Band* (Leipzig, 1920).

Schönhoven, Klaus, 'Der politische Katholizismus in Bayern unter der NS-Herrschaft, 1933–1945', in Martin Broszat and Hartmut Mehringer (eds), *Bayern in der NS-Zeit*, v (Munich, 1983), 541–646.

Schramm, Martin, *Das Deutschlandbild in der britischen Presse 1912–1919* (Berlin, 2007).

Schüddekopf, Otto-Ernst, *Linke Leute von Rechts. Die nationalrevolutionären Minderheiten und der Kommunismus in der Weimarer Republik* (Stuttgart, 1960).

Schuhmacher, Wilhelm, *Leben und Seele unseres Soldatenlieds im Weltkrieg* (Frankfurt am Main, 1928).

Schulze, Hagen, *Weimar: Deutschland, 1917–1933* (Berlin, 1994).

Schumann, Dirk, 'Einheitssehnsucht und Gewaltakzeptanz: Politische Grundpositionen des deutschen Bürgertums nach 1918', in Hans Mommsen (ed.), *Der Erste Weltkrieg und die europäische Nachkriegsordnung* (Cologne, 2000), 83–105.

Schwarzwäller, Wulf, *'Der Stellvertreter des Führers' Rudolf Hess: Der Mann in Spandau* (Vienna, 1974).

Service, Robert, *Lenin: A Biography* (Cambridge, Mass., 2000).

Sheffield, Gary, *The Somme* (London, 2003).

Sheldon, Jack, *The German Army at Passchendaele* (Barnsley, 2007).

Showalter, Dennis, ' "It All Goes Wrong": German, French, and British Approaches to Mastering the Western Front', in Purseigle, *Warfare*, 38–72.

Sinz, Heinrich, *Geschichtliches vom ehemaligen Markte und der nunmehrigen Stadt Ichenhausen* (Ichenhausen, 1926).

—— 'Die letzten vierzig Jahre der Judenschaft in Ichenhausen (1906-1946)', in Manfred Gromer (ed.), *Erinnerungen an Stadtpfarrer und Dekan Heinrich Sinz* (Ichenhausen, n.d.), 45–85.

Smith, Helmut Walser, *The Continuities of German History: Nation, Religion, and Race across the Long Nineteenth Century* (Cambridge, 2008).

Smith, Jeffrey, *A People's War: Germany's Political Revolution, 1913–1918* (Lanham, Md., 2007).

Smith, Leonard, *Between Mutiny and Obedience: The Case of the French Fifth Infantry Division during World War I* (Princeton, 1994).

—— 'The "Culture de guerre" and French Historiography of the Great War of 1914–1918', *History Compass*, 5/6 (2007), 1967–79.

—— Audoin-Rouzeau, Stéphane, and Becker, Annette, *France and the Great War* (Cambridge, 2003).

Snape, Michael, *God and the British Soldier: Religion and the British Army in the First and Second World Wars* (London, 2005).

Solleder, Fridolin, 'Die Judenschutzherrlichkeit des Juliusspitals in Würzburg', in Karl Alexander von Müller (ed.), *Beiträge zur Bayerischen Geschichte: Festschrift für Sigmund v. Rietzler* (Gotha, 1913), 260–304.

—— contributions to Solleder, *Westfront*: 'Einer der 12. Kompanie', 48–55; 'Erster Winter', 79–94; 'Führerliste', 369–80; 'Das Neue Jahr', 97–105; 'Der Stellungskrieg bei Fromelles', 152–78; 'Das Vaterland ruft', 1–2; 'Verbrüderung zwischen den Fronten', 89–94; 'Zwischen zwei Gefechten', 120–9; 'Zum Geleit', pp. vii–xii.

—— (ed.), *Vier Jahre Westfront: Geschichte des Regiments List R.I.R. 16* (Munich, 1932).

—— 'Der Einbruch der Engländer beim Listregiment', *Bayerische Heimat*, 16 (1934), 92.

Spatny, Emil, 'Kämpfe am Hohenzollernwerk', in Solleder, 'Westfront', 179–88.

SPD-Ortsverein Ichenhausen, *Festschrift zum 75-jährigen Gründungsjubiläum des SPD-Ortsvereins Ichenhausen* (Ichenhausen, 1982).

Stadtarchiv München (ed.), *Biographisches Gedenkbuch der Münchner Juden, 1933–1945*, Band 1 *(A–L)* (Munich, 2003); Band 2 *(M–Z)* (Munich, 2007).

Stark, Gary, 'All Quiet on the Home Front: Popular Entertainments, Censorship, and Civilian Morale in Germany, 1914–1918', in Franz Coetzee and Marilyn Shevin-Coetzee (eds), *Authority, Identity and the Social History of the Great War* (Providence, RI, 1995), 57–80.

State Museum of Auschwitz–Birkenau, *Death Books from Auschwitz: Remnants* (Munich, 1995).

Statistisches Reichsamt (ed.), *Statistisches Jahrbuch für das Deutsche Reich, Band 1914* (Berlin, 1915).

Steinert, Marlis, *Hitler* (Munich, 1994).

Stern, Fritz, *Dreams and Delusions: The Drama of German History* (New York, 1987).

—— 'Lessons from German History', *Foreign Affairs*, 3 (2005), 14–18.

—— 'Fear and Hitler's Instant Subversion of Freedom', lecture, Council on Foreign Relations, New York City, 4 March 2008; www.cfr.org/publication/15691/fear_and_hitlers_instant_subversion_of_freedom_video.html

Sternhell, Ze'ev, *Neither Right nor Left: Fascist Ideology in France* (Princeton, 1995 (1983)).

—— *The Birth of Fascist Ideology* (Princeton, 1994 (1989)).

—— 'From Counter-Enlightenment to the Revolutions of the 20th Century', in Shlomo Avinieri and Ze'ev Sternhell (eds), *Europe's Century of Discontent* (Jerusalem, 2003), 3–22.

Stevenson, David, *Cataclysm: The First World War as Political Tragedy* (New York, 2004).

Stibbe, Matthew, *German Anglophobia and the Great War, 1914–1918* (Cambridge, 2001).

Stiegler, Carl, 'Aus meinem Tagebuch', in Solleder, *Westfront*, 113–16.

Stiehler, Anne Marie, *Die Geschichte von Adolf Hitler: Den Deutschen Kindern erzählt* (Berlin, 1941).

Stöhr, Fritz, 'Zahlenmäßige Zusammenstellung der Verluste', in Solleder, *Westfront*, 381–5.

Stone, Norman, *Hitler* (Boston, 1980).

Strachan, Hew, 'The Morale of the German Army, 1917–18', in Cecil and Liddle, *Armageddon*, 383–98.

—— *The First World War*, vol. i: *To Arms* (Oxford, 2001).

—— 'Training, Morale and Modern War', *Journal of Contemporary History*, 41 (2006), 211–27.

Stürmer, Michael, *Das ruhelose Reich: Deutschland 1866–1918* (Berlin, 1998 (1983)).

Tapken, Kai Uwe, *Die Reichswehr in Bayern von 1919 bis 1924* (Hamburg, 2002).

Thamer, Hans-Ulrich, *Verführung und Gewalt: Deutschland, 1933–1945* (Berlin, 1986).

Toland, John, *Adolf Hitler* (New York, 1976).

Tubeuf, Anton von, 'Das Regiment hört auf den Namen Tubeuf', in Solleder, *Westfront*, 275–88, 292–310.

Ulrich, Bernd, 'Die Desillusionierung der Kriegsfreiwilligen von 1914', in Wolfram Wette (ed.), *Der Krieg des kleinen Mannes: Eine Militärgeschichte von unten* (Munich, 1995), 110–26.

—— *Die Augenzeugen: Deutsche Feldpostbriefe in Kriegs- und Nachkriegszeit, 1914–1933* (Essen, 1997).

United States Holocaust Memorial Museum (ed.), *Hidden History of the Kovno Ghetto* (Boston, 1997).

Unruh, Karl, *Langemarck: Legende und Wirklichkeit* (Koblenz, 1986).

US Bureau of the Census, *Population of the 100 Largest Cities and Other Urban Places in the United States: 1790 to 1990' (=Population Division Working Paper No. 27)* (Washington, 1998).

US General Staff, *Histories of Two Hundred and Fifty-One Divisions of the German Army which Participated in the Great War* (Washington, 1920).

Verhey, Jeffrey, *The Spirit of 1914: Militarism, Myth and Mobilization in Germany* (Cambridge, 2000).

Vogel, Rolf, *Ein Stück von uns: Deutsche Juden in deutschen Armeen, 1813–1976* (Mainz, 1977).

Vogt, Stefan, *Nationaler Sozialismus und Soziale Demokratie: Die sozialdemokratische Junge Rechte, 1918–1945* (Bonn, 2006).

Wakefield, Alan, *Christmas in the Trenches* (Stroud, 2006).

Walter, Dirk, *Antisemitische Kriminalität und Gewalt: Judenfeindschaft in der Weimarer Republik* (Bonn, 1999).

Wasserstein, Bernhard, *Divided Jerusalem: The Struggle for the Holy City*, 2nd edn (New Haven, 2002 (2001)).

—— *Barbarism and Civilization: A History of Europe in our Time* (Oxford, 2007).

Watson, Alexander, ' "For Kaiser and Reich": The Identity and Fate of the German Volunteers, 1914–1918', *War in History*, 12/1 (2005), 44–74.

—— 'Culture and Combat in the Western World, 1900–1945', *Historical Journal*, 51/2 (2008), 529–46.

—— *Enduring the Great War: Combat, Morale and Collapse in the German and British Armies, 1914–1918* (Cambridge, 2008).

Weber, Eugen, *Peasants into Frenchmen: The Modernization of Rural France, 1870–1914* (Stanford, Calif., 1976).

Weber, Thomas, 'Anti-Semitism and Philo-Semitism among the British and German Élites: Oxford and Heidelberg before the First World War', in *English Historical Review*, 118/475 (February 2003), 86–119.

—— 'Studenten', in Gerhard Hirschfeld *et al.* (eds), *Enzyklopädie Erster Weltkrieg* (Paderborn, 2003), 910–12.

—— *Lodz Ghetto Album: Photographs by Henryk Ross* (London, 2004).

—— *Our Friend 'The Enemy': British and German Elite Education before World War I* (Stanford, 2008).

Weinberg, Gerhard, 'Einleitung', in Weinberg (ed.), *Zweites Buch*, 15–39.

—— (ed.), *Hitlers Zweites Buch* (Stuttgart, 1961).

Weintraub, Stanley, *Silent Night: The Story of the World War I Christmas Truce* (New York, 2001).

Weisgerber, [Albert], 'Bei Gheluvelt', in *List Regiment*, 18.

Weiß, Dieter, *Kronprinz Rupprecht von Bayern (1869–1955)* (Regensburg, 2007).

Weiß, Katharina, 'Die Biographie meines Urgroßvaters Jakob Weiß', unpublished Facharbeit, submitted to the Gabelsberger-Gymnasium Mainburg, 2007.

Weitz, Eric D., *Weimar Germany: Promise and Tragedy* (Princeton, 2007).

Wenzl, Josef, 'Ein Feldpostbrief über Neuve Chapelle', in Solleder, *Westfront*, 118–19.

Whitehead, Don, *The FBI Story* (London, 1957).

Wiedemann, Friedrich, contributions to Solleder, *Westfront*: 'Atempause', 231–6; 'Auf den Vimyhöhen', 262–4; 'Das Gefecht bei Fromelles', 214–27; 'Gesundheitszustand und Verpflegung', 201–3; 'Ruhetage in Somain. Einsatz in La Bassée', 266–73; 'Die Sommeschlacht', 237–55; 'Unsere Stellung bei Fromelles', 204–6; 'Der zweite Kriegswinter bei Fromelles', 189–201.

—— *Der Mann, der Feldherr werden wollte: Erlebnisse und Erfahrungen des Vorgesetzten Hitlers im Ersten Weltkrieg und seines späteren persöenlichen Adjutanten* (Velbert, 1964).

Wiegand, Richard, *'Wer hat uns verraten . . .': Die Sozialdemokratie in der Novemberrevolution* (Freiburg, 1999).

Wilcox, Vanda, 'Discipline in the Italian Army, 1915–1918', in Purseigle, *Warfare*, 73–100.

Wilke, Fritz, 'Schiedsgericht und Völkerleben', in *Deutscher März: Zweite Liebesgabe deutscher Hochschüler* (Kassel, 1915), 100–7.

Williams, John F., *Corporal Hitler and the Great War, 1914–1918: The List Regiment* (London, 2005).

Williamson, Henry, *Goodbye West Country* (Boston, 1938).

Wilson, Trevor, *The Myriad Races of War: Britain and the Great War, 1914–1918* (Cambridge, 1988).

Winkler, Heinrich August, *Der Lange Weg nach Westen: Erster Band* (Munich, 2000).

Winter, Jay, and Baggett, Blaine, *The Great War: The Shaping of the Twentieth Century* (New York, 1996).

—— and Robert, Jean-Louis (eds), *Capital Cities at War: Paris, London, Berlin, 1914–1919* (Cambridge, 1997).

W[itt], V[alentin], 'Ausmarsch', in *List Regiment*, 7.

—— 'Einstellung der Freiwilligen', in *List Regiment*, 5-6.

—— 'Die Gefechte bei Gheluvelt und Becelaire', in *List Regiment*, 15–16.

—— 'Messiners-Betlehem-Ferme', in *List Regiment*, 25–9.

—— 'Oostaverne—Wytschaete', in *List Regiment*, 31–8.

Wolffsohn, Michael, and Brechenmacher, Thomas, *Die Deutschen und ihre Vornamen: 200 Jahre Politik und öffentliche Meinung* (Munich, 1999).

Yelton, David, *Hitler's Volkssturm: The Nazi Militia and the Fall of Germany, 1944–1945* (Lawrence, Kan., 2002).

Young, Robert, *Under Siege: Portraits of Civilian Life in France during World War I* (New York, 2000).

Zeiss, D., *Unterrichtsbuch für den bayerischen Infanteristen und Jäger* (Regensburg, 1913).

Ziblatt, Daniel, *Structuring the State: The Formation of Italy and Germany and the Puzzle of Federalism* (Princeton, 2006).

—— 'How did Europe Democratize?', *World Politics*, 58 (2006), 311–38.

Ziemann, Benjamin, *Front und Heimat: Ländliche Kriegserfahrungen im südlichen Bayern, 1914–1923* (Essen, 1997).

—— 'Enttäuschte Erwartungen und kollektive Erschöpfung: Die deutschen Soldaten an der Westfront 1918 auf dem Weg zur Revolution', in Jörg Duppler and Gerhard Gross, *Kriegsende 1918: Ereignis, Wirkung, Nachwirkung* (Munich, 1999), 165–82.

Zuckerman, Larry, *The Rape of Belgium: The Untold Story of World War I* (New York, 2004).

Zuehlke, Mark, *Brave Battalion: The Remarkable Saga of the 16th Battalion (Canadian Scottish) in the First World War* (Mississauga, 2008).

Films

Das schreckliche Mädchen, directed by Michael Verhoeven, 1990.

Joyeux Noël, directed by Christian Carion, 2005.

Knopp, Guido, and Remy, Maurice Philip, *The Rise and Fall of Adolf Hitler*, episode 1, ZDF/History Channel, 1995.

The Trench Detectives, Channel 5 series, Season 1, Episode 1: 'Loos'.

Websites

www.ancestry.com

www.araratcc.vic.edu.au/fow/holocaust.htm ('Survivors of the Holocaust')

http://avalon.law.yale.edu/wwii/blbk106.asp – Yale Law School, Avalon Project

www.iglesialuterana.ec/historica.htm – Lutheran Church of Quito

http://www.pbs.orf/historian/hist_wohl_06_hitler.html – 'The Great War and the Shaping of the 20th Century'

http://wahlen-in-deutschland.de/kuBayern.htm

http://wahlen-in-deutschland.de/kuRbbNiederbayern.htm

http://wahlen-in-deutschland.de/kuRbbOberbayern.htm

http://wahlen-in-deutschland.de/kuRbbOberpfalz.htm

www.wahlen-in-deutschland.de/wlBayern.htm

Newspapers

NB Newspapers articles consulted in archives are not separately listed here.

Bild

General-Anzeiger für Elberfeld-Barmen

Illustrierter Beobachter

St Louis Post-Dispatch

St Louis Star-Times

New York Times

Der Spiegel

Sun

The Times

Die Volksgemeinschaft

Index